# Humanitarian Solutions in the 21st Century

**Series editor:**
Larry Winter Roeder, Jr.

For further volumes:
http://www.springer.com/series/11580

Larry Winter Roeder, Jr. • Albert Simard

# Diplomacy and Negotiation for Humanitarian NGOs

Springer

Larry Winter Roeder, Jr.
South Riding, VA, USA

Albert Simard
Defence R&D
Ottawa, ON, Canada

ISBN 978-1-4614-7112-7 ISBN 978-1-4614-7113-4 (eBook)
DOI 10.1007/978-1-4614-7113-4
Springer New York Heidelberg Dordrecht London

Library of Congress Control Number: 2013936075



Printed on acid-free paper

Springer is part of Springer Science+Business Media (www.springer.com)

# Foreword

The book is an impressive manual of multilateral diplomacy and full of interesting and useful information and anecdotes.

Sálvano Briceño
Chair
Science Committee, Integrated Research on Disaster Risk, IRDR;
Senior Advisor
Global Earthquake Model, GEM;
Former Director
International Strategy for Disaster Reduction, UNISDR, 2001–2011

I am confident that the book will be enormously helpful to organizations and individuals who need to invoke diplomacy skills as part of their role, be that vocationally, or as a volunteer. As an NGO or charitable organization, one of our greatest "weapons" is diplomacy and used with tact and discretion and where possible, in partnership with local or central governments, presents perhaps the best chance for success. This book should be seen as a valuable addition to any organizational library and any front line negotiation management should be encouraged to utilize the content as part of their project planning and implementation procedure.

Trevor Wheeler
Former Director for Near-Eastern Affairs
WSPA, World Society for the Protection of Animals

Believe me; I think it will be useful, helpful for all of those who are not familiar with the "diplomatisches Parkett", as we say in German.

Dr. Johann Georg Goldammer
Senior Scientist
Max Planck Society for Chemistry, Biogeochemistry Department

I admire your desire, discipline and fortitude to make diplomacy practical and useful for the larger humanitarian community. I am pleased to contribute to your considerable effort.

Sharon Rusu
International Affairs Consultant, Strategic Planning Facilitator
UNISDR;
Former Director
ReliefWeb.int

Globalization has inevitably expanded the role of non-governmental organizations (NGOs) and their impact on perceptions of national, regional and international interests. They are the key new players in defining national and international public policy. Those that will succeed in this new environment must master a range of new skills including how best to engage in international diplomacy. Diplomacy, traditionally the domain of government representatives, entails a very broad range of skills that begin with defining, balancing, and choosing between often conflicting interests, and determining how such interests can be made compatible, realized, served, preserved, and expanded. While much has been written on Diplomacy, teaching literature on this subject is sparse. Larry Roeder has now made a major contribution toward filling this gap. By combining in-depth research with his own extensive international experience, he has put together an essential read and reference book for those NGO leaders, managers, and negotiators that hope to operate successfully in the new global environment. His book concentrates on tested diplomatic techniques that can be used to maximize impact and influence. Recognizing the vast variety of contexts and challenges those involved in such work will likely face, his work describes a broad range of techniques and provides a series of descriptive real case examples upon which to draw.

Victor Comras
Minister Counselor, Retired
US Department of State

# Preface

The world faces urgent and formidable tasks in almost every domain related to the condition of humankind. What were once dismissed as local matters have now become of universal concern … NGOs contribute greatly to the arousing of awareness and channeling of concerns … They also have a principal function of operating and taking direct action in their own right (MacAlister-Smith, 1995). This book is for NGOs and all civil society organizations.

The book began out of a project Mr. Roeder did while serving as the Policy Advisor on Disaster Management at the U.S. Department of State. Knowing Roeder had worked with many humanitarian NGOs, some friends of his suggested crafting a handbook on diplomacy for NGOs. Roeder then joined WSPA, a British NGO with a focus on animal welfare. His goal was to convince the international intergovernmental community to humanely protect livestock that poor farmers and refugees need for a living or for food. A number of people he met while with WSPA had the same suggestion about the need for a handbook on diplomacy; so after completion of his contract, and at the recommendation of the UN's Food and Agricultural Organization (FAO), Springer had Mr. Roeder finally author the book on diplomacy. Animal welfare and conservation NGOs are often small organizations with little experience in the field.

Following that experience, some of Mr. Roeder's former colleagues recommended creating a more comprehensive version for the humanitarian community, recognizing that for purposes of this discussion we are throwing a large tent out that includes operational NGOs that might work in a refugee camp, as well as those that advocate for better standards or those that lobby for peace, the protection of cultures, and economic development. The book is intended to do three things.

(a) *Manifesto:* Suggest that all NGOs regardless of size, should engage in diplomacy, though because of the costs, some smaller ones will need to work in coalitions. The entire book does this; but Chap. 1 is the main introduction to the concept.
(b) *How -To*: Provide tactics on negotiations and diplomacy, including an understanding of protocol with governments and International Organizations, as well

as donors, conferences, information management, etc., as tools. Chapters 2, 3, 4, 5, 6, 7, 8, 9, 10, 11, 12, and 13 cover those topics and include a model for managing a diplomatic initiative.

(c) *History/Precedent*: Some feel NGOs should simply focus on negotiating safe passage into a zone and then deliver services like medical care or road construction; but there is also a rich history of NGOs involved in diplomacy, going back to before World War I. Though Chap. 1 and other chapters also deal with this topic, History and Precedent are a special focus of case studies in Chaps. 14, 15, 16, 17, 18, and 19.

The effort is co-authored by an American and a Canadian, and draws on advice from over 45 international experts, a true team effort. Team work has been important, since diplomacy is not owned by any one country or expert. Indeed, the authors propose it is not exclusive to governments. For NGOs, diplomacy can be about obtaining permission to enter a war zone, perhaps from armed non-state actors, or gaining permits for relief supplies without duties. It is also a negotiation with local or national figures to protect human rights, or with the UN to change a rule, or fellow NGOs and the Red Cross movement to build a coalition to protect political prisoners or to foster development, many humanitarian actions. The authors also think it is about multilateral diplomacy, negotiating with the UN, its Specialized Agencies and Funds, non-UN international organizations like OECD, and NATO, perhaps the Arab League. Indeed, now is an especially good time to link NGOs and modern multilateral diplomacy. The modern form began almost one century ago with the end of World War I and the advent of the League of Nations. NGOs played an important role back then, and increasingly do so today in this important, evolving, and very complex arena. NGOs need to do more and be on the stage alongside the best diplomats any government or the UN and the Red Cross have to offer, preserving and building a better world.

To help, the authors drew on their own experiences, as well as historical precedent and the best diplomatic practices needed by even the smallest NGO to convince any organization or government to accept their policies and the written language to implement them. They also proposed an approach to prepare the NGO diplomat for the unexpected. In other words, this is a manifesto, history book, and manual all in one, encouraging NGOs to negotiate true change.

There are about 1.5 million NGOs in the USA alone, covering a myriad of topics, not all strictly humanitarian, plus millions more around the world (U.S. Department of State 2012). While "humanitarian NGOs" are the main audience, any CSO (civil society organization) can benefit from this book, as well as mediation practitioners who work with armed non-state actors (ANSAs). Indeed, it is recommended that in addition to ANSAs formally agreeing to follow international standards of behavior by signing Deeds of Commitment, they too use this book. It just might reduce some violence.

Whatever an NGO plans to do with governments or international organizations, this guidebook will be helpful, to include something of the skills known as "protocol," and much about the rules, procedures, and funding opportunities.

South Riding, VA, USA
Ottawa, ON, Cananda

Larry Winter Roeder, Jr.
Albert Simard

**Larry Winter Roeder, Jr.**

**Albert Simard**

# Contents

# Chapter 1
# Why Learn "NGO Diplomacy?"

**Extract** This chapter explains why NGOs need to be engaged in diplomacy in order to cause strategic change, especially in an increasingly multilateral world. Historical precedent is provided.

## 1.1 What is NGO Diplomacy?

> The decision to engage in humanitarian diplomacy is not a choice, but a responsibility. Humanitarian Diplomacy Policy, the IFRC. (IFRC 2009)
>
> The 20th century was in its infancy when Woodrow Wilson announced the League of Nations and an end to isolationism at an NGO Conference sponsored by the Committee to Enforce Peace on May 27, 1916. The league was to be the mainspring of a reorganized international system. In the speech, Wilson said as well we are "participants, whether we would or not, in the life of the world. The interests of all nations are our own also. We are partners with the rest. What affects mankind is inevitably our affair as well as the affair of the nations of Europe and of Asia." (Seymour 1926, pp. 293–295)
>
> Speaking of Medical Diplomacy, "If we are going to help people whose lives hang in the balance, we need to reach them. This means negotiating with government officials, high-ranking military officers, clan elders and rebel leaders." (Neuman 2012) MSF, USA, 2012.

"NGO diplomacy" means the effort by an NGO or NGO alliance to convince a government or some other entity to do something very specific. That could be to change language in a United Nations resolution, to convince an armed non-state actor to permit an NGO to provide medical assistance, or perhaps to negotiate changes an international convention. It might be what happens in the Arctic Council, which has as six nonvoting members, NGOs representing indigenous peoples and

L.W. Roeder, Jr. and A. Simard, *Diplomacy and Negotiation for Humanitarian NGOs*, Humanitarian Solutions in the 21st Century, DOI 10.1007/978-1-4614-7113-4_1,

advancing sustainable development, research, and conservation in the Arctic.[1] It could be a negotiation between NGOs to create an alternative to government treaties, as happened in 2012 in the Rio+20 Conference (see Chap. 15). Increasingly, it could be the negotiations required by NGOs to gain agreement from armed non-state actors to sign a deed of commitment to obligate the combatants to abide with international norms that otherwise only exist in state-to-state treaties (see Sect. 7.5). A new opportunity for such NGO diplomacy will arise in 2015 at a summit of disaster experts and governmental ministers in Sendai, Japan, to discuss and agree on the successor arrangement to the Hyogo Framework for Action. NGOs need to be there and in the preparatory conferences to make technical presentations and to directly influence the new framework agreement.

Lobbying (see Sect. 12.5.3) can be the best approach for a small or new NGO to build a reputation; NGOs need to be at the table with government and international organization negotiators, placing their own words into the pivotal documents of history, UN resolutions, treaties, and the like in order to reduce conflict, bolster the global economy and the environment, and protect all humans from abuse. Some sources suggested that NGO diplomacy should be about practical things like obtaining visas and work permits to move relief supplies. That is important, but Sabeel Rahman at Harvard is also correct when he argues that NGOs are often too apolitical in order to be efficiently operational. Studying democracy in Bangladesh, Rahman suggests "the NGO sector as a whole has shifted away from its initial focus on promoting political mobilized and accountable government, to the apolitical delivery of basic services. The result of this 'depoliticization' of NGOs is an accelerated erosion of democratic institutions in Bangladesh" (Rahman 2006). **Recommendation**: NGO diplomacy is about the practical day-to-day issues *and* advancing strategic change.

Proponents of "real politik" often argue that government officials must avoid spending their time viewing the world as it should be, instead focusing on how it really is and what is in the special interest of their government—focus on techniques, not vision. Instead, consider that NGOs are the people, and while NGO diplomats should be fully cognizant of the real world and be skillful in practical technique, they should also never lose sight of their vision of a better tomorrow, not let it be clouded by politics or the need for operational funds. This is especially true today because the world of the twenty-first century is full of deadly maybes that cry out for cleverer solutions than those that have usually come from governments. Some estimates indicate that conflict impacts over half a billion people in over 45 countries; countless more are poorly protected from natural phenomena. Governments must govern and NGOs need to be a valued partner to keep governments connected to the will of the people—in the end, governments and the UN and other international organizations are there to serve the people.

[1]The Declaration on the Establishment of the Arctic Council is governed by the Arctic Council Rules of Procedure, and observer status in the Arctic Council is open to non-Arctic States; intergovernmental and interparliamentary organizations, global and regional; and nongovernmental organizations that the Council determines can contribute to its work.

Since the founding of the UN, NGO conferences have also presented major opportunities for diplomacy and especially to make major policy statements on behalf of civil society regarding issues of global concern. As an example, in September 2009 the 62nd Annual NGO/DPI Conference was held in Mexico City[2] on the critical topic of disarmament. To prepare, a Committee of Experts was established in the New York and Mexican communities of NGOs, with the charge of coming up with possible speakers (the American NGOs insisted on gender and geographic parity) as well as a draft outcomes document to be adopted by the conference as a whole. The document was then distributed to the attending 1,300 delegates and adopted by voice vote. In addition, it was carried by the Foreign Minister of Mexico to the UN Security Council (Mexico was then a member) which was chaired by President Obama of the United States and read into the official minutes.

A good historical example of NGO-to-government negotiations in an environment of high drama happened in 1919 when the Deutsche Gesellschaft für Völkerrecht (German Society for International Law) formed from the ashes of the Great War. It consulted directly with the German government, asking them to agree to the NGO's draft convention to the soon to be created League of Nations (which the government concurred with and used as their own negotiating position), and then the NGO also took that text to the Paris Peace Conference and tried to convince the American delegation and others to agree (Chap. 19), (Niemeyer, *Draft of a Constitution of the League of Nations* 1919; Hestermeyer 2012).

One of today's most important NGOs, Save the Children (UK), also emerged from the violence of World War I and between the formation of the League of Nations and the United Nations; other NGOs began to surface at intergovernmental conferences, notably the World Economic Conferences of 1927 and 1933, where they lobbied on key issues relating to protectionism, relative to wheat, sugar, and wine. There was also the role of the Rockefeller and Carnegie endowments; the former provided funding for research activities; the latter sponsored a library at the new League HQ in Geneva, the Palais des Nations. And finally, there were the many NGOs who lobbied for what is now called human rights, such as the protection of women and children or to outlaw slavery (Clavin 2012). A more recent example was the effort of a coalition of governments and NGOs to pursue "the Ottawa Process," which led to a treaty to ban landmines, which 123 countries eventually ratified.

[2]Organized by the UN Department of Public Information (DPI) in partnership with the NGO community, the DPI/NGO annual conferences have been held since the founding of the United Nations and are jointly organized by DPI and NGOs accredited to UN/DPI and the Department. Attending are host government officials, representatives of industry, the United Nations, and usually over 1,500 NGO representatives from around the world. The 2007 conference in New York focused on climate change and was the first time an actual declaration emanated from the proceedings. This was shared with the Secretary General and numerous governmental leaders. The 2008 Paris Conference focused on the 60th anniversary of the Universal Declaration of Human Rights. The 2010 Melbourne Conference focused on global health as it relates to the millennium development goals. The 2011 Bonn Conference focused on sustainable development.

Without NGOs like Handicap International (France), Human Rights Watch (USA), Medico International (Germany), Save the Children (UK), and Care International (UK), there likely would not have been a treaty.

## 1.2 NGOs as a Force for the Sovereignty of People

Soren Kierkegaard said "there is a time to be silent and a time to speak" (Kierkegaard 1939, p. 5). NGOs often speak very loudly with public protests and on-the-ground research unfettered by national politics. This keeps the UN community informed, especially on practices like female genital mutilation, mass killings, and other practices that a government might not wish to be made public. In fact, NGOs have been at the heart of important multilateral negotiations and diplomacy since the nineteenth century, especially in the peace and environmental protection movements, as well as in sustainable development, human rights, and humanitarian relief operations in response to wars and destructive forces of nature. NGOs have also negotiated directly with governments to allow their own participation in international conferences, for example, the 1972 Stockholm Conference in Human Development (more than 250 NGOs participated), the 1992 Rio Conference (more than 1,400 NGO participated) and 25,000 private citizens participated as well in parallel sessions, the 2002 World Summit on Sustainable Development in Johannesburg (3,200 NGOs participated), and the 2005 World Conference on Disaster Risk Reduction in Kobe to which 40,000 private citizens participated. Though in smaller numbers, influential NGOs also helped develop the League of Nations, the first major international organization of the modern era, and have helped evolve the United Nations as it is known today into something that doesn't just represent governments but humanity.

> "I am prepared to say that the State is an individual, a moral individual, and is subject as such to the moral law. I believe that through the development of a mysterious but essential capacity of our nature, human beings can join together and make themselves, for one reason or another, into a corporate whole, and having done so they assume a new character, ceasing to be wholly and solely an aggregation of units, and becoming a new entity, subject to its own moral laws end moral duties." Lord Robert Cecil, British Under Secretary of State, 1915–1919. (Cecil 1923, p. 13)

The authors propose that while the covenants of the UN and the League of Nations are between governments, they were not created solely to support countries or governments. For many framers, they also were meant to protect the sovereignty of peoples, who give governments their authority. This point was echoed by Prime Minister Vittorio Orlando of Italy when he said during the Paris Peace Conference, "We are not establishing a League of Governments but a League of Nations" (Miller, *The Drafting of the Covenant* 1928a, p. 166, Vol 1). Some see the sovereignty of states as a problem, such as Lord Lothian (Ambassador to the USA) who indicated in 1938 that sovereignty is an insuperable obstacle to peace (Streit 1940, p. 53).

Declassified papers of Leo Pasvolsky, one of the drafting officers of the United Nations Charter, show that that the American team at Dumbarton Oaks discussions was not just considering the protection of states. They also considered the concept of world government. In the end, just as with the League, the UN is not a government nor is the General Assembly a world legislature. That said, it is useful to learn that in the briefing documents were the ideas of former US Supreme Court Justice Owen J. Roberts who spoke in favor of a "supernational government" with a simple Bill of Rights and a judiciary to hear disputes between private citizens and the government. They remind us of comments by former British Prime Minister Ramsey MacDonald who saw in international organizations a place for public debate (Howard-Ellis 1928, pp. 114–115). In other words, a UN, by whatever name, should not just be for States or governments; it should also be for the people, the common shepherd, or the wealthy tycoon (CSOP 1943b, July 23).[3] Owens and the "American Team" at Dumbarton Oaks were also influenced by an NGO that emerged from the readers of Union Now by Clarence K. Streit, who called for a Union of the democracies (CSOP 1943b, July 23, pp. 26–27)[4] and himself was influenced by George Mason, a US constitutional framer. Streit did not want leagues and was frustrated by the destructive power of nationalism, so instead of advancing a League of Nations model, his idea was to unify the democracies of North America, Europe, and the British Commonwealth into one democracy. David Hunter Miller disparaged of the name League and wanted instead an "Association."

One of today's oldest NGOs is the Fabian Society, founded in 1884 by leaders like George Bernard Shaw. It founded the Labour Party in the UK and later greatly influenced Jawaharlal Nehru of India and Lee Kuan Yew, the father of modern Singapore. In 1916, one of its leaders, Leonard Sidney Woolf, would write of how international government should be managed. Like others, Woolf wanted a democratic world, but understood they could not force autocratic governments to join nor force governments to be democratic. Democracy had to evolve from within by exposure to the world. He also desired a world authority representing the people in order to end war, but recognized that this was, in the then-current state of social evolution, a utopian fantasy. For practical reasons and understanding that a vast array of governmental systems then existed, he surmised during the "Great War" that a future international government would have to be made of representatives of states (Woolf, *International Government* 1916a, pp. 105–107). The founders of the League of Nations and the United Nations came to the same conclusion. Both organizational charters were agreements between states, but the people were also given a kind of voice by allowing NGOs to have association. In fact, NGOs were given an official status in the UN structure as a voice for civil society. It is important to note in this context that the UN Charter begins with the words "We the Peoples of the United Nations Determined." Why? The Paris Conference actually did consider establishing a Congress directly representative of the people, but as noted, the idea

[3]Owens was also chair of the *Atlantic Union Committee, formed in 1949 by the Federal Union, Inc., an effort which helped lead the way to NATO.*

[4]CSOP is Commission to Study the Organization of Peace.

was dropped. This then led to NGOs banding together through the International Federation of League of Nations Societies,[5] which said "The success or failure of the League depends on public opinion" (Joyce 1978, p. 163). The Federation met annually in different world capitals, much like the annual NGO conferences sponsored by the Department of Public Affairs of the UN and the DPI/NGO Executive Committee. Thereby, NGOs were then and are now spreading the message of peace.

The difference between state sovereignty and the sovereignty of the peoples is one of the great debates of international law, diplomacy, and politics which will not go away and why NGOs need to be involved in multilateral deliberations,[6] why the innovative concept of deeds of commitment makes sense, why NGOs should not only advocate for change but also should negotiate real change. Lobbying is very important and can change domestic political dynamics in such a way as to encourage governments to do the right thing, but negotiations create agreements, laws, and regulations. NGOs were part of the life of the League of Nations, often participating in meetings and in committees, lobbying, and negotiating. Recognizing that precedent and with the insistence of US Secretary of State Stettinius, the participation of NGOs in the United Nations was enshrined in the UN Charter in 1945 under Article 71 of Chap. 10, which created the Economic and Social Council (ECOSOC). ECOSOC was tasked to consult with NGOs on matters that concerned it. Forty-one NGOs were granted consultative status with ECOSOC in 1946. By 1992, the number had grown to more than 700, rising to 3,500 in 2011 (ECOSOC 2011). Still, hundreds of thousands of NGOs operate around the world, often with not enough resources to go to meetings in New York or Geneva. In addition to ECOSOC, some NGOs have a relation with the Department of Public Information (DPI) and with the many specialized agencies and funds of the UN, as well as non-UN international organizations. In other words, multilateral diplomacy is now living in the age of the NGO diplomat and an engaged civil society.

## 1.3 NGOs in the Multilateral World

To study modern multilateral diplomacy, go back in time to find a world system destroyed by World War I and a new system with the Treaty of Versailles in 1919. They were both created by governments, often for their own interests, though there was also a general cry from the people, often represented by a fairly small NGO community, for a new world order to reduce war. Great demonstrations filled the streets of Berlin and other cities infused by the vision of Woodrow Wilson, a vision then dashed by the vindictiveness of Versailles and what some called the Broken Star, the League of Nations, though it did many great things. Then, emerging from World War II arrived another global structure. This one, the UN era, was born from

[5] Situated first in Bordeaux, then in Brussels, then in Brussels and Geneva, and finally in Geneva alone

[6] See discussion in Sect. 1.2 on Sovereignty and the New World Order.

**Fig. 1.1** Multilateral talks April 1919 (Collection LRoeder)

the San Francisco Conference. This was also largely negotiated by governments, with NGO input. Its aim was to answer the call of Dante, who in 1309 called for all nations to live under one law (Joyce 1978). The Cold War followed and then the fall of the Berlin Wall, allowing the birth of a new age of uncertainty. By then NGOs had grown in large numbers and now are everywhere, and their numbers are increasing, as is their scope of operation. NGOs are in a position to help the disadvantaged who have emerged over the last half century without the taint of partisan politics and thus can be invaluable partners with governments and the multilateral community. Better yet, governments and the multilateral community can be their partner (Fig. 1.1).

Opportunities for NGOs to engage in the multilateral sphere rapidly expanded after World War II when the so-called developing world began throwing off the shackles of empire and exhibited an "ambition to modernize, to pull level with the more developed countries" (Ward 1962, p. 112). They also felt a right to equality, which led to much political and economic turbulence but also confusion and much conflict; many of these nations either became client states to the big powers in the Cold War or were left forgotten because they were not strategically important. But with the fall of the Berlin Wall in 1989, most in the foreign affairs community felt the world was about to enter yet another new era of uncertainty and an increased number of crises, especially from repressed indigenous peoples in the former Soviet Union. Conflict was also emerging from the populations of former client states who wanted political and economic parity, yet again, opportunities for NGOs.

A fresh model for NGO participation in multilateral affairs, what some call a multi-stakeholder approach, was invented at the UN Earth Summit in 1992. This was formalized in Agenda 21. "The Summit is blueprint of action to achieve sustainable development—acknowledged and codified those stakeholder sectors into nine 'Major Groups' Women, Children and Youth, Indigenous Peoples, *Non-Governmental Organizations* (NGOs), Local Authorities, Workers and Trade Unions, Business and Industry, the Scientific and Technological community, and

Farmers" (DESA 2012a). These groups have participated in each annual meeting of the UN Commission on Sustainable Development (CSD) and in subsequent review processes, such as the 2002 World Summit on Sustainable Development in Johannesburg. They speak at most plenary meetings and hold consultations with governments on substantive issues, receive official documents, and distribute their own material, often as professionally as any world power. They organize side events and build coalitions through meetings among themselves and partnership with governments and UN agencies. In other words, while the organization of Major Groups is hardly perfect, it recognized the central role of NGOs, and that's important, since the prophesy of change predicted in 1989 has certainly proven true; today it is easy to predict a continuation of economic and political turbulence, even if the reasons are different. Natural phenomena and the strains of energy demands are increasingly stretching the sustainability of all societies. Genocide still exists, as do ordinary civil conflicts, and failed nation states, which will be explored in this book.

Fortunately, governments, the UN, OCED, and other international organizations and the Red Cross movement have been planning for the changes. They understand that to do the job of stabilizing and improving the global political/economic map requires preparation and coordination. Sometimes work must be done between governments that don't like each other, also with international organizations. This book argues, like Rio, that to assemble the stool of stability, one leg must be the NGO world. Thus, in keeping with Rio, this book is primarily for the community[7] of humanitarian NGO's (nonprofit nongovernmental bodies) that deal with those uncertainties, often at risk to their lives. In other words, this book is both an operational textbook and a manifesto for action.

## 1.4 NGO Independence

NGOs have not always been independent of governments; today to be accredited by the UN, that's a legal requirement, though true independence is a question of degree; donors demand results. Some like the Carter Center are led by former world leaders and are very influential, which was the pre-World War II model. Often NGOs are single issue and more often than not small and run by local leaders. Those small NGOs are needed in the world of diplomacy.

> **Example of a Major International NGO: Doctors without Borders MSF –** ***Medecins Sans Frontieres*****:** " Negotiation and diplomacy are at every level in MSF to support the operations. It goes from the person responsible on the ground for a project negotiating with local authorities, to the head of mission negotiating with national authorities in particular

[7] "Community" in this context is defined as anyone associated with a broad political or civil rights movement, such as the humanitarian movement, from private donors and volunteers to staffs in NGOs, private corporations, academic institutions, government agencies, or international organizations.

the Ministry of Health, to the headquarters, including the representation team of the IO negotiating with governments, embassies, international organizations and in multilateral platforms. All those negotiations are done with the aim to ensure a safe, independent and indiscriminate access to people in need, to deliver quality healthcare. For MSF negotiations involve providing impartial assistance in and raise awareness of the violence of war, responding to the consequences of the neglected public health problems or caring for populations who have been deliberately excluded from social and healthcare systems.

MSF is a worldwide movement of 23 associations that manages projects in more sixty countries. It is also composed of 5 operational sections that are directly managing operations on the ground, with the financial and human resource support of the other sections. An international office has been set up to create platforms for the meeting, dialogue, collaboration and coordination of operations among the branches as well as to defend and promote the common interests of its members (Tronc 2012).

Every year MSF saves over 10 million people from death and abject misery.

## 1.5 What Is Humanitarian?

What makes an NGO "humanitarian" is debated; the authors include any which "aim to protect people, their rights, cultural artifacts and livestock, from war and national phenomena, or wish to advance sustainable economies, negotiate agreements to protect internally displaced persons or refugees, or craft national or international standards that save lives and actually reduce the risks of disasters and conflicts, whether with local or national governments, the UN, the International Red Cross and Red Crescent Movement, or international organizations. These NGOs might also be involved in nation building, advising transitional societies on economic development, spreading anti-viral medicines, etc. They might be large, international NGOs or more likely might a small NGO trying to help a local community," as was done in the great Galveston disaster of 1900 (Lester 1900). The diplomacy NGOs need to use is an art form and a science, as well as a tool for fostering the principles and rights embodied in the Humanitarian Charter (McConnan 2000)[8] (McConnan, *The Sphere Project* 1998).

## 1.6 A Model for NGO Diplomacy

This book introduces relevant tools of diplomacy, as well as case studies drawn from government, IO, and international NGO experiences, such as the famous Tampere Convention on the Provision of Emergency Telecommunications, which

[8]The Humanitarian Charter binds humanitarian agencies to basic principles of care and minimum standards, which when taken together define the level of service any human should receive in an emergency. The principles are (1) the right to life with dignity, (2) the distinction between combatants and noncombatants, and (3) the principle of non-refoulement (not returning a refugee to a place of harm).

NGOs helped develop. The Convention also provided P&I's (privileges and immunities) to NGOs under certain circumstances. There is also a mix of broad theory, such as a discussion on failed nation states, and practical advice such as on how to manage daily life at an international conference. Case studies are also provided on contemporary situations like dealing with armed non-state actors and on historical events like the formation of the League of Nations; they all illustrate what has failed and succeeded. The case studies deal with both NGOs and governments; the lessons are always valid for NGO diplomats or any of the major groups under Agenda 21. Various types of agreements are discussed that even a local NGO might achieve, e.g., treaties and memoranda of understanding, with their pros and cons. In some cases, the tools are delegation management concepts so that an NGO delegation can be as effective as the delegation of a world-class government. Protocol is an essential tool, so the student will learn how best to address an ambassador or minister. International conferences and the use of the media are also dealt with, so too where to find funds. A critical tool for any diplomat is intelligence and knowledge management, which are explored in depth in their own chapters, using real projects as examples, like ReliefWeb,[9] the UN's premier disaster response site and a project that emerged in part from the NGO experience in Rwanda, and PreventionWeb,[10] which deals with preventing crises. Underlying all of this is the concept of cross-NGO coordination, which is the norm in humanitarian crises, as well as development (Currion and Hedlund 2011, January ).

Crafting a memo, treaties, resolutions, and conventions among ambassadors and ministers in the United Nations is a main focus because they require negotiation; the work of diplomacy encompasses far more than negotiating an instrument. What if an NGO specializes in economic development and wants to help a nation build a sustainable import/export formula? Potentially, that might require negotiating with many different ministries, those of the nation in question and its trading partners. In addition, there is the international banking community like the World Bank Group, international organizations like the UN Development Program, and organs of the United Nations like the General Assembly, the later which might be used to draw attention to a development need or to set regional standards that avoid predatory practices. This idea of avoiding predators is crucial. Economic historians describe Albania in the 1930s as a victim of Italian investments aimed at creating "La Quinta Sponda D'Italia," the Fifth Coastline of Italy. A bit earlier, Firestone Rubber did the

[9]ReliefWeb.int. This is the UN's main source for timely, reliable, and relevant humanitarian information and analysis. The staff (Kobe, Geneva, and New York) scans the websites of international and nongovernmental organizations, governments, research institutions, and the media for news, reports, press releases, appeals, policy documents, analysis, and maps related to humanitarian emergencies worldwide. This ensures the most relevant content is available on ReliefWeb or delivered through a personal channel. They also produce maps and infographics to illustrate and explain humanitarian crises.

[10]PreventionWeb serves the information needs of the disaster risk reduction community, including the development of information exchange tools to facilitate collaboration. Information regarding the design and development of the project together with background documentation can be accessed here along with some services that have been put in place.

same to Liberia in 1925 when, with US agreement, it gained a concession of one million acres in order to raise a quarter million tons of rubber, more than half the world's production at the time.

Though the world is different in the second millennium, fewer invasions and fewer colonial problems, the same kind of predatory abuse could happen in a country like Somaliland and might happen in post-revolutionary Zimbabwe, North Korea, Byelorussia, Iran, or Syria. The Firestone deal essentially made Liberia a corporate colony and child labor camp, and that particular issue is still a problem (Moon 1939, pp. 109–110). Somaliland was in the past nothing more to the British Empire than a vehicle to export camels to British Yemen. For Somaliland to prosper, it needs an export market for its livestock, as well as a market for tourists. Were it to build highways or rail links between Ethiopia and its port, it could also be a major trade facilitator. But its past threatens its future (Kahin 2010). The nation is desperately poor, and the security situation in greater Somalia is terrible. Somaliland could become a wealthy nation; it is capable of reversing the impact of past abuses. However, because of its poverty, it must rely on sympathetic donors and investors, many of whom are governments and multinational corporations like the mineral extraction industry. Traditionally, negotiations to solve these problems are done by governments, but because they usually have their own strategic interests, NGOs can be an effective alternative. But to be effective they should master the techniques of negotiation and protocol discussed in this book, from the sequential tactic to other efforts.

### *1.6.1 Recommendations: Not Rules Cast in Stone*

This book provides a model; nothing is cast in stone. The "recommendations" are instead practical guidelines based on the experience of many people; each organization or private society must choose its own path based on its own resources, individual philosophy, and local legal constraints.

## 1.7 Historical Precedent

Though published nearly a century ago, a paper from 1922 is a great place to show why diplomacy should be a tool in any NGO's kit of skill sets. At the age of 77, elder statesman and Nobel Prize winner Elihu Root wrote to the American people at a time when most citizens in his country had little interest in diplomacy. It was also 2 years after the US Senate rejected Woodrow Wilson's League of Nations. Former Secretary of State Root understood better than most that a new age had been born from the womb of the Great War, and America was responsible for the baby's success. This meant Americans had to learn the business of diplomacy, especially multilateral diplomacy (Root, *A Requisite for the Success of Popular Diplomacy* 1922, September). Root had an action plan aimed at energizing America to get behind strong governmentally led diplomacy, which he was right to demand. If diplomacy had been more effective or the League of Nations better designed and supported, perhaps World War II could have been avoided. The irony is that some of the most interesting diplomacy from this early part of the century came not from governments but from NGOs. Today, humanitarian development NGOs and many other kinds are increasingly the valued lifeline between abject penury and sustainable development and between starvation[11] and survival. That is certainly true in Somalia in 2012 and was true in 2008 in Burma (Myanmar) when NGOs responded to Cyclone Nargis. Many NGOs from a broad spectrum of disciplines, from animal welfare to nursing, sat in very constructive, professionally managed NGO-led meetings in Bangkok, tried to figure out the best way to save a nation that had almost overnight turned from a rice exporter to an importer. At the same table were UN officials and government diplomats working as full partners. That is more typical than unusual.

The value of NGOs was certainly known in Root's time, especially the exploits of the Red Cross movement; though humanitarian assistance was not a new concept, it was still novel for NGOs to engage in multilateral diplomacy when attempting to create and manage massive relief efforts. The modern origins of this kind of diplomacy, what many NGOs do today, are often traced to Herbert Hoover who, 8 years before the famous journal article, was a self-made financial success living in London. To save the civilians of Belgium from starvation, Hoover crossed the North Sea into Germany over 40 times to negotiate permission to conduct relief. He did that as a private citizen, not a government diplomat, and undertook so many humanitarian efforts that it has often been said he saved more lives than any single person in world history.

When war broke out on the European continent, Hoover and other humanitarians were asked by the US Embassy in London to form an NGO to assist Americans fleeing advancing German forces.[12] They serviced over 100,000 Americans, doing what consular services do today; then Belgium fell. Before the collapse, Belgium had been a food exporter, but the occupation caused starvation. Whereas the Red Cross established by Henry Dunant in the nineteenth century was focused on prisoners of war, for which it rightly received the Nobel Prize, Hoover established on his own initiative one of the first true international humanitarian relief NGOs (the first according to some experts) in order to deal with the civilian side of conflict.[13]

[11] Unfortunately, the ICC (International Criminal Court) only defines intentional starvation in warfare as a crime when conducted in armed conflicts. However, the UN Security Council expanded the concept to include internal conflicts when it condemned the intentional starvation of Somali civilians (S/RES/792, 1992).

[12] Hoover said he was asked by his government to help, but Robert Skinner, the US Consul General in London at the time, where Hoover lived as wealthy mining engineer, recalls that Hoover actually volunteered, needing no request to come to aid of his stranded countrymen.

[13] The International Red Cross and Red Crescent Movement is now the world's largest private relief network for civilians who are victim to any form of disaster and pioneered legal protections for civilians as a result of armed conflict. Its members are not NGOs, for they are by international and national law "auxiliaries to the public authorities in the humanitarian field," but they operate under conditions similar to NGOs in many countries. The international institutions, ICRC and IFRC, are recognized as international organizations by the UN and many governments.

**Fig. 1.2** 1925. Nansen tests food at refugee camp (Courtesy of National Library, Oslo, Norway)

This NGO became known as the CRB (Committee for the Relief of Belgium) which was steadfastly neutral in the conflict and thus was able to provide relief to over nine million starving Belgian and French civilians. It also raised funds, negotiated "treaties," and coerced governments into action.

Unlike now when many NGOs receive large donations from national authorities, Hoover did not (Chap. 17). There was no OFDA (Office of Foreign Disaster Assistance) or any similar concept. So Hoover developed a multimodal fund-raising strategy, and over the course of 4 years negotiated with governmental diplomats, politicians, businessmen, and private citizens to raise the funds and establish the logistical means to feed Belgium. He actually raised over $1 billion in today's currency, provided over 5 million tons of food, and fed more than 9 million victims of war. Hoover's administrative overhead would be also the envy of any of contemporary NGO—less than 1 %. To understand the difficulty of his task, remember that Hoover did this in a war zone. The CRB also had a flag, his ships navigated subpacks, and his NGO negotiated treaties, and Hoover had diplomatic immunity, the latter nearly impossible for an NGO to achieve today. In other words, the new century had just begun and the use of diplomacy by NGOs other than the International Red Cross and Red Crescent Movement to save lives had been demonstrated (Fig. 1.2).

Despite his "later failures" as president, Hoover was a remarkable man who continued after the war to organize the relief of millions of Europeans and as Secretary of Commerce used government resources to save millions of Russians from starvation in the winter of 1921, 1 year before Root's article. He also showed that NGO coalition-diplomacy could operate effectively on a large geographic scale, in his case by both NGOs and governments working as a team. Between 1914 and 1923, Hoover's various private and government efforts saved tens of millions of lives and raised over 50 billion dollars in today's currency, gaining him the nickname of the "Great Humanitarian."

Though he did save millions abroad, Hoover is often attacked because at the advent of the great depression (a term Hoover invented), he could not intellectually break from the common practice of public self-reliance and offer quick, massive, and urgently needed government support to his own citizens. His successes and his failures however are very much a useful beginning for this book, just as his diplomacy was a useful opening for NGOs on the world stage. Governments can't do everything, sometimes they need NGOs. Conversely, sometimes NGOs need governments, for example, in the gathering and analysis of space-based data so critical to effective operations, exemplified by the chapter,[14] or the logistical support of military airlift as was done in Myanmar by the US Air Force, which flew in feed for livestock supplied by the World Society for the Protection of Animals (WSPA). Had that not been done, cattle would have died. Cattle are the tractors of Myanmar and bring in the rice. If they had died, there would have been widespread human starvation.

## 1.8 Dr. Fridtjof Nansen

Our story on NGO diplomacy began by using Herbert Hoover, an American businessman who created an NGO and became an example of a great humanitarianism. However, by no means is humanitarian diplomacy and advocacy an American domain. Humanitarianism is an international story with heroes from all countries. Another example from Hoover's time that still influences us today is that of Dr. Fridtjof Nansen,[15] a famous Norwegian arctic explorer, diplomat, and oceanographer. Nansen was also one of the fathers of modern Norway and helped negotiate his country's independence from Sweden. Unlike Hoover, he projected himself as a neutral when it came to international crises and was willing to work with any government or political system. As a result, he in many ways projected what the author's believe should be the perspective of NGO leaders. He used those qualities to great advantage as the first High Commissioner for Refugees, qualities that led him to be

[14]After the UNISPACE III conference (Vienna, Austria), July 1999, the European and French space agencies (ESA and CNES) initiated the International Charter "Space and Major Disasters", with the Canadian Space Agency (CSA) signing the Charter on 20 October 2000. Its origins, at least in part, lie with GDIN (the Global Disaster Information Network), which was initiated by Vice President Al Gore and his National Security Adviser, Leon Fuerth. "The International Charter aims at providing a unified system of space data acquisition and delivery to those affected by natural or man-made disasters through Authorized Users. Each member agency has committed resources to support the provisions of the Charter and thus is helping to mitigate the effects of disasters on human life and property." This was a similar dream by some GDIN members.

[15]The authors wish to thank the staff of the Nansen Institute and Associate Professor Carl Emil Vogt, University of Oslo, for their assistance on researching Dr. Fridtjof Nansen.

awarded the Nobel Prize for Peace. His office on Refugees, founded after Nansen's death to his honor, would also win the Nobel Prize.[16]

One of Nansen's first great acts was to develop a plan to repatriate prisoners of war after World War I. The Red Cross Committee took the initiative and they involved the League of Nations. The Secretariat of the League (it seems Philip Noel Baker personally[17]) contacted Nansen and wanted him to take care of it. When Nansen stepped in as the League of Nations High Commissioner, the Red Cross Committee had already negotiated a deal between Soviet Russia and Germany concerning the repatriation. Nansen and the League of Nations provided the political support needed, money (from Britain mostly), and ships (mostly confiscated German ships released by the British). Though Nansen did not start the initiative, he was a very important intermediary between the Soviet government and the West. He also had important contacts in British politics and was an effective leader in the humanitarian circles built around the League of Nations and the Red Cross Committee. Nansen's efforts repatriated over 427,000 prisoners from both sides of the conflict.[18] No prejudice was demonstrated based on nationality.

One exploit which brought Nansen into philosophical tension and partnership with Hoover was the rescue of starving millions after the war, especially during the Povolzhye famine in 1921–1923. It was the worst famine in Russian history and on the heels of a turbulent revolution which set the Western world politically against socialism.[19] The Soviet Union was then essentially a failed nation state struggling for sustainability. Doctors starved while treating armies of victims and former

---

[16] 1925 Photo of Nansen is at a summer camp in Kumajri, Armenia, for orphans run by an American NGO known as Near East Relief, organized in response to "the Armenian Genocide" at the urging of Ambassador Henry Morgenthau, Sr. in Constantinople. Their desire was to prevent the extinction of the Armenian people. Though an NGO in the sense that it was a nonprofit entity, it was created with the advice and support of the U.S. Department of State and President Woodrow Wilson and continued operations up to 1930. The NGO was credited with supporting 132,000 Armenian orphans from Tbilisi and Yerevan to Constantinople, Beirut, Damascus, and Jerusalem. The man to the right in the dark suit is Dr. Joseph Beach, Director of Near East Relief in the Caucasus; the photographer is unknown. Photo was provided courtesy of the Norwegian National Library. Reference email 6/4/2012 from Claes Lykke Ragner, Head of Administration and Information Fridtjof Nansen Institute, Norway.

[17] Noel-Baker helped create and manage the League of Nations and participated in the Paris Conference. He was principal secretary to Lord Robert Cecil who drafted the covenant, held senior posts at the League, and was an adviser to Fridtjof Nansen in his prisoner-of-war and refugee work

[18] The prisoners concerned were Russians in German camps (Russians, i.e., from the Tsarist Army of different nationalities) and on the other hand Austro–Hungarians (from the former Austro–Hungarian Empire of different nationalities) and in somewhat smaller numbers Germans (from the former German Empire). A small number of prisoners and civil internees were of other nationalities.

[19] It was estimated that upon the completion of World War I, over 160 million people were suffering from famine throughout allied and occupied territories (House and Seymour, *What Really Happened at Paris*, 1921).

aristocratic women washed train stations. The famine not only placed at stake the lives of millions but also the very survival of the revolution. After the armistice Hoover become head of the American Relief Administration, a government agency which would prove to be invaluable in saving Russian lives, so in the spring of 1919, Hoover and Nansen met about a joint effort to provide relief to the Russian civilians (Nansen 1923, p. 23).

Hoover had a genuine humanitarian interest in saving Russians; by then he was also a government man, and Washington also had an interest in undermining the communists, so the policy of relief could be seen as part of a partisan strategy. Nansen took the opposite approach; regardless of who ran the Soviet Union, the priority was to save lives, even if the repressive regime survived. He then used personal diplomacy to convince Wilson and the leaders of France, the UK, and Italy to support a food relief effort. The allies however envisaged a cessation of military operations, making movement of relief supplies easier. Though it sounded an innocent-enough and common-sense requirement, the open disquiet of the allies with Socialism meant that in the minds of the Soviets they would have to leave themselves open to attack by monarchist forces and others trying to overturn the revolution (Nansen 1923, pp. 28–33).

Regardless of what we might think of the barbaric violence of the Soviets, the government had an operational reason to be nervous; it was "assailed by the armies of Admiral Kolchak in the East, General Miller in the North, and Generals Denikin and Krasnov in the South; and by Estonians, Czechs, Finns, Germans, Latvians, Lithuanians and Poles, as well as nationalist movements in Ukraine and the Caucasus. British, French and Americans had also intervened to support the opponents of the Bolshevik regime" (Breen 1994). One is reminded of the violence in 2007 which forced 200,000 to flee the Somali capital of Mogadishu, walking with little water and no food across great expanses of desert in search of safety for their children. Millions of dollars of aid was available for assistance but the situation was too unstable for relief workers, resulting in many diplomats calling for a ceasefire, like German Foreign Minister Frank-Walter Steinmeier (German Foreign Ministry 2007). The point made to the combatants was that the safety of unarmed civilians should be more important than their political struggle.

Somalia was different than Russia in 1920 of course, though the rebels in Somalia in 2007 surely feared foreign intervention and the older conflict represented the classical split that often occurs between government and NGO or IO assistance and why some NGOs refuse to receive government funding. There was no way to force the Soviets to cease hostilities without a major expeditionary force, which no one wanted to do (any more than a few generations later was their appetite for an invasion of Somalia). Fortunately, diplomacy in 2007 was more successful. Meaning, no disrespect to Mr. Hoover, whose great works are admired, relief provided by humanitarian NGOs and international organizations to victims of a flood, epidemic, or conflict should not be part of a strategy to destroy a government, no matter how repressive—though it is totally appropriate as a separate political action for NGOs and international organizations to work against repression, as many did regarding Syria in 2012.[20] In addition, it is also totally appropriate for donors to demand accountability and measures to prevent the diversion of assistance to armed elements.

Just like Hoover, Nansen regularly negotiated with government leaders. While he never negotiated directly or even met Lenin, he interacted indirectly at the highest levels. For example, he worked with the official responsible for the prisoners of war, Aleksandr Ejduk; the Peoples Commissar for Foreign Affairs Georgij Chicherin; and Chicherin's deputy Maksim Litvinov. In addition, he met with top Bolsheviks like Felix Dzerzhinsky and Leo Trotsky. Unfortunately, although Nansen had successes in this venture, he couldn't acquire enough capital.

Despite some funding issues, on August 15, 1921, Nansen was asked at a conference of the IFRC (International Federation of Red Cross and Red Crescent Societies) to be High Commissioner for the new International Committee for Russian Relief (ICRR). Hoover's American Relief Administration also participated in the conference, as did NGOs like the American Friends Service Committee and the International Save the Children (UISE), supported by the British Save the Children Fund. The Americans reportedly felt Nansen was naïve over his approach to the Soviets. That was an error. A complete read of Nansen's *Russia and Peace* depicts a man sensitive to the political abuses that led to the Bolshevik Revolution but with a distain for the economic theories of the revolution's master. In any event, the Americans and British had the funds to do the job and Nansen was able to reach an accommodation with the regime requiring complete control of the relief effort to avoid diversion. Starvation was averted for millions. This also points to another problem in relief operations. They require money, and money often does grease the wheels of diplomacy (Fig. 1.3).[21]

Another famous Nansen achievement with an impact on today's world was the resettlement of White Russians who fled Bolshevik Russia and then the resettlement of stateless civilians until World War II. The Red Cross helped the White Russians but was overwhelmed by the number of refugees, so Nansen stepped in; many displaced were also stateless and thus without passports, so he devised the Nansen passport in 1922, versions of which are still in use today. This was started on July 5, 1922, by arrangement with 16 member governments of the League of Nations. Nansen designed the passport, which was then agreed to by the Council of the

[20] A caution is worth mentioning. How will the affected government be able to distinguish one kind of NGO from another? Will they consider NGOs working for political overthrow or reform as legitimate military targets or criminals? Or will political activities be permitted? These are questions the Study Team must examine. In Canada, it is illegal to raise funds for charitable organizations that also have a terrorist branch. If the affected government or one of its allies declares the NGO a terrorist body, will that impact it's legal standing back home? The Study Team must also examine the question from these additional angles.

[21] December 1921 photo was personally taken by Fridtjof Nansen in order to document the horrors of the famine. Photo is courtesy of Norwegian National Library, per email from Claes Lykke Ragner, Head of Administration and Information, Fridtjof Nansen Institute.

**Fig. 1.3** Three children died of hunger, Russia, December 1921 (Photo by Fridtjof Nansen), (Courtesy of National Library, Oslo, Norway)

League of Nations on July 20. The states then recognized the passport, with Britain and France among the first. By 1942 more than 52 countries recognized the documents, which were issued by the Red Cross and were the first international refugee travel documents. About 450,000 Nansen passports allowed stateless persons to travel and live normally. Following the war, citizenship laws in many nations made it hard for refugees, including millions of ethnic minorities, to become citizens; the Nansen travel documents became a real boon. Thanks to Nansen's influence, he was also able to convince the newly formed ILO (International Labour Office) to help these unfortunates find work.

Nansen continued his humanitarianism, such as saving thousands of Greek refugees on the Smyrna coast, pushed there in the postwar resettlement of Turkey. He organized a comprehensive refugee program to save these people, with the backing of the League, and by 1935 the Nansen International Office for Refugees at Geneva was offering help to a million refugees, including many who fled the Saar when it was returned to Nazi Germany. The work then continued to 1938 to serve Jews and other victims of Nazi oppression. Today, the Nansen Medal is the highest award conferred for distinguished service to refugees by the UN High Commissioner for Refugees. The legacy of Mr. Nansen is seen today as the international community continues to face refugee and internally displaced person crises such as the self-inflicted destruction of Yugoslavia which produced millions of refugees and internally displaced. As this book is written, thousands of refugees sit in camps across the Syrian border, hiding from the indiscriminate bombing of their cities. How they are treated without recourse to their political party or affiliation is a legacy of Nansen and his partner NGOs, the Red Cross Movement and the League of Nations.

Going deeply into the intrigue and politics of relief relative to Russia would warrant a different book, but even just scratching the surface provides lessons for humanitarian NGOs. The humanitarian NGO community must be willing to partner across international boundaries and with any useful entity that will operate in good faith, to set aside "small politics" in the interest of the greater welfare of people. In other words, as the founders of Save the Children believed, saving innocent civilians trumps the risk of appearing to support repressive regimes. A second premise is that precisely because partners often come into an emergency or development scene from different political perspectives, diplomacy is the glue that forms effective partnerships and builds bridges of common interests for cooperation. The effort of diplomacy is constant, not static. NGOs need to choose their partners, but it is rarely a good idea to go it alone. It is also important to partner outside one's own community.

This doesn't mean that all relief efforts need to be impartial. UNSC/Resolution 1401 linked humanitarian assistance to regime change and national building in Afghanistan. That made NGOs which supported the Resolution potential targets of the Taliban; partiality or its appearance is dangerous. However, despite MSF being opposed to linkage and valiantly trying to provide neutral assistance through a hospital, some staff members were murdered in June 2004. Similarly, ICRC staff members (also politically neutral) were murdered in the Eastern Democratic Republic of the Congo in April 2001.

# Chapter 2
# A Practical Model for Diplomacy and Negotiation: Steps 1–3—The Preliminary Stage

**Extract** Chapters 2 and 3 propose a specific model for NGOs to consider when engaged in diplomacy. Steps 1 through 3 in Chap. 2 focus on the pre-negotiation period when proposals for negotiation are considered. Of special attention are the concepts of the study group and the decision memo. The former is a team that examines whether a diplomatic initiative is feasible and may present a plan of action. The latter is a tool for more senior decision makers to examine options presented by the Study Team, as well as the risks and potential rewards of success.

## 2.1 Introduction to the Model: Three Phases

There are three phases to any negotiation: (a) pre-negotiation, (b) actual negotiations, and (c) post-negotiation or implementation. Chapters 2 and 3 cover a practical model for these activities. Chapter 2 covers pre-negotiation work and the process of deciding to engage in a negotiation. Chapter 3 covers the negotiation process, with recommendations on the formation of a delegation, as well as strategy and tactics. This chapter also includes thoughts on how various international instruments like declarations can be of value to NGOs. Chapter 4 covers the post-negotiation period, which often means finding ways of implementing an agreement or, in the case of an unsuccessful negotiation, rethinking the process. This model also contains a structured series of steps across the chapters to manage the phases, each of which involves many players, especially the "team leader" and the "chief negotiator." In this book they are different people because the functions are different, though circumstances could justify combining them; however, regardless of the circumstances, keep in mind that the roles are different, even if done by a single official (Fig. 2.1).

L.W. Roeder, Jr. and A. Simard, *Diplomacy and Negotiation for Humanitarian NGOs*, Humanitarian Solutions in the 21st Century, DOI 10.1007/978-1-4614-7113-4_2,

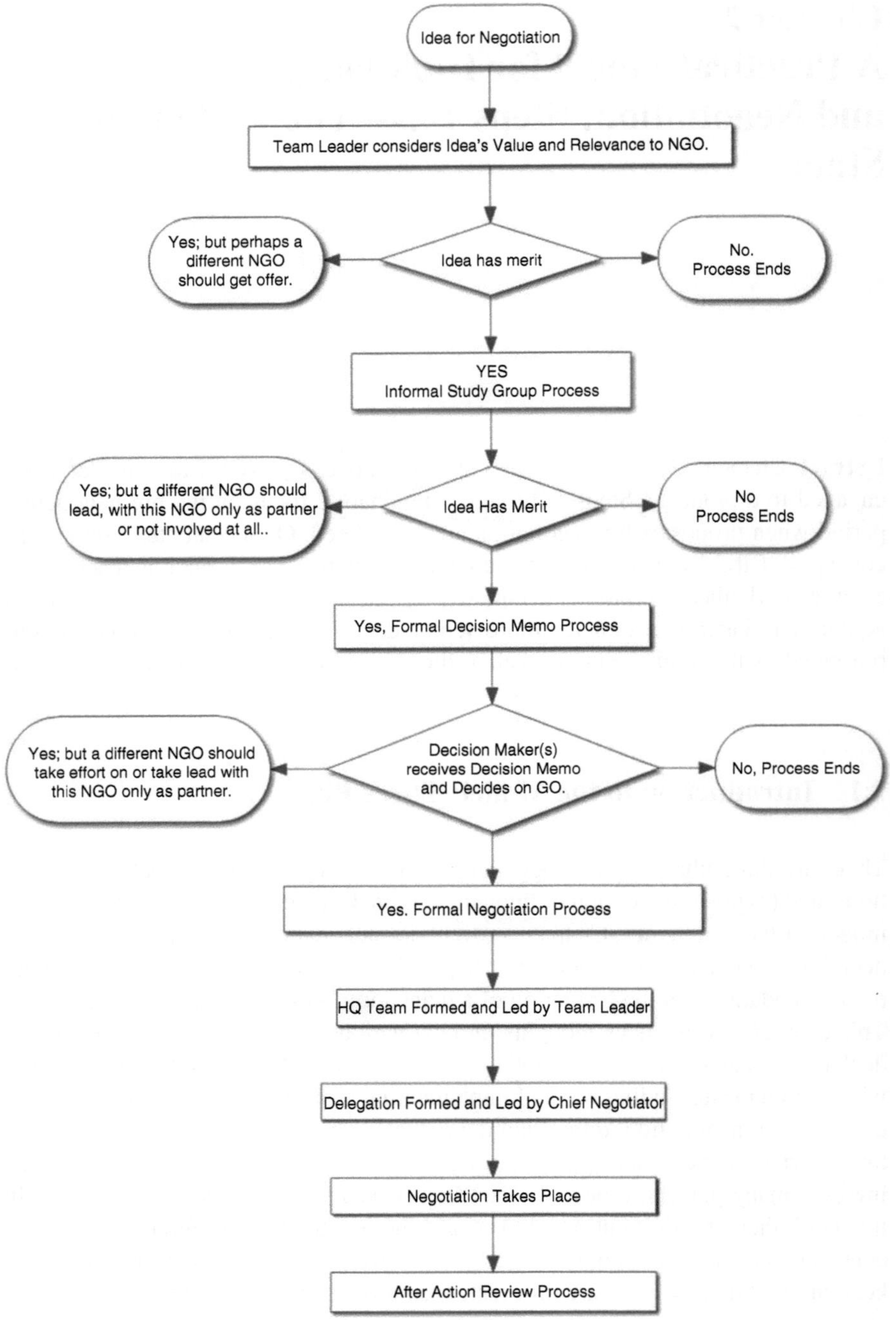


**Fig. 2.1** Model for managing new ideas

This book concentrates on how NGOs of any size and the Major Groups described in the UN's Agenda 21[1] strategy can use diplomacy to create strategic change, as well as gain agreement on important tactical issues. **We want to emphasize that any NGO of any size should be able to use our techniques, though those with fewer resources and smaller staffs may need to operate in coalitions. Coalitions are not a sign of weakness. They actually can build a stronger program by combining the relative strengths of many players, so large or small; we recommend all NGOs consider them.**

The approach we suggest also requires engaging in what are known as Track Two and Multi-Track diplomacy techniques (see Sect. 7.2). One expert with extensive experience in the Red Cross and the European Commission (ECHO) said "for many humanitarian workers diplomacy comes second to humanitarian principles and that agencies are having difficulties finding the correct balance between the two." The authors believe that the two concepts are actually not contradictory and can be done in balance. It is certainly also true that diplomacy is often uncertain and can be very frustrating. There is no magic pill, but NGOs who engage in true diplomacy have the opportunity to influence true behavioral change. What we propose is a model to consider accomplishing that goal.

Many NGOs specialize in lobbying, frequently an effective tool for change. One of the most famous and interesting such NGOs was WSP (Women Strike For Peace), which in November 1961 mobilized 50,000 women to enter the streets of America in order to strike against nuclear proliferation and to encourage effective peace negotiations between the Soviet Union and the United States. The strike was unprecedented and showered a public light on the national security risk to children from milk polluted by above-ground nuclear tests (Swerdlow 1993). Although such activism is truly heroic and needed, formal negotiations are also needed to build on attitudinal changes caused by lobbying and to achieve better local, national, and international rules, standards, and penalties. Those achievements could put an end to nuclear proliferation policies which can unintentionally harm the environment or lead to nuclear holocaust. Negotiations with political and administrative leaders can also put a stop to intentional harm, such as child abuse, solitary confinement of prisoners, gender abuse,[2] and torture, or establish minimum income levels and standards for treating refugees. In the conservation arena, intentional harm is an issue requiring negotiations to end specific practices like whale hunting, bear baying, and cock fighting. In the cultural arena, more effective rules and standards of care could deter abuse of historically and culturally important artifacts like the famous Buddhas of Bamiyan بت های بامیان, two monumental statues carved out of mountainsides in the sixth century AD in Afghanistan and later blasted by Taliban tanks. Historical artifacts must be protected from looting (Cuno 2008), an important humanitarian

[1] Agenda 21 is "a comprehensive UN plan of action to be taken globally, nationally, and locally by organizations of the United Nations System, governments, and major Groups (including NGOs) in every area in which human impacts on the environment" (DESA 2009).

[2] In 2012 one of the emerging gender abuse issues has to do with prejudice against transgender women, a scientific condition that is still poorly understood by many humanitarian professionals.

issue because this activity helps us retain the definition of who we are as a people. In other words, lobbying and diplomacy are partner tools. In a coordinated humanitarian strategy aimed at fostering sustainable societies, each partner may have a slightly or even dramatically different mandate but should be willing to work collaboratively for a common goal. In that vein, the best way to preserve fragile societies is to not just look at the preservation of people as biological entities. The book takes the position that the entire environment must also be protected; in addition to lobbying, that requires actual diplomacy between nonprofits and governments, as well as international organizations. This is one of the reasons that we encourage the use of NGO coalitions. They add monetary and staff resources. They also build a strong political fabric and encourage fresh thinking.

The handling of livestock in emergencies provides an excellent example for a coordinated humanitarian strategy, in this case linking humanitarian and animal welfare NGOs, UN agencies, and national authorities. Burma uses cattle instead of tractors to harvest rice, so when Cyclone Nargis struck in 2008, it left a path of destruction across the country and seriously threatened the rice crop, especially when thousands of cattle were wounded. One of the coauthors worked on relief coordination out of Bangkok supporting veterinary teams sent to Burma, including veterinarians from New Zealand, Australia, and Asia, which worked in partnership with the UN's Food and Agriculture Organization (FAO) and local government officials. If the cattle's condition had been left unchecked, the people would have starved and Burma could have become a net importer of rice instead of keeping its traditional role of net exporter. That required animal welfare experts working alongside doctors, nurses, and other humanitarian professionals. In some countries like Albania in 1991[3] and Somaliland in 2012, over 80 % of personal income came from livestock. Indeed, of the billion poorest people in the world, over 800,000 totally depend on livestock for a living. In other words, protecting livestock is a tool for protecting the human economy; yet often animals are at risk, not so much out of neglect but due to the moral conflict of balancing human and animal needs. Burma shows that a balanced, holistic approach is needed for humanitarian development. To develop that strategy, NGOs from traditional humanitarian sectors like public health and gender protection sat in meetings with animal welfare experts in Bangkok and developed a common plan of action. They recognized that modern relief operations often require going beyond the protection of the human body. They must include the entire human economy and culture "as a system." The same point could be made for integrating the protection of historical monuments, centers of learning and record keeping, places of worship, industrial centers, etc. Protection of people in crisis also has to be about more than just protecting the body from rape or a country from plunder. *It must be about the protection of the wholeness of a civilization.*

**Gaining agreement that an NGO will be part of the overall strategy requires defining permitted work, the territory in which it is done and protections provided NGOs doing the work. Doing that kind of negotiation is <u>diplomacy</u>, not lobbying.**

[3] When Roeder went to Albania during the fall of communism, he examined the quality of labor so that proposals could be made to improve the quality of life that did not require jobs to which Albanians could not apply.

**Case Study of a Coalition: Solitary Confinement in 2010**

The treatment of prisoners, be they prisoners of war, political prisoners, or criminals, has long been an area of NGO concern, e.g., by the John Howard Society. In January 2010 in the US state of Maine, the American Civil Liberties Union tried to end the practice of solitary confinement, but their mandate was broader, so they reached out to the National Religious Campaign Against Torture in Washington DC, knowing that the NRCAT had recently included solitary confinement in US prisons. NRCAT itself gets involved in different states for a variety of reasons, sometimes because there are already legislative efforts underway that they want to support or sometimes the NRCAT has a strong membership presence in a particular state and they ask them to take the lead in starting something if someone else like the ACLU already engaged.

In Maine, legislative advocacy[4] had already originated with the ACLU of Maine (the ACLU headquarters has a National Prison Project which advises the state affiliate offices—so many of the state ACLUs have taken an interest in this issue). The ACLU reached out to NRCAT for help, which in turn activated the Maine Council of Churches to engage the Maine religious community. There has also been a long-time Maine Prisoners Advocacy Coalition made up of prisoner family members, former prisoners, and other prison rights advocates in Maine, and they certainly have played a large role. Psychology and psychiatrist organizations also got involved, which was very powerful.[5] Although this is a domestic example of a coalition of allies, it could just as easily have been anywhere in the world on a regional or broader issue. Following the success in Maine, NRCAT is replicating its work in California, Colorado, Illinois, New Jersey, New York, Oregon, Pennsylvania, Texas, and Virginia.

## 2.2 Steps to Success and Managing Costs

To make the kind of changes we propose, bilateral negotiations (NGO to government, NGO to UN, etc.) will be needed, which can be tough. Multilateral ones are the most difficult; yet they are often the most needed for the NGO community. That's because they can change the status quo across borders and regions. Negotiations might consist of initiatives conducted in the United Nations General

[4]Although the bill did not pass, the immense momentum that people of faith and other advocates initiated against solitary confinement did pay off. The legislature required the Maine Department of Corrections to review its use of isolation and report its findings. Accordingly, the department prepared a report that listed many recommendations to improve due process and other policies related to the placement of prisoners in solitary confinement. Prompted by those recommendations, the newly appointed department Commissioner, Joseph Ponte, cut the number of prisoners held in solitary confinement by over 70 % in 2011.

[5]The diverse coalition of organizations included the NRCAT, the Maine Council of Churches (MCC), the Catholic Diocese of Portland, and other organizations like Maine Civil Liberties Union, the Maine Association of Psychiatric Physicians, Portland NAACP, Maine Prisoner Advocacy Coalition, and the Maine Psychological Association.

Assembly (UNGA) to insert language an NGO cares about in a resolution to end torture or efforts in regional bodies like the UN Economic Commission for Africa (ESA), based in Addis Ababa. Each effort will involve a mix of governments, international organizations, other NGOs and industries, etc. These negotiations might even be done through a series of bilateral discussions that lead to large-scale negotiations in a special conference such as the one that led to the ban on land mines. Our proposed model can help any NGO of any size do those kinds of negotiations.

### *2.2.1 Step One: Is the Initiative Worthwhile and Feasible?*

At the start, most diplomacy concepts lack cohesion. They are "ideas" and potential for constructive change, so they often need to be distilled and practicality challenged. To help, a team leader knowledgeable about his or her NGO's priorities and limits should ask, "Is the concept worthwhile from a policy point of view and is it practical?" Most ideas will be worthwhile; what about the second part?

To answer the question, the team leader should insist that the strategic aim of the proposed negotiation be defined as narrowly as possible and fall naturally within his or her portfolio, e.g., shelters for disaster victims, abused women, flood relief, torture, and protecting historic sites. The goal should be worthwhile from a policy angle, perhaps to end all rape, but is the goal practical? Can one negotiation achieve the goal on a global scale or even create a practical mechanism to do the same? Perhaps a more manageable goal would be to have a regional or provincial limit. Some have accused the negotiators who created the League of Nations and the UN as failing. Each did generate an international organization, but neither ended war. While that's true, remember that the goal wasn't to instantly end war. It was to create a workable structure to reduce conflict, eventually ending war. Looking though that prism of gradual elimination, even though we still see conflict, perhaps the negotiations succeeded at least regarding global conflict. Only the future can tell if all war can be eliminated.

Assuming the goals are judged achievable in principle, practicality can have another meaning. Many diplomatic initiatives are "mega-projects" with many moving parts that depend on smooth interaction. A good example might be to negotiate a national banking system. To achieve the overall policy goal, distinct negotiations on different parts may have to take place by different delegations or officers within one delegation. Some may prefer helping commercial versus private borrowers or supporting exporters instead of domestic traders. That complexity will require significant coordination in the team so that no one negotiation undercuts another. Does the NGO or coalition have the required discipline and skills, or is it better to focus on a specific part? Then keep in mind that other parties may focus on the other issues that compete, i.e., enabling provincial lending structures in advance of a national system.

If the team leader feels that the project is not feasible as defined, then the decision is either to recommend no further action or perhaps (and often more likely) to

**Fig. 2.2** A typical study group is informal, allowing a free exchange of views ((c) LRoeder 2012)

define the project more narrowly, making it easier to achieve at the negotiation table and reasonable to manage in the implementation stage, perhaps focusing on a small region versus a nation for example. Once the team leader concludes the effort is worth consideration as an official project, then it goes to step two, a study group.

### *2.2.2 Step Two: The Study Group Process*

Coordinating relief operations or major diplomatic initiatives are major challenges, in part because of the diversity of issues, NGOs, governments, and international organizations involved. Coordinating a common diplomatic position within the bureaucracy of an alliance is no less of a challenge, and it is often the most difficult thing to accomplish in a negotiation project—more than the actual negotiation in the field. That's because each partner office within an NGO or alliance partner brings different strengths and agendas, even if aiming for a common strategic goal. This is true whether at HQ or in the Field. A study group can help map out the path or paths to a successful strategy (Figs. 2.2 and 2.3).

Hans Zimmermann from OCHA told us this story.
Coordination is indispensable, but partners will only cooperate if they derive a benefit from it. An example from Liberia: Some visitors from UN HQs expressed their surprise after sitting in at a coordination meeting I had convened—because all the NGO and UN agency leaders working in Monrovia attended. How did I convince everybody to participate? I told

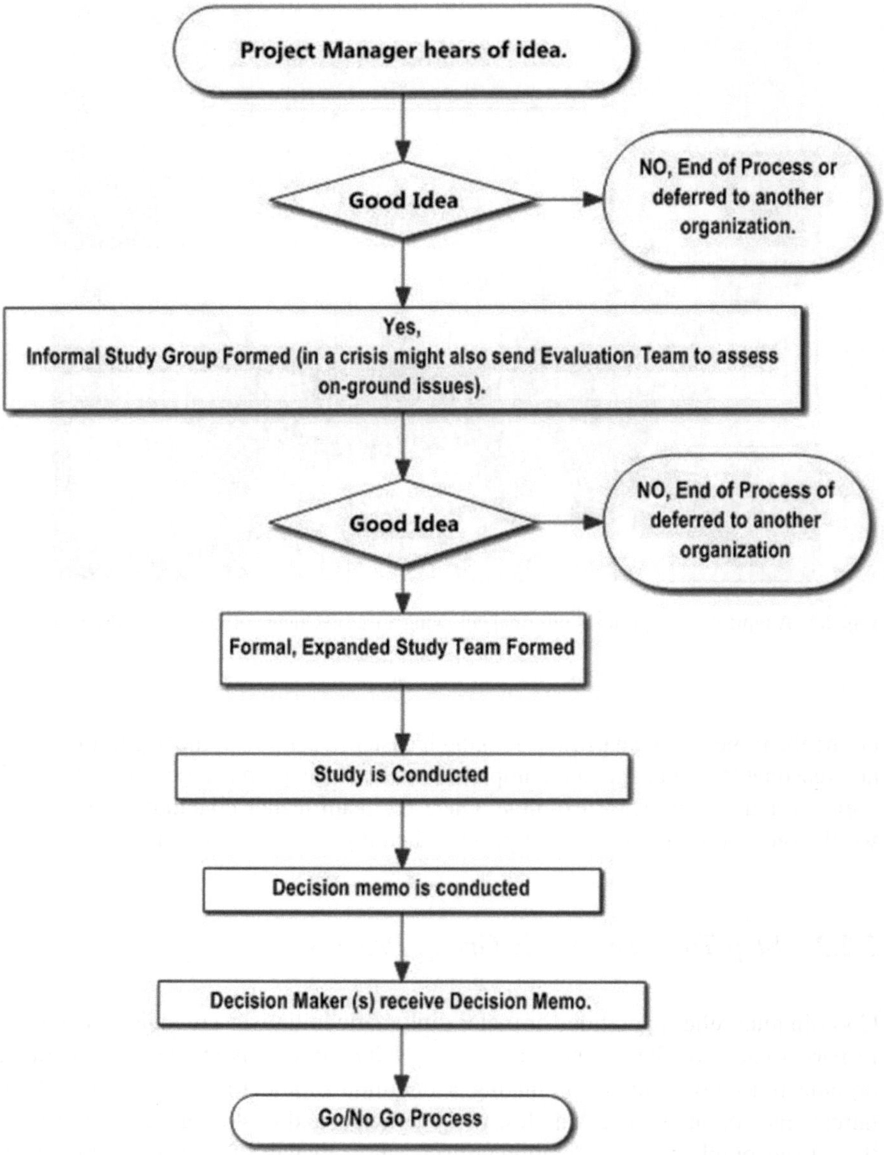


**Fig. 2.3** Study team process

them my "secret": These meetings were the only opportunity to get help from each other. My office had the only working international communications (an early Inmarsat "A" telephone and Telex line—at 50,000 dollars for the equipment and 8 dollars per minute for calls, communications was unaffordable for any NGO at that time). The Red Cross had the only functioning medical service, ships chartered by WFP brought the only diesel fuel available and operated the only gas station in town, and so on. Coordination was vital for everybody, and everybody understood that. Coordination brought added value, and attending the meetings was not seen as a waste of time (as such meetings often are) (Zimmermann 2012).

The initial discussion about possibly negotiating an agreement could easily have happened through an informal gathering of friends from different NGOs that share a common agenda. Perhaps they all work on food security issues, though from different angles. The model has the team leader form a study group to refine the proposal, initially using staff from the team leader's NGO, because its reputation will be on the line. The friends might also be invited. On the other hand, if the NGO is already working within an alliance, the members should also probably come from a variety of friendly NGOs. Regardless, hard questions about the project's goals will help define negotiation boundaries and reality. The questions are very much the same as initially examined by the team leader, but a larger group is now involved, consisting of:

- *Negotiation Expert.* The negotiation expert is just an adviser and need not be the actual officer chosen to lead the negotiations.
- *An Administrative Officer*, as well an expert on communications, both with experience in international negotiations.
- *Officials* from the fund-raising office.
- *Topic experts*, perhaps a legal adviser, perhaps a regional office in order to deal with issues of context.[6] Some study groups will have subcommittees dedicated to specific parts of the puzzle, drafting, administration, background studies, etc., all reporting to a master committee. Whether this occurs or not is entirely a matter of choice and usually dictated by the complexities of the issues, other special circumstances, and the availability of resources and time.

**Note** As described, this model may appear to work best for a long-term concept, like negotiating a declaration or setting up a public diplomacy campaign, and because fact finding can take time, some may consider it too much for an emergency operation; however, though time is compressed in emergencies, the same essential concepts exist, the same need to ask proper questions before making a go decision. Indeed, in an emergency, there may even be a larger need to delay action until an assessment mission can report back on the actual on-the-ground situation. See discussion on Operation Gwamba.

If feasible, the topic experts should also bring representatives of the targeted audience into the discussion. For example, if the idea is to protect transgender refugees, consider inviting transgender survivors; their experiences will put the issue into perspective, though getting the interviews will take time and delay a final decision on the initiative. Livestock can't talk for themselves, native herdsmen or commercial ranchers might. The point is that when designing policies to implement in any particular region, one must keep in mind local norms. It is fine to try to change such norms, but keep in mind that if the proposed policy is going to receive resistance from the residents, perhaps for cultural or religious reasons, that can seriously impact the project's sustainability.

---

[6]Some will be tempted to exclude offices that are only tangentially impacted by the subject to be negotiated. Caution is urged. A study group can become unwieldy if too big, but its results might be disrespected by those left out of the discussion. There is no metric here other than the founders of the study group must try for as representative a group as is practical, and before deciding membership, first weigh the potential negatives whenever someone or some organization or office is left out.

**SWOT** Essentially, the study group does a SWOT analysis. Some version of this analysis will also reappear in the decision memo, and then after negotiations are concluded, the team reassembles to review how negotiations went. All SWOT analyses are about the same.

- Strengths*:* Characteristics of the idea that give it an advantage over others; even if the negotiation succeeds, what about the team that might be assembled to implement the deal? What are the team advantages?
- Weaknesses that place the initiative as a concept and team at a disadvantage.
- Opportunities: These are external forces that could help, perhaps some political movement in a targeted country that could build local allies.
- Threats: These are *external* forces that could inhibit the project, perhaps a local disease outbreak, religious/cultural constraints, and economic sanctions.

When doing the SWOT analysis, use our Situational Matrix tool or a similar device.

**The Options** The study group has three options: (a) drop the idea as not feasible, (b) turn it over to a more appropriate NGO or group, or (c) decide to ask the lead NGO's decision maker to make the effort an official project, with all of the implied financial and political ramifications. Every NGO has a different decision maker, perhaps the CEO for a small one, perhaps a senior manager who can commit staff and money across office lines, and perhaps even a board, depending on the size of the endeavor.

### *2.2.3 Two Sets of Questions Need to Be Asked in Steps One and Two*

**Question Set One for the Team Leader and Study Team**

1. **What is the negotiation's purpose?** The first question is one of definition. What is being accomplished? While most NGOs involved in negotiating an end to the use of land mines wanted to also end war, the negotiation was about the former, not the later.
2. **Why is the idea relevant?** Even if laudable, if the negotiation is not a good fit with the organization's mandate or resources, perhaps another NGO should lead. After all, no one NGO can do everything. In other words, this is about strategic thinking. Frequently a department in a for-profit corporation will focus on the inherent value of its product, then when trying to move the larger corporate machinery to expand sales not taking into account the many other products made by the corporation or not taking into context whether there are enough consumers to buy the department's widget. Just because a product is good doesn't mean people will buy it, as the Ford Motor Company discovered with the Edsel. If the management of a for-profit corporation doesn't ask the same kind of question and do the proper studies to answer the question correctly, it risks expending enormous resources with no return. Do that enough times and a corporation will go bankrupt. A nonprofit corporation must think in similar terms, even though the motivation isn't profit.

3. **Is the world ready for the idea?** Even if a good concept, is the world ready for it? Would it be better to start small and build? Perhaps an agreement to protect a plant species in one country because of its food value is a better first step than trying to convince the world to protect the species everywhere, even though that may be the underlying, strategic aim.
4. **Who are the potential allies and foes?** Who or what might benefit or be harmed, and why? Who or what is undecided about the idea, and why? As any politician will note, an undecided person or organization is an opportunity to gain an ally. Foes can be turned around sometimes by understanding their problem and providing a solution. That's the basis of legislative negotiation in any Parliament. Try using a situational awareness tool such as that described in Chap. 3. Remember as well that the "who or what" includes animals, people, structures, industries, and organizations.
5. **What has happened before and why?** Precedence helps define probabilities of success or failure, the required resources, types of allies, and required tools. However, lack of precedence does not mean a no-go.
6. **What price failure?** Can the lead organization or coalition handle a loss of income or reputation if the negotiation fails?
7. **Are lengthy negotiations feasible?** Persuasion is a process, not an event. Will the NGOs staff, allies, and donors stick with the project if it takes a long time? Is it affordable?
8. **Is the public supportive?** If not, a public diplomacy effort may be required.
9. **What resources will be required, what people and money?**

These questions are not usually done in an afternoon, though in an emergency of course, they are done with dispatch. This is about positioning the initiative in a strategic context and building a path to success, so finding the best answers may well require a lot of preparatory work, for example, advance informal consultations with experts outside the lead NGO and its allies—just to get all of the facts straight. Another preparatory work that will have to take place will be *recruitment of financial donors*; they probably won't join without seeing the study first. They mostly come in after the decision memo phase; the decision memo must reflect the feasibility of them joining and under what circumstances. Consideration of recruiting allies also takes place before the decision memo phase; if traditional friends are reluctant to share resources and reputation, the decision memo must reflect that.

**Briefing Tabs** The study group should develop short Briefing Tabs that explain crucial elements of the proposal as background for the decision memo. For example, if the NGO wants to prevent abuse of women in a province, one paper should locate the province and explain the history of abuse. There is no hard rule on length; short Tabs are preferred because decision makers and delegates to a conference will have limited time to read. In looking for precedence for similar bodies, we discovered that the study group used by the U.S. Delegation to the Paris Peace Conference developed pamphlets of 10,000–15,000 words; that was far too much to use in a conference room, so negotiators relied on a small three-ring binder with position summaries known as the Black Book (US Department of State 1942a, p. 11). A single page is best on each issue, certainly no more than five for a very complicated issue, plus illustrations, maps, etc. It did make sense for the U.S. Delegation to the Paris Conference; they were trying to redesign a world, with borders that were bound to be controversial.

### 2.2.4 *Question Set Two: How Will the Goal Be Achieved?*

**A: Does the NGO or coalition have the resources, experience, and training in multilateral negotiations and strength of will to sell the initiative in tough times?** (Use the *Data Fusion Matrix in* Sect. 3.1). If all of these are not present, the lead NGO risks, weakening its other programs and its reputation; this is not an argument against being bold. Brave policies are needed in the humanitarian world, and an organization reluctant to take calculated risks should not do diplomacy. However, if analysis shows success is not likely, it may be more appropriate to redefine the mission with achievable goals that lead over time to a significant strategic objective. Caution and asking tough questions are thus hallmarks of the wise. Put another way, suppose that the goal is to amend the charter of the Organization of American States (OAS) in 5 years. The amendment is intended as well to protect all farms in Latin America from genetically modified seed. In such a case, while the goals are laudable, they might be unattainable with the resources, allies, and skills at hand. The goals are laudable, might be unattainable with the resources, allies, and skill sets at hand. A more prudent approach might be to narrow the scope or lengthen the time line, perhaps establish a set of intermediary agreements or precedents that can be a framework for a long-term plan. Prudence may not have the high drama of "trying for it all" at once or the spirit of "punching above our weight," but remember the clients, especially if they are unable to speak for themselves. That is the job. Which is more important, ego or success? Multilateral diplomacy should not be driven by fund-raising or bragging rights. It should only be about success.

**Expectations** Once goals are set, donors will require success within their definition of a "reasonable time frame," so will political allies. An example could be preventative diplomacy. In order to prevent ethnic strife from erupting into war, dispute resolution measures will be required, perhaps poverty eradication programs and efforts to reduce corruption and inequity in the social or economic fabric, perhaps building bridges between opposing factions or tribes. One NGO or coalition is unlikely to be able to handle all of that, so the team should examine the overall context into which the negotiations are set, and then establish a plan that manages expectations, keeping them realistic. The HQ Team should also be comfortable with donor time lines as well as those set by the Study Team in the decision memo. This is very important because once on the road, if it becomes obvious success would not occur as planned without more resources; it may prove difficult to acquire more funding, forcing budget reductions of internal programs, which can undermine internal morale and donor support for the rest of the NGO. Failure of a strategic objective under those factors can allow another NGO to take over elements of the lead's corporate portfolio, and since its reputation might be damaged, there is a risk of not acquiring a second try for other strategic goals. Put another way, the Delegation needs to understand what level of support it will receive from the HQ team and its donors. Not every negotiation is of the highest priority, and every negotiation will have budgets and time lines. The decision memo should identify these things.

**It does not take a genius to call for action.**
**Genius is turning action into victory.**

**B: Assess your allies' abilities and willpower and those in the multilateral community, industry, or particular governments which have a contrary point of view.** This isn't about finding "something wrong." NGOs are diverse, even within a common field of endeavor, so a discussion of their distinctions is an appropriate action that could avoid future problems. Just as self-analysis of a lead NGO's resources, core mission, and abilities must be objective and accurate, so too the analysis of allies and those who differ must be demanding and unrelenting. Not taking the time to study and fully grasp their true strategic objectives risks failure for the project. These questions should be asked very early on before any potential ally is engaged and answered in the study and reflected in the decision memo. After all, even friendly NGOs compete for scarce resources and, in order to protect their reputation and their own ability to garner support for future projects, will be jealous of "their territory." European and US NGOs typically see cooperation with governments differently, with American NGO's being more willing to work with governments. While international NGOs and indigenous NGO should collaborate, they operate within different political orbits, so the inherent political, cultural, and economic stresses will be different. That can have a major impact on cooperation, in a sensitive diplomatic initiative, to say nothing of the fact that local NGOs often do not want to be "told what to do" by an international NGO. If the negotiation is going to involve field negotiations, international and indigenous NGOs might also have differing ideas about appropriate counterparts with which to cooperate.

- Just because one or more allies agree with the lead NGO's general goals "in principle" does not mean they will agree with a specific text the chief negotiator eventually decides to accept. If the allies then disappear will the final agreement matter; if the lead NGO feels this problem is going to happen, it may have to leave the defecting allies behind and push ahead. However, to keep the rest of the alliance in place and lay a foundation for a sustainable agreement, one that will be implemented, the lead NGO must also engage the donors and the public by managing their perceptions of the decision. Controversy does not mean failure. In fact, controversy is often inevitable, so perception management is nearly always essential and must be planned for in the public diplomacy part of the strategy.
- When picking allies, ask if they are chosen for political wisdom, technical knowledge, or negotiating skill. Will their abilities make them strong enabling partners; or are they mainly "names" to provide political credibility or access to funding?
- Will a disagreeing government or coalition member try to damage the lead NGO or its reputation? What is the plan for a counterapproach?

**C: After reviewing points A and B, ask to what extent the true objectives of the other players are compatible with each other's and that of the lead.**

- If the opponent's strategic objectives and those of the lead are perceived as totally incompatible, there is a risk of total failure because grounds are lacking upon which to build a viable compromise without also violating core principles. The solution for this problem is often to find compatibility by repackaging the question.
- If individual objectives differ between members of an opposing coalition (quite common), that is an opportunity to create "wedge issues," perhaps even compromises that do not undermine the core values of the team but can divide the loyalty of the opposition.
- Conversely, if the lead NGO's strategic goals rank as only tactics for an ally, which is often the case, the ally may depart from the field at a critical juncture, and especially if it feels its own strategic goals have already been met or could be more effectively met by different tactics. Always try to predict those goals in advance.

**Note** One of the most famous examples of why carefully choosing allies is important or at least understanding them (since you can't always choose your allies) and why compromise is also important was the negotiation for the Treaty of Peace that ended World War I. More will be said about the treaty in the Appendix; in simple terms, the conference had two purposes: to end the war and to establish a mechanism to prevent future wars, this to be called the League of Nations. On its face, the two purposes were complementary; in reality, they conflicted in dramatic fashion. Wilson mainly focused on the second goal, though he clearly cared about the first. The French, who had suffered the most in the war, primarily were interested in the first goal, and the president of France probably would have been happy to walk away with just that. As a result, looking at Wilson as a Negotiation Leader,[7] his team had divided loyalties. Wilson's genius was coming up with the League and tirelessly negotiating it into existence, a noble deed; to achieve his goal, he had to compromise his core values with the French, who demanded total military capitulation from Germany and economic annihilation. John Maynard Keynes,[8] who traveled in post-War Germany and was considered one of the preeminent economists of his age, argued that Wilson agreeing to excessive reparations would lead to a future war with Germany (Keynes 1920). David Hunter Miller, legal adviser to the U.S. Delegation, also recorded in his daily diary a lunch meeting with Keynes and others where he offered his own opinion that moderation was required for reparations (Miller, My Diary At the Conference of Paris 1924, p. 34 and 71). In the end, the compromise did achieve an agreement to form the League but perhaps at the high cost of denying its purpose.

---

[7] Wilson was psychological leader, but the negotiations were a summit, each head of state or government sitting as equals.

[8] Keynes was the official representative of the British Treasure at the Paris Peace Conference until June 7, 1919, when he resigned believing that terms of the treaty, especially the reparations being demanded of Germany, would lead to the ruin of Europe.

This question of ethical compromise caused one member of the U.S. Delegation to resign and the Secretary of State to later privately declare the League pointless. As an example, consider the Shantung issue 山東問題; Japan seized the Chinese province from the Germans and demanded control. China wanted the land back, which was the birthplace of Confucius,[9] but Wilson went along with the Japanese, fearing that otherwise they would drop out of the conference. As a result, China felt slighted and refused to sign the treaty, leading members of the U.S. Delegation to be upset because the claim to the land was based on secret treaties, a concept of international law Wilson had been against.

The lesson for NGO diplomats and Study Teams to take from how the Japanese and French demands were handled is that even if the lead NGO's strategic goals are in full harmony with an ally's, there is still the risk that the ally will depart the field if the lead's means to achieve the common goal are felt to be incompatible with the ally's ethical frame or primary strategic goal. This does not mean the lead is unethical; Wilson was not unethical, but different NGOs with common strategic goals can still have different reasons for their existence or for being a part of a coalition. Ignoring that reasoning when an alliance is forged will create surprises at the wrong moment. Perhaps the lead wishes to work with a government or company that an ally refuses to communicate with. One of the most important ways to use this question is to determine if incompatibility is a problem of perception. What if (for either opponents or allies) the perceived differences can be bridged through careful wording that builds a paradigm where all objectives are perceived as compatible—even if different. If that paradigm shift can be achieved, the chances of success are increased. Of course, as in the Paris accords, Wilson had no choice but to work with France, though some have said Wilson also did not effectively use his military strength as a lever. In addition, the deal with Japan was more about economics and American desires to expand trade in Asia and the Pacific.

**D: Having answered question A in the affirmative and understood B and C**, the team should examine the tools to be used by the yet selected Chief Negotiator. (See discussion on role of Chief Negotiator.)

A lead negotiator for any topic makes the actual field decisions under the supervision of the Chief Negotiator, not HQ, but it is good for the Study Team to examine the following options in advance. To achieve strategic objectives in a negotiation, the negotiator will need to use persuasion, compromise, or direct action (threat, media stories, lawsuits, public diplomacy, etc.), using the right tool at the right time. This is why the Chief Negotiator should be experienced, especially when pitted against well-resourced institutions like governments. They have the power and the will, unless those strengths are reduced through "public diplomacy."

**The Study Group does not decide which tactics will be used, but does need to examine their potential value and make recommendations to a Decision Maker(s), with corporate responsibility.**

[9] This was also the birthplace of the 1900 Boxer Rebellion.

## 2.3 The Study Team

A project manager (*referred to as team leader throughout)* will pull together an *Informal Study Team* of interested parties and decide after discussion about whether an initiative makes sense to bring to the attention of senior management for approval. As seen in Operation Gwamba (see Sect. 13.4), in an emergency situation this process speeds up and often involves sending out an evaluation team to report back on the situation. The term "Study Team" is generic and the period of operation will be dependent on circumstances; but whether deciding to intervene in a crisis or considering a long-term negotiation, some analysis will be needed by a team of experts before the decision maker(s) initiate action. Otherwise, the NGO risks major failure and in some cases will unnecessarily risk the lives of its teams, to say nothing of wasting funds.

Once the Informal Study Team agrees, a project should advance to the next level, sending a decision memo by an expanded *Formal Study Team* to senior management who makes the GO/NO-GO decision. Senior Management includes the CEO of an NGO or the CEOs of an alliance of NGOs, probably also the directors of financial resources, media offices, etc. Whereas the *initial team* mainly had a substantive interest and needed to answer the practical question of whether the initiative was a good idea, management has a fiduciary responsibility and must protect the reputation of the NGO(s), both of which protect an NGO's sustainability. In addition, other projects could be impacted by the proposed initiative. The decision makers are also busy, so should not be in the Study Team. Further, because their responsibilities are corporate, the Formal Study Team must take the time to gather all of the facts and analysis required to make a decision; therefore it consists of officers from any relevant office.

### *2.3.1 The Study Team Must Ask Hard Questions*

Throughout this book are references to the various tasks a Study Team will encounter such as preparing a Communications Package that will enable the Delegation to effectively project its point of view. In addition, much reference is given to asking hard questions about potential adversaries. Disaster can emerge from the failure to dispassionately do this. The point here is that while the initiative may be laudable, if success is impossible or hard to obtain, the team as a whole and certainly the decision makers must be made aware. It is also important to understand "the other side" or the views of partners, not simply to discover weakness that is to be exploited; also locate common ground upon which both may walk. With this in mind, consider International Humanitarian Law (IHL) as an example of a field of work full of controversy. More will be said about IHL in a later chapter. For now, however, in order to illustrate the importance of analysis, the terror bombings of Dresden on February 1945 is raised as precedent.

### Hard Question Example: The Question of Dresden as Precedent

The fire bombing of Dresden has always been controversial, with good people disagreeing on whether what happened was a war crime, a crime against humanity, or just a terrible act. It is therefore a relevant event for preparing NGO diplomats for today's struggles involving violent risks to civilian populations in today's conflicts, be they international like the breakdown of former Yugoslavia and the invasion of Iraq or domestic disputes like the civil war in Syria. The discussion can be preparation for a study of the use of drones in the war on terrorism. With allegations of brutality come assertions of illegality; so envisage that an NGO coalition might wish to examine a contemporary conflict and say that the leadership is criminal and then try to convince a court in a friendly country or the International Court of Justice (ICJ) to take action against that leadership. One can always seek a political solution against a brutal regime of course, but what of criminality? Can a brutal leader or military officer be put on trial? The problem is that just because an act is deplorable or brutal doesn't make it illegal under international law. Brutality should always be deplored and can in itself be enough to warrant political action; but before an NGO attacks a government or some other entity as being criminal, make sure of the facts and the underlying law, not just the facts. Also, consider the range of opinions the community of historians and legal experts may have reached with the same facts.

To understand Dresden, start with Guernica, an essentially unarmed city in Spain bombed by the Germans just before World War II. The attack helped Franco win his civil war. There were two minor arms factories in the city; both were intentionally not bombed, whereas the rest of the city suffered so as to demoralize the civil population and influence the government to fall, what has been called by many experts a "terror attack." The attacks on Nagasaki and Hiroshima had similar purposes, not to destroy a major military target but to terrorize a national population and its government into submission. In the case of Dresden, this was one of the great German cultural centers and an "open city." Refugees fleeing the Russian advance stuffed its apartments and basements, and thousands of wounded German soldiers lay in hospitals and clinics. There was also a large POW presence. The city was destroyed by a firestorm created by massive British bombardments specifically designed to create the storm. The numbers of casualties are in dispute; but tens of thousands probably died. Dresden was also a communications hub for rail and did have an industrial complex; but the focus of the bombing was the cultural heart, a group of buildings and streets that were visited by generations of wealthy Americans and Europeans on their grand tour of Europe.

Any of these examples—Guernica, Hiroshima, and Dresden—bring strong emotions to the table, which is exactly why they are raised. Whether the attacks were required as a matter of military necessity is questionable; but in the heat of anger over the killing of civilians in a war, can analysis be accurate—the killings were illegal? Certainly, all the acts were very cruel. But all to one extent or another shortened a war. Didn't that save innocent lives? some experts ask. One shudders at the inevitable loss of military and civilian lives if Operation Olympus, the plan to invade mainland Japan with ground troops, had gone forward.

**Recommendation** The events are brought to the fore to note that they were controversial and that despite many decades having past, scholars still disagree, except that emotions are still very raw to this day. When contemplating an initiative on such an action, the Study Team should have on hand experienced legal counsel to offer an opinion and to continue to provide guidance to the NGO Delegation during the negotiations or field operation. Some experts are of the opinion that these events were not war crimes, arguing that it was not unlawful at the time to attack unarmed civilians; others feel very differently, that the bombings were crimes against humanity, with one expert saying that "international humanitarian law (IHL) has held that the indiscriminate killing of civilians is a punishable crime for several thousand years (Lamb 2012)."

Readers are reminded of the Hague Convention of 1907, which dealt with the bombing of undefended cities. Experts agreed when Guernica was bombed that the act was horrific and had seized the world's attention, but as discussed in meetings in the League of Nations, the application of international law on this point was unsettled (Lapointe 1938, Sept 14). Though there were military targets in each city, Dresden was not particularly defended and was also a hospital for German soldiers, a sanctuary for German refugees, and a POW location for allied soldiers.[10] The Convention of 1907 is still in force, in particular Article 25 on land warfare. Based on that, some experts consulted for this book felt Bomber Harris (Commander of the UK's Bomber Command and designer of the Dresden attacks) did indeed commit a war crime. However the UK did not sign the Convention, so other experts would opine that the UK was not bound by it. The United States did sign but did not ratify, so the same logic may holds.

In other words, though the slaughter of many thousands of civilians may have been repulsive, for US and British forces, bombing of Dresden might not have been a crime, whereas the German bombing of Guernica certainly was, since Germany had ratified the Hague Convention. Further, in 1938 by unanimous consent, the Assembly of the League of Nations passed a resolution on the "Protection of Civilian Populations against Bombing From the Air in Case of War (Assembly of the League 1938, September 30)." While bombing a train station, rail lines and munitions factories would be legitimate; some would argue that Dresden was less about that than killing civilians (residents and refugees from the Russian front) and unarmed soldiers (convalescing from battle). In other words, the bombing of military targets was an excuse, not a primary reason. If that's true, the bombing may have indeed been a crime. After all, the UK was then a member of the League.

The story however isn't as simple as signatures. Upon the close of World War II, the allies set up International Military Tribunals to prosecute major war criminals. These took place in Nuremberg and Tokyo and declared the principles embodied in the Hague Convention, and Regulations on Land Warfare of 1899/1907 had, by the time of the outbreak of the World War II, been so widely accepted by states that they had become part of *international customary law*, Jus Cogens (compelling law). In addition to formal written international instruments, Jus Cogens is considered a primary source of international law by the International Court of Justice, the UN, and

[10] The novel Slaughterhouse Five by Kurt Vonnegut is based on the bombing, by the way. He was a survivor of the bombing.

many member states, though its application will vary. In other words, if bombing Dresden violated Hague in the context of "international customary law," the decision makers could be brought to justice, perhaps the same for the destruction of Rotterdam and more recent attacks by the President of Syria on his own citizens.

Underpinning the discussion is the tension between law and contemporary morality, since that is what drives emotions like the revenge of Versailles, which led to an overreach in economic sanctions, setting the stage for the rise of the National Socialist Party in Germany or the Boxer Protocol of 1901[11] which led to the downfall of imperial China, abuse by Japan and western powers, setting the stage for the rise of Communism in Asia. In this hypothetical example, an NGO decided to pursue justice because of moral outrage. But are there moral counterarguments? Do they have equal weight or at least should they be considered? Even if the team doesn't agree with the premise of a countering moral argument, it must be studied and understood. To do that, the authors consulted Marshall De Bruhl, who wrote a modern history of the Dresden incident. His book *Firestorm* includes an examination of the motivations behind the attack and some of the allegations of criminality. De Bruhl is considered an apologist for Bomber Command, concluding that no crime was committed because the bombing was required. De Bruhl also rejects Hague. In a discussion with the authors in 2012, De Bruhl said that "the relevant clause about aerial bombardment from the first of the Hague Conventions—the one in 1899—follows: *The Contracting Powers agree to prohibit, for a term of 5 years, the launching of projectiles and explosives from balloons, or by other new methods of a similar nature.* By "other new methods," one assumes someone had in mind the newly invented airplane. So it seems the Hague Conventions of 1899 and 1907 said little about and did nothing to forestall the bombing of civilian populations. That said, I think linking Guernica and Dresden is just too facile. The first, we are told, was terror bombing pure and simple. And conventional wisdom has it that the Dresden raid was the same—a myth reinforced by Kurt Vonnegut and the disgraced historian David Irving. Indeed, I believed it myself when I first embarked on the research for *Firestorm* (De Bruhl 2006). But after months of research and reading through mountains of files at various archives, most notably the RAF files at the Public Record Office at Kew, I realized I was on the wrong track. Dresden *was* a militarily important city in Eastern Germany. The raids were a logical continuation of the air campaign to destroy Nazism and bring about the surrender of Germany. Another military historian, Frederick Taylor, has made the same argument. He and I both agree that the destruction of this beautiful city was one of the great tragedies of the war. But we came to the same conclusion ultimately. Dresden was a logical and necessary target" (De Bruhl, *Discussion of the Dresden Attack* 2012).

De Bruhl is making the argument, which justified the uses of nuclear power against Japan, that even though the loss of civilian life and culture was horrific, the acts shortened the war and the ends justified the means. But even were such an

[11]The *Boxer Protocol of* September 7, 1901, was between the Empress Dowager of China and an alliance of nations that had invaded China in part to rescue diplomatic legations in Peking during the Boxer Rebellion. The powers were Austria–Hungary, France, Germany, Italy, Japan, Russia, the United Kingdom, and the United States.

argument logical, did the bombing shorten the war? Not likely in the case of Dresden. A better plan would have been to bomb oil fields, strategic factories, and rail lines. But even if De Bruhl was correct, is it ever permissible to cause such mass destruction of civilians? In this case, the Study Team must ask hard questions, be prepared for all counterarguments—offer reasonable answers as well.

### 2.3.2 *Keeping Your Cool*

Important initiatives draw great minds and strong personalities, and this often will cause frictions, even feuds. Be aware of this when assembling the Study Team and the delegation. The key is to understand that friction happens a lot and surprisingly will involve what are otherwise the best people; so preparation is encouraged. As an example, both Dr. Simard and Mr. Roeder were heavily involved in the development of GDIN, the Global Disaster Information Network, an idea proposed by Vice President Gore and his National Security Adviser, Leon Fuerth, to save millions of lives a year and billions of dollars in property damage from natural phenomena by sharing satellite-based information and facilitating the development of techniques such as GLIDE, a universal tool for disaster data sharing fostered by an NGO named the Asia Disaster Recovery Center (ADRC) (ADRC 2004). Government experts, NGOs, UN experts, contractors, and academic centers were involved in the Study Team (which went by a different name), and at times emotions ran very high when a member did not get his or her way. The same thing happened with ReliefWeb, a project that evolved out of the Rwanda crisis and involved NGOs (see Chap. 18). It proposed a brand new way to significantly lower the costs of emergency management and sharing information. The Inquiry (see Sect. 14.2) created by President Wilson[12]" to help create the League of Nations had so much internal tension that a feud erupted between major players.[13] The lesson here is to be prepared to manage the problem, because if the project is important, the best minds will want to be a part, and that inherently means tension as great intellects clash, looking for the best ideas.

## 2.4 Step Three: The Decision Memo—Go or No-Go?

Assuming that the informal study group feels the project should move forward, the next step is to create a decision memo. Any part of the NGO that might be impacted should clear[14] the memo, as well as potential allies, to see if they want to be a part

[12] The Inquiry was formed on September 1917 (Mezes 1921).

[13] The British had a similar committee often named after its chairman, Lord Phillimore, but more properly called "The Committee on the League of Nations," which created the first government formulation on March 20, 1918. There was also a French committee under Leon Bourgeois, which formulated an outline on June 18th. The Italians did not start serious thinking on the postwar period until Armistice.

[14] Review and comment on

of the project and if the roles and goals are acceptable. **Recommendation:** The model in this book like any recommendation, a suggestion for a frame of mind, not a rigid construct never to be amended. The same point is true about personal anecdotes by the authors. They are offered to lend legitimacy to proposed ideas; each Negotiator must use his or her own judgment.

The decision memo has the operational function of asking the appropriate Decision Maker(s) for an actual GO decision. This has to be someone with proper authority to commit the reputation of the organization and its capital and human resources, e.g., the CEO, Director of Disaster Management, the Director of Programs, whatever works for the NGO. There are only four options from a decision memo: (a) decide not to proceed, (b) refer for further study, (c) ask someone else to take the lead, or (d) commit.

Before the decision memo is written, the study group needs to have conducted a comprehensive assessment of the issue at hand and the options available through a SWOT analysis. A good way to think of the decision memo is a simple, bare-bones explanation of the issue and a tool upon which to build a plan, since it will decide not only whether the project moves forward or not but also who is in charge, the reason for negotiations, and their substantive boundaries. In addition, the memo must identify some metric that defines success. Metrics like the establishment of democracy are often hard to define in the social sciences; to the extent possible, the memo should do this in a very few sentences. Brevity will be important since the communications officer (see Chap. 12) will use those metrics as part of briefing packages or a Media Kit; fund-raising officers will use them with donors. A metric could be a ceasefire between tribes or an agreement to protect a specific amount of forest, a species of animal, or vaccinate a certain minimum number of internally displaced persons. A metric could also be a larger goal like vaccinating all of the people leaving a province from a drought, accompanied with interim goals dealing with levels of vaccination over a period of time. Finally, will there be an exit strategy, for example, does the project envisage a permanent presence by the NGO alliance in a province, or does meeting a metric mean declaring success and moving on? **A caution:** Metrics is mentioned because the concept comes up often and has been tried for decades now by both (then) USIA and the State Department. In the opinion of many experts, no truly perfect method has yet been found; actual success is (at best) measured at the medium and long term.

Although steps one and two might take some time, a decision memo could take a month[15] or so to prepare because so many people are required to clear it (see Clearances in Definitions). Every NGO that might be a partner and any office in the lead NGO that could be impacted should clear. Steps one and two map out strengths and weakness of potential coalition partners. In step three, the team is asked to help the Team Leader refine analysis of the opposition. If all three steps are not taken, the lead risks different parts of his or her organization or alliance working for their own interests and making unreasonable demands, even undercutting coordinated positions

---

[15]Obviously in a crisis, all steps are speeded up. An example of this is seen in the case study of John Walsh and his Operation Gwamba in 1964, which is described later in this book.

during critical negotiation phases. Always keep in mind coalition integrity, what strengthens it and what could damage it. To flesh out options for discussion and fairly adjudicate disputes, use a formal clearance process and a chain of authority (see Clearances in Definitions). Some will see this as overly formal and it might not work for all NGOs, but it does save time and confusion in most instances. Size also matters. No matter how complicated the issue needing negotiation, the decision memo should contain no more than two full pages of substantive text. Make it a memo to the Decision Maker(s) from the Team Leader asking for a specific decision.

**Note for Decision Makers** Inherent in the discussion of decision memos, the upcoming chapter on "intelligence" and the chapter preceding it on "knowledge management" are a call for NGO Chiefs to plan for the future. That may seem obvious; it isn't too many, beyond the need to consider how to pay for programs, to survive, and how to solve today's issue. The Informal Study Team proposed in the model asks the question of whether the objectives of a diplomatic initiative actually relate directly to the mandate of the NGO or its alliance. Also, are the times or circumstances right for the initiative?[16] In addition, but predictably, the problem being "solved" may be short term, perhaps how to protect the elderly from cyber abuse in a particular region of the world. But the decision maker, when considering the choice "to GO," also needs to consider what the world will be like in 20 years and whether the proposed initiative does more than solve an immediate problem; does it also fit into a rational long-range strategic objective? You can't plan for every eventuality; if you only plan for midnight, morning will surprise you. decision memos should have in mind the next strategic problem down the road, not just the immediate hurdle.

The following shows how such a memo might be crafted for a fictional conference proposed for Paris in 2015. Keep in mind that decision memoranda should simplify understanding. Instead of inserting lengthy explanations in the main body of the memo, relegate explanations to attachments, often called "Tabs."[17] The basic memo should be a lean statement of logic and consequences with a few essential facts. If the decision maker doesn't know anything about the topic, he or she can use the tabs to study details. The sections of the memo are as follows:

- Question for Decision
- Importance of Topic
- Essential Factors
- Background
- Decision Checklist

[16] Timing is critical in diplomacy. Even if an idea is a great one, if the time is wrong, it won't happen. The idea of a community of nations collaborating in order to reduce war isn't new; but if President Wilson hadn't pushed it during the negotiations for the Treaty of Peace, the organization would not have happened. If President Roosevelt hadn't advanced the UN when it did, the public zeal would have waned as well.

[17] The term TAB is common in the memoranda world and comes from industry where small tags of material are attached to something and contain information about the object. Other people might say Attachment or Tag.

- Clearances (see definition chapter)
- Tabs (if any)

Instead of a subject line, as is normal in memoranda, ask a question or Issue for Decision.

**Question for Decision**

**Sample Text (1):** Whether to negotiate a declaration in the UN General Assembly to protect woman from rape in the ethnic Sutu camps of East Bangorania, Europe.[18]

**Sample Text (2):** Whether to agree to a specific plan in Tab C to build an NGO coalition to insert language protecting Sutu women (Description in Tab B) in the outcomes document at the Yokohama World Conference on Human Rights Reform. A key element involves inviting Ambassadors and UN officials to an event hosted by the new coalition July 20.

**Importance of Topic to the NGO**: A few sentences as to why the issue is important to the NGO's mandate, financial posture, etc., to include the strategic goal, e.g., eliminating rape in the camps.

**Essential Factors**: This is a list of key points. Some will be basic such as the date of an event, but others will be short distillations of analysis from the Tabs. Let the Tabs resolve questions, about what will work and why, and alternatives. The Essential Factor section is a short understandable statement, details to be found in the Tabs. Examples of essential factors might include the scope of violence in a country and a nutshell description of faction leaders, warlords, etc., and their aims; are those aims negotiable? What NGO equities are at risk, such as the protection of children and the nature of the threat to those equities by each faction in the conflict? Another factor would be an explanation of what else has been done or is being done by other players, if any, to ameliorate the situation.

**Background Tabs**: Most decision memoranda keep the summary background to essential bulleted facts or a concise paragraph. The drafting officer will be tempted to be verbose in the main memo, fearing that the decision maker "won't get it." Resist the urge and use the Tabs for critical detailed background papers, e.g., a backgrounder on the ethnic group, statistics on rape, background on precedence, and information who might oppose the initiative and why, as well as who will support and why. There is no limit on the number of Tabs, but it is usually wise to keep the number short. The length of each should be no more than a page, though studies can be attached. They should also follow the essential factors; if a conflict is the issue, a good Tab would explain its political/cultural and economic roots. Is corruption involved, resistance to transparency? In countries like Syria in 2012, there is an elite group. Who are they? What do they control and how? How do they abuse and reward other groups? Are there uneven economic dimensions between ethnic groups?

---

[18] We have chosen a fictional tribe and region on purpose.

**Decision**: This section is for the decision maker

(a) Approve.
(b) Disapprove and why/questions for further study. The explanation is usually just a few penned in comments.
(c) Suggest an alternative route. This is spelt out by the decision maker in a few sentences.

**Note**: Another approach for the decision section is to present a couple of options, especially if the team is split over separate approaches. In this instance, each option should be expressed as a sentence and have its own Tab for explanation.

**Clearances (see Definitions)**

- Each office or scientist in the lead NGO with a major potential interest in this topic should clear the memo, assuring the decision maker that the paper has been properly reviewed. (If a coalition is used, then one representative for each coalition partner clears.)
- Clearers cannot be afraid to defy common wisdom. They must be able to ask tough questions without their loyalty being questioned; it is not important whether the clearer is correct rather that he or she had a chance to speak honestly. Respect dissent and the dissenters will respect the mission. That is especially true if the negotiation involves a multiple NGO team. As any soldier would say "people, not plans, make victories."
- This is less an HQ document than a team effort. If the lead NGO has regional offices, the impacted ones also need to clear it in full (see Clearances in Definitions).

**Sample Tab Headings**

- Tab A: Funding and Policy Importance of Topic to the lead NGO and the larger NGO community
- Tab B: Specific language proposed for final conference outcomes document or Resolution, etc.
- Tab C: Plan to energize relevant NGOs which operate in the region
- Tab D: Plan to energize key governments, including proposed meetings
- Tab F: Brief on the Tribe and Women
- Tab G: Proposed budget (Note: Every initiative needs to have a cost associated with it, so that the overall impact on other programs can be assessed. This Tab should also consider what other NGOs might contribute, what they will extract for such funds). What if consensus Is Impossible?

Given that a decision memo is a form of peer review, it will inevitably be colored by the different perspectives of each participating person or agency. Consensus will not always be possible; however, while the team leader should try to massage differences, for the memo to reflect an honest appraisal, if one party or group insists on their minority option, it needs to be reported. The decision maker then chooses the final action. After all, just because the majority has an agreed position does not make it the correct course of action. In other words, while a lack of consensus is not optimal, sometimes the same facts just lead people to different directions. The team must respect dissent and, ultimately, also follow whatever direction is given by the decision maker. Formalistic as that sounds, this process is essential. The problem of course is that while it is fine to have a decision maker decide disputes, unhappy partners may also disappear at this point if they do not like the results. The team leader's job is to minimize the risks of this not happening.

### *2.4.1 The Off-Ramp*

There always needs to be a potential off-ramp. Study Teams developing field operations/negotiations in particular should remember that international NGOs are visitors and that any project needs a political off-ramp to avoid the Bremer model. When the United States invaded Iraq, it created a potentially destructive power vacuum, since Iraq was no longer a counterpoint to Iran. If anything, the new Iraq may become a friend to Iran. That's both a political and economic issue, political because while a period of internal stability might be entered into, a powerful, radicalized Iran with nuclear weapons is a clear and present danger to the region. It is also important to understand that when an international presence is administering, as happened in Kosovo, Iraq, East Timor, etc., it is filling a power vacuum. This inherently creates a tension between the needs for long-term democracy and early stabilization. Transitional authorities must see themselves as temporary stewards of a highway to success, and that highway must have a well-designed off-ramp so that the indigenous population eventually rules, even if imperfectly.

However, any initiative needs an off-ramp, a set of understood conditions that suggest moving on to something else. This might be because the initiative is a success and no more work is required or that the required work should be done by others, or perhaps even that at some point, success is deemed impossible or impractical.

## 2.5 Delegation and Negotiation Staff Decisions

Both for reasons of budget and management, the Study Team should recommend the makeup of the delegation and the HQ team.

### *2.5.1 The Delegation*

More will be said of the various potential delegation officers in other chapters, but it is worth noting here that because of the complexities of nearly any negotiation, there are often many specialist officers required to support the initiative, social events to attend, speeches to make, and interviews to give, as well as time-consuming bureaucratic processes. The model proposes using such specialist officers as a team leader, a chief negotiator, administrative/protocol and communications officer, and a legal adviser . For a cash-challenged NGO, especially a small, local NGO, the requirement for such a large team can seem daunting; if NGOs act within coalitions and if each specialized officer is seen as a *function* to be accomplished instead of as a person that must be funded by one NGO, then much can be accomplished. Although a legal adviser is important, for example, this officer might come from a partner NGO or be provided by a law firm on retainer. The point is to have access to relevant, accurate legal advice. Further, one person can do more than one task, or tasks can be handled through partnerships in a coalition or by HQ staff. Government diplomats are frequently being sent as a "Delegation of One" to international conferences or to the field. In those instances, they take on each role or have someone do the job for them. When Roeder served as the United Nations Affairs Director for a British NGO, he often found its delegations to be very well staffed; the delegations of other much smaller NGOs were effective because they were backed up by a team. When Roeder went to speak to armed non-state players in South Sudan for his government or the UN, he was the sole field representative; he had administrative/logistical help. Once in Sudan, a UN official provided a vehicle, a field tent, and a car. In 2010 when he went to Somalia to visit the president and local leaders in the north; he had just one partner from his NGO, shared functional responsibilities and used partners in Somaliland such as local government officials as well as members of civil society to help move the project forward. They also went into the field, having coordinated their approach with many experts outside their own NGO and after having developed a strategic set of goals based on study.

The delegation team is led by a chief negotiator who reports back to the team leader.[19] The chief negotiator makes the decisions in the field, with coordinated guidance developed initially by the Study Team and during the process of negotiations by the HQ Team. An administrative officer should handle administrative matters so that the negotiator(s) can do their job, and a communications officer should deal with the press, set up interviews, train members how to interact with the media, etc. However, these functions do not need to come from a single NGO. A communications officer might come from an NGO local to a conference, someone expert in the local media. A partner NGO back at home might provide administrative support. Everything in this book presupposes that success depends on teamwork. Further, it is important to remember that there are parallel functions back at the HQ team. For example, just as the delegation needs a dedicated communications officer for its own efforts, a communications officer back at HQ needs to

[19] Something to keep in mind is that team members are not perfect; everyone has flaws; but sometimes, you just have to work with specific people. Even presidents have found this to be true, such as Harry Truman who on assuming office had to work with Edward Stettinius, whom Truman inherited from Roosevelt. Truman felt Stettinius wasn't imaginative and intended to replace him' but the San Francisco Conference that led to the formation of the United Nations was about to occur, and a quick change wasn't a good idea, so Stettinius was kept on as head of delegation—with full powers. As it turns out, he was excellent.

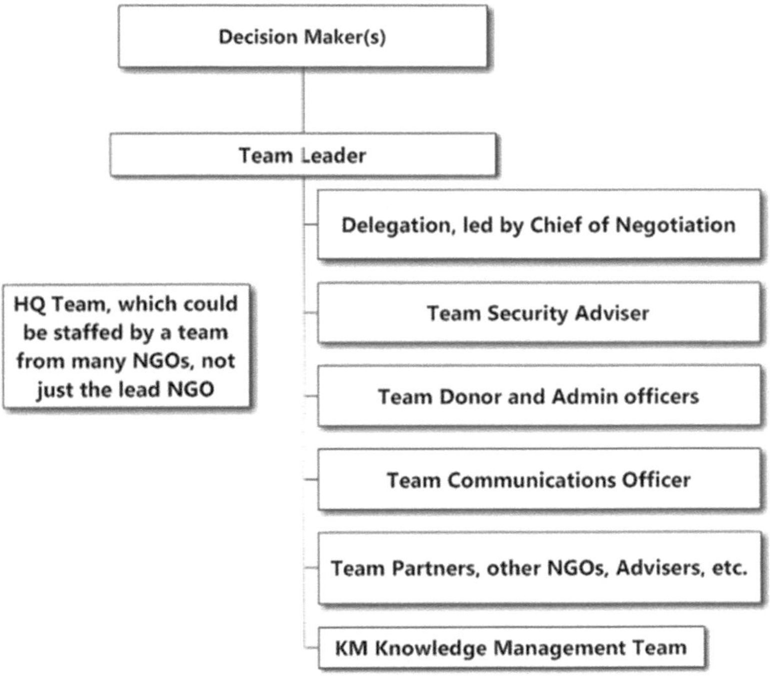


**Fig. 2.4** HQ team chart

manage public diplomacy and similar communications issues for the overall project, which might include efforts in many countries other than where the delegation is working. Those efforts in far-off places might, in turn, be led by partner NGOs; in fact they very likely will be.

### 2.5.2 *The HQ Team*

Assuming that the decision is a go, in addition to recommending the makeup of the delegation, an HQ team is formed, led by the team leader, consisting of members of the Formal Study Team.[20] The team leader manages HQ team and the project as a whole, keeping the alliance together and managing the flow of resources, and arranges coordinated instructions, as needed (Figs. 2.4 and 2.5).

[20]This was the model used to develop GDIN, the Global Disaster Information Network, a public–private partnership of NGOs, governments, contractors, and universities started by Vice President Gore's staff.

**Fig. 2.5** Delegation chart

## 2.6 Why the Lengthy Decision Process?

Because of the grandeur of multilateral diplomacy and the obvious potential gains for an NGO, particularly when pursuing a global change in practice, a CEO may consider that the simple act of engaging in diplomacy will convey to donors that the NGO is a serious player worthy of contributions. But donors expect success, so can the NGO succeed? The question needs to be quickly asked before anything happens; it is one of the first questions asked at each stage of the process by the project manager, the Informal and Formal Study Teams, and the decision maker(s). The question can't be asked too often. Keep in mind that a successful bilateral or multilateral negotiation is a major corporate undertaking that will demand a lot of resources and strong will. Does the NGO or its coalition have those resources and that will? Because the answers might not be obvious, the step-by-step decision-making process is needed, if for no other reason than to protect an NGO's reputation, its financial resources and its ability to raise enough funds for its work and to map out a successful path.

Don't worry about the size of your NGO. You can always compensate for size by building coalitions, using the comparative advantage of many partners. But do ask for clarity. The initial review by the project manager and Informal Study Team is needed because decisions to engage in negotiations often have no special starting point other than a desire to do good work. Many people in the NGO from the CEO to a staff officer or the NGO's natural allies also may have the same approximate idea, e.g., a convention to eliminate torture, or an initiative to protect a religious group from persecution, or perhaps a negotiation to set aside government land to be a special kind of farm needed to feed people, perhaps a regional development strategy. All of those ideas require a cohesive decision process to avoid a failed negotiation. That's why we have proposed our step-by-step model, a specific methodology to convert the informal chatter into useful action, then guide the action to success. Other models are certainly possible; experience has shown that this approach works. Although every NGO will have its own culture and process, the steps should be considered in some form, as they are based on proven success. Underlying them are also theories of protocol, fund-raising, and conference delegation management covered in the other chapters, all of which must be sewn together to make one coherent negotiating strategy that takes into account major policy issues that pose any threat to the initiative, with recommendations to resolve the issues.

# Chapter 3
# A Practical Model For Diplomacy and Negotiation: Steps 4-6 – The Negotiation and Implementation Stages

**Extract** Chapters 2 and 3 propose a specific model for NGOs to consider when engaged in diplomacy. Chapter 3 focuses on steps 4–6 in the model: position papers and delegation tactics and management. This covers the negotiation period as well as the post-negotiation period. In this period, the NGO might reexamine its process if negotiations fail or focus on ways to gain implementation if the negotiations succeed.

## 3.1 Introduction: Three Phases

There are three phases to any negotiation: (a) pre-negotiation, (b) actual negotiations, and (c) post-negotiation or implementation. Chapters 2, 3, and 4 cover a practical model for these activities. Chapter 2 covers pre-negotiation work and the process of deciding to engage in a negotiation. Chapter 3 covers the negotiation process and implementation stage, with recommendations on the formation of a delegation, as well as strategy and tactics, or, in the case of an unsuccessful negotiation, rethinking the process.

## 3.2 Step Four: Position Papers, Delegation Guidance

If the **decision memo** authorizes the recommended action, an agreed set of **position papers** sets out coordinated guidance for the team's delegation and should be arranged on each topic being negotiated. It therefore needs to be assembled by the Study team. With the delegation members assisting, the delegation arrives at an international conference or bilateral meeting. The position papers state who the chief negotiator is and provide formal coordinated guidance for the delegation on each issues,

L.W. Roeder, Jr. and A. Simard, *Diplomacy and Negotiation for Humanitarian NGOs*, Humanitarian Solutions in the 21st Century, DOI 10.1007/978-1-4614-7113-4_3,

papers used throughout the event. The delegation must know the package inside and out, lest their diplomatic opposites take advantage of their ignorance.

These products are similar to a decision memo in size and format, except that while the decision memo might only reference specific text to be negotiated and summarize strategic goals, the position papers flesh out the specific boundaries of acceptability, the issue's background, and strategic rationale. However, despite the additional detail, they still must be crisp and understandable. That way, if the chief negotiator becomes sick, requiring others to negotiate, it won't matter; the position papers will have spelled out what needs to be known and how the positions were arrived at.

**Be Reasonable** When drafting a position paper, some topic specialists, wanting to protect their interests, may be parsimonious when defining acceptable negotiation boundaries, but that advice could also cause failure in the real world. In the Middle East, carpet makers are renowned for their detail; they will be the first to admit that only God is perfect. Don't let perfection prevent success. Achieving practicality has to be a top priority for the negotiator and team leader; they should have reasonable boundaries, not a straitjacket of impossible goals or text. In addition, if a strong minority emerges when developing the position paper, its viewpoint must be reflected in the draft version that goes to the decision maker(s), meaning that the position paper be in final coordinated form before going into the delegation binder, leaving no lack of clarity. A collection of position papers are a delegation's bible, especially for an inter-NGO delegation, so anyone involved, including officers[1] from allied NGOs, must be involved in clearing. Even if everyone on the team has the same science background, each office involved may have different, preconceived notions of victory, its own individual definitions, and values. A position paper makes sure there is a reasonable understanding of the route to be taken; otherwise, a lack of clarity can emerge which inevitably leads to disaster on the ground.

**Short and Simple** Each issue should be simply written and no more than two pages in length, though Tabs are allowed for detailed background papers. This will be an especially important tool if the delegation is made up of representatives from different parts of the lead organization or draws officers[2] (see Chap. 1, footnote 2) from other NGO, so allow 2 months' time for clearances to be completed before departure. That will avoid misunderstandings once the delegation hits the ground. If the position papers cannot be fully agreed, then the final version is decided by the decision maker. Note that the risk here, of course, is that if consensus is not reached, the losing partner may defect.

[1] Some organizations use the term "officer" to mean the lowest rank. This book defines the term to mean everyone from the CEO to the lowest official. All delegation members are officers, though in diplomatic jargon, the head of the delegation to a UN conference is usually the delegate, with the other members being called alternative delegates.

**The following is a sample format for a position paper being used at a fictitious World Conference on Gender Equality in Berbera, Somaliland, in 2015.**

**Delegation Name** Coalition for Gender Protection (CGP)

**Venue** World Nation Building Conference (WNBC), Berbera, Somaliland, January 24–25, 2015.

**Issue** Whether to insert a sentence in the outcomes document of the WCNB calling a democratic convention on gender equity throughout the new country of Bahore, East Africa.

This was a contentious issue in the drafting committee in Berlin last August. Some governments and international NGOs insisted on such a convention to decide equity, in keeping with promises made by the Revolutionary Governing Council (details in Tab B). Other governments and some indigenous NGOs believe forcing gender equity too fast will be seen by minorities as an attack on their culture, which if successful will divide the country and foment violence just as the country gains independence (details in Tab C).

**Note** Notice how the Definition of Topic paragraph straightforwardly lays out the issue and the controversy; it does not take a side. Keep such a paragraph neutral, a simple statement of facts. Details on the Controversy are in Tabs.

**Delegation Goals** The GCP supports broadening gender equity right across the new country as essential to building a sustainable democracy, as well as to allow for the protection of livelihoods for all genders. Research on the society (Tab D) indicates that while speedy equity will be problematic, a delay would be institutionalized in minority-managed provinces, making inequity entrenched. However, if the cost of gaining agreement to an immediate granting of equality to the country is impossible, the coalition could agree to a road map leading to such status so long as a plebiscite is allowed within 3 years and supporters are protected in the minority provinces.

**Note** The delegation Goal paragraph is clear, as is the goal's rationale, so too a fallback position and its boundaries, and a Tab is provided with a detailed supportive study. Once again, the basic paper is not the place for detailed rationale. Instead, it is a ready to use "quick reference guide" taken by members of the delegation to the floor. In-depth rationale or background is reserved for the Tabs.

**WNBC Agenda Items** Gender equality is likely to come up under each agenda item. An agreed NGO coalition definition is in Tab A; however, defining "general equality" for purposes of the conference will be the purview of the Drafting Committee as it prepares the outcomes document for final adoption (Drafting Committee Chamber, Room 12, Randolph Hall; delegation Lead Officer (Mary James of Gender Two); Reporting Officer (Robert Meadows of Hybrid Economies).

**Note** Every conference has an agenda. In advance of the event, a delegation should figure out which item is an opportunity to build an understanding of their priority topic. It is entirely appropriate to craft a position paper for each agenda item, setting out a specific set of goals within a larger strategy. In the case above, gender equality is important and will come up repeatedly. Because the definition has not been agreed by the conference, a specific negotiating lead officer has been charged with that task in the Drafting Committee and another to report on the results of the discussion. However, those officers can't be in every room, covering every agenda item or committee (which may have many agenda items), so recognizing that one officer has charge of the definition issue as a whole, other officers will deal with other aspects of general equity in each item. To avoid confusion, all need to be listed and each given a cell phone in order to coordinate efforts by text or call, even e-mail if they have a smart phone, for example.

**Addressing the Root Causes of Farm and Pastoral Range Vulnerabilities** The matic Session 1:10, Room 45A, Randolph Hall. Lead Officer—Pearl White Sanctuaries United. **Note**: Notice that the agenda item isn't about gender, because the topic can impact gender issues, or because mishandling gender issues can harm farms and pastoral ranges, a member of the NGO coalition will lead.

**Background on Why the Topic Is Important to GCP** GCP member NGOs are involved in gender equality issues around the globe and support establishing gender equity in the constitutions of new governments. We should avoid any language that causes an excessive delay in gender equity say but also allow practical, verifiable processes to pull a society behind the idea over a reasonable time.

**Talking Points**

1. The coalition supports establishing gender equity in the constitutions of new governments.
2. While being culturally sensitive is important, excessive delays in granting equity will result in institutionalizing the marginalization of females and have a deleterious effect on the economy.
3. Excessive delays in granting gender equity are also inappropriate in that it violates agreements made with the Revolutionary Council during their struggle for independence, especially the Bangor Protocol (text in Tab E) which recognized that the revolution must protect its citizens from all forms of abuse and give them equal access to livelihoods and the permanent national political process, while at the same time protecting cultural diversity.

**Note** The idea is to have a few simple points to make in opening statements or to the media. As the negotiations progress, the delegation will need to use its best judgment for further statements and methods, making sure that when possible, such statements are cleared by the team and the communications officer.

**HQ Contact** Often, the flow of a conference can lead to uncertainty about how to deal with a fresh initiative by other delegations. And despite all attempts, sometimes the rationale behind cleared language can be uncertain in the light of real-world negotiations. As an aide, each position paper should list the Author and contact information, as well as who cleared the paper and their contact information. Ordinarily, one person does the drafting (usually the lead NGO for the topic), and an authorized representative from each participating NGO clears the document.

## 3.3 Step Five: Binders and Reports

The next step is to negotiate, management of which is the responsibility of the chief negotiator. That officer coordinates the creation of the position papers and manages the delegation, including supervision of the delegation binder, choosing tactics to suit the fluidity of negotiations, and deciding what to accept or not, within the agreed boundaries. He or she also manages the After-Action Report at the conclusion of the negotiations but before the team returns to HQ.

While this is going on, the team leader remains at HQ and is generally not part of the delegation, as that will cause confusion of responsibility. Instead, the team leader is the negotiator's liaison in HQ and is responsible for keeping the coalition together back at home, initiating supportive public diplomacy as needed and ensuring that appropriate resources are available to be rapidly deployed as needed.

### *3.3.1 The Delegation Binder*

To ensure that every member of the delegation knows who is doing what, the substance and strategy of negotiations, and any important administrative matters, a dedicated binder of information should be provided for any meeting or conference. The binder should contain the following items (for those not wishing to print paper, make the binder a set of PDFs to be placed on each delegate's laptop). Ordinarily, this is managed by a member of the delegation, supervised by the chief negotiator, but coordinated with the Communications and Administrative officers.

**Elements of a Delegation Binder**

- Agenda and program.
- Meeting documents. These were created prior to the event, like preparatory reports.
- List of delegation members and a short biography on each. The biography could be a critical piece of information when dealing with the media.
- List of hotels, mobile numbers, and e-mail addresses. This is very important if someone needs to be reached during the event. It is usually best if the entire delegation is in one hotel.
- Provisional list of all conference attendees. Many conferences develop these in advance. Make sure the delegation carefully reviews the list to identify potential allies or obstacles relative to your delegation goals, then prepare a short paragraph explaining the opportunity or potential issue.
- delegation position papers on each issue, as well as the decision memo.
- delegation's background papers, the detailed analysis used to help in debates.
- delegation action chart
- Instructions for handling the media
- Administrative information on the conference; examples are the following: (a) Maps and directions to the conference site(s), social events, hotels, trains, and

airports. (b) Immunization and visa requirements. (c) Internet and mobile phone availability. (d) Interpretation and translation services.[2] (e) Catering. When hosting an event at the conference, the official catering services will usually be used. Investigate well in advance, as some NGOs have very strict dietary requirements. See "Food at Receptions and Other Social Events" in the Protocol Section. (f) Security. Is a badge required and how to get it; what are the restrictions? In some cases, NGOs are not allowed in government delegation only rooms. (g) Visa requirements. (h) Announcements. (i) Security. How to handle publicity out on an event. (j) Others.

**Note** The binder is very sensitive and must be protected. Limit access to the delegation.

### Note: Delegation Action Chart

In a conference, there might be many agenda Items being covered. In that case, make a short report covering the entire conference and short reports on each agenda item. Two or more items can be combined in one report as well, but no report should be more than two pages in length. One page is best. Assuming there is more than one officer in the delegation, a chart could be developed that clearly states who is doing what on the delegation, as well as back at the HQ team.

| Agenda item/topic | Draft resolutions/ sponsors | negotiator | Committee | HQ action officer | Tasking comments |
|---|---|---|---|---|---|
| Conferences often have more than one agenda item. This column is for the title of the item | A single agenda item can have more than one draft resolution. A separate row should be given to each | Who is the lead negotiator for each draft? | Draft resolutions usually start in a committee | It is often a good idea to assign someone on the team under the lead of the team leader who will coordinate answers to questions from the delegation | There are often opportunities for NGOs to make statements, and each draft resolution for which the NGO wants to take action should have an HQ-cleared position paper. This column explains who does what |

[2] Interpreting is paraphrasing—the interpreter listens to a speaker in one language, grasps the content, and paraphrases with his or her understanding. A translator can write in the target language, understands the culture, and can provide an exact understanding. Documents are translated. One thing to be certain of is that when a document from a conference meeting has been published, the translation is accurate. It can happen that words or phrases in one language can be misconstrued. National delegations regularly look for such errors. It makes sense for NGO delegations to do the same unless there is only one official language.

## 3.4 Chief of Delegation and team leader

The chief of delegation should be a trained, experienced negotiator and will also manage the position papers and the delegation. This officer must also have reasonable authority to make decisions in the field. The delegation's chief of delegation is the overall delegation manager, even though there may also be other negotiators on deck. Even in a situation where the chief of delegation doesn't do hard negotiations, he or she is responsible for all decisions, so for purposes of this book and to avoid confusion with terms, the chief of delegation is referred to as the chief negotiator. This role is seldom held by the team leader, who has other responsibilities in HQ that generally supersede his/her need to also be in the field. The team leader probably does know the topic well and certainly needs to be an experienced lobbyist in order to hold the coalition together, but does not need to be skilled at multilateral negotiation. In other words, the two are a team, one in the field and one in HQ, each supporting the other. For example, since the chief negotiator will focus on negotiations, he or she should not worry about funding, though obviously stay within the budget. The team leader focuses on fund-raising instead, who hopefully will have accessed the donor's commitment to a project before setting forth (see discussion on fund-raising).

A good chief negotiator has courage, is innovative, and has good judgment, which includes the ability to place the agreement into a larger context, while at the same time protecting coalition interests.[3] To coalition NGOs, the agreement might be the most important thing on their agenda, but at the UN or in international conferences, the topic of interest to the coalition might be barely noticed by governments or other NGO when placed in the larger scheme.

The chief negotiator should also be prepared to make a deal, not just talk; be ready to develop concrete agreements, adjust differences, and line up support; and be willing to compromise without losing his or her moral core. This often means making hard choices. If the delegation head is also a topic expert, that is great, but irony is that in the real world, the combination of skills and deep knowledge isn't always required, so long as the positions being negotiated and the rationale behind them are well understood and documented and if the delegation is backed up by experts. In other words, experience from seeing diplomats in many multilateral settings shows that the chief negotiator does not always need to be a top expert at the

[3] Some of finest negotiators we met were former Assistant Secretary of State Hal Saunders, who ran the Near Eastern Bureau during the Iran hostage crisis. Another would be Judy Learner of Peace Action, that of NGO's United Nations representative and an adviser to this effort. Judy knows far more than most about the field of peace and why negotiations to promote an end to war are important. Another example would be George F. Ward Jr., Coordinator for Humanitarian Assistance in the Office of Reconstruction and Humanitarian Assistance and a senior official at the US Institute for Peace.

negotiated topic so long as HQ's position is understood, especially the boundaries of acceptability (Zone of Possible Agreement or ZOPA in diplomatic parlance). Real-time or at least good access to experts and HQ is however imperative. That's another reason why smooth communication with HQ is important, since an alternative to the sought agreement may be needed,[4] and to avoid confusion why the decision memo and position papers must be done well—papers the chief should have participated in developing.

The chief should believe in the general cause. For example, in a negotiation about post-conflict economic development, the chief should be a strong believer in the principles of development; if one of the agenda items is about the relative merits of Islamic banks versus conventional banks, the chief need not know the intricacies of Islamic jurisprudence (he will have experts on hand for that discussion); his briefing material should at least let him know that an Islamic banks's primary function is less about shareholder profits than being a tool to enable Muslims and their businesses to comport themselves successfully in conformity with Islamic teachings. In the 1980s, a number of diplomats met in Paris in a special committee called CoCom[5] to negotiate rules protecting technology used to test the efficacy of nuclear weapon explosions; the diplomats were not physicists. They were instead well-briefed generalists who understood the topic, the risks associated with failure, and a lot about the techniques of negotiation. Engineers back at HQ drafted the position papers and background material together with the diplomats, coming to an agreement on goals and boundaries. These "position papers" were not just scientific or engineering documents on the potential risk of a technology. They also reflected a complex political/economic calculus that protected domestic industries from diversion, while expanding exports within the context of the contemporary global political structure, in other

---

[4] Sometimes called BATNA (Best Alternative to a Negotiated Agreement), a BATNA needs to be kept in mind just in case negotiations do not succeed, perhaps even to suggest to the other side. After all, even the very best trained and skilled negotiators can fail. Just look at the decadelong Palestinian–Israeli discussions which have enjoyed the attention of generations of the world's best minds, without a final solution.

[5] An agreement was reached in 1948 by American allies to control the export of strategic goods to the Soviet Union and its allies. All of NATO eventually joined, except Iceland in January 1950 when the arrangement was managed by the "Consultative Group" or CG. Japan joined in 1952, followed by Greece and Turkey in 1953. To implement policy decisions of the CG, the Coordinating Committee for Multilateral Export Controls (COCOM) was created which continued to operate through 1994 to regulate trade in sensitive technologies between western economies and the communist world. The idea was export controls would limit the short-term striking power of the Soviet Union by restricting trade in both military goods and industrial goods that could be used to expand the military complex. It was credited with helping bring down the Soviet Union, despite many weaknesses because it dramatically increased the cost of modern technology in the Soviet Union in particular at the same time as they were trying to expand their military. CoCom was replaced with the Wassenaar Arrangement on Export Controls for Conventional Arms and Dual-Use Goods and Technologies in Vienna. Its focus was "rogue states." That arrangement still exists. What makes this relevant in the context of this book and the obligations of CoCom never rose to the level of a treaty arrangement. Technically, they were voluntary.

words reflecting the needs of other agencies and departments. Negotiations nearly always require coordination among many sectors or organizations. Exports of sensitive technology were therefore often allowed, some with potential risk, but only if the negotiators and engineers jointly agreed that safeguards were appropriate. But the non-engineers did the negotiating for the most part.[6] The engineers and diplomats were a team that jointly crafted "decision memos" and "position papers" that enabled the diplomats to seal an appropriate deal but always with an expert on hand "to keep science and engineering sound."

Some NGO executives we consulted disagreed with the philosophy behind CoCom negotiations and so many other technical agreements, fearing that if negotiating decisions were not made by a topic scientist, then an NGO's "moral compass" would be at risk. That could lead the delegation into making make ethical compromises in the name of expediency, but this is a false fear, if the team is managed properly.

**chief negotiator Needs to Be Briefed Well and Doesn't Always Need to Be a Topic Scientist** If the previous concern expressed by the Program Director were valid, foreign ministries would have armies of diplomats on hand. Instead, they usually only have a small corps of trained negotiators *supported by topic experts* to handle any number of technology trade agreements, conservation agreements, and other negotiations.

### *3.4.1 That Which Deflects from True Success Is Failure*

If the chief negotiator simply threatens, the other players may turn away or take counteraction against the lead NGO or even the coalition. The chief must then play "defensive ball." Advancing is more difficult because the initiative has been given to the other side. The chief negotiator's NGO might earn money from donors by using threats, perhaps even save some animals, which is always good, but sustainable success will be temporary due to loss of a true paradigm shift.

When defining the skill sets of any negotiator, look for someone who understands that compromise is ethical, if done properly and at the right time. But if all the delegation does is to bend to the wind, it also fails. A delegation ought to know its moral boundaries and use its resources sparingly—but use them if needed. A program director in a major NGO indicated that compromise is never acceptable, "since it lowered ethics." That is a misperception. Compromise is nothing more than the ethical editing of a negotiating position to meet another party's needs while retaining core principles. Let us not forget that prior to the Munich debacle of the 1930s, the terms "appeasement" and "compromise" were not viewed in the pejorative.

[6]There were exceptions to this rule. A number of engineers were also very fine negotiators in their right, generally from the defense, commerce, and energy departments.

Unfortunately, now they are part of the common vocabulary of defeat, but any professional diplomat knows the modern public view is unwise. There is no greater an authority on this than Winston Churchill, who was an advocate for compromise in its proper time:

> The declaration of the prime minister that there will be no appeasement commands almost universal support. It is a good slogan for the country. It seems to me, however, that in this House it requires to be more precisely defined. What we really mean, I think, is no appeasement through weakness or fear. Appeasement in itself may be good or bad according to the compromise. (Morgenthau 1968)

Understanding the true nature of ethical compromise is very important in negotiations. Some experts have argued that if a compromise is expected, it is best for the negotiator to use the tactic of presenting an extreme position. This is not correct. Humanitarian negotiators are not buying a rug. Don't start from weakness; do be honest. Compromise is alive and well in the UN. Use it in a positive way. Without it, the former Yugoslavian Republic of Macedonia would not be a UN member. One of the successor states of Yugoslavia, the landlocked former province, called itself Macedonia; Greece objected to that being its UN member name, saying Macedonia was part of Greece so a compromise was found. Because it is natural to narrowly define people with whom a team wishes to negotiate or whose behaviors must change, negotiators may discard, even unknowingly, information that does not fit a preconceived perception. That can lead to arbitrary knee-jerk responses or when considering reasonable "logical alternatives," calling them "ethical compromises." The classic allegory for this in negotiation theory is Aesop's "Fox and the Grapes." A fox wanted some grapes, but could not reach them and so rationalized that he really did not want the grapes, they were not tasty, and moved on instead of looking for a solution (Aesop 1955). Just because a government is tough on an issue does not mean an argument cannot be made to improve things. In addition, a delegation may have to bend a little in its position, but that does not mean it has to undermine its ethical foundation.

Of course the highlight for some contrarian delegations is to find the right "compromise word or phrase" and then insist on their formulation. In other cases, the negotiator may run into delegations that will never bend, in hopes that you will. In this case, the solution is usually to be sensitive to the room's atmospherics and the personality of the other delegations. Compromise can be a powerful tool to move a cause down the road, and if the delegation chooses that route, the action should be packaged as compromising "in the spirit of consensus," but remember that not everyone plays fair. Compromise is not always going to win points. Saying no to the tough guy may seem rigid, but sometimes that is what it takes.

**Recommendation** Pick a tough negotiator; also make sure the dispute requiring compromise is not over poor language, meaning that the other has not just misunderstood the chief negotiator's viewpoint due to a difference of language or jargon.

**Persuasion starts any debate** and will be used throughout the multilateral process; it's the face of diplomacy. This is where the chief negotiator links objectives in order to bridge what before seemed irreconcilable differences, often repackaging concepts and language by "reframing the question." But the other arrows in the delegation's quiver are almost certain to be used at the appropriate moment to keep momentum going in the right direction. When dealing with each other, governments sometimes use coercive persuasion to win their argument: (a) a demand, (b) the creation of a sense of urgency, (c) threats of punishment for noncompliance, and (d) promises of incentives. This happens a lot in the Security Council, but most NGOs cannot go about coercing national authorities, at least not at the same level; however, the concept is not without precedent.

In the early years of World War I, the United States was still a neutral power, and a private citizen named Herbert Hoover had created an international NGO to provide food to starving Belgians. The country was occupied by German forces, and the British Navy blockaded the coast.

**Note** Blockades such as were used on Belgian ports are known in international law as a "close blockade," which historically has been used to prevent ports from receiving food and other goods. The argument is that food will be diverted from civilian use to that of a belligerent armed force. The British Navy had a long history of using blockades to force arbitration of disputes, known as Pacific Blockade[7] when there is no actual war. There are thus no neutrals, since there is no war. But in an armed conflict such as existed in World War I, there can be neutrals, and a belligerent Navy will sometimes prevent neutral commerce access to blocked ports (Hogan 1908).

Unless neutral ships could bring food across the lines, there could be massive human tragedy; the British military argued that German occupation forces were responsible for feeding the civilians. Some British citizens like Eglantyne Jebb and Dorothy Buxton (sisters) were incensed over UK-imposed blockades in 1919, which they said were starving children, and later in reaction to the forthcoming blockade on Soviet ports. In response, the sisters formed **Save the Children**, a storied NGO still in existence. In sympathy, George Bernard Shaw remarked that he had no enemies under the age of seven. It is worth noting here that the sisters' NGO did something, up to then unknown, they engaged in modern public diplomacy in the UK by buying space in newspapers to not only raise money but also coerce the government by changing the public attitude, which in turn they hoped would change the heart of the government. Hoover, when speaking of his own effort in Belgium, addressed the British prime minister very directly and threatened to destroy American sympathy for the British cause unless relief was permitted. What he said was that England only had American sympathy "because America feels sympathy for the Belgians." He then threatened to send a telegram to US newspapers the next day documenting British intransigence "I will send the telegram at once, and tomorrow morning the last vestige of pity for England in America will disappear. Do you want me to do it?"

[7]Pacific Blockade as a recognized tool of international law went out of practice beginning in 1907 at the Second Hague Convention, which agreed to provisions of the Convention respecting the Limitation of the Employment of Force for the Recovery of Contract Deeds.

The British prime minister responded "You told me you were no diplomat, but I think you are an excellent one, only your methods are not diplomatic" (Nash, *The Life of Herbert Hoover: The Humanitarian 1914–1917* 1988, p. 70).

Hoover knew that the USA was split over support for the UK and that the large German–American population opposed the war. Even influential congressmen like Richard Bartholdt of Saint Louis were speaking out against the war and in defense of German interests (Bartholdt 1930, pp. 359–371).[8] In other words, the US entry was not certain. Though Hoover's direct coercion was successful, he was less adroit at indirect methods. Lloyd George was Chancellor of the Exchequer and at one point threatened to put an end to the relief operations. Instead of overt threats, Hoover turned the coin on the British minister by noting the point of the war from England's perspective was supposed to be about promoting democracy, ending autocracy, and protecting neutrals. Even if England were to win the war, if Belgium was destroyed, London would have a hollow victory, whereas supporting American relief efforts would craft a perception of British generosity that would "outlast the bitterness of the war." Hoover had spoken without notes for 15 min on the topic; Lloyd George not only changed his mind but became an ally. This was indirect coercion because George also knew that London was increasingly depending on American aid to stay afloat, and the American public was truly stuck on saving Belgium. Causing starvation in the most democratic of nations on the continent would not help US–British relations (Nash, *The Life of Herbert Hoover: The Humanitarian 1914–1917* 1988, pp. 84–85).

Direct legal action could take the form of lawsuits. They can cost a corporation dearly in terms of funds and reputation. Physical direct action could be used as well, so long as it is within law. It is a fact that governments might consider that in the case of Sea Shepherd, the NGO did the world a service by saving many whales from a horrible death, essentially by costing Japanese whalers many millions of dollars, reducing the economic viability of their illegal acts—without breaking international law nor the laws under which their ships are flagged. But that analysis is controversial.

In certain circumstances under the theory of "persuasion," the chief negotiator could imply that there are other NGOs which will respond to a negative position through direct action against private national interests. Such threats need to be carefully couched as though the delegation is trying to avoid conflict; otherwise, the negotiations will come to a quick end. The stated goal is to look for a solution acceptable to both parties. Keeping in mind that raising forms of coercion can be very counterproductive, reformulate the argument as a design for effective NGO persuasion. In other words, this is about "communication."

[8] Bartholdt had also been nominated for the Nobel Peace Prize in 1914 because he had founded the American group of the Inter-Parliamentary Union in 1904. He was also president of the Inter-Parliamentary Council, and he promoted international law and arbitration. The nomination was supported by 59 members of the US Congress and a letter from Andrew Carnegie (Source: Nobel Prize Nomination Database).

(a) Instead of a demand, the NGO has an "ask,[9]" perhaps a resolution on protection of the subset of internally displaced persons that are women, or even all IDPs,[10] of which there are perhaps over 25 million in the world, forced to migrate due to war or natural phenomena that can cause disasters.[11]
(b) There must be urgency or importance to the issue, like helping an ambulance NGO move into a war-torn country, or governments will not take the time. They are very busy. Remember that if they do not take the initiative seriously, the NGOs' interests are placed at greater risk.

A and B lead to (c) and (d). Instead of threats or punishments, the lead could explain that if (a) is not done, there will be unintended dire consequences. Perhaps the women in question will be killed or raped, or if about livestock, perhaps the camels are essential for food or job security. Perhaps the issue has to do with ecological balance (not killing certain snakes in order to preserve banana crops), some issue of great import to the culture, even if the grounds for the government doing good acts have little to do with the rationale for the NGOs' existence. The incentive for the government is "the positive result of supporting the initiative," e.g., more people are fed, poverty is averted, or ecological balance is restored. However, the chief negotiator need not care why the government, the UN agency, etc., agree to support the initiative. They can have their own reasons. What matters is that the initiative moves forward.

## 3.5 Coordinated Instructions

Whenever government diplomats go into the field, they travel with "coordinated instructions," meaning that the agencies or offices the diplomat represents (HQ team for an NGO) negotiated a common approach. In the cases of NGOs, this would be

[9]The term "ask" is common to negotiations and refers to what a negotiator is trying to achieve, perhaps a sentence in a resolution, an entire resolution, or even a declaration.

[10]Internally displaced persons

[11]NGOs have a strong interest in the protection of IDPs, but follow through can be a true legal challenge, to say nothing of the politics. The problem is that IDPs don't cross international borders, so regardless of the reasons for displacement, they are not legally protected by the Refugee Convention, yet their vulnerabilities are the same as refugees. The Guiding Principles on Internal Displacement do elaborate the legal protections IDPs should be entitled to under existing humanitarian, human rights, and refugee law, but the principles lack the authority of a UN mandate. This is a serious issue which needs adjustment, and NGOs should play a major role in the process since it is often they who provide assistance. However, NGOs involved in negotiations about IDPs do need to keep in mind that it is also unlawful under the Geneva Conventions to forcibly displace anyone based on their ethnic, religious, minority designation, or politics. The Convention on the Rights of the Child prohibits arbitrary separation of children from their parents, and the Universal Declaration of Human Rights and the Covenant on Civil and Political Rights provide not only freedom of movement but an implied freedom to refuse evacuation.

done by the Study team. The job of the delegation, regardless of personal feelings, is to follow those guidelines. This book proposes the same idea for NGO diplomats. decision memos and position papers clarify the mission and set rationale boundaries. If the delegation is asked to go outside the boundary, then they need to ask for permission from the HQ team[12], but this also means some flexibility is required in order to allow the chief of delegation room to maneuver. ***position papers are guidelines, not straitjackets. In other words, like combat, diplomacy is about managing uncertainty***.

The chief negotiator needs authority to make on the spot decisions. Not everyone agrees. One NGO leader insisted that negotiators should not make any decision without explicit approval with HQ. The same advice was uttered by a young Air Force officer when Roeder was working as an International Commodities Economist in his early days at the Department of State. The Air Force officer was an engineer who saw things in very black and white terms. But professionals in the art of negotiation agree that's immature. In both instances, the officials were looking for "perfection or nothing." In order to avoid a constipated negotiating style and failure, trust the chief to know when to call HQ, and trust any negotiator under the chief to coordinate topics within the delegation team. What if the conference is in a midday time zone when HQ is fast asleep, yet a decision must be made? This is why preparatory work by the Study team is so important and why the position papers and their background Tabs must be well prepared. The truth is that the delegation Binder Tabs should be enough to the initial guidance for a delegation needs. Judgment, not calling HQ repeatedly, is usually the wise choice. But remember, as any soldier also knows, most great plans change instantly the second boots hit the beach head and face reality.

## 3.6 Tactics

### *3.6.1 Have a Draft In Hand*

It is usually preferable to place in front of other delegates your draft text. That way the others are editing your paper, not the other way around. Of course, this might not work. Many other delegations may have the same idea, but even if they don't choose your draft, having a draft will act as a handy shorthand framework for interventions by your delegation, sort of a checklist.

Having a reasonable text prepared is how the United States handled the Tampere Convention and by convincing others to use the American text as the template. NGOs can't always do that on their own when in a multilateral setting. If a member state does agree with the NGO's positions, it might propose its own language. Keep in mind as well that regardless of whether the NGO in its own right or through a friendly state presents a formal paper for negotiation, if the NGO does have

[12]Don't forget that the decision memo and the position papers are not developed in a vacuum. The delegation members helped develop those documents, so the process of writing and clearances should enhance understanding of the desired goals and acceptable alternative options.

concepts to propose, it must also have in mind how to implement them. Otherwise, other powers that choose to run with the concepts may use their definition of terms, perhaps not in total harmony with the NGO. If that happen, it will be harder to return to the original intent. In other words, get back to Step one. If you are crafting a structure to change a pattern of behavior, it doesn't matter if the negotiators use your text. If the end result will achieve your goals, that's what is important.

### 3.6.2 "What Is Our Mandate?" Delegations

A chief negotiator need not always be a topic expert in all instances; this is because training and good briefing usually trumps the difference in knowledge—with some exceptions. Sometimes using non-experts is a tactic to slow things. Assuming a group of governments or NGO agrees to meet on an issue, if they do not know the topic well, they may send envoys that use procedural debates to delay while their boundaries of negotiating latitude are sorted out. On the other hand, some government or NGO delegations will almost always send experts, like the Swedes or Germans, who will likely come to the negotiating table with preset goals and a well-briefed team. Expect hard questions that may require going outside your instructions and may require coordination with HQ. That can be the other's tactic to test your abilities and the flexibility of your mandate.

If the names of the opposite delegates are known in advance, research their negotiating tactics; also have the team back at HQ deeply research the priorities of the opposites' government or agency. This will enable you to point out how your priorities can advance the other's goals. This tactic was used a lot when trying to protect livestock through conventions and resolutions. When talking to diplomats from poor, heavily agricultural societies, even if the opposite knew nothing about animals, it wasn't hard to show that humane treatment of cattle or some other livestock could reduce poverty and disease and increase the GDP. On the other hand, if an articulate, well-organized delegation wants to go on a slightly different azimuth than your own, the crowd may follow. In that case, the chief must be prepared with arguments and meet in advance with influential delegations. Make sure everyone is on the same "compass heading" or policy direction.

Once past the "what is our mandate" phase, the next step is to negotiate an actual text. Here it is important for the chief to remember that he or she is leading an NGO delegation, not that of a government. To bring governments over, it often is a good idea to keep the rationale short and tight, keeping the "ask" simple.[13] If negotiating a resolution, perhaps a few sentences are best in order to capture the gist of the "ask" to build steps of individual "asks" on a stairway leading to a complex document, because of its either language or politics. Especially if the outcome is an instrument

[13]By "ask," we mean the result you are aiming for. Keep an "ask" simple, especially in field negotiations, when the plainest language and as few words as possible are usually best. That way, the message is most easily understood, and the "ask" can appear to benefit the other's interests.

of length like a declaration, the team might engage a "neutral party" to manage introduction of the language, perhaps a member of the G77 or if the negotiation has a steering committee, its chair. If a friendly neutral party proposes a text, there could be less fighting, especially if the other governments are unused to dealing with NGOs on the particular topic. If a "contact group" has been created, the negotiator could ask the group to agree on a text and present it. Often, that is the best idea, but it only works if the contact group has matured to the point that they are prepared to handle such responsibilities (see Contact and Steering Groups for more details).

### *3.6.3 Moral Suasion*

Decisions in international organizations and conferences can have collateral consequences in theoretically unrelated areas; thus those collateral issues must be considered. Be prepared for "moral suasion" in the hallways to be used by national delegations during informal discussion in order to urge the chief negotiator to show that NGO priorities suit the opposite's "legitimate humanitarian needs." As an example, animal protection NGOs have a moral compass that says that animals should live a reasonably natural existence, so they often use moral suasion to achieve results, similar to NGOs protecting the environment, low-income people, or any other topic. Clients deserve the attempt, but the effective negotiator also knows moral suasion will not always work; have other options as a fall back. Civil rights advocates argued in the 1950s that Jews and Blacks in America should be allowed access to any golf club or hotel, often were disappointed. Illustrating this point is *Gentleman's Agreement*, a 1947 movie by Elia Kazan's starring Gregory Peck as a writer who pretended to be Jewish to find out about anti-Semitism. Abolitionists also used moral suasion in advance of the American civil war to argue for ending slavery; they too were disappointed to learn that economic and cultural arguments were more powerful, with some turning to violence, feeling that the new strategy was justified and itself morally persuasive, an argument not dissimilar to that of the anti-whale hunting NGO Sea Shepherd.

The bottom line is that any NGO delegation must be driven by ethics and purists will use the "moral compass" argument to push for "moral suasion" as the ultimate tool; a chief negotiator must also operate with a clear eye and understand when this works and when not, when it is better to use economic and cultural arguments, even coercion. This is not arguing that an NGO delegation give up moral imperatives. To the contrary, exposing wrong is important for its own sake, which is why humanitarian organizations like Medicins San Frontieres (MSF) were founded and argued that one cannot divorce relief from politics.[14] There must, however, also be practicalities.

---

[14]Médecins Sans Frontières (MSF) is an international, independent, medical humanitarian association that delivers emergency aid to people affected by armed conflict, epidemics, disasters, and exclusion from health care. MSF offers assistance to people based on need, irrespective of race, religion, gender, or political affiliation. MSF's work is based on humanitarian principles (Tronc 2012).

Is a delegation actually advancing its cause and changing the status quo for the better or just being pure to policy? If the delegation is not moving the ball down the field, it is failing its clients.

### 3.6.4 *Coercion*

Despite von Clausewitz, the authors do not ascribe to the theory of negotiating known as a Carthaginian Peace.[15] **Observation:** the foundation of a durable peace is not about physical victory. Peace should be through negotiation, yet much of the language of negotiation comes from the philosophy of war and defeating the opposite, and negotiation and lobbying can at times look like combat. After all, the goal of any negotiation is to change the status quo, and that usually means corporations or societies must also change, often at a financial cost.

The question then is asked, is coercion moral or ethical. The authors suggest coercion can be an appropriate form of negotiation as an alternative to violence; however, the recommendation is to pursue civil suits, peaceful demonstrations, perhaps using public diplomacy to cause the public to stop buying a company's products when it operates in a racist or demagogic regime. After talks failed, public diplomacy was used very effectively in the 1980s to coerce companies into not using purse seine nets to catch tuna, a practice that caused many thousands of dolphins to drown. The campaign began when the International Marine Mammal Project created a consumer boycott of tuna to attack the bottom line of US tuna companies, a struggle which took on a global scale when biologist Sam LaBudde smuggled a video camera onto a Panama-flag tuna fishing vessel in the Pacific and shocked the world with his imagery of dying dolphins. Though probably an illegal trespass, that direct action led to a massive consumer boycott, which coerced the industry into agreeing to dolphin-safe standards direct coercive action was probably much more effective than a continuation of traditional non-coercive diplomacy.

Charter revocation is also an effective technique used against abusive corporations, though it can be quite difficult to accomplish. This could be a tool to be used against international corporations that operate in violation of civil rights in developing countries when the local government either refuses to take action or unable. If an American corporation is found to have bribed foreign officials, both corporate executives and the firm itself can be prosecuted. Recommendation: When supporting emerging governments, counsel them to develop strong civil litigation laws that protect the indigenous population.

---

[15] Derived from the historic destruction of the city of Carthage by the Roman Empire in 146 BC, in diplomatic parlance, the term Carthaginian Peace relates to a coercive negotiation that destroys one side to the advantage of another. The most famous modern example of this would be the Treaty of Peace closing World War I.

Another more recent example of the use of peaceful coercion would be the campaign to end prolonged solitary confinement. In the opinion of many experts, this is an inhumane, counterproductive, and costly incarceration technique in which prisoners are placed in an isolated cell for 23 h a day with only 1 h of exercise, alone. It is used throughout the United States; in Maine, the practice has been greatly diminished because as part of the negotiation with the prison system, an NGO coalition including the National Religious Campaign Against Torture (NRCAT), the ACLU of Maine, prisoner rights, and mental health advocacy organizations documented that the practices in Maine met the international definition of torture. They threatened to go to court to have the practice declared unconstitutional under the eighth amendment of the United States Constitution. Instead of risking costly litigation and potentially forced reforms under a court order, the corrections department relented to the coercion by agreeing to review its policies and make good faith recommendations for reforms. The recommendations were implemented, and now solitary confinement is used only as a last resort. Prisoners used to spend years languishing in solitary confinement. Today, those few prisoners who are placed in solitary confinement are released after 40 days on average (Rice 2012).

Litigation or the threat of litigation is a peaceful coercion method that should always be considered. It is a favorite tactic of the American Civil Liberties Union (ACLU). In the case of the Maine Department of Corrections, once threatened with a lawsuit over its practices, the department saw the project could be costly to them, especially because of budget limitations, and if they lost, solitary confinement would become unconstitutional. There had also been litigation finding that placing mentally ill prisoners in solitary confinement is unconstitutional since it exacerbates their illness. In those instances, the court may impose an order, and all organizations are loath to receive orders by the courts on how to run their facilities, so the threat of litigation can be a powerful influence.

Legislation can also be coercive. In the case of Maine, the NGO coalition against solitary confinement brought legislation that would have ordered the department to make certain reforms (setting limits to the amount of time someone can be in solitary confinement, their review process, etc.). That legislation did not pass, a mandate did to study and recommend reforms. The department was left with a choice—actually make the reforms on their own terms or risk that the coalition would eventually negotiate legislation with a mandate for more humane confinement practices.

The anti-solitary confinement coalition succeeded by using peaceful coercion in the form of lawsuits and legislative initiatives with friendly legislators; they also approached their opposites with respect, understanding that in successful negotiations, even if the opposite has done bad things, NGO diplomats must avoid thinking in terms of enemies and allies; those concepts immediately color the perspective on what the others will say, their willingness to agree or implement a deal—and those perceptions might well prove wrong at a critical moment. First, try reframing the argument. That avoids a discussion where two knights impale each other on logical spikes. In addition, thinking in terms of "the enemy" leads to what in game theory is called a "zero-sum" situation. In "zero-sum," only one player can win and only at the expense of the other. No matter what is thought of the other players' motivations, try to work within "non-zero-sum," or win–win formulation, where both players leave perceiving that they have gained something. In zero-sum, after the losses and gains are added up, nothing has changed. As in football, the aim of negotiations is to move the ball down the field (von Neumann and Oskar Morgenstern 1944). The coalition applied game theory properly and gained a major victory for civil right. This is not to say that direct violent coercion doesn't ever work of course, so let's examine Sea Shepherd, which is a direct-action NGO combating whaling by Japan, and secondly WikiLeaks and Anonymous, which work against secrecy in government and industry.

Another form of coercion that is used against regimes like Thailand, Sudan, etc., is the political protest. It isn't always effective against autocratic regimes like China, especially those that believe in political repression, but could be used effectively in democratic countries like Greece that imposed strong austerity measures. Think of coordinated protests as tactics in a larger negotiation strategy leveled against a government or a corporation. The thing to keep in mind is protests and strikes occur all over the world, nearly every day. To be effective, they must have a well-defined audience, have appropriate media attention, and have specific goals. Also keep in mind that these events are generally part of an asymmetric battle against a wealthier, more power foe that sometimes has police and military tools to respond. **Question for the Study Team**: Is the protest sustainable? The Occupy Movement proved ineffective and unsustainable in many eyes because it didn't evolve in a true political movement like the Tea Party initiative in the United States.

**The Case of Sea Shepherd, a Direct-Action NGO** Combat can seem sensible; the brave assaults by the NGO Sea Shepherd on Japanese whale hunters in the south Atlantic in many minds fit the definition of a jus ad bellum or "just war," certainly to animal rights NGOs, because their "cause is demonstrably just." Whale hunting is without a doubt a cruel, painful, needless form of killing. In fact, it easily could be defined as torture because of the implements used and how they are used. The decision to use direct action for the protection of whales has been called a last resort because Japan refused all peaceful persuasion, and the resort to direct action was called "just" because no other avenue was apparent and the intention "was right." Similar proponents will also argue for Sea Shepherd that the end is proportional to the means, which do not harm humans, only an industry. On the other hand, Japanese legal scholars argue that direct action NGOs initiate wars without being a proper authority. The preference is for peaceful negotiation; but it needs to be said that the legalistic argument by Japan about proper authority misses the point and places the government of Japan at an operational disadvantage in the struggle with Sea Shepherd.

Japan sees itself as being in a position of strength in the struggle because it is a national authority, it has a navy and police, and international law is on its side.[16]

[16]As of the writing of this book, the CEO of Sea Shepherd is a fugitive from a German court, trying to extradite the officer for trial in Costa Rica on various maritime charges.

What Japan apparently has not understood is that Sea Shepherd is actually the party negotiating from strength, as are other similarly direct-action NGOs with governmental agencies, by using Japan's perceived strength as a weakness. Sea Shepherd understands that Japan's position is unpopular with many governments and even with many in the Japanese population. The NGO's negotiation strategy to change the status quo is to use a protracted, limited conflict to overcome Japan's overreliance on order and international law. This reliance may make Tokyo ill-prepared psychologically for the fatigue of an extended struggle to support an internationally unpopular market for whale meat. Revolutionaries like Mao Tse Tung would call this tactic "the never-ending struggle." Nations prefer to meet on the battlefield and "decide" or meet in a negotiating room and "agree." Revolutionaries like Sea Shepherd, or national insurgencies think asymmetrically, which gives them an advantage and certainly comes across as combat.

The authors oppose violent direct action but do recognize it as a tactic by some NGOs; instead, the preference is for peaceful negotiation. That can include nonviolent coercion. Certainly, the questions in this case for a decision memo must be "is the war or conflict winnable" and "what is the definition of success?" After all, NGOs generally have fewer resources than governments and large corporations; in the case of Japan's hunt for whales, some question if Sea Shepherd has a reasonable chance of success. It is all about definition. One could argue that while total success for Japan means a total end to whale hunting, success in the context of Sea Shepherd could simply be measureable drops in whaling on a slope that points to eventual eradication. That definition allows for a sustainable struggle which will be considered worthwhile on moral grounds alone so long as there actually is a measureable decline in whale deaths. If this occurs, the tactic will probably be supported by donors. One could also argue in fact that Sea Shepherd has indeed done that because they have saved many, many whales and are heroes to millions of lovers of whales, but scholars on successful methods of changing policy will also argue that diplomatic means proposed in this book are appropriate more often, that alternatives are possible, and that there is a dangerous precedent set when civil society takes the law into its own hands.[17]

**The Case of Irresponsible Action** Both WikiLeaks and Anonymous have a moral premise worth discussion, even though both have committed unethical practices that undermine their credibility and their cause. The authors are strongly opposed to their tactics, even though secrecy in government often leads to abuse of power, civil, and human rights. Some forms of civil disobedience by "NGOs" can also lead

[17] Armed non-state actors (ANSA) sometimes violate international law, like attacking civilians. This is often done in order to rebalance the relative strengths of state forces versus those of the ANSA. The justification is that tactics that violate humanitarian norms are tactically acceptable because they avoid military defeat. While the authors respect the need for coercion as a tactic and encourage interaction with armed non-state actors when done to protect innocent people, the authors reject any violence against civilians.

to innocent people being harmed. Also while secrecy can undermine democracy, the practical fact is that to properly serve the people, governments sometimes must negotiate in secret and have secrets and intelligence services. There is no question that secret agreements can also undermine global peace, as seen by the circumstances that led to World Word I, but sometimes secret deals are also needed in the interest of the greater good. Understanding that, the authors recommend oversight to avoid abusive secret deals. One of the American lead negotiators for the League of Nations said in his notes, "It is necessary, I think to do away with the abominable custom of espionage, but to abolish it and leave some dishonorable nation free to surreptitiously prepare for war would be a mistake" (Miller, *The Drafting of the Covenant* 1928a, pp. 13, Vol 1). That's why checks like the courts, activist NGOs, and the media are important. Ultimately, the people are the counterpoint to governmental agencies because governments serve the people, *but common sense is also required.* The practices of WikiLeaks and Anonymous endanger lives without truly protecting the people.

**Recommendation** Some scholars assert that the tactics employed by Sea Shepherd are unethical, but others disagree; the question needs to be asked however because "just cause" and "proportional means" are matters of interpretation that can lead to chaos. Indeed, many governments see direct action organizations like Sea Shepherd as "extreme" (OSOC:US Department of State 2008). But characterizing such direct action, NGOs as terrorist may miss an opportunity. The question should not be whether Sea Shepherd or similar NGOs are immoral or justified; rather, what are the driving reasons behind their actions? Further, the authors argue that well-executed traditional diplomacy can reduce conflict between nations. NGO diplomacy which includes coercion by pacific means should also reduce the need for violent direct action. That's a primary mission for NGOs, *to build sustainable understanding through peaceful means.*

### *3.6.5 Chatham House Rules*

Preparatory work for a negotiation often deals with controversial topics, opinions, and players. This might take place during a study group discussion or in actual bilateral discussions. The problem with controversy is that the players may feel vulnerable about expressing true opinion, fear it will be reported in the press or to higher authorities. Chatham House Rules will only work when there is an element of trust between the players; this can be a very useful mechanism in bilateral talks or in discussions with victims, anywhere the contacts desire privacy. The concept originated in June 1927 at the Royal Institute of International Affairs and goes as follows "When a meeting, or part thereof, is held under the Chatham House Rule, participants are free to use the information received, but neither the identity nor the affiliation of the speaker(s), nor that of any other participant, may be revealed" (Chatham House 2012).

### 3.6.6 The North–South Problem

When it comes to negotiations, the term "north–south" is increasingly understood as pejorative, creating an assumption that north is better than south. Indeed, in the pre-Rwanda Crisis days, northern NGOs were often accused of ineffectively transferring skills to their southern partners. Instead, the humanitarian community should think of local and regional NGOs as important partners, deserving equity. Forget about whether an NGO has a staff of five or five hundred or whether it operates in a village or national capital. Focus on its service, professionalism, and knowledge. By following that rubric, the relationship of all NGOs around the world can be defined in a way that builds broad bridges to significant funding and policy change opportunities. This north–south issue is pervasive in relief literature, and if something isn't done about it, rules, declarations, and charters will largely be western and implementation not necessarily the most effective. To counter the problem, at Rio + 20 in June 2012, the coalition of civil society bodies insisted that any proposal from their group for Sustainable Treaties includes both north and south partners (People's Sustainability Treaties 2012a).

There is already a rich set of often ideas in the NGO community. One particular problem however can impede progress. There is a geographic and wealth disparity in the representation of NGOs at UN meetings, with the vast majority coming from wealthy North America, Australia, and Europe. NGOs from "the north" have more money, and their staff is often better trained in the complexities of multilateral policy making and implementation. Northern NGOs do fantastic work[18] of course, but there are many southern NGOs that the larger humanitarian community never hears from. This disparity in participation translates into a disproportionate level of influence between the regions and diminishes the effectiveness of the global intellectual treasury. Since so-called southern NGOs don't have enough buy-in, why should they follow the advice of the "north?" The "north" does not have all the answers, yet one senior official from an influential European NGO told us he could not take seriously anything a Sudanese NGO suggested because anyone who survived in Sudan "had to be tainted by the government (Confidential 2008)." Another NGO official setting up an initiative alliance told us that all that they wanted for alliance members were large NGOs with money, which again meant northern economy NGOs. The argument was that while the myriad of small, local NGOs provided services, their narrowness of focus, financial resources, and training in emergency management made it inappropriate to engage them in large operations, even in their own region, unless they had a subordinate role. Those attitudes are unfortunate and antiquated. Engaging such NGOs provides fresh thinking and "cultural intelligence," which is essential in negotiations.

While it is also understandable to focus on NGOs linked to royalty, retired politicians, or the rich, culling the south will retard the intellectual quality of any dialogue. It is simply the wrong thing to do. The so-called southern NGOs sit in

[18] Heifer International works with the Batay Community in remote Paracelis, Philippines, on livelihood protection (Heifer, 2010b). Another example is Endangered Species International (ESI) which is fostering research and conservation activities to preserve endemic freshwater fish in partnership with local fishermen in southern India (ESI 2010).

remote villages of Brazil and Africa and elsewhere where people and culture are often at great risk but should stand as equals in New York and elsewhere with the major NGOs. After all, what is developed in the UN, the World Bank, or with the IFRC and other bodies will directly impact the "least influential among us." But that won't happen unless all NGOs are brought more fully into the fold.

In fairness, the staff of a tiny youth advocacy NGO in Somaliland is less apt to be able to travel to meetings in Europe or New York than a similar NGO from Copenhagen or Little Rock, Arkansas. A special project of the umbrella bodies might be to pull into the conversation even the smallest NGO from the remotest part of the planet. It may prove to be too expensive to pay for all of them to attend meetings in New York or Europe or even Nairobi; their ideas must be brought forward, some of which could be held in multilateral meetings in their regions.

#### 3.6.6.1 Reframing the Question

To maintain good relations in negotiations, try to avoid situations where one player appears to be in a superior position to another. That can create a dangerous psychology, which is why many negotiations happen at a round table, to maintain balance. Suppose the chief negotiator makes an "ask" but the other party says no. It might be tempting to walk away or complain about the other's tactics or motivations. Instead, change the conversation's tone by reaching out to the other and express interest in a "mutually satisfactory agreement." The chief could suggest an informal discussion to see where interests are shared (linkage) at the end of which the lead might express understanding of the opposite's underlying goals, even though there is a disagreement on tactics; the lead then suggests a fresh start. What this boils down to is changing the nature of the game from seeking the best position on the chess board "combat" to jointly solving a problem, "reframing."

#### 3.6.6.2 Dealing with an Unreasonable Opponent

A form of threat is not to be flexible and exude a willingness to pull up stakes. Suppose NGO GoodStock is negotiating with the Ministry of the Interior of MoreGrowth, a land beset by annual storms and frequent earthquakes. GoodStock wants to shelter livestock during emergencies. MoreGrowth agreed to meet but then took an inflexible position, saying "animal shelters must be very distant from urban human shelters, out in the country. Either we agree on that premise, or we can go no further." Their inflexible position might make it tempting to build a massive public diplomacy campaign against the government. This can work in very dramatic ways, as happened in November and December 2004 when tens of thousands of Ukrainians protested fraud in the presidential elections. The effort was nonviolent and so effective that the Ukrainian Supreme Court nullified the election and call for a repeat runoff.

Instead of walking, GoodStock could present a counterproposal. But what if MoreGrowth rejects the counteroffer by just reasserting their original proposal? Every situation is different of course, but at this point, GoodStock should be cautious about compromise, as MoreGrowth, knowing that the balance is gone, might see the tactic as weakness, and then push harder for more compromise. Meanwhile, GoodStock is faced with the very real operational problem that in the land of MoreGrowth, no emergency animal shelters exist. Should GoodStock accept MoreGrowth's proposal and call it a day just to gain something?

There is no simple answer to this quandary, but since a public diplomacy campaign might be seen adversely by MoreGrowth, causing the government to dig its heels in ever more strongly, one approach could be to redirect/reframe the conversation. Perhaps the following will work. "I see that your approach is important to you. Help me understand why you insist on rural shelters." The atmosphere may change due to GoodStock's seeming willingness to hear the government out, perhaps add that it represents a coalition of NGOs wishing to provide care to animals in a crisis without cost or sanitation issues to MoreGrowth. MoreGrowth is then asked to explain their concerns in that context. If MoreGrowth's delegate takes the bait, the conversation has been changed or reframed into a mutual problem-solving exercise. Both parties will now probably want an agreement, thus become more cooperative, with each player laying out a plethora of points. Each time MoreGrowth makes a point, it provides GoodStock valuable information and a chance to respond with a counterproposal that takes into account MoreGrowth's concerns. In other words, by changing the conversation into a meeting to address MoreGrowth's concerns instead of just those of GoodStock, this altered atmosphere offers opportunities. Perhaps the government is just worried about labor costs and security. Roeder faced this very problem when talking with the Arab Red Cross/Red Crescent societies in Tunis and then suggested that NGOs could manage the livestock corrals and provide all the care. He also pointed out that if the owners were in close proximity, they could help, which would reduce their stress, since they would know where to find their livestock. The Arab Red Cross/Red Crescent societies agreed that such a solution could provide the refugees some hope of taking their livestock back home after the crisis abated. In other words, the fresh approach addressed their concerns of reduced labor and monetary resources, enabling them to agree to allow animal shelters next to refugee and IDP camps.

#### 3.6.6.3 Troublesome Governments

Some governments have terrible human rights records, one of the largest issues of the day, and it often means that to achieve good ends, an NGO diplomat must work with unpleasant governments or organizations. There are anti-Semites who challenge the holocaust and "soldiers" you will have to negotiate with who might easily have been raping and the day before; keep in mind that the negotiation is not about them as individuals. It is about the client, like the children abused by the Ugandan warlord Joseph *Kony*. In other words, a delegate must park his or her personal dislikes; smile, while keeping one's moral compass pointed north; shake the hand of people who can help; drink their tea; smile; and negotiate. Keep the goal in front, not the other guy's idiosyncrasies, and you will reach your goals. If that means talking to diplomats from a country with an awful record, that is the price of success—so long as talking translates into a better world. On the other hand, if an NGO tries to isolate a government, they will isolate the NGO, and that could hurt clients.

## 3.7 Interdisciplinary Complexity

Modern NGO delegations are going to find that negotiations are becoming increasingly complex and that different disciplines need to brought together to support a cause, not only knowledge of one topic like refugee housing; what might first appear to be "unrelated topics" often turns out to be interconnected. As a result, the Study team needs to understand the larger context of a negotiating strategy, and the team leader will have to place coalition issues in a larger context while the chief negotiator manages the evolution of the negotiations, not constantly referring to HQ for guidance. In other words, decisions might not just be about the ethics that advanced the initiative. While the team might want governments to agree with their ethics, the important thing to keep in mind and what must drive the negotiator in the talks is actually changing the status quo in a specific way; the reason for governments and international organizations getting involved is less important than that they make the changes. Moral fusion will come later. Syria offers an example. In 1914, Syria was home to a myriad of secret societies, with their own agenda, and many in touch with Arab movements throughout the Middle East. Try to imagine the complexities of negotiation for European powers trying to undermine Turkey. They had to figure out what was motivating each society and try to convince them to join a larger context of independence. Similarly as of the writing of this book, the groups fighting the central authority want independence, but it is hard to differentiate what each will want after independence or who or what is influencing them. That sort of understanding will be essential in order to arm them or provide other support. It can't just be about "independence." What if the process arms a future despot?

## 3.8 Standard Rules of Behavior

Every industry has standards of behavior; no more true than in the humanitarian community, which has the SPHERE standards[19] developed in cooperation with governments, the UN, and the International Red Cross and Red Crescent Movement. The key point is that these rules were initiated by humanitarian NGOs, not the other way around as a way to define how a partnership between NGOs, governments, the UN, and International Red Cross and Red Crescent Movement will work.

[19]"The Sphere Project is a voluntary initiative that brings a wide range of humanitarian agencies together around a common aim—to improve the quality of humanitarian assistance and the accountability of humanitarian actors to their constituents, donors, and affected populations. The Sphere Handbook, Humanitarian Charter and Minimum Standards in Humanitarian Response, is one of the most widely known and internationally recognized sets of common principles and universal minimum standards in lifesaving areas of humanitarian response. Established in 1997, the Sphere Project is not a membership organization. Governed by a board composed of representatives of global networks of humanitarian agencies, the Sphere Project today is a vibrant community of humanitarian response practitioners (SPHERE, Not listed)."

### *3.8.1 Do the Rules Always Apply? Challenge Axioms*

The novice might be forgiven to think that the rules of diplomacy are inflexible. Not true. Always take a moment to reflect before acting, because the normal documented approach is not always the best.

***Case Study: Albanian Transition in 1991***

In 1991, Roeder went to Albania as the first US government economic affairs officer since World War II and before diplomatic relations were established. The old leader was dead, and a peaceful takeover by the people seemed possible. Roeder did not know the language, but he had studied the country for 2 years in the Department of State as part of a group of officials looking for countries about to drop communism. Based on the work of an extensive Study team, he chose to travel around the land, meeting local officials, mayors, union bosses, etc., and regular folks. He was also given a local driver and interpreter. The driver was a former government driver with broad knowledge of the countryside and a trained bodyguard, the latter because of bandits. The other was a young university firebrand. Roeder also had two goals set by the Study team—to show that America cared about Albanians and to find opportunities for investments in order to build a sustainable economy and expand American trade and jobs.

One day, Roeder's team rolled into Shkoder and found a mob yelling at a burning office building. Another mob also stood to one side, considering their next action. Locals explained that the smoldering building belonged to the secret police and because they had killed some demonstrators, the citizens burned the structure, with the police inside! Cairns marked fallen marchers. The mobs also wanted to burn more buildings and then perhaps march on Tirana, the national capital. Meanwhile, another State Department team in Tirana was advancing democracy in the parliament, while a third was trying to create a peaceful demonstration in Tirana for the Secretary of State to attend. It was one of those moments when a decision was required, also caution. Roeder's instinct was to avoid mobs, and the driver also wanted to move away, while the interpreter wanted Roeder to lead the crowds in a peaceful march; Roeder felt neither was a valid option. Leading a march sounded romantic, but the marchers could also have been met by the army, leaving in shambles American efforts at peaceful transition. Departing also looked bad. Roeder's driver was just trying to keep him safe, but what kind of commitment to Albanian democracy would departure show?

This was in the era of pre-Internet and pre-smart phone, so a quick consultation with HQ or the teams in Tirana was impossible. Roeder decided to have his driver move the car to one of the cairns, essentially keeping the US flag between the two mobs. Leaving his colleagues behind, he then removed the flag from his hood and planted it in the center of a cairn, then left his business card on each. He then talked to the mobs, saying that America was with them, but spoke of Reverend King, who preached peaceful demonstrations. It was a weird moment, oddly quiet in fact, not knowing what would happen, but the call for calm and the promise of American support worked. Everyone clapped and shook Roeder's hands till they were sore. The transition was smooth, and when Secretary of State Baker arrived in Tirana, nearly every Albanian in the country was there, thanks to another State Department official who had been on the ground. For a year, Roeder received cards of thanks.

**Recommendation** Be true to core values but bend the rules when needed. Also, be ready to accept the consequences of failure. Roeder's actions could have backfired.

## 3.9 Using an Opponent's Strategic Objectives

A clever negotiator can turn the other's tactics into the actual "point of discussion" rather than battle over the other's strategic goals. Avoid threatening the opponent's viability "in their eyes"; instead appear to have compatible goals and sympathy. The opposite will be more willing to compromise, and, as a result, less apt to strike back. Example: Is the true objective of Tradeisstan's Agricultural Ministry to encourage farmers to use intensive livestock as a tool to save money and achieve a profit, or is the true objective to have profitable turkey farms? Is the strategic goal of Village X to sell bush meat, or is it only to earn enough money to survive?[20] Is Pooristan's strategic goal to produce meat, or are they trying to feed their population in the absence of alternative, socially acceptable food sources? Was France's strategic objective about destroying Germany or actually about some repayment of costs and the establishment of an effective political barrier to future war? This may never be known, but perhaps a collective security arrangement like today's NATO might have been a better compromise for the allies within the League Framework.

If an ally's strategic corporate ethics suggest they cannot support a government that the chief negotiator needs as an intermediary, can cooperation with the ally be achieved by repackaging the rationale? Example: A particular tribe in the forests of Bogistan is at risk from deforestation. In order to reduce the potential harm, the support of the G77 coalition of governments in Geneva is needed to insert language in a resolution of the UN's Economic and Social Council (ECOSOC). Time is critical. A year's delay will mean forestry roads would reach tribal areas, leading to contamination of the tribe's culture, a great loss to anthropology and the right of the tribe to privacy.

---

[20] Bushmeat trade in particular is a crisis not only for animal welfare/rights professionals and conservationists but also for those practicing sustainable development in that it threatens the ecosphere even more than the conversion of land to living space and is a prime source of animal–human disease transmission. Yet socioeconomic realities often work against this most ugly and cruel of trades. It is also the subject of both bilateral and multilateral diplomatic efforts by NGOs and governments.

A successful resolution could provide a mandate to the UN agencies funding lumber-based development in Bogistan. Unfortunately, it is also learned that this year's chair of the G77 coalition is the country of Badisstan, which has a horrendous human rights record and whose leader is being pursued by the International Criminal Court (ICC). The chief negotiator feels that the delegation must gain the support of the Ambassador of Badisstan because without his or her support, there is no hope of convincing the rest of the G77. Careful analysis reveals however that an NGO ally and donor to the initiative named GoodLands will refuse to collaborate with Badisstan. GoodLands loses nothing (no funds or supporters) by withdrawing, because they are a domestic NGO. They might even gain funds.

The chief negotiator on the other hand may lose the initiative, making it harder to attain future alliances or funding. Knowing in advance that this problem could be an issue allows the chief negotiator to develop a plan in advance, perhaps preserving his or her alliance by pointing out that cooperation in ECOSOC only means working with the "position of chair of the G77," not in any way endorsing the national practices of the government. This is exactly how the UN often works. If cooperation is neutral with regard to internal policies, it does not endorse governmental practices under indictment by the ICC—it just recognizes UN protocol realities.

Compromise certainly played an important role in the formation of the United Nations, and NGOs were often at the heart of the debate. Three major compromises were included in the charter: education, human rights (including the creation of a Human Rights Commission), and formal recognition of NGOs at the UN. As Stephen Schlesinger pointed out in his study of the UN's formation, none of those concepts were incorporated in proposals out of Dumbarton Oaks, yet today they are central features of the multilateral system. These great achievements came about because of direct negotiations between representatives of civil society and government members of the United States delegation and other delegations. The compromises are probably not perfect in many minds, and some NGOs were left out like the World Federalists, who more recently helped bring about the International Criminal Court; the main point is the UN isn't just a room for governments to talk and negotiate. Thanks to the early and effective interventions by NGOs and private citizens, the governments compromised, and the UN is now a space for everyone (Schlesinger 2003, pp. 123–126).

### *Case Study: Brazil and the Value of Precedent*

One way to convince an ally who is reluctant to work with governments is to provide examples of when such cooperation has worked, as in the following situation in Brazil. The Ministry of Agriculture, Livestock and Supply was looking for ways to publicize good agricultural practices in order to impress European importers. Local animal welfare NGOs approached the ministry with a solution—"traceable cattle," raised with good humanitarian practices. The ministry had troubles in the past with Brazilian farmers and European importers so decided to step up the monitoring of cattle with the help of an NGO partner in order to make sure humane slaughter training took place for county, state, and federal slaughterhouses and inspectors. Strict guidelines were developed with the NGO partner because the NGO managed to gain the trust of the authorities and supply a solution for both animals and the ministry. The project worked so well that Animal Welfare (AW) specialists were invited to take part in legislation review boards to update guidelines for raising cattle, pigs, and birds. This was a huge step for AW legislation in Brazil and was taken without a single threat or protest. This was all done by face-to-face bilateral conversations, after identifying key players and showing them enough argumentation and a balanced attitude. The NGO approach in this case was one of the advisors to the ministry, showing the ministry that the NGO could effectively help solve a problem that bothered both parties concerned (Antonio, *Review of Book Discussions* 2010).

## 3.10 Time Management

A critical feature of diplomacy is that, except in operational matters when time is essential, what is important is the deal's quality, not the time taken, so as resources dwindle and donors begin to pressure for results, being calm is critical for both the team leader and the chief negotiator, who should keep HQ and coalition members sensitive to the ebb and flow of negotiations and resist arbitrary deadlines. As part of the decision memo and position paper processes as well as the situational awareness exercise of examining those with whom the negotiator "will negotiate," determine to the extent possible if "time" is a critical factor for any player, including donors. Understanding this factor provides a strategic advantage. Misusing it can place a negotiator at a disadvantage. Executives who have expended many resources in an initiative often feel the compulsion to "finish this thing quickly." Donors can become anxious when an end is not in sight and resist more requests for funds. The team leader can also cause the chief negotiator to rush decisions in order that HQ looks effective, but a reactive strategy is inherently unstable and usually leads to poor decision making. This is not to suggest that things go on forever, but the entire team needs to analyze how long the process will be, understand that multilateral negotiations can be very lengthy, and, in rounds, constantly reevaluate their position. Both the team leader and the chief negotiator must keep everyone informed, so that if more time or an exit strategy is needed, all parties will be properly prepared and understand.

The need for reasonable time and patience cannot be over stressed. The Vienna Environmental Convention was signed by 24 governments, mostly from the so-called northern, industrialized nations. A deal was thought, therefore, to be inevitable. Unfortunately for the negotiating teams, when the southern, "developing economies" were finally engaged, they felt they had been left out and wanted more concessions. That happened at Rio when the conventions on climate change and biological diversity had to be signed by 154 nations. The truism is that with size comes complexity and delay, for example, the debate over the relative importance of natural and anthropogenic change, how to measure and control atmospheric composition change or predict ozone depletion in the atmosphere. Some of the most important goals of humanitarianism will require negotiations with just as many countries as Rio, but a negotiation even half that size can take many years to achieve. Both the team leader and the chief negotiator must keep in mind that progress towards success is what matters, not artificial deadlines. If the chief negotiator is making progress, instead of pushing to close negotiations, the team leader would do better to work with allied NGOs and build an effective coalition that can leverage negotiation successes by the delegation to push ministries in capitals to change their directions to their delegations. Failing that, perhaps a major public diplomacy program might be in order.

## 3.11 Other Points

- **Why is this important to your opposite?** If you can't explain this, you are dead. Giving them this information gives your opposite a reason to take the time to lobby for your cause with his government. Your issue is a product. What will your opposite gain by buying it?
- **Questions will be asked, partly out of curiosity and partly to test your knowledge, perhaps on precedence.** If the position papers and your own background are inadequate, don't resort to a guess. That can be disastrous for credibility. Just say you must check with HQ; don't forget, just because a fact seems trivial to you doesn't make it so to your opposite. However, do not become Commander Data from *Star Trek* and bore with a plethora of information. Only give what is needed to make the case.
- **Be a Credible Representative:** Before selling your position, sell yourself as a credible, honest representative. Your opposite might not understand your NGO, its coalition, or even the topic, but if your opposite believes you are a solid rep, you have established a basis for persuasion. In a shoe store, you want to know that you can trust the knowledge of the salesman, or you likely won't buy any shoes. This is the same concept, though it usually doesn't mean you must be a top expert—so long as you have access to them. Also credibility is directly proportional to your promises and ability to deliver. Don't commit to what can't be delivered.[21]

[21] "Diplomacy throughout comes in many guises. Some are apparent and stem from being diplomatic, but on its own, that is not enough. Many foreign government officials recognize raw diplomacy and may be suspicious of your intentions and reasons for invoking the art of tactful discussion. Diplomacy with foreign government officers often needs to be more covert and will likely materialize as compromise, cultural sensitivity, and a genuine willingness to proffer trust and credibility. In a number of Middle Eastern countries, it has sometimes taken several years for governments to accept our NGO as a full operational partnership. For example, the provision of statistical information or information relating to past activities would not normally be offered without a formal MOU or partnership agreement. This can only be achieved through the establishment of trust and organizational and personal credibility (Wheeler 2012)."

- **Use Coordinated Guidance.** One reason for coordinated guidance is that an NGO team is often made up many NGOs or different offices in an NGO, each with its own perspective. Be careful that your interventions do not unintentionally undermine your allies. This doesn't stop you from making suggestions, but keep in mind the guidance and why different points were agreed to. This is why we recommend, if possible, that delegation members (or least the negotiators) be part of the Study team. The negotiator might not be the world's expert on a position, but he or she will understand why the position was taken.
- **Equality.** National diplomats treat each other as equal. While not always realistic in NGO–government negotiations, the NGO negotiator does need to be sure he or she is treated equally by relative rank. In other words, the chief NGO negotiator is organizationally within the NGO system equivalent to a national Ambassador and speaks with similar authority for his or own NGO or alliance.
- **Personal Prejudice:** An NGO representative is a citizen of a state; therefore, keep in mind that the opposite may have a personal opinion of that country which colors his or her judgment. If that's possible, have a plan of action in mind.
- **Show Some Empathy:** This means understand the opposite's limitations, emotions, thought processes, and even the capacity to grasp.

## 3.12 Contacts and Cooperation

### *3.12.1 Cooperation with NGOs*

Cooperation is encouraged across types of NGOs such as those that are traditionally humanitarian and others dealing with the environment or development, animal welfare, etc. There also needs to be cooperation between all players in civil society and with governments, UN agencies or other international bodies. This avoids stove pipe operations like we used to see on livestock. Frequently animal welfare NGOs work in isolation from human rights NGOs, and as one human rights colleague once said to one of the authors, "we don't do animals." Both were wrong. A failure to deal with livestock can cause human starvation and poverty. Both humanitarian and animal welfare bodies need each other in many instances. The same could be said of many issues where in the interest of purity, some refuse to cooperate. That can result in failure to solve a very real problem. For example, those caring deeply about refugee rights should be willing to work with NGOs which do not have refugee protection as a primary goal if that would reduce suffering.

Private donors might send NGOs into the field to promote a specific issue, not to coordinate with other NGOs; yet coordination is essential and donor governments like the United States insist on coordination. Unless already set into the plan, like any other important decision (see discussion on decision memos), impromptu coordination may need to be cleared with HQ and interested parties, especially appropriate UN clusters. It will also often involve time and funding, but the investment is worthwhile. NGOs in Port au Prince in 2010 could not have achieved success without coordination with other NGOs, as well as governments, and the UN (Funai 2010). NGO successes in Bangkok during the Cyclone Nargis similarly resulted from cross-sector meetings among a range of NGOs. Though a voluntary process, collaboration and coordination will reap significant rewards because lessons are shared, as well as data on field conditions, background on government leaders and rules.

***Case Study: The 1974 Cyprus Invasion***

One of the more interesting cases of cross-sector cooperation involved the UN in 1974 during the Turkish invasion of Cyprus. The United Nations understood that livestock on the island were at risk and that, in turn, placed livelihoods at risk, so UNHCR, UNDP and FAO asked the International Society for the Protection of Animals (ISPA) to intervene. This was the first known instance of when a UN agency requested help from an animal welfare NGO. FAO was also involved in supporting NGO operations in 2009 in Myanmar in an operation where cattle were protected in order to protect the rice crop and prevent starvation.[22] Assistance was provided to Nicosia, Kyrenia and Limassol areas, with some staff flown to Cyprus by the RAF so that drugs could be provided veterinary surgeons (Roeder, *Diplomacy, Funding and Animal Welfare* 2011).

## *3.12.2 Cooperation with Corporations*

Like any nation, International Organization or NGO, private corporations will pursue their own interests. They often also have enormous resources and global networks. Finally, they have political influence. To understand this, study the history of economics and its influence on politics. Despite the existence of empires, local self-sufficiency was the common socio-economic trait until the end of the fifteenth century, which was very limiting. Then came national economies that replaced local ones, followed by the Industrial Revolution in the eighteenth century when national economies that evolved into global interdependent systems. Today, global corporations are largely free of the political bonds of nations and act in their own interests, even though they must follow national laws and regulations. But their goal is to gain profit through the control of industry, finance and transportation, be it by ship, airplane or the internet. Anything that reduces profits is a problem, and with that premise lays the foundation of cooperation. If an NGO can show that corporate assistance

[22] At the time, Roeder helped coordinate shipping of NGO purchased food to Burma on US Air Force planes based in Thailand. Non-animal welfare partners in Burma then picked the supplies up on arrival and conveyed it to the NGO staff in the field.

to a cause will help a corporation's public brand or bottom line, it may provide vastly more assistance than a government—and more quickly. Alternatively, going it alone will severely limit what can be accomplished in a connected world.

### *3.12.3 Personal Contacts*

Before seeking an MOU or other formal agreement with a humanitarian body or government, an NGO might find a member of the other's staff who is personally favorable to the NGO's strategic goals. That can reap rewards, such as keeping an NGO informed of developments relative to its issues; the official might even join an informal "contact group" of interested officers. Such "friends of *the Issue*" can also provide professional advice in their "personal capacity" on what tactics will work or not in a given context and even help the lead NGO contact officials in ministries during an emergency. For example, personal contacts with a variety of missions helped one source for this book convince the chair of the G77 to sponsor a discussion on an NGO issue, which meant the NGO had access to the entire membership.

Friendship is an important component of diplomacy and people who hold different political beliefs can make common parley, perhaps easier so, if they have already built a foundation of trust and friendship. It is often pointed out for example that one of the reasons the United Nations charter passed the US Senate, whereas the League's did not was that the head of the isolationists in 1945 was Burton K. Wheeler, who also was a close friend of President Truman (Truman 1972, p. 258). The lesson here is to make friends, even if you disagree with your opposite's policies. Indeed, NGO delegates that work long enough in the UN or one of the other important bodies should make a lot of friends, i.e., people that a delegate can probably partner with in workshops and programs. Keep in mind that trust is essential; a diplomat's reputation for honesty is the foundation of success. As Metternich said "Good diplomacy does not try to deceive, for one is never so easily deceived, as when trying to deceive others." Of course, Metternich lied all the time. Keep in mind, however, that officials in diplomatic missions work for their government, not for NGOs, and officials in UN agencies work for the agency. No matter how nice they are, confidentially is not assured. Anything said to these officials might be shared. In addition, public statements of support by officials do not always mean or imply official government endorsement. In fact, support for an initiative might be less about helping the NGO or its cause than promoting a hidden agenda.

In one instance, an NGO diplomat needed the support of an important African state in order to achieve a briefing. He was on friendly terms with an ambassador at the African state's mission to the UN, who finally agreed after many phone calls and a meeting over a meal. The briefing proved very helpful to the NGO's cause; at the same time, the NGO diplomat was realistic enough to understand that the mission did not care about his issue. Their government was having serious political problems with the international human rights community and the mission felt that agreeing to the NGO request would deflect attention from their problems. In the opinion of the NGO leadership, gaining the briefing helped their cause, so they went forward, it being understood that they never endorsed the country's human rights record. That is how things are done in the UN, and it is consistent with best practices performed by the humanitarian NGO community.

The issue happened in 2009 after Sudan expelled the international humanitarian NGOs; the International Court of Justice was after the president, but Sudan held the chair of the G77. An NGO officer in New York, remembering that he represented an NGO, not a government, felt it important to refrain from public comment on the regime's expulsion of the 13 NGOs responsible for half of all humanitarian assistance. Some NGO officials in his alliance wanted to make public statements of revulsion, and that was understandable given the genocide in Darfur, but had that happened, it could have provoked further expulsions and, in the NGOs case, set its particular issues back. At the same time, the NGO diplomat was quietly speaking to UN officials about being resolute; it being assumed they would not be tossed out. This was a safe bet based on the diplomat's earlier experiences in Sudan when he had to deal with the Khartoum regime and the rebels to the south. Encouraging contacts to do no harm involved a delicate dance; it was risky appearing close to the Sudanese since they might use a supposedly good relationship with a respectable NGO to counterweight damage they did to their own reputation. The only way to do it was to avoid stating anything good or bad about activities in Sudan, while focusing on the administrative role of Sudan's ambassador in the UN as chairman of the G77. That was Diplomacy in the most classic form.

#### 3.12.3.1 Is the Personal Contact Speaking for the Government, Agency or Corporation?

Suppose the first Secretary of the UN Mission for the Republic of Central Islands says she personally supports protecting the right of a particular oppressed minority to use its language in schools. The officer also says that she can convince her Ambassador to publicly support a declaration that your NGO delegate is advancing to protect this particular minority, a small indigenous tribe that lives in a flood prone country with few resources. The delegate also wants to do this in the Second Committee of the UNGA. Second Committee is the part of the UNGA that focuses on sustainable development, so this isn't a perfect fit; the First Secretary is very supportive, saying that the oppression of any minority threatens the "minimum rights and liberties of mankind." Precedence is even given, such as the 1860 French invasion of Lebanon in order to protect the Maronites from slaughter because this was a defense of "mankind as a whole" (Eppstein, *Ten Years' Life of the League of Nations* 1929, p. 115). How should you as an NGO delegate react?

It is always great to hear an ambassador or other senior official speak in public on an NGO's behalf. If donors know about the statement, this could also bring in more funding. But does the statement actually mean that the Republic of Central Islands will join the consensus on a resolution once it comes for a decision? The answer might be "no." Find out if the ambassador was speaking in her personal capacity, as they sometimes do, or on instructions from the government. If it was in her personal capacity, an NGO cannot say that the ambassador's government definitely supports the initiative. Reporting such support could in fact embarrass the Ambassador when her Foreign Ministry asks for clarification, at which time they might decide that "while the declaration is an interesting concept requiring consideration, the agenda item under which it would be considered is not appropriate for the topic. The recommendation is to table this issue (a parliamentary term for delay) until the following year when it can be discussed by the Human Rights Commission." UN Missions do not like fights, so unless there is another national sponsor for the declaration, this simple "official" statement by one member state requesting a deferral will likely kill the initiative for the entire year. **Conclusion:** Be very careful on how developments are reported and make sure that if the mission says something, it is also supported by the Foreign Ministry, which has the final say on all "official statements" by any UN mission. And in the case of the example, consider if the topic is even coming up in the right forum.

## 3.12.4 *Contact and Steering Groups*

### 3.12.4.1 Contact Groups

Once a set of personal contacts has been developed, consider asking them to join a "Contact Group," or "Friends of …", a tool governments and International Organizations regularly used to investigate a problem, and share ideas. Sometimes seen as a community of practice, role the groups play will vary with the issue. Be aware that the term "Contact Group" goes by many definitions in the diplomatic community, one which is "these are made up of delegates who have the trust of their groups and can convey to the president (of the UN General Assembly) a sense of the deliberations of each group, and can even help this officer guide the groups" (Leguey-Feilleux 2009, p. 231).

Another sort of contact group is assembled by governments in order to coordinate action during a breaking crisis, such as the "Friends of Syria Group" formed in February, 2012 to respond to the slaughter of civilians. Held in the middle of the some of the heaviest fighting, the goal of the inaugural meeting was to "focus on humanitarian aid and to help the disjointed Syrian opposition form a united and democratic alternative to the Assad regime" (LaFranchi 2012), an especially difficult task since China and Russia vetoed a peacekeeping force. Meanwhile, Arab neighbors were arming insurgents and the international community called for protection for humanitarian convoys. Such events must be attended by major humanitarian NGO's, since much of the work on the ground from driving trucks, to treating patients will be done by the NGO community.

For long-term crises and to develop a UN mandate for policy changes on development, the G77 is an essential forum. The G77 is organized differently than other contact group, and is often considered the biggest "contact group". If it agrees to something, that idea has a good chance of becoming UN policy, and it has been known to consider NGO initiatives. A smaller body is the Alliance of Small Island

States (AOSIS),[23] which could also be a venue for NGOs. AOSIS is an informal group whose members are willing to share ideas on a cause. This could be about any NGO initiative, such as a resolution or a project. In other words, use a contact group to discuss "bridging issues," or links between NGO priorities and those of member nations, "pushing the camel's nose into the tent."[24]

**A Caution on the G77** Much is made of the G77 in this book, because it is an important block of nations; however, they don't always operate as a block. Mexican diplomats have often said such blocks are on the out in ECOSOC and the GA, and that states will increasingly negotiate along ideological lines, rather than traditional blocks; that remains to be seen. Mexico is not a G77 member.

Keep in mind that before most missions participate in such discussions, they require instructions from their Foreign Ministry. This gets us back to statements of support by Ambassadors. Some NGOs have expressed the view that because a ministry has expressed sympathy for an issue, that is a statement of support by the government. Actually in the context of multilateral discussions in an International Organization, a real statement of support by a government must come from or be authorized by the Foreign Ministry. There are exceptions but for big global negotiations, Foreign Ministry support is required. It is their job to coordinate the government's opinion on foreign affairs matters and provide official instructions to their diplomatic missions.

As an example of another contact group, in June 2006, at the suggestion of the United States delegation to the UN, some Ambassadors in New York formed the International Contact Group (ICG) to examine the constitutional crisis in Somalia. It was initially led by the Norwegian and American missions to the UN and still exists, and now is led by the UN Special Representative for Somalia, who is based in Nairobi in the UN Political Office. The group meets at least twice a year and consists of "representatives from capital"[25] for Italy, Kenya, Norway, Sweden, Tanzania, the United Kingdom, and the United States together with the African Union, European Union (Presidency and Commission), Intergovernmental Authority on Development, League of Arab States, and United Nations. Notice that it includes both regional and donor nations (Norway, *UN Mission* June 2006).

Also consider the Contact Group on Piracy off the Coast of Somalia (CGPCS) has a very narrow focus. The ICG is informal, with no legal authority but much influence, due to its membership. The CGPCS, established on January 14, 2009, was called together with a limited focus on the illegal seizures of ships and crews. It was created as a result of a UN Security Council Resolution, No. 851, thus giving it special powers under international law. It contains both donor and regional powers

---

[23] Climatecaucus.net provided assistance to AOSIS in 2010.

[24] An old Bedouin proverb. If a camel can push its nose into a tent, the rest of the body will soon follow, but by bit.

[25] This term means that the representative is not based locally at an embassy or mission but instead is based in a nation's capital, perhaps at the Department of State or Ministry of Foreign Affairs, etc.

(Spokesman 2009, January 14). Yet another Somali group also exists, known as *Friends of Somalia*. This informal contact body was started about a decade ago by Norway and meets prior to Security Council meetings to share ideas and strategies. Like the other groups, it consists of regional and donor powers (Enge 2010).

In 2004 while at the U.S. Department of State, Roeder became increasingly concerned that livestock owned by refugees and the internally displaced was not being taken care of properly, thus threatening food supplies, jobs and the local culture; so he formed a "contact group" of government and NGO officials to talk about "animal welfare" and unite the communities behind practical solutions. By sharing ideas with professionals in the NGO community, state officials gained knowledge which made them comfortable with the concept and thus that is a good initial model for any NGO-based contact groups on concepts fresh to the UN; even for well understood concepts like reconciliation, which often takes the form of preserving the past as much as it does sponsoring dialogue. One could imagine NGOs with an interest in Kymer-Rouge atrocities as well as reconciliation in Cambodia forming a similar contact group with a friendly government, especially since as of 2012 no official Truth and Reconciliation process exists in that country, though there are courts that are trying former officials. However, reconciliation cannot be imposed on anyone from the outside. That kind of process takes a lot of time and requires trust, which will be slow to coming. This is where NGOs can make a significant difference, creating a climate for change, essentially facilitating a collaborative space.

Another contact group worth mentioning is called JUSCANZ (pronounced juice-cans). Its full membership varies a bit between Geneva and New York but generally includes Australia, Canada, Iceland, Japan, New Zealand, Norway, Switzerland, and the USA. In January, 2010, Israel also joined the group for sessions in Geneva, but not New York, Vienna, or Nairobi. JUSCANZ does not coordinate positions. They just share ideas in informal settings; unlike the EU and the G77, they do not coordinate policy decisions.

**Recommendation** When trying to advance an issue at the UN, it probably is a good idea to start, join or collaborate with an informal working group "interested officials" from UN Missions, UN agencies, and the International Red Cross and Red Crescent Movement and the World Bank, with the governmental and agency representatives providing informal advice and reporting back to their HQ with recommendations for further action. Such a group could also be helpful for surprise issues. For example, if negotiating a Convention, over time the members will become familiar with the topic and provide helpful contacts to NGOs on a range of topics. Roeder did that quite successfully with the mission of Israel with regard to the need to move agricultural supplies into Gaza during the Intifada.

#### 3.12.4.2 Steering Groups

Steering groups are sometimes formed as an alternative to contact groups. These are more formal than a "contact group" and have a specific focus of advancing a cause, not simply sharing information. Every situation is different; it is a good idea to start with a contact group as a tool for creating allies, then moving to a steering committee, since one expects all of the members of that body to have a common view point. These officials might be from diplomatic missions to the UN or some other international organization, or perhaps represent ministries from the capital, even be a mix; one principle must underlie everything, namely that the officials have authentic authority to represent their governments as a whole on the topic at hand. If they only represent their ministry, that can also be very helpful, sort of a fulcrum to budge the Foreign Ministry; however, without the Foreign ministry, their power to move the issue in the UN or other international for a will be limited.

## 3.13 Field Negotiations

Field negotiations can be about everything from convincing tribal elders to protect women who go off to collect water at risk of rape to discussions with armed non-state actors like the Kachin Independence Army (KIA)[26] to allow telecommunications for doctors. They are often about dealing with the denial of humanitarian assistance or access. They could also be negotiating with UN agencies, the IFRC, rebel forces or a government in order to obtain the information needed by refugees to return home or tend to their farms. In some cases like Herbert Hoover's saving of French and Belgian civilians from starvation during World War One, John Walsh's epic Operation Gwamba in 1964, or the Rwanda Crisis of 1994, field negotiations related to fast-moving emergencies may require amending the Study team time-frame, though its premises remain. In many cases however, field negotiations are also about making long-term change; then the time frame should work (Fig. 3.1).

Famed Humanitarian relief expert Hans Zimmermann remarked when discussing the study group framework in the book that "Diplomatic negotiations in the field can be very frustrating, and one should warn people not to lose courage! I remember only too well, how useless I felt when I spent whole days trying to negotiate the necessary permits for those who did the actual humanitarian work In Liberia in 1990/1991 and in Somalia a bit later. The relief workers from UN and NGOs would usually gather for some talks in the evening, and everybody could proudly report about having saved so many patients' lives, or having distributed so many tons of food to the starving population, or having made visible progress in re-building a school or a hospital—and I could only report that I had spent all day discussing with officials from the minister of whatever down to whatever bureaucratic level, trying to get permits for the relief workers to do their job or for a ship or plane to deliver relief goods. …. Results of diplomacy are not always directly measurable. Another discouraging experience was Ethiopia: obtaining permits and support from the

[26]Many armed non-state players are military wings of political movements. The KIA for example is the military wing of the Kachin Independence Organization (KIO) in Burma.

**Fig. 3.1** Cattle and Farmers in Indian Flood © 2008 (Courtesy GDIN Project)

government for assistance to the Sudanese Refugees (or even an exemption from import duties for relief goods for them) was next to impossible at the time when their own population suffered from an unprecedented famine. Understandable, but totally frustrating for me (at that time a UNHCR logistics officer)" (Zimmermann 2012).

MSF (Doctors Without Borders) had this to contribute: "MSF medical teams on the ground are in constant dialogue with local authorities (in particular the Ministry of Health), warring parties, and other aid agencies in an attempt to ensure the best possible medical care for patients and their communities and to reinforce the organization's operational independence. In 1999, when MSF was awarded the Nobel Peace Prize, the organization announced the money would go towards raising awareness of and fighting against neglected diseases. Through the Access Campaign, and in partnership with the Drugs for Neglected Diseases Initiative, this work has helped lower the price of HIV/AIDS treatment and has stimulated research and development for medicines to treat malaria and neglected diseases like sleeping sickness and kala azar (Tronc 2012)".

## *3.13.1 Know the Other Side*

Around the world, millions of people are in need of expert assistance by the NGO community. For example, in only a part of Southern Kordofan, Sudan, over 360,000

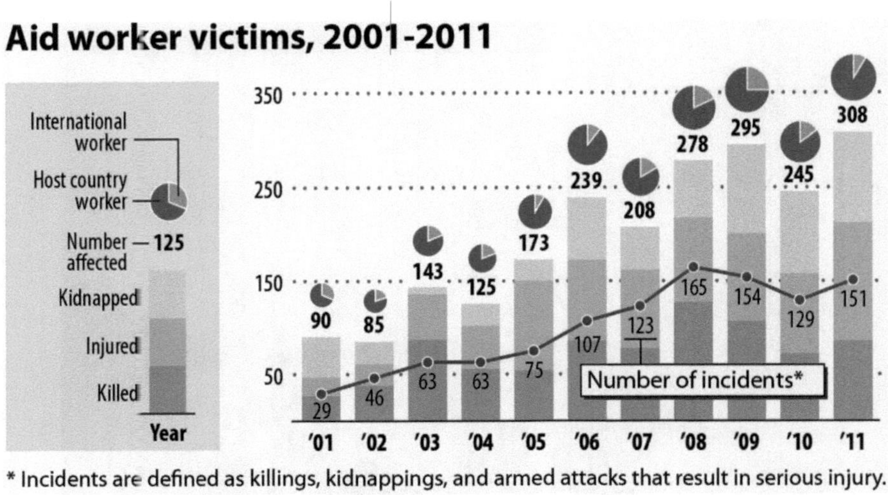


**Fig. 3.2** Courtesy, Dennis King, US Dept. of State 8/22/2012

people are either internally displaced or in some other way impacted by the violence (USAID/OFDA 2011). If an NGO is going to negotiate agreements to support these people, it should begin with the very best information, so before flying off for any negotiation, the study group should obtain a biography on the people to be met, especially if they are in the field. If an NGO negotiator understands the perspective of the opposite delegation's members, it will be easier to place the NGOs needs into a context relevant to the needs of the opposite. Of course, sometimes, biographies won't be possible, so it is a good idea to read up on the culture, which should be done anyway. If there is time, cultural immersion programs like at Heifer-International in Little Rock, Arkansas will also sensitize delegations to local thinking (Fig. 3.2).

Another requirement is to acquire a full security profile. "Since 2001, the number of aid worker victims who have been killed, wounded/injured, or kidnapped in security incidents has risen dramatically. The majority of these victims are national staff aid workers. Aid workers can be the targets of combatants or collateral casualties caught in the crossfire of conflicts, or they can be victims of criminal attacks, robberies, or kidnapping for ransom (*World Humanitarian Day 2012: Aid Workers in Harm's Way* 2012)." In other words remember that a dead or injured NGO diplomat can't support the cause.

An excellent source of information on risks is the Aid Worker Security Database (AWSD), which can be accessed through the professional resources section of Reliefweb. This tool records "major incidents of violence against aid workers," with incident reports from 1997 through the present. Initiated in 2005, to date the AWSD remains the single most comprehensive global source of this data, providing a much-needed quantitative evidence base for analysis of the changing security environment for civilian aid operations. Statistics provided by the AWSD formed the basis of a major study released in September 2006 by the Humanitarian Policy Group, of the

**Fig. 3.3** Bodyguard in Somaliland ((c) 2010 LRoeder)

Overseas Development Institute and the Center on International Cooperation at New York University as well as briefing papers and data updates in 2006 and 2009 (Humanitarian Outcomes Project). NGOs should also consult with the InterAction Security Unit, which has established practical guidelines and training tools.

But also keep in mind government sources such as those of USAID, which are available to the general public. During Hurricane Emily in 2005 that threatened Jamaica, in advance of the storm hitting that country, USAID developed a team that monitored data coming in from technical services like the United States Weather Service and crafted maps and situation reports for use by all NGOs. They monitored the situation from their Latin America and Caribbean (LAC) Regional Office in San Jose, Costa Rica, and the sub-regional office in Bridgetown, Barbados, as well as from Washington, D.C. In addition, they had a team in Barbados coordinating with local and regional disaster relief officials and the U.S. Embassy in Bridgetown regarding possible USG disaster assistance to the eastern Caribbean (Stone 2005). If an NGO wanted to go to Jamaica to work with local municipalities, in addition to negotiating that permission with the national and local authorities, the NGO should have well in advance studied which agencies inside and outside of the country have critical operational information and have developed a strategic relationship with the body (Fig. 3.3).

Remember the information matrix proposed in the section on knowledge management. Certainly one filter in field negotiations would be civil order. What is the crime level? Will anarchy impede negotiations? Will the host government provide police support, as it did for Roeder's NGO mission to Somaliland in 2010? Is the police force itself a problem, perhaps an abuser of human rights, and as a result might their protection might create barriers to success because of a perceived association? Unlike in a conference, field negotiations are usually not about committees and "word-smithing"[27] documents, perhaps no documents at all. Keep things simple.

### *3.13.2 Perspective*

Every negotiation is important and field negotiations can seem daunting because of the immediacy of a crisis or in a long-running emergency because around the team are people in terrible conditions who might not understand the rationale behind an NGO's actions, especially if it isn't dealing directly with food, medicine, etc., perhaps it is there to protect an ancient site or prevent environmental hazards. The American adventurer John Walsh, father of modern animal rescue, (Walsh, *Time is Short and the Water Rises* 1967) had to face that every day in Kabul when protecting the zoo animals after 9/11 (Walsh, *Discussion of Kabul Zoo Operation* 2011). When faced with those kinds of situations, where physical protection of people isn't the precise goal for the NGO, it is important to remember to put the NGO priority in the context of an overall theater strategy—to describe what is being done by the NGO as essential to a holistic approach to humanitarianism, perhaps for the survival of jobs. There will always be those who do not get the bridging argument, but if the team is honest and sensitive, it should work.

As any good decurity adviser will attest, perfect security is unattainable even for heads of state or government, so every NGO should have its own or security protocols, designed by a professional security adviser and something that dictates how to operate in an emergency and even whether to operate in a particular kind of crisis, e.g., an oil spill, nuclear accident, earthquake, or a state in conflict. They also need to be in harmony with the InterAction Minimum Operating Security Standards (MOSS). If the plan is to operate in a crisis, the first bit of diplomacy is not even about the substance at all, but how to enter and how to stay safe. In the case of the Kabul Zoo crisis, a major NGO alliance approached the US government for assistance in developing a security profile. Any NGO which plans to operate in a conflicted environment should certainly have a security firm on retainer to provide advice.

Peacekeeping forces often acquire SOFA (Status of Forces) agreements. While NGOs are unlikely to acquire anything so comprehensive, protections are possible when operating under the aegis of the Tampere Convention on the Provision of

[27] Word-smithing is a common term referring to the tedious effort in most conferences of working and reworking document many times over as numerous. delegations insist on specific words or phrases in order to protect a particular interest. This process can be very tiring, but is crucial since different cultures will have different ways of phrasing the same concept in the same language.

[28] *Examples:* References: (a) position paper of Dec 26, 2015 on Reconstruction Zones in Afghanistan for the February 24, 2016 – Berlin Conference on Aid Effectiveness. (b) Research Project on Targeting Aid to Provide Adequate Infrastructure by Paul Minor, Feb 10, 2009.

Emergency Telecommunications, which in certain circumstances, does provide legal protections to NGOs. Finding out if this is possible should be a priority goal for the team's legal advisor.

Deciding on bodyguards depends on the situation and how it would impact the negotiation. In South Sudan, Roeder was offered guards for protection against rebels, but he refused as that would have made him a target and in the case of Charles Gerang with whom he met, would have indicated a lack of trust. However, in Somaliland and Kenya, different politics dictated that he was sometimes accompanied by a uniformed soldier with an AK-47 and other times, a plain-clothes ministry official, expert in defensive driving. Inevitably, if an NGO is going to do work in a conflict zone or even a massive disaster, this question comes up. For the most part, if the guard is a government official, this can be a handy asset, particularly at highway check points, but it can also identify the NGO with the government, and that can be very dangerous. Think in a situational manner. To examine the fisheries near Berbera requires armed protection due to robbers. Driving around the port and town only requires a civilian guard, perhaps only an effective facilitator. But do not wait until arriving to learn these facts. The Study team should gather security intelligence in advance.

If an NGO is lucky enough to work with the UN in a crisis, it is usually protected by the UN Security System, which is designed by UNSECOORD in New York. The idea is to provide a coherent security profile for each area in which the UN and its implementing partners might work, and in each country is a Security Management team (SMT), with whom it is wise to coordinate. They will have the latest information on what is safe to do and with whom. They will also have advice on how to approach specific individuals. There are then a lot of dos and don'ts which anyone who has worked in a crisis is well aware of, camp security (whether guards or fences are needed), field security (movement plan and travel authorizations), cash security (carry only what is needed), crowd security, mine awareness, decisions on protective gear, and other factors.

In some cases, a security protocol will be required to face terrorists or kidnappers, as might be the case in Puntland (ر أ اض لذبط), a self-declared independent republic of Somalia. It declared itself independent in 1998; however, no state recognizes it. Puntland is also a focal point for pirates who attack along the coast of Africa, as far south as the Seychelles. Keep in mind that negotiating with rebels or even governments in a war zone is always risky, which is why security profiles exist, but many of the rules are the same as anywhere. Dress properly and exercise calmness and honesty. The negotiator should explain why the work is of added value to the local community, and if the negotiator's NGO is politically neutral. Let the people with guns do most of the talking, but the negotiator must not be afraid to state his or her case. Follow all of the normal rules. The irony is that if the other side is willing to talk, the negotiator will probably be alright—with certain exceptions. Just keep in the mind that the other side will be as nervous about the NGO as the NGO is about them.

## 3.14 After Action and Implementation

### *3.14.1 After-Action Report*

At the conclusion of the negotiation, a report should be written by the negotiating team while the results are fresh, and then both that team and the HQ team should consult on the way forward, looking at what worked or did not and why; then the cycle begins anew with a fresh decision memo. Without the "after-action report." there is risk of losing an accurate historical record. Every NGO involved in diplomacy or lobbying for that matter should have a central electronic file that contains such reports. That way, future negotiators will be a step ahead. Before drafting a decision memo or a position paper, read after-action reports from prior missions to see what worked or not, and why, all of which should be in the delegation Binder or least on a CD-ROM for reference (Fig. 3.4).

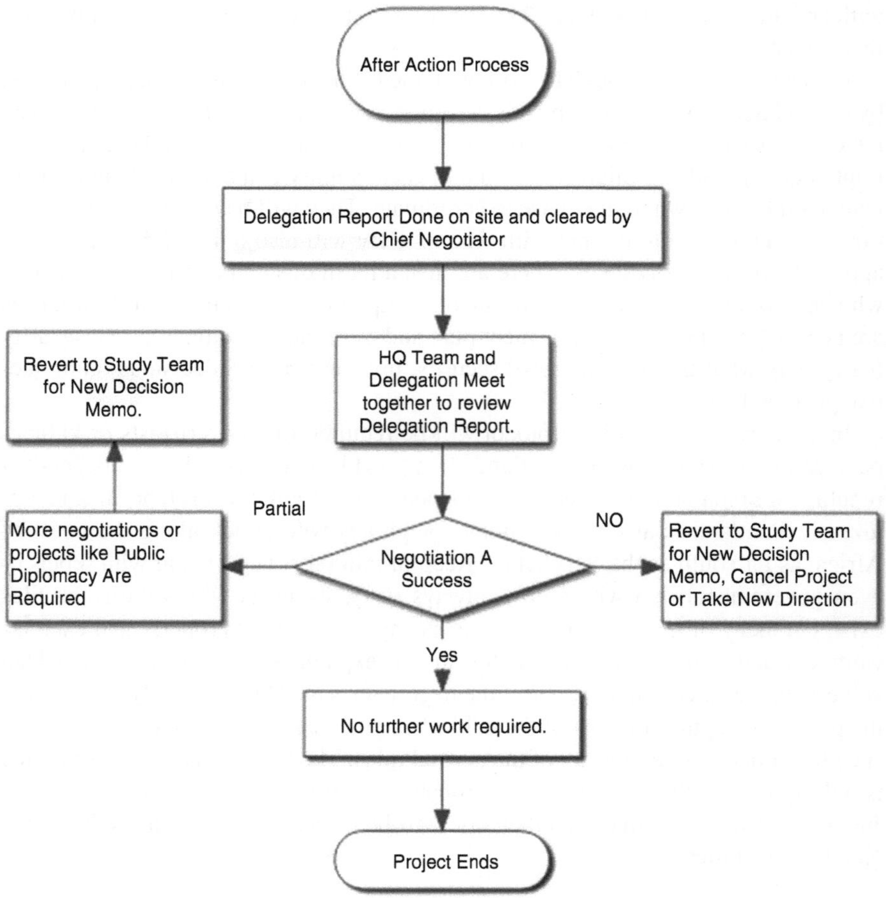


**Fig. 3.4** After-action process

An after-action report should be written before the team departs for home, whether the mission was to a conference, a meeting with fellow NGOs, a government, whatever. This is important so that information is fresh. One officer should do the drafting; each team member needs to clear the substance (grammar is not as important), because each member will inevitably have a different view on events. The chief negotiator is the approving officer for the report and the one who sends it to HQ or whomever or whichever else needs to see it, e.g., partner NGOs. Nobody loves paperwork. It is the action which is interesting, but decision memoranda, position papers, background tabs, and after-action reports are essential reference material. Doing these items well reduces paperwork and redundancy of effort. It also makes it easier to pick up the pieces later on, especially if the team members move on to other jobs.

**A basic format for an after-action report is as follows**

Fr: Head of delegation

To: HQ (name of person(s), if also to other agencies (names of persons there)

References: These are one-liners referring to past position papers and other relevant material. The idea is to minimize text in the report to precedent, etc., so no need to repeat *positions* in the report, other than a brief summary statement of goal(s).[28]

Subject: after-action report for the March 15, 2018, UN Conference on Dynamic and Inclusive Growth in Reconstruction Zones, New York.

**Summary**: Summarize the reason for the trip, what was accomplished and what did not go well. Keep it to one paragraph. The body of the report should contain the details.

**Body of Report:**

(a) List the delegation members and who led on which item, as well as who was delegation lead (remember that the report does not go out until it is cleared by the team members and approved by the chief negotiator).
(b) Report on what went well or not and why; but avoid an exegesis. The report should be written in the simplest possible language, covering all of the main points in concise and accurate terms that can be easily followed by the CEO of the NGO, even if he or she is not deeply familiar with the topic.
(c) If materials (reports, studies, resolutions, etc.) have been collected at the conference, list and explain their relevance.
(d) Recommendation for further action and why: keep to one paragraph.

### 3.14.2 After-Action Review Session

Upon return of the team to HQ, an "after-action review session" should be held with the HQ team and others as appropriate to discuss what went well or not and why—even if the consensus is that all goals were achieved. This discussion is led by the team leader and should lead to new decision memos deciding what next to do:

- Find ways of implementing the agreement, if one was made.
- Cancel project, if that is the consensus.
- Engage in new negotiations or perhaps public diplomacy efforts.

### 3.14.3 Implementing an Agreement

Negotiation is a process, not an event; and just because a negotiation was successful, the project probably isn't complete. Implementation may require years of work, projects, the expenditure of money and staff resources. The deal must be followed through, perhaps through "implementing legislation,"[29] or rules promulgated by existing legislative authorities, any one of which might require lobbying and/or further negotiations. It might be that the negotiations failed. Generally the best procedure at this stage is to replicate the study group process. A careful analysis could point to a more effective path to success if the project failed or a new path even after success at the negotiation table. Whatever happens must be sanctioned by a second decision memo. Even a successful negotiation will likely require the same process in order to map out the forward journey. Some of this certainly should have been considered by the initial Study team and decision memo; but whether the negotiations were successful or not, the playing field will have changed. Events will have happened; perhaps new alliances have been formed. A fresh, careful rethink will enable.

In order for policies agreed at a strategic level like the United Nations to actually bear fruit, some implementing agreements may be required on a local, national or even regional level. The trouble is that as one NGO informed us, sometimes "laws are not enforced because there is no infrastructure to do it" (IFR, 2010a, October). This observation is very important because it points to the importance of using NGOs at all levels from local to international to advocate for an implementing structure.

As an example of the complexity of implementation, consider that for NGOs to negotiate strategic agreements, they often must work with regional bodies like UN agencies or even non-UN bodies. An NGO involved in the reconstruction of disaster-affected states across a region like North and South America might need a regional deal brokered by the OAS (Organization of American States[30]). Recognizing that

[29] This legislation provides government officials the authority to implement or enforce a law.

[30] The OAS is not a UN body; but works in association with the UN.

national legislation and political structure and philosophies on reconstruction in the region will frequently differ between governments, before the multilateral negotiations took place, the NGO coalition should have lobbied for "common multilateral principals" that could be implemented by national legislation, e.g., not to trade in endangered species, or identify a strategic framework to promote fragile environments. Even though that was likely done, the same process in some form will also have to be done at the completion of strategic talks. The advantage of gaining agreement to principles versus rules before the strategic agreement has been set is that one can avoid the natural resistance of governments against agreements that might impinge on their sovereignty. The UN and other multilateral bodies are not global governments after all. In this context, keep in mind that for the UN at least, "the sovereignty, territorial integrity and national unity of states must be fully respected in accordance with the charter of the UN (UNGA 1991)." In addition, issues like the rights of indigenous must sometimes be considered, as well as whether or not the other side will adhere to what they have agreed (see Sect. 6.7).

# Chapter 4
# Information and Knowledge Management

**Extract** This chapter explores the emerging role of information and its sister component knowledge management in the development and management of diplomatic initiatives. Diplomatic initiatives have both HQ and field teams, so this chapter shows how each component impacts the two teams so that they can interact effectively.

## 4.1 Introduction

**Note** For the purpose of this book, KM or knowledge management is a skill set any delegation member must acquire. In addition there should be an officer dedicated to handling KM requirements for the team. That person reports to the team leader, supports both the team as a whole and the delegation, and thus receives requests from the delegation. Any NGO should have its own KM staff that reports to the CEO or some senior manager. In practical terms, the KM officer for the delegation might or might not be a member of the home lead NGOs staff. It doesn't matter so long as that officer can always be relied upon when requests come in from the team or the delegation. The KM officer also handles supporting the "intelligence" requirements mentioned in Chap. 5.

> Approaches must be developed to find and distribute essential information to any disaster manager anywhere in the world. The most famous success story in this arena may be ReliefWeb, considered by many to be the finest disaster information website in the United Nations and a prime example of the innovative international teamwork that is required in this field. As a result of some of the information failures of the Rwanda Crisis, to say nothing of the failure of Media to cover the crisis, ReliefWeb was first conceived of by the Department of State. But AID, the UN, and many others in the NGO world were engaged. In addition, the idea that became ReliefWeb had deep roots in the emergence of the modern Internet age and the struggle to advance information management in Africa. ReliefWeb was launched in October 1996, after a prototype period, to serve the

L.W. Roeder, Jr. and A. Simard, *Diplomacy and Negotiation for Humanitarian NGOs*,
Humanitarian Solutions in the 21st Century, DOI 10.1007/978-1-4614-7113-4_4,

> international relief community, becoming an essential newspaper and search engine and a stimulus for NGOs and other crisis organizations to post information on a common platform (Holmes 2004, March 18).

The information and knowledge revolutions are changing the way the world lives, works, and does business, how children are educated, how research is conducted, and how people are entertained (G7 Secretariat 1995, Feb 25–26). An economy in which the basic resources are information and knowledge is fundamentally different from one in which the basic resources are land, labor, and capital (Martin 1996). Rather than trading atoms in the form of objects, markets are trading bits, in the form of knowledge (Negroponte, *Being Digital* 1996, p. 255). These societal-scale revolutions affect all institutions, organizations, and disciplines everywhere, including humanitarian assistance NGOs. Stop or impede the flow of information and knowledge and an NGO cannot function. This chapter describes what NGOs need to do to adapt to the new world order and how they can benefit from it.

The knowledge society is about much more than making information easier to publish and more widely available. It is about more than creating, managing, and using knowledge as a core economic resource. A few examples demonstrate the scope and importance of this global revolution.

- The 2010 "Arab Spring" showed that, because of social media, it has become very difficult for dictators to hide the truth from those they govern or to prevent massive assemblies of their citizens. It is also equally difficult to hide events within their borders from the outside world.
- In British Columbia, Canada, tens of thousands of cell phone images taken by witnesses during the 2010 Vancouver hockey riots allowed police to investigate incidents, identify perpetrators, arrest those responsible, and charge lawbreakers.
- A major corporation hired hundreds of experts, paid them to write encyclopedia articles, and used its industry dominance to market an online encyclopedia. At the same time, a global collaboration involved experts who voluntarily wrote articles for free. They were made available to anyone, anywhere, at no cost. Fifteen years after it all began, the encyclopedia no longer exists and Wikipedia is the largest and most successful encyclopedia ever created.
- An intelligence video was posted on YouTube that showed allied forces defending a small outpost in Afghanistan against an attack by insurgents. In presenting the actual event to the outside world, it countered the claims of innocent civilian casualties spread by the insurgents.
- Cell phones helped emergency responders during the Haiti earthquake. People trapped under collapsed buildings were able to call outside and direct searchers to their location. Cell phones also helped by automatically pinpointing witness reports with GPS. Social networks helped with relief efforts by diverting supplies from areas with excess to areas where they were needed.

Key characteristics of the Knowledge Society that affect all NGOs include:

- Accelerating pace of change and decreasing half-life of knowledge
- Increasingly complex issues—sometimes beyond the capacity to know
- Less time for analysis, synthesis, and decision making
- Engaged citizens and donors who want more organizational transparency

- Growing importance of communities, networks, and global connectivity
- Information overload, in which filtering is more important than finding
- Collaboration becoming essential because no one can do it all

Rather than focusing on the emerging knowledge society as challenging and not well understood (which it is), NGOs should consider that they are well positioned in the new order. Most NGOs (particularly those for whom this book is intended) are relatively small. Being small, they are nimble; they can sense, adapt, and respond quickly because they are not constrained by large bureaucracies, infrastructure, and policies. They are used to collaborating within larger networks of similar NGOs. As a rule, they tend to be more open than governments; it is in their nature.

To benefit from these advantages, however, NGOs must understand the emerging knowledge society. The knowledge management literature began with a handful of pioneering authors in the 1970s and has grown to thousands of books and articles today. Important general texts include Nanaka and Takeuchi (1995), Davenport and Prusak (1998), O'Dell and Jackson (1998), and Dalkir (2005). This chapter compresses many key ideas into an overview of important questions. What are data, information, and knowledge and how does an NGO acquire, manage, and use them to achieve their objectives? How does an NGO learn what it needs to know to accomplish its mission? What are the benefits and methods of sharing information and knowledge? What practices enable an NGO to increase the value of what it knows and use that knowledge more effectively? Finally, how do collaboration and negotiation work, and how does an NGO capture value from these activities? These questions lead to knowledge management principles and practices described in the next section.

## 4.2 Management Framework

There are many ways to organize the information and knowledge services that are needed to support humanitarian assistance provided by NGOs. One is an emergency management framework of before, during, or after an event. Before an event, the focus is on planning and preparation; during an event, emphasis shifts to response, interaction, or participation; whereas after an event the primary activities are mitigation, recovery, and rebuilding. The times can also be relative. If an NGO is seeking funding to respond to an event that has already occurred or a situation that exists, before refers to planning and preparation prior to responding. The categories should be viewed more as trends rather than absolute. For example, mitigation normally begins during an event and is likely to continue afterwards.

This framework can also be applied to negotiation in a meeting or conference, at which an important negotiating goal becomes the "event." NGOs plan for, participate in, and debrief after events. Extended negotiations, involving a sequence of meetings or conferences, can be managed as a series of events.

This chapter identifies 12 types of information and knowledge work that an NGO is likely to undertake. These are listed sequentially, relative to an event, in the first column of Table 4.1. All types of work are not needed for all events. An NGO should identify what work is needed for a specific event and its associated services.

**Table 4.1** Management framework for humanitarian assistance

| Work needed | When done | Knowledge service | Knowledge management | Type of content |
|---|---|---|---|---|
| **1. Understand the context** *(institutions, laws, economy, customs)* | Before | Searching, synthesis | Content, sharing, collaboration | Information, knowledge |
| **2. Know the situation** *(domain, resources, infrastructure, environment)* | Before | Searching, analysis, synthesis | Content, sharing, collaboration | Data, information |
| **3. Manage funding** *(donors, proposals, partners, administration, reporting)* | Before | Funding marketplace, funding database | Content | Data, information |
| **4. Manage contacts** *(expertise, representatives, sources of supply)* | Before/during | Contact directory | Content, sharing, collaboration | Information, knowledge |
| **5. Interact with others** *(communication, feedback, communities, networks)* | Before, during | Individuals, communities, social networks | Content, sharing | Information, knowledge |
| **6. Collaborate** *(social context, knowledge flow, technical support, organization)* | Before, during | Communities, engagement, leadership, collaboration space | Sharing, collaboration | Data, information, knowledge |
| **7. Negotiate agreement** *(pre-negotiation, negotiation, post-negotiation)* | Before | Searching, analysis, synthesis, Contact directory, negotiation DB | Content | Data, information, knowledge |
| **8. Capture experience** *(conference, response)* | During | Event database | Content, sharing | Data, information |
| **9. After-action review** *(administration, efficiency, effectiveness, outcomes)* | After | Activity/project database(s) | Content, collaboration | Data, information |
| **10. Report activities** *(projects, events, accomplishments, outcomes, issues)* | After | Activity/project database(s) | Content, sharing | Data, information |
| **11. Learn and adapt** *(individual, community, organization, change)* | After | After-action review | Sharing, collaboration | Knowledge |
| **12. Categorize positions** *(delegates, organizations, countries)* | After/before | Voting database | Content | Data |

The second column identifies the time, relative to an event, when the work is primarily done. Before includes planning and preparation; during includes response, interaction, and participation; and after includes mitigation, recovery, and rebuilding. Note that some work may span more than one time category. The third column lists the high-level information or knowledge services that are needed to support the work. These three columns provide the overall framework for this chapter.

It is helpful to describe the underlying principles and practices that support specific knowledge services. These are identified in columns 4 and 5 of Table 4.1. Knowledge management (column 4) identifies the primary generation of KM involved: content, sharing, and/or collaboration. Three types of content are considered here: data, information, and knowledge (column 5).

Table 4.1 shows that every type of work needs content management, eight types require sharing, and six types involve collaboration. Clearly, all three generations of knowledge management are needed to support the full range of knowledge work in an NGO. Although some KM practitioners emphasize the glitz and glamour of third-generation social networking in support of collaboration, without first- and second-generation services in place, collaboration has no foundation and cannot achieve anywhere near its full potential. Similarly, eight types of work require date, 10 require information, and six require knowledge. Again, all forms of content are needed to run an NGO, and each must be managed according to its attributes.

## 4.3 Knowledge Management

In two decades, knowledge management (KM) has evolved through three generations (content, sharing, and collaboration (Dixon 2010)). The three generations of KM provide a framework for organizing current best practices.

The first generation of KM focused on content (data, information, and explicit knowledge). Explicit knowledge has been expressed, captured, and codified in documents and procedures. NGOs can manage content as an asset (intellectual property)—something that is owned or held by an organization. Assets can be managed in a structured way, for example, as data in a database or information in a library. All forms of content must be captured, organized, preserved, and made accessible. Differences arise in the methods used to execute these functions for data, information, and knowledge.

The second generation of KM emphasized sharing and using tacit knowledge. Tacit knowledge is personal knowledge, in someone's head, that is influenced by individual beliefs, perspectives, and values. We can promote, facilitate, and support the exchange and use of tacit knowledge, for example, with a directory of expertise or community of practice, but we cannot manage it using the same structured methods as are used for content. Some tacit knowledge cannot be made explicit. For this knowledge, NGOs must manage relationships and social opportunities to transfer knowledge between individuals or from individuals to groups through conversations, dialogue, or other forms of interaction.

A third generation of knowledge management is evolving that emphasizes collaboration and synergy among communities and networks to create and share knowledge. This generation of KM can be seen as using technology to support core NGO activities. Social interactions and interfaces can be formal or informal and are largely based on voluntarism. They can be encouraged and facilitated but not managed in a traditional structured way. NGOs must support conversation, collaboration, and communities to facilitate capturing and leveraging new knowledge generated in the turbulence of cyberspace.

Al Simard in *Knowledge Services: A Strategic Framework* (Simard 2012) provides a comprehensive state-of-the-art framework for and discussion of contemporary knowledge management practices founded on the three generations of KM. Much of this chapter is derived from this work.

A number of knowledge management principles developed by Kurtz and Snowden (2003)[1] reflect the diverse, unstructured, and ephemeral nature of knowledge:

- Knowledge can only be volunteered, it cannot be conscripted.
- We only know what we know when we need to know it.
- In the context of real need, few people withhold their knowledge.
- Everything is fragmented.
- Tolerated failure imprints learning better than success.
- The way we know things is not the way we say we know things.
- We know more than we can say, and we say more than we can write.

These principles highlight aspects of knowledge that most people are vaguely familiar with and yet that pose challenges to management's traditional structured comfort zone. The degree to which we can manage different types of knowledge and knowledge work depends on the degree to which we can structure, integrate, and manage people, systems, work processes, governance, and knowledge. The degree to which knowledge and knowledge work are not manageable depends on the extent to which they tend towards intangible, tacit, and ephemeral states. The next section lays a foundation for knowledge management by describing various forms of content, in general, and knowledge, in particular.

### *4.3.1 Content*

A key challenge for knowledge management is the difficulty of defining what is being managed, reflecting a lack of consensus among KM practitioners. Everyone knows what knowledge is, but no two people seem to agree. Webster's Dictionary has nine different definitions for information and another ten for knowledge, some of which are in terms of each other (not to mention data), so that either can mean

[1] http://www.cognitive-edge.com/blogs/dave/2008/10/rendering_knowledge.php

almost anything. Further, authors frequently interchange terminology, which adds to the confusion. In this book, we refer to three types of content:

- ***Content*** is a collective term for data, information, and knowledge. Content is an embedded value, in the form of a pattern, message, or signal contained within the three forms of content.
- ***Data*** are recorded, ordered symbols or signals that may carry information and patterns. Data managers acquire, organize, preserve, and provide access to data, databases, data repositories, and data warehouses. Data are organized into elements, files, data sets, databases, and statistics.
- ***Information*** is meaning in context, arising from processing, interpreting, or translating data to extract an underlying message or pattern. Information managers acquire, organize, preserve, and provide access to information in information bases, repositories, or libraries. Information includes documents, reports, images, maps, brochures, presentations, or multimedia recordings. Records are content that is specifically related to running an organization.
- ***Knowledge*** is an understanding, resulting from analysis or synthesis of data or information to reveal cause-and-effect relationships that help to explain and predict natural, technical, or social phenomena. Knowledge managers acquire, organize, preserve, and provide access to knowledge through knowledge bases, knowledge repositories, or communities of practice. There are four categories of knowledge: authoritative (approved), explicit (documented), tacit (mental), and innate (talent).

**Authoritative knowledge** has been approved for internal use within an organization or for external use by others, in cases of legal or regulatory control. Authoritative knowledge includes laws, regulations, policies, rules, and procedures. It can be used by everyone because it has been codified and analyzed in a business context to ensure that it is collected, coordinated, used, and recorded as part of running an organization. Authoritative knowledge is transferred throughout an organization through direction, policies, reports, guidelines, and communications.

**Explicit knowledge** has been expressed, captured, codified, and stored in reproducible media. It is the tangible result of knowledge work. Explicit knowledge can be managed by an NGO as assets. There are many types of explicit knowledge, including:

- Books, publications, documents, and reports
- Photos, diagrams, illustrations, and drawings
- Presentations, speeches, and lectures
- Computer algorithms, code, and software
- Decision tools, decision-support systems, and expert systems
- Stories, lessons learned, and recordings

**Tacit knowledge** is personal knowledge, gained through observation, experience, or practice and stored in the mind of an individual. Tacit knowledge is also embedded in communities and an NGO's culture. It is the invisible accumulation of experiences. Tacit knowledge cannot be "managed" in the same sense as explicit knowledge, but it can be leveraged as an essential capacity for performing knowledge work. There are many types of tacit knowledge, including:

- Awareness (acquired by being informed)
- Skills (acquired through practice)
- Practical (acquired through training)
- Formal (acquired through education)
- Mental models (knowing how things work)
- Expertise (knowing what works and what doesn't)
- Experience (knowing what happened previously)
- Judgment (knowing the best way)
- Wisdom (knowing why)
- Social (knowing how to relate to people)

Tacit knowledge must be captured and transformed into explicit form to be manageable. This begins by identifying and prioritizing what should be captured. Some tacit knowledge is held by many individuals and doesn't need to be captured. Other knowledge loses its value rapidly and there is little point in capturing it. Not all experience is equally important and emphasis should be on the highest-priority knowledge. Critical knowledge held by one individual should be continuously captured. The consequences of unexpectedly losing such knowledge can be substantial. Lessons learned and best practices should be documented and disseminated as they occur.

**Innate knowledge** can be thought of as a form of talent. From an organizational perspective, talent is a naturally recurring pattern of individual thought, feeling, or behavior that can be productively applied. Unlike skill, which can be mastered with practice, talent cannot be taught or transferred although it can be demonstrated. Talent can only be used by the individual who has it. Talent is important to creativity, inventiveness, and innovation. Many factors can affect talent, including engagement, communication skills, interpersonal relationships, and ability to reason. Talented people tend to learn faster, are more productive, and build stronger relationships than average individuals.

The next section begins by describing first-generation knowledge management—knowledge assets.

### *4.3.2 Knowledge Assets*

To manage knowledge assets, NGOs need to understand them in all their complexity. Organizations need to know where they are, how they increase or decrease in quantity and value, and how management can affect their value and usefulness. They need to be able to measure the value of knowledge and represent it on a balance sheet. Most organizations are still learning how to manage intangible assets, which are becoming increasingly relevant in the knowledge economy. A number of books have been published on managing knowledge as an asset, including Edvinson and Malone (1996), Stewart (1997), and Andiressen (2004). Managing knowledge assets involves five activities: acquisition, organization, mapping, preservation, and repositories.

An NGO's stock of knowledge determines its short-term ability to accomplish its mission. There are two ways to increase the stock of knowledge—create new knowledge or acquire existing knowledge held by others. Most NGOs will emphasize acquiring existing knowledge through capture, inventory, and importing. Capture codifies internal content on reproducible physical, mechanical, analog, or digital media. Inventory gathers, classifies, and describes existing content that is owned by an NGO. Importing brings external content into an NGO.

An unstructured collection of knowledge is of little use to an NGO. A systematic structure is needed for organizing knowledge assets. This is typically done through classification, which involves categorizing, assigning, or sorting knowledge into systematic classes, categories, or structure according to subject matter. There are three types of classification schemes. *Single* criteria, such as subject index, alphabetic list, or taxonomy, have the advantage of a simple structure coupled with the disadvantage that they are not well suited to complicated subjects with multiple relationships. *Multiple* criteria use metadata to classify content according to more than one attribute. Multiple criteria provide flexible structures that enable combination searches with multiple terms. Conversely, they are more complicated for nontechnical users to understand and for information specialists to manage. *Unstructured* schemes, such as full-text indexing or folksonomies, enable totally unstructured searching. Their advantage is infinite flexibility in organizing and searching content. Their disadvantage is the difficulty of doing an exhaustive search or finding specific content due to inconsistent terminology.

Mapping knowledge relates what an NGO knows to what it needs to know to accomplish its mission. Mapping knowledge is discovering the constraints, assumptions, value, and uses of available knowledge and finding opportunities to leverage existing knowledge. There are three aspects to mapping knowledge. Knowledge *needs* describe what needs to be known and/or accessible to accomplish an NGO's program objectives. This would seem to be a straightforward task, but it often requires significant effort to complete. Knowledge *gaps* document the difference between available knowledge and what is needed for supporting business lines or program objectives. *Prioritizing* knowledge involves ranking its relative importance to an NGO. This is important because not all knowledge is created equal and an NGO does not have the resources to manage everything.

Preservation links an NGO's past, present, and future. Past knowledge that was not preserved is not available today, and present knowledge that is not preserved will not be available tomorrow. Delong (2004) describes the consequences of lost knowledge along with techniques for its preservation. Preservation is preventing the irretrievable loss of content throughout its life cycle by managing it in permanent physical or electronic media. Preservation involves three functions. *Archiving* is storing content in physical or electronic repositories for safekeeping and subsequent retrieval. *Maintenance* is keeping content in its original state, preventing loss or decline, and safeguarding it from damage, vandalism, or theft. *Migration* is transferring content from obsolete storage media to long-term stable media, which is absolutely essential for digital content.

A repository is a physical or digital place where content is deposited, stored, searched, and retrieved. A database adds data-processing functions such as extraction, manipulation, calculation, and analysis. Managing a repository begins by designing an architecture to organize the content in a logical way to facilitate search and retrieval. Operation requires content storage devices, servers to run the management application, and connectivity to internal and external networks. Finally, a software application is needed to manage the repository or database. Three interfaces are needed to access the repository—one each for content entry, user access, and administration. A multi-criteria search engine is needed to find content, using a variety of search terms. Finally, view, print, and download functions are needed for content retrieval. The repository should also include security features to ensure that content is protected from malicious or inadvertent misuse, modification, or loss.

### *4.3.3 Sharing Knowledge*

Knowledge in a file cabinet or in the mind of an individual involves a cost to create or acquire but represents only potential value or usefulness to an NGO. The actual value is only realized when knowledge is used to accomplish work. This means that knowledge must "flow" from its source to where it is needed. Knowledge sharing can be mandated, but the extent of sharing generally depends on generosity and altruism or the expectation of reciprocity on the part of those who have knowledge. Incentives are usually needed to motivate those who have knowledge to share it with those who need it.

Dalkir (2005) lists a number of organizational benefits of knowledge sharing. Sharing allows knowledge to be leveraged for more than its original purpose. It enables knowledge to be reused without having to be duplicated. Sharing permits knowledge to "flow" from its source to where it is needed; it builds an organization's collective capabilities and relationships. Finally, sharing individual knowledge with others is the first step of the social process through which an organizational learns.

Creating an environment that is conducive to sharing requires removing or minimizing a number of behavioral and cultural barriers to sharing. The natural human tendency to control or hoard content for personal benefit must be minimized. Providers must be able to trust that those who access their knowledge will use it appropriately. They must also feel safe that it will not be used against them. Providers must also feel secure that it will not be distributed beyond the intended recipients. Finally, ways must be found to overcome the difficulty of explaining complex ideas across subject-matter boundaries.

Table 4.2 lists three approaches to providing incentives to encourage and promote sharing (Stoyko 2010). In shifting from compliance to engagement, individuals shift from behavior (what you do), through attitudes (what you think), to willingness (how you feel). That is, from observable, external, interpersonal responses to unknowable, internal, voluntary responses. Similarly, organizational

**Table 4.2** Individual and organizational outcomes of different approaches to incentives

| Approach to incentives | Individual response | Organizational results |
|---|---|---|
| Compliance | Behavior | Functionality |
| Motivation | Attitudes | Productivity |
| Engagement | Willingness | Creativity |

results shift from functionality (do the work), through productivity (do it efficiently), to creativity (do something new). That is, from hard, measurable, and enforceable outputs to soft, subjective, and recognizable contributions.

Compliance emphasizes extrinsic incentives, such as pay, job security, duty, work ethic, and penalties. Compliance is appropriate in areas such as manufacturing, the military, the law, regulations, and policies. It generally results in quota-based, minimal threshold, standardized, unchanging results. Motivation emphasizes managing people through incentives, such as ambition, challenges, bonuses, rewards, and recognition. Motivation is appropriate for increasing organizational efficiency, productivity, and quality resulting in evolutionary (quantitative) improvements. Engagement emphasizes intrinsic incentives such as meaningfulness, sense of ownership, self-esteem, enjoyment, and self-satisfaction. Through engagement, people personally commit to and become truly involved in a task or activity. They do so not because they are told to, or they expect something in return, but because they want to, because they enjoy doing it. Engagement can result in creativity that leads to revolutionary (qualitative) changes.

Shifting to an organizational scale, Simard (*Disaster Information Service: A Proposal* 2005, Jan 18–22) identified a number of benefits that would accrue to content providers in a Global Disaster Information Network:

- Sharing broadens *awareness and reach* of the provider's knowledge and increases its visibility, influence, use, and impact.
- Providers will develop a *reputation* as an active and knowledgeable community participant, thereby promoting collaboration and group synergy.
- Feedback from recipients *informs providers* of knowledge needs and how it is being used, which, in turn, increases the *relevance* of the provider's work.
- Increasing awareness of the provider's knowledge and reputation encourages *partnerships and leveraging* of existing resources and capacity.

**Explicit knowledge** has been captured in reproducible media such as documents, presentations, or drawings. There are three ways of sharing explicit knowledge. *Dissemination* involves passive, one-to-many, one-way transfer by pushing content to recipients. This approach is used for increasing awareness or understanding of an NGO's positions, activities, or accomplishments. *Accessing* content is an active, many-to-one, one-way transfer through users pulling content to themselves by going to a repository or physical location to search for, find, and retrieve content. *Exchange* involves active, one-to-one, two-way transactions. Exchange usually involves trading intellectual property, such as accessing and downloading a document from a repository.

Sharing explicit knowledge often takes place through information or knowledge markets, such as ReliefWeb, and the OCHA Consolidated Appeals Process, which may include facilitation and brokering. Facilitation is providing logistical, administrative, and/or advisory support to knowledge providers, users, and/or market transactions. Brokering is arranging or negotiating transactions, agreements, or contracts as an agent or intermediary on behalf of both providers and users.

**Tacit knowledge** is personal knowledge, gained through observation or experience, which is influenced by personal beliefs, perspectives, and values. It exists in the minds of individuals and is often difficult to transform into explicit knowledge. Although it is less manageable and more difficult to share, knowledge in the minds of people may be the majority of an NGO's knowledge as well as most valuable to the organization. Several methods can be used to share tacit knowledge:

- Conversations, discussion, and dialogue *(colleagues or peers)*
- Questions and answers, problems and solutions *(novice/expert)*
- After-action review and lessons learned *(event or activity/group)*
- Capturing, documenting, interviewing, and recording *(expert/facilitator)*
- Brainstorming, spontaneous ideas, and group synergy *(group/facilitator)*
- Advising, briefing, and recommending *(subordinate/superior)*
- Teaching, educating, training, and instructing *(teacher/student)*
- Storytelling, narratives, and anecdotes *(teller, listener)*
- Explaining, demonstrating, showing, and describing *(technician/user)*
- Mentoring, guiding, and leading *(leader/apprentice)*
- Presenting, lecturing, and speaking *(speaker/audience)*

People overwhelmingly prefer sharing tacit knowledge face-to-face, especially when negotiating. This is because humans are hardwired to interpret visible and audible clues that accompany and enhance the intended meaning of spoken words. Face-to-face encounters also greatly facilitate establishing mutual trust, an essential prerequisite for sharing tacit knowledge. That is, trust on the part of the recipient that they are receiving valid knowledge from someone who knows a subject, and trust on the part of the provider that what they are sharing will only be used appropriately. Note that the level of trust is usually minimal during negotiations.

Individuals can share tacit knowledge anywhere that people can meet—in an office, a hallway, the street, via telephone, or e-mail. A key advantage of one-on-one conversations is that, once trust is established, the knowledge being shared tends to be more honest and straightforward. The provider is less concerned with appearances, avoiding mistakes, and who might be listening. Many significant breakthroughs begin life as a sketch on the back of a restaurant napkin! Be aware, however, that in adversarial, security, or diplomatic situations, people may not be authorized to freely share their knowledge.

There are many events that support sharing tacit knowledge among individuals and groups, including conference calls, meetings, workshops, conferences, symposia, site visits, classrooms, communities, and networks. The chief advantage of physical interaction is enhanced transfer of meaning and understanding; the chief disadvantage for distributed participants is the high cost of travel. For interactions in cyberspace, the advantages and disadvantages are reversed.

### 4.3.4 Communities of Practice

Communities of practice (CoP) are becomingly increasingly important in the workplace. They are key to knowledge creation and sharing in a networked world. Although communities cannot be managed in a traditional sense, they can be promoted, encourage, and facilitated. Wegner (Wegner et al. 2002) and Saint-Onge (Saint-Onge and Wallace 2002) describe communities of practice in some detail.

Communities are becoming increasingly important because they are well suited to getting work done in the fast-paced, ever-changing knowledge society. Further, while increasingly complex issues require greater specialization, the half-life of knowledge is getting shorter. Only a community has the collective breadth and depth of experience and knowledge needed to keep up with the increasingly rapid pace of change.

The primary benefit of CoPs is the increased diversity and range of experience that they bring to any activity or dialogue. Although diversity often increases the effort needed to achieve a mutually agreed result, the improvement to the solution is almost always worth the extra effort. Communities can be particularly effective in addressing complex issues in which participants often know more than they can express or document. Having personally led three successful community projects involving complex issues, Simard estimates that the final result was twice as good (more creative and robust) than what any individual participant could have produced by themselves.[2]

Informal, unstructured communities of practice should not be confused with formal, structured committees. The central purpose of communities is to generate and validate creative and innovative ideas that would not likely arise from traditional committees. The central purpose of committees is to develop structure and processes to implement new ways of working and to integrate them into the organizational infrastructure.

Communities typically consist of 10–50 members. They are self-organized, self-governed, and self-managed. A mutually agreed purpose determines community objectives while consensus-based norms guide behavior and practices. Communities create new knowledge through collaboration and dialogue. Communities support their members by helping with work, solving problems, providing expertise, and facilitating learning.

Communities of practice do not replace organizational infrastructure or functions. They contribute to organizational success through timely and rapid sharing and collaboration to address complex problems or emerging issues. There are three types of community structure: informal, supported, and structured. Informal communities tend to be more democratic, dynamic, and creative, whereas structured communities tend to be more committee like and are more likely to produce outputs that have organizational impact.

---

[2]Crafting an access to knowledge policy for a science-based agency, understanding knowledge services provided by government departments, and developing a modeling framework for a regulatory agency

Ultimately, members are the community. But all members do not participate equally, nor do they consistently adopt the same roles. Membership roles vary with the subject and even over time, as the dialogue shifts over different aspects of an issue or situation. Community members can be classified into five categories based on the extent of their participation:

- ***Conveners***—Establish, lead, and oversee community or network sites.
- ***Authors***—Create, post, or upload original content on community or network sites.
- ***Participants***—Review, comment on, respond to, critique, or edit content posted by authors.
- ***Joiners***—Connect to communities or social networks by maintaining their profile, and occasionally participating.
- ***Spectators***—Read, view, or listen to content posted by others ("lurkers").

Communities have individual and collective behavior and attitudes that strongly affect community effectiveness and can make the difference between success and failure. In informal communities, those who negatively impact the community or ignore community rules of conduct are ignored or removed by the community itself without appeal to higher authority. In contrast, structured communities, with invited or assigned participants, must carefully select members at the outset.

**Positive Behaviors**

- *Dialogue*—a free-flowing exchange of ideas facilitates synergy.
- *Trust*—is essential to enable participants to present honest views.
- *Safety*—controversial opinions will not be externally attributed to participants.
- *Meritocracy*—the best ideas rise to the top, based on their merit.
- *Equality*—all opinions and points of view are solicited, valued, and equal.
- *Outliers*—are sought after because they likely represent innovative ideas.

**Negative Behaviors**

- *Discussion*[3]—mutual pounding on opposing points of view impedes synergy.
- *Debating*—in which someone wins and someone loses inhibits creativity.
- *Arguing*—until opponents are worn down leads to withdrawal.
- *Agenda*—representing an external constituency impedes progress.
- *Positioning*—authoritative declarations preclude meaningful interaction.
- *Assuming*—superior knowledge patronizes and disengages participants.
- *Majority*—voting yields plain-vanilla averages of current opinions.
- *Consensus*—the lowest common denominator acceptable to all participants.
- *Groupthink*—rarely rises above the status quo.

[3]Discussion has a similar root (… + *quatere* – to shake) as percussion and concussion.

### 4.3.5 *Social Networks*

A network is an interconnection among large numbers of people, communities, or organizations with common interdependencies, interests, or purpose. The Internet, with its global connectivity among virtually everyone, everywhere, all the time, has raised the idea of "networking" to heretofore unimaginable levels. Networks have become embedded in every aspect of society—from communications and transportation to work and recreation, to governing countries, and sustaining the planet. A number of authors have described networks and social networking, including Kelly (1998), Allee (2003), Tapscott and Williams and Anthony D (2006), and Anklam (2007).

Networks range from hundreds to millions of participants. Because networks can be huge, it is impossible to know more than a small percentage of the members. Consequently, there is a loss of trust and safety—two key community attributes. Participants must be cautious about what they post in a network, as some teenagers and employees have learned, to their regret. Conversely, size greatly enhances the possibility of synergy and emergent knowledge. For example, it has been observed that no computer bug is impossible to find and fix if there are enough eyes looking at it. Similarly, many apparently intractable problems have previously been solved by someone who is unknown to the person with the problem.

Organizational participation in networks is typically through individuals who participate in external, national, or global networks related to their profession or areas of interest. As such, they perform an interface function—in the sense of monitoring the environment and bringing external content into the organization, as a form of informal intelligence gathering. Interface roles range from "gatekeepers" who passively bring external content to the attention of those who have an interest in it to "conveners" who actively promote the adoption of external content in the organization.

With this brief background of knowledge, management principles, and practices, we are now in a position to consider various types of knowledge work done by an NGO and how the work can be supported by knowledge services.

## 4.4 Knowledge Work

We identify twelve types of work done by NGOs that can be supported by information and knowledge services. They are described in an approximate order in which they are done—before, during, or after an event (response to an emergency or stage of a negotiation process). Although most services could support either response or negotiation, not all services are needed for all projects or activities, depending on the specific work being done.

This section is divided into bite-sized chunks of information and knowledge work for ease of understanding. The real world, however, is not so easily categorized. Boundaries between tasks are, in fact, fuzzy and blend into one another.

It will quickly become apparent that all types of work are connected to several other types of work and that all services support multiple types of work. Thus, searching appears in several places, as does storing documents in databases, and interacting with people. In essence, managing information and knowledge are highly integrated processes that can support much of the work done by an NGO.

### *4.4.1 Understand the Context*

The first task generally undertaken when establishing a humanitarian assistance project or beginning an activity is to be aware of and understand the institutional, legal, economic, and social context in which the work will be done. Understanding the context in which an NGO will be working is not only essential to success but also necessary for knowing what must, should, can, or cannot be done. This activity generally takes time, so adequate lead time must be scheduled in the planning process.

Understanding the socioeconomic context of a country in which an NGO has not previously worked is a two-stage process, beginning with awareness. Increasing awareness can be done in either physical space, cyberspace, or both. Searching published literature can yield a great deal of background information about a country. Information published by reputable sources is likely to be reliable. However, substantial time and effort will be needed to read and filter relevant information from various sources. Further, the information may not be current, and it is unlikely to include sufficient detail to plan a specific project or activity. Published content is, however, a good place to begin research.

There are many places to look for published content, including libraries, academic and professional journals, conference reports, and the media. It is important that the source of the information be considered when evaluating content. Is it known to be reliable, unbiased, and objective, or is it promoting an agenda? Was the information produced for a different purpose than its intended use, such as promoting tourism or investment rather than presenting facts? Answers to these questions are key to evaluating published content.

Searching the Web is likely to provide more up-to-date content. Web search services, such as Google,[4] can identify a wealth of sites that provide information about a country. Wikipedia also provides articles with links to sources and related content. Even more than for published literature, however, it is critical to consider the source when searching for, reviewing, and evaluating Web content which will have widely variable quality assurance. Governments are not the only organization that uses the Web to promote a particular position or agenda.

Most Web content is relatively brief. This can significantly reduce the time needed to assimilate it, but it is more likely to be superficial relatively to what is

[4] http://www.google.com

needed for a specific situation. Further, Web content tends to emphasize the positive side of a country—good for tourism—but not necessarily what an NGO needs to know when planning a project in a new country.

From a technical perspective, all that is needed for searching the Web is a computer with a Web browser that is connected to the Internet. Technology is not enough, however. The person doing the searching is more important. They must have a good sense of where to rapidly find content and for filtering masses of irrelevant material. Good judgment is also essential for interpreting and evaluating what they find. An ability to synthesize diverse material into a coherent whole and produce well-crafted reports related to the proposed project or activity are also important.

Once socioeconomic information for a country has been compiled, it should be corroborated, to the extent possible, through one or more country and/or subject-matter experts. A draft country report and/or or presentation that integrates the content should then be prepared. The information should then be validated in the context of the NGO's organizational and operational procedures by an internal group or community to provide diverse perspectives. A final country report is then prepared and submitted to decision makers for consideration. It is also stored in the NGO's country database for future reference and possible reuse. See Sect. 4.4.5 for additional detail on external interaction and community validation. See Sect. 4.3.2 for information on managing a repository or database.

### 4.4.2 *Know the Situation*

Understanding the context within which an activity or project will take place provides essential background information and knowledge. When an event occurs, an NGO needs data and information about the specific situation (sometimes referred to as "situational awareness"). To "know" is used here in the sense of being informed, or being aware, rather than in the sense of understanding, which is a deeper kind of knowing. When an event occurs, there is precious little time for learning and reflection.

An NGO needs to quickly mobilize data and information about an event. Ongoing monitoring systems are invaluable in this regard. ReliefWeb is an excellent example of a global information system designed to increase awareness of humanitarian events and issues.[5] More specifically, Simard and Eenigenberg (*An Executive Information System to Support Wildfire Disaster Declarations* 1990) describe an automated executive information system that predicts the daily probability of large forest fires to support wildfire disaster declarations in the United States. Similarly, the Canadian Wildland Fire Information System provides daily national forest-fire danger maps, fire-behavior predictions, large-fire locations, and reports of current and historical fire activity.[6]

---

[5] See: http://reliefweb.int/?gclid=CNeglezM6bACFWkCQAodYzDL1Q.

[6] http://cwfis.cfs.nrcan.gc.ca

Without access to a monitoring system, a highly focused search and filtering process is needed to sift through masses of content. If an NGO does not have a previously developed country file, they will have to obtain that information from another organization that does. There is no time to produce a background report.

Here, searching begins by contacting subject-matter experts and acquiring explicit and/or tacit knowledge from them. They should be able to answer questions or point to the answers. The key is that experts do not have to search or learn; they know. See Sect. 4.3.3 for detail on sharing explicit and tacit knowledge and Sect. 4.4.4 for managing a list of contacts. Interacting with known, trusted experts provides confidence in the accuracy, quality, and reliability of the received data and information. Although there is always some to considerable uncertainty in rapidly evolving situations, this will likely provide as good content as is available at the time of the query.

When there is considerable uncertainty about the situation, one strategy would be to wait until it stabilizes before taking well-reasoned action. If waiting is not an option, it would be prudent to minimize risk by conducting scenario analyses and developing "what-if" contingency plans. In chaotic situations, in which little is predictable, the best operating strategy may be to minimize planning and react to events as they occur; in other words, act, sense, and respond (Kurtz and Snowden 2003). In such cases, the team leader or chief negotiator must have considerable experience and good judgment to properly apply existing knowledge in new situations. This is, in effect, a definition of wisdom.

For emergency response, an NGO needs current information about the infrastructure in the immediate area. For example, are roads and bridges passable? Is the telecommunications network functional? Will the field unit have to be self-sufficient? How will large quantities of supplies be brought to the disaster site? What local resources are available to provide services? They also need to know something about the environment in which they will be working, such as weather and field conditions and whether protective clothing and/or vaccinations will be needed. They will need briefings from subject-matter experts to advise on technical issues related to the specific situation. Finally, they will need to be aware of local customs and culture to prevent inadvertently causing offense.

For a conference or other negotiating event, situational awareness emphasizes knowing the participants in the process and their positions. What laws and agreements are in place that must be respected? What were the positions/voting records of individuals, organizations, or countries on this and similar issues? What is known about their needs and wants, constraints and possibilities, and, ultimately, their likes and dislikes? See Sect. 4.4.12 for more detail on categorizing positions.

Whether for an emergency or negation, data and information about an event must be integrated into a holistic view. This is then interpreted in the context of the NGOs mandate and the desired outcome for the proposed response or activity. Then, a synthesis document or report is prepared, including recommended actions. The document is submitted to decision makers for consideration and stored in an event database for future reference and possible reuse.

### 4.4.3 *Manage Funding*

One of the most important aspects of humanitarian assistance is funding because without funding, an NGO cannot operate in a meaningful way. Although voluntarism can significantly leverage funded programs, by itself, it tends to be ad hoc, except when managed, as part of a larger undertaking, by funded organizations. Seven aspects of managing funding are considered here: finding and selecting sources, knowing the rules, preparing proposals, storing documents in a funding database, negotiating with donors, administering funds, and reporting to donors.

Funding begins with finding potential donors. An NGO could use broad search techniques such as those described in Sect. 4.4.1 (understand the context) or targeted techniques as in Sect. 4.4.2 (know the situation). Alternatively, an NGO could begin by considering one or more of the funding agencies identified in Chap. 9.[7] A global humanitarian funding marketplace would greatly facilitate this process.[8] Once potential funding sources have been identified, they should be prioritized, based on compatibility between donor interests and the purpose of the proposed activity or project.

Preparing a proposal begins by downloading or physically acquiring and becoming familiar with the rules, constraints, restrictions, procedures, and proposal evaluation criteria used by the selected donor(s). This normally includes the use of a proposal template. If there is a template, it will be necessary to have a personal computer, compatible office application software, and know how to use them. If there is no template, a proposal outline should be prepared, using a word processor, which includes all the headings referred to in the proposal evaluation criteria to ensure that all required information is included. The proposal should be reviewed by someone other than the author to ensure its accuracy and completeness prior to submission.

An NGO is not an island. Other NGOs will also be preparing funding proposals. Some may directly compete with yours while others will indirectly compete by accessing some of the limited funding. Think of funding as an ecosystem with limited resources or as a "competitive market," in which an NGO would be wise to know its competition. There are many open sources of information about other NGOs such as annual reports, public websites, and project reports.[9] These can provide background information for developing a funding strategy. Better still, joint submissions by more than one NGO in a partnership are generally stronger and favored by donors over those from a single organization.

---

[7] See, for example, http://ochaonline.un.org/cap2006/webpage.asp?Page=1243.

[8] Two examples of global social networks that facilitate exchanges between people with problems and those with solutions are as follows: http://www.innocentive.com and http://www.crowdsourcingdirectory.com.

[9] We do not condone any illicit or unethical methods of gathering intelligence.

Here the work involves finding NGOs with similar or related mandates that operate in the same funding market (Sect. 4.4.1), determine whether they are potential competitors or partners (Sect. 4.4.2), find contacts for potential partners (Sect. 4.4.4), and negotiate with representatives (Sect. 4.4.7). Information about both competitor and partner NGOs should be organized and stored in an NGO database (Sect. 4.3.2). This avoids having to redo market searches and analyses as well as provides immediate information during emergency events or crisis situations.

Once a proposal has been drafted, it should be stored in a funding database. This will greatly facilitate review and revision. This will also enable it to be reused at a future date rather than redoing the research, recompiling the information, and rewriting a new proposal from scratch. The database should have three components—categorized information that has been acquired about the selected donor to enable searching; attached documents, such as the proposal, related to funding; and links to related project content.

The database should be structured to be searchable using a variety of criteria, such as donor name, mandate or domain, contact information, geographical area of interest, typical funding amounts, and key constraints or rules. It should also include previous experience with the donor, such as project submissions, funding received, and financial considerations, as needed. Any criteria that are likely to be used to identify and select one or more potential donors from the database should be included as a field. Criteria for each donor should be categorized to facilitate searching, using indexes, keywords, subject categories, taxonomies, or other methods, as appropriate. Full-text searching of documents is both inefficient and yields inconsistent results. See Sects. 4.4.8 (capture experience) and 4.3.2 (assets) for more detail on managing a database.

After a proposal has been submitted, some negotiation with donor agencies may be needed. This will likely be in the form of recommendations or requests from the donor, for example, to delete, modify, or add elements to improve the proposal from the donor's perspective or to coordinate with similar or related proposals. Having the proposal stored electronically will facilitate this process. Note that version control for evolving documents is essential to ensure that the latest version is always used.

After a proposal is accepted, there will likely be negotiations with the donor to prepare a contract, memorandum of understanding, or some form of agreement to ensure that the NGO delivers what it promised. Traditionally, this would involve traveling to the donor's location and spending some time together, negotiating face-to-face. Today, this can be done electronically over a distance if both parties have access to a common collaboration website (see Sect. 4.4.6—collaboration). Prior establishment of trust between the parties is particularly important when negotiating contracts electronically. Major funding agencies will likely have established joint work spaces to facilitate preparing contracts. If not, there is always e-mail for electronic documents or snail mail for physical documents. Any negotiated agreement and supporting documents should be stored in the funding database, with links to the project database.

Funds must be administered properly and reports provided according to the terms and conditions of the agreement.[10] This will likely require a commercial accounting application. Depending on the size of the NGO, the amount of funding received, and donor requirements, this could range from simple accounting software to a full-fledged financial system. There needs to be built-in accountability to document that expenses were approved by the appropriate authority. The advantage of such applications is that they include built-in reporting functions for whatever data is likely to be needed. Also, for NGOs without internal accounting expertise, once set up, such applications transform simple journal entries into full-fledged financial reports. An NGO could also process electronic invoices or scan paper ones and file them electronically. This greatly facilitates subsequent auditing which is often also required. Finally, it is important that the accounting application includes links to related databases, such as donor agreements and project management.

All donors will require periodic reports of project expenditures. These can range from monthly, through quarterly, and semiannually, to annually, or any combination of time periods. This is where the primary benefits of accounting or financial software are realized. Once a report format has been set up, and the ongoing bookkeeping completed, it takes little more than the click of a button to produce a report. All reports should be stored in the financial database to enable future access and audit.

### *4.4.4 Manage Contacts*

Much of the work of an NGO requires contacting people either inside or outside the organization. When an organization exceeds 30–50 employees, it becomes increasingly difficult to be aware of what everyone does or who does what. Someone may need to talk to a subject-matter expert, a representative of another organization, or a sales agent for a supplier. A contact directory provides a powerful electronic equivalent of an old-fashioned rolodex.

A directory of contacts is like the yellow pages of a phone book. Rather than being organized alphabetically by name, it organizes people by subject (expertise), organization (representative), or service (supplier) or any other criteria that are needed by an NGO. Further, electronic directories can be easily structured to search by multiple criteria—not just one.

A contact directory should have an entry page (or landing or splash page) that describes the directory, provides links to help files or demonstrations of how to use the directory, requests users to login, and asks users to select what they want to do: data entry, search, or administration.

---

[10] See, for example: http://www.aidtransparency.net/.

For internal contacts, the directory should be linked to the employee database so that individuals do not have to enter (with possible errors) data and information that already exist within the organization, such as name, telephone number, e-mail address, organization, job title, position, and language. External contacts can be provided direct access to a Web-based submission form (with appropriate security safeguards) or someone within the NGO who knows the individual will have to enter the data and information to the extent that it is available. When contact data on external individuals is maintained in a directory, the individuals should have access to their information and be permitted to modify it as they deem appropriate. If direct electronic access is not possible for security reasons, they should receive a copy of their information via e-mail.

From an architecture perspective, the directory should be structured differently for different types of contacts. Individuals should only see and have to fill out information for their type of contact. For expertise, the directory could include education, areas of expertise, current and previous job descriptions, projects worked on, committee assignments, community memberships, publications, presentations, and links to individual websites or blogs. Organizational representatives would emphasize their position in the organization, current duties, their role, supplemental information about themselves, and links to organizational and personal Web pages, as appropriate. Supplier agents would focus on the goods and services they provide and links to sales catalogues and organizational websites of interest to the NGO. Individuals should be reminded, semiannually, via e-mail, to verify and update their contact information.

There is also an administrator interface that permits adding, changing, or deleting individual data. This may involve fixing directory malfunctions, correcting content errors, or removing entries that have expired. In addition, individuals may not be permitted to enter certain information, such as "official spokesperson" or management approval of individual data. An administrator might also manage a temporary "holding" file pending approval of entries or other management action.

The search page enables people to find contacts. Users are offered a choice of what they want to search for and how they want to search. A search hierarchy would begin by selecting search by a person's name or type of contact. If name is selected, a name box appears, the user types in a name, and the system returns a list of all matching entries. Selecting a name links to that person's information.

If the user chooses a contact type, a list of types appears. Selecting a type returns a list of all criteria for that type. A user then chooses one or multiples search criteria and the system returns a list of all matching entries. Selecting a name from the list links to that person's information.

A contact management system can be easily developed from scratch, using open-source software.[11] It can also be purchased commercially as a stand-alone application. Alternatively, many vendors offer employee and expertise directory

[11] For example, see: http://www.slideshare.net/Al.Simard/directory-of-expertise-and-skills.

functionality as part of larger groupware applications. The latter is usually integrated with a set of office applications which greatly facilitates integrating various types of work. In such cases, simple "out-of-the-box" implementation will usually be sufficient for most NGO needs.

### 4.4.5 Interact with Others

There are many reasons why an NGO needs and/or wants to interact with external individuals, communities, or organizations, such as communicating a position to stakeholders, sharing information with partners, compiling intelligence about an event or situation, or soliciting feedback on a proposal. Interaction may take the form of one-way communication, one-on-one sharing, community dialogue, or participation in a global network.

**Communication** involves disseminating (pushing) content to stakeholders outside the NGO or posting it on an open website so that they may access (pull) it to themselves. Many organizations compete for attention and influence in a marketplace of ideas. For example, government agencies, private companies, and NGOs all want recipients of a message to believe that their position on issues is the most appropriate. Messages are crafted to balance facts with positioning the organization. The balance ranges from predominantly positioning (political statements) to predominantly factual (peer-reviewed publications). Communications require formal review and approval and follow approved formats and guidelines. Communication techniques include interviews, press releases, brochures, presentations, informal documents, formal reports, and publications.

**Feedback** is a two-way process involving a request for comment from an NGO to a person, group, or organization with interest in and knowledge of a subject coupled with providing a way for them to respond. This may involve, for example, a survey of opinions on an issue or a draft document with a request for comment prior to submission. Increasingly, this is being done electronically through a website that includes a template for answering survey questions or submitting comments. Potential respondents are usually contacted through an e-mail that includes a link to the feedback website.

**Sharing** is transferring or providing access to content without an expectation of reciprocity, whereas exchange includes an expectation of reciprocity, fee, or other considerations. There are two equally necessary but very different aspects of sharing—technology and motivation.

Although sharing still takes place by transferring paper documents or other physical media, today it more often involves electronic content. There are many technologies that can support sharing, including e-mail, chat rooms, bulletin boards, online forums, blogs, microblogs, social networking, and sharing websites. Websites that support sharing are a form of database consisting of access management, uploading, search, and retrieval (see Sect. 4.3.2—assets).[12] Sharing sites are primarily intended for transferring content rather than creating or modifying it.

Knowledge sharing can be mandated, but the extent of sharing depends more on generosity and altruism or the expectation of reciprocity on the part of those who have knowledge. They must be convinced that they should share it with those who need it. Because sharing generally benefits the recipient more than the provider, incentives are usually needed to motivate sharing. Incentives include:

- Communicate and promote desired sharing behavior.
- Design physical and virtual spaces that encourage conversations.
- Conduct on-site and online training on how to use sharing tools.
- Managers must lead by practicing good sharing behavior.
- Implement recognition and reward programs for good sharing behavior.
- Reinforce desired behaviors and discourage undesired behaviors.
- Encourage people to collaborate and work in communities.

## *4.4.6 Collaborate with Others*

Collaboration is working together with others in a primarily intellectual activity to satisfy mutual interests and achieve compatible goals. As used here, the term "cooperation" emphasizes physical activities or tasks, such as jointly responding to an emergency or crisis. The distinction between sharing and collaboration is that sharing provides access to existing content whereas collaboration involves joint creation of new content. The distinction between collaboration and negotiation (Sect. 4.4.7) is that collaboration involves little or no conflict between participant goals, whereas negotiation usually involves conflicting goals that require mutual compromise. In essence, collaboration approaches agreement as a partnership. Collaboration involves three phases: social context, technological support, and post-collaboration.

### 4.4.6.1 Social Context

Successful collaboration is about relationships. It depends primarily on individual, community, and cultural relationships that, taken together, provide a social context conducive to successful collaboration. Desirable attributes include candor, openness, voluntarism, trust, and diversity, in pursuit of joint creativity. The social context for collaboration is classified into four levels: attitudes, behavior, relationships, and culture. Hargrove (Hargrove 1998) describes the social aspects of collaboration in some detail.

---

[12] For example, http://www.slideshare.net/Al.Simard/slideshows is designed to share presentations.

**Attitudes** involve personal feelings, emotions, or mental positions with regard to a fact, state, or purpose. They also involve a readiness, preparedness, and willingness to become involved in and commit to collaborative work. Attitudes strongly affect individual behavior which is observable. They can be influenced through engagement, counseling, and positive interaction, such as feedback, listening, and mutual agreement. Positive attitudes include enjoyment, candor, honesty, openness, altruism, and ethics. Negative attitudes include negativity, hostility, arrogance, selfishness, deception, and closed mindedness.

**Behavior** relates to observable conduct, action, or response of an individual to stimulation or their environment. Positive behavior is manifested through desired sharing, participation, and collaboration practices of an individual. There are three approaches to providing incentives: compliance, motivation, and engagement. Compliance involves external approaches, such as policies, rules, performance review, and job security. Motivation uses reward systems, such as challenges, bonuses, awards, and recognition, and engagement uses internal approaches, such as a sense of ownership, meaningful assignments, self-satisfaction, and enjoyment. Compliance is least effective for affecting behavior and engagement is most effective.

**Relationships** refer to desired behavior and interactions within a community or group. Positive relationships and behaviors include dialogue, trust, safety, equality of participants, a meritocracy of ideas, searching for outliers, and synergy. Negative relationships and behaviors include debating, arguing, promoting an external agenda or position, assuming superiority, majority voting, consensus building, and group think. Community dynamics can be guided through mutually agreed rules of conduct, group norms, fostering positive relationships, and community support.

**Culture** focuses on shared attitudes and beliefs, values and social norms and goals, and practices that characterize an NGO. Kotter (Kotter 2002) identified eight steps that were necessary for changing an organization's culture: sense of urgency, guiding team, uplifting vision, communications, empowerment, short-term wins, persistence, and nurturing. A collaborative cultural includes diversity, flexibility, freedom of expression, transparency, and learning.

#### 4.4.6.2 Technology Support

The increasing need for speed, complexity of issues, diversity of expertise required, and wide dispersion of collaborators have made digital technology an essential element of collaboration in the knowledge economy. Collaboration is increasingly taking place online using collaboration technologies.[13] Such technology allows anyone

[13] See http://en.wikipedia.org/wiki/Main_Page for the largest encyclopedia ever produced. It is the best example of what has been accomplished through collaboration and the open-source technology used to support it.

with access to a site to post documents and to modify documents posted by others. Another feature is that the rapid turnaround of ideas enables collaborative documents to be produced in days rather than weeks or months. There are five aspects of technological support for collaboration: a collaboration site, accessibility, network, site security, and operations.

**Collaboration Site** is a website that is used by members of a group or community to share existing content, present and discuss ideas, organize and manage work, and jointly create new content. Typical site functions include a document repository, posting content (blog), discussion areas, and a work space for jointly creating content (wiki), a directory of expertise, a search engine, and support functions, such as a calendar, announcements, task manager, and links.

**Accessibility** is the extent or degree to which content on a collaboration site can be easily acquired, delivered to, downloaded, or received by participants. The site must be easily accessible to all members through a Web browser and a user-centric main page. Participants may include people from outside the NGO who access the site via the Internet. Although the latter poses additional challenges for network and site security, access must remain easy for authorized external users or they won't voluntarily participate. User training, help files, and a help desk can greatly facilitate use of the site by participants.

**Network** is the communications technology that connects dispersed communities, organizations, or large numbers of people, with common interdependencies, interests, or purpose. An internal site must be connected to an intranet, local area network (LAN) or a wide-area network (WAN). A site with external members must be connected to the Internet and a domain name server (DNS).

**Site security** involves controlling access to a website and its content; architecture and operating procedures that minimize the risk of sabotage, damage, or loss of functionality; and redundancy that enables rapid recovery of the site and its content. Security must balance the need for protection with ease of access and use. Inadequate security poses a risk for an entire network, while a site that is difficult to use won't be.

**Operations** are activities, work, or functions associated with installing, running, maintaining, and upgrading a collaboration site. It also includes life-cycle management of the site as well as planning for and implementing disaster recovery and business continuity in the event of damage, failure, or loss of content.

#### 4.4.6.3 Organizational Work

Collaboration results in potential value for all participants, just as a rising tide raises all boats. To capture the value, an NGO must bring the content inside the organization, add internal value to the common product, and adapt the content to its operational needs and practices. It is equally important that procedures are in place to move the content from collaboration through the NGO's decision-making process to obtain approval for action. In other words, an NGO must be prepared to sail on the high tide. There are three stages of post-collaboration organizational work: documentation, storing, and recommendation.

**Documentation** adapts collaboration outputs to the organizational structure in preparation for making recommendations to decision makers.

**Storing** documents and recommendations in a collaboration repository makes it available for sharing and possible future reuse (Sect. 4.3.2). As a precursor to decision making, it may also become part of the record of decision.

**Recommendations** transfer collaboration outputs to the NGOs authoritative hierarchy for decision making. When the recommendations are approved, the explicit knowledge becomes organizational knowledge.

### *4.4.7 Negotiate Agreements*

Negotiation is a dialogue, discussion, or bargaining between two or more persons, groups, or organizations, with mutual interests but conflicting goals, requiring compromise to reach an understanding, resolve differences, gain advantage, produce an agreement, satisfy various interests, or craft outcomes. A classic example is that of a buyer and seller who want to do business (mutual interest) but the seller wants the highest price possible while the buyer wants the lowest price possible (incompatible goal). Negotiating a service contract is similar. Both parties benefit from reaching a fair agreement, but the contractor would like to do the least amount of work for the largest fee possible while the NGO would like just the opposite. MCormack (1995), Malhotra and Bazerman (2007), and Fisher and Ury (2011) provide good descriptions of the negotiation process from different perspectives.

Negotiation is both the most important and complex activity undertaken by an NGO: important because it is core activity that supports almost everything that an NGO does and complex because it involves many different elements of KM coupled with significant uncertainty. Unlike collaboration which emphasizes a partnership approach to creating knowledge, negotiation emphasizes an adversarial approach to reaching an agreement. Recognizing this difference at the outset is critical to ultimate success because the two processes are very different. Voluntary sharing of tacit knowledge is, for the most part, absent in negotiation. Any information that provides a bargaining advantage will most likely be withheld or it may be misleading. In fact, some negotiating tactics are specifically intended to elicit information from the opposite side without their being aware that they "let something slip."

Negotiation focuses on producing situation-specific intelligence about the opposite party, establishing a position, reaching a mutually acceptable agreement, and recommending organizational approval. The main phases are pre-negotiation, negotiation, and post-negotiation. The phases are renamed here, for clarity, as preparation, bargaining, and organization.

#### 4.4.7.1 Preparation (Pre-negotiation)

Like so much of life, the greater the preparation, the greater the chance that negotiation will be successful. The more that is known about the opposite party, the better a negotiator can present their side of the case and counterarguments made by the other side. The less the uncertainty there is about a situation and its associated facts, the less the risk of being surprised during negotiations. Preparation includes six steps: preliminary analysis, recommendation, determine goals and strategy, compile information about the opposite and the situation, interpret the information, and establish a position.

**Preliminary analysis** (*such as we have suggested by the Study Team*) determines whether a negotiation is desirable, feasible, and likely to succeed. Since a significant amount of effort, involving several individuals, is likely to be needed to prepare for negotiating, it is useful at the outset to conduct a preliminary analysis to support a request for approval to proceed. Some organization may allow for this step to be skipped when the need for negotiation is obvious or the process is likely to be straightforward.

**Recommendation** involves preparing a briefing note, paper, or report summarizing the situation and the opposite party in a negotiation along with a recommendation to proceed or not (***what we call a decision memo***). It may also include recommendations to collaborate with others in a joint negotiation. If negotiation is approved, continue; if not, the process ends.

**Determining goals and strategy** begins by establishing overall goals. The goal statement should specify intended outcomes as well as the nature of the agreement (MOU, contract, letter, etc.). This is followed by determining the strategic purpose of the negotiation, such as securing an agreement, or building a long-term relationship. These, in turn, affect the negotiating strategy, for example, win–win and win–lose.

**Compiling** involves searching for, acquiring, and assembling content related to the organizational context of the opposite party and about the situation or issue being negotiated. This typically employs focused context and situational intelligence gathering (Sects. 4.4.1 and 4.4.2) coupled with as broad a range of related content as possible. The latter minimizes the risk of surprise during the negotiation and reduces the level of uncertainty. Compiling typically also involves a significant amount of one-on-one conversations and interactions (Sect. 4.4.5) to elicit as much information about the opposite party and the situation as possible.[14]

---

[14] As previously, illegal or unethical methods of compiling content are not condoned by the authors. A substantial amount of information can be compiled through the open literature and the Internet. The key is in knowing where to look and how to extract patterns from relevant but seemingly unconnected facts.

**Interpreting** is construing, conceiving, or explaining the meaning and implications of content related to the opposite organization and the specific issue or situation to be negotiated from the perspective of supporting a negotiation position. This involves both analysis of relevant facts and synthesis of scattered bits and pieces of information to reveal overall patterns.

**Establishing a position** is generally accomplished through internal collaboration (Sect. 4.4.6) and/or study. It starts by determining the "Best Alternative to a Negotiated Agreement" (BATNA) which identifies the preferred action that could be taken if an agreement cannot be reached. This is determined for your organization and estimated for the opposite party. This is followed by determining the "Zone of Potential Agreement" (ZOPA) for both parties. The upper limit of the zone identifies the most that you are willing to concede, in the while the lower limit estimates the most that the opposite party is likely to concede. The region between these two limits denotes the boundaries of the "negotiation space." If there is no "positive space" between the two limits, the negotiation is unlikely to succeed and should not proceed. The position should be documented in a negotiator's briefing book and a negotiation database on a notebook computer.

#### 4.4.7.2 Bargaining

Bargaining involves discussion, debate, and sometimes argument between two or more parties with the intent of reaching a mutual agreement. Although fairness is desirable, particularly when a long-term relationship with the opposite party is important, it is not necessary. Bargaining is not sequential; everything connects at the center of multiple two-way interactions in a hub-and-spoke process geometry. Although there is a tendency to test assumptions and maximize benefits earlier and counter deception or emotions after they occur, any process can affect the course of the discussion at any time. If negotiation involves a sequence of sessions, the overall process would link a sequence of individual bargaining processes.

**Bargaining** is the core of negotiation. There is a body of literature on methods and tactics that will not be described in detail here. For more information on bargaining beyond that presented in the previous chapter, see MCormack (1995), Malhotra and Bazerman (2007), and Fisher and Ury (2011). Bargaining is a quintessential human process, involving points made and countered by both parties. Each party explores areas of uncertainty and tests assumptions about their opposites through carefully crafted questions and answers. They also search for unknowns in their perception and understanding of the opposite party's position. There are techniques specifically intended to positively rather than negatively influence the opposite party. The same holds true for detecting and dealing with deception, mistrust, and unethical behavior from the opposite party. Finally, there are tactics for countering emotional behavior or differences in the relative power of the two parties.

Bargaining should be undertaken by a trained, experienced negotiator supported by a subject-matter expert and a support staff. The negotiator should have immediate access to researchers (the Study Team) who can quickly compile and interpret content related to new information that is revealed during the negotiating process. They should also have immediate access to an organizational manager (team leader) to discuss and approve changes beyond the previously established position. An initial position may be revised by returning to the preparation phase and very quickly (within hours or overnight) repeating the steps used to develop the original position, using the new information. Bargaining concludes by drafting and signing the negotiated agreement by both parties.

#### 4.4.7.3 Organizational Work (Post-negotiation)

Negotiation is not finished when the agreement is signed. Organizational work is needed to approve the negotiated agreement. There are four stages: after-action review, documentation, storing, and recommendation.

**After-Action Review** is a structured process for evaluating what occurred during a negotiation, why it occurred, and how it can be done better in the future. It is undertaken by those involved in and responsible for the negotiation. Such reviews can also support accountability on the part of those involved. The after-action review formalizes organizational learning.

**Documentation** involves writing and submitting a report of the after-action review of the negotiation.

**Storing** negotiation documents, the agreement, and recommendations makes it available for sharing and possible future reuse (Sect. 4.3.2—assets). As a precursor to decision making, it may also become part of the record of decision. The agreement is then submitted to the NGO's decision makers for approval.

### *4.4.8 Capture Experience*

Whether responding to an emergency or participating in a negotiation, it is important that information be captured as soon as possible after the experience to minimize the loss of important details. Event notes could be recorded in a paper journal, a tape recorder, or on video, particularly if time is at a premium. This will require subsequent transfer to a document or a database. It will also be difficult for anyone other than the person directly involved to access the information in near real time.

An electronic event journal, available to everyone participating in a project, eliminates the need for transfer and provides immediate availability of content. By automatically including the time when notes are recorded and the person recording, such a system provides a comprehensive record of what happened, when it happened, and who to contact. This is invaluable for after-action reviews, demonstrating due diligence, post-event follow-up, or investigations.

Major event command and control centers typically have built-in journal entry capabilities for every member of an operational team. However, most NGOs operating in the field won't have such capacity. Developing or purchasing this capability on a small scale is not a major undertaking, however. It is basically a database designed to facilitate content entry, retrieval, and sharing.

As much information as possible should be automatically entered by the system to minimize data entry time. Automatic entry would include the time, date, event name, location of the event, and other general information as appropriate. The user would log in and select the type of entry, such as purchase, task assignment, and discussion note.

Ideally, as many content categories as possible would be preprogrammed in a list to facilitate rapid selection with a mouse click. Each type of information should have a built-in template with required and optional fields. A user should only see the template associated with the type of information that has been selected. The user would enter specified data or a text description of an experience and log off. A maximum entry length could be programmed to prevent unnecessarily long descriptions. The task here is to rapidly capture brief descriptions sufficient to trigger subsequent memories when full reports are being prepared. The system should also have a capacity to upload photos or videos from mobile phones or similar devices. Once entered, only the original author or a system administrator would be allowed to modify the data to prevent accidental or deliberate deletion or change after the fact.

The system should have a capability to notify selected users that updates of interest to them have been posted. This will eliminate time spent searching through content that isn't relevant to a specific activity. Most of the people involved with the project should have access to most of the information in the event journal. Conversely, access to sensitive content could (should) be restricted to specific individuals; content-specific as well as general access control capability should be included in the event journal system.

Although multiple computers at an event could each be preprogrammed for specific content entry (as they are in hardwired, fixed command and control centers), the flexibility advantages of anyone being to use any available computer for entry or searching outweigh the disadvantage of users having to identify themselves and select a few additional fields before entering content. Finally, the event journal should be searchable, able to respond to queries, and generate preprogrammed reports.

### *4.4.9 After-Action Review*

Evaluation is compiling, reviewing, and assessing criteria and indicators of an activity or project to determine the extent to which it was successful. Evaluation provides key inputs to project documentation and reporting. Evaluation consists of four criteria, listed in order of increasing importance and difficulty of measurement: administration, efficiency, effectiveness, and outcomes. It is neither necessary nor desirable to evaluate all indicators for all criteria—only those that are most relevant to a particular project.

**Administration** concentrates on management considerations, such as staffing and budgeting. Indicators for administrative evaluation should be determined when an activity or project is established so that they can be monitored, entered into an administrative database, and extracted at the time of evaluation. Administration can be easily measured with standard responsibility and accountability indicators, such as:

- Management processes completed correctly and as scheduled
- Degree to which actual expenses match the planned budget
- Proper human resources management practices
- Quality and timeliness of project communications
- Extent of compliance with policies, rules, and procedures
- Reflecting organizational values and ethics

**Efficiency** emphasizes productivity, in terms of the amount of effort needed to deliver outputs. Efficiency is a useful evaluation criterion that is only slightly more difficult to measure than administration. Efficiency indicators should be determined when an activity or project is established so that they can be monitored, entered into an activity or project database, and extracted at the time of evaluation. Efficiency measures could include:

- Actual cost
- Human resources used
- Technological infrastructure employed
- Work processes followed
- Time and effort required

**Effectiveness** focuses on project accomplishments in relation to goals and objectives. Effectiveness is the capacity of a project to produce desired, decisive, or useful outputs or results. Effectiveness indicators should be determined when an activity or project is established so that they can be monitored, entered into an activity or project database, and extracted at the time of evaluation. Effectiveness is somewhat more difficult to measure than efficiency. Effectiveness indicators include the extent to which:

- Intermediate milestones and deliverables were achieved.
- Project outputs were produced as planned.
- Goals and objectives were attained.
- Results were communicated to interested parties.

**Outcomes** evaluate the contribution of project outputs to resolving a problem or addressing an issue. Alternatively, outcomes are results or impacts of using outputs to solve a problem or influence an issue. Outcome indicators should be determined when an activity or project is established so that they can be monitored, entered into an activity or project database, and extracted at the time of evaluation. Outcomes are the most important evaluation criteria but are also the most difficult to measure. Outcome indicators could include the extent to which an activity or project:

- Improved existing NGO processes or productivity
- Increased the visibility and recognition of the NGO

- Supported, influenced, or affected a negotiation
- Influenced awareness, attitudes, or behavior of stakeholders
- Reduced the risk from potential disasters or crises
- Mitigated the impacts of a disaster or crisis
- Increased the well-being of affected individuals

### 4.4.10 Report Activities

All NGOs must report periodically to their donors. They also want to keep stakeholders and interested parties informed of their activities and successes. There are several types of reports that might be needed, such as an annual report for the NGO, annual and progress reports for individual activities and projects, and plans and work schedules for the coming year. These may incorporate financial and budget statements, or separate reports might be needed for this information.

At the time of establishing an NGO, a number of foundation documents are normally prepared. These could include a charter, a business case, a governance structure, a strategic plan, and a communications plan. These are prepared using the same methods and services as are described in this section, except that compiling content requires a combination of broad and focused searching as described in Sects. 4.4.1 and 4.4.2, respectively, rather than simply be an extraction from a database.

Preparing reports begins with compiling content. If an NGO has established a context database, a situational database, a funding database, an activity or project database, and an event database, and they are kept current, compiling content for a report is a fairly straightforward matter of search and retrieval. Without one or more databases or out-of-date content, compiling content for a report can become an onerous, time-consuming task. Further, some useful content will probably have been permanently lost due to fading memories.

The next step is to draft the document. Drafting may begin with consideration of the strategic purpose, direction, or thrust of the report, as, for example, in the case annual reports in which each year presents a different view of the NGO. In most cases, a report template is helpful in that it outlines what should be included in each type of report. Templates can range from a simple outline, to pre-formatted macros for a word processor, to a fill-in-the-blanks form. Office application software, such as a word processor, graphics, and spreadsheet, is essential. Version control is recommended to keep track of changes and ensure that the most recent version of a document is used.

The document is then reviewed. This could be done through a collaboration site in which reviewers can change the content, as in a wiki; a sharing site in which reviewers can view or download the document and comment publicly, as in a blog; or via e-mail with reviewers replying with comments for consideration by the author, as in tradition. The author then revises the report and repeats the process as often as necessary to achieve a consensus, subject to a report submission deadline. The report is then submitted for approval by the appropriate authority, and once approved it is stored in a report database. Finally, it is distributed to recipients or made broadly available, as appropriate.

### 4.4.11 Learning and Adapting

Organizational learning is essential for adapting to changes in an NGO's environment. In the rapidly changing twenty-first-century knowledge society, the speed with which an NGO learns and adapts is critical to its continuing relevance and sustainability. Organizational learning is a three-stage social process: (1) assimilating existing information and knowledge by individuals, (2) validating individual learning in an organizational context by communities or groups, and (3) institutionalizing group learning through organizational decisions. Organizational adaptation implements learning or anticipates future trends. Haeckel (1999), Hamel (2000), Kanter (2001), and Kotter (2002) provide good descriptions of change management and organizational adaptation.

**Assimilation** involves an individual becoming aware of existing facts, information, or knowledge that they did not previously know. Awareness comes through various methods, such as self-learning, teaching, training, presentations, demonstrations, or experience. Methods of assimilating tacit knowledge by individuals are listed in Sect. 4.3.3 (sharing). Assimilation can take place through either physical or online approaches. A need or want to learn results in interpreting the new content in terms of what a person already knows, followed by committing it to memory for future use.

**Validation** determines the extent to which individual learning is useful in an organizational context. Validation and endorsement are done by groups such as communities of practice, committees, or work groups. It is typically based on characteristics, attributes, or standards that provide a basis for evaluating, judging, and deciding that individual learning is appropriate for organizational purposes. Validation is supported by a collaboration site and after-action reviews.

**Institutionalization** occurs when group learning is transformed into organizational action. Documentation involves preparing written or multimedia documents that describe what was learned, its relevance to the organization, and the recommended action. Documentation is supported by office applications and document templates. Storing lessons learned in a learning repository (Sect. 4.3.2—assets) makes validated learning available for future use in recurring similar situations. Recommendations propose organizational adaptation, based on what was learned. Preparing recommendations are supported by office applications. A decision to implement proposed changes completes the institutionalization process.

**Adaptation** is modifying organizational processes, functions, or outputs based on organizational learning or in anticipation of changes in the NGOs environment. All organizations must adapt to current or anticipated changing environments to sustain themselves. Techniques described in Sects. 4.4.1 (understand the context) and 4.4.2 (know the situation) can be used to monitor trends and emerging issues of interest to an NGO and to produce actionable intelligence (a form of learning) that supports recommended organizational changes.

Adaptation begins with a change management plan outlining how an NGO will transform itself from its present state to a desired future state. Like renovating a house, adaptation is often more difficult than building from scratch. This is because an NGO has to dismantle existing systems, develop new systems, unlearn existing practices, and learn new practices, all while continuing normal operations. Having a blueprint for designing, developing, and implementing change at the outset will minimize the risk of unanticipated problems that will become increasingly difficult to overcome as a change initiative progresses. Once a plan is developed, adaptation can be managed just like any other activity or project.

### 4.4.12 Categorize Positions

When the Study Team plans an NGO's negotiating position and strategy, it is important to know previous delegate, group, organizational, and national positions on various issues. Although negotiation and voting may take place in a closed session, the results are often available on public sites. By acquiring results from a series of votes and entering them in a voting database, it is possible to analyze the data and identify voting trends and patterns. These can be used to identify potential negotiating allies and adversaries as well as partners or competitors for funding.

Voting data is only an indicator, however. It may reveal partial truths or it could be misleading. One needs to understand the underlying context of a voting pattern and the particulars of a specific vote. These may be partially explained through contextual or situational searches mentioned previously.

Voting patterns are not likely to be fully understood only through open sources of information, however. It is more likely that one-on-one conversations with knowledgeable individuals will be needed. Here, trust and security become essential. Anything that might be revealed in such conversations must be treated as confidential.

Confidential information should not be entered into a database unless it is very well protected by comprehensive security measures. For example, responsible merchants now delete credit card numbers after a transaction has been completed because the liability of a potential leak, despite the low risk and security safeguards, is simply too great. The best security is an "air gap," in which a system has no connection to the outside world (except users, who can be compromised). Although this is typically used by high-security organizations, it is likely to be infeasible for NGOs and impossible in the field. Anything less, however, and determined hackers, particularly if they are state sponsored and the target is sufficiently interesting, will eventually break through a firewall or simply steal a computer. In this respect, cyberspace and real space are the same!

One only has to consider the impact of WikiLeaks[15] to realize the potential harm that could be done to an NGO's credibility should an unwanted leak of confidential information occur. Further, a security breach may be entirely unintentional. All it takes is an accidental click on the wrong e-mail address, a document left in an

[15] See http://en.wikipedia.org/wiki/Wikileaks for a detailed discussion of WikiLeaks.

airport, or a cell phone left in a restaurant. Unfortunately, the information society is a double-edged sword. The enormous social advantages are countered by equally substantial criminal disadvantages that will do harm anywhere that they find a weakness.

## 4.5 Integration

Knowledge work and knowledge management are highly interconnected. All types of knowledge work interact with other types of work. As well, some knowledge services are needed to support all categories of knowledge work. Table 4.3 shows the extent to which knowledge work and knowledge services are interconnected.

Table 4.3 should be read from top to bottom. The presence of an "x" in a cell indicates that the work listed in the vertical column needs the work indicated in the horizontal row to accomplish its objectives. For example, knowing the context also requires managing contacts, interacting with others, collaboration, and preparing a report (column 1). It also requires all five knowledge services.

**Table 4.3** Interconnection between knowledge work and knowledge services

| Knowledge work ↓ | Context | Situation | Funding | Contacts | Interact | Collaborate | Negotiate | Capture | Review | Report | Learn | Voting |
|---|---|---|---|---|---|---|---|---|---|---|---|---|
| Context | | | X | | | X | X | | | X | | |
| Situation | | | X | | X | X | X | | | X | | X |
| Funding | | | | | | | | | | X | | |
| Contacts | X | X | X | | X | X | X | | | | | X |
| Interact | X | X | X | | | | X | | | | | |
| Collaborate | X | X | X | | X | | | X | X | | | |
| Negotiate | | | X | | X | | | X | X | | | |
| Capture | | | | | X | | | | | X | X | |
| Review | | | | | X | | X | | | X | X | |
| Report | X | X | X | | | X | X | | | | X | |
| Learn | | | X | | X | X | X | | | | | |
| Voting | | X | | | | | | | | | | |
| *Services* | | | | | | | | | | | | |
| Database | X | X | X | X | X | X | X | X | X | X | X | X |
| Web portal | X | X | | | X | X | X | | | | | |
| Search | X | X | X | X | X | | X | | | | | |
| Office app. | X | X | X | X | X | X | X | X | X | X | X | X |
| Security | X | | X | | | | X | | | | | X |
| | 9 | 9 | 12 | 3 | 12 | 8 | 12 | 4 | 4 | 7 | 5 | 5 |

Three types of work are highly interconnected with everything else (12 connections out of a possible 17): funding, interaction, and negotiating. Funding and negotiation are core activities for any NGO and interacting with others supports almost everything. Four types of work are moderately interconnected with everything else (7–9 connections): knowing the context, situational awareness, collaboration, and reporting. The first two are key to undertaking a project, the third is central to execution, and the fourth is administratively essential.

Five types of work are less interconnected than the other two groups (3–5 connections): maintaining contacts, capturing experience, reviewing activities, learning, and classifying voting. However, even these are not isolated. And the interactions are not necessarily symmetrical. For example, although maintaining contacts is only connected to three types of knowledge services (vertical column), seven types of work need contacts (horizontal row).

The fact that the same or similar types of services, such as office applications, are used for different types of work suggests one generic application will suffice for all uses. Conversely, although many specific databases have been identified, each should be a module within a larger system of database. This allows interaction among individual databases coupled with tailoring each database to its particular use. A modular architecture has the additional advantages of allowing sequential development of individual databases as well as maintaining and upgrading any component without affecting an entire system.

The implications of the strong interconnectedness are that no aspect of knowledge work or services can be designed, developed, or implemented in isolation from the rest. Overall goals, objectives, and scope are essential to define the work to be done. A blueprint is important to show how everything connects to and interacts with everything else. A plan is also necessary to outline a logical development sequence, including milestones and deliverables.

The best approach is to start small but think big by undertaking low-risk, high-priority, project-scale development that yields early deliverables within the context of an overall strategic direction. This approach also minimizes the risk of failure and allows for learning as you go. The history of large IT and system development is littered with the remains of large projects that failed or fell far short of expectations. This lesson is best learned from the experience of others rather than personally.

## 4.6 Conclusions

In today's fast-paced, ever-changing, increasingly complex knowledge society, information technology, coupled with good data, information, and knowledge management practices, enables small NGOs to effectively participate on an intellectual par with large, well-established organizations. Conversely, the same technology and practices have become essential for an NGO to participate in a meaningful way and increasingly to succeed, grow, or lead in their chosen area of interest.

This chapter describes a dozen types of information and knowledge work done by humanitarian assistance NGOs and the types of data, information, and knowledge services needed to support them. The cost of most of these applications has dropped to a level where most NGOs can afford them. Further, many are available from open sources at little or no cost, other than that for implementation and operation. Proper use of these practices can greatly leverage limited NGO resources and increase the chances of success in the twenty-first-century knowledge society.

# Chapter 5
# Security, Risk Analysis and Intelligence

**Extract** This chapter explains the role of a security adviser and the need for intelligence, especially risk profiles, and the need to trust but verify contacts and their information. A tool for developing profiles is provided with a link to an expanded version on a website associated with this book. Proposals for special reports are recommended as well as case studies.

## 5.1 Introduction to Chapter Five

A ***Security Adviser*** assesses the physical and political risks to a negotiation and must be an expert at threat assessment and situational analysis, provides solutions to weaknesses, and is able to recommend cancellation of a trip, if the risk is unjustified. It might be a staff officer from one of the alliance NGOs or an adviser from an umbrella body like InterAction. For purposes of this book, the security adviser reports to the team leader on risk analysis for the negotiation; this officer might also accompany a delegation to the field if the mission is risky. In the latter case, the officer reports directly to the chief negotiator.

## 5.2 The Need for Profiles: And Using a Data Fusion Tool to Help

Profiles are studies attempt to understand the underlying problems and prospects for success tensions in a country or population. As an example of the kind of study that might fit into a profile, consider political and economic tensions which population growth and dispersal can cause. Such a study may be useful to describe the urban versus rural and migratory populations, as well as the job market and relative desires

L.W. Roeder, Jr. and A. Simard, *Diplomacy and Negotiation for Humanitarian NGOs*, Humanitarian Solutions in the 21st Century, DOI 10.1007/978-1-4614-7113-4_5,

of the different populations. Keep in mind that cities and towns will likely absorb all future population growth from now until 2050 and perhaps beyond, effectively doubling the world population of 1950 by the year 2050. That's going to cause new societal stresses in many countries, especially those with few job opportunities, a lot of ethnic strife or poor health, and educational standards, discussions on which fit into a profile. Regarding population alone, in the 1970s, there were only two cities with populations over 10 million; in 1990, there were ten. In 2012, there are 23 mega-cities, and in 2025, there might be over 37 (DESA 2012a). In other words, there is a rapid process of urban concentration. Not only people concentrating into urban settings alone, which places stress on the rural areas, cities with more than one million inhabitants will increase their share of the urban population, often in the developing world, while cities with less than one million inhabitants will have a declining share of the urban population. This increased, centralized demand will place a major strain on local, regional, and global resources, to say nothing of the indigenous? What about on countries where NGOs work? That has to be part of the analysis of any country profile.

A political crisis can have many parents, poorly managed population growth being one. A profile requires illuminating all factors that lead to instability—in other words, true intelligence, the kind of information, for example, gleaned by the Famine Early Warning System or by analyzing reports that come in every day on ReliefWeb. Had that been done more effectively in the past, there would have been better warning of the impending crisis in Rwanda, and perhaps it would have saved thousands of lives. Various NGOs did provide a warning of human rights violations; the United States leadership and others did not listen well enough.

While the NGO community should be emotionally connected to human tragedy by the images that flood in from the social media, the ones that drive moral outrage and are good fuel for driving action, NGOs must also always be analytical before taking action, to try to understand the causes of disaster even while the images are used to raise funds and other resources. For many in the NGO community, the first instinct upon watching the attacks on the town of Homs by the Syrian Army in 2012 was a desire for a no-fly zone. Some wanted to begin bombing Syrian military forces. However, any specific policy decision to intervene in a crisis should be based on intelligence and true analysis. A bombing run in early 2012 was impractical and risked creating a regional war. The nations supporting the revolution didn't know at first who they would be supporting and if those forces might even be worse than what needed to be replaced. It is better to work with the international community and negotiate some sort of umbrella for the civilians, as well as send in intermediaries like Kofi Anan, though his project did not fare well. The project team wanting to enter a crisis or building an alliance of NGOs and agencies to support their cause needs to carefully develop a security package and as a profile on each ally. The project team also needs to develop a profile on itself, to decide if it or its members are the best professionals to deal with the issue.

The population analysis/profile we offered at the start of this section can be time consuming to generate. Often it is better to hire a contractor for the work; however, much information on every country is being collected all the time by many sources that can be condensed into useful bits. Those "bits" can then be used to develop a "snapshot profile" that will help the Study Team decide whether to become involved at all or how to wisely choose allies. For that exercise, NGOs may wish to consider using a well-designed *Data Fusion Matrix*. Such a tool, if it is maintained,[1] can provide donors, policy makers, and analysts an understanding of overlapping interests and quickly identify potential partners that either won't be appropriate or might be problematic. This is another kind of profile.

- The same kind of questions can be used when deciding whether or not to set up an operation. By defining the operational space in which an NGO might operate, this approach greatly simplifies decision making on resources, when or where to deploy and who best to send by identifying overlapping interests or the lack thereof.
- Even if several answers might suggest that an NGO can or should operate in a specific situation, others may argue against that, perhaps regarding resources, talents, and other issues.
- Even if circumstances might inhibit work in a specific situation or country, that might not prevent support for other NGOs that can. For example, an American NGO expert in a disease might not be able to enter Iran but could fund a different NGO that is able to enter.
- The questions presented here can help any NGO self-define its own "operational area or space" (Fig. 5.1) in a database, allowing donors to find the right NGO for an emergency or to negotiate a declaration. Keep in mind that the questions posed in this exercise are samples. Depending on the nature of the work usually conducted by the NGO, the questions may vary. The goal is to be able to show why an NGO is or is not the right fit to an emergency.
- When disasters strike or the call goes out from the public to help, it is not always easy to know which NGO is the best fit for a task. The immediacy of any crisis, especially a major emergency, also stimulates NGO instincts to leap to the rescue, but if black bears are the species most at risk, does it make sense to send relief workers who focus on wolves?
- Even if the NGO is properly trained for the crisis, like flood management, other factors might prohibit work, perhaps infectious diseases like Ebola or a fast-moving war. Perhaps local terrorist groups are targeting relief workers.
- Humanitarian Relief and Development NGOs regularly work in all of these stressful situations, but not every NGO can do everything.
- Before a donor gives money or an NGO negotiates an agreement to enter a territory, or perhaps creates an alliance to negotiate something, it is best to ask some hard questions that define what is called (Fig. 5.2) "operational space."

---

[1] *A caution with this idea* is that keeping data current required data maintenance, probably by constantly contacting many sources, NGOs, academics, commercial and government experts, the UN, etc. Nobody likes an administrative burden and this kind of work won't be easy. It will require hours of work and some cost. However, if allies or collaborate, then tools like the Data Fusion idea proposed in this book can save money and time as well as ensure that policies are defensible and sustainable.

**Fig. 5.1** Roeder and colleague use map to plan flood rescue in the Sinai ((c) LRoeder, 1986)

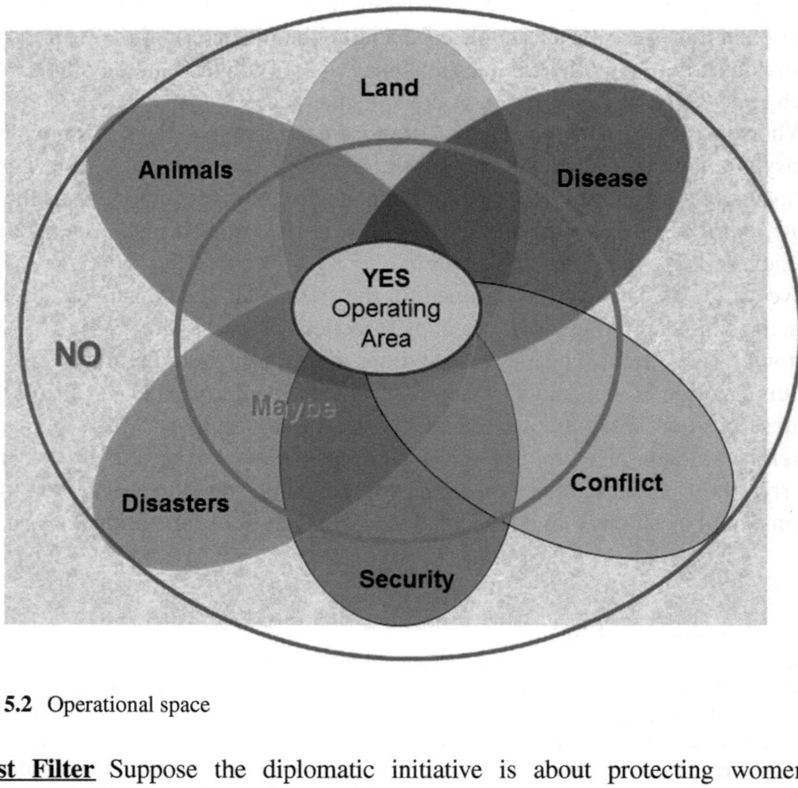


**Fig. 5.2** Operational space

**First Filter** Suppose the diplomatic initiative is about protecting women in Country X. The first filter when deciding on an operation is often whether or not, regardless of any other circumstances, the NGO or its partners can conduct any operations in Country X. Even if the NGO or its potential partners focus on protecting women, if one of the partners has a policy of only working in a different region of the world, then that NGO may not be a good fit. After all, even if the NGOs share general moral objectives, resources are limited. The issue might be more nuanced in that an NGO might be willing to share knowledge, not money.

**Second Filter** A second filter deals with work focus. Women often look after livestock in the developing world, so it might be natural to seek partners with animal-welfare NGOs when seeking to protect women. Assuming Filter one shows that the country or region in question is appropriate to the targeted NGO, they might well see a direct synergy and often would; at the same time, their donors may have restricted their work to livestock disease work, so while the staff might be sympathetic, their mandate and resources might not allow an "overlap of interest." Often the reverse is seen; when an animal welfare NGO wanted help from a development agency, the officials said "we don't do animals" until it was demonstrated that helping livestock reduced poverty. That created an "overlap of interest."

**Third Filter** Assuming that the first two filters have identified potential partners that are willing to help protect women in the targeted country or region, other filter questions may identify problems. For example, if the women are suffering from a type of disaster, it may be that the potential partner doesn't have the expertise. Experts in drought management might not be the right people to engage in a crisis where the risk is rape. That's an important filter for either a negotiation or an expedition. Similar filters might focus on conflict regions, whether the country is a failed nation state, etc. There is not one set of filtering questions. The point here is that when deciding to reach out for partners, before reaching out to them, ask relevant questions. Are there circumstances under which there is no overlapping interest? If so, that partner is risky. That doesn't mean they will never work out; knowing the risks ahead of time is crucial for planning a diplomatic initiative or an operation.

**Behind Each Filter Are Other Questions** For example, a filter on conflict might indicate that the current situation is stable and thus acceptable for a field trip; don't stop there. Under what scenarios might the conflict escalate and how will that risk the negotiations?

## 5.3 Case Studies

### *5.3.1 The Relationship of Drought and Political/ Economic Crises in Africa*

> The 1984–1986 droughts in Africa resulted in the continent's most severe famine in recorded history. Countless lives were saved by the massive outpouring of assistance from around the world. The US response to this crisis was larger than that of any other donor nation as a result of the concerted efforts of numerous government agencies, private voluntary organizations (NGOs), businesses, and US citizens (Brown et al. 1987).

Those who served in the US military in the Horn of Africa in the early 1970s understood that the region was a potential disaster; yet many were surprised in 1984 and 1985 by the great famines in Ethiopia, Sudan, Chad, and elsewhere. Underlying the pitiful images of starving refugees and the displaced, images that drove many westerners to action, were long-term trends that often did not get the required attention, the "big picture," so to speak. The general public saw an urgent need to ship food; professionals also saw the underlying causes of political disharmony and famine, the scope of potential death and economic destruction, soil erosion, deforestation, and desertification. Indigenous security forces and rebels often did not follow normal rules of civilian protection, often there were just too many people chasing too few resources. The carrying capacity of the land wasn't enough for the needs of the population. By 2012, more than 40 % of the region's population is still undernourished, with perhaps as much as 70 % in Eritrea and Somalia. Taken together there are over 160 million people living in Djibouti, Ethiopia, Eritrea, Kenya, Somalia, the Sudan, and Uganda, and nearly half live with extreme food shortages. And the problem isn't just the intersection of overpopulation and nature. Often there are corruption, factions, warlords, abusive governmental structures, persecution, and waste. This is absolutely where NGOs should be working. As the great nations like China, Russia, the United States, and parts of Europe see their economic equities threatened, they will take action that they deem appropriate to their national interests. Too often in the past, however, that led to other abuses as poor nations were caught up as political pawns. On the other hand, while not all NGOs have been neutral and some proselytize when it's inappropriate, they usually operate with purer motives and work to balance uneven economic dimensions in the ethnic makeup of countries, because it is the right thing, not because it is in the national interest of their own country. To do that well requires more than training and money; it requires developing an intelligence profile on the causes of the crisis, either man made or natural, more often a combination and well-developed profiles on the local actors, the people, and organizations with whom the NGOs must negotiate. Every Study Team should create such profiles.

### 5.3.2 *The 2009 Swine Slaughter in Egypt*

In 2009, pigs were being culled in Egypt to stem the rising tide of swine flu. This was an animal welfare issue because the slaughter was cruel and not needed; it was also a humanitarian crisis because the effort seriously placed the Copt minority at a disadvantage. NGOs did try to stop the slaughter and actually went to the agencies identified as the lead in the printed rules of the road to lobby for a change in policy and even to negotiate new health rules; they failed. Some of the international NGOs involved did not realize that Egypt had been in a state of emergency for years, and as a result only the president had the real power in emergency situations, not his ministers. An in-depth analysis might have led the NGOs to approach the president directly. Not having considered the potential for an alternative approach, they did not. No one can now say if President Mubarak would have reversed his ministers; real analysis of "intelligence" by experts might have provided a more viable path to success, which in their system meant to the chef de cabinet, and working up from there. The sense after asking around with the NGOs involved was that the intelligence leading up to the strategic approach to avoid the president was based primarily on a compilation of answers to these basic questions:

- **What were the Egyptians doing?** A cull.
- **Who made the policy?** The prime minister and his cabinet.
- **Who is described in the Constitution as having authority for such matters?** The prime minister and the ministers of health and agriculture.
- **Was the policy based on science?** Not according to OIE and WHO.
- **Was the policy based on prejudice against an ethnic minority?** Perhaps. Some experts indicated that the flu scare was just an opportunity to harm the Coptic minority, which has also suffered since the Egyptian revolution.
- **Could public diplomacy have turned public opinion around?** Perhaps. Not all Egyptians agreed with the policies.

Due to the urgent need to act before the entire herd was slaughtered, NGO research at least in one major international NGO went no further than an Internet-based glance at Egyptian Law, not an in-depth analysis of information provided by topic experts. That prevented the development of true intelligence and constipated the policy process. The resulting hypothesis was that the only route to saving the pigs was public diplomacy in the media or lobbying the prime minister and his ministers. That was certainly a reasonable route in the abstract in most countries, but while hindsight is 20/20, the proposal in such a future situation is to challenge the axioms before making a final decision. The 2011 revolution in Egypt changed things dramatically in that country, and it is hard to know what rules will emerge. If the political structure had remained, the recommendation would have suggested considering possibilities of decision making not described in the Constitution. No one probably ever called the chief of staff to President Mubarak. Now that Egypt is entering an entirely new era, NGOs wanting to engage the system would do well to build a Study Team with country experts to examine in detail the mechanics and politics of the new government, as well as the evolving social system. In the case of Egypt, changes in government and society are likely to be in continual flux for years. NGOs wanting to work on development projects in the Sinai, for example, will definitely see a dramatically different political scene and new risks in the indigenous population from only a decade ago. **Note**: That can seem a daunting task for an NGO. Just as with the Data Fusion idea we proposed in Sect. 5.1, any analysis undertaken Monday might be outdated by Friday. Periodic updates are highly recommended. Our recommendation for most NGOs is not to try to do this alone. Use partners like the UN ReliefWeb project or other NGOs. In other words, share the burden of data collection and analysis.

### 5.3.3 Civil War

Before an NGO decides to intervene in a civil war or even lower levels of civil unrest such as in the Sinai Peninsula since the fall of the Mubarak regime, the Study Team should go through the same rigor a government does, asking hard questions that not only expose physical risks, but also political and economic causes. In Syria in 2011–2012 many of the national authorities and western NGOs who wanted to help the civilian population were uncertain about which organizations were sustainable, what their politics were, and which to support in general. The same was true for vulnerable groups like women. There was no doubt that women played a role, leaders like Suhair al-Attasi. Until early 2012 when she fled Syria for Paris, she lived in Damascus and ran the Jamal Atassi Forum group on Facebook, which called for political reforms in Syria and the reinstatement of civil rights and the cancellation of the emergency law that had suspended constitutional rights since 1963 (Al Jazeera, 2011). Another is Razan Zaitouneh, a Syrian-based human rights lawyer who also maintains a Twitter account for public diplomacy purposes and as of the writing of this book is in hiding, for fear of arrest by the Syrian government.

The question when dealing with any rebel force or political activities is "what are their motivations and who fronts them?" In Syria, the opposition is made up of Christians, Kurds, Druze, and other minorities, and some are members of the Syrian National Council (SNC). The question early on was whether the SNC was truly inclusive or overly influenced by one minority over others? Even some Alawite are being to lose interest in the government (Sands 2012). Be cautious and do not allow the urgency of a crisis to prevent analysis. Providing weapons, money, or moral support to the wrong group can make a crisis worse, not better. Entering a crisis without a proper security profile could place NGO relief workers or negotiators more at risk, not less.

### 5.3.4 The Sinai Peninsula in 2012

As an example of a current conflict where this approach would be helpful, consider the Bedouins of the Sinai Peninsula.[2] With the fall of President Mubarak, a power vacuum emerged in the Sinai which directly impacted the Bedouins, who have never been treated well. Ancient Egyptians called them *mesh-wesh*, which meant sand fleas. Modern Egyptians consider them little better. Consider a development NGO with a focus on indigenous populations. It might wish to negotiate an assistance program for the Sinai Bedouin with the emerging governance structure in

[2]Mr. Roeder played with Sinai Bedouins as a child, then lived near them while serving in Egypt as a civilian observer in the MFO (Multinational Force of Observers), where he taught Bedouin culture, and subsequently has maintained personal contact with a number of tribe members, some of whom were consulted for this book.

Egypt. If so, then the NGO would need to ask some very hard questions in order to avoid political land mines, not only in Cairo but also amongst the tribes, which would require discussions with the tribes.

The tribes of the north are more connected to Bedouins in Palestine and Gaza than the tribes of the South. There are two loose confederations, one each for the north and south portions of the peninsula; they don't coordinate. The Bedouin in the north are accused of many things, like smuggling and terrorist attacks in Sharm, Dahab, Nuweiba, and Taba, though not all the accused are likely guilty. What has emerged in the north is an independence movement, and because they rely on different economic indicators than the Southern tribes, which rely entirely on tourism, the north feels freer to act.

Though some politicization has taken place in the north, in the south, the tribes generally deplore violence, except for an instance when two American female tourists were "kidnapped" near St. Catherine's Monastery. The aim of those Bedouin was the release of some men of their tribe from prison. The ladies went on a five-star desert safari with guns. They were treated nicely. But still, those kidnappers got into much trouble with their fellow bedu from the Southern Tribes, as the action hurts their reputation and could scare away tourists. On the other hand, the Northern Tribes do not depend on tourism income, so a bad reputation doesn't hurt them the way the bedu in the south were hurt. The Northern Tribes want an independent Sinai with a Bedouin government; the bedu in the South were satisfied in February 2012 because each tribe's sheikh is now represented in the maglis issha'b (parliament). They now have more power and responsibility in their own territory. Some hard questions would need to examine sources of income and trends in political activity.

### 5.3.5 *Poland in 1982*

An historical case study may prove useful in understanding the thought process relative to intelligence as it relates to NGOs convincing external powers to pressure a repressive regime. **Recommendation**: Whether or not the target regime will moderate its stance, NGOs need to speak out about violations of human rights. At the same time, behind the scenes in HQ, as NGO representatives reach out to UN agencies or friendly government ministries to ask for support, they need to answer practical questions about the effectiveness of those measures. That will help determine the kind of resources expended and where. Consider 1982 in Poland, known as the *Stan wojenny w Polsce*.

The repressive regime felt threatened by internal forces, especially massive demonstrations, and on December 13, 1981 declared martial law and continued this status until July 22, 1983. The same evening, the labor movement Solidarity was banned, as were other movements; their leaders were arrested; and tanks and infantry moved into the streets. By 1981, it was clear that the government was going to impose Martial Law. Although they were wrong to do so, it was also clear to many that civil society organizations would not be able to directly change their minds.

However, across the globe pro-Solidarity demonstrations were going on, and by 1985, one NGO-led demonstration in Washington, DC was even graced with a speech by the President of the United States (Reagan 1985), but it took 3 years for that to happen. Why? First, why was Martial Law invoked? It is always important to ask why something happens and to do it in an impartial, analytical way, even if the actions are horrible. In 1980, Solidarity had won the right to strike through the Gdansk Accords[3]; by December, 1981, Poland was in sharp economic decline, the Solidarity movement was rising quickly, and central authority had been weakened. Many poles were calling for free elections which might have ended Communist rule. At a minimum that would have resulted in an accommodation or sharing of power between the pro-democracy movements and the central authority. Just as in 2012, Iran is concerned about losing the Syrian government as a client and its influence in the Gaza Strip, in 1982 the Soviet Union worried about Poland withdrawing from the Warsaw Pact, with Soviet influence becoming collateral damage throughout Eastern Europe. Both Warsaw and the west feared Soviet military intervention, as happened during the Prague Spring in 1968. This was definitely possible because the Polish Communist Party was in disarray. Some argued that because the Polish army took over, promised that civilian institutions would remain and arrested pro-democracy leaders, that action prevented an invasion and possible civil war. In other words, the coup leaders were not going to give up power, for fear of invasion, which would have been far more awful—at least that was an argument. The army could easily have sided with the people, but instead it retained the old order. So what about friendly European governments? Could civil society have convinced them to moderate the Polish army?

The United States and its allies could have imposed massive economic sanctions in response to the repression, but sanctions are often regressive, with the poorest people hurt first. Further, Moscow had too big a stake in Warsaw to allow the regime to fail; so the Soviet Union provided over a billion rubles in aid right away. The other Eastern European regimes also feared that Polish democracy could lead to what might now call an early Arab-Spring. Even Western European governments were reticent about being too politically aggressive; they wanted democracy of course, and they feared the Warsaw Pact. This was after all during the Cold War; the public was in favor of supporting Solidarity. At the same time, important nuclear weapons talks (INF) had begun just before the announcement, and real progress was being made as a result of the *Walk Through the Woods* talks. If the crisis in Poland was to cause INF to stop, many believed that would cause real growth in intermediate-range nuclear weapons which would foster an existential threat to all civilization. In other words, the Polish crisis was second fiddle to the potential for killing SALT talks, the limitation on strategic missiles. The point of this history lesson is that no political act is simple. An NGO back in 1982 wanting to change the political situation in Poland would have been wise to take the economic and military realities into

[3]Gdansk is the former Free City of Danzig, formed by Napoleon Bonaparte.

context, especially when talking to donors. However, that doesn't mean do nothing. On the contrary, the very complexity of such a situation never means to give up; it means that an NGO alliance in that situation would plan for a long-term struggle for freedom in Poland and constantly probe for opportunities. Similar situations can be expected in the future.

## 5.4 Possible Annual Reports

*In addition to profiling conditions in a country, it is also a good idea to track what other NGOs and other potential partners are doing. This isn't about trying to take advantage of competition. We are recommending the development of "annual reports" to keep track of your own progress, avoid confusion in-house and unneeded duplication between NGOs and other potential partners.*

NGOs like to compete with each other and within their organization between departments; the argument in favor of compartmentalization is that each program has its own purpose, so full communication between offices or NGOs is not needed, perhaps not even desirable, but that is often a formula for disaster. Confusion and costly duplication can occur in an NGO when unconnected parts are working on similar projects with different elements of the UN or some other organization. Similarly, if two NGOs are doing exactly the work, this might reduce the chance of effectively finding solutions to new problems.

In our opinion, this kind of compartmentalization can reduce synergies and cost savings and usually should be avoided. In addition, if a lot of NGOs are working in field but not collaborating, the team leader must understand that coordination of effective negotiation positions may be harder. One office in an agency might help more than one program in an NGO, perhaps one at HQ and one in a distant field office. Therefore, both an HQ officer and a field officer in the same agency could be unaware of each other. UNESCO is a good example.[4] Its many offices include disaster management programs, especially disaster risk reduction education and science. Other parts focus on indigenous people, on conservation, etc. If an NGO or alliance does all of those things, it is important everyone know what the others are doing. But there are hundreds of multilateral agencies with thousands of programs, and there are many thousands of NGOs who do similar work. How does one track all of this activity in order to avoid unneeded duplication, perhaps identify gaps? Perhaps an "Annual International Organization Report" could solve this problem. Were such a project to occur, it would have to be developed by one NGO or academic institution for the benefit of everyone, but we feel it could be very useful. Though not exact parallels, governments like the United States produce annual reports on their work

---

[4]UNESCO is a UN specialized agency established on November 16, 1945, and headquartered in Paris.

with the UN and other international bodies. Using that tool, an NGO can see which US agencies are handling a topic and what they accomplished. A variant of that tool which focuses on an NGO's work could be very handy.

### 5.4.1 Annual International Organization Report

It is worth knowing that in the case of the government of New Zealand, they produce an annual handbook on the United Nations that shows what a lot of member states are doing on similar topics (NZ Ministry of Foreign Affairs and Trade 2012). We have just recommended in Sect. 5.3 that an NGO might find it useful to develop an annual public report on its own work. Doing an NGO variant to the New Zealand report would also be useful for the entire field. A network of partner NGOs like GenNet or humanitarian umbrella bodies like InterAction and CoNgo could develop similar annual surveys of NGO participation in the UN, its agencies; the Red Cross; and other international bodies. The word survey is very important. One document can't cover everything all NGOs do; projects and major achievements should be "summarized," reducing the document's size, cost, and workload. Any NGO should have a similar internal report for its staff, but this coordinated report would help the entire community and suggest opportunities for new avenues of work and funding. It could help the community at large avoid duplications and assist constructing meaningful alliances and donor opportunities. Such a document could also offer a sound historical record, helping future generations of NGO diplomats understand precedence and best practices. It could also review how negotiations were handled and recommend tactics.[5]

### 5.4.2 Annual Voting/Consensus Practice Guide

As part of the annual report project, a *Voting Practice* database could be of huge value for all negotiators across the humanitarian NGO spectrum. The idea would be track how issues related to humanitarianism and NGOs are handled by the UNGA or any other agency and include the actual text of documents voted on or dealt with by consensus, both draft resolutions and final texts. In some cases, explanations of

[5] *A Caution*: There will be a natural urge to push back on the administrative burden imposed by doing regular reports, but to be clear, we do not want to overburden NGOs. They should be out doing their work; the reportage we are discussing is intended to enhance, not impede work. Also, reports like the variant of the New Zealand handbook or the Annual Vote Guide discussed in Sect. 5.3.2 could be done under contract for all NGOs by a single academic institution or NGO for the benefit of the rest.

votes are provided by governments or comments in support of or against a resolution reached by consensus. All of the "legislative history" is important as background material for future negotiations by any NGO considering an initiative. This is exactly the kind of research a Study Team might generate or that might be conducted on an annual basis by an academic entity or NGOs to help the entire community.

When doing such a report, keep in mind that international organizations do not vote on most issues. They use consensus, partly to minimize the divisiveness that could come from a majority outvoting a small number of governments. If that happened enough, the minority might depart the body. In the long term, such a process would destroy the UN from within. In other words, while resolutions requiring consensus might be "weaker," than otherwise and not please everyone, they have the moral strength that comes of universal agreement. However, just because a country does not vote, does not mean it approves. In addition, votes also happen on very contentious topics, as happened in 2005 when the United States called for a vote on a resolution in the Committee on Human Rights (CHR-61) dealing with the right to development. In its statement of explanation, the United States agreed to the concept but insisted on voting NO because the resolution called for a legally binding instrument on the Right; that would have required Senate approval, which was unlikely.

## 5.5 Doveryay, No Proveryay Доверяй, но проверяй: Trust but Verify

Throughout the book, we have worked against confusion. It is never a good thing, and accurate and clear reporting is crucial to Study Teams and decision makers, especially when dealing with governments. Many humanitarian NGO's like InterAction and CARE are used to reporting at international conferences. A word of warning, for novice NGOs is that reports written by NGO activists at intergovernmental conferences sometimes don't agree with assessments of the government participants. This is not to say that NGO representatives must agree with government representatives on perceptions of progress; but if they do not, that's at least a warning flag. On the other hand, as happened at Rio+20, many NGOs disagreed with the recommendations and reporting by governments and made their own unilateral declaration.

A good example would be the Universal Declaration on Animal Rights "proclaimed" at UNESCO. Internet reports show the declaration was proclaimed at a UNESCO meeting. If true, that would have been a very big coup; yet that agency's legal affairs office never heard of the declaration. Probably an activist did "proclaim" something at a meeting; it was never on the agenda, nor recorded as a formal document. If an NGO wanted to gain publicity for their declaration, perhaps to advance a new constitution in Sudan, for example, even if the international organization doesn't recognize the instrument as having been coordinated, the NGO should present it to an agency public affairs officer. That way, it would at least be reported as a publically submitted document, even though it won't have the stature of an official document. On the other hand, some international organizations like

ECOSOC, an organ of the UN, allow participating NGOs to initiate resolutions and influence the agenda, which is an even better approach because it might receive official government support.

Negotiations are often done directly in large groupings like the 1990 London preparatory meeting for the Montreal protocol when 95 heads of delegation met in secret, without supporting staff. Negotiation also often happens in face-to-face meetings or small groups outside the limelight of conference halls, away from the crowds. The London Conference on Ozone did set the stage for Montreal, but mostly deals are made in small negotiations, often in informal settings like a coffee table. Whereas formal negotiations in conference halls are orchestrated, this informality can lead to mistakes. Remember that when talking to an Ambassador, indeed any diplomat, that this official symbolizes a country's sovereignty, the officer is the personal representative of the head of government. There are different opinions on confidentiality. Some contacts suggest that relationships can be developed with governments that are totally confidential in nature. Others believe that to be naïve, that no matter how strong the personal relationship, NGO contacts must assume that anything said to a government person could be reported back to their ministry. In other words, there is no such thing as an off-the-record conversation. That does not mean contacts are dishonest; a national diplomat's first objective is to serve his or her country, not the NGO. Keep even the friendliest gesture in context. The same goes for discussions with the representatives of other NGOs.

Sometimes the problem is miscommunication. In any emergency there are often dozens of accounts on any one incident; it is often necessary to say things three or four times before the facts sink in. People are scared or stressed in a fast-moving and confusing environment. Generally, no two people will see the same incident the same way, and that is true for impartial witnesses as well as those with an agenda. It is also the same phenomena when talking to fellow delegates at the Vienna Café in the UN in New York on the bottom floor right down from the main conference rooms. The lunch break has started. The national delegates are grabbing a quick snack, perhaps a cigarette (even in these times), and an NGO delegate wants to know what happened to the language he proposed to advance discussions between tribal and national justice systems. A national delegate in the Fifth Committee was kind enough to introduce the NGO language, and others said they were supportive. Things were going well until one national delegation opposed the motion for an obscure parliamentary reason, and then, other delegates changed their mind. The NGO delegate needs to know why and is in a hurry to formulate a strategy with his team before the afternoon session starts up. Unfortunately, six people may have talked to him, each with a different spin.

Most delegates want to help, are friendly, honest, and forthcoming, but the mind is selective. Just as a displaced person in Homs, Syria running from a helicopter gunship in 2012 might not know how fast the helicopter passed over his street at night or from where it came, it is not an easy thing for a professional to estimate, the mind of a busy delegate will hear selectively and remember less. To winnow the truth from accidental exaggerations and false analysis, a delegate needs to place himself in the shoes of the interviewed. How good is their command of the subject matter? How good are their language skills, especially if they did not put their translator headsets on? The NGO delegate might speak English, but do the others understand? Does a government have its own point of view that could color a colleagues' response? This is all about the need to develop intelligence in advance that can be used to make a decision.

Delegates sometimes "guess" in order to be helpful; they mean no harm but have a lapse in memory and do not want to disappoint or mislead when asked a specific question. Be prepared for a check. In one instance in 2009, Mr. Roeder, then a director in a British NGO, asked a very junior delegate from Central America a question about the G77, if the group was apt to support his idea. The delegate said no, unless her ambassador supported the notion, which she said could be arranged. Roeder then mentioned that another ambassador felt the idea would fly. She quickly said the other government was not in the G77 and that he needed to follow her advice. The only problem was the other government actually was a very active member of the G77, which Roeder verified moments later on his smart phone. She made an innocent mistake, guessing the truth in order to seem knowledgeable and essential; Roeder then had to wonder what else might be in error about her statements. The reverse truism is true. Do not guess. If you do not know the answer, say that you will find out. You cannot know everything.

A version of this problem is "false friends," which one expert consulted for this book regularly encountered. Delegates may tell an NGO that they will agree with an issue, but then their country votes a different way, perhaps in a secret ballot. This is why "vote tallying" is an important function of any delegation, even when decision making is by consensus; "you can be sure that some of your yes votes are not really yes. They are false friends." Recommendation: Доверяй, но проверяй (Doveryay, no proveryay) Trust but verify.

# Chapter 6
# Legal Matters

**Extract** Chapter 6 outlines the duties and need for a legal adviser. Also highlighted are a variety of core issues in international law, as well as general legal terms and concepts that can be problematic in any negotiation.

## 6.1 Delegation Legal Adviser

NGOs who engage in serious negotiations should have on call a legal adviser who is expert in international law or the laws to be negotiated, e.g., environmental or human rights law. This person doesn't need to be a permanent member of the staff but should at least be a trusted person on retainer. This is totally separate from lawyer used for contract or personnel law, though they too are important. To gain an understanding of how important this matter is, consider the debate over Article 10 of the covenant in the League of Nations, where the issues were colored by politics, as well as questions of domestic and international law. In the model we propose, the legal adviser is also a key member of the Study Team, laying out any legal problems and possible solutions in the decision memo and position papers.[1] If a lawyer is not available, try to have "on call" a practitioner in international law, perhaps a retired diplomat with experience negotiating international rules.

[1]Consider the complex negotiations that led to the Paris Peace Conference ending World War I is a good example. Each issue and suggestion had a political and legal context. To understand how each connected, a prominent lawyer named David Hunter Miller was assigned the job in 1918 to study every political statement made by President Wilson on foreign policy and analyze the relationship of those points to international law, as it pertained to the specific negotiation being undertaken. That way, when the negotiating team met with other delegations, it was fully prepared. In a much smaller way, this is how any negotiation is done – study the legal implications of every policy recommendation.

L.W. Roeder, Jr. and A. Simard, *Diplomacy and Negotiation for Humanitarian NGOs*, Humanitarian Solutions in the 21st Century, DOI 10.1007/978-1-4614-7113-4_6,

Many law firms and law libraries relevant to humanitarians exist that deal with everything from environmental law, to the protection of culture, refugees, the internally displaced, children, women, the disabled, land mines, etc. The trouble is that small NGOs often can't afford lawyers; any humanitarian NGO, from a clinic for poor children to a major supplier of food for flood victims, needs legal advice, either in-house or through access to a law firm. In-house is best, since the attorney will learn the unique aspects of an NGOs interests and priorities; that can be too pricy for many NGOs, unless the expert works pro bono.

The first thing to ask when consulting someone for a specific legal opinion or advancing some new legal principle is if he or she is an attorney or legal scholar, or at least an experienced practitioner, not just someone who worked in a law firm. Some say that financially challenged NGOs can make do with a law firm intern for the basics. One NGO examined for this book used that option in order to save money, but this is usually a bad idea. While interns may be inexpensive and knowledgeable, if the person is not a lawyer or at least an experienced practitioner like a diplomat, that officer is not qualified. Use the real deal.

## 6.2 Sanctions and Legality

### *6.2.1 United Nations Sanctions*

The UN General Assembly can't impose international law, though its Sixth Committee does consider matters of law. As a result, some have posited that the no part of the UN can enact binding rules of international law. Actually the Security Council can through the UN charter, Chap. 7, sanctions. Another way of looking at the legality of an initiative proposed by an NGO is to consider whether what the NGO wishes to provide is prohibited by multilateral sanctions. The UN Security Council does impose trade and travel sanctions in many situations, which might prevent citizens of certain countries from traveling or certain goods from entering, some as simple as a laptop. A lawyer or the NGOs UN delegate can determine this by inquiring for details of sanctions regimes from the Security Council's secretariat.[2]

[2] Some trade restrictions are commodity based in order to avoid types of conflict, such as multilateral controls on missile components or on chemical precursors. Chemical precursors can be otherwise perfectly legal chemicals that might be used in an industry, but are known to also be used in the creation of chemical weapons. As a result, when exported to certain countries, they are "controlled" by requiring a license. All states participating in the Australia Group are parties to the Chemical Weapons Convention (CWC) and the Biological Weapons Convention (BWC) and strongly support efforts under those conventions to rid the world of CBW (Government of Australia 2007).

If the UN has imposed sanctions, there will be a Sanctions Committee that sets the rules, and the rules are always published; also keep in mind that individual countries might impose additional unilateral sanctions.[3]

### 6.2.2 *National Sanctions and Restrictions*

**Sick Meat** In the United States, nearly 400,000 "meals ready to eat" flown to Little Rock by the United Kingdom in response to Hurricane Katrina[4] had to be quarantined in a warehouse because they contained British beef, banned by American health regulations (Agence France-Presse 2005). Someone did not check the laws before doing a good deed. What if someone's health had been impacted? A resulting law suit could easily have bankrupted the NGO.

National sanctions can impact both international commerce and travel by NGO staff members, e.g., in the case of Cuba, since it can be very hard to travel from the United States to Cuba or to some Arab states from Israel, vice versa. In addition, sometimes exports are controlled, even without the UN being involved. In 1985, Angola was in the middle of a violent civil war, and the United States became concerned that exports of Lockheed L-100's might be diverted to military purposes; any application to export was reviewed by an interagency panel that included representatives of the defense department and other agencies. The point here is that a development NGO might well want to export such planes in order to distribute peaceful supplies, like Lutheran World Relief did in Sudan; just because a UN sanctions regime doesn't exist and the purpose is humanitarian, doesn't mean the export will be approved or processed quickly.[5] In such a situation, an NGO may find that in addition to conducting negotiations in-country, it must also negotiate with the exporting power, the country that controls the technology.

---

[3]Russia and China refused in the UN Security Council to allow UN sanctions against the repressive regime in Syria; so in April, 2012 a contact group called the Friends of Syria, led by the United States, recognized the rebel movement created their own individual sanctions, and established their own Sanctions Committee.

[4]A Canadian warship was the first foreign aid to arrive in New Orleans.

[5]In the United States, the review to consider approval of controlled items can take months, when they are controlled for national security reasons. Keep in mind that controlled goods also include intellectual property. In the Canadian military, it takes about 4 months to process a request to export controlled goods, which can be a real problem for an NGO wanting an export license.

### 6.2.3 Sanctions on Non-State Entities

In 2010, the Supreme Court of the United States in Holder v. Humanitarian Law Project ruled that organizations providing international law training to bodies branded as terrorist groups by the US Department of State are committing a crime (18 U. S. C. §2339B(a)(1).), even if the organization is not a US person (US Supreme Court 2010). Ordinarily, this might not seem a problem, except that in its efforts to reduce mines, the NGO Geneva Call trained the Kurdistan Worker's Party in international law; the KWP has been branded a terrorist body. This means Geneva Call could be considered a criminal body under US law. They have also been banned from entering the Turkish territory for the purpose of contact with KWP. In our opinion, this is a bizarre legal decision, as it avoids the concept of intent. The training is innocent and harms no one, and the ban seems to violate the US 1st Amendment right of free speech. How are professional humanitarian NGOs to be able to convince rebel groups to follow peaceful practices if they are not allowed to have contact?

### 6.2.4 International Courts

**International Court of Justice (ICJ)** The ICJ superseded the Permanent Court of International Justice in 1946; it is essentially the "legal advisor" of the UN system, so NGOs should try to understand what it has covered, everything from territorial rights, the right to asylum and the right of passage over foreign territory to issues of nationality, reparations for damages and appeals against administrative tribunals in the UN and the International Labor Organization.

**International Criminal Court (ICC)** The ICC is not a UN body, although its indictments can have severe impacts on operations in countries with which an NGO may wish to collaborate, e.g., Sudan in 2009 when the President of Sudan was indicted for crimes against humanity, while Sudan was serving as chair of the G77. That might be a problem if the Security Council or another multilateral court were to make rulings favorable to the interests of the NGO; the ICC might be a venue for the NGO and its alliance to take action.

> The ICC, governed by the Rome Statute, is the first permanent, treaty-based court established to help end impunity for the perpetrators of the most serious crimes of concern to the international community. The ICC is an independent international organization. Its seat is at The Hague in the Netherlands. The international community has long aspired to the creation of a permanent international court, and in the twentieth century, it reached consensus on definitions of genocide, crimes against humanity, and war crimes. In the 1990s after the end of the Cold War, tribunals like the International Criminal Tribunal for Rwanda were the result of consensus that impunity is unacceptable. However, because they were established to try crimes committed only within a specific time frame and during a specific conflict, there was general agreement that an independent, permanent criminal court was needed. On July 17, 1998, the international community reached an historic milestone when 120 states adopted the Rome Statute, the legal basis for establishing the permanent ICC. The Rome Statute entered into force on July 1, 2002 after ratification by 60 countries (CICC 2012).

Not every government recognizes the ICC, such as the United States, and the US delegation to the UN has on many an occasion deleted resolution language referencing the ICC for fear that if the US supported the final draft, it might be seen as legal precedence and impose an obligation. We feel the US government and others made a mistake on this, so using the reference in a resolution may be appropriate, but a word of caution is wise. This point is mentioned in particular because so many NGOs are involved in the protection of victims of human rights violations and will want to cite precedence of understood violations of international human rights law found in numerous international instruments like the ICC, but also the Universal Declaration of Human Rights (article 8);[6] the International Covenant on Civil and Political Rights (article 2); the International Convention on the Elimination of All Forms of Racial Discrimination (article 6); the Convention against Torture and Other Cruel, Inhuman, or Degrading Treatment or Punishment (article 14); and the Convention on the Rights of the Child (article 39).

**Note** Some in the humanitarian community feel that the emphasis of the ICC on justice can be an impediment to achieving peace and ending death and suffering. Protagonists are less likely to negotiate if the outcome for one will be a jail cell. One offered "there is a key tension between justice and peace between the human rights and humanitarian communities (Source 2012a)," whereas another offered he was "in favor of accountability, which the ICC theoretically advances. I understand the tensions, but some societies have managed to negotiate these tensions while achieving a reasonable outcome from both a humanitarian and a justice perspective --- South Africa, for example. In other cases, men with blood on their hands have achieved power with little accountability --- see Afghanistan. Ultimately, I think the lack of justice erodes the ability of societies to come together after conflict and encourages impunity. But the ideal situation is when the moves and processes that advance the justice process are internal rather than external (Source, *About ICC* 2012)."

**Recommendation** Whether or not the NGO wants to support the ICC, when engaged in international agreements of any size, have a qualified legal adviser at hand, even if only on retainer. Keep in mind the countervailing opinions on legal instruments and institutions.

**The future** of international laws, rules, and principles in disaster environments is at the heart of the Disaster Law Program being managed by the International Federation of Red Cross and Red Crescent Societies. Guidelines for the program, known as IDRL, were approved by governments and National Societies sitting together at the International Conference of the Red Cross and Red Crescent in 2007, and work is proceeding on a model law which will help iron out many inconsistencies in national laws and remove serious obstacles in the way of the speedy delivery of humanitarian assistance after a disaster.

---

[6]UDHR was adopted by the UN General Assembly on December 10, 1948. It elevates measuring of human rights to all people and to a common standard.

## 6.3 Words Matter

### *6.3.1 Cultural Sensitivity*

Being culturally insensitive can be disastrous. Many NGOs are trying to end the practice of solitary confinement in prisons by negotiating directly with prison staffs and legislators. Though experts feel solitary confinement actually amounts to torture, in the United States, NGO negotiators are wary of using that term when dealing with corrections staff. The reason is that the staff will interpret the use as disrespect and assume the NGO negotiators are "out of touch" with the realities of running a safe prison. The term can be helpful when messaging the public as part of the public diplomacy campaign, but can turn off corrections staff at the negotiating table (Rice 2012), and in the end, they need to be brought on board to implement "change."

In another example, the UN Transition Assistance Group in Namibia (UNTAG) was set up in 1989 to supervise and monitor free and fair elections for the territory, once a German colony and then a League of Nations/United Nations Mandate controlled by apartheid South Africa. UNTAG used a lot of clear information-sharing tools in order to build confidence in the process such as a T-shirts with anti-intimidation messages, flyers, and graphics. The project almost floundered when in an overabundance of impartiality, some media products were translated into Afrikaans. Non-white Namibians were very disturbed by that development though virtually everything was also translated into 13 Namibian languages by the national broadcasting service of South Africa.

Certainly being culturally sensitive can reap major rewards. In 1964, John Walsh's epic rescue operation in Suriname was partly successful in gaining local volunteers and hires because he accepted false names, due to religious considerations (Walsh & Gannon, Time Is Short and the Water Rises, 1967, p. 65). In 1991, Roeder was in Albania during a time of great unrest. Towns south of Tirana were suffering some violence, though mostly when they saw the American flag flapping on Roeder's car, the population waved hands with the V for victory sign. Still some feared civil war, a wild cat strike at the Vau i Dejës dam near Schodra, and some other dams threatened to shut down the electrical grid for the entire country. That would have meant civilian workers fighting armed soldiers. And while westerners were pushing hard for political progress, there were those who felt that foreigners did little more than talk.

One night while walking near his hotel after a meeting of store owners, a gang of teenagers threw stones on the ground and then surrounded him, and it appeared he was about to leveled; he showed his diplomatic passport and asked to be escorted to a mosque. The street thugs had mistaken him for a Russian, but the passport calmed things, and the respectful reference to the mosque also helped (Roeder 1991). This may not work so well in some places today; however, it is true that in most mob situations, showing fear is emotional gasoline and explosive. Instead, be respectful and calm. In a more pleasant situation in 2011, Roeder had addressed a crowd of over 1,000 Muslims in Virginia on the need to register to vote. To demonstrate his sincerity, he pulled out a small Koran his father gave him as a child in Egypt. Roeder is a Christian, but since his father was a diplomat serving in Cairo, he felt that his son should visit a mosque to start understanding how the majority of Egyptians lived. Roeder saw children of his own age reading the Koran. His father then gave him a Koran and asked him to read it cover to cover and on that day in the fall of 2011 pulled it out. The physical book is sacred in Islam, and they are often passed down from generation to generation, much like family bibles. When he told his story, the entire congregation rose as one and clapped. Being calm and sensitive matters.

### Case Study: Cultural Sensitivity in the Middle East

As any NGO that has worked in developing countries knows that mishandling animal populations can spread disease and cause property damage to humans. But how to handle the problem while remembering that cultural sensitivity is paramount; any infringement or criticism of cultural or religious aspects of a program could well result in a polite but firm rebuttal of negotiations—even with something that might seem as benign as animal control. One consultant brought out an interesting example. Cities in a GCC (Gulf Cooperation Council) country were overrun by feral cats, which could damage property and spread disease that harmed people. The method of population control was inhumane by western standards and also unsuccessful. For example, major culls often provide a false impression of population reduction. After a respite, the population just grows out of control. To deal with the problem, a TNR (trap, neuter, and release) NGO program was suggested to the government. The NGO looked at the western methods and decided that from an Islamic optic, that approach was barbaric and a mutilation of an animal which the population revered and held in high esteem. In other words, there was a clash of cultures. To resolve this dispute required some clever diplomacy. Using statistics, the NGO showed that preventing unwanted births in the streets was kinder and more effective than large kills. Cultural atonement was utilized by sending a delegation from the country concerned to a neighboring country which had successfully implemented similar program. The success of the cat program was followed by an attempt to introduce a humane stray dog control program, also very sensitive in the local culture. This had to be undertaken while giving respect to the issues of handling and transportation of dogs. Without going into detail, suffice to say that all the skills outlined above had to be utilized to find an acceptable compromise which would be seen as beneficial to the government, the local human population, and the animals concerned without compromising the religious and cultural aspects of the local society.[7]

### Case Study: Farmwatch and Brazil

As a culture, Brazilians tend to be more on the side of conciliation and negotiation of differences instead of frontal confrontation, fielding such great international

[7] Stray Animal Control Case study submitted by Trevor Wheeler, former Director for Near East, WSPA.

diplomats and humanitarians as Sérgio Vieira de Mello.[8] Words still matter. An international NGO started to work in Brazil with the premise that it would change the country's huge farming system. The first attempt was called "Farmwatch." With a name like that, the project went nowhere because the term raised suspicions among farmers, importers, exporters, and the Ministry of Agriculture. Everyone thought of being monitored by an NGO, instead of the NGO acting as a friendly partner. To resolve the situation, the program was redesigned and the name was changed to "Farm Animal Welfare Program;" all the material was reworded to reflect their focus, and that led to an unprecedented gain of credibility with the government and other partners. Farmers welcomed the revised program because their farming process became more in tune with European importers; it was essentially the same "Farmwatch" program with a different name.

## 6.4 Generic Problem Words and Phrases

Every country has some sort of constitution, even if unwritten, so the job of a treaty affairs office or its equivalent (in the Foreign Ministry ordinarily) is to study whether an agreement violates its Constitution, even if policies are compatible. This was one of the big problems in the United States with the League of Nations. Article 10 of the covenant appeared to obligate nations to help (even provide armies) to fellow members suffering from external aggression. That was seen as unconstitutional; only Congress declares war, not the Executive Branch. Opponents saw article 10 as violating US sovereignty because it theoretically turned over to a world government the power to send US troops into an unwanted conflict, perhaps even command of the troops to the League. The truth is that the League's covenant also gave member governments the power to veto any League action (High_Contracting_Parties 1920).[9] Perhaps because the president's efforts to inform the public and rally support were ineffective, ratification did not happen, a mistake Roosevelt did not repeat. To gain American agreement to the UN, the US government and NGO allies like the Woodrow Wilson Institute engaged in a massive and successful media campaign. Many feel that two of the reasons the United States senate rejected the League was a failure of leadership by Wilson to effectively convince both parties of its value and to effectively engage civil society to act as advocates, though there were NGOs trying to mount their own public diplomacy effort to convince American public of the value of the League. The story fortunately was different with the UN. Roosevelt, followed by Truman, both worked hard to unify both parties and build up civil society support.

---

[8] Farmwatch Case study submitted by G. S. Silva Augusto Antonio, former Country Director of WSPA in Brazil.

[9] This is still a complaint today; but actually the UN has no power to compel member states to offer armed forces; further UN command is only nominal. All troops contributed to a UN force, even though it has a theater commander, report to national authority and can be withdrawn at any time.

With regard to Senate support, when Truman took the Presidency just days before the San Francisco Conference, he specifically had his Secretary of State regularly confer with Republican and Democratic Senators (Truman 1955, p. 303 and 358).

It is wise for NGOs to avoid such problems at the start by asking questions about a nation's constitution and ratification process, avoiding binding obligations unless that is essential. The authors suggest any major multilateral agreement (binding or not) also requires that when the study group develops a negotiating plan, it should propose a coalition of NGOs that includes influential bodies in governments that might oppose or be leery of the agreement.

The following words and phrases often cause problems, but there will be others and not every government will be of the same opinion, so the study group should research these points.

- **Shall or Will Versus Should.** In a nonbinding document, in clauses that urge that certain action be taken, most governments will prefer "should," which is optional, as preferable to "shall" and "will," which are binding. In Australia, the issue is often between the words "should" and "must" (Phillips 2011).
- **Ensure.** This word connotes an intention or obligation to "guarantee," a concept most treaty affairs offices oppose in nonbinding documents.
- **Party.** This word can be problematic when outcomes documents are not contractual undertakings. A government is "not a party" to a nonbinding agreement, in other words.
- **Agreed or Agree** to are words that should be entirely avoided unless followed by the term "in principle," which makes the agreement voluntary and nonbinding, unless you want a binding agreement.
- **References** to international conventions or other legal instruments are often included in outcomes documents because they refer to precedence, which can be excellent. Care should be exercised in that a convention or binding legal instrument is only binding to those that are party to the agreement. If an NGO is helping to draft an outcomes document and such a reference is included when the NGO does not endorse the agreement, make sure that language is also included to parse out those the NGO doesn't like. Otherwise, it may appear that the NGO has agreed in principle to the problem instrument.
- **Assistance and Resources** are words NGOs might wish included in an outcomes document, especially if financial and political support is desired for an initiative, but be aware that donor nations will be suspicious, of an obligation for foreign assistance or financial support instead of voluntary aid, especially if the assistance impacts the budget of an existing program (see PBI).
- **Technology Transfer.**[10] This topic has been an important element of diplomacy for generations, but in particular since World War I. Some nations and NGOs

[10]For decades, Technology Transfer has been a term of art covering any kind of information in any format, patented or not, copyrighted or not, which can be used or adapted for use in the design, production, manufacture, utilization or reconstruction of articles or materials.

make an egalitarian argument that everyone had a right to the latest technology. Some have even said "patents" are monopolistic tools of industry.[11] This had even led to a movement to make music available for free to all by simply downloading. Of course, inventors and industrialized nations tend to disagree, arguing that in order to develop a technology or drug, enormous intellectual and monetary resources have to be expended and that royalties from patents and copyrights are the only way to guarantee a proper return on investment. However, many G77 coalition nations argue for liberal technology transfer rules; so the UN General Assembly and ECOSOC forums have become platforms to argue for a breakdown of technology transfer barriers. Even with the fall of the Berlin Wall, this struggle continues. **Recommendation:** NGOs should avoid being pawns. The best medicines and rescue techniques for people or buildings all require some level of technology; some patents, so does risk reduction, reducing the potential for harm from weather, storm surge, and other hazards. One way to avoid this issue is for the industry to collaboratively develop technologies that are intended to be shared, not sold. It could be something as simple as Heifer's development of a rolling plastic barrel with a hollow center to help people push massive amounts of water, rather than carry pails uphill. The technology may be duplicated without royalty.

As recently as 2008, "China's Premier Wen Jiabao urged developed countries to transfer climate-friendly technologies to China and other developing countries, and he called on the international community to establish a fund and mechanism for overcoming technology transfer barriers" (DESA 2008). There is definitely a moral imperative to encourage the transfer of technology, especially in disaster risk reduction, water management, and climate change. Such transfers could save many people and structures from harm, but NGOs are urged to be cautious in the wording of any resolution they might join, to avoid their priorities being distracted by debates over property rights. This can often be resolved by taking care with the language and working closely with the delegations of manufacturing nations. **A Cautionary Note:** The point of preparedness and risk reduction is to reasonably prevent an overwhelming event. Doing it right depends on science, the technology Wen Jibao wanted transferred, and politics. But while many knew that the level of protection in New Orleans was not adequate for a major hurricane, is the same true for the super storm that hit York and New Jersey in 2012? *Sometimes, even the best intentions mixed with the best science will reap mistakes*. There are no guarantees in risk reduction.

- **Upper and Lower Riparian states' Rights.** Development NGOs are certain to run into this issue, a form of landownership that impacts drinking water, transportation, farms, and wildlife, especially in droughts. In many countries the upper riparian user cannot cut off the lower, but does retain rights of reasonable use.

[11] One of the great intellectual property ironies is that the Cotton Gin, which revolutionized labor markets and the cotton market in the United States, was never patented.

Unfortunately "reasonable use" might mean that the upper riparian's development initiatives, e.g., gold and coal mining, could take place. However, coal and gold mining can poison water, perhaps in pasture lands of lower riparian states used by livestock used by displaced persons. Some have said the 1997 UN Convention on the Law of the non-Navigable Uses of International Watercourses is an appropriate source for applicable law, but be aware that not all states agree. Further, the convention is only applicable to those that are party to the convention.

- **Migrants: The Internally Displaced and Refugees.** It is critical that when delving into initiatives involving policies relative to such people, the Study Team use experts. An initiative otherwise supported in concept could fail because of a poorly chosen phrase or word. For example, migrants often want some consular protection while in motion, but the right to consular protection doesn't always apply. Take, for example, a migrant about to cross a border illegally and is stopped short in international waters. It is argued by some that since the alien was detained outside any consular district, a "right to consular notification" does not apply, even though most countries would accommodate.
- **Non-Self-Governing Territories.** The UN defines non-self-governing territories as regions where the people have not yet attained a full measure of self-government, this topic is considered annually by the Special Committee on the Situation with Regard to the Implementation of the Declaration on the Granting of Independence to Colonial Countries and Peoples (Committee of 24 or C-24) and by the Special Political and Decolonization Committee (Fourth Committee) of the UNGA. Questions of American Samoa, Anguilla, Bermuda, the British Virgin Islands, the Cayman Islands, Guam, Montserrat, Pitcairn, Saint Helena, the Turks and Caicos Islands, and the United States Virgin Islands all come up within the context of a resolution confirming the right of self-determination. Representatives of these bodies will appear in UN meetings, but NGOs need to remember that although the UNGA may consider that a territory should not to be a part of a state, the state controlling that territory might ignore the call, the exception being when made by the UN Security Council, as happened to Italian Somaliland which Italy had to give up in 1960. Some, like American Samoa, might have its own visa structure. Puerto Rico, Tahiti, and Bermuda are other examples of territories often mistakenly called countries. They are actually integral parts of the United States, France, and the UK, not countries, thus incapable of independent binding foreign policy decisions. Can the President of the United States negotiate a treaty with Iran? Yes. Can the Governor of Colorado? Not without permission from the Department of State. **Recommendation:** Be careful about inviting subnational authorities to an international conference. They often do attend, and in the United States, the Native American tribes often go to UN meetings, but their authority is limited.
- **Rights of the Indigenous.** Internationally there is the Declaration on the Rights of the Indigenous, which emerged out of the 1994 UN General Assembly and called for a Decade on the Rights of the Indigenous in coordination with the Commissioner on Human Rights. The Committee on the Indigenous may offer opportunities for NGOs to make their case directly to

indigenous populations at the annual conference of the Indigenous in New York, but keep in mind that the indigenous protect their traditional rights in order not to lose their culture. Depending on the country, the indigenous have different rights. In the United States, the Rights of the Indigenous are enshrined in domestic law such as the Tribal Law and Order Act of 2010 (NCAI 2010) and treaties with native tribes, as well as state laws. **Recommendation:** It is essential to work directly through Tribal elders or civil rights bodies like the National Congress on American Indians (NCAI). **Example of a Potential Conflict with Indigenous Rights:** An NGO contact for this book wanted to outlaw aboriginal hunting of sea mammals on the grounds that such hunting is inhumane. The NGO has a point about the inhumane nature of the hunt; however, in the United States, at least, Native American tribes and, in Canada, "first nations" have "treaty" rights to hunt on their reservations,[12] "rights" that a fresh international agreement signed by the federal government cannot overturn unless the treaties are altered. If the NGO wants to change those hunting patterns, it will have to negotiate directly with the tribes as well as the US Department of the Interior or perhaps the National Congress of American Indians (NCAI), America's oldest civil right body, to foster talks (Pevar 2004). Similar issues exist in other countries with indigenous peoples. In Canada, problems can occur when the federal government wants to run a pipeline through first nation's lands, and the natives say NO! In addition, there is the Akwesasne reserve that spans Ontario and New York near Cornwall and is used to smuggle contraband because neither country has jurisdiction on their side of the St. Lawrence River.

## 6.5 Value of Written Constitution

NGOs might be asked to provide advice on new national legal instruments, which is an opportunity to insert their own thinking on policy structures. Although NGOs are not traditionally the author of national constitutions and every nation's tradition will be different, the authors tend to lean on the side of recommending a written constitution and suggest that when NGOs are involved in any aspect of nation building,[13] they take the opportunity to influence this process, even to the point of recommending language to government decision makers. There are plenty of examples like that of Syria where written rights are ignored; still, a written document is a contract with the people that lays down basic rights and obligations. It should be endorsed by the

[12] In Canada these are called tribal lands. In the United States, some tribal lands are not in official reservations, which is the source of controversy.

[13] Although nation-building is a common term, it better to refer to state-building, given the different definitions of state and nation; however, we have retained the term nation-building due to popular usage.

public through a referendum, and that, while it needs to be culturally sensitive, should also include all of the human rights incorporated in international law as a basic foundation. To arrive at that document, scholars from academia and NGOs that advance the rule of law should be part of the delegation.

In order to build a sustainable economy, the point of a constitution is to imbue the country with the rule of law relative to the markets, what's allowable and what's not, authorization for ministries to establish regulations, break up either public or private monopolies, protection of the environment and good contract law, as well as a regulated market and banking system. The basis for all of that comes from the constitution.

It is also important to remember that NGO advisors are just that; they can't, nor should they try to impose their national system on the local population; advice is influence. An example might be Somaliland, which has three systems of justice. One is Sharia (Islamic law); there is also secular law derived from Italian and British colonial origins and traditional common law. These legal systems "coexist in a non-harmonized tangle (UNTV 2006)." In addition, according to the United Nations, some ninety percent of practicing legal professionals in Somaliland have no formal training in all three disciplines. The result is an uneven justice system. To solve that problem, the United Nations development program has been advising on lawyer and judge training and uses the University in Somaliland's capital for classrooms, clearly a market for NGOs.

## 6.6 International Humanitarian and Human Rights Law

There are plenty of laws that relate to international conflicts, but field negotiators in such upheavals like Afghanistan and Iraq are more often going to face severe violations of humanitarian and human rights law within internal conflicts like the civil struggles related to Arab Spring, in parts Sudan and Somalia.[14]

### *6.6.1 International Human Rights Law (IHRL) Always Exists*

It applies to all persons subject to a state. There are derogations in times of conflict or a "public emergency," of which natural disasters and armed conflicts are two. Freedoms of movement,[15] speech, liberty, and security and association can be

[14]For this section, the authors want to thank in particular Ambassador Christopher Lamb (Australia), former Special Assistant to the Secretary General of the IFRC, and Kit Hope, Sr. Associate, International Humanitarian Law Dissemination, American Red Cross.

[15]Freedom of Movement, which includes humanitarian personnel (UN, Universal Declaration of Human Rights, p. Art 13) (Covenant on Civil and Political Rights 1994, p. article 13) (UN 1994).

suspended, but only to the extent required by the exigencies of the situation. These are permitted under a variety of treaties such as the International Covenant on Civil and Political Rights, the European Convention, and the American Convention on Human Rights. There is however a core set of rights that are never suspended at any time under any circumstances.

Human Rights Law has a long history, e.g., the French Declaration of the Rights of Man and the Citizen in 1789 and the American Bill of Rights adopted in 1791. More recently, the League of Nations made human rights a central feature of its work, as has the United Nations. Discussed elsewhere in this book, the work of Nansen comes to mind in this context. He cared deeply about minorities and refugees. The League also did a great deal of work on women, sexual trafficking, and children, to say nothing about drug control, health, and the rights of workers protected by the ILO (International Labor Organization), which was formed by the League of Nations.

General Human Rights are also emerging, which should be of interest to NGOs, namely, the right to development,[16] peace,[17] a healthy environment;[18] the body of required instruments is still in development. One of the areas of Human Rights Law that recently emerged and has a direct bearing on those NGOs engaged in emergency management is how it treats gay, lesbian, and transgender persons. "On September 14, 2012, the United Nations human rights office released a new 60-page booklet on sexual orientation and gender identity in international human rights law. The publication, "Born Free and Equal (OHCHR 2012)", sets out the source and scope of state obligations under international human rights law to protect the human rights of lesbian, gay, bisexual, transgender and intersex people. Drawing on almost two decades' worth of UN research, guidance and jurisprudence, the booklet focuses on five core areas where state action is urgently required – from protecting people from homophobic violence, to preventing torture, decriminalizing homosexuality, prohibiting discrimination, and safeguarding freedom of expression, association and peaceful assembly (Cianfarani 2012)."

This particular aspect of international law was also the subject of considerable, UN, Civil Society Organization, and NGO member, discussion in 2012 in the Gender and Disaster Network (GDN); some members were concerned that transgender victims of conflict and natural disasters were not always receiving the care they deserved. GDN is an educational project initiated by women and men interested in gender relations in disaster contexts. It emerged from an early-morning meeting during the

[16]Development often causes harm to the rights of the vulnerable, surely a paradox since most humanitarian NGOs do profess the values of sustainable development. The solution, and a core location for NGO effort, is to reaffirm that development is a right of every person, not just the society. In other words, we need to link the human right of participation in development policy packages. This makes a person, rather than the state, "the central subject of development." See UN Declaration on the Right to Development.

[17]See UN General Assembly resolution 39/11 of 12 November 1984, "Declaration on the Right of Peoples to Peace."

[18]"Environmental protection shall constitute an integral part of the development process," Rio Declaration, Principles 1 and 4.

July 1997 Natural Hazards Research and Applications Center workshop in Boulder, Colorado, and then became the major outcome of the "Women's Disaster Research Caucus" meeting convened by Barbara Vogt the same month. The original focus was on (1) how to network more effectively, (2) how to promote young women professionals, (3) how to promote women and gender issues as legitimate research topics, and (4) how to use web-based resources for communication. Those are still its main focal points, and the organization has proven to be a valuable forum for a wide range gender issue, as the topic has developed since 1997, with gay, lesbian, and transgender issues being but one example. The authors recommend that NGO officials belong to such groups. Not only do they allow for a diverse dialogue on complex topics that bring out the latest academic and scientific thinking, they can also be an effective, informal "expert group" within a Study Team.

In the case of gay, lesbian, and transgender topics, GDN was able to explore various aspects of this community as "potential victim" and recommend remedies. However, more than that, the system was able to show how this community is also an asset in emergencies. A crucial point is to have these capacities recognized by the larger community and other stakeholders of DRR. It then becomes possible to integrate those capacities into local action planning, reduce discrimination within the community, and provide tangible evidence for advocacy at the policy level. As an example, JC Gaillard,[19] one of the experts in the system, was able to document that the contribution of transgender people to DRR is neither passive nor helpless in time of disasters. This expert's initial practical and research activities conducted in the Philippines, Indonesia, and Samoa all showed that transgender and other gender minorities displayed significant capacities which often reflected their particular skills and roles in everyday life and their ability to swing from male to female chores. For example, Filipino *baklas* often spontaneously collected relief goods and organized daily routine activities in evacuation centers. In Indonesia, during the eruption of Mt Merapi in 2010, *warias* offered free haircuts to evacuees to help them keep their dignity in time of hardship. In Samoa, *fa'afafine* played a crucial role in organizing rescue and relief activities during and after the 2009 tsunami (Gaillard 2012).

### *6.6.2 International Humanitarian Law (IHL) Only Exists in Conflict*

In fact, the law is specially designed to deal with conflict and to protect those who do not or no longer can take part in hostilities. The basic sources of IHL are the Geneva Conventions of 1949[20] and their additional protocols of 1977 and 2005.

[19]Dr. Gaillard is a Senior Lecturer, School of Environment, The University of Auckland/Te Whare Wānanga o Tāmaki Makaurau.

[20]GC1 deals with wounded and sick on land. GC2 deals with the ship wrecked, wounded, and sick at sea. GC3 deals with prisoners of war (POW). GV4 deals with the treatment of civilians.

**Common to the Human Rights and Humanitarian Law are**

- No discrimination based on race, color, sex, or religion
- Right to life
- No torture
- No cruel treatment
- No humiliating of degrading treatment
- No slavery
- No retroactive application of the law

### 6.6.2.1 The Geneva Conventions of 1949 and Their Additional Protocols

The Geneva Conventions are essentially four treaties and three protocols.[21] Taken together, they are the legal standard for the humanitarian treatment of the victims of war—what is often called "disinterested aid," including internal conflicts as in Darfur and Syria. In other words, it doesn't matter who the victim is or on what side of a conflict. The Geneva Convention means the agreements of 1949. Those were negotiated following the World War II. Those agreements are also seen as updating three treaties (1864, 1906, 1929) and adding a fourth (1949) which defined the rights of civilian and military prisoners during war, highlighted by the abuses of the axis powers. The 4th Convention also provided protection for the wounded as well as civilians and noncombatants in and around a war zone. The Hague Conventions are also noteworthy since they deal with instruments of war (First Hague, 1899; Second Hague 1907), and the Geneva Protocol on the Prohibition of the Use in War of Asphyxiating, Poisonous or other Gases, and of Bacteriological Methods of Warfare, 1929).[22] *See discussion of Australia Group.*

### 6.6.2.2 Seeking Guidance

Even though the protections accorded to NGOs in the field which are unassociated with the UN or the International Red Cross and Red Crescent Movement are limited, it is important for any field negotiator to be aware of Human Rights and Humanitarian Law and use that knowledge to protect innocent civilians from harm. The Study Team should certainly seek guidance from expert legal counsel about relevant international legal instruments prior to entering a failed nation state or an internal conflict. However, if the NGO negotiator is having trouble and an impartial humanitarian organization like the ICRC, the IFRC, or the Red Crescent is present,

[21] From a legal perspective, there is no legal difference between a protocol or a treaty. A protocol is a form of treaty that derives from another treaty, often implementing a change.

[22] Not to be confused with the Geneva Protocol for the Pacific Settlement of International Disputes.

it is a good idea to ask for their assistance. This is because they have the right to render aid to parties to a conflict, per common article 3 of the Geneva Conventions.

## 6.7 International Instruments

In diplomacy, sustainable change is often accomplished by negotiating specific instruments, a Memorandum of Understanding, called an MOU, perhaps a Declaration or Convention, even a Resolution, as was done in Tunis in 2007 when the Red Cross agreed to support the protection of livestock. Lobbying is the art of changing the minds of policy makers to allow such negotiations to go forth. Thus, one of the most important elements for the decision memo is to choose the instrument, unless it is simply language in a conference report to act as precedence for some future action. Whatever the instrument's form, it must have a defined, practical purpose and be seen as the most appropriate tool at that time to achieve the purpose.

The best start to making sure an instrument is coherent and effective is to involve all of the stakeholders. To take a holistic approach to humanitarian relief and recovery, this means not only stakeholders involved in the physical protection of people but also many specialized NGOs and industries involved in protecting culture, the local economy, the environment, etc. They cannot be ignored, otherwise they might get in the way of implementation, and even if they don't, the instrument won't have the benefit of a broad agreement. They too lobby governments, negotiate laws, and have resources and thus can be helpful allies or harmful foes. To return to the abortive Farm Watch program in Brazil, it was launched against a huge industry, with exports alone from the beef, chicken, and pigs industry expected to pass US$ 30 billion in 2011. The first approach meant: "I want to destroy your business," thus creating an enemy with major cash resources. By "repackaging," the enemy became the partner. (Antonio, *Discussions on NGO diplomacy* 2010).

### *6.7.1 Note on Drafting an International Instrument*

There is no reason why NGOs can't draft and propose treaties, whether the traditional sort between governments such as the demining convention or the nontraditional civil society variety that emerged at Rio+20 in 2012, but use clear language so that the purpose the instrument is obvious.

The first part of most instruments is the "preamble". Like a book's introduction, it sets the document's tone. Look at the United States Declaration of Independence. As Archibald MacLeish noted in a memo to the Secretary of State in June, 1945, it is the first few sentences that captured men's hearts. A preamble should be like that, soaring language that captures the meaning of the rest of the document, "not constructed like a cross word puzzle out of political and academic odds and ends

(MacLeish 1945, June 8).[23]" Keep in mind as well that in so much as the preamble is a summary of the rest of the document and to the extent that the document is a binding instrument, the preamble had juridical status. Make it clear.

Depending on the issues, a Study Team may well have committees and subcommittees, especially since large committees are difficult to manage. This approach was used very effectively by Die Deutsche Liga für Völkerbund in 1919 (Sect. 12.6) when formulating a draft constitution for the League of Nations and by the team advising President Roosevelt on the postwar effort. The Study Team (a series of committees that went under a variety of names) contained a drafting committee which met in July, 1943 to establish the first draft UN charter (CSOP, 1943a). The group was a part of the Division of Political Studies in the Department of State and consisted of only 11 people with a range of political and work experiences. Leo Pasvolsky, special assistant to the president, managed the entire study group. Several were experts in international law, with one an expert on the relationship of international law to domestic jurisprudence. One had been Commissioner General of the League of Nations pavilion at the New York World's Fair in 1939–1940. One was a political scientist with expertise in agriculture. One was a philosopher and follower of Reinhold Niebuhr, an ardent anticommunist and anti-utopian. One was an expert on human rights, others on the League of Nations experience and the foreign policy of Woodrow Wilson, that being the previous experiment in multilateral diplomacy. Pasvolsky's work would of course be edited and reedited many times; the model of work was sound, same for Die Liga; if an NGO or NGO alliance wants to develop new international law or amend international law, they should craft a drafting committee within the larger Study Team and even specialized topic teams.

### *6.7.2 Will the Instrument Solve the Problem?*

Before deciding on an instrument's format, the organizing parties should agree that it can actually solve a real-world problem. In addition, decide if a binding document is needed. Nonbinding documents require less work and procedures than do binding ones. They are not generally registered with the UN Secretariat and are NOT true treaties, but do have moral force since governments sign them. Binding documents have the force of international law.

**Binding International Instruments** Various binding instruments are called treaties, conventions, covenants, charters and protocols. MOUs can be as well. They are all much the same thing from the standpoint of law, each an obligatory document signed by governments and perhaps international organizations. Some have even called conventions more of a tradition and not an instrument as such. The terminology usually relates to the function; protocols are usually supplementary or perhaps

[23] Archibald MacLeish was an attorney, editor, poet, and Librarian of Congress.

an important addition or change to an existing instrument, perhaps instructions on how to operate under the original instrument.[24] Conventions are usually broad standards of behavior such as the 1982 Convention on the Law of the Sea (UNCLOS). Before deciding that either a convention or a protocol is a treaty, make sure it truly is obligatory and also understand when the instrument goes into force, usually once a certain number of signatures are ratified by national legislatures. charters and covenants are usually the constitution of a body, e.g., the charter of the United Nations or the covenant of the League of Nations.

#### 6.7.2.1 Nonbinding International Instruments

These are essentially statements of policy. They often have moral authority, but can't bind governments. Resolutions are often nonbinding, especially those of the UN General Assembly, though the resolutions of the UN Security Council are binding. They can also be declaration, MOUs, charters, etc. In other words, the nature of an instrument isn't in the title, but rather in the words and their obligation.

#### 6.7.2.2 The Tampere Convention

The Tampere Convention on the Provision of Emergency Telecommunications provides a successful example of government and NGO delegations answering basic questions and achieving binding international law. The concept of Tampere emerged, in part, from discussions in the amateur radio community about ways of protecting communications during emergencies—talks that evolved into a true convention unanimously adopted by the delegations of the 60 governments that participated in the Intergovernmental Conference on Emergency Telecommunications (ICET-98), in Finland, June 1998. The NGO organizers at the ground level worked hard using public diplomacy via the amateur radio NGO system, as well as direct bilateral discussions with governments. They felt that emergency relief workers entering a foreign disaster often faced excessive entry fees and licenses to use communications equipment, as well as a lack of security.

Although the Convention had a strong link to ARRL (American Radio Relay League), it was technically a result of an intergovernmental conference on emergency telecommunications convened by a UN entity (UNDRO[25] at that time, the

[24] A good example would be the 1924 *Protocol for the Pacific Settlement of International Disputes*, which was submitted to the League of Nations to guarantee collective security, in some respects as NATO does today for its members. It was called a protocol because the intent was to amend the League, was submitted by Edvard Beneš founder of modern Czechoslovakia, and created a series of sanctions against aggressor nations. It also provided an arbitration mechanism for the peaceful settlement of disputes, through the Permanent Court of International Justice. states refusing arbitration were aggressors under the protocol. Though supported by France, the instrument failed due to British opposition.

[25] United Nations Disaster Relief Organization.

predecessor of DHA[26] and then OCHA[27]), in Tampere, Finland, in 1991. This conference adopted a document called the “Tampere Declaration”, which called for an international convention. The actual text was then drafted by a team working with Prof. Fred Cate of Indiana University School of Law, under a project funded by the Annenberg Foundation. The point here is that success requires coordination with civil society, governments, and the UN, a process that led up to adoption and ratifications until 2004. Technically, and this is common, the main NGO ARRL only had observer status, so formal negotiations were among governments. Cate and others were “national experts,” in this case ARRL and IARU (International Amateur Radio Union); that doesn’t diminish the fact that this essential international law could not have happened without NGOs.

To grasp the importance of the Convention, imagine a doctor or dentist in a remote region without access to reliable satellite phones who needs to send a colleague to a nearby flood zone for a complicated operation. The colleague has never conducted such an operation and wants to consult with an expert in HQ. This problem came up a lot in rebel controlled South Sudan in the 1990s when the United States and the UN were setting up ReliefWeb. Neither Khartoum nor the rebels allowed satellite phones, which made it hard to ask for help and thus endangered patients. The existence of inadequate telecommunications resources is a real-world situation that happens frequently. On the other hand, neither a national authority nor a rebel force would want to lose control by letting NGOs inadvertently pass on sensitive information about the military or economic situation. So how will those competing interests be served in a way that allows the doctor to do his or her job? The solution in 1998 was Tampere, a convention that finally came into force in 2005 and provided rights, responsibilities, and privileges to both NGOs and governments.

### *6.7.3 Leverage*

Leverage is often needed to bring governments to the negotiating table because conventions and other instruments are expensive and difficult to negotiate. Governments will also go to great length to protect their own interests. Because conventions, declarations, and other instruments often impact International Organizations, industry, academia, and NGOs, they too will often be present or influence negotiations through their own public diplomacy campaigns. The best way to garner enough political will to negotiate these instruments is to have precedent, perhaps past resolutions from relevant bodies calling for such action. A sense of urgency is also helpful.

[26]Department of Humanitarian Affairs.

[27]Office for the Coordination of Humanitarian Affairs.

At the time of the Tampere Convention negotiations, urgency was in the air, due to lessons learned during the 1994 Rwanda Crisis when 800,000 men, women, and children perished. The US government had great difficulty reaching NGOs on the move in Rwanda, and that problem was placing many relief workers, a million war victims, the environment, and Rwanda's mountain gorillas in great peril. A simple matter of poor communications was partly to blame, but part of the problem was also a reluctance to share information. The Tampere negotiators did initially consider UNGA resolutions as precedent for the instrument, but more was needed. There had already been more than 50 international regulatory instruments, including the Constitution of the International Telecommunication Union (ITU) saying there was an absolute priority accorded emergency life-saving communications. The focus was traditional protection of people; it could just as easily be about any aspect of humanitarian relief, such as saving cultural treasures or livestock. The ITU had also passed its own resolutions. The Proceedings of The International Conference on Disaster Communications (Geneva 1990) addressed the power of telecommunication systems in disaster recovery and response, and the Tampere Declaration on Disaster Communications (Tampere 1991) called for reliable telecommunication systems for disaster mitigation and disaster relief operations and for an international Convention on Disaster Communications to facilitate such systems.

Although precedence was important, resolutions did not have the force of international law, meaning that UNGA resolutions are not binding on governments. Meanwhile, relief workers could not take their critical communications gear across borders. In other words, getting back to the hypothetical example, the doctor was not able to move across the border with his radio to communicate with medical specialists in the outside world. In such a situation, the safety of the relief worker is at risk, so too the clients to be served, be they refugees, IDPs, or anyone else. To solve this problem, a group of Western powers and the United Nations Office for the Coordination of Humanitarian Affairs (UN OCHA) decided that the only solution was to advance an NGO-inspired binding convention. Government leaders had the additional requirement that the convention was of no value unless governments in the middle of entrenched conflicts like Sudan also agreed to the final text. This is a basic rule of thumb in such negotiations. No declaration or convention is worth much unless the countries which should sign, do sign. A global declaration or convention without G77 support is of limited value. An instrument protecting the environment, a species, refugees, or cultural artifacts is also of limited value unless the signatories include impacted countries.

### 6.7.4 *The Authority to Negotiate*

Beyond deciding on the form of agreement, do the negotiators "across the table" have the authority to make a deal? Consider a hypothetical agreement to protect sensitive farmlands in order to protect food security. One might think if the US Department of Agriculture or a European Ministry of Agriculture delegate expressed support for an outcomes document on this topic at a conference, that such a statement represented an official endorsement by the government. That assumption would be wrong in many countries, unless the Agriculture Department official possessed permission from the Foreign Ministry[28] to make an endorsement. This rule that the Foreign Ministry or Department of State must allow for an international agreement to take place is normal. It is also the basic rule in the United Nations or most international organizations. **Recommendation:** Before the Chief reports that an initiative actually has a government's support, the delegation should make sure that the official saying so has the authority by asking that officer to approve a publicity statement. If he or she "clears" the statement, that is a good indication.

In the United States, permission to formally negotiate a binding agreement is handled by the Department of State's Office of Treaty Affairs, through a process known as Circular 175, by which the Secretary of State authorizes the negotiation and conclusion of international agreements. The office also regularly reviews hundreds of draft nonbinding instruments to ensure they do not contain unintended legal obligations. In virtually every nation, the Foreign Ministry or its equivalent has the final say below the head of government for deciding on treaties and similar international instruments. In some cases, these ministries will delegate authority to another ministry, but a wise Team Leader and Chief Negotiator always check to see how these matters are handled in government(s) before entering a negotiation.

When negotiating an international instrument with Sudan, unknown to the UN or Roeder, the Chief Negotiator for the United States Delegation, although the Sudanese negotiator was a full minister, he did not have full powers from the Ministry of Foreign Affairs. Because of this, Roeder had to do a separate request to the Minister of Foreign Affairs to agree to the deal.

In the United States, there is a separation between the Executive and Legislative branches, so the "Circular 175 procedure" process was begun in 1955 as a tool of the Executive Branch to avoid policy clashes with the Legislative Branch, as well as constitutional clashes with the Judicial Branch and the states, which, like in Australia, have their own constitutionally protected rights. In essence, the procedure deals with the constitutional provision of limited or full powers to sign treaties that the president will send to the United States Senate for possible ratification, what is called in American jurisprudence "advice and consent." Similar systems exist with nearly every government. This is important for every NGO to understand since under international law, a binding agreement can only be negotiated by someone with "full powers," and such powers may only be issued by heads of state or foreign ministers. The process is generally very complex, meaning it involves clearances (see Definition/Explanations appendix) by many departments or ministries because not only are matters of substance being considered but in many cases the constitutional limits of government as well. For example, the US government cannot negotiate

[28]In the United States, the Department of State is the same agency as a Foreign Ministry in a parliamentary system like that of the United Kingdom.

away rights to its citizens guaranteed by the US constitution. In federal systems such as Germany, Australia, Canada, and the United States, provinces or states also have rights. So too do indigenous peoples by treaty. There is nothing unique in this. Many governments have constitutional structures that require a form of ratification. Therefore, it is also important to understand that even if the Negotiator has "full powers," that doesn't always mean that the signature on the document, even by a head of government, will be the final word.

As a result, certain types of agreements might have to be negotiated at a sub-federal level, at least in part. There are also fiduciary responsibilities that must be considered. Will the text obligate the government to spend money, perhaps to implement a program such as protecting a historically significant site or perhaps an agricultural project. In the United States, the negotiator must also consider potential environmental impacts and whether the agreement might undermine other treaty obligations, such as those with native peoples to hunt on their reservations or to protect their religious artifacts and ancient burial grounds from acquisitions by museums. In addition, if implementing legislation will be required, that too must be considered. All of these things must be examined by any delegation, which is one of the reasons multilateral diplomacy is so difficult. There is always the chance for surprise, for countermeasures by an opposing delegation. Even if something makes sense to a doctor or mine-clearing NGO, that does not mean it will or even can be agreed to by a particular national authority (Office of the legal adviser 2010).

The same considerations do not generally apply to documents that are not binding under international law, like resolutions and some declarations. The same is true of statements of intent or documents of a political nature like a statement of support by an Ambassador. Some legal procedure will be required to determine that the instrument is not binding, but if the determination is that the document is nonbinding, then the process of negotiation is much easier.

### *6.7.5 Memoranda of Understanding (MOU)*

An MOU can be a treaty, such as the one between the United States and Germany in 1990 concerning the rights of the US Air Force in Berlin after Germany unified. The instrument was signed by the US Ambassador to Germany and the German Secretary of State, and then registered with the UN secretariat as a treaty, pursuant to Article 102 of the charter (UN Treaty Office 1990). Whether binding or not, MOUs are very useful to set down an institutional framework, terms of partnership, or a joint understanding of an issue. In Canada, once the MOUs are in place, they permit cross-jurisdictional cooperation without administrative hassles. In fact, right now, they are the only way that the Canadian government can share controlled goods without a lengthy review.

NGOs are more apt to see MOUs as an agreement with a government or International Organization that outlines areas of cooperation. This is an important negotiation, a CBM, or "confidence-building measure," for future instruments such as a declaration. An example would be the 2008 agreement and follow-up in 2009 to the Convention on Migratory Species (CMS), to provide special attention to four species of shark because of their "unfavorable" conservation status. These species are in grave danger, and while Humane Society International (HSI) was unable to achieve a mandatory treatment, it was at least able to harness attention, now considered a first step on the stairway to mandatory law (Regnery 2010).

There is no one format for an MOU; mainly the idea is to keep the language simple and clear, and do not promise what cannot be delivered. A sample MOU follows between the Director of Disasters for the Organization of African Unity (OAU) and the fictional Society for Sustainable Agriculture Development (SSAD).

> The Office of Emergency Management of the OAU and the SSLD agree to collaborate on issues of common interest and concern.
>
> This *Joint Letter* establishes foundations for collaboration in programs to reduce risks in agricultural zones of the Republic of Zimbabwe, thus supporting the Millennium Development Goals (MDGs) established by the UNGA[29] and the Hyogo Framework For Action.
>
> OAU and SAD agree to jointly design processes to reduce risks in zones of mutual interest and restore meaningful livelihoods after emergencies or during long-term crises like droughts. OAU and SSAD also agree to develop synergies towards common goals based on respective comparative advantages. Annual meetings between the chief executives of the organizations will review cooperation and set directions for collaboration in the period ahead.
>
> Signature blocks for Secretary-General, OAU, and Chairman of the Board, SSAD.

### *6.7.6 Resolutions*

Resolutions take two forms. One is a "stand-alone or independent" resolution, and the other is "inserted language" into an existing resolution, perhaps one that comes up and is agreed each year on a general topic. Resolutions are a great way to convey a mandate, especially so in the UNGA, but also in any of the UN agency or other multilateral bodies discussed in this book. Further, in the case of the "inserted language," a national mission to the international organization might not have to seek Foreign Ministry support, unless the language negatively impacts existing policy.

The United Nations is made up five organs, the UNGA being the only one where every state is represented and is on an equal footing. Its resolutions are not binding but can have enormous importance such as the 2012 recognition of Palestine as a nonvoting observer state like the Vatican. In that great assembly, the Republic of the Seychelles has the same vote as the United Kingdom or Australia. The UNGA in turn has six committees on which may any or all of the member states may sit. Each

[29] Footnotes are often used in MOUs, due to the familiarity of the participants with the topic.

committee deals with draft resolutions within their own topical mandate and in turn reports draft resolutions to the full General Assembly revised draft resolutions for general consideration. In the UNGA, most resolutions begin in committees, though some start in the General Assembly. The list below provides a breakdown of the UN General Assembly committees.

- **First Committee**: Disarmament and International Security—a good place to amend laws of war.
- **Second Committee**: Economic and Financial—where sustainable development is handled.
- **Third Committee**: Social, humanitarian, and cultural, where the ending of bull-fighting or the relationship of livestock handling and refugee camps could be discussed.
- **Fourth Committee**: Special Political and Decolonization. Primary focus is decolonization, Palestinian refugees, human rights, peacekeeping, mine action, outer space, public information, atomic radiation, and University for Peace.
- **Fifth Committee**: Administrative and Budget. Where Program Budget Implications (PBIs) are handled (see case study on PBI's). The Fifth Committee also approves "*informals,*" essentially preconference drafting sessions for major UN conferences. NGOs wanting to influence a conference need to participate in both the *informals* and the actual event. Besides its own agenda, the fifth must also unanimously agree on the budgetary implications of any UN conference, a process that began in the 1980s when faced with a budgetary crisis; peace-keeping funds were used to cover other UN needs.
- **Sixth Committee**: Legal—a good location for discussions on definitions of terms; also the implementation of international law. For example, for those NGOs interested in implementation of the Hague Convention for the Protection of Cultural Property in the Event of Armed Conflict or any aspect of the rule of law, this is a good location to network.

*A stand-alone resolution* is a resolution on a narrow topic that and therefore can provide a focal point for a fresh subject or some topic that has received little attention, but it is also the hardest to achieve, one reason being that it requires calling for a new agenda item. To achieve such a resolution, a government usually starts in a committee of the UNGA or perhaps in ECOSOC. Generally governments find it easier to amend an existing resolution because it is associated with a previously agreed agenda item; that means the topic has already been accepted as important. While an NGO can certainly introduce a stand-alone resolution through a friendly government, amending an existing draft is easier.

#### 6.7.6.1 Amending a Resolution: Possibility One—Sustainable Development

Resolution on sustainable development deals with protecting jobs and food security as well as protection against hazards. They can be the easiest way to introduce a new idea because every year there is a set of sustainable development (SD) resolutions in UNGA which emanate from the G77 coalition. Even if the main point of the resolutions does not deal with the topic of interest to an NGO, if it can in any way support the basic notion, then supporting the narrower topic could be included as a line item in the resolution. As an example, in 2009, as part of support for UDAW (Universal Declaration on Animal Welfare), WSPA tried to insert language in a resolution implementing the Rio Summit, and it received quite a bit of support from the EU member states, a handful of G77 members, as well as a variety of western nations outside of Europe. Unfortunately, China (a G77 member) opposed the edits on very narrow procedural grounds, namely that since animals were not mentioned in Rio, they could not be part of implementing resolutions. Though the facts were accurate, the objection was too narrow an interpretation of protocol; this objection can be overcome in time. Still, it is a reminder that whatever the issue, the NGO delegation needs to carefully review past voting performances and statements by important national delegations in case they decide to intervene. Sometimes, the solution is simply to choose narrow language that doesn't achieve everything an NGO wants, but achieves an agreement to some of "the ask," and then build on that agreement in future years. The leaner agreement would then be UN policy and precedence to advance large projects and major declarations. The suggestion for major conferences like Rio and for other events is to keep any proposed language for consideration in "outcomes documents" simple.

Keeping the language simple can enable it to fit in a number of resolutions having to do with sustainable development; then, it has the best chance of being adopted and then used as a lever to develop a formal Contact Group of G77 and western UN missions to advance a broader consensus.

#### 6.7.6.2 Amending a Resolution: Possibility Two—Disaster Response

Another group of resolutions that might be amended to serve an NGO are the many which have a disaster aspect, especially those related to recovery from a war or man-made or technological event. Every year the G77 advances in the UNGA an Omnibus resolution on disaster management. In addition to topically narrow resolutions, given the relationship between livelihoods, food security, and people, an Omnibus resolution could be the perfect place for inserting language of interest to an NGO, especially if the topic relates to the response phase of emergencies or about refugees and internally displaced persons (IDP) camps. Language to be inserted in an UNGA resolution or an IASC statement for this topic could be very helpful when trying to gain an actual UN mandate for action, either a political mandate through a resolution or an operational mandate through an IASC statement of agreement.

#### 6.7.6.3 Amending a Resolution: Possibility Three—Disaster Risk Reduction

Linking a topic to Disaster Risk Reduction may also be worth considering. This can be done by coordinating with a sponsoring government (as with any resolution) or with the Special Representative of the Secretary General on Risk Reduction, or the secretariat of the United Nations International Strategy for Disaster Reduction (UNISDR). As with disaster response, there is a UNGA resolution on this topic every year, so this provides another opportunity. Resolution language could cover such topics as reducing risks to almost anything from storm surge, high winds, and earthquakes for clinics, barns, and other shelters, placement of livestock away from high-risk livestock (Huertas and Murillo 2007).[30] And if an NGO wanted to do this with another international organization, certainly UNESCO comes to mind,[31] which is a leader in reduction education. In addition to UNESCO there are also UNICEF, WFP, FAO, WHO World Bank, UNDP, and several other UN agencies, all working on disaster risk reduction and members of the ISDR in Risk Reduction. Completely outside the UN orbit is OECD, which does studies on a regular basis on risk reduction. One of the most interesting is "Disaster Information Needs of Ethnical Minorities," which was conducted in 2004–2006 (Secretariat 2006). Essentially, OECD (from an economic perspective) and ISDR (International Strategy for Disaster Reduction) from a global strategic perspective have concluded that governments and civil society must improve how they anticipate, prevent, or mitigate crises and how they will respond, hopefully as partners instead of competitors. As disasters increase mainly due to climate change and in numbers, as well as an expansion of human and social vulnerability in urban and coastal areas, it will become more urgent that all sectors in society focus on reducing risk and vulnerability rather than just preparing to respond to disasters—which is a clear body of work for NGOs, both in operational terms, as lobbyists and as negotiators of relevant international instruments.

#### 6.7.6.4 Elements of a Resolution

Most international instruments have a common structure which offers many opportunities for NGOs in influence policy through insertion of a key word or phrase. In the case of resolutions in particular, the first part contains Preparatory Paragraphs that explain the problem being handled by the instrument and provide precedence, following by Operative Paragraphs that suggest or direct someone to do something.

**Example**

**Preambular**: Reaffirming that discrimination on the basis of sex is contrary to the charter of the United Nations, the Universal Declaration of Human Rights, the Convention on the Elimination of All Forms of Discrimination against Women, and other international human

[30]The concept of sustainable or risk-resistant heath facilities, water, and sanitation systems was a major focus of the 2005 World Conference on Disaster Reduction and the 2005–2015 Hyogo Framework for Action. As noted in the introduction of this book, a new opportunity for NGOs will also arise in 2015 when governments meet again in Sendai, Japan, to discuss and agree on the successor arrangement to the Hyogo Framework for Action that ends in 2015.

[31]UNESCO has its roots in the League of Nations. The precursor was the International Commission on Intellectual Cooperation.

rights instruments, and that its elimination is an integral part of efforts towards the elimination of violence against women.

**Operative:** Stresses that women should be empowered to protect themselves against violence and, in this regard, stresses that women have the right to have control over and decide freely and responsibly on matters related to their sexuality, including sexual and reproductive health, free of coercion, discrimination, and violence. (HCHR 2004)

The entire package is negotiated in the form of a Draft Resolution proposed by sponsoring governments in informal drafting sessions and then in formal committee meetings, where they emerge as Revised Draft Resolutions to be considered by a plenary body such as ECOSOC or the UN General Assembly. There can be exceptions; that's the rule. Since many resolutions come up every year, sometimes with only minor editorial changes, NGOs should consider proposing language in ECOSOC (where it is allowed) and work with governmental delegations in the committees of the UN General Assembly to insert words or sentences that are considered helpful to the cause.

One vivid instance of an NGO asking for language happened in 2003 when Roeder was approached by a lobbyist for the Millennium World Peace Summit. She had already contacted the US embassy in Tel-Aviv and wanted support for language for a resolution on religion or rather to declare as a "crime against humanity," any violence perpetuated on the basis of religion. Although the woman was a lobbyist for an NGO, some governments were also in support of the idea. The lobbyist wanted UN General Assembly support, and if not possible, then UN Security Council supports. This was clearly a case where the NGO had not effectively used the model for diplomatic initiatives, otherwise she would have been aware that September was late for a government to propose a unique resolution, and the subject was not one then considered topical by the Security Council. Still, it was correct to find the action-officer responsible for coordinating voting. Although the resolution died, it began with a good premise, which was that conflict should not begin on the basis of religious tenets. However, it was also clearly aimed directly at one religion, Islam, and therefore had no chance of success in the G77 and would have caused far more trouble than it could have cured. Roeder's thinking was that instead of focusing on religion which was usually just a political tool to rally around a conflict, it is usually better to use resolutions and UNGA debate to focus on the true causes of conflict, which usually had less to do with religious choice than poverty, corruption, and prejudice.

#### 6.7.6.5 Are There Too Many Resolutions?

Many resolutions repeat themselves over time, e.g., a set of resolutions in ECOSOC that emerged in 2003 agenda item 41, Strengthening of the Coordination of Humanitarian and Disaster Relief Assistance of the UN. Their goal was to call on the UN General Assembly and development assistance elements of the UN to support humanitarian assistance to Tajikistan, Timor Leste, the Democratic Republic of the Congo, the Federal Republic of Yugoslavia, and Somalia. Much of the text was verbatim from previous years. In addition, UN Ambassadors were being asked to seek UN help for a range of man-made disasters or those caused by not preparing properly for a natural phenomenon, and rather than treat each crisis as a separate agenda item, to lump it all under a broader heading of "humanitarian assistance." The United States government and some other donor nations resisted this tendency, preferring that such individual needs be taken up in the governing bodies of UN agencies, in other words the International Organizations like UNHCR or UNDP that had a field presence. Many negotiators complained in fact that the time it took to negotiate these calls for help was long and that result was unhelpful, certainly less helpful than working directly with a UN Agency. On the other hand, nations in need felt this was the one way, other than annual addresses to the UN General Assembly by their heads of government, that broad attention could be given to their plight.

This was one of the times Mr. Roeder strongly disagreed with his own government and in September, 2003 criticized the tone of the complaining. In his view, nations have a right to use the General Assembly as a venue to vet their issues. That was a point after all for creating the League of Nations and then the United Nations. If democracy meant anything, Roeder felt the government should be more sympathetic and less strident. In one case, a fellow officer in the Department of State calling the repetitive resolutions "mindless," a term Roeder called most inappropriate, though he did agree that the government should diplomatically work with the fellow member states to limit resolutions to those that were necessary. In other words, he was sympathetic to the rationale behind the complaint but felt the approach was a bit undemocratic and not helpful to building peaceful relations. In fairness, the US Delegation is staffed by some of the most overworked diplomats in the UN. Despite being the largest delegation to the UN, because the US makes a practice of negotiating everything, people come in very early in the morning and stay late into the night and try very hard to meet anyone who asks for help. They have a daunting task, so perhaps it is no small wonder that some would complain of the workload posed by repetitive resolutions.

### 6.7.7 *Conventions and Treaties*

A treaty is essentially a contract between governments that assumes obligations, and if a party fails to meet those obligations, it can usually be held liable. Conventions are essentially a form of treaty. Indeed, protocols, covenants, and exchanges of letters can also be Treaties, though not necessarily so. It is certainly true that negotiating a Convention, indeed any treaty, requires a huge amount of effort and funding, and it can be binding or not. An example of a specific animal-related convention is CITES (the Convention on International Trade in Endangered Species of Wild Fauna and Flora).[32] Another convention, which was not adopted, was on USAR

[32]CITES is an international agreement between governments. Its aim is to ensure that international trade in specimens of over 30,000 wild animals and plants species does not threaten their survival. NGOs are heavily involved in this work as observers.

(Urban Search and Rescue). USAR teams are used to extract people from collapsed structures from earthquakes or other phenomena, and there was particularly after 9/11 an interest in better standards for USAR. However, after looking over the Convention and the reaction of governments such as Japan, the UK, and a few others, the US government decided that a Convention was not needed. Instead, some of the negotiators decided a UNGA mandate (resolution) would be more appropriate asking all disaster-prone nations to participate in the UN's efforts to standardize how Urban Search and Rescue was handled. The remaining participating governments agreed with this approach, and Turkey presented the resolution at the UNGA. The point here gets back to the basic question. CITES was urgently needed to avoid mass extinctions of rare species; in the case of USAR, experts agreed that a lower-lever mandate was sufficient and easier to achieve.

**Note** NGOs don't have generally treaties with governments; they can negotiate contracts or agreements, though historians often cite as an early example three "treaties" between Hoover's CRB (Committee for the Relief of Belgium) and the German High Command, which allowed for extraordinary access to occupied territories. These authorized the CRB to feed civilians in occupied France and pledged not to divert supplies. The Germans also permitted Americans to station themselves in the territory in order to supervise food distribution, but under German watch (Nash, The Life of Herbert Hoover: The Humanitarian 1914–1917, 1988b, p. 109). Though historians have characterized these agreements as "treaties," they are really MOUs.

Unlike an MOU which might be between governments or between NGOs, or some mix, a Convention is nearly always an agreement between governments, not the public, since governments are the public's representatives. If an NGO wishes to develop a Convention the Study Team should carefully consider whether such an instrument is worth the effort. One way to do that would be to consult with the Fifth Committee of the UN General Assembly and explore whether their experts think the support of a group of governments is possible. This should come from every major UN region and include influential governments that have significant direct interests in the topic of concern. It is also important to include the G77, the UN's largest coalition; International Organizations like UNEP; or even the International Red Cross and Red Crescent Movement, if their mandates are impacted. It is also worth noting that with regard to any convention, the parties may fluctuate because of geopolitical changes such as unification of the Federal Republic of Germany and of the German Democratic Republic on October 3,1990 or the division of a state as happened to Czechoslovakia on January 1, 1993, into the Czech Republic and Slovakia.

### 6.7.8 Declarations

Declarations can be binding or nonbinding agreements. One common form would be a proclamation of intent or a petition signed by an NGO or individuals declaring that something (refugees, women, farm, animals, etc.) deserve a standard of care. Such a proclamation could be used to encourage states to take action.

The Pennsylvania Declaration of April 1, 1970 was a "self-declared" proclamation by the University of Pennsylvania Museum of Antiquity and Anthropology that it "would purchase no more art objects or antiquities ... unless the objects are accompanied by a pedigree." This was the first such instrument of its kind and was intended to influence an entire community, prevent the buying of objects stolen after disasters and wars, thus making the university a tool to preserve fragile cultures. Later the same year a UNESCO Convention was signed aimed at the same goal, and similar instruments have followed since. So, although the Pennsylvania Declaration only directed the University of Pennsylvania, it influenced many other institutions—however, not all agree with it. (Penn Museum)

While individual institutions like NGOs can issue declarations, when in the context of international law, a Declaration is generally an agreement between states (nations) and/or International Organizations (because their members are states). Subnational authorities such as territories and colonies or individuals do not usually sign such instruments because they do not enjoy rights and obligations under international law; they also cannot engage in foreign affairs unless their "state" agrees. Since the war crimes trials of World War II, states have also provided that individuals have some responsibility relative to human rights, an emerging body of law. Individuals have been making declarations for a long time, the most famous being, perhaps, the US Declaration of Independence proclaimed in 1776 by private citizens (armed non-state actors) that they and the colonies they represented were independent and had a right to be so. Of course, they had to fight for that declaration to be recognized in a treaty signed by states. There is not any international law saying that an agreement between individuals cannot be called a declaration, and as the Pennsylvania Declaration shows, such an act can be influential. NGOs must understand however that it would not have the same legal standing as an agreement between "states" and International Organizations, with the exception of contract law. In other words, signatories might be bound to each other and subject to suit in court if the contract was broken. Whether that is possible will depend on the local legal system.

Some declarations are nonbinding, such as the Universal Declaration of Human Rights (UDHR). This is important to understand when deciding to advance a Declaration; though not binding, they are important. UDHR sets down an agreed standard of rights for human beings that have been enshrined in domestic law around the world. Nobel laureate John Polanyi considered UDHR as more important than the Magna Carta because of its global impetus and breadth of claims (Polanyi 1999). Therein sits the potential value of a declaration signed by states, assuming enough do it, to be recognized as a global standard for whatever issue is of concern to the NGO and its alliance. If enough nations enshrine the concepts in domestic law, binding international rights could follow.

A detailed discussion of two important animal welfare declarations is discussed in a companion book, which can be models for humanitarian NGOs to use (Roeder, *Diplomacy, Funding and Animal Welfare* 2011). One was called the Universal Declaration on Animal Welfare (UDAW) and the other the Universal Declaration of Animal Rights (UDAR). Despite similar names, the two are very different in style and substance. UDAR is a statement of principles, signed by people, though if a government wanted to sign, it could do so (Belair 2009). In contrast, UDAW is a nonbinding agreement between governments associated with a public petition. Both want to be models for performance. Unlike UDAR, upon which no government has expressed an opinion, some governments have agreed to UDAW "in principle." This example is raised because of the common misunderstanding that when a government has agreed to something "in principle," it has formally agreed to adhere to the instrument. Not so. The term "in principle" does not mean agreement to an actual text, but rather a general agreement with a policy. That's nonbinding in any court of law.

## Case Study: The Ankara Declaration

The Ankara Declaration is an example of an important nonbinding agreement versus a binding international instrument.

On April 28, 2000, a body of experts, industry officials, contractors, military officers and government, UN, and IFRC officials gathered in Ankara at the suggestion of the American, Mexican, and Turkish governments. The purpose was to make more formal some understandings which had been reached on the use of disaster information over the course of the previous 12 months following a similar conference in May, 1999 cosponsored by the Mexican and American governments in Mexico City. The Ankara conference also pulled in the results of a July, 1998 conference in Washington, DC, hosted by the US Department of State and the Office of the Vice President. Many of the participants were also NGO officials, as well as representatives of industry. The conferences were under the umbrella of a then unincorporated project known as the Global Disaster Information Network (GDIN). Following much discussion, the participants agreed by consensus on the text of "The Ankara Declaration," which had been drafted by Al Simard. Was the Declaration binding?

The point of the Ankara Declaration was to state the importance of information-sharing networks to mitigate the effects or extent of international disasters and provide principles that governments and other entities might follow to facilitate the transmission of disaster information. Though important, the Ankara Declaration was not binding international law. There were several reasons. Only representatives of governments and IOs (as defined in this book) when acting on instructions can develop international law. Many of the representatives were from civil society and so did not have that legal "competence" or authority. Further, the governmental and IO representatives, while they were attending on instructions and in some cases could authorize funds for GDIN activities, when joining in consensus on the Declaration (just like the rest of the conference), were operating in their personal capacity, much like the President of Costa Rica when he signed the Animals Matter Declaration crafted by WSPA. As a result, no government incurred a legal obligation (McLeod et al. 2000, June 8). This does not dilute the importance of the Declaration. Indeed, the Ankara Declaration influenced the development of a number of disaster projects over the years as well as three more international disaster conferences in Australia (2001), where it was decided that GDIN would obtain a legal existence; Italy (2002); and Washington, DC (2004), by which time the international element of GDIN had been incorporated as an NGO. Many of the participants became leaders on major future disaster initiatives, drawing on the Ankara principles for inspiration.

#### 6.7.8.1 Universal Declaration of Human Rights (UDHR)

The Universal Declaration of Human Rights is considered to be one of the important bodies of international law (Danieli et al. 1999); is it binding? Certainly the original intent was that the Declaration would become a standard or statement of goals to be pursued, though unfortunately, in our opinion, not binding international law. Indeed, the official position of the US government, as conveyed to the US Delegation by the Department of State, said "in the view of the Acting Secretary of State, the declaration of human rights should not be so phrased as to give the impression to individual citizens or governments that there is a contractual obligation on the part of governments or of the United Nations to guarantee the human rights enumerated in the Declaration. In fact the Declaration is largely a statement of aspirations rather than established facts (Glen and Symonides 1998)." The nonbinding nature was a creature of the politics of the time, and as many human rights NGOs have pointed out, unfortunately been used by despots to push back on "infringements of sovereignty," noting that this particular Declaration is not binding. Nonetheless, it is a powerful statement that can be used to put pressure by "moral suasion" on governments and armed non-state actors, and in 1968, the United Nations International Conference on Human Rights agreed that the Declaration "constitutes an obligation for the members of the international community" to protect and preserve the rights of its citizenry.

### *6.7.9 Treaties*

What matters in any negotiation is the result: A higher standard of care for an identified interest such as refugees. The terms for the most common major international instruments are defined differently by separate scholars and governments. Under United States law, a treaty is any international agreement by whatever title that receives the "advice and consent of the Senate," so Conventions and Treaties are usually the same thing. The United States Constitution also says under Article II, Section II that the Senate must provide advice and consent to ratify treaties negotiated and agreed to by the president or his agents such as the Department of State. (USC 1 - US CODE 1 - U.S. Code - Title 1: General Provisions 2004)/.

In order to be considered a treaty by the United Nations, Article 101 of the UN charter requires that the instrument be deposited with the secretariat; otherwise, both the UN and the International Court of Justice will ignore it.[33] Other bodies like the Red Cross have their own rules. Some would argue that if a declaration like UDAR were registered with the UN Secretariat, it would be a treaty, making that a rationale for moving the instrument through UNGA and then depositing with the UN Treaty Office (Berridge 2005). The truth is a bit more complicated. While it

[33]This is an important remnant of Woodrow Wilson's 14 points and the League of Nations, recognizing that secret treaties partly led to World War One.

might indeed be technically correct to call instruments deposited with the UN Secretariat treaties, the member states might not manage them as such, and a document endorsed by the UNGA might not even be accepted by the UN Treaty Office as a true treaty. Treaties are also not binding on governments that do not sign and accede, so even if the UN accepted an NGO initiated Declaration for deposit, a government like the United States would not consider it a treaty unless it "had to be sent" to the Senate for advice and consent, which they might not consider was needed, in other words, if compliance was voluntary. The United States and other powers will generally also not consider a treaty if it can't be verified.

### *6.7.10 People's Treaties*

Not technically treaties in international law, "People's Treaties" are signed expressions of support or declarations signed by private citizens or bodies of civil society like NGOs or even private corporations and schools, calling for an international action. This might be a treaty like the one aiming to eliminate antipersonnel mines. At the same time as 122 governments signed the actual Ottawa Treaty banning antipersonnel mines, a People's Treaty was put forward on December 3, 1997 in Ottawa by Mines Action Canada (MAC). It was an instrument for citizens to sign to show solidarity. Similarly, in 2008 on the final day of the Dublin Diplomatic Conference on Cluster Munitions, the Cluster Munitions Coalition, in collaboration with Mines Action Canada, re-launched the treaty in order to encourage more states to ban the weapons as a result of built-up public momentum. Similar types of "People's Treaties" might be the Universal Declaration on Animal Rights (UDAR) that has already been mentioned or the People's Treaties proposed to come out of Rio+20 in 2012. What they all have in common is that they are nonbinding civil society declarations in support of a cause. They also have the goal of influencing governments to take a binding action, in other words a version of public diplomacy to an extent, but also a genuine effort to change the attitude of ordinary people.

A caution on such instruments is that if they are going to be effective, they must be focused and have well-developed goals. If in conjunction with an international conference, the recommendation to drafting officers is to integrate into the process and try to influence the official outcomes document. Even if that proves impossible, if the organizations or people involved do not at least engage the "official players" in a non-hostile manner, then the instrument may lack sufficient credibility to be truly influential. The instrument need not agree with the official outcomes document at all; it is important to be "diplomatic" in the approach. Balancing language acceptable to the NGO community while also respecting government and UN language and goals may prove difficult, but it is important to make the effort. Finally, as with any instrument, define the problem clearly and who is involved, as well as the proposed solutions.

### 6.7.11 *Protocols*

From a legal perspective, there is generally no difference from a protocol or a treaty. Protocols are usually a form of treaty that derives from another.

Readers are reminded of the discussion of the Kellogg–Briand Pact, which is still international law, although the pact is mainly a moral statement. There are no sanctions to be imposed on violators. This perhaps isn't surprising, as a separate initiative which failed also tried to outlaw war as a policy, but it proposed to impose sanctions for violators. The case of the Geneva Protocol is relevant in this context because it is an example of a new government renouncing the signature of a prior government to an international accord. This could happen again today, especially regarding fresh governments emerging from failed nation states or revolutions.

The Geneva Protocol's formal name was the Pacific Settlement of International Disputes. It pledged signatories to engage in disarmament and to renounce war in favor of peaceful means of settlement. Many members of the League supported the Geneva Protocol, and initially it did receive the votes of all 47 member states on October 2, 1924. This was at the 5th General Assembly. Had the protocol, which had been largely drafted by the US government, succeeded, it might well have averted future conflicts; however, on March 2, 1925, upon the recommendation of Imperial Defense and feeling the proposed protocol would undermine security in Europe, the newly installed conservative government of Stanley Baldwin refused to ratify the agreement the previous government had voted for the previous year. This caused the effort to fail (British Cabinet 1925, March 2). David Hunter Miller of the US Department of State and coauthor of the American text placed particular blame on the UK for the failure of the negotiations (Miller, *Declares British Foes of Protocol* 1925).

## 6.8 The Impact of Program Budget Implications (PBI)

*(See also* Sect. 9.11*)* An example of inserting language in a preexisting resolution draft was the 2006 proposal by Save the Children, Human Rights Watch, and other NGOs to support the rights of the Child (Cecchetti and Becker, *Proposal for the 2006 UNGA resolution on the rights of the Child* 2006, October 2). This is also an example of why it is important to consider PBIs. The draft language emanated from the NGO Group for the Convention on the Rights of the Child to the NGO Advisory Panel on the UN Study on Violence against Children (VAC). Attempts were successful in advancing their cause, but they did not achieve all of their goals right away.

The principle recommendation was a request to provide a mandate for a Special Representative on VAC, but this was not accepted in 2006. Unfortunately, "in 2006 there was not enough appetite in the diplomatic community in New York for the appointment of a new Special Procedure (technical name encompassing special rapporteurs, experts, representatives, envoys, etc.). The Human Rights Council was reviewing existing ones and the countries did not want to create a new one in the midst of the review." (Cecchetti, *Discussion on the VAC* 2012). This was despite the fact that the call was among the key recommendations included in the UN Study on VAC conducted by Paulo Sergio Pinheiro, the independent expert of the Secretary General on VAC. The same issue came up with OCHA in 2003 when the UN Emergency Relief Coordinator (ERC) felt the need to have resources to deal with surges like a sudden onset disasters. To deal with the issue, the ERC wanted to reclassify several posts to higher-level positions, as well as establish a new Deputy Assistant Secretary General position. While most major donors were sympathetic to the problem, the solution chosen by the ERC required a permanent additional expense in the budget and change to the PBI (program budget implication), which they felt was unneeded and some were unwilling to support.

Budget and other administrative concerns meant that the NGO coalition on children had to wait until 2008 and the position had less of a mandate than Save the Children wanted, but it was much more than they had before. "During 2007 Save the Children decided to launch a petition amongst the child rights NGO community to support the call for the appointment of the Special Representative of the Secretary General on Violence Against Children (SRSG/VAC) and managed to have over 1,000 signatory NGOs. Meanwhile, lobbying continued in NY, including by Sergio Pinheiro whose mandate was renewed for 1 year to prepare a progress report of the UN Study. And Save the Children was successful in 2007 in that the UNGA adopted a resolution calling for the appointment of the SRSG/VAC for a period of 3 years. The budget came from voluntary contributions, rather than from the regular budget, which was the only reason the UNGA could come to agreement. In other words, the compromise meant no direct UN budget implication (PBI)." (Cecchetti and Becker, *Proposal for the 2006 UNGA resolution on the rights of the Child* 2006, October 2) In the meantime, a new UN Secretary General was appointed, which delayed the process of appointing Marta Santos Pais. Two resolutions (2008 and 2009) by the Human Rights Council and one more resolution (2009) by the GA were adopted to call on the Secretary General to appoint the SRSG/VAC. This finally happened in May 2009 with the post taking effect as of September 1, 2009. The mandate runs until September 2012. As a result, the Secretary General appointed Marta Santos Pais of Portugal as his Special Representative on VAC at the level of Assistant Secretary General.

This NGO resolution initiative took several years to achieve success, despite the organizers following all of the rules. The reason was in part because the PBIs were not first resolved. However, the program is now entirely funded—though by extra-budgetary money. The delay did not result from a lack of importance to the UN. Protecting children in one form of another has been part of the UN's agenda for decades, especially over nutrition, education, sexual abuse, and child soldiers. The problem was simply that unless enough governments feel that a negotiation is urgent, there are usually so many things being negotiated at the same time that any one effort might take years, especially if even one government has doubts. To mitigate against this risk, the NGO community kept "their ASK" small—only a few sentences in a larger product—feeling a small request would be easier for the delegations to digest.

## 6.9 Sovereignty, the New World Order and Implementing a Deal

Sovereignty comes up frequently in this book because it can be an inhibiting factor to international NGOs conducting or implementing in-country diplomatic initiative, e.g., talking to political dissidents and lobbying for change with the public. It is no small matter for NGOs to consider when advancing an international agreement. Territorial integrity was at the heart of the League of Nations and is considered by many as a core function of the UN. In fact, Article 2(7) of the UN charter says "nothing contained in the present charter shall authorize the UN to intervene in matters that are essentially within the domestic jurisdiction of any state." Only crimes against humanity transcend this concept.

Even though the practice of the UN protects member states, many of the UN's founding fathers, especially in the Commission to Study the Organization of Peace (CSOP), lived through World War I, a conflict caused by nationalist and probably corporate greed, and they also lived through the horror of World War II. Those global disasters convinced the founding fathers of the need for a "new world order," as they put it, which diminished the role of nationalism; many of these founding fathers (and mothers to include Eleanor Roosevelt) saw the concept of sovereignty as inherently a threat to democracy and human rights. Today there is further development in the continuum of a fostering of popular sovereignty, e.g., the effort by Civil Society Organizations, to include NGOs, to negotiate their own treaties, and to develop their own strategies—though this still must be done within the context of a state framework.

The League of Nations and the UN both had a tension, to avoid creating a super-government or single sovereignty, but also to diminish at least in part the unbridled traditional sovereignty of nations to undertake heinous atrocities. People around the world wanted no further wars and demanded that their voices be heard; what was the right approach? After World War II, some felt that in addition to states being party to the UN, so too should NGOs, even if they could not sign the charter. Some also felt that the International Court of Justice needed to not only litigate disputes between nations but also between people and nations (Hillmann 1988). This was the view of some involved in the development of the League of Nations and its precursor, the Interparliamentary Union, and national politicians like Congressman Richard Bartholdt of Saint Louis, Missouri[34] who also felt that for the world to reach a comprehensive peace, "nations must surrender a measure of sovereignty to a

[34]Formed in 1889, the Interparliamentary Union (IPU) (now in Geneva) was the first international political organization, whose aim was to promote international arbitration and world peace. Members of the IPU like US Congressman Bartholdt saw it as a challenge to traditional sovereignty, born of the Treaty of Westphalia, when the modern state was invented. To Bartholdt, sovereignty was antithetical to democracy. The goal of the IPU was to compel governments to resolve disputes by means of peaceful settlement and arbitration. IPU therefore the initiative of Tsar Nicholas II who had called the Peace Conferences was held at The Hague in 1899 and 1907. The IPU was also instrumental in setting up what is now the Permanent Court of Arbitration in The Hague.

"High Court of Nations," … lest conflicts perpetuate at the will of one government or a strong leader" (Bartholdt 1930, p. 175). German economist Gerhart von Schulze Gaevernitz (Schuze-Gaevernitz 1919) proposed to the US Delegation to the Paris Peace Conference that the League of Nations have an Assembly for the people, much like the US House of Representatives. In fact the idea of an assembly of the people or at least of Parliaments instead of executive branches of governments was also proposed by the International Labor and Socialist Conference in Berne, Switzerland in February, 1919. However, though at least one member of the US Delegation saw some value in the proposal, it was deemed impractical by Wilson and the delegation, as were the other ideas proposed by the conference (Miller, *The Drafting of the Covenant* 1928a, pp. 272–275, Vol 1).

While the foreign policy of most governments is to preserve sovereignty, there is also no rule that prevents an NGO from postulating a different point of view in defense of self-determination or freedom, such as arguing for the independence of Somaliland, or as happened at Rio+20 in 2012, and collaborating on a series of "treaties" as an expression of popular will (see cases study 12.3).

Before going to the UN, one approach a Chief Negotiator might consider on a broad regional or global basis is to start with individual national agreements, negotiating specific language; then when enough national rules are enacted that are similar in intent, use them as precedent for stronger or clearer voluntary multilateral principles in the UN, which might be the subject of the negotiations just discussed, perhaps through the instrument of a resolution. But if the NGO has previously taken sides on unrelated conflicts in which the governments are involved, they might not cooperate.

Assuming that a set of similar national rules has been negotiated over time, this can led to confidence in using them as international principles for the negotiation of a binding multilateral agreement or treaty. Remember however that any agreement must be implemented, whether binding or voluntary instruments. When done with a corporation, which is increasingly a practice, they are only as good as long as the corporation sees a business advantage. In the case of governments, many agreements can't be administered without "national implementing legislation." The Team needs an implementation plan so that if negotiations work, next steps are evident and in a budget.

## 6.10 Rights of Indigenous Peoples

With nearly 400 million indigenous peoples spread around the world, a discussion of their rights[35] is both a compelling topic for NGOs and complicated. The topic easily goes back to the 1920s in multilateral diplomacy suffering in the League of

[35] The word "peoples" is significant in that it conveys the notion of community.

Nations when placed against state sovereignty. The Speaker of the Iroquois Confederacy tried to get the League to consider their grievances against Canada; while some members of the League were sympathetic, the decision was that this was a domestic dispute outside the competence of the League: Thus a precedent was set. However, the rights of the indigenous have since been gaining recognition in the international arena. This includes a 1971 ECOSOC resolution that authorized the Subcommission on the Prevention of Discrimination and Protection of Minorities to conduct a study on the problem. Following publication of the study, a UN Working Group on Indigenous Populations was formed under the UN Commission on Human Rights, which has become a great platform for discussions on the tension between the rights of states and those of the indigenous. This included debates over cultural integrity, self-determination, political autonomy, and other topics. That effort led to 1993 being designated "The International Year for the World's Indigenous People," and then, a decade was declared, which led to the development of a UN Declaration on Indigenous Rights.

Despite those advances, there is still a significant tension between the efforts of the indigenous to expand their rights and efforts by states to limit the meaning of self-determination. Generally, declarations by ECOSOC or the UN General Assembly are thought to have a higher standing than those by the UN specialized agencies and funds such as the ILO (International Labor Organization), which had a series of instruments on rights. The adoption by the UN General Assembly of the "Declaration on the Rights of Indigenous Peoples" on September 13, 2007 was significant. So too was the vote. Usually votes in the General Assembly are by consensus; in this case, the vote was 143 in favor to 4 against (Australia, Canada, New Zealand and the United States), with 11 abstentions (Department of Public Information • News and Media Division 2007). The explanations of Yes and No votes limited the right to self-determination in order to protect the rights of the state and defined limits regarding individual versus collective rights. As an example the government of Australia when explaining its NO vote said it

> supported and encouraged the full engagement of indigenous peoples in the democratic decision-making process, but did not support a concept that could be construed as encouraging action that would impair, even in part, the territorial and political integrity of a State with a system of democratic representative Government.

## 6.11 Non-ratification or Non-implementation

Even if a country's Chief Executive signs a negotiated text, the government might not support it. Depending on the system of government, the legislative branch may have to concur with the executive, even if the Foreign Minister or his equivalent approves. Legislative branches have said no in the past, e.g., when the US Senate failed to ratify the Kyoto Protocol of 1997, which aimed to lower greenhouse gases or after World War I when it failed to ratify the Treaty of Versailles. The failure of the European Constitution is not exactly parallel, but just because a government like

France is supportive does not mean a treaty will be ratified. Always check the government's system to see if further work may be required.

Since the point of any negotiation is to change the status quo for the better, analyze whether the target government (s) or agencies/corporations are willing or are able to implement the deal. This analysis comes before negotiations even start and continues as the negotiations evolve. Implementation can require years of post-negotiation work, requiring more staff from the coalition, not just the lead NGO, and in some cases a government to enact "implementing legislation." In the case of industry, one assumes corporations will have an easy time of implementing, or they would not have made the agreement. As for governments, existing rules may allow government agencies to enact fresh implementing rules or practices, which is also often the situation with International Organizations.

**Case Study: The Struggle Against Driftnets**

In July 1989, saw the culmination of years of effort to end driftnet fishing with the promulgation of the Tarawa Declaration, followed by a Convention on the Prohibition of Driftnet Fishing in the South Pacific at Wellington the same year, and then the UN General Assembly adopted the concept by consensus in Resolution A/RES/44/225 (UNGA1989, December 22). The resolution called for a moratorium on pelagic driftnet fishing. Although a deal had been made, driftnet fishing continued, probably due to the high profit as well as the practical point that the high seas are difficult to patrol. Finally after much pressure from Human Society, the USA, Earth Trust, and other NGOs and governments, in May 1992, a binding treaty on Fisheries Surveillance and Law Enforcement in the South Pacific Regions to enforce the Wellington Convention was completed at the 22nd Forum Fisheries Committee meeting in Niue and signed by the 12 member states of the South Pacific Forum and Palau (Earthtrust and Driftnets: A Capsule History from 1976-1995 1995). The UN's ban on driftnet fishing was a win for NGOs involved in conservation, but the struggle continues. It will be up to NGOs, the UN, and governments working together to make the ban totally work.

Never assume that because a government should implement an agreement, that they will, or that implementation would not take surprising turns. In 2010, France got into trouble with the European Commission for the way it expelled Roma migrants. According to the government of France, their process was in keeping with their duties under the EU's free movement directive, but according to officials in the EC, France was incorrect. The point is not whether either party is right or not rather that implementing laws or rules do not always look the same. **Bottom Line:** Once the primary negotiation is complete, if fresh rules, laws, or customs are needed to implement it, the Study Team should have developed a follow-up campaign (Castle 2010).

# Chapter 7
# War and Peace: Roles for NGOs

> *"Peace cannot be kept by force. It can only be achieved by understanding."*
>
> Albert Einstein

**Extract** Chapter 7 extends the discussion of legal concepts in Chap. 6 with a special focus on the law of war and the potential role of NGOs with peacekeeping officials. A discussion is provided on the rewards and risks related to interacting with armed-non-state players, as well as an understanding of the concept of the Veto in the United Nations. The importance of neutrality is given much attention, as well as multi-track diplomacy.

## 7.1 Law of War

> The winning of the war is but the first stage in the winning of the peace. Wars are not fought for their own sake, but for the sake of determining which of the protagonists will shape the peace that follows. (Pasvolsky, *The Problem of Economic Peace After The War* 1942)

> "War between nations should be outlawed as an institution or means for the settlement of international controversies by making it a public crime under the law of nations." Idaho Senator William Borah, US Senate 1923 (Howard-Ellis 1928, p. 329)

> Arnold Toynbee made a point many years ago about the anti-war movement; "Its first embodiment in the League of Nations … failed to save the world from … the General War of 1935–45. At the price of this further affliction, we have now bought a fresh opportunity to attempt the difficult enterprise of abolishing war through a co-operative system of world government. Whether we in our world will succeed in achieving what no other civilization has even yet achieved is a question that lies on the knees of the Gods." (Toynbee 1947, p. 285)

L.W. Roeder, Jr. and A. Simard, *Diplomacy and Negotiation for Humanitarian NGOs*, Humanitarian Solutions in the 21st Century, DOI 10.1007/978-1-4614-7113-4_7,

One area in particular where NGOs are valuable in today's world as a moderating influence is in conflict management. Nations and international organizations tend to examine political conflict or environmental damage through the lens of politics and international law, yet that kind of thought process stovepipes nations into groups of "rogue states," potentially subject to economic or military sanctions by the UN Security Council or an international court.[1] That's very confrontational and such terminology or sanctions exclude, rather than include. NGOs, while they can be very confrontational (see discussion on Sea Shepherd), are mostly bridge-builders, advocating for change without confrontation, and because they are everywhere, especially when working in coalitions, they can be an engine for preventative diplomacy by sharing critical information needed to avoid disasters like Rwanda. They can also mediate between antagonists and in the fields of agriculture, the environment, health, and development bring the best minds in the world behind altruistic goals.

Aside from natural phenomena, little harms humanity and its institutions like war. It is an essential area of NGO diplomatic activity that interfaces with all aspects of humanitarian concerns and increasingly a study of barbaric, internal conflict. *Diplomacy and Animal Welfare* explored how the law of war impacts livestock and the impact on food security and livelihoods (Roeder, *Diplomacy, Funding and Animal Welfare* 2011). What made that research relevant to any humanitarian NGO interest was the discussion *Jus ad bellum*, criteria that render a war just. The Prussian military expert von Clausewitz argued that war was a natural process to resolve disputes and that under certain circumstances it was just or *Jus ad bellum*. However, since 1945 the UN Charter has reserved conflict to self-defense or as authorized by the UN Security Council. Once war breaks out, another concept known as *Jus in Bello* takes over. That concept deals with the morality of the conduct of the conflict and thus offers potential opportunities for addressing many aspects of humanitarianism.

Under the proportionality principle of *Jus in Bello*, it is reasonable to use proportional methods against armed combatants, and accidental damage to civil property is permissible, even inevitable. However, "unnecessary collateral damage to property" is illegal unless that property is a tool of war—such as dropping cluster bombs in neighborhoods or farms. NGOs should want to protect refugee camps, hospitals, farms, museums, etc. Unless the humanitarian asset in question is a "tool of war," intentional or reckless acts against the assets in conflict are also illegal. To make this theory work will mean testing proportionality in a high international court. It will be controversial, as there is a long history of armies moving through farms, but when the farm is the target and not incidental to the military operation, legal action might be worth examining. Especially regarding the protection of farms, this litigation could be used to defend the UN's core mission of reducing poverty and hunger but would also be useful for protecting a library, a statue, or other cultural artifact essential to preservation of culture. We are not saying such litigation would be easy, but even if the UN or other bodies do not protect certain assets for their intrinsic value,

[1] The League of Nations also had a sanctions regime under Article 16, but no power to enforce, since any member nation could veto direct action. There was also no Security Council.

making an argument to protect them under *Jus in Bello* has moral weight, especially for farms. After all, protecting farms can be logically connected to the principle that people have a right to food and a standard of care. While those rights are not well articulated in law, they must be considered relevant to negotiations, and a successful ligation using *Jus in Bello* could be precedence.

The 1954 Hague Convention for the Protection of Cultural Property in the Event of Armed Conflict (UNESCO 2010) covers "immovable and movable cultural heritage." The authors propose that it should also include zoos, museums, structures of cultural and historic importance, and farms which are central to jobs and food security.[2] This conversation also relates directly to the Rome Statue of the ICC used against Sudan's president in 2009, when he was indicted for crimes against humanity, in that the starvation of humans or destroying livelihoods (jobs) is illegal. Of interest to NGOs that focus on livestock and conservation, the concept of protecting livestock specifically came up in 1982 in the case of the relocation of Nicaraguan Miskito Indians and the destruction of their property and livestock by their Government, then trying to control counterrevolutionary activities. The Inter-American Commission on Human Rights required compensation for lost livestock.

These precedents should lay a legal foundation for cooperation between the traditional humanitarian, development, and agricultural NGO communities and by extension other areas of work that relate to humanitarianism like the protection of historic sites. This is especially true given the increasing recognition by humanitarian practitioners to include livelihood protection in emergency management, not just the protection of human lives The reason is simple. The inability of people to return to their lands and follow their previous lives fosters conflict and social upheaval (Feinstein International Center 2009). In contrast, failing to properly deal with this issue can cause tension and violence, as seen in the summer of 2005 in Uganda and Kenya when livestock received less and less water and food, due to a severe drought. The situation became so bad that on a Tuesday morning in 2005, Borana tribe raiders broke into a northern Kenya school in Turbi. Using machetes and AK-47 assault rifles, they slaughtered 22 children and 50 other villagers, all members of the rival Gabra tribe. This massacre resulted from ongoing rivalries worsened by drought-stricken livestock herds upon which both tribes depended. For five consecutive seasons prior to 2005, the winter rains all but vanished in much of East Africa, triggering violent competition for water, grazing land, and food. The extended drought resulted in a 50–80 % loss of livestock, mostly cattle, which meant that many rural families were below the minimum threshold to support life. Consequently, violent livestock raiding became a huge regional problem that extended to Sudan and Somalia (Lal 2006).

Related to this conversation is the concept of crimes against humanity, which is an area where NGOs have a long history in public diplomacy and bilateral/multilateral diplomacy, sometimes on their own and sometimes in partnership with

[2] We would not include farms used for illegal activities such as the growing of poppies, despite their import to the local economy.

governments. As an example, consider genocide. Unfortunately, many consider genocide an atrocity from history, something from the Nazi regime of Germany or the rule of Stalin in Russia rather than a crime of the present; that is not so. Go back to the Convention on the Prevention and Punishment of the Crime of Genocide and its origins (Cohen and Albright 2008). The treatment of Darfur by Sudan and the Nuba people of South Kordofan clearly qualify as genocide. One could also make the argument against Khadafi when describing how he treated dissidents or how Syria currently treats its people. Frequently it is the NGO community and the media that sees firsthand what atrocities take place on the ground, and if there is one community that needs to develop the art of diplomacy, it is the NGOs, in order to safely negotiate passage through rebel hands or access to trouble areas through government agencies.

## 7.2 At the Peace Table

Peace negotiations have ordinarily followed "Track One" diplomacy. Under that scenario, negotiations are conducted by the leaders of combatants and mediated by regional organizations or neutral governments. That began to change in the 1970s when "Track Two" and "Multitrack" diplomacy, emerged. Track Two is a term coined by a former US diplomat named Joseph Montville and a psychiatrist named William Davidson who wrote about the concept in Foreign *Policy* (Montville and Davidson 1981–1982, Winter). This track uses informal interactions between NGOs, universities, or religious bodies. This was also the approach taken by a group Roeder managed when designing a proposal for resolving the Palestine question, in their case engaging influential, pro-peace Palestinian-Americans to convince the PLO not to attack Israel and instead engage in mutually beneficial negotiations (Sizer et al. 1982).

Following the articulation of Montville's theory, Ambassador John W. McDonald expanded the concept and created a series of other tracks that eventually were combined into what is now commonly called Multitrack diplomacy, which involves everyone, governments, international organizations and NGOs, etc. (McDonald 1991).

McDonald's nine tracks are:

- Track 1—Government
- Track 2—Nongovernment/Professional
- Track 3—Business, or Peacemaking through Commerce
- Track 4—Private Citizen, or Peacemaking through Personal Involvement
- Track 5—Research, Training, and Education
- Track 6—Activism, or Peacemaking through Advocacy
- Track 7—Religion or Peacemaking through Faith in action
- Track 8—Funding, or Peacemaking through Providing Resources
- Track 9—Communications and the Media, or Peacemaking through Information

Despite the work of Montville and McDonald, NGOs are not often enough at the negotiating table, though it does happen in places like Liberia.[3] While there is no question that governments and international organizations have a special role in such negotiations and offer aspects of legitimacy to combatants that can't be provided by civil society such as membership in the UN, World Bank financing, and economically beneficial trade, NGOs should have a larger role. As noted in this book's Introduction, they saved millions of lives in Belgium and Russia during World War I when NGOs directly negotiated with governments, and their role was also essential in the development of current international instruments like the Convention on the Prohibition of the Use, Stockpiling, Production and Transfer of Anti-Personnel Land Mines and on Their Destruction, also known as the Mine Ban Treaty, or the Ottawa Convention. NGOs like Peace Action should be at the table with governments in crisis negotiations because they don't represent governments and thus are less apt to have hidden agendas. While international agreements are by their nature made by "states parties," NGOs can be a central and effective player in identifying acceptable political–military frameworks to which combatants or contesting powers might agree.

The goal of any negotiation, be it about sustainable development or peace, needs to be realistic and durable. NGOs increasingly have the expertise to help. A good example would be Gilgit Baltistan, where NGOs have been very effective. Most of the humanitarian work done in education and health has been done by NGOs. If the schools run by NGOs are excluded, then literacy rate will fall to almost nonexistent for females and less than 15 % for males. Any socioeconomic, cultural, and environmental development that has been done at a microlevel has had great contributions from NGOs. At some point, funds used by NGOs in Gilgit Baltistan were much higher than the government's annual budget (Sering 2012).

Another situation where NGOs could play a significant role in both public diplomacy and Track Two-type direct diplomacy would be the current conflict with Iran where a repressive theocratic regime is likely developing nuclear weapons and the parallel crisis in Syria where a repressive minority regime is trying to destroy a popular but disjointed intifada. Governments do what is in their own self-interest or at least what they perceive to be in their own self-interest, so it is entirely possible that Israel might attack Iran's nuclear sites. Israel is a tiny country and very vulnerable to conventional missiles, to say nothing of strategic ballistic nuclear devices. But if Israel attacked Iran, this could weaken Israel and strengthen Iran and Syria, as well as terrorist organizations in the Gaza, the West Bank, and Lebanon—whether or not the sites are successfully destroyed! The reasoning is that Iran's ally Syria has

[3] The Mano River Women's Peace Network (MARWOPENT) is an NGO formed by women of the Mano River region (Guinea, Sierra Leone, and Liberia) to promote their participation in peace processes in Africa and specifically in the Mano River region. MARWOPNET has participated in a variety of peace summits in the region and encouraged dialogue between combatants in Liberia by meeting with faction leaders during the war. It participated in the Liberian peace negotiations held in Ghana in the summer of 2003 and was a key signatory member of the Comprehensive Peace Agreement for Liberia.

a robust, well-disciplined tank force; lots of missiles; an air force supported by a massive air-defense system, as well as a large infantry. There are also Iranian naval vessels in Syrian waters. So it is entirely conceivable that soon after the Israeli attack, Syria might attack Israel to support their ally, assuming that the civil war doesn't overwhelm Damascus. Repressive regimes (or politicians) often attack external forces when they are threatened by internal politics, in order to coalesce the population. Similarly short-range missiles from Gaza and Southern Lebanon might start raining over Israeli villages. Western governments would get sucked in of course, and after the dust settled, two repressive regimes would possibly be on stronger domestic political ground and many Israelis will have died and probably some Americans. Hard-line political groups like Hamas also might be strengthened. The Security Council will probably be split, as usual. This is all conjecture of course; it is however a reasonable scenario. We need NGOs to help!

The authors propose that large NGOs like Peace Action and smaller indigenous NGOs in the Middle East craft a coordinated argument against war, an approach created using the Team technique in Chap. 1. On the one hand, as Montville envisaged, NGOs could be effective middlemen with governments, when politically neutral, though that's very dangerous in Syria and Iran, less so in Israel and neighboring Lebanon. And while a politically neutral NGO can be quite useful in many situations, there is also a need for more partisan NGOs that can speak directly to abuse, as many do. Either way, the approach should include a public diplomacy campaign using social media in order to build public support against war both inside and out of the combatant nations. Doing this might avoid much death and destruction. Not taking this coordinated approach may well cripple the intifada in Syria and the political opposition in Iran. In other words, they have to be part of the complex project. Those counter-repression forces for good are needed to prevail past the current crisis in order to achieve a long-term, practical peace in the region. A war definitely could harm their chances.

## 7.3 Neutrality and Working with or Avoiding the Military

Some NGOs refuse to work with the military, fearing loss of political neutrality. While neutrality might not be an issue in some disasters, especially related to natural phenomena, in politically charged crises, it is usually important to appear neutral when providing relief supplies. That said, unlike an operational NGO perhaps that is providing assistance to victims, an advocacy NGO may be on site to lobby for changes in welfare policies, to push for environmental policy changes, etc., and therefore may need to be a partisan. The thing to remember is that in a conflicted environment, neutrality can be protective, whereas partiality or bias can endanger. Plan this out in the study team.

Even a totally neutral operational NGO may find the military an essential partner. The military often provides hospital support in disasters (Haiti), transports food and supplies (Burma, *during Cyclone Nargis and Georgia in* 2008), and gets involved in rebuilding civil structures like schools. At the same time, there is a perception by some that military forces can pervert humanitarian assistance by using it selectively to achieve political objectives while ignoring the basic humanitarian principles of independence and impartiality.

NGOs need to also be aware that there are guidelines for Civil–Military operations which were designed by the UNOCHA, in cooperation with operational NGOs and relief agencies. Despite the operational advantages of military support, a basic principle of civil–military cooperation is to use military assets only as a last resort. Especially in response to a natural disaster, it is also best that such assets be used in support of local emergency management. They should also be need based, neutral, and impartial—the situation may be different in a conflict. In addition, military personnel assisting in such missions should be unarmed and in national uniform, as happened in Cyclone Nargis. The details of such guidelines are too lengthy for this handbook. They are based on suggestions by InterAction, the International Red Cross and Red Crescent Movement, and OCHA. NGOs should also contact those agencies for the latest thinking.

As already noted, US Department of Defense is increasingly involved in emergency management, and this has begun to worry many NGOs. As far back as 1995, the US Department of Defense paid for some of the expeditions into Sudan to explore using ReliefWeb as a nonmilitary humanitarian information tool.[4] Today, 25 % of US humanitarian and development expenditure is controlled by the military. There has been an incredible expansion of their role, and it goes beyond places where the USA is a belligerent. As the US Navy ads now say, the military is supposed to be "a global force for good" (Charny 2012). Keep in mind that the military, civilian peacekeepers, diplomats, and NGO officials are seen in crises all over the world, be it a conflict or destructive natural phenomena[5], and these players have very different characteristics. Their chains of command are different, as is their governance, jargon, and the communities they represent. It is also clear that as they are all going to meet in the same field, NGO diplomats need to understand the differences, so that, taking into account the NGO's mission, the team knows what to avoid or take advantage of.

Unfortunately, but reasonably, some leaders in the humanitarian NGO community have become increasingly concerned that Western militaries in particular are so heavily involved in relief and development that they might subsume civilian AID agencies like the European Community Humanitarian Office (ECHO), USAID, and the US Department of State's Refugee Bureau. Military engineers build civilian structures, sometimes alongside civilian contractors who might be considered

[4]Other expeditions in that time frame were funded by the US Department of State, Bureau of International Organization Affairs.

[5]The term *natural disaster* is often misused. It should refer to a natural phenomenon that overwhelms the capacity of person or society to cope. A hurricane however isn't always a disaster. It could bring rain that saves crops and cattle or drowns a city. Whether the strong winds or storm surge actually create a disaster is really all about preparedness and context.

legitimate targets of combat. This creates confusion between those military forces that fight on one day and build on another versus civilian relief bodies that protect the environment, cultural icons, refugees, or IDPs every day. What is the distinction between combatants and noncombatants? This is a really big issue for Canadian and American forces, as well as those of other nations, and should be as well for NGOs associated with those forces.

To an extent, some confusion is inevitable since military forces have stronger logistical support structures than does the civil sector, sometimes the only ships available for evacuations or sending supplies. There is no NGO with a USNS Comfort in its inventory,[6] a major life saver after the Haiti earthquake and other crises going back to 1990 (Webmaster). The plain fact is that in order to save lives, one uses what resources are available. During Cyclone Nargis, animal welfare NGOs flew supplies on US Air Force planes in the same cargo bay as traditional humanitarian goods; it saved money and sped relief that prevented starvation and protected the rural economy. Without the military, the NGOs would have had to pay for ships and that would have meant delays and fewer supplies. In Haiti, the largest relief body was the US Armed Forces. That kind of cooperation is perfectly appropriate; what about conflicts like Iraq and Afghanistan? It is usually appropriate to say thanks for help; unless neutrality isn't an issue to the NGO, it should avoid being so imbedded as to convey political sympathy with one side or the other. If not careful, the NGO could be designated a legitimate military target by one of the combatant sides. This is all about context of course, understanding on the hand that the more an NGO works with a military force, the harder it also is to prove neutrality, yet given the reality of war, cooperation can significantly reduce overhead, allowing funds that would have been used for trucks, ships, and planes to be used for the purchase of medicine, food, and other support items.

## 7.4 An International Army and Peacekeeping

NGOs are not going to form peacekeeping forces or international armies, but they could influence how they are formed and the future of peacekeeping operations. As an example, in 2008 a prominent American peace NGO (Citizens For Global Solutions[7]) advocated for the establishment of a permanent international peacekeeping force. Citizens call their idea the United Nations Emergency Peace Service

[6]Built as an oil tanker in 1976, the vessel is now a mobile field hospital ship used by the US Navy, often in response to natural disasters.

[7]With roots in the 1940s, by 1974, two major organizations, the Campaign for UN Reform (CUNR) and the World Federalist Association, both which have combated war, tyranny, and injustice and have strongly supported the UN, formed a united NGO called Citizens for Global Solutions, with HQ in Washington, D.C. It promotes its work through grassroots and government advocacy and education. public diplomacy is a key factor; and unlike most NGOs, it has a Political Action Committee (PAC) that supports political candidates.

(UNEPS) (CGS 2008). Citizens and other NGOs and private citizens in the past have suggested that if the United Nations had a permanent armed force, it could be quickly deployed to evacuate civilians from a conflict or even separate belligerents—perhaps even if the government of the land said no. Perhaps such a force could have saved lives in Rwanda or Syria, if it had appropriate resources and the right authority. Citizens are actually following in a long line of pacifist NGOs and those in governments, which for generations have looked for ways to end war, some by advancing the concept of arbitration, others through the use multilateral sanctions, and still others through a formal standing League of Nations or UN army. Would it ever work? Would it do the job or be misused? Those are central questions for an NGO study group to consider, and they are worth exploring in this book.

### 7.4.1 Operational Advantage

Prior to citizens, Australian Army Major A. W. Gunder (Gunder 1995) posited in 1995 that an international army would be advantageous because it could be quickly deployed to any trouble spot. More recently in cases like the Syrian crisis in 2011–2012, it has been suggested that an international force could provide cover for evacuating citizens. In addition, reflecting on genocides in Nazi Germany, in Darfur, former Yugoslavia, Pol Pot's Cambodia, and now in Syria, many people like the idea of using such a force to take collective action against regimes that commit crimes against humanity. In other words, instead of the United States and other great powers forming a coalition, let the UN do it for all of us. The counterargument however is that this places too much faith in the UN which is incapable of quick, decisive action. Even NATO is too slow at times. It has been argued, for example, that in the case of Rwanda, the United Nations officials in New York were too slow to respond to calls for international forces to intervene in the conflict or to allow the UN forces to defend the Tutsis.

During preliminary talks on the creation of a UN, Nationalist China actually proposed that the UN have its own air force (Group of Military Representatives to the Dumbarton Oaks Conference 1944, October 3). Their view was that Security Council planes could then be dispatched to immediately stem aggression, though probably they had Communist China in mind, which underlines the risk. One nation's rescue squad is another's invader. Instead of an air force, British and Americans at Dumbarton Oaks however said a better, less expensive operational model was for nations to possess designated contingents that could be called to duty by the Security Council. In other words, they did not disagree with the basic concept, just the methodology. Their model is used today. Nations like Fiji, Colombia, and others have long deployed designated contingents, which both raises revenue for them and bolsters standardization of operations. Keep in mind however that the forces can always be withdrawn. While they will report to a General from another nation, governments always retain the right to instruct their "international forces" to ignore orders and act under "national instructions."

Others agreed with the Chinese, perhaps reflecting the politics that emerged from the emotions of surviving a global conflict. Supreme Court Justice Owens Roberts, speaking before the American Bar Association, felt there had to be a strong police force to support the UN (Oaks 1943, p. 10). Further illustrating the political environment of the time, in the United States Senate, the Ball–Burton–Hatch–Hill bipartisan resolution[8] (S.Res.114) emerged, which provided for "the assembly and maintenance of a United Nations military force to suppress military aggression (Oaks 1943, p. 11). One imagines they had a future Japan or Germany in mind." But who decides what aggression is? Who gets to deploy the force? Could it be used against a nation which had taken a preemptive strike to prevent aggression, thus undermining the concept of sovereignty (Chap. 1.2) or the right of self-defense? This is, however, not a political position that would survive in the Senate in 2012; the overall question is very relevant when considering the potential threat of long-range missiles and nuclear weapons in Iran. A policy of force is two edged.

When trying to negotiate a concept in the present, it is always useful to know if someone tried to negotiate it in the past. Following World War I, Léon Victor Auguste Bourgeois[9] proposed that the League of Nations have an army, but his idea wasn't to deploy the force to trouble spots around the world. He wanted to protect France from a future armed Germany (Walters 1952 (reprint 1965), p. 61), though they did not insist on the idea. The French also considered asking American troops to defend the French border, a precursor to today's UN peacekeeping forces and the MFO,[10] which separates Egypt and Israel (Bartlett 1944, p. 118). Disarmament has long been considered one of the best ways of preventing war. But during the disarmament talks of 1931, worried about future German aggression, France would not consider reductions in her own naval and land forces without the establishment of an international force under control of the League of Nations. If the French actually wanted a force, they should have insisted on it in Paris; it was too late later, for example, in 1932 when they proposed that all nations set aside their biggest weapons, bombers, battleships, heavy guns, etc., to be placed at the disposal of the League, along with a standing international police force and earmarked national forces to be called up on need to reinforce the police (Walters 1952 (reprint 1965), pp. 444, 502–504).

---

[8] The sponsors were Joseph Ball (R-Minnesota), Harold Burton (R-Ohio), Carl Hatch (D-New Mexico), and Lister Hill (D-Alabama). The conservatives in the Senate were very worried about becoming entangled in wars they had no interest in, similar to the conservatives in Wilson's Senate a generation before. These conservatives were led by Republican Senator Robert Taft, son of former President and Chief Justice William Howard Taft. Similar bills today in any government would also have to be negotiated between competing political parties and philosophies within the parties.

[9] A one-time French prime minister, he was a strong advocate for the League of Nations as the protector of peace. He called for compulsory arbitration, disarmament, economic sanctions, and an international military force.

[10] The MFO or Multinational Forces and Observers is not a UN peacekeeping force. It is its own international organization.

The French were reacting to the pain they received in a global war, just as were others at Dumbarton Oaks a generation later; even before the advent of World War I, as far back as 1914, the directors of the NGO *New York Peace Society* considered the idea of an international force when they formed a study group called the Plan of Action Committee, which had the express purpose of examining how an international police force might be formed as part of a League of Peace. The Plan of Action Committee met promptly and recommended that a conference of neutral powers be convened and a movement formed to induce belligerents to attend. While consideration of an international police force did continue,[11] the specific idea of a neutrals conference died because the participants reported to the Executive Committee (the decision maker) that due to real-world events, such a conference wasn't a practical idea for the times. That is precisely what study groups need to do, recommend if an idea is practical or not and, only if practical, move forward (Bartlett 1944, p. 31). However, the efforts did have a positive effect; it led to the formation of the NGO called the League to Enforce Peace (LEP), which became one of the two biggest NGO champions of the League of Nations concept, the other being the British League of Nations Society. The LEP, which was led by former President Taft, wrote directly to President Wilson on February 8, 1919 on the subject, pushing hard for a League of Nations, with at least military sanctions.[12]

### 7.4.2 *The Saarland and the First Multilateral Force*

To settle a crisis in the Saarland, the League of Nations deployed the first international force under the aegis of an international organization.[13] By way of background, the Versailles Treaty imposed huge economic sanctions on Germany, forcing the country to pay reparations, which included losing the Saarland area of the Rhineland. This property was governed by a League commission for 15 years, enabling France to use proceeds from coal sales to pay off reparations. The Nazis eventually came to power and then the Mandate became a sanctuary for anti-Nazi Germans. Of interest to today's NGOs wanting to observe elections, the League then decided on a plebiscite in the Saarland to take place on January 13, 1935.

---

[11] Theodore Marburg, a Baltimore-based peace activist, felt that a voluntary international court could not induce peace, so it would be necessary to form an international police force or standing army of the League of Nations (Bartlett 1944, p. 36).

[12] Similar NGOs existed elsewhere, the Swiss National Association for the League of Nations, the German Liga fur Volkerbund (discussed on Chap. 19), British League of Nations Union, Canadian League of Nations Society, as well as bodies in France and the neutrals. One of the authors, Mr. Roeder, is proposing to do a separate study on this entire group of NGOs as part of a book on the history of Peace NGOs.

[13] See also the Leticia incident between Colombia and Peru in 1932, mediated by the League and the Straits Commission, 1924–1936.

That way, the citizens could democratically decide their own fate, stay in the League, rejoin Germany, or join France. There was general animosity against France, and the Catholic Church was in favor of Germany, important given the large Catholic population. However, joining Nazi Germany was a different thing than the Weimar regime, so it was distinctly possible that the largely German population might vote to stay in the League. To combat that, Joseph Goebbels organized a reunification campaign which created awful conditions for Jews in the Mandate. Disorder occurred, threatening the legitimacy of the plebiscite. Complicating matters, Germany withdrew from the League in the winter of 1933–1934.

The situation eventually became so grave that the British commissioner for the Saar threatened to call in French troops to maintain order, and France indicated they would heed the call. That one unilateral action, designed to protect the peace, could have produced a flashpoint for war. Germany called the move illegal, and Britain was not willing to support such a force unless a coalition participated and unless Germany agreed. Italy, Denmark, and the Netherlands agreed to join the mostly British force, and then Hitler supported the initiative. The force of about 3,000 troops from Britain, Italy, the Netherlands, and Sweden moved into the Saarland just before Christmas, 1934. They supervised the vote on January 14 counted by 300 neutral tellers (Brind 1935, October 26).[14] The result was to rejoin Germany, a position accepted quickly by the French government.

### 7.4.3 *Misuse of a Force*

As seen from the Saarland example, an international police or army could have operational value and there have been many examples of temporary UN forces through the years. But could a permanent force, even if valuable, be misused? The German legal scholar Lass Oppenheim, who some see as the father of modern international law, examined this very question, asking *Quis custodiet ipsos custodies*? Translated liberally, this meant who will keep in order those who are to keep the world in order (Oppenheim 1919, pp. 46–47)? It was a fair question and timely then, as the League hadn't yet become a reality. Conservative political elements in the United States today often complain that a UN army could subvert national sovereignty. Like the French before at the Paris Peace Conference of 1919, Mr. George Nicoll Barnes, a Labor Party member of the British delegation, worried that an aggressor country could move quickly, so he wanted provision for a permanent international force "ready to strike against an aggressive state (Department of State 1942a, p. 226)"; however, a typical rejoinder was made by Wisconsin State Senator Herman C. Schultz who said it was illogical that armies could enforce peace.

[14] Readers are encouraged to read the report (unpublished) in the League of Nations Archives in Geneva because it was influential on the use of future UN forces and on the observation of plebiscites.

He was also of the opinion that a League army would become the tool of foreign dictators (Schultz 1919), the same fear offered by Oppenheim.

Theodore Roosevelt also proposed a similar idea in his Nobel Prize Lecture (Roosevelt 1910); he wasn't about neutrality. Roosevelt was worried about communists and saw the United States as the central force in such a police, which meant that such a force would not have been impartial. By 1950, some journalists also saw the idea of a permanent UN force in terms as a counterweight to world domination by the Soviet Union or as one put it, a force of 50,000–100,000 that could put out the small fires of the Cold War; no such force would be put into action without authorization of the UN Security Council (Gannett Editorial 1950). Once again, they risked doing what Oppenheim feared, creating a tool for international despots.

The framers of the United Nations also worried about abuse, which they addressed in the UN charter, which does give the Security Council the power and the responsibility to take *collective action* to maintain international peace and security. But neither the League before it nor the UN today have ever had the authority "to force governments to form armies." Any UN armies are voluntary and, even when they operate under a UN mandate, retain their national link, meaning the country of origin can take them back when needed. NATO also does peacekeeping, and there is an independent peacekeeping force in Egypt and Israel called the Multinational Forces and Observers under its own non-UN international organization, in which Roeder served as a civilian observer. In each case, NATO, the UN, and the MFO, while the international organization has operational control over the collective force, the armed forces follow national command instructions. In other words, none of the international organizations has its own permanent army; what if they did? In theory, the entire Security Council might form a force to invade a country like Syria (unlikely, due to the veto); just because a war is declared doesn't mean people need come. It is also doubtful that NATO would engage except to arm rebels. Again; governments can't be forced to participate. Taking these ideas into account, in 1948 then Secretary General Trygve Lie posited that it was a political impossibility. It might still be. Of course, he had also proposed creating a small, dedicated "United Nations Legion."

### 7.4.4 *The Veto as a Positive Tool*

It is interesting in this discussion to consider the veto itself. In the League, any member could veto action; in the UN, only the permanent five (Russia, USA, UK, France, and China) can veto in the Security Council, though since decisions are made by consensus, there is in effect a kind of veto held by all nations in the General Assembly of the UN. How did the formal veto process come to pass? At Dumbarton Oaks, this topic was considered one of the most important before the negotiators. The British felt that parties to a dispute not be allowed to vote, but it was understood as well that the principal states would withdraw if a decision went against them and the United States Senate would oppose provisions permitting the Security Council to vote against the United States. Despite the fact that protocol would prevent the council from dealing with crises to which the permanent members were party, most other disputes could be handled, and it was felt that if a dispute involving one of the principles could not be handled in the UN, a coalition of powers outside the organization could deal with it, perhaps NATO (American Group at Dubarton Oaks 1944, August 10). This, what otherwise might appear to be an arcane discussion, is relevant in 2012. Russia may be arming the Government of Syria and the United States and others may be providing arms and nonlethal support to rebel forces. In June, 2012 the Syrian government shot down a Turkish warplane off their coast. Were such acts to continue, under Article 5 of the NATO charter, Turkey might ask fellow members of NATO to go to their defense, which would mean potentially that US, British, and French forces might find themselves in combat with Russian forces—clearly a matter for the Security Council; any permanent five could veto the proposals of others. What happens?

### 7.4.5 Conclusions

A small specially trained, permanent international police force or army might be of operational value to protect refugees and evacuees, if authorized by the Security Council; less certain is the viability of a permanent ***army or air force***. Like Franklin Roosevelt, who considered this idea for the UN, our view is that armed forces should be under national authority, lest some future UN abuse them; in other words, Oppenheim had a legitimate worry. But this then is why the topic is raised in the book. It is exactly the kind of important debate where NGOs like Citizens and others could provide intelligent input and advocacy, and perhaps, given the special political crises of this age, propose a new model which would be accepted by the UN. Today over 54 NGOs are on record in support of Citizen's idea, including the National Association for the Advancement of Colored People (NAACP), Human Rights Watch, and the Presbyterian Church (USA) (Valkarie 2011).

The concept of a permanent police or military force does raise important sovereignty issues: What about the people? What about their sovereignty? Will they lose their rights through abuse of such a tool? Could a small legion complement, not replace existing peace operations, be deployed immediately, and not have to wait for lengthy Security Council debate? We are doubtful that the permanent five members of the Security Council would agree. In addition, some pacifists would also not want an international standing army that could strike immediately before proper analysis takes place. The plan as envisaged by a study group created in 2003 by GlobalSolutions however would have appropriate rules set up to make a volunteer-based force work well, protecting people. For one thing, it could not be deployed without a mandate from the Security Council. Practical uses are obvious, perhaps to create a humanitarian corridor for civilians in conflicts like Syria or to protect villages that have been decimated in parts of Sudan. However, for this to happen, much public diplomacy will be required by NGOs if civil populations are to support the concept and lobby their governments to agree. And nothing will happen unless the permanent five nations of the Security Council agree, since any one of them can veto any action.

## 7.5 Working with Armed Non-State Actors (ANSAs)

The chapter has discussed working with military forces and using diplomatic coercion, as well as the activities of unarmed direct-action NGOs like Sea Shepherd, but not armed non-state actors. In some cases, to enter a crisis zone, travel documents must be obtained from rebel forces.[15] Is it appropriate to deal with them or any armed non-state actor (ANSA)? This is one of the most important areas of work for NGOs in the twenty-first century and an essential activity to reduce violence to civilians, e.g., *al-Shabaab in Somaliland,* if only to permit the passage of medical and food supplies to unarmed civilians. It is of course also an area in which the international Red Cross movement has worked since the nineteenth century (Fig. 7.1).

> *at least half the belligerents in the most widespread and most victimizing of armed conflicts around the world, i.e. non-international armed conflicts, are non-state armed groups. (Bellal and Casey-Maslen, Rules of Engagement 2011)*

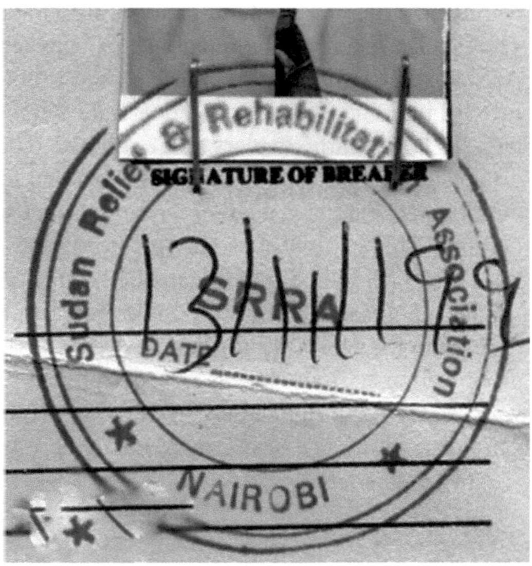


**Fig. 7.1** South Sudan Travel Pass © LRoeder 2012

[15]Figure 10 is a1994 travel document of the Sudan Relief and Rehabilitation Association (SRRA), the humanitarian agency of the Sudan People's Liberation Movement (SPLM). (Courtesy, LRoeder)

Geneva Call, a prestigious NGO in Switzerland, helped with this section. They primarily focus on armed entities that operate outside state control and that are motivated by political goals. That definition would exclude armed groups with a strictly criminal motivation like the mafia and drug cartels or others strictly or loosely to a state apparatus such as mercenaries or private security companies. This book interprets the Taliban as an armed non-state player, but are they also a terrorist organization[16]? What about Al-Qaeda, which every government sees as criminal and terrorist? In some situations, Geneva Call has discovered that it is difficult to distinguish between a state-controlled paramilitary force and an autonomous pro-government group. Where collusion exists, Geneva Call believes that the state should be held accountable for the actions of these de facto state agents. "The conduct of a person or group of persons shall be considered an act of a state under international law if the person or group of persons is in fact acting […] under the direction or control of that state in carrying out the conduct.[17]"

Prior to South Sudan gaining independence, an armed insurgency controlled the land; they were also a non-state actor that issued entry permits, like any government. Sudan called them terrorists. Many in the international community called them freedom fighters. In Darfur, violent armed groups also appear to be working under the control of the national authority. In Afghanistan, an insurgency emerged against the government elected in 2002. That insurgency is collectively called by the UN Assistance Mission in Afghanistan (UNAMA) "anti-government elements." It includes individuals and armed groups of diverse backgrounds, motivations, and command structures, including the Taliban, the Haqqani, Hezb-e-Islami, and others. The precise nature of the relationships between the different armed groups within Afghanistan and in neighboring Pakistan is not known (Bellal et al. 2011, March). In 2012 in South Sudan, armed non-state actors might simply be rival tribesmen. In late 2011 and early January 2012, around 6,000 fighters of the Lou Nuer ethnic group attacked the remote towns of Pibor and Likuangole and numerous villages in the troubled Jonglei state after days of clashes with the rival Murle tribe over cattle rustling. This caused over tens of thousands to leave the Pibor region (MN/HN 2012) (UN Mission South Sudan 2012, January 19).

Our point is that there is no single, universally accepted definition of armed non-state actors, ANSAs. Some describe them as "terrorists" or "bandits," while the groups often self-describe as "freedom fighters," "liberation movements," or tribal warriors trying to right a perceived wrong. Humanitarian and human rights organizations tend to use less controversial terms such as "armed group," "armed

[16]Though the Taliban has committed acts of terrorism by most definitions, such as the attempted assassination of Malala Yousafzai in Pakistan in 2012, the organization is also part of the complex negotiations aimed at peace in Afghanistan.

[17]When mercenaries or security companies operate under a Letter of Marque or by contract with a government agency, the government should be responsible for their activities.

opposition group," or "armed non-state actors.[18]" What these terms have in common is a neutral terminology that captures the idea that the groups use armed means to achieve their goals and do not operate within formal state structures, though there is some debate over whether all groups challenging the state's monopoly of violence should be included, regardless their objectives, level of organization, and degree of independence from states (Decrey-Warner 2012).

There will be many times when in order to reduce violence, to evacuate people, or to provide essential services such as education and health care some kind of specific agreement with an armed non-state actor will be required. In addition, such groups need to be aware of international norms. Indeed, one useful point of persuasion is to explain that if the group wants international recognition, it will need to comply with international norms such as the treatment of prisoners, even though the group isn't a signatory to a treaty, a tactic Mr. Roeder used when working with rebel elements in Sudan in the 1990s and which Human Rights Watch (HRW) used more recently with peaceful protestors in February 2011 and with rebel forces. In addition, in September 2011, Amnesty International warned the National Transitional Council (NTC) to cease reprisal attacks and arbitrary arrests (Bellal and and Casey-Maslen, *Rules of Engagement* 2011). Roeder was in Sudan either on diplomatic missions for the US government or the UN and did not have authorization to gain rebel signatures on a written agreement akin to a deed of commitment; which he lamented. The reason was simple. That would have a level of official recognition beyond what either the US government or the UN was capable at that time; NGOs like Geneva Call could do this, negotiate such deeds of commitment and then publish them in Geneva much like the UN publishes state-to-state agreements.

Be careful however that government partners don't consider such "collaboration" a crime. Any cooperation with groups designated a Terrorist is a crime in many countries, even just sharing information on international law; if such discussions are to take place, the NGO or coalition would be well advised to first consult with an attorney and perhaps arrange for separate agreements with state actors. That could avoid difficulties downstream. Assuming that the conversation is to move forward, also keep in mind that because an ANSA is not normally recognized as a combatant under international humanitarian law and so faces prosecution for having taken up arms under the national law of the state that captures him or her. Use of the Chatham House Rule may help; this will require considerable trust and as already stated may not may immune from national prosecution the NGO mediator.

---

[18]In a study for the ICRC, the authors used the following working definition of an armed non-state actor: "any armed group, distinct from and not operating under the control of, the state or states in which it carries out military operations, and which has political, religious, and/or military objectives. Thus, it does not ordinarily cover private military companies or criminal gangs, although a study by the US Senate Armed Services Committee 'uncovered evidence of private security contractors funneling U.S. taxpayers' dollars to Afghan warlords and strongmen linked to murder, kidnapping, bribery as well as Taliban and other anti-Coalition activities'. See Committee on Armed Services, 'Inquiry into the role and oversight of private security contractors in Afghanistan', Report together with additional views, US Senate, 28 September 2010" (Bellal et al. 2011, March).

The Geneva Call approach is unique and useful, as it attempts to convince armed bands to adhere to international norms by having a representative sign a covenant to do so. However, when negotiating with rebels, they might point out that because they are not representative of a state, certainly not one signatory to any convention, they are not liable to the international community. The authors disagree. As a result of the evolution of conflicts in the late twentieth and early twenty-first century, the understanding of the applicability of law has also evolved, to include those under a "responsible command." Armed non-state actors are covered when their actions constitute atrocities, referring as precedence to the "Martens Clause" of the Hague Conventions of 1907 which aimed to protect basic principles of humanity and conscience (Ticehurst 1997). Also as precedent, consider the UN Security Council, which under International Humanitarian Law, established ad hoc tribunals for Yugoslavia and Rwanda and referred cases to the International Criminal Court, which investigates crimes against humanity.

# Chapter 8
# Failed and Weak Nation-States

**Extract** This chapter examines the phenomenon of failed and weak nation-states and why NGOs need to take a more prominent role in negotiations, leading to sustainable economic and political structures. A comprehensive analysis of the macro/microeconomic factors would be a book in itself, a project which is being considered. There is no specific recipe for success or reconstruction; for any NGO to be able to do this will require coalitions and a study group described in Chap. 1, as well as access to seasoned economists and experts in econometrics, as sociologists and area specialists.

## 8.1 Introduction

What is meant by failed and weak nation-states[1]? Some countries function in a weakened state because of factors such as a lack of water or encroaching desertification. They also might not have manufactured products, raw materials, or agricultural goods to export in order to generate income for services. Tribal enmity, greed, or despotic regimes also produce weak states. The economic and social tensions inherent in weak societies often reach a breaking point that leads to armed conflict, further diminishing infrastructure like roads, hospitals, and schools. That will lead to further economic disparities, more corruption, social injustice, and a decline in taxable income. That leads to a government that is unable to pay for services, which in turn can lead to a

[1] A state is a political and geographic entity, e.g., the Vatican or the United States. A nation is a cultural or ethnic entity, e.g., the Kurdish nation. A nation-state exists when the two concepts coexist. However, the terms are often mixed up in popular language. We have made an effort in this chapter to distinguish between the two, but not elsewhere.

L.W. Roeder, Jr. and A. Simard, *Diplomacy and Negotiation for Humanitarian NGOs*, Humanitarian Solutions in the 21st Century, DOI 10.1007/978-1-4614-7113-4_8,

humanitarian catastrophe as internally displaced people or economic migrants cross the border. As seen in the former Republic of Yugoslavia, ethnic cleansing may increase, and as seen in 2012 Syria the rulers will become despotic in order to maintain order. Cuba is also a weak country, as is Burma and Byelorussia, and as Cambodia was under Pol Pot. All were or are functional or, to one degree or another, weak. North Korea fits this definition. Freedom is almost always curtailed to some extent. Egypt is uncertain, as it rises from the political ashes of revolution.

Failed states go another rung down the political ladder. There might be no government or just a hollow shadow that barely controls the capital. Warlords and armed non-state actors rule (see Sect. 7.5) when the population becomes radicalized and the government fails to perform its basic tasks, such as self-defense. Rulers tend to be autocratic and ignore democracy. Judiciaries tend to do the biding of the executive, and the bureaucracy only serves the executive, not the citizens. Infrastructure tends to fail, including hospitals, telecommunications, transportation, water storage, power, and schools. Disease spreads. The poor become poorer or, as in Puntland, turn to piracy and organized crime.

NGOs can help an emerging nation turn from failed or weak to a strong, functioning entity, yet the needs are often vast. Part of the solution must be to enhance the capacity of the government to provide essential services in a fair manner. Central ministries must begin to function; so in the new Republic of South Sudan, this means in addition to the people inside its borders, the government may need help receiving requests in the capital of Sudan, proper for certificates of nationality. Once these people repatriate to the south, they will need jobs, so one of the first efforts of the new government must be to build a viable economy. This chapter suggests NGO-led diplomacy could help, not only because of the expertise they often bring but, quite simply, they don't represent governments, and thus are less apt to have hidden agendas, nor as many competing agendas. But to do that requires a strategic plan and partners.

The model for initiating diplomatic action in Chap. 1 proposes that before deciding to engage any major effort, NGOs should form a Study Team and take into account the knowledge management and risk reduction concepts in Chaps. 2 and 3. When doing that, NGOs should consider if they can play a role in Failed/Weak Nation-states, especially in the economic sector, meaning more than simply being conduits of foreign aid from wealthy donors like USAID and ECHO, aid that maintains a basic living, basic survival. NGOs, regardless of their specific field, could make revitalization of the society the heart of a strategic effort in a way that fits cultural norms. Economics has often been the cause of conflict and social instability, and it will also be at the base of any long-lasting solution to development; indeed the failure of the League of Nations to effectively deal with economic matters led to issues that underpinned the World War II. The authors suggest stable, socially responsive states are essential to a peaceful, global political/economic structure, states founded on building sustainable markets for local products and local jobs. The formula for success must link market statistics and normative politics, articulating the will of the people through an agreement between the governing body and the citizens, as well as international donors, and, thirdly, the ability to meet expectations. This is so-called modern "Nation Building,[2]" the struggle to achieve the

Millennium Development Goals (MDG) that has been set by the international community. So whether an NGO is engaged in protecting livestock, reducing violence, or advancing gender equity, how does its mandate fit into the larger skhēma? Can it work through a coalition of NGOs (local and international) and directly negotiate with governments for positive change, not just lobby? Coalitions bring strength of numbers and knit what otherwise will be a disparate set of interests into a single development fabric. They can also bring enough political capital to allow an NGO to be accepted at the negotiating table.

Don't underestimate the importance of the UN system of agencies, bilateral aid agencies, and international financial institutions (IFIs); NGOS can also be in nation-building! In 2006, in their Program of Action for the Least Developed Countries for the Decade 2001–2010, the Interparliamentary Union (IPU) highlighted the role of NGOs in helping LDC parliamentarians to properly represent the will of the people. The IPU also suggested that governments enhance dialogue with civil society by regularly meeting NGOS recognizing NGOs (IPU 2006). In 2010, the Intergovernmental Authority on Development (IGAD) of the IPU also said "Non-Governmental Organizations (NGOs) are serving as "valuable and cost-effective intermediaries between central agencies and community groups," and "The self-organized efforts of NGOs ... to improve the situation of the people, promote their interests and defend their rights, are a vital element in the Region's economic and social progress (IGAD, N/A)."

As noted by Victor Comras, NGOs are increasingly becoming involved in the legislative aspects of nation-building, influencing laws, regulations, and the constitutional process in major states like Canada and in less developed states. They also provide technical assistance, macro- and microeconomic training for government officials and the private sector alike, which Roeder saw as far ago as 1991 when he was stationed in Albania as an international commodities economist developing a national development plan.[3] One could imagine a development NGO like Heifer doing this where livestock is essential to the export market as well as food security. Such markets often use child labor, so a coalition might also have as members NGOs that protect that sector. Sometimes there is also no national Veterinary service, or only an ineffective one, so in such a hypothetical nation, a development NGO

[2]Although nation-building is a common term, it is better to refer to state-building, given the different definitions of state and nation; however, we have retained the term nation-building in this book due to popular usage.

[3]NGOs quickly sprouted up in the United States to help the Albanians as they transitioned from a communist to a democratic society. Partners for democratic change, founded in 1989, started their work in 1991 and today it is represented by a local version Qëndra për Ndryshim dhe Manaxhim Konflikti (QNMK). Also in Albania at the time, there was NDI (National Democratic Institute), a nonprofit, nonpartisan, nongovernmental organization that supports democratic institutions and practices in every region of the world. In addition, IRI (International Republican Institute) was there, a nonprofit, nonpartisan organization that in its own words advances freedom and democracy worldwide and the rule of law.

wanting to improve farms might form a study group with expertise in local culture, child labor, local jurisprudence, and appreciation for the intersection of religion and law. Heifer is a very large NGO which might not need a coalition; a small NGO probably would use a coalition to staff the study group and the delegation.

An economist in a developing country when looking at the overall economy, and using a simple econometric formula, might argue that child labor keeps overhead down and profits up; the UN is trying to end child labor, so in addition to lobbying for things like a national veterinary service in order to increase the quality of meat for exports and domestic food, the coalition might engage in public diplomacy to change the attitude of the public of acceptable norms. That could encourage the public to ask its government to invest in education, keeping children out of pastures. Having a coalition doing this will be more effective than just one.

While not advocating that NGOs use threats in negotiations except as a last resort, if the new government feels it needs foreign buyers to purchase its livestock, it may listen to coercive tactics if the NGO coalition can convincingly show that a continuation of abuse child labor conditions might lead to few buyers, especially if the goals of the government don't comport with the MDG or Millennium Development Goals, which are:

- Eradicating extreme poverty and hunger
- Achieving universal primary education
- Promoting gender equality and empowering women
- Reducing child mortality rates
- Improving maternal health
- Combating HIV/AIDS, malaria, and other diseases
- Ensuring environmental sustainability
- Developing a global partnership for development

The authors suggest any strategy linking a coalition must support the MDGs, which represent an agreement on goals among 193 UN Members States and over 23 international organizations to achieve by 2015. With origins in OECD (the Organization of Economic Cooperation and Development), the World Bank, and the IMF (International Monetary Fund), the MDG came about through the Millennium Summit which crafted the Millennium Declaration in the year 2000. Unfortunately, while some nations have met their goals, many have not. There is a high degree of poverty in the world, and all of the other problems exist to some degree. Probably over 40 nations are failing and NGOs are not often enough at the negotiating table; though it does happen in places like Liberia[4] and in Southern Sudan, where the National Democratic Institute over many years in partnership with USAID has

[4]The Mano River Women's Peace Network (MARWOPENT) is an NGO formed by women of the Mano River region (Guinea, Sierra Leone, and Liberia) to promote their participation in peace processes in Africa, and specifically in the Mano River region. MARWOPNET has participated in a variety of peace summits in the region and encouraged dialogue between combatants in Liberia by meeting with faction leaders during the war. It participated in the Liberian peace negotiations held in Ghana in the summer of 2003 and was a key signatory member of the Comprehensive Peace Agreement for Liberia.

conducted studies that provided the only reliable public information available on Southern Sudanese attitudes about the self-determination, in other words the basis for fostering normative policy making in a new country (USAID 2012a).

While there is no question that governments and international organizations have a special role on multilateral negotiations and have aspects of legitimacy not held by NGOs such as membership in the UN, as well as relatively vast resources, NGOs should take an even larger role than they now possess. In the discussion of Herbert Hoover in the Introduction and Chap. 12, the potential for NGOs directly working with governments was shown by Hoover's effort to save millions of lives in Belgium and Russia during World War I, and their role was also essential to the development of international instruments like the Tampere Convention in the 1990s and the demining Convention.[5] Industry and commerce also have a role to play, because of their financial resources and networking. Indeed, one of the first NGOs accepted by the UN was the Chamber of Commerce.

### *8.1.1 Coalition Building with Local NGOs*

Garnering local knowledge is essential before engaging in any activity in a failed nation-state; one of the issues to be examined by the study group is who are the local NGOs and what is their political orientation? Are their objectives compatible? Do they have the resources or credibility? As an example, in Belarus in 2009, the Polish minority came under stress to the point that the government of Poland directly complained to the government of Belarus. Many NGOs were supportive of the regime and many were supportive of Polish interests. This book takes no sides; this kind of divide will be common, so a careful study should take place before contact. Regardless of the quality of your NGO's ideas, the decision to partner with a local NGO will likely bring both allies and antagonists. To be effective, true intelligence is needed, as defined in Chap. 3.

## 8.2 A Common Political and Economic Vision

Econometrics will have to be part of the discussion for a study group to create a baseline upon which to make economic development recommendations in the decision memo.[6] From its Greek origins, the term means economic measurement; econometrics is a fairly new term,[7] even if modeling isn't, and important when studying failing states,

[5] **Convention** on the Prohibition of the Use, Stockpiling, Production, and Transfer of Anti-Personnel Land Mines and on Their Destruction.

[6] A decision memo is the instrument used by an NGO's CEO to decide action, having examined the proposals made by the study group.

[7] While Ragnar Frisch probably invented the term, it was not in common usage until the 1960s.

which are increasingly popping up. As an example, no country is totally self-sufficient in all raw materials, so in order for the United States to build certain high-speed military aircraft, it needs to import platinum. Another example is tantalum, which is used in capacitors and extracted from columbite–tantalite in conflict areas of Africa.

Understanding a nation's strategic needs and shortages is very helpful when considering how to build trade, especially since even if a mineral exists in large measure, the economic advantage is only a potential if no one is buying; so a good starting point is to ask about the balance of trade as well as the GDP or gross national product, in other words for the later, the national output of goods and services as compared to the neighbors and traditional trading partners[8]. However, while questions on trade can highlight weaknesses and strengths and the GDP gross figure might show great disparities between nations, it is not the whole story. Also needed to know is the GDP per capita, but even that isn't enough since it won't show the economic benefits gained by individuals, nor disparities based on class, political party, etc., which are also essential factors in any failed state with major economic disparities between classes, regions, and tribes. What is the per capita income and why? How does the mission of the NGO or its coalition fit into that?

**Normative Politics** NGOs will be particularly useful ferreting out the perceptions of the local culture; the indigenous should have the same rights as anyone else, but their perceptions of procurement and consumption, which are cultural, will be different than urban dwellers. The latter will buy food in a grocery store and the former perhaps will hunt, fish, and gather. Ethnic groups, religion-based communities, and the indigenous may focus less on the math of modern economics than to protect languages and identity, as with the First Nations of Canada and in the United States with Native Americans and Native Alaskans—in any country with indigenous peoples. So while econometrics is a discipline which, through mathematics, measurements and detailed analysis can establish useful models that link the complexities of a nation's economy as a whole and then forecast the future, and while NGOs involved in advancing sustainable development will need to be tap into that knowledge base, math is not enough to tell the entire story or predict politics. Most international policy makers agree that there is a right to food, for example; they would then look at a failed nation in terms of hunger statistics, malnutrition, etc.; that might miss the indigenous' perception of normative politics. This is where an NGO initiative could fit in, to negotiate for cultural sensitivity in decision making by aid suppliers. It isn't that the models are not useful. They are a crucial risk analysis tool; but no model is perfect, a point with which econometricians agree. Math is also not politics. While the experts from the World Bank and other financial institutions push useful econometric-based predictions and advice in order to build jobs and income, NGOs, especially community-based NGO, must demand full implementation of the right to food, and that may create a political conflict. The landless will want access to land. The indigenous will want to protect traditional land titles. Indigenous fisher

[8] The UN Statistical Yearbook may be a good source.

folk will fight against industrial fishing which raises national income but can destroy local culture. If the NGOs can both understand the underlying basis of the economy and the people's political and cultural desires, they can add balance to the equation, decisively help the local players, and propose language and concepts for inclusion in constitutions and ministry mandates that make sense. That is their true role.

So, the conclusion is that while the government must have accurate facts and draw on science-based analysis, it must also take into account the people's will. This doesn't mean econometrics and politics should be countervailing forces however; the point of life is to pursue one's own rational self-interest, and rationality requires facts. If the policies of a new administration are rational, not simply greed driven, that leads to a morality that respects the rights of others, and if a society can be allowed to move in that direction on its own, then the state can do the same, pursue economic, political, and security policies that are rational and peaceful. Of course, this requires perception, which will be tempered by prejudice and tradition; so NGOs involved in advancing a failed nation-state must also advocate for (which is very hard) education, forgiveness of past sins (as is happening in Rwanda), and intellectual freedom, the kind that comes from the people's will expressed through a democracy respecting all rights, not only of the majority, not of course should it go to the extremes of philosophers like Ayn Rand.

Since the people's will is important, the next question usually asked when a failed state like East Timor, Albania, Somalia, or Libya moves to a new period is what form will the fresh government take, e.g., Somaliland, which is gaining increasing international support? The trouble is that often places the cart before the horse. The American Architect Louis Sullivan once said, form follows function. The same is true about national economic reconstruction. The decision on a precise new governmental structure in a failed state is less urgent than identifying societal priorities and identifying required structures and resources to achieve them. An economy will be one priority. After all, without a functioning economy, no money will be available to pay for governmental services like roads, dams, and schools or a security service; so instead of recommending a specific form of government at the start of the reconstruction phase, e.g., parliamentary democracy or a federal system, NGO advisors should help the country coalesce behind a common national economic vision. Finally, what emerges from that process will be the foundation upon which to erect the architecture, through a separate agreement, of a sustainable and acceptable overall governmental structure to enable the priorities, which absolutely must include civil rights for all.

## 8.3 A Framework That Is Inclusive and Avoids Retribution

Arriving at the best overall framework (which may require experiments) is a complex negotiation that should not be dictated by outside forces. It can be facilitated by expert NGOs through a meaningful dialogue between former and transitional governmental supporters and the commercial/industrial world and the entire public, including previously marginalized minorities like Albanian gypsies of Albania or Egyptian Copts, each with its own self-imposed, often conflicting goals and time frames. That also means avoiding retribution and allowing the participation of members of the "Ancien Régime" who have not committed crimes against humanity. Agreeing on that inclusive philosophy will help advisory nations avoid mistakes like the economic sanctions[9] regime against Germany after World War I that was a factor in the Weimar Republic's failure and kindling to the fire of National Socialism.

**Note** The economic sanctions of the Treaty of Versailles are generally acknowledged as unintentionally fostering a political environment that helped extremists. It is interesting to note in November 1917, two months after the formation of "The Inquiry" and seven months after the United States entered the war, Newton Baker, Secretary of War, recognized that overly punishing economic sanctions would likely generate a Germany of the future worse than caused World War I (US Department of State 1942c, p. 25). Similarly, in a note to Colonel House dated Dec 3, 1918, from David Hunter Miller, he noted concerns over the risks associated with turning Germany into an "economic slave" (Department of State 1942c, p. 334). However, it was also deemed impossible by Wilson to achieve the League without agreeing to French demands for severe sanctions. Wilson surmised that the evils inherent in the treaty were outweighed by the potential for good inherent in the League of Nations (Keynes 1920, p. 240). Given what that decision on Germany might have helped cause, the *lesson for NGO negotiators is to consider the potential long-term repercussions of any compromise (or perceived compromise) on core principles, even if it meets immediate operational needs, e.g., to achieve an agreement.* ***It is a very important ethical question***. (See Chap. 14.)

A mature framework can also give rise to inspirational thinking like George Marshall's reconstruction plan. However, while not proposing any specific governmental architecture—all societies are different—one goal for any new country should be a functioning democracy. Of course, there aren't many examples today like the Weimar. History does march on, and thus despite the attack on Kuwait on Iraq and the post 911 wars in Iraq and Afghanistan, transitional societies are more apt to come from societies that have collapsed without an invasion, like Somaliland, or perhaps the republics of the post-Soviet era, which are slowly and painfully evolving, perhaps an imploded North Korea or a post-rebellion Iran. They will also come as a result of the march of

[9]Economic sanctions are usually a regressive tax on the poor of repressive states, since no dictator will allow himself to be weakened and will instead rob from the disadvantaged and blame the sanctions regimes, not his or her own policies. Still, they can cause positive change as in the cases of Rhodesia and South Africa, both of which Mr. Roeder, one of the authors, worked on. It can also be argued with some justification that costs associated with economic trade restrictions imposed by the west on the Soviet Union hastened its decline. Woodrow Wilson felt they would inhibit war, and so made them an element of the League, though that failed. However, sanctions regimes are not perfect, and removing them not always popular. In 2012, the United States government dropped many sanctions imposed on Burma, to the dismay of many human rights organizations such as Human Rights Watch, feeling the move undercuts Aung San Suu Kyi's effort to democratize her country (DeYoung 2012).

self-determination that led to independence for South Sudan, and which may lead to independence for Darfur, though not without bloodshed. In a land like Darfur in 2012, over four million people (a mix of refugees and IDPs) are impacted (USAID 2012, April 4), and since much of the conflict has been a genocide, that is going to result in a call by indigenous leaders for retribution, much as Clemenceau demanded because the damage and public harm inflicted on France by Germany. It doesn't matter that France was a state and Darfur is a region. Historical examples are pertinent for today and teach that one should avoid extreme retribution as demanded by France, Australia, and others at the Paris Peace Conference and keep in mind the ethical consequences of long-term decisions. Just that consideration led to the United States refusing to bill Italy $20 billion in reparations after World War II, instead deciding to provide financial aid in order to stimulate reconstruction and democracy (Thorp 1947, June 1).

Though the examples of Egypt, Libya, and Syria of 2011/2012 might not appear to say this, the easy part of transition is the removal of a despotic, ineffectual government. People who don't like each other will partner to accomplish that goal, hopefully without too much interference by outside forces like Al Qaeda and its ilk. What is needed then is to translate that common political goal into a common economic and political vision for the future. That will be hugely difficult in many contemporary societies that are tribal like Libya or where there is a disconnection between religious beliefs and modern economic principles. This is clearly where NGO coalitions are needed, partnering indigenous and international NGOs, because local experts will be needed to find the political bridges that enable a government (local, provincial, or national) to be coherent, fair, and capable of achieving that vision, a government that can pull even a fractured society like Somalia or Libya into a "common mission of mutual success." Particularly when emerging from civil war or long-term political conflict, the formula for national reconciliation in the twenty-first century will be very complex and full of road bumps, as definitely seen in Afghanistan. Perfection is impossible; a workable concept is however doable if the players engage in an open and fair negotiation. In other words, the people's wishes need to be at the heart of the conversation, which is why this book calls for democracy and heavy NGO participation. Struggling populations will often suffer prejudice or despots for generations; eventually the hot steam must be released. Aiming for a permanent democratic structure allows the best opportunity for people to express their own self-interest.

## 8.4 Democracy Can Be a Quality Control Tool for Economic Policies

If people fully engage in a true marketplace of ideas (assuming accurate information is freely shared), they will be able to reject shoddy economic and political proposals. The phrase "fully engage" is essential, which requires freedom and literacy, though radio, television, or image-laden t-shirts have been used successfully in low-literate societies. All people want to determine their own fate, to control their own resources, and to be democratic at some level; but this doesn't mean only under of a system of government whereby the executive reports to a parliament, itself elected by the people, though that's a fair institutional construct and one to which countries should aspire. Democracy is the institutional manifestation of free will for the common person, the inherent; some would say genetic desire of all to seek their own destiny. This is controversial, especially since the traditional view is that democracy began in Athens, Greece, about 508BC; this desire can be traced back to early tribes and clans, which were generally egalitarian, small societies of a few hundred or less. They often democratically chose their leaders, as do tribes today, like in the Sinai. Things evolved with the advent of agriculture, commerce, and specialization.[10] Decisions were too complex to handle by consensus, and differences between tribes, religions, and cultures caused tensions which could only be settled through conflict or negotiation between state leaders.[11] That led to autocrats, dictators, and kings; when information was freely shared, demands for change and democracy rose up, at least among those who got the information. In other words Greece was not the birthplace of democracy; it was the birthplace of a method of democracy. Today when Twitter, Facebook, and other social media share information, average people become empowered with information and plan on how to use it for constructive change, as do the illiterate from radio, and with that empowerment, push for their rights. Of course, for a democracy to work well, it requires a social bargain; even the smallest tribe is built on a circle of desires and ideas broader than that of any one individual, which is why democratic systems vary from Greece to indigenous tribes, to America, to England, and to Egypt. In addition, pure unfettered majority rule can lead to tyranny, which is why the first ten amendments to the US Constitution exist, to protect the rights of the minority from being destroyed by the majority. As seen in the violence surrounding the publishing in 2012 by Google/YouTube of a repugnant anti-Muslim film, different cultures will look on free expression and its allowable range differently. Spending time explaining this theory is important because there are those who push back on democracy, saying it won't work in a society where that isn't a tradition. They say it should be a lower priority, not necessarily. If the urge for democracy is inherent in humanity, then it makes sense to advance it everywhere, while still being sensitive to the local culture and traditions; a major role for NGOs today is to bolster this natural human urge by fostering the effective sharing of information on economic, social, and political issues—especially in weak or failed states.

NGOs should urge weak or broken states to permit information sharing and teach basic economics, as well as to be critical of political posturing. That can be hard to accomplish in an autocratic society, even in democratic America where the electorate tends to join political tribes (parties) and not think outside the box, often lazy to the point of believing even the most ridiculous statements by partisan television and

[10] This is generally called the Neolithic revolution, though the sequence of events has recently been challenged, due to archeological findings in the Fertile Crescent.

[11] Tension between people having a tribal identity with a clan, a culture, or a religion can definitely be destructive, even while rewarding, and is not dissimilar to the tensions inherent in competing national structures.

radio commentators. To deal with that, NGOs should push fresh thinking. One approach is to influence conference outcome documents; more than 1,000 NGOs from more than 80 countries attended the World Food Summit (WFS) in 1996 and agreed on a statement, "the globalization of the world economy, along with the lack of accountability of multilateral corporations and spreading patterns of overconsumption have increased world poverty (Windfuhr 1998)," and called for more direct NGO action. But conference statements are relatively easy to accomplish. What about making changes on the ground in transitional societies?

Weak and failed nation-states are often thought of as transitional societies (going up or down); sometimes they even have official transitional governments mandated to take the society to the next level, as happened in East Timor when the UN ran the show or the elected Transitional Libyan government in July 2012. To help the rulers acquire a sustainable society or for the average person to acquire the knowledge to join his or fellow citizens in building the economic and governmental framework of the future, the job partly starts in the schools, so suggest NGO-based community organizers who can parse fact from fiction. In a post-revolutionary society, especially when the revolution or breakdown of society is violent like in Libya and Egypt, that's often dangerous work, especially while old and new political factions vie for authority. In 2012 many of the forces that defeated Gadhafi feel disproportionally represented in the new government; so the work of NGO is essential because unfortunately and far too often the effort is not well managed. If the provisional authority is weak or corrupt, strong leaders can turn a victory for freedom into a tool for despotism. That phenomenon led to communism when the Czar fell in Russia and almost led to Communists taking control of post-Imperial Germany in the 1920s. In fact, Bavaria did briefly turn Marxist. Once in power in Russia, China, and their satellite states, the Communists tamped free expression and instituted demand economies that were fated to fail. In a store, instead of being able to choose from a variety of shoes, only one design was available. Quality control also fails, such as in Communist Albania where the manufacturer of hard alcohol routinely bottled its products with loose tops! There was no competition, no need to improve. While citing an example of an early twentieth century revolution might seem odd in the early twenty-first century; witness today's post-Soviet Central Asian republics which have generally been slow to distribute wealth and social benefits to the poor. The economically desperate have begun to feel nostalgia for the Soviet system, partly because these new societies have not been given universal education, health care, and jobs. They also want a free media. They do have more religious and cultural freedom; armies of unemployed will inevitably lead to political unrest, as in Iran. In China in 2012, 25 million people will join a workforce that isn't accommodated with sufficient meaningful jobs. Half of those will have higher education. Perhaps as many as ten million will move to cities from rural locations. If China doesn't provide them employment, this will create major political risks; can today's Chinese Communist Party provide the required economic and political flexibility (IANS 2012)? The same risk of political mismanagement exists today as it did in old Russia. In Egypt, there has been far more commercial choice than in the former Soviet states; their revolution also brought political repression and excessive control of the markets by the government. This doesn't just happen in repressive societies. Even strong capitalists in vibrant democracies like America and Europe can be terrible economists, as seen with the housing market in America and its handling by major banks. The common problem is a "failure of governance," which is a key area where NGOs can be very influential when guiding national, provincial, and local governments. Indeed, when the term "democracy" can be problematic, **"governance"** may be a good alternative, since sustainable governance will require involving all levels of society.

**Governance** will mean different things to different people, as does the term democracy. From the perspective of a politically conservative economist, a government's purpose is just to craft an efficient economy (though government clearly also has other purposes—which is a source of major debate); market equilibrium only comes when demand equals supply, the price the market will bear being the equilibrium price. Put in simpler term, every market has buyers and sellers. A buyer in a village grocery store takes a cereal box off a shelf when he or she buys it, a good the seller placed on the shelf for the buyer to purchase and which will be replaced with some of the sales revenue. A seller is also a buyer, in this instance of the cereal box from a different seller, and onward. When demand meets supply, there is equilibrium and the prevailing price is the equilibrium price. The trick is sell the cereal for enough to raise funds to reinvest in new cereal and pay salaries, rent, and other overhead, without the price point being so expensive that buyers walk to the competition. Keeping in mind the impossibility of pure equilibrium, what NGOs to transitional societies need to advise is how to foster a society where purity is north on the political compass, a society where families are net savers, companies are net borrowers, the government's budget is balanced, and net exports are near zero. Again, that's textbook modern economic theory and a fantasy world for the immediate future in many countries, like Somaliland, and many developing countries. Still, it must be a long-term national goal that is explained to the public so they understand the direction and provide a popular mandate. If they accept, they may take the time to achieve the goals, which is necessary since a government must build the right banking infrastructure early, the elements of a free market society early, and avoid paying for critical services with backbreaking debt creeping in (Koo 2008). Some argue that business is not concerned with equity or public safety. "Let someone else pay the downstream cost of pollution; maximize profit—the heck with risk to workers and consumers." Not all businesses feel that way; when a government agency, especially in a fresh government, wants to impose food safety regulations on producers, there will be a large fight (except perhaps right after consumers die from food poisoning, and then only because the ensuing lawsuits are often painfully expensive!) or food riots that lead to smashed windows. A social contract is a cost that doesn't contribute to the bottom line. Business is about maximizing shareholder value this quarter—sustainability can seem irrelevant to the quick profit and run investor. That's why regulations are essential to protect society from corporate greed, such as denying collective bargaining in order to maximize profits.

Being these points in mind, NGO advisors with a strong economic and social background are needed to push a society into a sustainable direction, to convince its leaders to create a fair social bargain between the estates of society. Once the society decides on its economic goals and overall structure, the daily political struggle will be to use practical rules and governance to minimize corrupt or inept bankers and businessmen. Modern banking and investment rules will be needed as well as professional supervision, perhaps through a central bank. On the other hand excessive government controls or nationalization[12] will cause price and quantity distortions, too little for one thing and too much of something else. This takes us back to the stage of civilization after the advent of agriculture and commerce. People allowed autocrats to rule because they were ignorant and the strong controlled the facts. To avoid reverting to that system, democratic institutions such as the vote won't be enough to stop excesses by corporations or governments of today if the people don't know the facts—hard in an illiterate society or one in which the government controls the media; so once again, NGO advisers should argue for institutions like schools and unfettered radio that can guard against an asymmetry of information between government leaders, the corporate world, and the citizens. In other words, the schools must teach economics, and the new society must be provided a free flow of information in newspapers, television, radio, and the Internet. While it is certainly true that even in a literate society the average citizen may have little clue of how the national or world economies work, schooling and the sharing of information through public media can make a difference, perhaps avoid the pyramid schemes that led economic collapse in Albania, for example. Even an illiterate society can learn and make better choices, if information is shared appropriately.

Still, while every state can eventually become democratic and reach towards market equilibrium, each won't do it right away (Diamond 2006), nor does democracy mean immediate wealth for all, so NGOs in weak and failed states need to help manage expectations and understand the difference between theoretical and practical equilibrium. India is the world's largest democracy, yet also one of the poorest. Peasant democracy is happening in China, but the national government insists on one-party rule. Hippler said "we do not know what is required for a society to move from a traditional and authoritarian basis to the establishment of democratic institutions and representatives institutions" (Hippler 2008). The authors suggest *good governance and openness are required and must be the daily mantra of the NGO advisors.* Without that, the mix of ministries, laws, and system of government, no

[12]Nationalization, especially that of industries that exploit mineral resources like oil, are often couched in political rather than economic terms, removing foreign controls and restoring control over the national patrimony, which is the accumulated wealth of a national economy. However, it isn't always a bad arrangement. When companies are first in, they might demand an excellent deal that in the long term provides an unfair share of income for the government or its citizens. That's why in 1957 AGIP (Azienda Generale Italiana Petrole) agreed to absorb exploration costs, and share profits equally with the National Iranian Oil Companies over the decades have had to make similar arrangements, especially after OPEN was formed in 1960. Eventually, many countries took over all foreign stock, e.g., Kuwait in 1975. Development NGOs in the business of advising weak or failed states today might remind relevant authorities that with a total takeover comes responsibility, especially in highly technical areas, which when handled poorly will reduce production and profits, one of the reasons Saudi Arabia phased in control with ARAMCO.

matter how cleverly designed, risk becoming institutions of economic and political repression. By being open to its population, trust is built as well as forgiveness for honest mistakes. That also encourages normative economic policies.

**Positive economics** is the study of facts: who is paid, what, and why. What is the impact of a policy on labor availability or salaries? **Normative economics** deals with ethics. Do the answers gained from asking fact-based questions (positive economics) suit the social framework of the transitional society (normative economics)? For example, while interest-bearing loans might provide economic benefits for investors, does the culture have moral qualms about such loans, e.g., in strict Islamic societies? Another way to look at this is that while the diplomacy of governments and nonprofits (the focus on this book) is intended to lead to clearly understood written agreements upon which people can act, many people act in their daily lives on a "common consciousness and conviction" (Reddies 1851, p. 275), which might be based on culture or religion or some combination. That common, normative construct should not be ignored.

**Recommendation** Fostering normative policies is essential to peaceful societies that want to avoid artificial economic disparities. What's the risk? While the Boer War helped British mine owners, did it help average British citizens in the UK, or for that matter the average South African native? No. Instead, there was a steadily broad divide between the haves and the have-nots in the UK and Africa. Has today's cobalt and diamond wealth been fairly distributed in Zaire? No. That kind of economic divide can lead to political unrest, not only in South Africa a hundred years ago but around the planet today. NGO advisors do need to foster a business-friendly government, must one that avoids the pitfalls of corporate greed. With the invention of the company as a legal "person" during the industrial revolution, they began to accumulate wealth on a par with nation-states, and today multinational corporations have boards with members from many nations and wealth and influence greater than entire regions. Building on the personhood concept, in the United States, corporations have even begun competing with citizens in civil rights like free speech, a troubling development.

Of course, corporations are not people. They are controlled by people, and the boards of large multinational commercial enterprises will want to be involved transitioning a weak or failed state into a sustainable one, especially if large mineral deposits are available like oil, and all firms (large and small) will demand political space in order to protect growth. Fair enough; will normative policies be left in the dust? Large corporations have always been influential to the march of nationalist wars, in some cases even the fomenter; now in the post-Cold War era, investors are arguing for a different form of empire with "international multinational board-led corporations" in the seat of power, using the natural resources of those "backward societies" to gain corporate economic advantage and—very dangerous—in local elections trying to influence results. In other words, as societies transitioned from dependencies on national authorities, new dependencies on commercial powers have emerged. Many corporate leaders naturally worry that unbridled raw national politics are potentially harmful to profits, due to the unpredictability of popular politics that are not driven by science or the cold bottom line.

Some have extrapolated from Adams Smith to a new imperial formula, and the father of modern economics did strive for a global market of peaceful merchants trading in fair competition. But what if national authorities interfered? Would multinational corporations have to step in and manage things? That's one conservative political theory that pushes hard for minimal government. The management and identification of scarcity and efficiency are pillars of modern economics, as Smith noted. Governments waste, the argument by some corporations goes, and great economists or businessmen avoid waste; in the case of the British, Smith felt this meant avoiding wasting energy on conquering lands of little value. The investment did not provide a profit. There is certainly much truth in the allegation. So the answer is not to be antibusiness. Business creates jobs and raises the taxes needed by government to fund services. At the same time, in order to maintain balance, the transition should establish governmental entities that regulate corporate behavior but keep rules to the minimum required. Regulations should protect both the people and commerce, not be a disincentive to economic growth.

On the other hand, what if normative social policies contradict those of the corporate world? While it is not the business of NGOs to homogenize the globe, and while fostering a diversity of cultures is good, there are also universal norms, e.g., freedom of religion, the right to collectively bargain, the right not be abused based on race, sex, or age, rights that have become stronger, thanks to the advent of the League of Nations and the United Nations. Also, what if there is excessive or unrealistic public demand? It is all very well to call for listening to the people so that policies are normative; what if the people call for a flawed economic vision? In other words, simply wishing for prosperity won't make anyone rich. In the 2012 presidential campaign in the United States, one candidate called for establishing a colony on the moon—laudable in decades to come perhaps, farcical in the near future, given America's available resources and its many expensive needs. Some agri-based, poor nations might want to be an industrial powerhouse within a decade fueled by nuclear power plants or massive hydroelectric dams. That's often unrealistic, especially if huge unsupportable loans are required and there is not the educated or trained workforce for the plants or the consumer base to buy the products. A slower, more pragmatic approach would be required. NGOs advising the government or transitional authority(ies) needs to help the people; the rulers and local industry understand what is doable in the near term, even if they have a great idea for a distant future. This is a huge ask, but today's NGOs are up to the task, if they work in coalitions of local and international players, if their study groups (see Sect. 2.2.2) examine the big picture so that proposed policies fit within a practical strategy.

## 8.5 The Case of Egyptian Economic Development

Egypt could be a good case study of advising the population to be cautious about investing too fast, especially when agricultural resources do not meet the requirements of population consumption. New democratic governments for countries like Haiti, or some future North Korea, might see rapid industrialization as the solution to elevating their constituents out of poverty. In fact, an angry, freed populace probably will make such demands; if the transition is not done wisely with an optic on future debt management, it can lead to an even bleaker economic posture. It is generally better to argue for first developing a diversified agricultural market since there might not be an immediate market place for local manufactured goods, especially if the country is competing against more experienced industrialized states on its borders or nearby. On the other hand, it is often a good idea to improve consumer goods production since they are relatively inexpensive to buy and will enhance the standard of living.

Whatever is done, debt management will be important. Egypt developed a plan of action for the period 1960–1970 to address poverty and the food supply; the plan failed because excessive public consumption, which rose 89 % in 5 years, could not be supported. Private consumption and earnings in the same period were paltry. Domestic savings were not enough to finance investments. This particular plan was picked especially because it dealt with a fresh "transitional" government. Egypt's anti-Monarchial revolution was only 8 years old, and the new leaders chose nationalization as an important tool. At the start of the Egyptian revolution was massive agricultural "reform" through excessive governmental intervention. The financial institutions were also nationalized, as was the Suez Canal by 1956. By 1960, most major industries were government owned, creating a system that though since improved, still causes economic instability to this day. A good example of massive capital investment would be the controversial Aswan Dam which had many benefits but created huge debts and political obligations, as well as environmental damage. Financial aid was also unreliable and dried up from Libya when Nasser rebuffed Gadhafi's overtures for unification. The country became unable to repay loans used to buy Soviet weapons and finance capital improvements. On the plus side, the plan Egypt chose to elevate itself certainly followed what its leaders felt were normative politics; the hard fact is that government receipts did not equal expenditures. Even knowing the risks, Egypt refused to hold down rising governmental consumption. The lesson is that while fresh governments must employ normative policy making—act on the will of the people—they also must be practical and recognize that services and goods have a price. A government can't borrow its way into prosperity unless the receipts from investments reap savings that can pay off the loans, with interest. Unfortunately for Egypt, that did not happen. NGOs advising transitional bodies should argue against repeating those mistakes. The public should keep expectations realistic and give industry and government a practical mandate for action.

## 8.6 Inform the Public

The public needs to understand that no country is without scarcity; to avoid the disparities of predatory government or corporate policies, as discussed earlier, the population, not just the government, must have at its disposal the right information to understand practical economics, in the schools and the media. Further, there must be an integrated strategy that links a practical identification of needs with technical assistance, credit, and/or direct funding. Those were key recommendations Roeder

**Fig. 8.1** Roeder in Borama, Somaliland, 2009, inspecting road construction needs (© Roeder, 2009)

made to transitional powers in Albania in 1991, the first US government economist to visit since World War II. In school, economics is defined as the efficient management of resources, labor, or infrastructure in order to cost-effectively produce and market goods that others need. That's right out of Adam Smith; in the real world, it is also human nature for people to look after their own self-interest to the disadvantage of others (just as do corporations and governments) and that has often led to nothing more than the management of resources to benefit the few. And of course there is the investment side of government, in other words funding roads and other infrastructure projects; often in failed nation-states, emerging governments don't have the funds nor a tax base to raise funds. Somaliland is a case in point. While first conceiving of this book, Roeder went to the breakaway Republic in 2010 to study its civil rights and economic infrastructure. Infrastructure was truly struggling. In the northern provincial capital of Borama, for example, known for its investments in health services and higher learning, the roads were very poor. Ambulances could not safely transport patients, and consumers could damage their vehicles trying to buy products. It was also hard to keep stores provisioned; yet the central authority in Hargeisa, the national capital could not afford to build proper modern roads. Out of frustration, expats who returned from working in Saudi Arabia and local businessmen formed an NGO, a nonprofit with the aim of building roads. It was an audacious plan; lacking sufficient funding to buy modern earth-moving equipment, with the permission of the city and provincial government, the NGO attracted local volunteers and cheap labor to break rocks, lay tar, etc. (Fig. 8.1).

Jeffrey Sachs has proposed that the world needs “development that meets the needs of the present population without comprising the ability of future generations to meet their own needs” (Brundtland 1987). Achieving that goal in transitional societies will require helping both the public and the private sectors as part of an integrated strategy, and negotiating an agreed structure early on that inhibits the natural tendency of governments and corporations to monopolize power and resources (empire building) to the detriment of the population and instead fosters fair balance between the four estates (media is number four). The fair balance will only happen if the population is educated about the risks of imbalance, of trying to do too much with too little resources, same of course for government officials and the private sector.

Another way to look at normative policy making in a transitional society is setting a bargain. The people who contribute to the success of the economy must benefit from that success, not just the wealthy, the workers, and middle class. There is nothing wrong with the very top growing wealthier from their incomes and investments; society must be fair and offer an opportunity for everyone else to struggle less with costs, to not rack up more and more debt just to keep up. At its best, modern economics is not only the study of how to achieve a fair profit. Transitional societies do need to be pro-business and companies can’t operate at a deficit; transitional economics must also be about “the study of those resources in order to benefit the people as a whole in the short and long term, be about sustainable development, to take the long view, while at the same time keeping all of society informed of the measures taken, the rationale behind them, and the government’s expectations.”

To understand the opposing stresses of investment and labor at the street level and why ignoring normative pressures is dangerous, one might read *The Jungle* by Upton Sinclair. The book did not simply cause Theodore Roosevelt and the new progressive movement to revamp meat safety rules; the novel also displayed in very graphic terms the plight of nonunionized labor and showed the public the dangers of not appropriately treating the middle class. A good counterargument might be that in countries of mass unemployment, the example of *The Jungle* isn’t relevant because jobs are needed, period; but that is shortsighted. The novel took place in a time when people were desperate for jobs and took anything in order to gain some income, regardless of danger. In the butcher factories described by Sinclair, not only was the beef of questionable quality; the working conditions were such that the workers cut off body parts due to accidents. It is easy to say, give them jobs; however, also remember the precepts of the ILO (International Labor Organization), a specialized agency of the UN dating back to the League of Nations. The first ILO convention in 1919 adopted rules limiting work hours and insisted on rest periods. In addition, the ILO of 2012 argues under their SafeWork program (ILO 2012) that decent work must be safe work. In order to reduce the incidence of diseases and accidents Sinclair reported on a century ago, the UN agency is advocating that every state implement national occupational and safety standards which comport with international labor standards. NGOs work directly with the ILO on the development of such standards and should also bring these ideas to the public space in developing nations.

## 8.7 Equality of Opportunity and Good Governance Create Stable Politics

Modern economics needs to be about raising all boats, not just fiscal equality but equality of opportunity, which can lead to better fortune and sounder politics. Illustrating the point, in 1981/1982, a group of thirty-one experts posited the proposition that "Granting the Palestinians a state in the West Bank and Gaza would give the community a powerful stake in the outcome of any peace process. The predictable objections of the "rejectionist" Palestinian minority would be manageable" (Roeder et al. , *Palestinian Autonomy and the Jerusalem Question* 1982a). It was the political corollary to sustainable development, meaning that giving Palestinians a stake in their own economy would undermine political extremism—important since this was an exercise in normative policy making, not only as a means to help the Palestinians but also as a strategy to support Israel's peaceful existence. "Once at peace, Palestine, Israel and the … region can maximize their economic potential. Peace and statehood are essential elements of prosperity" (Blitzer 1982) (Kimble 1982 (Spring)). The Study Team proposed a Transitional Executive Authority (TEA) to arrange for the return of Palestinians and appropriate investments in sectors like agriculture, particularly food processing. Of course, their philosophy was predicated on a model using UN and Western power assistance to foster good governance that respected both the private sector and civil society and reconcile combatants, even supporters of the Ancien Régime, meaning in the Palestinian context, those who wished to destroy Israel, and by doing so, to bring peace to Israel and Palestine. The study group's findings were distributed to US diplomatic missions, but someone then leaked them, and then much media coverage took place in the Jerusalem Post and Arabic-language newspapers. Yasser Arafat even expressed an interest through Edward Said[13] of considering the ideas; Secretary of State Al Haig disagreed politely, and the process died.

One way to approach good governance in a new transitional society like Syria perhaps would be to assemble a team of non-crony experts, instead of leaders just asking best friends for advice, seek the best minds available. That might be a fantasy in some of transitional societies, especially when tribally based. A head of state or government must consider the views of representatives from each sector of society, religious and ethnic minorities, etc.; the principle is a good one because the issues, especially when dealing with economics, can be complex, for example, should there be massive tax breaks for industry and private citizens, an idea with roots in the theories of John Maynard Keynes, in order to build up corporations. Consumers might use money otherwise transferred to the government to buy corporate products, thus creating demand and lower stocks, which in turn means more workers

[13]Professor of English and Comparative Literature at Columbia University and a leading, progressive light in the American–Palestinian community. Personal friend of one of the authors. Arafat passed on his interest in a note to the Department of State through Said and the author.

must be hired, reducing national unemployment. The point here is not that Keynes would be right in all cases; rather if a transitional government is willing to be bold and reach out of one's inner orbit, using real experts with fresh ideas that could be understood by the people, such a government could create a bond with the population and create a mandate. Too often, transitional leaders won't do that. Ideas matter. Openness matters. So does governance. So does inclusion.

Where transitional governance was done right was in East Timor (Timor Leste) under the visionary UN diplomat Sergio Vieira De Mello, Transitional Administrator for East Timor. Had he not been assassinated in Iraq, he likely would eventually become UN Secretary General. East Timor became independent in 1999, 7 years after the Rio Earth Summit on sustainable development. It had been brutally ruled by Indonesia since 1975 after 400 years as a neglected Portuguese colony. In 1999 the occupation ended after the people of East Timor voted for independence. Unfortunately, Indonesia left under a scorched earth policy. But because of Sergio's open, imaginative leadership, the East Timorese were able to move forward to success and create the current state. The story is not over and the country is still in transition with many difficulties due internal governance; as Sergio remarked in 2001, he was able to gain popular agreement to his restructuring plans because he approached the problem slowly and with the population in mind—normative politics (de Mello 2001).

But back to the peace point, investments aimed at economic development must include settling political differences and finding jobs for people who lost them when the state changed. If they are homeless or jobless, the Transitional Authority will have begun a counterrevolutionary movement. What this means is to prioritize investments neither in poverty alleviation, controlling inflation, etc., nor in national reconciliation. The investments must be in all of those activities. Choosing one over the other is a false choice. That kind of calculus will be tough to manage, especially since some of the players will not be fully trusted, like the Taliban in Afghanistan. They need to be brought into the conversation and be treated fairly; at the same, do they share common goals, even if they say so? That's a tough question to answer at times.

# Chapter 9
# International Funding

**Extract** Chapter 9 covers the role of funding as fuel for diplomatic efforts, what donors look for and how to find them. Special attention is given to potential benefits as well as conflicts of interest that can arise from receiving funds from governments or commercial institutions.

## 9.1 Introduction

Money is needed to run any initiative, yet nearly all nonprofits are facing financial pressure, and while the global economy may be improving, the pace is slow, and the global financial crisis has meant a decline in personal giving, shifting the targets, and perhaps some policy influence to government agencies and international organizations, as well as foundations and corporations. They too have pressures and thus in return for their support will increasingly demand accountability. There are other books that deal with fund-raising from private citizens, especially in this climate. The context here is how to ask for money from governments and the international donor system. Is it even acceptable to accept their money, and if so, how does an organization attract the attention of the UN and its international organizations, the International Red Cross and Red Crescent Movement, the World Bank, the European Commission, or government agencies such as USAID? They are all potential donors that could significantly change the fortune of any cause; the field is very competitive.

L.W. Roeder, Jr. and A. Simard, *Diplomacy and Negotiation for Humanitarian NGOs*, Humanitarian Solutions in the 21st Century, DOI 10.1007/978-1-4614-7113-4_9,

## 9.2 Who Receives Government Funding?

In a survey of 1,000 animal welfare NGOs for a parallel book, some which operate in humanitarian emergencies, the primary sources of funding were private individuals, followed by international NGOs, and then local governments, national authorities, academia, industry, and foundations. On the other hand, with regard to the humanitarian NGO members of InterAction, most accept US government funding, and many of the major organizations are heavily dependent on such funding. Especially true in that case are the International Rescue Committee, CARE, Mercy Corps, and the International Medical Corps. World Vision also accepts large amounts of US government funding, but has a remarkable global private fund-raising operation, so their overall percentage of government funding is rather low. The most significant InterAction member that does not take US government money (or any government money, for that matter) is Oxfam America. But their international affiliates, such as Oxfam GB, do take government funds. Other NGOs that do not take government funding are the so-called "peace church" agencies, such as American Friends Service Committee and the Mennonite Central Committee (Charny 2012).

Governments with healthy economies certainly have money; some humanitarian and other NGOs believe receiving such funds may impinge on their political neutrality, an important issue for MSN (Medecins Sans Frontieres or Doctors Without Borders),[1] which receives over 90 % of its funds from nongovernmental sources. This is a complex issue. While the potential of great funding offers hope of great results, there are also ethical and political questions to be answered. In the end, each NGO must develop a fund-raising strategy that suits its mandate and backers and does not simply change goals with available funds. A valid question is will collaboration with donors inhibit or enhance "effective change." The authors suggest the criterion for success should not be a graph that shows income gains and losses, though there is nothing wrong with NGOs who as a matter of principal do not accept government funds. NGOs are after all nonprofits driven to do good deeds; the success graph must show real change in whatever field of work the NGO operates.

In the parallel survey local American humane NGOs told us usually don't take corporate funding, the view being it is very hard to find a company not involved in exploitative practices. About 9 % of the respondents around the globe did just that however and 35 % accepted funds from foundations that often were managed by corporate leaders, the same problem faced by any NGO in any field. If a government

[1]MSF (not a member of InterAction). MSF determines people's needs by conducting its own evaluations on the ground. More than 90 % of MSF's overall funding comes from millions of private sources, not governments. This goes up to 100 % for certain contexts like Afghanistan. This allows MSF to act and speak independently from any pressure and to stay outside the cluster system initiated by the United Nations coordinating humanitarian actions. The organization does not take sides in armed conflicts, provides care on the basis of need, and pushes for independent access to victims of conflict as required under international humanitarian law (Tronc 2012). That said, it does criticize governments and non-state actors.

agency foments war, is collaboration with an NGO like Peace Action ethical? Fair question, and not dissimilar to the one faced in the example of having to deal with the chair of the G77 when his government's president was indicted for human rights violations. That collaboration was justified; is such partnering always ok? It is all about the situation and the facts at hand.

Some donors will want to help NGOs in order to help their image; if they also want the NGO to do something it doesn't like, read the contract. There is no question that association with certain donors presents potential problems; if the contract asks an NGO to do something that violates its ethical foundation, don't do it. Unless there is truly something unethical about the donor, accepting the monies as a tool to accomplish a great good that otherwise would be unattainable is fine. The same logic holds for any donor, government agency, corporation, or international organizations.

The truth is, in the United States anyway, it is rare for humanitarian NGOs to reject federal funding; however, there are over 1.5 million NGOs in the United States alone that cover any conceivable issue, and most do not receive federal funding, even though there is no restriction on it nor on receiving funds from foreign governments (depending on the government in question). Other governments may have different rules. Further, there are few political restrictions either, though some activities will prevent an NGO from gaining the full range of nonprofit tax benefits, and that may inhibit donations. Most countries restrict foreign NGOs from operating in their territory without a license or to receive funds, something the Study Team needs to keep in mind. Further, the USA and others will restrict the use of funds from certain activities (see discussion on prostitution).

## 9.3 Sustainable Funding

Sustainable donations are perhaps an even bigger problem than whether a donor is politically problematic. This is because most programs need financial stability, to be able to regularly pay for what is needed. If the team leader can't project sufficient revenue, that can turn off political allies. It is possible to get grants for such initiatives from international NGOs, governments, the public, or foundations for short projects. But if the donations are not sustainable, that can pose a serious problem. To gain sustainable funding, not only must the donor mix be reliable, the NGO should show its programs have been effective. Donors to diplomatic initiatives will realize that a high-stakes project can reap major rewards, but they are also risky, so a sign of NGO stability isn't its bank account balance; it is the reputation of the NGO.

Since even traditionally reliable donors can turn funds off in these economic times, the best advice is not to rely on a sole source for a diplomatic initiative; that is probably too much vulnerability. Some NGOs such as GOAL Ireland rely on governments for a lot of their income. On the other hand, as YouthBuild USA discovered, it does not make sense to have the majority of funding from one agency or government, for the simple reason that if they pull their funds—perhaps just for fiduciary reasons, not politics, the NGO's economic viability can be placed in doubt.

In other words, NGOs should diversify donors and donor types. One little NGO on Saba in the Caribbean does not have enough staff to do professional fund-raising. As they put it, they can barely keep up with their work, but if an NGO can build a large diversified donor portfolio, such as has been done by the Heritage Foundation, it can also afford to turn down donations that have strings attached and focus on fulfilling its mission at the same time.

In one case examined for this book, to keep a core project alive, an NGO accepted funding from a single private donor who received the majority of his funds from Internet gambling, who then reneged, which put the NGO into a financial crisis; based on the promise of those inputs, the NGOs HQ made capital investments it could not honor. The gentleman in question originally made a multiyear pledge, but was unable to fulfill it after the first year. There is nothing a charity can do in that case in most countries because a gift is a voluntary transfer of property— not a legal obligation. Though charities should have a letter of agreement or MOU, which outlines the charity's responsibilities to the donor and the terms of the multiyear pledge, one doesn't try to force donors. It is, of course, difficult for the charity who was counting on that money and it means that another donor must be found or the program must be modified or delayed, which can destroy a diplomatic initiative. It isn't wrong to seek funds from a gambler and a diplomatic initiative could be a fascinating idea for an unorthodox donor to consider, but the team leader needs to first carefully consider the risks.

Another thing to keep in mind is that governments often pledge money for projects and fail to come through. As is seen by studying UN and OECD records of government pledges, governments have often been slow on delivery, and accounting can be surprising. Sometimes a government also double counts its development and disaster assistance donations, according to Stoddard Ahmad of OECD, who has expressed some pessimism over development aid funds after examining money pledged by Italy, Japan, and France in 2010 (Bryant 2010).

## 9.4 Political Taint

Although as has already been pointed out, there are times when dealing with troublesome governments is the right thing to do, one can't ignore how another's politics might taint the recipient when seeking donations, especially when trying to fund a sensitive diplomatic initiative. After all, there are governments with questionable policies who need the support of reliable, well-known "Western NGOs" in order to burnish their political identity. Sudan, Myanmar, North Korea, Zimbabwe, and Syria come to mind. They are all under huge international pressure to correct humanitarian practices that run counter to international norms. In this vein, local NGOs in repressive countries may have to be careful not to anger the government or they might be shut down. An NGO not headquartered in one of those countries could lobby such governments for changes in policies or to allow fund-raising, often a sensitive matter; this doesn't always work, as seen in Egypt after President Mubarak's regime collapsed.

## 9.5 Donor Rules

Barbara Harrell-Bond asked an important question in her 2002 article in UNHCR's *Humanitarian Review* journal, which is whether humanitarian work can be made "humane." Her argument is that because of donor rules, humanitarians must lower their moral compass and, instead of providing what victims need, provide what donors desire (Harrell-Bond 2002). Some of this is likely true, and it is certainly true that international donors have rules that must be followed, but usually this need not cause any ethical issues, though in some cases like the US ban on prostitution, the rules were ill-designed (Hoffman 2010). For the most part, the rules are really only intended to make sure money is not wasted.

Registration is one common rule, especially for major donors such as WFP, FAO, and USAID. To receive money from USAID, NGOs must be registered, have audits, and prove they are a nonprofit and spending money wisely. With UNICEF, the system also requires registration and a screening process on reputational risks, accreditation with ECOSOC, availability of annual reports, and audited statements. Those are common-sense rules for nearly any donor; if the team leader for a diplomatic initiative is seeking funding and his or her NGO hasn't already registered, keep in mind that the process can be slow. There are also limitations on which countries where money can be spent or on advancing religion or working with a listed terrorist organization. Keep in mind on the last point some terrorist organizations have "arms" that do perfectly respectable work; if the two are tied legally, receiving their funds, even for a proper project, is often illegal. Further, if the UN Security Council restricts dealing with certain countries or entities, member states of the UN are obligated to restrict their donor funds, so while a member State of the UN might ordinarily fund an initiative, perhaps not if it entails work physically in a listed nation.

### *9.5.1 Political Pressure*

Rules are often just intended to make sure transactions are honest, transparent, and meaningful. Some governments may also put political pressure on NGOs, but NGOs are not forced to sign a contract. Of course, in order for an NGO to move forward, it does need money and may feel forced by its own situation to sign contracts for work with stipulations to which it otherwise would not agree. One example might be ***The Ban on Prostitution:*** Since 2003 in the Bush II administration, an anti-prostitution pledge requirement has been imposed by the US government, initially on foreign-based nongovernmental organizations and since 2005 on US-based nongovernmental organizations who want federal grants to do humanitarian, anti-HIV/AIDS work abroad. The government's position was that improving the lot of prostitutes helps the trade, which is described as sexual slavery. The policy was then protested as counterproductive in early 2005 by CARE, the International Rescue Committee, Save the Children, and the International Center for Research on Women, which called the policy counterproductive and not science based, essentially a version of the Volstead Act of the 1920s which criminalized the sale of alcohol.

Their protest was then followed by hundreds more NGOs in May of the same year. The NGOs argued that they did not support the trade at all, however, had to help prostitutes live safer lives; otherwise, there would be an inevitable spread of disease. They also wanted to lower the social stigma so that former prostitutes could reenter society. Eventually, NGOs sued in the Federal Court, where oral arguments were heard in January 2012 on the constitutionality of the ban.[2] The US policy also saw pushback from Brazil which turned down anti-HIV/AID funding, their view being that sex workers were part of the program to combat disease. Indeed, Brazil has been cited for success in reducing disease. Similarly, in Calcutta the Sonagachi Project[3] (which started in 1992 with World Health Organization funding) has been cited by the World Bank, using science as the basis of aid policy (Mas de Xaxàs et al. 2008).

This is one of those issues that actually split the NGO and CSO community, with largely faith-based NGOs supporting the ban in what some have described as a "moral crusade," with over 100 NGOs supporting the pledge, feeling strongly that prostitution must be abolished and that decriminalizing prostitution would spread disease. Some of the most important of these groups were the Christian Medical Association, Concerned Women for America, Family Research Council, the Salvation Army, World Relief, and others. In Nigeria, this would include the Daughters of Abraham Foundation (DOAF).

### 9.5.2 Intelligence Gathering

The authors suggest NGOs, governments, and IOs need to share operational information with each other so that relief operations are safer and more economical. That was the basis behind the US Department of State's ReliefWeb project and why it partnered with UNDHA (UN Department of Humanitarian Affairs), now OCHA. Further, to the extent that it is safe, governments need to declassify information for the same reason, especially products derived from satellites, which was one of the reasons for the GDIN (Global Disaster Information Network). On the other hand, NGOs should not be asked to gather intelligence for governments. That will place humanitarians in unneeded risk. But if a donor provides a lot of funding to an NGO, do they have the right to know who is executing the contract? Therein rests a growing tension between donors and NGOs.

---

[2] The constitutional issue was that USAID said to get USAID funds NGOs would have to espouse a policy of opposition to prostitution which would limit their ability to use non-USAID funds to work with prostitutes. One of the two courts which heard the case agreed that USAID was unconstitutionally attempting to compel speech.

[3] Sonagachi is one of the oldest and largest red-light districts in the city.

During the Bush II administration, NGOs had to provide information on their national employees, what has become known as a "partner vetting system," which required NGOs receiving government funding to supply lists of names of their own staff, as well as any staff and board members of local partner organizations. In Somalia, there was also talk of being forced to supply names of key suppliers and contractors. Partner vetting is in place in West Bank/Gaza, and the current Obama administration has also attempted to impose it in Afghanistan. Congress has also mandated a pilot of PVS for the Philippines, Kenya, Guatemala, Ukraine, and Lebanon; however, attempts to impose it in Somalia were withdrawn in the face of the famine. Given Congressional interest among some members and the fact that the Obama administration has also sought to impose it, it looks like PVS is here to stay. We'll see what happens with the pilot and whether the next administration will then try to make PVS mandatory in all contexts and whether it creates problems (Charny 2012). It is certainly very controversial and something to examine in the second edition of this book.

**Bottom Line** The point here is that donors will try to advance their agenda through aid; it won't always just be about providing food, medicine, and shelter. NGOs are not forced to take the funds or sign contracts; if an NGO's primary source of funding does come from such a government, this could be problematic. It is a potential risk NGOs should consider.

**Being Too Specific** A particular weakness in donor funding can be that it is aimed at a specific project, rather than a concept. For example, Roeder sometimes had to go before Congressional staffers to argue for funds and they wanted specificity, due to the fiduciary responsibility of senators and representatives to the taxpayers to properly authorize expenditures. Some of that was looking for accountability, wanting to measure success; it was also hard to acquire funds for coordination to improve overall strategic planning among NGOs. That's a mistake. Just as governments need strategic planning, the project team also needs to think that way and finds resources to make it happen. This was a problem in 2004, for example, when UN officials asked for a pledge to help fund the upcoming World Conference on Disaster Reduction in Kobe, Japan. Roeder wanted to do so; the funds had already been committed elsewhere, so funds had to be reprogrammed, and that meant asking the Senate and House appropriations committees for permission prior to making a pledge, even though no experts saw a substantive problem. Fortunately, the funds were approved; there was no guarantee.

## 9.6 Being an NGO Donor

It is always useful to have a minister fly in from capitol to support your initiative. It is a strong sign of support. Similarly, if a diplomatic mission to the UN were to host a reception in support of an initiative, that event could be a great networking opportunity. Unfortunately, many diplomatic missions to the UN are very small staffs that are overwhelmed by work and the costs of doing ordinary business, so support for an NGO diplomatic initiative might go no farther than friendly, strategically placed statements. Many ministries in impoverished nations also are unable to meet the expense of sending senior officials to the UN to support an NGO initiative, even if they believe in the concept. Instead of asking them for money, why not pay their way to the conference? Done the right way, it isn't bribery. It is facilitating them, since they will also do other work. A suggestion is that if a reception would help to advance the cause, then it is a good idea to arrange for the G77 or some other coalition or perhaps one or two friendly UN missions to "sponsor," but the NGOs cover costs. What the mission gets is visibility and a networking opportunity. The NGO has the aura of "endorsement." The same is true for friendly ministers. Ministers often want to go to New York or some other important capital. Cover their air fare and a hotel room. In return, they speak at your event and do their business. Everyone wins.

In addition to funding receptions, briefings by government experts, etc., another approach for NGOs is to use international conferences to develop mandates; however, keep in mind that conferences can be expensive both for NGOs and small governments. As an example, NGOs were often charged $8,000 (US) to hold public forums at the World Conference on Disaster Reduction (WCDR) in Kobe Japan in 2005 (Horekens 2004). Why not combine efforts and find a formula for an intergovernmental conference to support an NGO cause that also provides governments an opportunity to advance their own issues? Such conferences will have reports and resolutions, and if worded right, those instruments can attract international donor institutions.

The truth is that implementation of some NGO initiatives might be too expensive for a government, perhaps modernizing agricultural production or allowing collective bargaining. It is important then sometimes at the study group stage to understand the local commerce. What sustains it and would the initiative have a negative impact? If so, can the NGO bring resources to mitigate against the cost? Could the NGO help facilitate a World Bank loan? In many instances, the decision memo will need a Tab describing the nature of local economic activity, any decline in per-capita income, unemployment, and the nature of production and trade.

Microfinance and small grant programs from NGOs to local communities can also be useful to change policies. After all, if poor local villagers are receiving aid from an NGO to change their agricultural techniques, or methods of education, or to build roads that bolster local markets, it stands to reason that they will also lobby their government to support the policies espoused by the NGO. For that logic, consider the research of Muhammad Yunis, winner of the Nobel Prize for Economics in 2006. Often called the banker to the poor, Yunis cited in his book *Building Social Business* the 1989 Grameen Fisheries and Livestock Foundation as a precedent. The project was set up to administer 1,000 fish ponds in northern and western Bangladesh that were not working anymore, due to poor government management. By 2009, Yunis and his people had brought together over 3,000 people into a group that produced 2,000 t of fish per year. "For many in Bangladesh, livestock was the only hope." Seventy-five percent of the 150 million people in 2008 Bangladesh depend on that source of income to some extent. "In 2002, a livestock program was added providing training, vaccination, veterinary care and support services for poor women to become dairy farmers" (Yunis 2010, Bari 2008). Projects like this start small and can totally change the way a microculture handles an issue. If an individual NGO or coalition funded such a project through local governments, that can create political allies which might inform the national authority of the worth of the NGOs ideas.

Another creative approach to funding is to tie an initiative to a high-priority, perhaps already well-funded humanitarian-oriented projects related to disaster recovery, development, drought resistance, flood sustainable agriculture, or hunger management. During the World Conference on Disaster Reduction (WCDR) in 2005, participating governments came to realize that poor farmers and businessmen will act impatiently. If a shanty town on the coast of South Africa is washed away, it will be rebuilt just as shabbily as before unless external donors invest in disaster-resilient shelters. Local NGOs, especially shelters and local advocacy groups, can quickly identify the needs. Why not use such a situation to fund a pilot project to solve an international organization priority. That will draw additional funding? As an example, suppose an NGO wants to improve the income levels in a developing country and learns that an IO is interested in improving the operational safety of industrial plants in the same country, a study by the NGO that the international organization might use would examine the local societal work patterns and natural phenomena that are hazards to technologies used by the plant. If the pilot is successful, it becomes documentation for a diplomatic initiative. Having been shown by the pilot project to be useful, the initiative might have an easier time of being funded in its own right.

## 9.7 Red Flags

### *9.7.1 Program Budget Implications (PBI)*

One way to pay for a fresh initiative is by changing program budgets, but this can be a serious problem if the program is funded by core UN budget monies. In the UN and many other international organizations, these are called Program Budget Implications or PBIs. No UN resolution will be considered in either ECOSOC or the UNGA if PBIs are not considered. Similarly donors to international bodies will demand that their secretariats flag increases in core budgets. Every organization has methodologies for handling budgets, and in the UN system (which uses a biennium) governments cover them, and major powers such as the USA and the UK cover a percentage of that budget, often making them enemies of PBIs. Any increase in the core budget increases their financial exposure. Initiatives with a potential PBI are reviewed by UNGA's Fifth Committee and then by the Advisory Committee on Administrative and Budgetary Questions (ACABQ). Unless the UN's major donors feel that the initiative is worthy of changing the budget, it will die if it negatively impacts the budget. **Recommendation:** Avoid supporting any PBI when negotiating an agreement with the UN, even if the supporting governments like the idea (unless they are major donors).

The approach to the PBI problem is to have the resolution endorse a project's value while requiring that it be managed through extra budgetary funds. This is because the same governments that do not support PBIs often unilaterally provide extra budgetary support to programs. One project Roeder pushed this way was ReliefWeb.int, the UN's most successful disaster information project. It has always been funded from extra budgetary sources, yet it has grown from a project requiring a few hundred thousand US dollars a year to several million a year and three offices. If enough donors agreed to support an NGO concept and it had the support of influential members of the G77 coalition of nations, such a project could be endorsed and effectively funded.

What we have described is the cautious approach, but keep in mind that politics can change international attitudes. As an example, whereas some PBI issues came up after the WCDR conference in Kobe, Japan, in 2005, by 2012 major governmental investors began to see the value of mainstreaming disaster risk reduction into sustainable development—in other words, targeted increases in program investments could bend the curve of future costs.

### *9.7.2 Global Public Goods*

The Global Public Goods (GPGs) concept can be considered for funding regional or global NGO projects, something developing countries and the UNDP (UN Development Program) understand as an alternative to PBIs. A local public good is a lighthouse, which protects ships entering a harbor from sea or a satellite early warning system. The beneficiaries do not pay for the service, but someone must, yet there is no internationally agreed definition of GPGs or payment methods. Usually, it comes from a coalition of governments or foundations. From an NGO perspective, GPGs might apply to cross-border concepts like fighting diseases that can be spread by vectors such as insects or rodents or cross-border water supply systems. An example of how to finance such a GPG could be a carbon tax proportional to a country's level of carbon emissions. Since 1 t of coal gives off approximately 5,700 lb of carbon dioxide, it is easy to calculate the pollution by measuring consumption. Anything that can be measured can be taxed, so this is an emerging environmental idea for both reducing carbon emissions and funding public goods; however, using international GPGs in this way is controversial in nations like the United States where goods such as health care are provided by both the state and the private sector, whereas there is an international movement for all health care to be a GPG.

### 9.7.3 International Taxation

This concept is similar to the GPG minefield and emerges rather regularly in negotiations involving G77 nations as a way of funding a project, but NGOs are wise to be wary of it as a method of paying for their initiatives; like PBIs, it is not voluntary. Even if some supporting government proposes international taxation for covering implementation of an NGO supported concept, the taxes will probably be geared towards taxing the wealthy, and wealthy governments will likely oppose the tax, possibly killing the initiative. Also remember that some nations have laws that prohibit making voluntary contributions to the UN if it imposes taxation. There is an exception. The burden of international taxation normally is intended to fall on wealthy donor nations, but if the impacted nations were willing to set up some kind of "voluntary regional scheme," this might be an achievable proposition. In that case, all of the impacted governments have agreed in advance, but this is a major ask.

### 9.7.4 General Things to Avoid or Keep in Mind

When approaching governments in particular for grants, it is very important to have the NGO's tax papers and audits in order, usually for the preceding 3 years. In addition, donors will want to know what percentage of funds is used for fund-raising and administrative matters versus actual services. A charity that spends only 33 % of its revenue on services is very inefficient. Donors will want to see 70 % or better of revenue spent on services. As for raising funds, a charity should spend 10 cents (US), a dime, or less to raise a dollar of revenue. Salaries should be in line with industry norms for the size and type of organization; the US government frequently restricts their funds from going to salaries or anything other than a bit of administration. They and most donors focus on services. ReliefWeb.int is a good example. This was initially funded by the US government out of reprogrammed money. In other words, the Department of State went to Congress and asked permission to reallocate authorized money from another project. Congress never had a problem so long as the money did not go to salaries.

The money provided by governments is in turn may be based on some formula, reimbursing X amount of dollars to the NGO multiplied by the number of people served. Most of the time, grants are also competitive. In that situation, the request for proposals (RFP) will establish a service, criteria to compete, and a maximum budget. Depending on the rules, grants can be more flexible on how the funds are spent so long as the service is delivered on time and within budget. The key thing to remember is that since grants are competitive, evidence must be presented as to the ability of an NGO to perform a task like education of children or a reduction in rape.

## 9.8 Finding the Money

Donors are increasingly demanding open development, meaning that they want to participate in the governance of donations. They are also demanding access to accurate data with which to make evidence-based decisions on whether funds are being properly used and also want the ability to contest common assumptions; in other words, increasingly they are challenging secret decision making "by experts." This is one reason that the IATI (International Aid Transparency Initiative) was created in Accra, Ghana, in 2008. It aims to make information about aid spending easier to find, use, and compare. Those involved in aid programs will be able to better track what aid is being used for and what it is achieving. This stretches from taxpayers in donor countries to those in developing countries who benefit from aid. Improving transparency also helps governments in developing countries manage aid more effectively. This means that each dollar will go as far as possible towards fighting poverty (IATI 2011). In other words, this is a crucial tool for both a transitional government and the people whom it is supposed to serve and is critical NGOs either wanting funds to help clients or wanting to know how well others have performed. Other sites like ReliefWeb.int are similarly crucial as reliable sources of operationally relevant data.

Humanitarian NGOs also need to be aware that funding is often/usually also based on assessments which are frequently joint efforts to discern needs and the resources required to meet those needs. As an example, in Southern Kordofan, Sudan, where over 300,000 people are displaced, assessments are made by a mix of officials from UN agencies like IOM (international organization for Migration), UNICEF (UN Children's Fund), WHO (World Health Organization), and the UN Department of Safety and Security, as well as Government of Sudan officials. Per the other discussions on sovereignty, it is important to note that UN agencies can't go into Government of Sudan-controlled territory without permission of Khartoum or the UN Security Council. Each agency will also have its own assessment methodologies, the results of which are merged into a common understanding of needs, which then translate into calls for assistance. Donor governments also do the same thing, like the UK, US, Norwegian, and Swiss governments and ECHO (European Commission's Directorate-General for Humanitarian Aid and Civil Protection), as well as NGOs, in the case of Sudan, organizations like the IMC (International Medical Corps), which screens for malnutrition.

Unfortunately, while there are tools to help NGOs know who or what is donating, there is unfortunately no single tool, agency, or website to do that job. A proposal for the humanitarian NGO community might be to fund such an effort in order to benefit everyone, perhaps by creating a specialized Donor Identification NGO. Such an NGO would need to identify and coordinate the availability of reliable funding across the entire international donor community in support of the entire humanitarian NGO community—a daunting task. Were such a service NGO to be created, instead of competing with other NGOs by having its own operational projects, its mandate should be to identify funding opportunities and projects needing support from the NGO community. That way, the entire community will be better informed, regardless of the NGOs size or geographic location, thus creating enormous efficiencies in finding donors and probably in the delivery of services as well. Every NGO needs its own donors, but any funds it acquires will mainly be used for its own end—which is entirely appropriate. A central service can facilitate a consolidated approach benefiting the broader community. Right now wherever there is a UN emergency, the NGOs, governments, and international organizations involved do surveys to assess resource needs and funding requirements. These consolidated statements are then placed into one public database called the Consolidated Appeals Process (CAP), managed by the Office for the Coordination of Humanitarian Affairs (OCHA). However, the CAP doesn't cover all humanitarian needs. A coordinated NGO effort could augment this process for its clients, making the identification of the broad spectrum of humanitarian needs and resource requirements easier and also avoiding duplication and waste.

After a crisis occurs, emergency managers from the host government, the UN, EC/ECHO, USAID, and other agencies, send out assessment teams, which develop statements of need and proposed budgets. A lot of humanitarian-related needs are not regularly tracked by CAP, livestock needed for food security and job, damaged historical and cultural structures, etc. A coordinated service could augment the database. Donors pledge against these consolidated needs statements, e.g., France might pledge €5 million towards a road project and one could imagine other donors pledging to protect schools, anything that relates to preservation of lives, culture, food security, and jobs, assuming CAP had the data. The point here is that NGOs can make proposals for those funds to be applied to them in order to accomplish the stated need. Without the CAP, NGOs might not even be aware of the potential funds. This suggests that a coordinated NGO service could broaden the needs universe and NGO opportunities, as well as donors. The potential for funding under such a system is enormous. Since 1992, well over 100 donor countries have provided more than $42 billion for over 330 appeals through CAP to address the needs of people in more than 50 countries and regions. Think of the opportunities if the identification of the universe of needs is broadened and better advertised.

Related to this question of knowing what projects do exist, there are a number of other websites NGOs need to study, all designed for the humanitarian development and relief community that a team leader (Chap. 1) could use as a starting point for funds.

**Financial Tracking Service** This UN site can be found on ReliefWeb.int and explains how well appeals are being funded and whether or not pledges are being fulfilled. Ministries and other organizations need help both before an emergency to reduce their risks and after a disaster strikes in order to effectively respond and build for a more sustainable future. FTS tracks needs, who pledges to help, progress made, and if the pledges for financial assistance were met (UN_OCHA 2010b).[4]

**Good Humanitarian Donorship Initiative (GHD)** In the mid-1990s, NGOs, the Red Cross, and United Nations agencies involved in humanitarian assistance decided to create their own specific guidelines, define their responsibilities and rights under international law, and set standards against which they could be accountable. An outcome of this work was the Sphere Project. The point was that donors would be more likely to provide funds to NGOs which operate in an open, transparent manner that also increased professionalism. All humanitarian NGOs, regardless of professional focus, meet those standards (GHD Initiative 2010).[5]

**Online Project System (OPS)** The United Nations asks humanitarian NGOs to use the OPS to bid on a project or propose their own project, while some NGO projects will be so specific that OPS would not list them, especially when taking the big-tent approach to what is considered humanitarian.[6]

**Central Emergency Response Fund (CERF)** This is primarily a cash-flow mechanism allowing UN agencies to access funds rapidly while waiting for donor pledges to be transferred—important since pledges often are often slow, being tied to fiscal years than actual needs. The CERF also does not directly fund NGOs (UN_OCHA 2010); however, NGOs can be funded by projects funded by CERF.[7]

### *9.8.1 The European Commission*

Within the EC, the Humanitarian Aid Department (ECHO) is definitely a body that NGOs should consider. It is the service of the European Commission responsible for humanitarian assistance. Various directorates in the EC are also likely potential sources for development opportunities. Probably the best approach is to ask for targeted project funds. Project funds related to appeals are also a good approach with ECHO; it provided in 2009 nearly a billion dollars in assistance in a wide range of emergencies, a lot of it directly to NGOs. The range of projects can vary topically as well, not just disaster assistance but also risk reduction. In Somaliland in 2010, they funded a project to provide disincentives to youths turning to radical groups. ECHO also funds capacity building in international organizations. In 2010, the Foreign Affairs Council of the European Union asked ECHO to build a food security program to help the more than one billion poor people who are food insecure (ECHO).

[4]Thanks to UN/OCHA staff for help on this.

[5]Thanks to UN/OCHA staff for help on this.

[6]Thanks to UN/OCHA staff for help on this.

[7]Thanks to UN/OCHA staff for help on this.

#### 9.8.1.1 Credentials and Who Decides What with the European Commission

European governments and the European Commission are very friendly to humanitarian issues and major donors; it is important to understand how to communicate with the EC in a UN context and who makes decisions. One of the first surprises is that the EC is not accorded the same status as member states. That's because the EC is not a state, only its constituent members. This means that an NGO wanting to work with the EC should also develop relations with member state foreign ministries so that they guide the EC Representative to the UN. For most humanitarian issues, this won't be a problem; it might be for niche issues like animal protection, even though protecting livestock reduces poverty and hunger, the latter an especially critical issue in 2012 with over one billion people starving across the globe. NGOs also need to work with the EC office in New York, Geneva, Rome, or wherever negotiations are going on; keeping mind that while member states value the EC's participation as an Observer to the UN, those normal observer rights, combined with representation through the EU (European Union) presidency, are considered the boundaries of their authority. The EU does try for full representation, what is called "additionality"; governments like the United States will resist, insisting that representation be made through the EC Presidency, which is a UN member state. That delegation will then speak on behalf of the community as a whole. The most EC officials will get its accreditation by the Credentials Committee as members of the delegation of the country holding the Presidency. There are exceptions in multilateral bodies, such as the Australia Group, which tries to prevent the spread of chemical weapons.

Despite these challenges, the EC is a welcome and powerful partner. Having them on an NGOs side is a plus. A suggestion is to have an NGO representative to the UN make him or herself well known to the EC Observer Mission to the UN, the mission holding the Presidency (which rotates) and missions of EU member states thought to be most helpful to the NGOs positions. However, be aware that the New York Mission of the EC might not set negotiating policy on certain issues done by the EC Observer Mission to the United States in Washington, DC, specifically through the office that handles Food Safety, Health and Consumer Affairs. This office gets its instructions directly from Brussels. It is the same for the Australian and New Zealand delegations to the UN. Their Washington embassies develop guidance on specific topics.

Many NGOs tackle the issue of EC positions in the UN by first approaching a relevant topical council like the Agriculture and Fisheries Council in Brussels to support their initiative. That Council in turn might pass a resolution "of support in principle for the development of the initiative." The resolution in question might then be sent to the Council of Europe, which also might pass a similar resolution, this time going even further, such as "unanimous support to the development of X initiative." That resolution is then passed through Washington to the EC Observer Mission to the UN or perhaps through the presidency. This might seem a victory. Every member state of the EU will now vote for the initiative! After all, the Council of Europe voted unanimously! Unfortunately, the victory may be illusory. "Agreements in principle" happen all the time in multilateral diplomacy. They do not mean "agreement in fact" or "agreement to actual text." The EC office in New York may well first call around to the various EU member state missions and ask them to inquire as to how far their governments feel this issue can go or to consult on text, even when support for a topic is clear.

Suppose that an NGO initiative is a text of some sort, perhaps to protect indigenous swamp people, and that text is in the form of a draft resolution, a Declaration, even a Convention, and the Council of Europe said "unanimous support to the development of the text." This is a very strong language indeed; it doesn't mean that Brussels blessed the text, only "its development." The NGO will have an ally in the EC; the member states will need to vote (unless they have conveyed competency to the EC), and while they might agree to the concept of "developing language," they just as easily can disagree on a particular set of words or agree to text changes that totally undermine the intentions of the initiative, from the perspective of the NGO. The NGO will still need to return to the individual governments and seek support for the "specific text."

Some do feel that one might not need to go back to governments for support of specific text when a minister in the Council of ministers is empowered to commit his or her government. In other words, the minister's signature "is the signature of the whole government"; at least that's the argument. Moreover, each minister in the Council is answerable to his or her national parliament and to the citizens that parliament represents. "This ensures the democratic legitimacy of the Council's decisions." All that is true, except that in the example cited, the only thing the Council agreed to was a concept, not specific words. It is very important to pay exact attention to the words of any communiqué from Brussels.

Though it can seem an arcane point of international law for an NGO to consider, the topic of "additionality" is important, especially as the European Union is expanding, as is its governing structure. It is also important because European Union member states are among the most productive and progressive in the UN system. The whole question of the legal status of the EU is changing and it may be soon that not just the EC but the EU gains "legal personality," with competence over new topics in the UN. In such a situation, the EU might have the right to exercise the votes of the member states. In such a circumstance, the assumptions above will change, and negotiations on an "agreement in principle" or "an agreement to develop" could be held directly with the EU, the advantage being not having to negotiate with each member state individually (Maier 2010a).

### *9.8.2 International Organizations as Donors*

Engaging an international organization is very similar to engaging ministries, missions, and embassies. Many NGOs like writing to the Secretary General in order to short circuit the process and speed and ask for funds or political support. This can work if the NGO has excellent personal connections, but without such an advantage, it almost never succeeds. It is usually best to first find out who in the organization has primary responsibility for the topic of focus and build a relationship from the bottom up. When writing to a national agency like the US Department of State about wanting funds to help with the food security issues of migrating women in camps in Mauritania, instead of communicating directly with the Secretary of State, write to the Assistant Secretary of State for the Bureau of Population, Refugees, and Migration (PRM), perhaps the Director for Mauritanian affairs. Once the right officer is found in the organization, build a relationship and ask questions about the organization's mission, how NGOs interact with it, and whether funding for projects is possible. If the subject officer is convinced of the value of an NGO's proposals, then it has a permanent supporter at the working level.

**Note** We are not recommending that NGOs never write to heads of government or government departments, only that in most cases, such letters won't get to the intended target. However, if the NGO has a direct connection, it should consider using it. In the case study of Herbert Hoover's rescue of Belgium, he had already developed relationships with senior members of the media, the British prime minister, the US Ambassador and other senior officials. For Hoover's NGO, direct contact with senior decision makers worked very well and sped relief. In fact Hoover directly challenged the British prime minister on decisions as a social and intellectual equal, and gain positive results. (Nash, *The Life of Herbert Hoover: The Humanitarian 1914–1917* 1988b, p. 69)

Consider UNHCR (the High Commissioner for Refugees). Instead of going to the High Commissioner in Geneva, while Roeder was serving as an NGO official, he used an officer who worked on food security and livelihood protection schemes. The UN official became Roeder's advocate and introduced him to many other officers in UNHCR with related interests. Now if the NGO needs the support of the High Commissioner, it has a trusted subject expert to support proposals. Another reason to do this is that staff officers last longer than CEOs, who frequently move on.

In addition to finding out which office(s) might cover an NGO's areas of focus, check the website out for information on collaboration with NGOs and funding projects. Most IOs have a special section on interaction and, like the World Food Program (WFP), have developed brochures that cover rules and funding opportunities. Also, fully review the many areas of interest by the IO before making the first appointment. Doing that due diligence will say to the new contact that the NGO is serious. After all, the contact might not be the only official that can help.

It is also important to know that IOs are organized like commercial corporations, except that instead of a board of directors made up of important private investors and talented corporate leaders, each IO has a governing body made up of government representatives. Governments are usually the primary donors and the keepers of the charter, so it is important to understand their point of view, keeping in mind that if the agency decides to fund a project, a member government might as well. And if one of the governing body governments is an ally of the NGO, that government can also lobby for NGO interests.

Most work with an IO is done with the secretariat, which, follows the political guidance of the governing body and manage the IO. The bottom line is that IOs are not just technical bodies. They are political. Sometimes the Secretaries General (Chief Executive Officers) give personality to their organizations, like Achim Steiner of UNEP or Kofi Annan, who used to be the UN's Secretary General. The IO is a living organism, so it is important before engaging it that its mission and daily pulse be understood. If that is done, partnerships will probably open up.

For NGOs interested in collaborating with international organizations on emergency management response or prevention issues, go to ReliefWeb and PreventionWeb (http://www.reliefweb.int or http://www.preventionweb.net). Both are excellent resources managed by OCHA and portals to explain what NGOs and IOs are already doing. ReliefWeb operates under a UN General Assembly resolution. That kind of research will be invaluable when making a first appointment.

# Chapter 10
# Meetings and Conferences

**Extract** *Highpoints*: The focus is on the preparation for meetings and international conferences, as well as their management and how to use them to advance diplomatic initiatives. Great attention is given to the role of conference secretariats, special committees, and staff. In addition, the roles of Administrative and Protocol Officer are introduced.

## 10.1 Why Hold Private Meetings and Attend Conferences?

Regarding the modern multilateral system, it used to be said by the League of Nations that it was a model for *diplomacy by conference*, a system of dialogue used to settle disputes or the need for international standards. The same could be said today of the United Nations and of many international organizations like OECD or the Red Cross movement and NGO conferences led by the DPI/NGO community[1] based in New York or the conferences led by InterAction in Washington, DC; ICVA; and CoNGO in Geneva, New York, and elsewhere. Conferences offer a major platform to use a single moment in time to impress many governments and institutions, especially useful to an NGO alerting the global community to a solution. In addition, people, institutions, and governments with which one might not otherwise associate attend the conferences. As an example, NGOs worried about the treatment of female migrants in a country might not have permission to cross the border; conferences offer an opportunity to either reproach governmental behavior publicly or meet privately with governmental representatives. Such "private meetings" happen during the preparatory stage conference, as part of the daily life of international organizations or in "the margins of a conference" (Fig. 10.1).

[1]UN Department of Public Information Non-Governmental Organizations

L.W. Roeder, Jr. and A. Simard, *Diplomacy and Negotiation for Humanitarian NGOs*, Humanitarian Solutions in the 21st Century, DOI 10.1007/978-1-4614-7113-4_10,

**Fig. 10.1** Entering a conference hall (© 2012 LRoeder)

## 10.2 Short Meetings

Even a simple meeting requires serious preparation, if not a formal decision memo. That's because in any international conference, the most effective meetings are often held in corridors and side rooms. However, these side events can be as formal as those held in a mission; some sort of set of questions needs to be asked very similar to that needed for a major decision:

1. **Is a physical meeting needed**? Reporting at the end of the year that an NGO representative saw 20 diplomats might look impressive, but was anything learnt or the status quo changed? Did the meeting raise money? That is what matters. If a representative just wishes to impart information, a letter with attachments is often just as effective, perhaps phone calls or e-mails. In fact, personal diplomacy involving phone calls is often an excellent alternative to physical meetings, being quicker and not requiring travel.
2. **Why this particular mission**? There is only so much time, so what makes this venue important versus the others? Who will be visited? Does the contact have authority to make decisions?
3. **Understanding**. Does the person visited understand your NGO's concerns or the basic topic? If not, bring solid briefing material.
4. **New issues**. What new issues might the contact person raise? For example, if you are asking them for help, what happens if the contact asks for assistance on something? Be prepared.

5. **Is there an appointment**? Do not just show up. Set a date, time, and venue to allow the person being met to prepare and set up an agenda in advance. Make sure there is enough time to achieve the key goals. Request the meeting in writing and then follow up with phone requests. Be on time.
6. **Venue**. UN missions change, and some missions occupy more than one building. Make sure the address is correct. If time is available, scout the location in advance. Start with the Blue Book, which is published every September by the Protocol and Liaison Service of the UN.
7. **Report on the meeting**. HQ and other parts of the lead NGO need to know what happened and understand any recommendations the representative might have or new issues. That means notes must be taken, often a problem for a negotiator. A suggestion is that someone should be charged with note-taking; if that's impossible, once the meeting is over, be certain to immediately jot down all important points from memory, and if more than one delegation member attended, compare notes.
8. **Get items in place**. The right handouts in the right order keep meetings smooth.
9. **Keep it simple**. Have no more than three goals in mind. Contacts are busy.
10. **Ask if the person being met has questions**. Orally summarize any agreement in case the person met has a different interpretation.

## 10.3 International Conferences

### *10.3.1 Why Attend?*

International Conferences[2] and Seminars are:

- A great way to introduce a diplomatic initiative. Many such events have small meeting rooms or opportunities to raise ideas; if an NGO isn't certain how well an initiative's packaging will be received, a low-key test bed could be a carefully selected conference that deals with a related topic.
- Often the best way to advance a full initiative; to convince a large group of governments, international organizations and other NGOs, industry representatives,

[2]By way of interest, the first international conference to which the United States officially participated was the 1853 Maritime Conference in Brussels in 1853. Sponsored by the US government, it was established to create a uniform system of maritime meteorological observations. The conference was a technical conference due to the subject matter. Of course, many international conferences had been held before then with US government and NGO officials as observers or in their personal capacity. The United States also intended to officially attend the 1826 Panama Congress, but one delegate died at the sea, and the other was unable to attend while the event was in session. The first truly diplomatic conference was the First Red Cross Conference in Geneva in 1864 "Conference international pour la neutralization du service de santa militaire en champagne." American NGOs did however heavily participate in conferences, e.g., the General Peace Congress of 1851 in London and the 1848 General Peace Conference in Brussels.

and donors; and to formally support ideas through resolutions, declarations, and other public means.
- An excellent way of showcasing the inherent value of an NGO.
- Not a final destination rather a transit point in a long process, often the result of years of negotiations and the beginning of many more, sort of a milestone like the Earth Summit in Rio de Janeiro in 1992, otherwise known as the UN Conference on Environment and Development.

International conferences and various forms of multilateral diplomacy have been around for a very long time. It is worth noting that in 1916, Leonard Woolf, working with Bernard Shaw, remarked that diplomats had a tendency to narrow negotiations in conferences to "the arrangement of the details of settlements already arrived at by negotiations" (Woolf 1916a). A century later, that is still often true. Frequently, the real deals are made in preparatory conferences, leaving summits and the named conferences to endorsements, which is why NGOs need to attend both. Don't just wait until the deal is sealed. Be part of the process from the beginning. NGOs need to attend conferences and seminars if they want to collaborate and influence the UN system, the International Red Cross and Red Crescent Movement, the World Bank group, or other humanitarian international organizations. That way, NGOs can help develop broad-based agreements or at least learn what others are doing. Some will have a very narrow geographic focus such as in 2012 when a member of the Gender Network (GDNET) set up a seminar "on woman's rights and acid throwing of women in Pakistan," with a focus on the District of Lodhran, Pakistan (Baloch 2012, April 10). However, even though such a seminar is small, it can have a major impact on a local topic and be an energizer for larger regional and international conferences.

Though few in number in the early days of the UN, regional and international conferences have increased in frequency and are a popular tool for all international organizations and major NGOs, often have prime ministers and presidents in attendance, and are an exciting opportunity for old-fashioned lobbying and diplomacy. The World Conference on Disaster Reduction (WCDR) was attended by the Emperor and Prime Minister of Japan and high-level delegations from 160 governments, along with 40,000 interested delegates from NGOs, Universities, media, and industry. Forty-seven thousand attended the 1992 Earth Summit in Rio and 50,000 debated the rights of women in Beijing in 1995. But they don't have to be large to be useful. A much smaller Global Risk Forum (GRF) hosts the International Disaster and Risk Conference (IDRC) on a biennial basis in Davos, Switzerland, and those meetings are an outstanding opportunity for experts and managers from NGOs, international organizations, and governments to meet in an intimate setting well suited for real interaction.[3]

[3]The purpose of the Global Risk Forum is to "bridge the gap between science and practice, to promote the worldwide exchange of know-how and experience, to target solutions and promote good practice in integral risk management and climate change adaptation for an improved understanding, assessment and management of disasters and risks that affect human safety, security, health, the environment, critical infrastructures, the economy and society at large, to provide and manage a network for decision-makers, practitioners and experts from politics, government, IGOs, business, science, NGOs, media and the public" (Amman, Goals of the Global Risk Forum).

Some scholars will argue that conference diplomacy is different from multilateral diplomacy, unless the conference consists of only one or two governments; that is too precise a parsing. Conferences are usually but not always about making a deal. They are also often about convening experts to discuss the latest science or decide upon the usefulness of a project or to explore an idea, e.g., the sustainable risk reduction meetings of OECD, which convene experts to develop experiments that show how to avoid tomorrow's potential disasters. But whatever the reason for the conference, it will be a great venue for some NGOs to network and lobby, and it is also important for someone on the NGO staff to track conferences through the various UN secretariats or through NGO umbrella bodies like ICVA, CoNGO, and InterAction in order to find which will be of the most value.

Although like the opening meeting of the Friends of Syria in February 2012, conferences are often led by senior officials, even Ministers—supported by middle-level staff, this isn't always so, as seen by the 2001 Reykjavik Conference on Responsible Fisheries in the Marine Ecosystem, which was led by middle managers (FAO: Corporate Services, Human Resources and Finance Department 2001). Either way, virtually any such conference presents networking opportunities. If an NGO is thinking of developing a diplomatic initiative, the team leader should consider sending staff members to related international conferences well in advance just to introduce themselves to participants. After all, they will be the ones who will decide their agency's policies on the topic of interest. Showing up shows seriousness of purpose, and exploratory conversations are bound to help a delegation refine thinking.

Especially for NGOs wanting to host a conference, another factor to keep in mind is that these events are very expensive, often costing tens of millions of dollars, when one combines the costs of the secretariat with travel costs of government, IO, and NGO delegations. In other words, when an NGO builds its annual budget for conferences, it probably will have to be very selective, especially given the current economy. As for attending, having been delegates to a great many of these events since the 1970s, the authors tend to think that the focus on costs by donor nations is overdone by many NGO managers. There is no question that conferences cost money; consider the opportunity costs of not attending as well as the values gained from networking and inserting positive statements in outcomes documents. This was the approach taken in 2004 when the government of Japan asked Roeder to support for the WCDR in Kobe. He was then the Policy Adviser on Disaster Management in the IO Bureau. Roeder insisted that the conference have a well-defined outcomes document that changed the status quo and that it be the beginning event of a decade of changes in risk reduction practices like the Earth Summit in Rio or the United Nations World Summit on Sustainable Development (WSSD) (Earth Summit II or Rio +10) in Johannesburg, South Africa. The Japanese ended up turning WCDR into one of the most important international conferences in history by creating the Hyogo Framework for action, an action plan for reducing risk.

NGOs are in the business of changing the status quo, through lobbying or negotiation; while budget staffs must be listened to, they should not be able to dismiss the networking and educational values of conferences. Such events pave the way for arguments that enhance lobbying and negotiation. It all must be seen as part of the same package. Even if an NGO is not there to advance specific language, it can build alliances. That can lead to an important negotiation at a later date. The NGO might also wish to use those events to build awareness of its issue years in advance and find potential supporters, not just among the institutional Decision Makers but the community at large.

Another reason to attend an international conference is to learn how an institution works. Perhaps an NGO wants to ask the World Bank Group to support a project, but the staff has never met a World Bank official. Before going to one of the banks in the group, the NGO should send staff to attend the Annual Bank Conferences on Development Economics (ABCDE). This series, which began in Washington, DC, in 1988, advances new theories of development and is an excellent platform to see what the bank, the UN, and donors are thinking. Without presenting any formal initiatives, the staff can learn a lot about development programs and procedures, enough to prepare for formal meetings or find donors.

Some NGO leaders told us they were worried about being lost in a large conference, that their ideas would not be noticed; that's a misplaced fear if the NGO prepares and performs well. NGOs are often being more effective than government delegations. Consider the 1997 Convention on the Prohibition of the Use, Stockpiling, Production and Transfer of Anti-Personnel Mines and on their Destruction is an international agreement that bans antipersonnel landmines. It is usually referred to as the Ottawa Convention or the Mine Ban Treaty and was concluded by the Diplomatic Conference on an International Total Ban on Anti-Personnel Land Mines at Oslo on 18 Sept. 1997. What makes this special to the NGO community is that while the Convention is an agreement between governments, NGOs began the initiative, in particular the International Campaign to Ban Landmines (ICBL), which helped draft the treaty. Indeed, the ICBL had a formal seat at the table in all of the diplomatic meetings leading up to the negotiations and then during the negotiations themselves. ICBL later was awarded the Nobel Prize for its efforts. And that's not the only example. There are many others (UNOG) (ICBL).

## 10.4 The Delegation Administrative and Protocol Officer

For reading ease, various functions have been combined into a single role of ***Administrative and Protocol Officer***; this officer furthers an NGO-led diplomatic initiative, not a general support for the NGO back home. Remembering as well that small NGOs have limited resources, this specific function might be accomplished by a single person or a group of people from allied NGOs, some physically a part of the delegation and others perhaps in an HQ; that will depend on many factors, intra-NGO politics, available resources, etc., and the nature of the negotiation. But for purposes of this book, the function of Administrative Officer will be treated as an official physically part of the delegation. In summary, the Admin Officer:

(a) ***Manages security issues:*** If there is no security adviser. That's very important in field operations and could also be crucial in a huge international conference, if only to reduce theft of laptops.

(b) ***Manages physical communications:*** This is everything from setting up Internet networks to acquiring cell phones. It is very important to maintain communications between team members, negotiating partners, and HQ throughout a negotiation; if an Internet room is provided on the conference site, check the reliability of the connection. What mobile phone system is used? Should mobile phone be rented for each member of the team? In Somaliland, three different SIM cards go into the mobile phone. Some countries just need one and others two.

(c) ***Sets up meetings:*** This could be arranging for a conference room or transportation to making sure everyone is in the same hotel, etc., and the proper briefing material is available for the delegation.

(d) ***Visas, maps, currency, and transportation:*** Frequently, no visa is required, but if the delegation is multinational, make sure the member have a visa in advance, if one is needed. Definitely, do not make the common mistake of obtaining a visa at the border. While many countries permit this, like Dubai and Kenya, significant delays can occur, as well as additional charges. In addition, a visa can be denied due to some misunderstanding. If a visa might be needed, best to obtain in advance, and if there is any chance the delegate may return, he or she should obtain a "multiple entry visa." Once the delegation leaves the airport or road entry point, transportation, currency, and maps will be needed. All of these should be obtained in advance by the administration officer. The delegation may also have to buy currency at the border if the host country has a "soft currency" and then sell the remainder on departure at an unfavorable rate.

(e) ***Budget:*** Every delegation has a budget. It is essential that the Admin Officer pay the bills and make sure that the delegation operates within its budget. It is assumed the HQ team has a parallel officer.

(f) ***Protocol:*** While every member of the delegation should be familiar with the rules of protocol, especially the chief negotiator, it is good to hand on deck an expert (see Chap. 11).

## 10.5 The Delegation Office

Small NGO delegations may not need a formal office, but a large delegation or any delegation planning on a lot of meetings, perhaps a party, may find it wise to rent space and install equipment. An office can also be used to stow large demonstration items like posters that would not fit in a hotel room. In some cases, the office will be on the conference site if a lot of use is expected during the day and in other cases at the hotel for after-hours work and meetings. This is a judgment and budget call. Some teams will even have dedicated phones, TVs, and computers installed to enable 24/7 (permanent) phone contact with home base or the ability to write reports, have late-hour meetings with the team, and watch breaking news. If a delegation can afford it, it should obtain a refrigerator for its own food and drink—much cheaper than a minibar and healthier. Make sure there is plenty of bottled water on hand, no alcohol.

## 10.6 Learn the Compound Layout in Advance

UN compounds often operate in old structures. The FAO HQ is in the Mussolini era Department of Agriculture Building in Rome. The main compound in Geneva was the League of Nations, but some structures date from before World War I. UNESCO and Nairobi compounds are confusing, as is OCED in Paris, so a suggestion is that if the delegation has never been to the building or compound, obtain a floor plan or find an escort; being late for meetings can kill opportunities. New York's main compound is deteriorating, so as a result of the UN Capital Master Plan (CMP), the entire complex is being renovated. Over half a century in age, the buildings are no longer safe or secure (UNGA resolutions 57/292, 60/282 and 61/251, and 62/87). With a projected cost over nearly $2 billion, the construction and renovation of the New York compound, begun in 2009, will continue for some years and impinge on NGO access, especially the ability to host meetings or social functions, and it is harder to display material. This is because of reduced available space and the right of national delegations to preempt NGO reservations.

## 10.7 Preconference Tactics

### *10.7.1 The Sequential Negotiation Technique*

There are several methods to prepare for a complex negotiation involving many players. The sequential negotiation technique is on. Suppose an NGO or coalition wishes to take on as complex a negotiation as upgrading the rights enjoyed by Internally Displaced Persons (IDPs), bringing them more in line with those enjoyed by refugees. Current handling of IDPs by humanitarians is covered by an IASC document known as The Guiding Principles of Internal Displacement, published by OCHA (UN OCHA 2004). See also *Compilation and Analysis of Legal Norms* (Representative of the Secretary-General 1996). While IDPs do have rights, the responsibility for IDPs largely rests with the national authority. If the internationally recognized rights are to be significantly expanded, that would require bringing on board many governments, probably from each region.

One reason multilateral diplomacy is hard is that many players are usually involved at one time, governments, perhaps NGO delegations, and international organizations, and it is a well-known fact that the more negotiating partners there are in one room, the harder it can be to come to consensus, to identify sticking points or even avenues for success. Often the negotiating partners will operate on rigid instructions from their capitals. For the hypothetical negotiation on IDPs, one needs to remember as well that in the UN, negotiations could involve all 192 member states, as well as many departments, international organizations, and influential NGOs. Some may not have much stake in a specific negotiation like upgrading IDP rights, but all can either vote or influence the vote. This can place a delegate at a disadvantage in the UN General Assembly or ECOSOC meeting. It can also be a disadvantage in a small conference setting. One mistake or fuzzy choice of words will be heard by all of the other delegates at the same time, and under the normal rules of procedure, once a delegate speaks, he or she must listen to everyone else's reply before speaking again.

Another way to look at this is while a delegate only gets one chance ordinarily to lay out the plan; the group which is listening gets many opportunities in a compressed space of time to misunderstand, change the meaning of the delegate's words, and undermine the initiative, even if unintentionally. Thus, due to the nature of such discussions, the underlying rationale behind contrary positions might not be as clearly understood to the NGO as would have been the case in a private bilateral discussion, where there is more give and take. Even if the delegates are friendly and use short statements, the wait for a second statement by the presenting NGO delegation can be very long. The group experience can then become one large, counterargument, with one constructive criticism feeding into others, a verbal tsunami that weakens an NGO delegate's ability to parse the subtle nuances presented by each individual player and then craft a reasonable stand that carries the day forward.

In one situation examined for this book, an NGO team leader consulted with the lead NGO's allies and required the chief negotiator to present an idea to a group of national delegates at the UN who were friendly towards the NGO coalition's general concept. Unfortunately, they were also unfriendly towards the way the package was framed. Though HQ had been forewarned of this problem by the chief negotiator, the team leader said the allies disagreed with the negotiator's assessment and needed to see their rendition of the package presented. That was their right of course. HQ always has the final say.[4] They insisted that the chief negotiator move forward with their formulation. Unfortunately for the initiative, the national delegates quickly talked the idea down, with one negative statement after the other in the space of about an hour, which was the maximum time allotted for the meeting. This is also something any negotiator needs to keep in mind. Time is a precious commodity, especially for UN missions. The staffs are usually very overworked.

The day was saved when the chief negotiator proposed a draft reformulation in the last minutes of the allotted time, but that could only take place after everyone had spoken. The delegates did agree in principle to the new formulation but were visibly upset over the initial tactic of presenting a package that had already been rejected in private meetings. As a result, the positive momentum which existed prior to the meeting was lost. Quite apart from the mistake of ignoring "intelligence," the team back at HQ had unwisely chosen a front attack approach, presenting the controversial package to a large group of decision makers with no time for serious debate. chief negotiators do make mistakes, so it was not unethical to require the chief negotiator to re-propose a rejected idea. However, given the intelligence the chief negotiator provided to HQ, which was based on many interviews in NY, if the HQ team felt strongly about its own formulation, a wiser approach might have been a "sequential negotiation," but it does require significant planning and expenses.

[4]We also need to keep in mind that the chief negotiator might have been incorrect. It does happen.

In the "sequential negotiation" technique, a chief negotiator can cause any one delegation to respond to his or her presentation in private, without any other delegation being aware of what the others have said. This tactic also allows an NGO delegation time to strengthen/refine weak points in its own position along the trail to a formal conference where the stakes are higher. Larger NGOs will have an easier time of it; small NGOs can definitely use this method if they pool resources with friendly NGOs in a coalition.

In the hypothetical example, once the team decides who to meet along the road (which requires much analysis), the KM (knowledge management) team should study the probable positions of the contacts. Then, starting with the friendliest and ending with the least, the chief negotiator should visit the appropriate ministries in each country (Foreign Ministry, plus expert ministries) or agencies. Preparation may also require engaging local NGOs for intelligence best contacts. The entire preparation process will be very time-consuming, probably involving much use of social media between partners.

Starting with the first contact, the chief negotiator examines the official's comments on the draft text, discusses alternative language, and enquires as to what the contact thinks will be the reactions of other governments or international organizations. *If the NGO cannot afford to visit all of the needed contacts, choose a representative sampling.* As the chief negotiator moves along the route, keeping HQ informed, the proposal will probably have to be adjusted with the team leader coordinating with allies. Assuming the allies agree to reasonable adjustments, now the chief negotiator can arrive at the office of the last contact with what is likely to be the strongest package. This also changes the psychology of the negotiations, because ministers, Agency leaders, and their staff will respect the expense and effort required for such a personal venture. Further, because the discussion of the draft proposal has been split across individual meetings instead of clumped into one, the NGO gets ten times as much time with contact. The players will also have reacted to their guest in private, thus giving the chief negotiator valuable intelligence needed to offer language adjustments without compromising values.

This is a tough economy, so the budget-meisters may balk at this idea, especially as the chief negotiator may have to entertain some decision makers along the route; when the budget officers complain, remind them of the discussion on challenging the axioms. Also remind them that by the time the last contact is visited, the NGO delegation will be talking to the toughest opponent with the advantage of language the others are likely to accept. That's the value of prior consultations. Even if the last contact does not concur with the revisions, this effort will gain the NGO delegation much respect, placing the NGO in a strong position at the conference:

> An alternative to physically conducting each session in person is to hold meetings online, using one of the many available video conferencing services like Skype or social-media. That technique is perfectly legitimate, especially when taking into account costs; nothing beats personal contact and the value of meeting over meals or short walks. It is similar to developing this book, which came about by taking parts to experts around the world before presenting the entire product for public consumption.

### 10.7.2 Building Allies in Advance

Tactics are situational. In the above case of the overly insistent HQ, a sequential tactic might have been an effective tool, but other methods can work just as well. Suppose an NGO team has worked for years on a text and a conference has been announced to agree on a final version. Even if the sequential method was used, do not assume that because the tour was made, the revised/improved text will be "the final word." Influential governments might propose a surprise text. Roeder had to do this regarding the Tampere Convention on the Provision of Emergency Telecommunications, which had been initiated by an NGO, the American Radio Relay League (ARRL), and supported by UN agencies, and some governments would not survive US Senate confirmation. At the time, he was in the Department of State, and the US government definitely supported the ARRL's initiative, knew they had engaged in a sequential process of their own, and felt that relief workers around the world desperately needed such a Convention. In addition, Washington supported the UN's efforts to advance the Convention, led by one of the UN's foremost experts in emergency management, Hans Zimmermann; however, the government was also determined to change the text negotiated by ARRL, this because legal scholars felt elements of it were unconstitutional. Wanting a successful conference as well as an agreement on an alternative text, Roeder, who was chief negotiator for the US delegation, linked up with the German, British, and Canadian delegations by telephone and e-mail in advance and agreed to a joint draft which was then presented to the UN and the interested nations and NGOs on his first day in Geneva in 1998. ARRL was a bit upset at first, as were some UN folk, but the alliance represented important governments, and instead of jumping in too early, the US team very carefully and gently explained its concerns in the context of being helpful, pointing out that while the US government was arguing for a different text, Washington's goals were the same as those of the conference participants. That bridging point was very important, not to appear arrogant but instead as a friendly power looking for a common solution. The group agreed to use the American text, and the conference moved forward with further edits negotiated over time. There is no reason that an NGO wanting to initiative a convention could not pursue the same tactic, if it is willing to absorb the administrative and cost burdens.

**Note** Preconference private negotiation is common and often essential. On the eve of the San Francisco conference that would create the United Nations, there was still uncertainty about key elements of the structure, especially on the nature of the Security Council, so in the spring of 1944 and just prior to a final drafting session at Dumbarton Oaks estate in Washington, DC, the US team consulted regularly with the governments of Britain, Russia, and China to fine-tune. Surprises by the main victorious powers at the conference could have been disastrous, especially as once the war was concluded, the energy required to craft a new global peacemaking governance body might have dissipated under the pressure to rebuild the world's economies (Schlesinger 2003, p. 47).

## 10.8 Stress Management

The most famous example of stress at a major conference is probably that of Woodrow Wilson, who seriously damaged his health at the Paris Peace Conference, then went on a tiring rail trip to sell the League to the media and the public. Towards the end, he suffered an incapacitating stroke. Stress is always an issue in a negotiation, no matter the age of the delegate. Take it seriously. Although successful negotiations usually begin at ground level, NGOs should eventually negotiate issues at the highest level of government possible, attend UN conferences, and attend diplomatic and local UN functions. Do not worry that an NGO delegation does not represent a government. The delegation represents a serious topic. That is justification enough. Stress management will be important, however, in order for the chief negotiator and the team to be in top form. Failure to do these things can result in serious mistakes that will seriously undermine delegation goals; after all, the delegation is a group of egos that might not necessarily be used to working together and, in another setting, might not even associate with each other. Experienced, longtime negotiators will expect deference and not wish to do minor tasks. It is perfectly natural, if disquieting. Expect tempers to fray, mood swings, depression, and excessive happiness, all part of being a member of a normal delegation.

### *10.8.1 Appropriate Assignments Give Order and Reduce Stress of Confusion*

A delegation chief should chair delegation meetings and agree on daily goals, as well as assign one or more agenda items to each delegation member. The delegation chief—or as formulated the function in this book, the chief negotiator—is in charge, but the team must work as a team, not a military unit. That requires leadership, not dictatorship. Typical assignments are (a) who reads a statement at the plenary sessions, (b) who negotiates which part of the text, and (c) who reports on progress. It is a good idea to have one officer tracking conference events and developing a daily report as a Microsoft Word document. Depending on the technical skills of the team, however, it may be wise to avoid spreadsheet and database software. As noted in the Chapter on Communications, also have an experienced Communications Officer.

The chief also needs to meet privately with each delegation member to make sure that person is relaxed and ready. If the member is new, it is good to ask why he or she is involved and for the chief to do the same. Share personal stories. Every member of the team will be full of zeal; taking the time to know motivation, strengths and perceived weaknesses, worries, etc., can avoid problems downstream. Plus, it shows that chief isn't just a boss. He or she actually cares. That will reap rewards when the going becomes tough, as it always does.

At the end of the day, the secretariat will make announcements, e.g., what is to be covered the following day? If they do not, some member of the delegation must raise the organizational placard in an appropriate plenary meeting and ask or personally seek out the secretariat. This is very important so that an important meeting is not missed the following day.

Predetermine what the team feels are the key issues and then track what other delegations say about those issues as the conference moves forward. These reports should not be verbatim; the idea is to develop a chart that shows in very simple terms what different NGO, IO, and government delegations think, perhaps in two or three words. Collating can be an effort, perhaps too much for a small delegation, but the effort of jotting down comments will be useful during the conference to identify potential allies or adversaries and be useful for research into tactics used at future conferences. There is no one way, whatever works best for the delegation.

A team breakfast meeting is a good idea, during which each member can digest a proper meal and report on his or her goals and what happened the day before. That way, the entire team has the big picture. This will also bring out disagreements; everyone should have a chance to speak, and all opinions need to be respected. This is also the time to link activities to the Journal if the delegation is at the UN. A daily UN Journal should also be examined, setting out meetings which agenda items will be covered in which rooms and at what times. Make this effort an integral item, but do not feel that the agenda must be taken in order. The chief negotiator or a designate should prioritize what is talked about.

When Roeder studied negotiations at the Foreign Service Institute, they taught to almost forget delegation members were humans rather almost as soldiers in the field, though as a former soldier, Roeder will tell you they are the most human of all. It is certainly true that one has to take care of the body. During the day, stay hydrated; keep coffee and tea intake low, and find time to exercise, perhaps by walking upstairs or in a nearby park. Delegates should avoid planning evening sessions and should put some healthy snacks and juice in their briefcase; negotiations can go well past the dinner hour. Be proactive. If there is a piece of an issue needing special attention, try to set up a meeting to deal with it as early as possible with the appropriate delegations.

### *10.8.2 Relax*

Each member should find quiet time at night where for 30 min of uninterrupted time, he or she can sort out what happened during the day. In the morning, the chief should then ask the delegation about progress on objectives and what can be done to further them. Everyone needs quiet time, as well as an evening dinner, dancing, or light drinks where the work of the team is not discussed. Instead, the conversation should act as a release, be about anything other than the work.

**Fig. 10.2** Luggage tag (Collection LRoeder)

## *10.8.3 Jet Lag*

Do not ask teams to go on a long flight and then participate in serious talks on arrival. Even governments make this mistake. A few times when leading team on trade issues, Roeder noticed delegation members from one agency that arrived in the morning were falling asleep by late afternoon. Those who had been there for 2 days were fine, but the sleepy members had produced nothing of value that day, all because their agency wanted to save money. A better idea is to make sure that the entire team arrives in the morning one full day before formal negotiations. Require each delegation member to get plenty of sun on day one. The longer the flight, the more days in advance to arrive. For example, a 12 h flight requires 2 days of rest (Fig. 10.2).

The team should not sleep on arrival, if they arrive in the day. Instead, they should get out and about, moving blood through the body. If a beach is nearby, swim. Make sure everyone eats well and is hydrated, and then have a light team meeting in the late afternoon to go over last-minute administrative or policy issues. That will start to refocus the mind. The team then needs to unwind, watch movies, eat lightly, listen to music, and relax. Do not crash the night before negotiations. "Crashing" is a term that means staying up a night studying or rewriting. If lots of work is needed, bring enough staff to do it, and do not kill chances of a good night's sleep. There are many dangers in crashing, not the least which is that if the team members just left a long flight and are tired, they can make serious judgment errors. On one mission examined for this book, the Chief worked with virtually no sleep and, then one evening, went into the delegation office to look up precedent. In the morning, a guard found all of the safes open! An NGO won't have access to classified information but might have sensitive information like negotiation fallback positions. You certainly don't want to leave those about.

Another recommended night action is to "organize the briefcase." This may sound silly; the chief negotiator would not think so the next morning if the team has to rush and at the conference site some member has forgotten a cell phone, conference pass, perhaps medicine, or position papers. Ten minutes of preparation the night before can save hours of worry the next day.

### *10.8.4 Delegation Size*

The temptation exists to send as many delegates as possible to a conference, workshop, or meeting. Remembering that NGOs are nonprofit organizations, it is wise to resist large staffs. In addition, many events limit delegation sizes. Not only that, but an NGO is limited on the number of temporary ground passes that can be issued by its official representative.

### *10.8.5 E-mail/Phone Communications*

Effective NGOs have always understood the importance of quick communications with members in order to share information or create an instant demonstration. In 1962 during the Cuban Missile Crisis, poor diplomacy at the time could have led to a nuclear holocaust, and domestic politics could have led to a continuation of atmospheric nuclear tests, resulting in deadly pollution. To sensitize the American administration to the desire of many citizens not to go to test weapons, the NGO Women Strike for Peace (WSP), barely a year old, organized a national call system between lead ladies around the country who would then call local women in their cell to mount instant demonstrations. Conservative politicians called them Communists. They in turn joked that they were actually capitalists because the call system increased the revenue of AT&T by tens of thousands of dollars a month (Swerdlow 1993, p. 71)! Today of course, a similar movement would rely on social media.

Just as it was important in 1962 for effective anti-war activists to have access to phones, it is very important for today's NGO delegation to be in touch with each member. Each should have a mobile phone capable of texting, e-mail, and even web browsing; don't treat the texting or e-mails informally. WSP's phone calls were private. E-mails and text messages are not. As delegates get to know someone, the language tends to become "familiar." That is natural, but an e-mail is actually a written record—no less than a formal letter—and should be treated with respect.

Also, keep in mind that parts of the conference building may have poor telephony. An example is the UN General Assembly in New York and some of the basement conference rooms. Cell phones will not always work there, though open computers for delegations are in the hallways. As for computers, any delegates leave their confidential instructions on the hard drive or in the trash bin or perhaps leave themselves logged into their e-mail account. NGO delegations need to avoid that practice, or one's entire strategy will be open to the world. Ambassador Mary

Mel French makes a good point that e-mail is often misused, and accidents can seriously undermine diplomatic efforts, for example, replying to all with a criticism when the intent is to only send to one. It can be very embarrassing (French 2010). The same could be said of social networking sites like Facebook or Twitter, which are useful as convening tools for demonstrations or to set up a simple meeting; they can also convey too much personal information. Keep in mind that the people you are being negotiated with are likely researching your team. Every bit of data on the Internet about a delegation member is potentially a tool for the opposing forces to use to undermine your positions. Paranoid as that might seem, it is true.

## 10.9 Outcome and Discussant Papers

**Discussant Papers and Handouts** Many international conferences base their plenary debate upon participant reports, or perhaps the conference might have working groups that provide an opportunity to present a paper. In addition, very often, papers by NGOs, academic centers, and think tanks are quite welcome, as they offer thoughtful, fresh thinking without committing a government's hand ahead of discussion. Such papers might be provided by academic centers, think tanks, NGOs, etc. As a result, in addition, to coordinating position papers, the Study Team should commission papers for presentation. That will also require getting a speaker on the agenda for either the Plenary or one of the subordinate discussions, perhaps a technical working group. The delegation might even consider sponsoring a working group for this purpose, though a larger audience might be had by participating in existing working groups both as discussants with a paper to present and as a member of the audience with ideas to be heard. Related to this is the matter of handouts, posters, and other such material. Virtually, every conference allows for some distribution of handouts and locations for posters. Especially if a discussant paper proves impossible to organize, then a handout might be a good alternative.

**Outcome Documents** Virtually every conference has an outcomes document that reports on conference accomplishments, perhaps lays out contentious issues, and often sets out proposals for further work. In most instances, it is essential that the NGO delegation do its best to influence the government drafting officers to include language supportive of the NGO initiative and, if no outcomes document is planned, to recommend that one be created. Suppose an NGO is interested in potable water, inserting language on drilling water wells in a country with little such water might be a perfect tool to highlight the issue in a country of concern to the conference attendees and then use that experience to foster work on a global or regional scale. Then, it might be argued that an agreed mandate was provided by conference participants for the action, and from such a mandate, international budgets are often built.

There are circumstances where NGOs or civil society in general has lost faith in government negotiations and, instead of trying to augment the outcomes document, will instead attend the conferences but just use the energy to foster a civil society movement. This happened in 2012 in the Rio+20 Conference. The distain of civil society may be such that they actually repudiate the outcomes document (see Chaps. 15 and 16).

### 10.9.1 *Example of Outcome Documents*

The 23rd General Assembly of the Conference of NGOs in Consultative Relationship to the Economic and Social Council of the United Nations (CoNGO) was held in Geneva, 5–7 Dec. 2007, at the International Conference Center in Geneva (CICG). For over 50 years, CoNGO has been an independent, international, nonprofit membership association of nongovernmental organizations. It facilitates the participation of NGOs in United Nations ECOSOC debates and decision making. CoNGO is most active at the major UN centers of New York, Geneva, and Vienna, but its work stretches out to all regions of the world. In 2007, the head of CoNGO needed a key note speaker on Climate Change, and as Climate Caucus had just been formed in New York with Roeder as one of the leaders, she asked him to speak.[5] Being asked to speak is always important, as it gives exposure, but instead of just agreeing to the request, Roeder asked to include comments on the impact of the climate on his NGO's issues. CoNGO's head agreed and also placed Roeder in the drafting committee for the outcomes document (CoNGO Conference on NGOs 2007b). The speech allowed a platform to push NGO's priorities, and because he participated in the drafting committee, the outcomes document "Call for Action" by the conference included endorsements of Roeder's issues. That was a lot to accomplish out of one negotiation; the end result was one of the oldest NGO alliances in the world agreed to make support another's issues as part of its official and effectively lobby for them as well.

## 10.10 Secretariat and Other Conference Bodies

### 10.10.1 *The Secretariat*

Conferences, international organizations, the General Assembly, ECOSOC, and other bodies have secretariats. The chief negotiator should get to know the secretariat very well. Depending on the nature of the negotiation and the importance given to it by governments, secretariats can be large or small. They are often made up of professional diplomats and international civil servants that provide continuity in the discussions as participating diplomats enter and depart with new assignments.

[5] Climate Caucus was a partnership of NGOs in the CoNGO and DPI/NGO alliances which examined aspects of climate change on everything from the impact on women to the indigenous.

A suggestion is to go to the G77 secretariat for advice on internal G77 rules or to set up appointments. As a treaty is being negotiated, the secretariat follows it, perhaps for years, staying connected with what worked or not over time. They serve the chairperson who may even have an elected Bureau (committee of conference members) elected by the negotiating parties to preside over plenary sessions and working groups.

In the context of conferences or official initiatives, the true client of the secretariat is the conference or the initiative, not home agency. It is their job to find a way to success, though not to advance a substantive agenda. As a result, a secretariat can provide clarity to NGO issues and be an effective mediator. The secretariat, through its chairperson, will also seek to find ways of stimulating collaboration between the parties. If an NGO delegation can appear to be useful to the goals of the secretariat, the secretariat can prove useful to the NGO at critical moments. In 2004 in preparation for the WCDR, the United States, Great Britain, and others regularly coordinated efforts with the secretariat in order to avoid duplication of efforts and to keep the secretariat informed. In return, the secretariat kept us well informed of preparatory developments as well, as it would have for any government who asked, especially regarding the roles of regional or interest groups like the LDCs (less developed countries).

**Recommendation** The NGO chief negotiator should introduce his or her team to the secretariat, share goals, and ask for guidance. In a real sense, the secretariat is there to help the initiative succeed; if the delegation can convince the staff that its issues are important, of added value, the secretariat will also help.

### *10.10.2 The Conference Chairperson*

An NGO delegation should meet the chairperson and secretariat to impress them that it intends to make a constructive contribution. They in turn will think of the delegation in a positive light; remember it when members put their hands up to be recognized. For example, in 2006, Roeder attended the International Disaster Reduction Conference (IDRC 2006) in Davos, Switzerland, an annual risk reduction conference held by the Swiss Government in cooperation with other governments, the UN, the Red Cross, and civil society. At the time, he represented a British NGO and wanted to gain some significant exposure for its issues, so well in advance of the event, he called on the conference host on a regular basis, impressing on him the link between his British NGO's priorities and sustainable development. This eventually led to Roeder being selected as an honorary conference chair, which in turn enabled him to present a major address on his topic to some of the most important risk reduction experts in the world (Roeder, *Linking Animal Welfare and Human Survival* 2006). He was also invited to the VIP dinner to meet with the Governor of Harbin, China, who expressed interest in cooperation. That kind of success is rare but doable if a chief negotiator is prepared to be persistent (Amman, *IDRC Davos 2006 Conference Brochure and Program* 2006), in other words another example of how making an investment can reap rewards.

## 10.11 Credentials Committee and Rules of Procedure

Most major international conferences have some sort of credentials committee to make sure people attending have the right to be there, and NGOs are generally handled differently from national delegations. Assuming such a committee exists and follows normal practice, NGOs asking to attend will be asked in advance to certify eligibility, according to rules set in place in advance (usually on the conference website), and then to announce the chief negotiator, the deputy, and other representatives, often called "alternate delegates or alternative representatives" (Fig. 10.3).

**Fig. 10.3** Credentials Desk ((c) 2012 LRoeder)

In some conferences, NGOs (especially those with ECOSOC accreditation) have the right to speak, even propose language changes to resolutions, which is a powerful tool to advance NGO initiatives. This has been done many times, and NGOs often are accorded nameplates, just like a national delegation. But this is not always the case. A delegation might only be allowed to speak in workshops or perhaps provide a short statement in plenary after national representatives and senior UN officials have spoken. The rules might also limit delegation size. Nevertheless, no matter how small, all of these opportunities are tools to elevate NGO policies.

## 10.12 Role of the Drafting Committee

What if along the way, a delegate becomes stuck on a contentious issue and no one seems ready to agree to specific words? This happened in the Tampere Convention negotiations in a later session in Finland. To resolve the dispute, Roeder asked the delegation of Singapore to lead a special drafting committee on the issue of contention. Singapore is famous for its skilled diplomats, and this proved to be a good choice. The committee worked its way through the nest of problems and crafted language that protected all interests.

Drafting committees are challenging, draining experiences, often called "wordsmithing exercises." Quality is more important than speed, so one member of the delegation should be in the drafting committee. Hopefully, the text is fairly simple; it may be, however, that the delegation is involved in a much larger effort involving many governments and NGO interests. It can happen that as many competing texts emerge, none work. In that instance, the drafting chairperson may seek a compilation text. This will be welded together by the drafting committee and need refinement. Most of the time, the chair will then insist that all future edits be proposed in writing. Warning: An NGO delegation must be careful that its interests remain in the compilation text, even if the words are not the same. Unless the fresh wording destroys its interests, the delegation should also be willing to "work with the drafting committee." They are charged with finding a text that will be acceptable to the conference as a whole; the concepts must be packaged as central. Sometimes edits are done live, the text thrown up on a conference room screen; participants then raise their hands and suggest changes. This is a great process, but be careful to have a clear explanation for recommendations. Any process of cutting and refining can actually create a complicated text because of unneeded verbiage. The delegates want to go to dinner and would not usually challenge anything strongly put. This can lead to a lot of words being inserted which, if the document is not about the NGO priority per se, seem satisfactory to the governments involved.

Warning: Read every word so that NGO interests are not accidently impaled. Also keep in mind that it might not just be government delegations to worry about.

Other NGOs will be around. At Rio, 15,000 private individuals were present, and similar NGOs do not always agree. At the 60th DPI/NGO Conference in New York, Roeder led the drafting committee for an NGO statement on climate change and had to wrestle with otherwise friendly NGOs over language.

## 10.13 Example of a Mega-Conference: The Rio Summit

Because conferences are uniquely useful vehicles for advancing NGO issues, the Rio Summit, the UN Conference on Environment and Development (UNCED), makes a good case study. However, NGOs cannot just look at a conference as an event. Like Rio, any conference is seen as part of a process. One also needs to examine the organization that emerged or might emerge from a conference as a potential tool for NGOs, such as the Commission on Sustainable development (CSD) which rose from Rio, and existing agencies impacted by the conference like UN Environmental Program (UNEP). Any major international conference could do the same, which is why Rio is a good model. Rio's outcomes documents were the Rio Declaration on Environment and Development and two treaties on climate and biological diversity, an authoritative statement of principles on forests, and an 800-page document called Agenda 21. The latter was a compendium of guidelines and recommendations for policies and actions by governments, NGOs, and IOs on environmental, economic, and social issues. The documents were negotiated by 182 governments, with 118 sending their heads of state/government. Many tens of thousands of NGO officials also attended. This is the wave of the future, big conferences with luminaries in attendance.

Remember that summits usually follow a long line of conferences and meetings, and the 1992 Rio summit was no exception; NGOs should enter the process early. For Rio, the process began with 1982 negotiations, leading to the 1985 Vienna Convention for the Protection of the Ozone layer, the 1987 Montreal Protocol on Substances that Deplete the Ozone Layer, and the 1990 revisions to the protocol. They were the first international agreements aimed at preventing harm to the environment. So, Rio has a legacy, but it also almost died.

The Tampere Convention negotiations were stalled for a few days when the US delegation argued for text changes, but in that case, the delay was done in the spirit of reaching a consensus. At Rio, negotiations almost fell apart when the US government refused to sign the Biodiversity Treaty. In addition, Arab delegates pushed for references to Israel's occupied territories, which, while important to Middle East peace, were not central to the environment. Oil exporting states tried to strip away language implying that petroleum was bad for the environment. Standing in the middle of that kind of debate, it may be hard for an NGO to be heard, which is why, for some conferences, the *sequential negotiating proposal* should be considered. Such a procedure could allow an NGO to acquire a fair, quiet, and detailed hearing in ministries free from distractions; perhaps NGO drafted language might then be incorporated into instructions from Foreign Ministries to their delegations.

The Rio Summit also represents the increasing encroachment of complex interlinking negotiations requiring an understanding of culture, law, and science; that offers opportunities for NGOs, though the intellectual logistics of handling this kind of complexity can be formidable for any delegation, which is why NGOs (large or small) often are more effective in coalitions. In 2008, Roeder led a discussion with the G77 on an NGO issue in New York and used scientific briefs by respected experts in the field to make the case (Lanier 2010). They were based on recommendations of a coalition and were very effective.

The Rio process led to the 31st Session of the Intergovernmental Panel on Climate Change (IPCC) and beyond. It was not one event, in other words process based on many years of work. For example, the Montreal Protocol alone took 4 sessions over 9 months. What this teaches when considering NGO initiatives is the importance of not looking at conferences as stand-alone events but as movements, with stepping stones, each an opportunity for NGOs to inject their agenda, even if the overarching theme of the conference process is not about an NGO's primary goals. In addition, because so many different conferences are related, no one NGO can staff them all, although a major foreign ministry might do so through its embassies and missions. NGOs should work with umbrella bodies like InterAction and in coalitions.

As a follow-up to Rio, in December 1992, the Commission on Sustainable Development[6] was established. CSD is a functional commission to follow-up implementation of the UNCED, also known as the Rio Earth Summit. Based at UN Headquarters in New York, CSD is composed of 53 UN members, elected to 3-year terms. During its first decade, the CSD met formally 4 weeks annually to consider specific sustainable development issues and to promote implementation of internationally agreed development goals. At the 2002 WSSD in Johannesburg, governments called for specific reforms of the CSD, including limiting negotiations in the sessions of the Commission to every 2 years, limiting the number of themes addressed at each session, and having CSD serve as a focal point for discussing partnerships that promote sustainable development, including sharing lessons learned, progress made, and best practices. NGOs have found a home in the CSD through implementation of Agenda 21. At the CSD's 11th Session (Apr–May 2003), members developed a multiyear program of work to address a series of "thematic clusters" and crosscutting issues, all opportunities for NGO interaction.

[6] Sustainable Development is a catchall for issues like risk management. In the past, disasters were considered temporary disruptions that could be managed only by response or their impacts reduced by technical interventions. Today, we know that risk management is intertwined with sustainable development and that risks like famine, epidemics, and economic depressions exacerbate the impact of disasters. This is one reason diplomacy can be complex. Will the proposed solution to one risk undermine efforts to solve others? Will the solution fit into a multinational grand strategy?

# Chapter 11
# Protocol

**Extract** Chapter 11 introduces protocol guidelines that can open many doors and place an NGO ahead of others for donations and political influence. Emphasis is placed on how to invite government officials to NGO-sponsored events and how to comport oneself in order to gain the best results. A basic concept is that in meetings, parties, conferences, and other events, the NGO representative is considered the symbolic representative of his or her organization in the same way as an ambassador of a country and, to an extent, is a symbol of all NGOs. The representative never acts along but on behalf of the NGO. Although protocol rules can seem artificial at times, they can be used to impress donors and policy makers.

## 11.1 Introduction

> Throughout the region in which I have worked for WSPA, the Middle East, diplomacy is essential, and the implications or consequences of a diplomatic faux pas in the region can at best set back or nullify a potentially successful project and at worst be construed as insulting and result in a hasty exit strategy (Wheeler 2012).

Many believe the protocol is about how to wear a white tie or where to put the seats at a formal dinner, perhaps about not wearing brown shoes after six or pearls in the morning if a woman or not looking at a watch during a party to avoid appearing bored (Boritz, *Email Discussion on Diplomatic Practice* 2010). Those concepts are not what this book is primarily about; there are many excellent books showing how to handle a receiving line, how to set a table, etc. There are also some great teachers like Nancy Mitchell of Protocol Partners in Washington, DC, who train national and NGO officials from around the world. This chapter received much advice from Ms. Mitchell, which is deeply appreciated because it is a summary of how to use the customs that diplomats are familiar with in order to advance NGO

L.W. Roeder, Jr. and A. Simard, *Diplomacy and Negotiation for Humanitarian NGOs*, Humanitarian Solutions in the 21st Century, DOI 10.1007/978-1-4614-7113-4_11,

priorities. In addition, officers in the secretariat of the US Department of State made suggestions, as well as the Office of International Conferences and the Office of Protocol. The Protocol and Liaison Service of the United Nations was very helpful, as were the works of Mary Jane McCaffree, a protocol specialist at the Department of State whose book has been a bible for diplomats for over 30 years (McCaffree and Innis 1977). A more recent and welcome addition to the essential collection is a book by ambassador Mary Mel French (French 2010). Finally, Joanna Morrini, Ceremonial Office, Protocol Directorate, Foreign and Commonwealth Office, and Moritt Boritz, a curator in the Danish National Museum, were both very helpful. There is also the *Protocol for the Modern Diplomat* by the Foreign Service Institute. Nearly every country has its own manual.

One of the most overused statements about "protocol" is that the term comes from the Greek phrase meaning "the first glue." As McCaffree points out, rules of protocol go back as far as Cyrus the Great in Persepolis, over 2,500 years ago; throughout history, even though the rules have changed, the intent has been the same, to help make and keep useful connections, which is how an NGO official should see protocol. In past times, ambassadors were important because they came from important governments; however, now the system is a meritocracy. The ambassador of even the smallest, least powerful nation like the Seychelles can influence major events because of his or her personal skills as a negotiator and a user of protocol. Thus, this is one of the most important tools for an NGO of any size when communicating with a diplomat, rebel, military official, and even a local political leader.

Communication between governments and the UN with NGOs is often strained because many NGOs are considered to be informal, biased, and uninformed in protocol—though not substance. Some are often called extreme. To overcome that barrier, every member of the team must comport himself as a diplomat, which Moritt Boritz once said meant someone whose personal characteristics are truthfulness, calmness, accuracy, patience, good humor, modesty, and loyalty. More precise and workable skills like self-control, an ability to formulate one's thoughts, an ability to read a situation, an instinct for discreet flattery, and a talent for making contact with people are also important (Boritz, *The Hidden Culture of Diplomatic Practice* 1998).

## 11.2 Attending Social Events

In the small-community environment of the United Nations HQ cities like New York, Rome, Geneva, Bangkok, and Nairobi in particular, NGO representatives will have frequent opportunity to meet ambassadors in meetings, social events, and major conferences. It is important to reach out to them, shake their hand, introduce yourself, and explain your mission, and it might relate to their own mandate. That simple act, especially if done regularly, will enable an NGO representative the ability to have personal meetings on NGO priority topics. The ambassador might also come to an NGO event. Similarly, the national diplomatic community in many countries is small and often welcoming to NGO representatives. NGOs need to make a point of attending national holiday celebrations and other events at embassies and other diplomatic missions, "becoming a regular part of the scene." That way, the NGO will learn who best to deal with on issues, and ambassadors and agency chiefs will be more apt to return calls.

## 11.3 Accreditation, Badges, and Business Cards

Before attending an event or trying to go to a meeting at an international organization, the representative often must be accredited in his or her own right or work for an accredited NGO. Every conference or meeting has its own attendance rules; the Admin Officer needs to learn them well in advance. In addition, some conferences will limit the size of a delegation. On the other hand, though attending an event might require some form of accreditation, many NGOs and UN agencies also foster discussion groups on the Internet, which require no accreditation (Fig. 11.1).

Assuming accreditation is needed, which office does it? A common misunderstanding is that the United Nations as a whole accredits NGOs. Not so, the UN is a conglomeration of institutions: organs, conferences, organizations, departments, and agencies, each with its own badge system. In each case, to be accredited, the secretariat should be consulted. The delegation needs to quickly figure out which UN entity it will visit and then decide if it must be accredited in more than one city; some agencies have both New York and Geneva offices. If an NGO is accredited to either ECOSOC or DPI, the badge will allow access to most UN facilities in NY, though special arrangements may be required in cases like UNHCR. National agencies around the world and the Geneva, Bangkok, and Nairobi UN compounds all have their own badge systems. DPI and ECOSOC badges can also be helpful for entering the UN compound in Nairobi and elsewhere, but prior authorization is required. Nairobi is home for the UN Environmental Organization (UNEP) and most relief operations in the Horn of Africa. In Rome, the World Food Program (WFP) and the

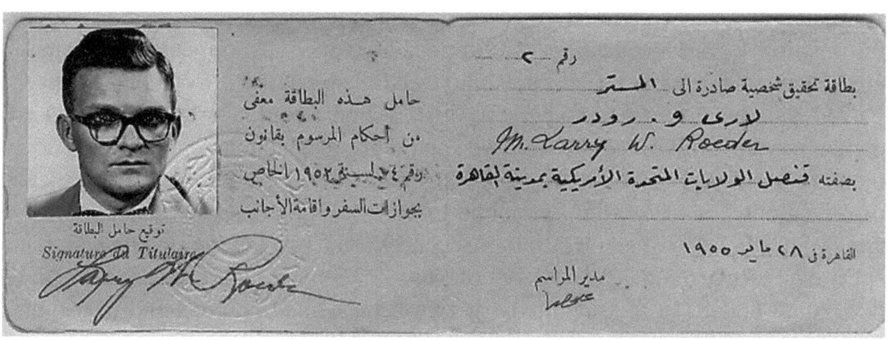


Fig. 11.1 Accreditation badge

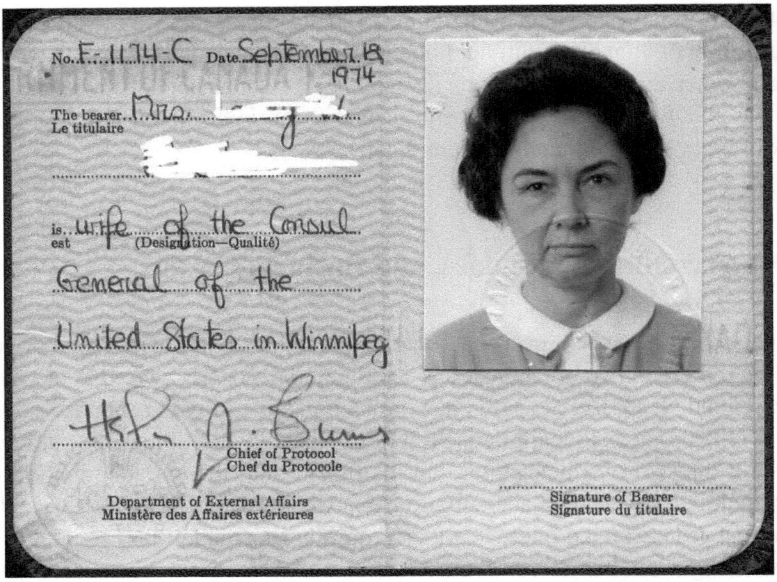


**Fig. 11.2** Diplomatic badge

Food and Agriculture Organization (FAO) are both organizations anyone interested in food security should get to know. Each requires separate grounds passes. Paris is home to UNESCO, which is responsible for protecting culture, education, and science, as well as the Organization of Economic Cooperation and Development (OECD) and the World Health Organization for Animals (OIE), the last two of which are not under the UN. A separate grounds pass is needed for each (Fig. 11.2).

If an NGO gains accreditation to ECOSOC, the badge will allow its representatives access to compounds in Geneva and New York and many of the UN agencies in both cities. Access is also possible for the regional economic commissions. Authority to do this is granted by Article 71 of the UN Charter. UN DPI: The relationship with the UN Department of Public Information (DPI) with NGOs is almost as old as that of ECOSOC. In 1946, The General Assembly, in its resolution 13 (I), instructed DPI and its branch offices to ". . actively assist and encourage national information services, educational institutions and other governmental and nongovernmental organizations of all kinds interested in spreading information about the United Nations. For this and other purposes, it should operate a fully equipped reference service, brief or supply lecturers, and make available its publications, documentary films, film strips, posters and other exhibits for use by these agencies and organizations." In 1968, the Economic and Social Council, by Resolution 1297 (XLIV) of May 27, called on DPI to associate NGOs, bearing in mind the letter and spirit of its Resolution 1296 (XLIV) of May 23, 1968, which stated that an NGO ". . . shall undertake to support the work of the United Nations and to promote knowledge of its principles and activities, in accordance with its own aims and purposes and the nature and scope of its competence and activities."

NGOs should try for ECOSOC and/or DPI accreditation, keeping in mind that not all UN agencies accept their badges, but be prepared for delays, as much as 2 years for ECOSOC and 6 months for DPI. For ECOSOC, there are limits on how many passes can be granted for a full year of access. If a staff member will only visit once a year, it is probably better to use "day passes." "Each NGO in consultative status with ECOSOC can designate representatives to obtain passes for the UN premises, valid until 31 December of each year. A maximum of five such passes can be issued for New York, 5 for Geneva, and 5 for Vienna, in addition to the chief Administrative Officer (CAO) and the President or chief Executive" (2 additional passes).

Don't abuse badges. Many NGOs try to use their DPI or ECOSOC pass to gain entry to emergency and disaster compounds in Haiti, Africa, and elsewhere. While this might work from time to time, it is illegal and the authorizing authority might remove the badge. On the other hand, the DPI or ECOSOC pass can authenticate bona fides, making it easier to obtain a local pass.

Whether meeting people in official meetings or social events, an NGO representative should have a bright, understandable business card. When abroad for a major event or an extended time, the back of the card should be in the language of the visited country. When stationed in Bangkok during the Nargis crisis, Roeder's card was in English and Thai, and when posted in France and Egypt was in French and Arabic, etc. The card's contents should include name, position, the NGOs name, and contact information. Business cards usually do not include honorifics, i.e., Mr., Mrs., Ms., or Dr., except for military ranks. (MD or PhD would follow the name when appropriate.) Society association letters are not needed in the United States, but this practice may vary in other countries and the British Commonwealth.

**Administrative Support** One thing that the various organizations mentioned to do is facilitate the distribution of literature for NGOs which can't attend meetings, and ECOSOC/NGO and DPI provide grounds passes and other administrative support to visiting NGOS. More help is needed to arrange for inexpensive housing and the facilitation of visas. Perhaps, working together, the NGO associations along with ECOSOC/NGO and DPI could develop a UN system-wide accrediting system, so that if an NGO is accredited to one agency, it is accredited to all. Badges issued by DPI and ECOSOC are very helpful, not universal across the various UN HQ sites.

**Note** In New York, a grounds pass should get the holder into ALL UN buildings whether there is a gate like DC1 and 2, the FF building on 45th Street, or 866 UN Plaza where there are many diplomatic missions. A New York grounds pass won't work in Paris at UNESCO. The NGO will need a local pass for the rue Miollis building and the main building. The New York pass will generally work in Geneva at the main gate, but other gates will stop NGOs. Saturday access in Geneva is provided by Pass Chalais—where participants register for special conferences—for that, Security will have a copy of color-coded special passes, so the officers know if you are an NGO, diplomat, etc.; these are needed for Saturday access. Rome, Bangkok, Nairobi, and other compounds have their own rules. Before heading out, it is best to examine those rules first (Jordan 2012).

## 11.4 Politeness, Trust, and Respect

Friends are not hard to make in the UN, in governments, or in multilateral bodies. Indeed, as trust is built, officials will help in immeasurable ways, but remember that a contact's first loyalty is his or her agency. Everything said, even in confidence, can be repeated. This does not mean that lies are appropriate, however. If you cannot promise something, do not. If you do promise something, complete the task. As an example, General George Marshall, usually considered the architect of the war in Europe during World War II, had to build trust with allies and potential adversaries, e.g., Joseph Stalin who said he would trust his life to Marshall. Even if a delegate strongly disagrees with the policies of the official with whom he is working, if trust exists, listening will happen (Abshire 2005).[1]

Conferences offer many opportunities for NGO delegations to speak in front of Ministers and ambassadors, and conference workshops are handy for fleshing out concepts and building working-level contacts. ***Keep It Crisp***. Too often, speakers read every word of a PowerPoint presentation or send an overlong report to HQ that does not truly capture the essence of what happened. If a delegation wants to influence, not just participate, it must translate complex concepts into short clear, practical explanations and recommendations.

Keep in mind that nonnative speakers in the delegation's language might fail to fully grasp what the delegation intends. Keep the vocabulary straightforward and speak slowly. A native speaker may think that he or she can choose the right word in a second, but politeness dictates that he or she gives the others time to work it out. However, also keep in mind that there are often shades of meaning behind words that can be lost in translation. If uncertain about the direction of discussions, feel free to ask questions.

A delegate should not jump in with the right word all the time. Let others develop their own ideas and particular choice of phrase because listening patiently conveys the impression that you actually care about the opinion of others, thereby giving your interventions more weight. Otherwise, an impatient NGO diplomat will appear to be dominating the discussion; keep in mind that sometimes an NGO delegate's best approach is to use like-minded NGOs or UN member states to make the same point. Remember that some delegations love being the one which finds the right compromise phrase or word; success isn't about who receives credit. It is about moving an initiative forward. Also, if the discussions have been in one official language, it isn't unusual for a delegate to require seeing the official translation in another official language before agreement.

This point about keeping it simple is very important, and one of the hardest things to teach a negotiator is to speak little and listen a lot. Whether at UN HQ or in the field, the person with whom a delegation is meeting is probably anxious to tell

[1]One approach around the problem of repeating confidential information is to resort to Chatham House Rules, but keep in mind that officials often "do repeat."

his or her story first, so let him or her. That shows sensitivity and provides a tactical advantage, since every time a delegate speaks, something is revealed about that person's knowledge and thinking process. Let the other side reveal themselves first. Listening also reduces tensions, by the way.

### 11.4.1 Understanding and Empathy

Leaving prejudices behind is important. Within reason, if a rebel promises something, the word will usually be kept, since the official may want to come back for something else later on. If an NGO team brings trucks of feed for cattle, it may be able to arrange for trucks of food for people. On the other hand, a delegate should not make the mistake of "understanding of where the other is coming from." The rebels will certainly be insulted. After Haiti's devastating earthquake in 2010, Roeder became involved in helping NGOs to enter the emergency. What they discovered were women being forced into prostitution for 50 cents just to buy food. In Sudan, he also regularly saw villagers whose feet had been blown off from land mines, and, in 2010 while on a mission for an NGO regularly, saw people in Somaliland living in terrible conditions. How can anyone who comes from comfortable conditions possibly understand their plight? Roeder related a story on this for this book about his last days in the US Army; while going through the International chiefs of Police Academy (IACP) training at Fort Bragg, he had to join civilian police patrols. One night, surrounded by drunks, he faced one who held a broken shard of bottle which was waved around to slit throats. Roeder's first words were a mistake, something along the lines that he understood the other fellow's issues. The drunk lunged, saying Roeder had no idea! He was right, of course. Roeder then said he could see the man was in pain and asked what was wrong. The question had to be asked several times, but the angry drunk finally calmed down, and eventually, his anger spent, he gave up the bottle. Very powerful lesson, there. Listening is empathic. Let the other person talk. NGO diplomats will find that while negotiations are usually very civil, especially when money, lives, or rights are involved, negotiators can be testy. As an example, during the Paris Peace Talks ending World War I, Premier William Hughes of Australia said if a shepherd had to mortgage his home because of the loss of income due to the war and then lost his home due to foreclosure, then Germany owed him reimbursement. The United States was opposed, so Hughes shouted, saying "Some people in this war have not been so near the fire as we British have, and therefore, being unburned, have a cold, detached view of the situation" (Lamont 1921).

The Americans smiled back. Smiling is important. A delegate need not worry about knowing anyone, but smiling keeps one alert and reduces tensions. It is also tougher for others to be confrontational if a delegate is considerate, even with staff members that do not perform up to expectations. In other words, never berate a hapless hotel clerk or waiter who makes a mistake or lose your temper at a meeting. Also, a diplomat will often have to take hard positions, strongly disagreeing with someone else's position; if a delegate smiles, other delegates tend to smile back and treat his or her point of view with deference. Never criticize someone in front of another diplomat unless it is accepted that the one being criticized will hear about it.

### *11.4.2 Thank You's*

Rituals surround thank you's. Always thank hosts the following day in writing or by phone. E-mail "thank you's" do not replace written ones, even in the Internet age. They are also signed without courtesy titles (i.e., Carlo Ponti, not Mr. Ponti). Local custom might allow gifts in certain circumstances, but it is better to stick to a handwritten note because they are actually read and in some cases can reap major rewards. In 1972, the President of the United States invited Roeder and the other members of his office to a reception honoring ambassador Philip Habib because his staff had supported Habib during a dangerous mission to Lebanon. Roeder then sent a handwritten note the following day to the President and First Lady thanking them for inviting the office into their home, and, a week later, the President called to chat. It turns out that the letter was only one of a few, so all of those correspondents received personal calls.

**Tips**

- Parents may be reluctant to leave children or pets behind when attending social functions; however, neither may attend unless invited, with some exception. Otherwise, never assume either is welcome.
- Avoid looking bored; do not look at a watch or smart phone.
- A guest being toasted should remain seated and does not drink to the toast. However, the guest does make a reply and offer a toast to the host.
- Leave a party at a reasonable hour (varies with each country). Leaving early is better than overstaying; briefly thank the host before departure. Custom also dictates that delegation members do not depart prior to the chief of delegation. This isn't just fluff; the chief in a national delegation represents a nation's sovereignty or an NGO delegation, the "flag" of an NGO or NGO alliance. The practical reason is that issues needing resolution happen at social events, and a chief needs to be able to make assignments. What if the chief learns at the event that the following morning another delegation will put forth a surprise motion? The chief needs to be able to assign one or more members of the team roles ASAP, not after he goes back to the hotel.
- There are cultural differences about casual conversation, so it is best to learn in advance what is appropriate. Definitely do not feel compelled to offer personal information. Even when working in a culture where these questions are permitted, do not ask them. Discussing children or food is rude in some cultures, not others.
- When mingling, keep casual conversations brief and mingle and meet as many people as possible.
- In some countries, an invitation for 8:00 p.m. means arriving precisely at 8:00 p.m. In other countries, it means no earlier than 9:30 p.m. To avoid awkward and embarrassing situations, ask questions in advance.

## 11.5 Gifts

Be careful of gifts and gift-giving. NGOs often leave medallions and certificates, which are free advertisements for whoever goes into the office. Also fine is giving flowers to a helpful delegation, but receiving gifts is generally a bad idea, especially large ones. However, if gifts cannot be refused, they should be accepted in the name of the NGO. Former Secretary General Kofi Annan showed how to do this in 2008 when Charles Garang, a rebel leader Roeder also worked with in South Sudan, offered cattle. Understanding that to refuse the cattle would have insulted the rebel leader; Annan said "I accept these cattle and would urge your leaders to keep them for me until that proper time when I would ask that they be slaughtered to feed the widows and children who have suffered so much through this conflict." Like Annan, find a clever solution that fits the culture (UN 2005).

One of the most common gifts is to offer coffee or a meal. Though an opportunity to quietly reflect on an issue, NGO representatives need to be aware that some governments place limits on the value of the meal being offered, lest it appear to be a bribe. The carefully selected bottle of wine or bunch of flowers can be an effective tool when invited to someone's home or in recognition of someone's efforts, but it is very important that the cost be modest and proportional to the deed. If wine is the gift, first make sure the recipient actually drinks alcohol. Even if you work for a wealthy NGO, expensive gifts send the wrong signal about NGO priorities.

Expensive gifts can also work in both directions. In May 1991 while on a mission to Albania to develop a fresh national economic plan, Roeder stayed at a tourist hotel. Food was very limited, potatoes, onions, a few tomatoes and cucumbers, only thin meat and kebob, and no fish, chicken, or many vegetables. Soup was consistently rice and mystery meat. At some point, he was then was offered an apartment in the residence of the prime minister, along with great food. Though the access would have been advantageous and the food a welcome change, Roeder refused due to the gift's magnitude, especially since the US government was trying to figure out which post-communist faction to support, the prime minister representing one.

As an example of what one might do, provide flowers to staff officers in the UN and diplomatic missions who go out of their way to be helpful. In one case, Roeder had been trying to attract the attention of an ambassador for two weeks with no success. He knew she was very busy, but it was essential that her mission host a meeting of delegations. Finally, he sent her flowers. She called that evening to apologize for not returning e-mails, engaged in a long conversation about the initiative, and agreed to host the meeting. Thirty dollars worth of flowers delivered personally to the office worked, but if he had spent $100, this would have been excessive. Another common gift is a large memorial coin from the NGO to be placed in an ambassador's office, something to advertise the NGO. The ambassador will feel honored, and every time the coin is seen, it turns into a free statement of support, but stay away from pens. That's tacky.

Many rituals and customs often surround gift meanings. The type, color, and number of flowers, for example, may have a hidden meaning. In Italy and China, mums are funeral flowers; think twice about bringing them to a dinner party. But in

Japan, placing a single petal at the bottom of a wineglass brings long life. A guest may be expected to bring a small gift, or it may be better to bring nothing at all. Once again, ask colleagues and coworkers about local customs.

## 11.6 Managing Perceptions

When an NGO delegate interacts with an ambassador, the delegate isn't just showing the face of his or her NGO, that delegate is putting a face on all NGOs. Roeder noted that growing up in the Foreign Service, every member of the family felt that any public action reflected on the entire embassy and America in general. Penny Laingen was the spouse of Bruce **Laingen, Charge´ d'Affaires** at the US Embassy during the hostage crisis in Tehran. Mrs. Laingen spoke on exactly these points in interviews in 1986 and 1990:

> The hostage crisis was a terribly public, international crisis, and when I was on television, I think I was, in the minds of the American people, the wife of the Charge d'affairs being held in Tehran. And how I behaved reflected…perhaps on the whole Foreign Service and other Americans abroad. (Fenzi and Nelson 1994, p. 217)

Laingen's point of view should be in the consciousness of any NGO delegate. NGOs bring a great vigor, intelligence, and imagination to diplomatic affairs, and they have been participating in the activities of international organizations for over a century. Refugees depend on NGOs and many issues like land mine destruction would not have happened without NGOs. The agricultural NGOs have also become an important part of the food security and livelihood protection network. As an example of good work in modern transitional societies, consider the efforts of NGOs in the societies of the former Soviet Union for the last twenty years, especially in nations like Turkmenistan, Uzbekistan, Kazakhstan, Kyrgyzstan, and Tajikistan. On the negative side, there is a growing disparity in those countries between the rich and the poor. Corruption is rampant and there is ethnic hatred, such as between the Kyrgyz and Uzbeks; counterbalancing the negative side of these transitional societies, local and international NGOs have been providing many useful services, some never seen before, like public diplomacy. Farmer and water usage associations and the like are emerging, and much of the work of these NGOs is done with the United Nations, the World Bank, and the International Red Cross and Red Crescent Movement and with donors like the ECHO and USAID. Every time an NGO official advances this good work, he or she builds up the reputation of all NGOs.

So, much has been accomplished by NGOs; the record of accomplishment has been uneven, which is why not every government or IO takes NGOs seriously. While the vast majority of NGOs operate as professionally as any world class government delegation, some overstate their success, not recognizing that initiatives that succeed in the UN, for example, are a result of government action, as much as civil society. Some forget about team work and see only the NGO world as the font of solutions. Indeed, one need look no further than CITES and the Land Mine Treaty to understand the importance and intellectual weight NGOs can bring. In the end, the world rises and falls together.

## 11.7 Receptions and Personal Entertaining

Professional government diplomats make entertainment a regular practice, at conferences, as part of the "business of business," which should also be the style for NGO diplomats. Inviting local diplomats and government and UN officials widens one's circle of friends among officials and private citizens who might advance an NGO's agenda or even identify donors. It also facilitates the informal exchange of information, affording others an opportunity to hear alternative views. Of course, when planning the event, carefully consider whom to invite and how formal or informal to make the affair, as well as local customs. Invite higher-ranking officials. Their schedules will be tight, but they still might consider a change of pace. Events need not be large, elaborate, or expensive. In many situations, a simple lunch or a backyard barbeque at a home is more effective and enjoyable than an elaborate dinner or reception.

Before considering holding a significant social event like a reception at a conference, question whether it will significantly influence voting, or in the case of a bilateral meeting, will it build support with the host government? If the expense is not likely to build such support, consider joining receptions belonging to other organizations. They can be just as effective for networking.

**A Caution** While holding a function can look appetizing to supporters, in these times of financial stress, if the event is not going to change votes, it may be more prudent to use those funds elsewhere. Some NGOs want to consider receptions because they give an appearance to the donors that the NGO is successful or powerful. While photos at a diplomatic function can produce the appearance of a vibrant, effective NGO, such pictures are not more effective than well-written reports to the donors on progress. There is a risk that such events will become propaganda, not cost-effective tools.

**Consider the Following at Personal Events**

- Is the proposed date appropriate? Any conflicts?
- What is social time in the host country? Will guests tend to be on time or late by custom?
- Weekday evenings are the most common times for official entertaining, leaving weekends and evenings for families.
- Review plans in terms of local food and drink preferences and entertaining space.
- How will the weather impact the event?
- What are the language abilities of proposed guests?
- Make a guest list that allows for both entertainment and policy advancement.
- Each member of the NGO should have target guests with whom to discuss issues.
- Invite diplomats and policy makers who might not share your opinions, not just the convinced.
- When sending an invitation to a formal event and/or official function, use official stationery cards, followed by a telephone call. It is also acceptable to extend an invitation by telephone and to send a reminder card as a reminder, but sending the card in advance gives guests who might not immediately be prone to attend an NGO event a chance to read why they should attend, perhaps to meet a national figure in the movement.

- Make arrangements well in advance if equipment is to be borrowed or extra helpers hired. Include security and parking arrangements here, if appropriate. During a presidential campaign, Roeder hosted an event in his house and used volunteers to organize local parking so that it would not disrupt the neighbors. After all, he had to live among them.
- For formal affairs, consider appropriate seating arrangements by taking into account the order of precedence of individuals in attendance. If confused, consult a professional protocol firm.
- Design seating arrangements after people arrive, not in advance, since some people would not respond, but attend anyway or accept but not attend. Invited guests will sometimes bring uninvited guests or arrive late. When it is crucial to have an accurate guest list, telephone the invitees to ask if they will attend.
- Name tags can be very useful for large informal events.
- Place cards are often used for formal dinners. When doing so, follow the rules of precedence. The male guest of honor sits to the right of the hostess, and the female guests of honor to the right of the host. If there is no plan, invite the most important guests to the host's table. These are done in order by social ranking.

The following is one ranking order, but this varies by country; to be safest, obtain a local protocol manual or call the Office of Protocol at the embassy of the country you will visit (Leki 2007).

1. Ambassador Extraordinary and Plenipotentiary
2. Ministers Plenipotentiary
3. Ministers
4. Chargé d'Affaires ad hoc or pro tempore
5. Chargé d'Affaires ad interim
6. Minister-Counselors
7. Counselors (or Senior Secretaries in the absence of Counselors)
8. Army, Naval, and Air Attachés
9. Civilian Attachés not in the Foreign Service
10. First Secretaries
11. Second Secretaries
12. Assistant Army, Naval, and Air Attachés
13. Civilian Assistant Attachés not in the Foreign Service
14. Third Secretaries and Assistant Attachés

- Informal parties could be family-style meals, buffet lunches, barbecues, picnics, and teas.
- Even though informal entertaining is relaxed, keep in mind that the NGO staff is working. A backyard event involving hamburgers and cold drinks requires as much thought as a white-tie state dinner. This is something any spouse of a diplomat will say.
- Make a list of people you and your staff should meet either at a personal event or an official reception, noting whether the contact has a topical responsibility, e.g., sustainable development and human rights perhaps the Security Council? Time is limited at a reception. Give priority to those covering critical issues.

- Place cards are used for formal dinners. When doing so, follow the rules of precedence. The male guest of honor sits to the right of the hostess and the female guests of honor to the right of the host. If there is no plan, invite ranking guests to the host's table.

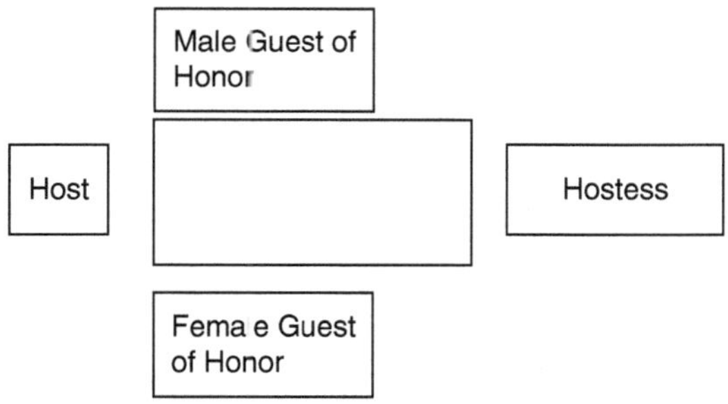


- Informal parties could be family-style meals, buffet lunches, barbecues, picnics, and teas.
- Even though informal entertaining is relaxed, keep in mind that the NGO staff is working. A backyard event involving hamburgers and cold drinks requires as much thought as a white-tie state dinner. This is something any spouse of a diplomat will say.
- Make sure to invite staff and friends from the NGO community and move the guests around, so they can talk to different people and have a good time, while sharing ideas.
- A buffet service is an excellent format for breaking down formalities.
- Some guests do not like to eat from lap plates, so tables are a good idea, but keep them to no less than six in order to stimulate conversation.

### *11.7.1 Use of Alcohol*

Many NGOs have rules against paying for alcoholic drinks, and some do not allow them at all at a function, even if the staff members pay. While that is an internal matter for any NGO, be aware that alcohol is often served during diplomatic functions at the UN, the International Red Cross and Red Crescent Movement, the EC, and the World Bank. The main exception is an event in an Islamic culture. However, no one is going to force a delegate to drink or think less of the official for not drinking, except perhaps in Russia or Japan where delegates are expected to drink or at least take the alcohol that is offered. Pretend to drink. Depending on the circumstances, it is usually best to quietly avoid alcohol at social events, perhaps only sip a glass of wine or a highball glass of mineral water and lime, the theory being an official event is work, not vacation, and the head must be kept clear. That method has much precedent (House 1926) and is increasingly normal. The real rule is never to overindulge at an event. If someone does get drunk on delegations, they should be sent back. Many CEOs do not care what employees do in their spare time; *never* do what the US Secret Service did in Cartagena in 2012.

## 11.7.2 Food at Social Events

Few issues are more controversial than food. Some people are vegans, vegetarians, or omnivores, and some meat eaters won't eat particular kinds of animals; regardless of any internal food policy, NGOs wishing to work with international organizations must be sensitive to local culture and understand that all IOs are a mix of omnivores, vegetarians, and vegans. This does not mean organizational standards need to be breached, but if a particular dietary style is to be offered at an NGO event, it is good idea to say so on the invitation card, and it may even be a good idea to provide a response card that allows the guests to note their requirements. Local cultural norms should also not be violated, e.g., providing pork or alcohol in a Muslim gathering, pork at a Jewish gathering, or beef at a Hindu party. On the other hand, when attending another's event, a delegate should accept offered food; unless he or she has some dietary restriction, then let the host know in advance. If a delegate cannot try a portion, just refuse with a simple explanation. However, if diet isn't a problem, consider new foods as an opportunity to explore a new culture and show it respect. Just keep in mind that in some cultures all of the served food should be eaten while in others a small portion is left on the plate.[2]

### 11.7.2.1 Flags and Uniforms

Many NGO officials are former military or government officials, perhaps former officials at international organizations, and may have been awarded official decorations that can be worn on civilian clothing. Doing so can be advantageous at a diplomatic function, though by wearing decorations, one might be conveying a partisan political point of view, so caution is advised. A precursor to the United Nations called the League of Nations discouraged its officials during time of appointment from accepting honors from their government or decorations received prior to joining (Joyce 1978, p. 77). The image was to be a servant of all humanity, not one nation.

Should the decision be to wear decorations, some experts suggest only doing it when the invitation says White Tie or Black Tie, "with decorations," and then of course wear them in correct order (French 2010); decorations have always been welcome at either Black Tie or White Tie events. It isn't required that the invitation allow it, but keep in mind that most decorations are issued in two forms, one for day uniforms and one for tuxedos. Wear the smaller tuxedo variety in the correct order and make sure the delegate was awarded the decoration. In the United States, wearing unauthorized decorations can be a criminal offense under the Stolen Valor Act of 2005. In addition to legal issues, the taking on of unauthorized titles or wearing unearned medals is considered a serious breach of protocol. Every country has its

[2] The companion book published by Springer on *Diplomacy and Animal Welfare* offers suggestions on humane standards.

Fig. 11.3 Private Collection of Larry Roeder

Fig. 11.4 Private Collection of Larry Roeder

own rules, so an NGO delegate wearing ribbons should wear them in the order of his or her own citizenship (Figs. 11.3 and 11.4).

White-tie events are the most formal of evening dress events in Western society, whereas a black-tie event is a normal evening affair. White House events are known to have both, and full state dinners are often white tie since the host and guests of honor are either heads of government or heads of state. Most formal events from inaugural balls to weddings to special receptions are usually black tie. For men, the jacket can be either black or white.

An NGO wishing to hold a reception or meeting for many missions may find it useful to display national or organizational flags on a wall or walking path. Keep in mind customary rules when doing this and that flags change. One approach is to consult with the UN in New York which has a flyer on the order of flags (Protocol and Liaison Service, United Nations 2010).

When displaying flags, be certain to be accurate. In 2010, a formal briefing and reception was held for the Foreign Minister of Somaliland at a hotel in Virginia, not long before Roeder headed to the country to meet the president. The event had not started quite yet when he noticed something odd about the national flag. It turned out the hotel staff had accidently turned it upside down, which is the international sign for distress. This kind of error is common, especially for horizontal tricolor flags, so in order to prevent such a breach of etiquette, a suggestion is that the NGO obtain a manual of flags. Even governments make mistakes. In 2010, the US government had to admit to an "honest mistake" when it displayed an inverted Philippine flag—which wrongfully signified that the Southeast Asian country was in a state of war—in a meeting hosted by President Barack Obama, no less. The Philippine flag was displayed upside down behind President Benigno Aquino III when leaders of the Association of Southeast Asian Nations met Obama in New York (Associated Press 2010).

Generally, the convention is that a national flag is only displayed on a car when the passenger is an ambassador; that's not always so. When Roeder was stationed in Albania, for security reasons, it was felt best if a flag fluttered on his car. Hoover's NGO did the same in occupied France in World War I (Nash, *The Life of Herbert Hoover: The Humanitarian 1914–1917* 1988b, p. 111). One caution is worth mentioning. A flag is a national symbol; bearing it can convey the wrong message and call into question an NGO's neutrality—especially since an NGO is never a national representative.

### *11.7.3 Other Issues at Receptions*

- Events held in a UN compound are often possible, but if after hours, there will be an extra security fee. All guests will be required to have a grounds pass.
- **When inviting VIPs, "staff the invitation**," meaning call the Mission or office and make sure that the assistant of whoever was invited receives a hard copy. If the NGO doing invitations has volunteers, do not mail any invitations; hand-deliver them a month to 6 weeks in advance. That is a lot of work, but if the guest is important enough, he or she is important enough to verify receipt of the invitation.
- **Event address**: Make sure the invitation has the right address, time, and date. Human errors happen. One of the experts interviewed for this book remembered suggesting to an NGO that they hold their reception in a hotel across from UN HQ and volunteered to make arrangements, but the HQ wanted to do it because it handled the budget. Unfortunately, HQ staff (not familiar with New York) used the address of another hotel with the same name on the west side of Manhattan. The UN is on the east side, so the invitations had to be redone. Human errors will creep into even the most organized event, so it is best to have a local person manage such matters, and if possible, have on the delegation one officer with that responsibility.

- **Mission address**: Publications exist in every capital in New York and Geneva showing who represents what mission or embassy and their address and contact information, but these items often change without any warning (Ad Hoc Working Group on Informatics 2010).
- **Reserving rooms**: Reserve a room for meetings or receptions 6 months in advance; national delegations and NGOs are doing the same. However, be aware that if the Secretary General or a national delegation wants the room, they will prevail, so have a fall back off-site venue.
- **Catering need not be problematic**: UNHQ in New York, UN agencies around the world, the International Red Cross and Red Crescent Movement, the EC, and the World Bank in Washington all have contracted catering services, called concessions. NGOs should definitely host receptions because it is a great way to build exposure, but remember to work with the concession, which may require using their food and cost structure—for reasons of security. Concessions are however used to international audiences and should be able to handle any diet.
- **Have a backup plan**: Arrangements should be made prior to departure by the delegation, keeping in mind the budget, since catering can be very expensive. Determine if rooms are available at the conference site or hotel, nearby restaurants, and in the case of the conference site if the conference caterer must be used.

## 11.8 Ambassadors

Getting to know ambassadors is essential. ambassadors to the UN can help move initiatives along, so too ambassadors to a nation's capital. For example, if an NGO wants the host government to agree to an international standard at the UN, while lobbying or negotiations will take place in New York or some other UN venue, and if a friendly government shares the opinion of the NGO, then it also makes sense to approach that nation's representatives to the target country; to ask their advice on tactics, who to approach in the local Ministries, etc.; and even to ask the ambassador to speak on the issue's behalf. So what is an ambassador exactly, and is it ever appropriate for an NGO representative to take on such a title?

In the American system, the president decides who is an ambassador, and this person must be confirmed by the Senate. The title is good for life. In UN agencies, goodwill ambassadors are also created, but they only use the specialized title while serving in that capacity. In the British system, the UK Government uses the title ambassador for the person formally accredited, through agreement by Her Majesty The Queen and the receiving government, as a head of a diplomatic mission in a non-Commonwealth country, whereas in British Commonwealth member countries, the head of diplomatic mission is known as a High Commissioner. There are a few exceptions, one of them being the Permanent Representative to the UN in New York, who is also called ambassador. There will be other systems as well; international custom and law connotes special meaning to the term ambassador; thus, it is considered inappropriate for an NGO official to use the title unless they have been authorized by a government or an IO. Exceptions are found in a number of European countries which use the title in an honorific fashion and in some countries that permit individuals to retain the title of ambassador once their tenure has finished (Morrin 2010); great caution is recommended. When researching precedent for this book, there was discovered one official in a small European NGO who took on the title of ambassador without ever having been granted the privilege by any IO or government. No protocol insult was intended; indeed, the otherwise inoffensive official just wanted to convey the diplomatic nature of her job; several proper ambassadors did however comment that her approach was "uninformed." Why? An ambassador symbolizes his or her country's sovereignty and is the personal representative of the head of government/state or IO (Leki 2007).

Keep in mind also that irrespective of the personal relationship an NGO representative might have with an ambassador, everything said to this person is likely to be reported back to the Foreign Office/Ministry/Department of State. There are no off-the-record conversations. ambassadorial duties include negotiating agreements (though often only with authority from the capital); reporting on political, economic, and social conditions; advising on policy options; protecting national interests; and coordinating the activities of government agencies and personnel in the country. The point on authority is particularly pertinent to an NGO because if an ambassador or some other official does not have instructions to support an NGO's cause, they might not have the liberty to be of help, no matter what they might say at a social event. In those situations, the best advice is to (a) ask to keep them up to date/brief on an informal basis and (b) lobby the Foreign Ministry in capital to provide instructions. Remember that regardless of the topic, without instructions from the Foreign Ministry, officials at an embassy or mission cannot do much.

Instead of using first names, always use the courtesy title, unless otherwise invited. ambassadors are addressed as Mr. or Madam ambassador, ambassador Jones, and Sir or Ma'am. Some countries do allow an ambassador to keep his or her title after retirement, but this is not always the case, and so NGO officials who used to be ambassadors should avoid using the title unless they are certain the practice is authorized. Officials below ambassador are called Mr., Ms., or Mrs., if marital status is known. Military officials go by rank, unless retired, then are called Mr. or Mrs., except for field and general grade officers, who generally are allowed to retain their titles (Leki 2007). The following is the American order of precedence: ambassador Extraordinary, Charge d'Affaires; Minister-Counselors; Counselors (or Senior Secretaries in the absence of Counselors); Army, Naval, and Air Attaches not in the diplomatic corps; First Secretaries; and Civilian Assistants (see also demarches) (Leki 2007).

When a country has more than one ambassador posted to multiple missions, the order of precedence among them is determined by the customs of their country. Keep in mind that officials not in the formal diplomatic corps are also diplomats if they hold a diplomatic letter or a diplomatic passport and are on assignment.

## 11.9 Invitations and Greetings

As the diplomatic community gets to know an NGO officer, invitation to receptions will follow. Cultural differences abound in issuing and responding to invitations, so it is often best to consult with local authorities in advance. As a general rule, unless the invitation is addressed to other family members, they are not invited, including the spouse. Do not bring someone you are dating to a working event, unless allowed. Do respond by phone within 2 days. If the card says "regrets only," no response is needed unless you cannot attend. In that case, it is important to regret. If the card says "rsvp," always respond.

A few common greetings go a long way, as well as some food vocabulary in the host language in order to get through informal social situations. Be aware that cultures can vary dramatically in how they greet people. In Albania, people nod for no and shake their head for yes. Bows, handshakes and kisses, and other forms of friendliness can be decidedly different. In the Arab world, it is not uncommon to see men showing affection by holding hands while walking. The appropriate distance between people can be quite different than in the West. In China, people stand close in order to show trust. The best advice is to ask about such customs in advance, so not to be surprised. When confused, just ask during an event. Hosts are always willing to respond to a guest who expresses honest interest in their culture.

Introductions are an important part of an event to exchange names. Keep it simple "Mrs. Clinton, may I present Mr. Lewis" is used in formal settings. In an informal setting, try "Mrs. Clinton, Mr. Lewis." Do introduce yourself, but just use your first and last name, never an honorific. It is also important for a delegate to add context that he or she is representing a particular kind of NGO. "Hello, I'm Dana Seagrams, Director for Disaster Management in the Society for the Protection of Cultural Centers in the in Gambia." Every culture has a way of asking how someone is and responding. Learn them, and keep in mind gender. When asking a male how do you do in Hebrew, it is Ma shlomkha? To a female, it is Ma shlomekh? Smiles and a casual hello can be appropriate in cocktail parties. When introducing several people, start with the person of the highest rank and women. Any NGO attending diplomatic functions should also have a set of stories that link humor and the NGOs core mission, stories that seem naturally told and are memorable (unless meeting the same people often!).

- When making introductions, tell each individual a bit of information about the other; this encourages conversation.
- Rise when meeting anyone or being introduced.
- Learn the rules of greeting and leave-taking. Failure to use them is considered a serious breach of protocol and extremely rude.
- Don't panic if you forget names. If that happens, just say something like "Good evening, I'm Jim Smith of Human Rights, International. We met last year at the Navajo Indian conference in Window Rock, Arizona, on the protection of indigenous cultures. Great to see you again." This reminds the other of the first meeting and provides a context in which to respond, and likely the delegate will

reintroduce himself. In other words, when unsure, begin by assuming the other does not remember you either. Give them a clue. On the other hand, if the referenced earlier meeting was wrong, this is not a problem. The other delegate will simply correct the error and likely provide lots of information.

## 11.10 Dress

The dress at most international conferences is Western business attire, but local clothes are also frequently worn, especially by indigenous guests or when making a cultural statement, and in some climates, local clothing is also more practical. To be effective and respected, know the right dress and customs at the event you will attend. When in doubt, call the local UN office, the embassy, or the Ministry or Agency which issued the invitation. If nothing else, this action alone will do much to reduce stress. International conference negotiations can run into 12–14 hours per day, so wear comfortable shoes. There is often not enough time to change clothes for evening receptions, so consider how to dress during the day to make sure it is appropriate for the evening. When the hotel is a long way away, it is a good idea to bring toothpaste and brushes, mouthwash and cologne, and any daily medicine. Freshening up in the middle of a difficult day can do much to rebuild spirits and energy (Fig. 11.5).

**Fig. 11.5** Suits are normal wear at diplomatic functions, but dinner jackets are welcome as well. © 2011 LRoeder

**Semiformal/Informal**

Appropriate for cocktail parties, dinners, some dances, the theater, the opera, and evening receptions:

- Male attire: dark suit, tie or bow tie, and dark shoes. Dinner suit is acceptable.
- Female attire: short cocktail dress, gloves are optional and rare to see, and high-heeled shoes or dressy flats.

### *11.10.1 Casual Dress*

In some countries, jeans or sportswear is often seen, also at casual functions in some diplomatic missions. However, if invited to a casual dress affair, be aware that not everyone means jeans and sneakers. Business attire is usually appropriate for an event specified as casual. But call ahead. Breakfast, lunch, daytime meetings, afternoon tea, and some receptions are generally considered casual, but the invitation should specify.

**Male Attire** Business suit (light or dark) or sports jacket and pants, tie or bow tie, and dress shoes or loafers (called slip-ons or slippers in other cultures)

**Female Attire** Business suit or daytime dress as well as pumps or flat shoes

**Head Coverings** This may be considered a requirement at some events. Wide-brim hats may also provide welcome and necessary protection from the sun.

## 11.11 Gender and Race

Gender roles can be very complex. Certainly as a topic of NGO advocacy, the community needs to acknowledge female strength and achievement and remind others of the importance of succeeding in the ongoing global struggle for gender equality empowerment. When about to enter a country for a negotiation or when engaging a diplomat or Minister from another country, inquire in advance about gender customs. Even regions in a country can vary, especially one with a wide diversity of ethnic and religious groups. When entertaining, spouses may have unexpected social rules in receiving lines or the dining table. Some cultures require clothing which in the NGOs land is not appropriate. Do not complain; instead, go along with these traditions, unless they are demeaning; show respect for local culture; and remember that the role of the delegation is not to change host country customs but to advance the NGOs' goals. When going to Mosques, for example, take your shoes off. Woman should not show bare legs there and must cover their heads. In an Islamic society, men should not offer to shake the hand of a woman, regardless of location. In any Islamic society, a man should instead wait for the woman to extend her hand to be shaken, rather than offering his hand first, and shake her hand only if she has given that signal. Men and women are unlikely to meet in a mosque since she would be on the women's balcony or rear seating area and he in the front or main floor, but even outside the mosque, this etiquette should be followed. If addressing mosque etiquette for women, you should make sure to say that any female entering a mosque should have something handy to cover her head (doesn't have a scarf, a jacket can be used); though non-Muslim (especially Western) women are not expected to follow this rule completely and may enter the mosque without a head cover if otherwise modestly attired, many women would likely feel more comfortable by having some form of head covering as a mark of respect for the location.

There are some exceptions. One expert consulted on this book noted that when dealing with some cultures, it is wise not to have a female as the lead of the team or delegation, even people of certain religions as lead can be a problem. While the expert's logic is understandable, it is being egalitarian to safely stretch local customs, if possible in those areas. If you are dealing with diplomats or officials used to working with diplomats, they will usually accommodate. Field operations are another matter. Never endanger staff just to make a moral point like this.

## 11.12 Speak Without Notes

In many situations, a formal written speech is the proper format for communications, especially when speaking on the record where an interpreter will assist; he will need the exact words. But what about impromptu speeches given at receptions and cocktail parties? In 1983, President Reagan and Roeder had a conversation about public speaking, and the President made an interesting point about storytelling. Roeder was used to reading speeches, long before Teleprompters, and, just a month earlier, had presented an academic piece on US trade options (Roeder, *US Policy Option on High-Tech Exports to the Soviet Union* 1983, March). President Reagan wanted Roeder to give a speech on Poland, something he would write. Roeder had actually suggested to him that he give the speech to counter pro-communist rallies on May Day, and he liked the notion, but eventually scheduling got in the way and Reagan wanted Roeder to do it instead (Reagan 1985). During the discussion, Reagan remarked that when he began running for office, he too did a lot of long speech reading but then decided that storytelling was a more effective way of getting the point across. To Reagan, it did not matter about the exact words so long as the basic idea was accurate, entertaining, and memorable. That was a very good advice, which should also work for NGO conferences and cocktail parties. Delegates are going to hear a lot of speeches, especially at conferences but even at dinner and cocktail parties. Instead of reading PowerPoint presentations or pages of speech, skip the props, except perhaps for one slide; practice the presentation three or four times; and then tell the story. The truth is that at conferences many read speeches are heard and forgotten. The passionate, from-the-heart speech will be remembered if it is well told.

## 11.13 Use of Language

### *11.13.1 Official and Working Languages*

**Working Languages** These are used in a conference room during negotiations or in the field. They can vary widely, from Swahili to Arabic. Although multilateral negotiations, especially in UN agencies, are mostly done in English, with intersperse of other languages, it isn't always so.[3] Have in the delegation at least one person who can speak and write in the main working language.[4]

**Official Languages** If the negotiation will result in a written agreement, the language chosen for the text is the official language. For practical reasons, since hundreds of languages exist, some international organizations also have a limited set of official languages for conversations. The Arab Red Cross and Red Crescent Societies use Arabic and English, whereas there are five official languages at the UN. If someone speaks in one, translation is often offered in the rest, but in any other, though translation from a nonofficial to an official may be offered. Further, the text must be in one of the official languages.

The French regularly insist on using their own language, and it is useful to note that at one time, the official language of diplomacy was French; that changed forever when the negotiators at Versailles agreed to British and American demands that the official languages of the League of Nations and its related bodies be both French and English (Miller, *The Drafting of the Covenant* 1928, pp. Vol I, pg 505). The truth is, change was on its way. As late as 1903, French was the official language of the Inter-Parliamentary Union, a precursor to the League (Bartholdt 1930, p. 214). However, choices of official language began to change by 1895 when a tribunal of arbitration was held in Paris to settle differences between Great Britain and the United States on the Bering Straits. To the surprise of the French arbitrators, the United States insisted on English, but President Harrison did agree that official languages could also be those of other participants (Cambon, *The Diplomatist* 1931, p. 113).

---

[3]Multilateral negotiations in the UN system, the World Bank, and the IFRC are generally in English, though the UN's official languages are Arabic, Chinese, English, French, Russian, and Spanish. The working languages of the General Assembly are English, French, and Spanish (in the Security Council, only English and French are working languages), which is why those are really the only two languages needed when meeting with delegations to the UN in Geneva and New York. But different organizations have different rules.

[4]When Roeder represented a British NGO in Tunis for negotiations with the Arab League and the Association of Red Cross and Red Crescent Societies, the discussions were entirely in Arabic, with simultaneous English interpretation, but IFRC talks in Geneva were in English with French and Arabic interpretation.

**The Bottom Line for the Study Group** The bottom line for the study group is to determine what languages will be used in any situation related to a project and be able to operate in those languages, have a translator, or arrange for the host to offer translation. Also agree on the official language for any outcomes document and make sure that before agreeing to a text, a true expert in that language translates[5] it. This person should also understand the subtleties of your language. If the translator does not fully grasp either language or the required terminology, e.g., jargon specific to the NGOs field of work, then serious mistakes can be made.[6]

Facilitators are also often used on field trips for getting through customs, interactions at farms, etc. Their role is to understand customary approaches to rules, often to smooth the edges, but a caution is in order because facilitators quite innocently can also take over a situation and lead a delegation where it does not wish to go. They also might miss something considered by the delegation as an opportunity. Perhaps the delegation wants to photograph a stable, but the facilitator might not understand unless briefed in advance. Ask lots of questions. Do not let them spend hours and hours talking to the driver or bodyguard. Some of that is needed to smooth local relations, but they will be more useful if they constantly interact with the delegation; ask questions, clarify needs, etc.

**Jargon and Speed** Even if English is a working language, not everyone will be native in English, certainly not jargon and colloquialism. Speak at a speed that is easy to follow.

**Simultaneous Texts** It is important that the text have agreed official language(s) and that whatever is agreed gets a good linguistic scrub. That will be especially important should you encourage governments to implement an agreed text. You do not want them to be confused over intent. Even NGO delegates who are expert in both official languages should keep both texts in front of them. It can be very helpful and create goodwill. It will also help sort through disagreements that arise from poor translation.

---

[5] "Interpreters" work with the spoken word and "translators" work with the written word.

[6] In this context, one of the interesting things highlighted by one of the surveys used in this book for research was the variety of language used for by the NGOs we contacted. While 70 % spoke English as a primary language, followed by Spanish, French, Arabic, and Portuguese, a lot of local languages were also primary. This illuminates several issues. For one thing, some of those NGOs will have trouble communicating in the UN or other international forums unless they have on staff someone who speaks a major UN language like English, which is sort of a lingua franca. But alternatively, they provide a rich tapestry of tongues that can be used to better understand the needs of local culture yet another reason for fully integrating them into the discussion on international rules. Many of the lesser used language are actually very important global languages, e.g., Russian, Italian, Greek, Swedish, Dutch, and Norwegian. Other languages were Navajo, Bahasa, Bosnian, Catalan, Estonian, Hindi, Marathi, Telugu, and others (IFR 2010a, October).

### *11.13.2 What if You Don't Speak Any of the Official or Working Languages?*

This can happen when a visiting dignitary shows up to make a speech, not actually negotiate. In these situations, a written statement is provided to the interpreter. In fact, common practice is to share any speech with the interpreters, regardless of the base language. It makes interpretation easier.

### *11.13.3 Trying to Change Text*

If you are dissatisfied with a proposed text during a negotiation, do not give up trying to change because you are an NGO. Governments do respect the point of view of NGOs, if they are well stated. Just make sure that interventions are seen as within a "spirit of consensus." That provides a positive spin. This is important because delegations that hold up negotiations without an excellent reason (from the perspective of the conference) can be "isolated," but it is needed to slow things up a bit while gathering argumentation, just ask the proposing party to "explain their proposed change."

## 11.14 Neutrality

A guiding principle of humanitarian affairs is that "humanitarian assistance must be provided in accordance with the principles of humanity, neutrality and impartiality" (UNGA 1991). In the real world, diplomacy is often partial, aiming to not just mediate between opposing forces but to cause specific change; diplomats, and especially NGO diplomats, need to be humane, meaning polite, even to representatives advancing offensive policy positions. For the most part, it is also best to be neutral in political fights—unless that is the point of the intervention. To be neutral, just be sensitive that language proposed by the NGO does not appear to be negative towards a particular country. For example, members of the Arab Group and the Organization of the Islamic Conference (OIC) regularly make efforts in New York and in conferences to insert language in resolutions and documents that explicitly or implicitly single out Israel for criticism. Unless the NGOs' mission is to criticize a policy like the slaughter of civilians in Syria, regardless of one's point of view, stay out of such a difficult situation. Such arguments are often distractions from a core mission like protecting women and children, though that can at times seem counterintuitive. This however does not mean being silent about abuses. MSF is famous for being neutral, not taking sides; they speak loudly in order to reduce abuse. "MSF's actions are guided by medical ethics and the principles of neutrality and impartiality; reserves the right to speak out to bring attention to neglected crises, to challenge inadequacies or abuse of the aid system, and to advocate for improved medical treatments and protocols" (MSF 2011).[7]

When thinking of knowing the other side, also keep in mind religion, especially when the negotiation is done in the field. What is the religion of the people with whom you will negotiate an issue, and how will they perceive you if of a different belief system? Humanitarian relief work isn't about advancing a religion. It is about reducing misery or building up an economy. Yet, even if an NGO intends to do the right thing, nothing can be more harmful that being insensitive. Witness the riots in Kabul in 2012 after US military forces accidently destroyed Korans. Or go back to the relief operations in Sudan, a country split between Muslim, Christians, and Animists. Too often religious NGOs proselytize, which is totally inappropriate in emergency settings. It is best to leave such things to the indigenous population, such as in Uganda where Catholics became Muslims during the Amin rule, and before then in order to go to a Catholic school, one had to be baptized. Even statistics on how many people are or not Christian is a political weapon. In other words, neutrality isn't just about politics. It is also about faith.

### *11.14.1 Neutrality Versus Sovereignty*

Being neutral has its limits. One of the great things about NGOs like MSN is that they will speak up when they see a real abuse; that brings risk. Government diplomats are banned from interference in the internal affairs of host nations by the Convention on Diplomatic Relations (Denza, *Diplomatic Law, Commentary on the Vienna Convention on Diplomatic Relations* 2008a), though they can certainly lobby government officials for changes, sometimes at the behest of their Foreign Affairs Ministries, spurred on by the public back home, themselves driven by public diplomacy advanced by NGOs. Indeed, the UN is not supposed to interfere in the internal affairs of nations, though the exception is when the state violates

[7] MSF reserves the right to speak out to bring attention to neglected crises, to challenge inadequacies or abuse of the aid system, and to advocate for improved medical treatments and protocols. MSF medical teams often witness violence, atrocities, and neglect in the course of their work, largely in regions that receive scant international attention. At times, MSF may speak out publicly in an effort to bring a forgotten crisis to public attention, to alert the public to abuses occurring beyond the headlines, to criticize the inadequacies of the aid system, or to challenge the diversion of humanitarian aid for political interests (Tronc 2012).

international norms, for example, committing crimes against humanity.[8] Diplomats do speak with political dissidents, though in private, but if he or she tries to impact elections or assist a dissident group, that's considered interference in internal affairs; though often the acts are justified, it can result in a Diplomat being declared persona non grata, since they can't be arrested. This is a reflection of the legal concept of the right to protect national sovereignty. If an NGO, particularly a foreign NGO, tries to do the same, they do not have diplomatic immunity and the staff can be arrested. I'm not arguing against interference, particularly in order to save lives; the context of this book is to advance diplomacy. How will being arrested advance diplomacy? It is a serious question an NGO needs to ask before engaging in this kind of direct action.

Lest NGOs think that a government's push back on NGO interference damages democracy, while in the real world, that's often certainly true, the very concept derives from historical actions to protect democracy. It all started with the French revolution, which created the Constitution of 1793 *Acte constitutionnel du 24 juin 1793*; the French people do not interfere in the affairs of other states; the people (very important here, distinguishing between the people and the state) do not tolerate interference by other nations in their affairs. This document, which grew out of the Declaration of the Rights of Man and of the Citizen of 1789, essentially provided for the superiority of public sovereignty over national sovereignty; interference by foreign powers was seen as an attack on the people as a whole. Again, in defense of freedom against totalitarianism, interference by NGOs can be a good thing; however, it can also be risky to the physical safety of NGOs in-country and can undermine diplomatic initiatives; take those issues into account.

## 11.15 Titles and Saying Hello and Goodnight

Forms of address for foreign government officials and people holding professional, ecclesiastical, or traditional titles vary among countries. To be current, check with the local embassy or UN office. Here are some recommendations on typical title.

### *11.15.1 Diplomatic Titles*

**Chiefs of Mission** In general Mr./Madam ambassador works fine. This also applies to an ambassador with a military title. Some diplomatic missions are led by ministers, in which case the form is Mr./Madam last name.

[8]This was a serious issue at the start of the League of Nations discussions, with the Swiss insisting that the League have no authority over internal affairs (Miller, Meetings With the Neutral Powers, 1928).

### 11.15.1.1 Government Titles

Once again, this can vary widely by country, so it is best to consult directly with the UN mission of embassy of the country in question. In most cases, the spouse of a government official does not share the official's title with his/her spouse (i.e., the president's spouse is Mr./Mrs. Reagan or Ms. Lincoln).

**Executive Branch**

- Mr./Madam President
- Mr./Madame Vice President
- Cabinet members are addressed as Mr./Madam Secretary except Mr./Madam Attorney General (Parliamentary systems use Ministers for Cabinet officers, but Federal systems like that of the United States of America do NOT have Ministers; instead, they have Secretaries, which are different in rank to Secretaries in the UK system).
- Below the rank of secretary, government officials are addressed by their own name: Mr./Madam Reynolds, not Mr./Madam Undersecretary. Sometimes undersecretaries, assistant secretaries, and deputy assistant secretaries are addressed as Mr. or Madam Secretary, but it is best just say Mr., Ms., or Mrs. as appropriate.

**Judicial Branch**

- Mr./Madam chief Justice
- Mr./Madam Justice. Keep in mind that below the chief Justice of the Supreme Court, justices are Associate Justices, whereas Appellate Judges are not justices, only judges. When in doubt, call the court HQ. Why does this matter? While most NGOs do not talk to the Judicial Branch, they probably should do, as those contacts can be very helpful towards understanding local legal customs.

### 11.1.1.3 Legislative Branch

In some parliamentary systems, the legislative and executive branches are combined, so it is possible to have a prime minister, who is addressed as Mr. or Mrs. Smith, Prime Minister of X.

- Senate—Senator Collins, not Mr. Collins.
- House—Mr./Madam Speaker of the House and Mr./Madam Rogers for a state representative. The titles "Congressman" and "Congresswoman" are becoming more common in social usage, but are not, strictly speaking, correct forms of address.

### 11.15.2 State and Provincial Government Titles

- Governor Collins
- Mayor Millville or Mr./Madam Millville

## 11.16 Letter Formats

### 11.16.1 The Démarche

A démarche is usually a written communication between governments or an international organization used to convey a complaint, to make an alert, or to state a position. NGOs don't do démarches by name; they often do the same thing in the form of a letter or memorandum, so it makes sense to use formats the diplomatic community is used to receiving.

The first rule is to use precise text and include any necessary phrases of courtesy for first-person notes or letters; the text should be self-explanatory, understandable, and independent of any other document or earlier correspondence:

- Do not use foreign words.
- Avoid abbreviations and little-known acronyms.
- Keep in mind that memoranda are not letters: too often, the forms are mixed, which is unprofessional. Make letters look like letters, not memos and vice versa. A common mistake is to insert a subject line on the top of a letter. This is an error because the opening paragraph explains the topic in a letter; a subject line is superfluous.
- Get the main point across in the opening paragraph. ambassadors and government leaders receive thousands of letters a year. They might not read past the first paragraph, so instead of using the opening paragraph to advertise your NGO, just state your request.
- Keep the main body of a letter to one and half pages or less, including the signature block, if possible. If a lot of background material must be shared, create one-page Tabs such as those used in decision memoranda. This is because the person written to will be busy. ambassadors would not read more than a page in the main memo, unless the issue is important to them, so this sense of importance also needs to be present.
- Never use window envelopes when writing to diplomats or government leaders. That is tacky and commercial and can result in the envelope being tossed out.
- Some NGOs make it a habit to put their logo on each page, probably thinking it is a great way to advertise. This is tacky.

#### 11.16.1.1 How to Address Letters

There are a number of formats that can be used in mailing letters, some more formal and elegant than others. The following format is recommended for the middle of the envelope, which should be orientated lengthwise.

## *11.16.2 Sample When Writing to Ambassadors to the UN to Be Included*

**Capacity** Always address the person in the capacity for which he or she is written. For example, if Ambassador Doe was the ambassador of Spain to the UN and/or ECOSOC, and the letter is about ECOSOC.

His Excellency

(Dr.) (General) John Doe
Representative of Spain on the Economic and Social Council of the United Nations
Street Address
New York, New York 00017, USA

Many ambassadors also represent their country in the Group of 77 at the United Nations, a very important block. If writing to an ambassador in that capacity:

His Excellency

(Dr.) (General) John Macintyre
Representative of Whatever to
The Group of 77 at the United Nations
United Nations Headquarters, Room S-3953 New York, New York10017, USA

## *11.16.3 Salutation for Ambassadors*

"Dear ambassador Doe" is sometimes used, but the best salutation for an ambassador is either Excellency or Dear Mr. (Mrs.) ambassador. When writing to someone of lower rank, usually start with Sir/Madam: Of course in situations where the person writing knows the person being written to, less formal approaches are often used.

### *11.16.4 Complimentary Close for Ambassadors*

Yours Sincerely is fine, but ordinarily it is one of the following. Just use the word "sincerely" or:

- Head of Mission, the last line is usually Accept, Excellency, the (renewed—if the Head was written to before) assurances of my highest consideration. Note: Highest is used because the ambassador is the personal representative of the head of state.
- Deputy Head of perhaps a Charge´ d'Affaires ad interim, the last line is usually Accept Sir/Madam, the (renewed—if written before) assurance of my high consideration.

### *11.16.5 Other Personalities*

#### 11.16.5.1 Position: The Speaker of the House

The Honorable Nancy Pelosi
Speaker of the House of Representatives
Washington, DC 20515

Salutation: Dear Madam Speaker
Complimentary Close: Respectfully or Sincerely

#### 11.16.5.2 Position: United States Representative

The Honorable James Doe
Street address (sometimes not in Washington) City, including zip code

Salutation: Dear Mr., Ms., or Mrs. Doe Complimentary Close: Sincerely

#### 11.16.5.3 Position: United States Senator

The Honorable Nancy Harriman Fidelity
United States Senate
Washington, DC 20510

Salutation: Dear Senator Fidelity
Complimentary Close: Sincerely

#### 11.16.5.4 Position: Cabinet Member (Minister or Secretary)

The Honorable Hillary Clinton
Secretary of State of the United States of America
Washington, DC 20520

Salutation: Dear Madam Secretary or Dear Minister, depending on title
Complimentary Close—Respectfully or Sincerely.

### *11.16.6 Memo Enclosures and Attachments*

If there is only one, do not number it if only one, say "Enclosure," not "Enclosures." Little details like that matter. This is where flyers are placed or long background paragraphs, perhaps a backgrounder on the NGO. Use this formulation and place it at the bottom of the page about two lines below the signature line.

Enclosure

Background on the Protection of Horses in Snow. Here is the formulation for more than one enclosure. Enclosures:

1. Background on the Protection of Horses in Snow
2. Background on Protection of Animals in Floods

Label the attachment (also called Tabs), for example, Tab One: Background on the Protection of Horses in Snow or Background on the Protection of Horses in Snow. Only number attachments if there are more than one, for example, Attachment One: Background on the Protection of Horses in Snow.

# Chapter 12
# Delegation Communications and the Media

**Extract**

Chapter 12 explores how to use press conferences, speeches, interviews, and social media to advance negotiations or to bolster an NGO's image at an event. Facebook and Twitter are explored, which are often effective public diplomacy tools in places like the Arab Spring. Communications is a key part of any diplomacy, and special care must be given to the words chosen to explain an initiative to reporters so that they understand its context. All of this means study groups often must create a working group on communications. The role of delegation Communications Officer is also introduced.

## 12.1 Delegation Communications and the Media

Suppose a G77 ambassador endorses an initiative by the Paris Wildlife Conservation Society to protect endangered species in the newly independent Republic of South Sudan. Donors will appreciate seeing a photo of the ambassador saying something nice about the initiative; what if the conference is about employment, not conservation? A clever approach might be to convince the media explain the concept in terms of jobs. For example, "the establishment of Boma National Park in Jonglei State also fosters real jobs through conservation." Such a story would give the NGO's efforts *relevance* to conference goals. Participants might then endorse the initiative. Such media stories in Internet blogs and niche sites could also be very effective in convincing society to lobby the government to support negotiating positions or fund a project (Fig. 12.1).

One of the important tasks for the Communications section on the study group is to identify who are the decision makers. Once they have been identified, NGOs can place op-eds and media stories in local media outlets to influence both the public and the decision makers.

L.W. Roeder, Jr. and A. Simard, *Diplomacy and Negotiation for Humanitarian NGOs*, Humanitarian Solutions in the 21st Century, DOI 10.1007/978-1-4614-7113-4_12,

**Fig. 12.1** Press conference ((c) 2012 LRoede)

## 12.2 The Delegation Communications (Public Affairs) Officer

This is often the delegation's public face with the media, though every delegation officer should be trained on how to speak. Sometimes called the Media Officer or Public Affairs Officer, or in the U.S. Department of State the public diplomacy Cone, for purposes of this book, the term Communications Officer is used.[1] The title is limited to the task of furthering an NGO-/CSO-led diplomatic initiative, not the other general efforts to raise funds or to extoll the general virtues of an NGO as a whole, though the officer likely will be seconded from such a staff. The assignment is mission specific in other words. An NGO's Director of Communications and Public Affairs would coordinate the organization's overall communications strategy; the delegation Communications Officer just handles delegation needs.

[1] The Authors are not saying that readers must use the term Communications Officer. They are speaking about a function. "Public Affairs Officer" is more common in diplomatic circles. In embassies, the spokesperson for the media is the Press Attaché while educational and cultural matters are covered by the Cultural Attaché. For most diplomatic staff people, "communications" officer denotes staff primarily concerned with the technical aspect of communications, i.e., computer technology; whereas in many NGOs Communications Officer mean Public Affairs Officer.

**Speaking in Plenary or Committees** The Communications Officer looks for opportunities to speak in committees or in the plenary session at conferences. A good example is ECOSOC, which rotates its meetings between New York and Geneva. Since 1996, NGOs in consultative status with ECOSOC had had the ability to make an annual oral statement at those sessions. The only requirement is that the statement relates to ECOSOC's focal theme for that session (ECOSOC 2011).

**Important ECOSOC Commissions to Consider for Speaking and Networking Opportunities**

- **Commission on the Status of Women (CSW)**
- **Commission for Social Development (CSocD)**
- **Commission on Sustainable Development (CSD)**
- **UN Permanent Forum on Indigenous Issues (UNPFII)**
- **The Commission on Population and Development (CPD)**
- **United Nations Forum on Forests (UNFF)**
- **Commission on Crime Prevention and Criminal Justice (CCPCJ)**
- **Commission on Narcotic Drugs (CND)**
- **Commission on Science and Technology for Development (CSTD),**
- **United Nations Statistical Commission (UN StatCom)**
- **The Human Rights Council (HRC)**[2]

**Telling an Accurate Story** Unfortunately, there are instances where telling an initiative's story failed to provide the true picture, perhaps in order to make results seem stronger than they actually were. Keep in mind that factual errors will damage the effort a diplomatic circles. When working with ReliefWeb, a pattern of false claims can also lead to a source being banned. While a certain clouding of facts might seem inevitable as passions rise with proponents or antagonists, sloppy reporting needs to be avoided, even if the truth may endanger donations. It is essential for the Communications Officer to ensure that the team projects accurate, well-understood news on a regular basis to the appropriate press.

To prevent such problems, a good delegation Communications Officer keeps a constant eye on delegation press reports for errors. The officer should also recommend corrections and preempt mistakes by sending press statements to the Regular Press Notes disseminated to the UN HQ in New York, Geneva, Rome, Bangkok, and Nairobi. The IFRC may also be a good choice, as well as the main humanitarian networks, the World Bank Group, and other bodies such as ASEAN. The same officer can also send such notes to agency media offices in the UN system, such as managed by the UN Department of Public Information (DPI).

A news story, regardless of the media, is a well told narrative that explains issues people want to know about or should. It should also grab the audience and pull them into the narrative, past the other stories they could just have easily chosen to read.

---

[2]Not a subsidiary of ECOSOC, but only NGOs in consultative status with ECOSOC may participate.

That's especially true at an international conference. Thousands of people attend those events, international conferences. You have seconds to convince them to hear you, and only a little more time to convince them your point of view is essential to them. It is the same for pictures. They need to tell a compelling, tight story, and if audio is used, it must be clear. So, how do you engage the media at conferences or bilateral events to help NGO causes or to facilitate change? How do you avoid the normal routine of just reporting the news, making your story another in a blizzard of fast-moving facts? At international conferences, unless the person being interviewed is a star, the media will mostly just want to summarize proceedings, which means NGOs are often ignored by policy makers. How to reverse that situation?

Many will just ask media to provide a bare-bones coverage of an event such as endorsement by an ambassador of an NGO's initiative. Nice pictures or a short note in the wire services can definitely be valuable for donors. This is a very common "Fifth Estate" role. But that limited approach can miss opportunities. Take reporters aside and build a positive relationship before the conference starts, to explain "the relevance of the initiative." In addition, while the NGO must not lose sight of its own values, explain the project in terms that relate to the values of decision makers, like ministers. How is the event connected to why donors and governments are attending? That way, conference participants might see the initiative as a tool to advance their own ideas.

**Communications Officer as Couch and Trainer** Some people are uncomfortable at a mike, standing on a platform or with the media, being interviewed or in press conferences. Before any delegation member speaks to the media, the Communications Officer should make sure that the speaker can do the job well with accurate information. Provide training as needed. Officers should not be afraid of press contacts (they are often a good source of information) and junior officers will be leaders one day. This means every member of the team must be properly informed if only to tell reporters they need to go to someone else for better information. In addition, each delegation member should see himself or herself as responsible for internal communication within the team. The Communications Officer coordinates this effort.

**Media Kit** The Communications Officer should develop a cleared Media Kit (also called a Press Kit) for distribution at events. This is usually a glossy flyer (but it need not be, journalists often equate glossiness with just being slick) presenting illustrative charts and photographs that highlight the NGO's initiative in the best light and in the context of issues considered important to a larger community. For example, a media kit on micro-finance at a risk-reduction event might show policies the NGO espouses as coping mechanisms to reduce loss of income in poor, seismic-vulnerable neighborhoods. The Press Kit should provide a contact person(s) for questions and include a set of questions a reporter might ask, accompanied by answers. A list of endorsements is also a good idea.

**Press Releases and Handouts** The Communications Officer creates press releases and distributes them to any media outlet or relevant Web/blog site, providing information on breakthroughs or general background. The importance of such releases can't be minimized. Interviews might not come, or even if they do, the interviews

**Fig. 12.2** Leave handouts ((c) 2012 LRoeder)

might not get much coverage; regular press releases can keep the story "on the air." A certain discipline will be required by the Communications Officer, making sure that information flows to him or her by a deadline, so that they can be distributed to media outlets and conference press offices or just placed on conference room chairs (Fig. 12.2).[3]

**Assets and Hazards** Another Communications Officer responsibility is to inform the team about the opportunities and hazards of the media contacts; this report should be a specific Tab prepared by the Study Team. As an example, if a delegation is going to a country to negotiate protection for historical properties, the Communications Officer should learn who controls the local media and what their attitude is on the topic. Is the media run by a ruling elite or the private sector? Who are the opinion leaders in the country in and outside the government, rebel factions, or industries?

## 12.3 Are Media Events Needed?

**Are Conferences and Interviews a Good Idea?** It is natural to consider press conferences and interviews as very important; unless they actually advance a negotiation or a larger strategic goal like funding operations, their usefulness is often

[3] At international conferences, handouts are usually left on desks just outside the entrance to a meeting; but often delegations are permitted to leave a flyer on each seat, which can be a great way of sharing an idea, perhaps draft language for a resolution or a press note.

questionable when related to a diplomatic initiative. The delegation Communications Officer must make sure they are relevant by sharing briefing points that will energize reporters and talking points that enable delegation members to effectively answer questions.

An international conference is usually attended by hundreds, even thousands of diplomats, ministers, NGO leaders, and other officials. Legions of reporters cover events, so it can seem essential to hold news conferences to advance an NGO's cause, if for no other reason than to grab the attention of the world stage. NGOs might even be tempted to use a media event to garner support for a resolution on an NGO's main topic of interest, perhaps during the UN General Assembly in New York. This approach can work; it doesn't always hold water, especially if the conference is not primarily focused on an NGO's priority topic.

**Note** If the press event is not carefully prepared, attendance will be below expectations; attendance is key at press conferences and can be a double-edged sword. It is hard work to attract journalists to a specific press conference. Some tricks help include the presence of one high authority on the subject, someone already familiar to and trusted by the press. Celebrities are another bait for catching papers' and TV editors' attention. If you are lucky enough to have either or both, your chances of a successful press conference or media event are greatly expanded. George Clooney on the Sudanese regime atrocities, as will be discussed further down, is the perfect example of a match that becomes irresistible to the press.

Will such a press event actually build support from governments or will it just end up as a way to convey forward motion to the donors? Unless the NGO issue in the resolution is considered important or newsworthy in its own right to governments, such a press conference usually makes no ripples with policy makers; if the aim is to change the political landscape, such an effort can be a waste of time and money. On the other hand, such an effort could impress the supporters back home. In that case, photos from the negotiations are apt to give the appearance of progress, even if none has been made, but delegations need to remember that a picture showing a group of reporters clamoring for answers to questions can also appear pretentious, unless the event was connected to what the donor or supporters care about. If such an image does raise expectations of future success with donors and create an initial infusion of funds, what happens if the resolution effort fails? The result could be loss of credibility which will hurt future requests for help.

### *12.3.1 Push for Relevance*

The influence of a well-executed media story on policy development cannot be underestimated on the public. As an example, the media could be very helpful in explaining that the protection of antiquities, sculptures, painting, and other arts of obscure tribes is crucial for the survival of a nation's culture or a region, to say nothing of major industrial societies (Lafarge 1946). Internet blogs and niche sites could be very effective in reaching diverse subpopulations within society and pushing them to lobby the government to support an NGO's negotiating positions, even fund work. NGOs should think of the media as a tool to advance diplomatic efforts, not just the short-term gain of a word or phrase in a document. Maintaining a long-term relationship with journalists is useful. They appreciate keeping this relationship with "sources," as they become reliable tools for a story, if they happen to be out of subjects on a specific day. Reporters will contact you to sniff something out for their day, and this is your chance to have an item to catch the reporter's attention. Many good stories have been aired or printed on slow news days. Do not try to compete with breaking stories in the White House or some serial killer being chased. This is called "hard news", and they will usually have priority over any diplomatic coverage involving NGOs. Those are long-term subjects that can be monitored along time and do not necessarily have to make today's assignments.

Press conferences are often essential, but context is important. Have something important to say and keep in mind the audience being influenced. If a senior UN Official or an ambassador is willing to endorse the initiative, this is a true sign of progress which might help in negotiations and definitely will impress donors. A press conference with just an NGO's CEO in attendance is not necessarily very interesting to reporters. This doesn't mean discouraging the use of press conferences and interviews. To the contrary, NGOs need to use every available avenue with the media, including press conferences to advocate for a cause in order to influence the public, governments, and international organizations. A well-briefed NGO official who is personable and articulate can be a very effective spokesperson on broadcast media or in press conferences. The truth is that if you rely on a single news conference to gain publicity for your ideas, you have already lost. You can never predict what would happen that day. Briefings might be a better avenue and can be very informal or public meetings which the reporters and public can attend: These work well if you have good and well-informed panelists. Peter Hulm[4] found that they enabled him to show that IUCN's species specialists knew more than anyone else (delegates or activists) at talks on trade in endangered species (Hulm 2012).

## 12.4 One-on-One Interviews

Reporters often do not show up for a press conference, being very busy, torn between many events. So unless the event is scheduled to announce hard news, do not expect a lot of reporters to attend, though the UN or conference site's press facilities might film the event for reporters who might watch later on. On the other hand,

[4]Communications Consultant at International Trade Centre, Geneva, with UNEP and many other bodies

**Fig. 12.3** Hallway diplomacy (© 2011 LRoeder)

one-on-one interviews with targeted reporters are often very helpful and easier to obtain. They do not have the glamour of a press conference, but do provide more time for a considered discussion. The real value is that because they are slow, they provide an NGO the opportunity to package its story in a way that sells causes to governments or other conference delegations. Also keep in mind that you have no competition when you have a one-on-one interview. The probability of the story to gain prominence is much, much greater (Fig.12.3).

## 12.5 Public Diplomacy, Propaganda, and Lobbying

Jargon often impedes progress, so using textbook terminology is not required; regardless of which terms an NGO chooses, keep in mind that other people may connote to a word a variety of meanings. Therefore, the Study Team should develop a specific policy and strategy on public diplomacy,[5] lobbying, and propaganda.

[5] Some will argue that when a member of the public of one nation-state advocates to the legislature of his/her own country on behalf of humanitarian principles being violated in another county (or some other issues), that's ADVOCACY/ACTIVISM. While true, those terms are too broad for this conversation; we are parsing Lobbying the government about changing policy from negotiating for specific language, which is Diplomacy, and making a distinction as well between convincing the public to change its own behavior, which is also advocacy and activism, and convincing the public to lobby for specific changes. In that case, the public is engaged in advocacy and activism; but the effort to convince them to do that is public diplomacy.

### *12.5.1 Public Diplomacy*

The vision of the United Nations is that governments are supposed to represent the people; to cause them to instruct their delegations to support NGO initiatives, NGOs need to change the people's will and turn it into a vocal advocate. Depending on the country of course, doing this can influence policy more effectively than a single NGO could by direct contact. This is what governments call public diplomacy (PD), what many in the NGO community call "lobbying." PD is parsed from lobbying. That will include placing effective stories in carefully selected print and social media, also broadcast media like radio and television, and op-eds. Which is more useful will depend on the region and country. Some budget officials will demand metrics to define success, evidence that the process is changing the status quo; that can be hard to do, given the nature of social sciences, and refined polling can be very expensive or impossible at times; nonetheless, experience has taught us that the technique can work.

The definition[6] of PD in this book is derived with permission from one crafted for government diplomats by Michael W. McClellan, Diplomat in Residence, the Gerald R. Ford School of Public Policy, Michigan (McClellan 2004): "*The strategic planning and execution of informational, cultural and educational programming by a humanitarian NGO to create a public opinion environment in a target country or countries that will enable target country political leaders to be comfortable with changing their political paradigm and thus make decisions that are supportive of humanitarian objectives.*"

Of course, the term public diplomacy can be looked at in different ways. President Reagan (Reagan, *Management of public diplomacy Relative to National Security (NSC-NSDD-77)* 1983) described public diplomacy as "those actions of the government designed to generate support for our national security objectives." Regan's State Department defined it as "20th century public affairs adapting traditional approaches both domestically and abroad to take account of modern communications technology." The truth, as others like Tuch observed in 1990, is that the definitions are contradictory and governments have many interests, economic, political, social, and cultural, all promoted through public diplomacy efforts. Tuch also asserted that governments do not practice "diplomacy"—traditional or public—with its own citizenry (Tuch and Kalb 1990). In addition, perhaps because diplomats use the term public diplomacy, it is often thought to have originated in the

[6]One might argue that anyone engaged in promoting an idea like protecting children from sexual predators or improving the welfare of animals is an "activist," but many draw a distinction from that word and "professional." For example, in the animal welfare world, MEAT and Livestock Australia (MLA) says the dedicated and effective work of "professionals" to improve animal welfare in countries to which Australia exports live animals has been overshadowed by the claims of "activists" determined to shut down the trade (Bettles 2012). By contrast, the members of the "activist" groups are often staffed by scientists and consider themselves as professionals who might describe MLA as activists for cruelty.

government, but it was actually coined by Dean Edmund Gullion of the Fletcher School of Law and Diplomacy at Tufts University (Kotok 2010).

One expert felt that "public diplomacy" may be better termed "public advocacy" for the simple reason that "public diplomacy" is a part of the diplomatic efforts extended by the government of one country towards another country's public, providing accurate information on the propagating country's society and values and on counteracting prevailing misperceptions. The authors chose to distinguish public diplomacy (PD) from public advocacy (PA), with PA including efforts to change public behavior versus PD which is specifically convincing the public to lobby the government to change its own mind. In addition, while it can be argued that a government doesn't partake of diplomacy on its own people, NGOs are not governments. Indeed, they are independent, extra-governmental bodies, often with an international agenda and staff. Increasingly, as seen at Rio+20 in 2012, they also see themselves operating on a higher plane, another reason why it is totally appropriate for NGO to conduct diplomacy of all forms.

**Example: Kellogg–Briand Pact of 1928 (General Treaty for the Renunciation of War)** Some would argue strongly that this treaty was an early example of how public diplomacy can work. The treaty's intent was to outlaw war as an instrument of policy, essentially compelling signatories to seek pacific means of settling disputes. It was first considered a bilateral agreement between France and the USA and became a multilateral international law that still stands.[7] It is also enshrined in US domestic law (US Department of State 2011). While the effort did not end war, it is relevant to this book because of how it came to be created. The story began with a letter to the American people by Aristide Briand, French Minister of Foreign Affairs, asking for an end to war as a measure of policy in dispute resolution. The letter was published in newspapers throughout the United States by the Associated Press on April 6, 1927, the tenth anniversary of America's entry into World War I (Associated Press 1927). As David Hunter Miller explained it, historian James T. Shotwell[8] developed the idea of renouncing war as an instrument of national policy and met Briand as a private citizen a fortnight prior when he essentially proposed the idea of the treaty. At first the press did not pick up on the proposal's importance; then private American citizens started a national discussion in the New York Times on April 25. Things heated up with organizations akin to today's NGOs sprouting up with their draft treaties to implement Briand's letter.

The result of the discussion was that the idea quickly entered the popular consciousness; with the proposals being advanced by the general public went well

---

[7] Fifteen nations signed the treaty in Paris on August 27, 1928, in order of signature: Germany, the United States of America, Belgium, France, the British Empire (except for the Dominions and India), Canada, Australia, New Zealand, South Africa, Irish Free State, India, Italy, Japan, Poland, and Czechoslovakia.

[8] Shotwell was a Canadian-born American History Professor who was a member of the Inquiry and played a significant role in the creation of the International Labor Organization and the concept of human rights protection a generation later in the United Nations.

beyond anything Briand envisaged. In the twenty-first century, this kind of public engagement is normal, the kind of energy that made the demining convention possible. However, in 1927, having such momentous ideas being pushed from the people up was an alien concept in America and Europe. Since this was a new phenomenon, Briand asked the Department of State if a treaty was something they also wanted. The timing was right. Distance had developed since the Senate rejected the Treaty of Versailles. With the public so strongly on board, the Department of State responded to Briand in the affirmative and the final product ended up being a multilateral treaty to which former enemies like Germany joined hands. Done a century ago, this specific experience in peacemaking influenced the UN Charter in the 1940s and should influence NGOs and the public today to engage in public diplomacy (Miller, *The Peace Pact of Paris* 1928, pp. 7–20 and 146–149). Another feature that may be of interest to NGOs pursuing treaties is that whereas such instruments often offer opportunities for signatories to withdraw, this one is perpetual. Treaties are also often considered to operate under the concept of *rebus sic stantibus*, meaning that the conditions that existed at the time of signing must continue in order for the treaty to continue. That condition doesn't exist in this treaty. The signatories can't withdraw.

**Example: Proposition 4** An example of effective public diplomacy would be the NGO-driven effort to negotiate the text of and also advance Proposition 4 (a specific body of legislation), taking advantage of California's unique legal structure encouraging citizen government, which was adopted by the voters in 1998 to protect pets and wildlife from cruel traps and poisons. The main backers were NGOs and private citizens (BallotPedia 2010).

**Example UNAMIR** (United Nations Assistance Mission for Rwanda) International organizations and peacekeeping forces also do this kind of work. UNAMIR[9] set up an independent radio station in Rwanda 15 months after the mission started in October 1993, about 10 months after the advent of genocide. Radio UNAMIR broadcast every day for over a year, and its credibility was very high, to the extent that the Security Council encouraged its continuation after the UN mandate was completed. Unfortunately, government officials did not agree, likely seeing the UN radio as a breach of sovereignty. Some scholars like G.R. Berridge however argue that UNIMIR's activity was nothing more than propaganda and that twentieth-century politicians coined the phrase "public diplomacy" to avoid negative connotations associated with propaganda in earlier years (Berridge 2005). What is certain is that if an NGO's website unreasonably stretches the truth in order to convince the public, then the advocacy is propaganda, not public diplomacy, which has to be truthful.

**Example: Animals Matter to Me** This is a program of WSPA, the World Society for the Protection of Animals (WSPA 2010a). The public campaign to gain support for UDAW (Universal Declaration on Animal Welfare) was launched in June 2006 and by December 2007 the president of Costa Rica, Oscar Arias, became the official one

---

[9]The **United Nations Assistance Mission for Rwanda**

millionth signatory; WSPA hosted celebrations in San Jose, Costa Rica, in March 2008 (Wiki contributor 2010). A million signature list spread across the planet was interesting, but electronic petitions are not acceptable to many policy makers because the "signatures" can be duplicated through multiple e-mail accounts. A million signatures in Costa Rica would have been a louder statement, or a list of e-verified signatures. A more authentic petition requires handwritten signatures and contact information so that its authenticity can be verified, or at least verified e-signatures. Both forms have value as public diplomacy tools, and the issue being supported by Animals Matter is a good one. Is WSPA's campaign effective? Only time will tell if it "creates the conditions under which government officials feel comfortable with a paradigm shift."

**Example: Somaliland** In 2012, members of a group on social media site LinkedIn decided they wanted to foster Somaliland's international recognition through petitions, and their approach could be a model. Instead of starting with large national petitions in the United States, which has a federal system, they decided to consider smaller petitions in individual states with large Somali-immigrant populations, then using the results to entice friendly state Senators and Representatives. Under this model, if the state legislature endorsed Somali recognition, that vote would gain the attention of Federal Senators and Congressmen, who could take the idea to the next level. On the other hand, the use of national petitions can be simpler in non-federal structures like the UK where only 100,000 signatures can cause an issue to be brought before the national Parliament.

#### 12.5.1.1 Exchange Programs

Another way of doing public diplomacy is to consider exchange programs, for example, NGOs worried about protecting women might invite government and civil society representatives to a country where women are well protected; expose these individuals to the policies being advocated in an environment that demonstrates their added value. Conversations of this kind can build understanding of an issue and trust in an NGO's motivations and expertise. A similar approach would be to invite editors or reporters from influential local media so that they can report back to their audiences.

#### 12.5.1.2 Managing Expectations

Although social media and other media platforms can create a quick, effective public opinion in favor of a policy change by the government (classic public diplomacy), it is recommended to think long term. Many NGO policy initiatives are intended to have a lasting impact, e.g., protecting fragile wetlands needed for fishing, food security, and jobs in Iraq. In many of those instances, the Study Team should consider crafting a coordinated, long-term public diplomacy strategy that runs for some time prior to opening direct talks. A year could reap significant rewards otherwise unattainable because it offers enough time to build public support to influence the government. On the other hand, jumping too fast may have the opposite effect.

Consider that while public diplomacy is an essential tool to change the political paradigm and an essential augmentation to diplomatic efforts, it is also important to understand the risks (Crutchfield and Grant 2008). What if the NGO is unable to deliver the goods? While it may be possible to gain support in principle from the public for a text from a draft document, aggressive "public diplomacy" can also raise expectations that what the public perceives as a "good text" is what will be final negotiated text. Since even the most talented negotiators can fail, before a public diplomacy campaign shares a draft text with the public, it must keep in mind the potential fallout if the final text must be amended to achieve governmental support. Instead of pushing out a specific text, it is sometimes better to ask the public to buy into a set of principles and leave the text to the negotiators. On the other hand, once in the negotiating room, the negotiator with the pen often has the most power.

## *12.5.2 Propaganda*

> The world seen at a cockeyed angle through the narrow lens of the political propagandist is a depressing and claustrophobic place. Winston Burdett (Burdett 1969)

What is propaganda for one organization is truth or at least well-reasoned political theory to another. The tension between the two interpretations can erupt into angry discord, something any NGO needs to keep in mind when discussing a nation's point of view. In the mid-1960s, the United States and the Soviet were locked in a deadly struggle while also negotiating reductions in arms, such as the 1963 Limited Test Ban Treaty, outlawing atmospheric nuclear tests as well as tests in outer space and underwater. Underground tests are also outlawed if they spread radioactive debris outside the territorial limits of the country where the explosion was conducted. This was a major issue for NGOs like the Women Strike for Peace (WSP) which argued that quite apart from the fact that nuclear weapons killed, the tests themselves were deadly. Unfortunately, the US government was distracted by the Vietnam War and political upheaval in the Dominican Republic, which caused the Soviet Union to begin saying that the United States was an aggressor nation. It finally got to the point that Secretary of State Dean Rusk said on December 9, 1965, "every time anyone stands in the way of Communist aggression, those who stand in the way are called aggressors. That is a standing pattern of Soviet Propaganda. It is built into their concept of the world revolution" (Rusk 1965, Dec 27, p. 1006) (Bureau of Public Affairs 1965, p. 581). Of course, they said as much about us.

### 12.5.2.1 Example of Propaganda: The Endangered Potomac River

In 2012, the residents of Washington, DC, were startled one morning by a headline story in the prestigious Washington Post which reported that Environmental News Service said "America's most endangered river is the Potomac" (Potomac River Most Endangered in America, 2012). The problem, as reported the following day,

**Fig. 12.4** Somali political rally ((c) 2010 Larry Roeder)

was that the NGO allegations were false, even though part of a well-meaning campaign to energize river cleaning. As the paper said, "Just because you're promoting a worthy cause doesn't justify distorting the truth." There was no scientific evidence to back up the claim; in fact the evidence showed that a troubled river was improving (McCartney 2012). These kinds of false accusations tarnish the reputation not only of the NGO making the report but all NGOs, in this case environmental NGOs.

Example of Propaganda: Misstating Meeting Results At a conference on Tourism in Africa, an NGO advocates for a regional agreement on export-oriented reconstruction zones (ERZ) in the Sahel and hosts a reception of national delegations to the African Union. But while some delegations do agree to discuss the initiative, they mainly want to talk about traditional tourism. Needing to gain more resources from its donors, the NGO then reports on its website that it scored a victory by garnering a meeting on Sahel reconstruction zones. While that statement might raise funds and even public support, the half-truth is just "propaganda." The ethical thing would have been to say that while the meeting produced positive statements by some ambassadors, more needs to be done to gain the full support of the AU, and statements by delegates at the reception have led the team to think this is possible (Fig.12.4).

### *12.5.3 Lobbying*

Some will want to use the term Lobbyist to describe all advocacy with the government; in some countries the term has very negative connotations, such as in the United States where it is associated with the corruption of public officials by "special interest" advocates. It is one of the reasons to avoid the term. However, at its best, lobbying is a core tool of democracy, giving private citizens and small NGOs the ability to effectively influence legislation through paid experts or alliances (Samuelson 2008). Nonprofit organizations can quite properly lobby lawmakers within limits without fear of losing their status in the USA but must avoid overt partisan politics. However, this kind of direct contact with legislators is not what the authors mean by "public diplomacy," which targets the government indirectly.

## 12.6 Why Talk to the Media?

### *12.6.1 Explainers of Truth*

To some, the value of public opinion to government policy decision-making process is overstated, it being too volatile, too driven by images, instead of facts—in other words, dramatic images from a crisis drive public opinion, not critical thinking. The public doesn't have time and isn't interested, anyway—according to some—and since the public isn't as well-informed as the government, the UN, etc., following popular guidance could lead to strategic blunders. In the early days of a rebellion against a tyrant, for example, the public will often be inflamed by violent repression; who are the people fighting the regime? Not always clear. This is why it is not an anachronism to say that the media has a special job of exposing truth. However, if a competent international media does not cover a crisis, be it a slow burn like a drought in an obscure country or a fast-breaking story like the burning of a diplomatic facility in Libya in 2012, then the global population can only rely on governments or advocates of issues to inform them, in other words, partisan informants who convey opinion rather than necessarily facts. NGOs must make it a priority within their public diplomacy/Communications program to directly inform the media with actual facts. While the public is often driven by images, distillations, or summaries of truth, and often don't want to read an exegesis, it is crucial in addition to a tight story that the media be given the full story so that their depiction will be less distorted. That's a role for the Communications Officer.

**Note** Ideally, this is a two-layer process, where there is a catch phrase and a summary for a first look and on a second layer, the full story. Time is precious in newsrooms and the reading is intense, so catching the journalist's attention is an essential part of the process of being noticed and becoming news. The full story as a start is

**Fig. 12.5** Photographer ((c) 2012 LRoeder)

a no-go. Too much text and too much information upfront are almost an imposition on the reader, and journalists are fast readers. If they find something that they can use in the catch phrase or the summary, they will go deeper into the text. Otherwise, they won't waste their time.

Even the truth can be problematic, as noted by an expert on animal welfare issues in the Middle East. Many animal welfare programs become humanitarian when they reduce diseases like rabies; what happens if the society doesn't understand? "In many countries we found a tolerable level of ignorance towards animal welfare rather than an intolerable level of cruelty. So, an understanding of why that ignorance exists and how to bring humane education to the table is far more productive with long-term potential rather than a public media exposure or criticism. Knowing the country you are working in and its culture is key to success in diplomatic relations. In one country or region where media headlines may cause embarrassment and invoke the desired remedial action may well result in termination of negotiations in another part of the world and the loss of a long awaited opportunity – perhaps forever!" (Wheeler 2012). Wheeler could have been talking about any concept of course, labor rights, protecting the water from pollution, earthquake standards for homes, etc. (Fig.12.5).

## *12.6.2 Protect the Media*

Even free democracies can toy with preventing a free press from working properly. During the great depression, America could easily have swung to dictatorship, given the huge domestic economic crisis. Many intellectual luminaries of the time pushed the idea, and indeed, columnist and presidential confidant Walter Lippmann said to FDR that "You may have no alternative but to assume dictatorial powers." He also did not feel that the public needed to know everything (Steel 1980, pp. 299–303) and argued in his column that the "danger we have to fear is not that Congress will give Franklin D. Roosevelt too much power, but that it will deny him the power he needs" (Lippmann 1933). Switzerland's love–hate relationship with the League of Nations led to the government refusing visas for many reporters accredited to the League, with some officials viewing the institution as a threat to Swiss neutrality (Dell 1941, pp. 352–353). The issue was so controversial that Switzerland would not accede to the Covenant without a referendum, which barely passed, though the citizens were very favorable to Wilson's points (Rappart 1931, p. 38). The American negotiator David Miller also agreed that the Swiss were very jealous of their neutrality (Miller, *The Drafting of the Covenant* 1928b).

While there might have been local tension, it is also true that the League's Assembly, which met once a year, relished publicity through the press and then by direct broadcast to the world via radio. The secretariat believed that its proceedings must be understood by everyone, so the League began to broadcast news by shortwave radio in February 1929 from a station in Geneva and then from its own station in the village of Prangins until 1939.[10] It is perhaps not surprising that in 1938 League passed the landmark "Convention on the Use of Broadcasting in the Cause of Peace," later adopted by the UN (UNGA C. 5.– 1954). If only the media had been more effective in informing the public about totalitarian regimes, sharing in-depth, easy-to-understand analysis that shows totalitarianism as a true threat to democracy. Hitler marched into Poland that year and the infamous Munich pact occurred. In 1938, only 117 journalists were accredited to the League, from 26 nations, and most did not live in Geneva, so coverage was very weak (Dell 1941, p. 340). Fortunately, FDR rejected Lippmann's proposal because the truth now as then is that dictators rarely give up power.

### *12.6.3 Engaging Journalists*

There are now thousands of reporters from most nations accredited to the UN at each of its major centers. They now cover every aspect of the UN's work and regularly note repression. The same is true at some proportion regarding journalists accredited to any international organization, whether small or large. There are also thousands of issues and thousands of NGOs trying to get attention. In other words,

---

[10]This almost did not happen. The League Secretariat wanted a shortwave radio to broadcast news to the world and, because the airport in Geneva in those days was rather small, wanted the member states to expand it in order to accommodate additional traffic. Switzerland agreed but was nervous about losing its image of neutrality. In addition, the member states in 1928, when this proposal was made, wanted to limit expenditures, an issue which comes up repeatedly in today's United Nations.

whereas with the League there was a dearth of interest in in-depth reporting, today the field is so competitive that it can be impossible to gain a reporter's attention. The great challenges for Communications Officers are to attract the international media in a highly competitive field, to effectively inform the public as part of a public diplomacy campaign, and to capture the imagination of decision makers in governments, the UN and international organizations. This is why it is strongly recommended that the study group develop a true communications strategy.

**Note** Inviting journalists to come and witness a particular situation is often very useful. There is nothing better for both the reporter and the organization than a visit, so the reporter can see something "in locus." As an example, endangered species are best seen in their habitat; cruelty against beggars in the streets is best witnessed and photographed by a team of journalists and photographers, so they can get as much out of a situation as they can. Refugees or abused women are best seen in person. The impact of the reporting becomes magnified by their own eyewitness account. This is way beyond what the best press release can do, without the physical presence of reporters or photographers. Many news organizations do not publish something they are not exactly sure how it happened, so an eye-catching photograph may lead to a lot of explaining on how that was done, and the stamp of authenticity will have to be on it before it is aired by mainstream media in any country with a free press.

### *12.6.4 How Much Is Shared?*

Reporters are in the business of telling compelling stories, so before contacting one, consider the item from his or her organization's perspective. For example, if your NGO is focused on protecting antiquities, will a reporter whose beat is refugees give your story the coverage it deserves? Perhaps; perhaps not. Just as you should study your opposite in a diplomatic initiative, so too the reporter. Who are the best contacts is a critical question for the Communications Officer, especially if the Chief Negotiator is trying to advance something like a resolution or the team leader is trying to raise funds for the initiative.

**Note** Check the publication in which you want to be published or the TV news channel on which you want to have a story aired, and look for the reporters who already have an interest in your specific field. In the case of Human Rights, the Climate, or any other issue, there are not only journalists who are personally involved in the cause, but many who make the subject a priority. The same is true for many other fields of coverage and issues. Find out who these reporters or editors are before suggesting a story to a newspaper or a radio or TV station. But also remember that most stories get their foot in the door through the Assignment Desk of the news organization, so becoming familiar with who are the Assignment Desk post holders is also very helpful if you do not have that extremely popular topic to "sell" to the paper or the station. These first sorters of news items to be covered can make a big difference in deciding what is going to be covered on that day. And on slow news days, you can come way up on their priority list of "stories to do today."

### 12.6.5 *Trust*

One source told us he doesn't trust reporters and related that UK papers were in trouble in 2011 and 2012 over hacking private **cell phones**. While the events were true, the hacking incidents were aberrations, not a pattern upon which to build a policy. They were however a teachable moment about mobile phone security; and some reporters do lie and make up stories, as happened in 2005 in New Zealand (SMH, 2005). Remember that reporters are human beings, and news organizations are run by personalities. Mr. Roeder has known many fine journalists over his career, some whom he consulted on a portion of this book; the vast majority are very honest and often the greatest of humanitarians because they will regularly risk their lives to get a story out. American correspondent Marie Colvin and French photographer Remi Ochlik were killed in the besieged Syrian city of Homs in February 2012 while covering the slaughter of civilians. Without reporters like those two humanitarian heroes, how could networks verify what is happening on the ground? How would the public be able to make a judgment? Both were highly respected professionals who protected their sources.

Reporters will ask for a lot of background information, some of it sensitive, so it is important to know that most reporters protect sources and will handle sensitive information very well; this isn't always the case. Use caution and know your reporter. During the Iran hostage crisis, several American diplomats escaped from the US Embassy to the Canadian Embassy. Non-American reporters told the Iran Working Group (IWG)[11] that they would not publish the story, fearing for the safety of both the hostages and the Canadians. Unfortunately, a famous American journalist would have told the story on television had not Secretary of State Cyrus Vance personally intervened. Roeder was then serving as the OIC of the evening shift of the IWG and had asked this same journalist not to reveal the alleged sensitive occupation of one hostage, fearing that the officer would be tortured; that issue had to go to the journalist's boss before the story died. In preparation for this book, the journalist, who is still very active, told Roeder he remembered talking to him, but not the second incident, only the intervention; he then offered that he honestly felt that back then he had simply been aggressive when asking questions. "We are as crafty as you guys," he remarked. The man did use terrible judgment thinking it would have been under any circumstances appropriate to reveal the location of a hostage. However, he is elderly now and at the end of his career. The point is that even a great journalist can have awful judgment; his excuse about aggressive questioning is also true for many reporters. The fact is, reporters are needed; they also need information and must verify its accuracy. In other words, if they think you have it, they will push hard. The solution for an NGO officer asked to grant impromptu interviews is to work with your Communications Officer and be very clear of what will be shared and what is too sensitive. Most reporters will understand, even if they press hard. For example, while it might be appropriate to reveal that doctors in a certain town are tending to

[11] State Department Group that managed the crisis

wounds inflicted by the government, it would not be appropriate to reveal the name of the doctors or the clinic's permission. The reporter will likely press for this information very hard in order to authenticate your information. Be cautious.

## 12.7 Media Accreditation and Access

International organizations and conferences have their own accrediting process, such as the UN system in New York which has the Media Accreditation and Liaison Unit (MALU). MALU assists in (a) Accreditation—a requirement for journalists wishing to operate at UN HQ in New York or Geneva,[12] (b) logistical assistance in the coverage of UN events, and (c) daily alerts on all open meetings and briefings or conferences at the UN. The Communications Officer should develop a relationship with MALU in New York and its equivalent in any other venues, in which the NGO may operate, to find out what is happening relevant to NGO activities and to discern which reporters are best to cover events. One way to make sure a story is written well is also to invite specialized reporters to cover it. Most reporters who cover the UN and related bodies have a professional focus on the environment, the economy, and security issues and, in addition, refugees, development, health, and technology. While they will grasp humanitarian issues, especially those regularly reported on, if the topic is less central to "their beat," they might not know how to package it. The Communications Officer needs to have a roster of specialized reporters who are likely to do a good job.

Accreditation at UN events can be a real problem. At UN conferences, no double accreditation is allowed (e.g., as press and delegate or as press and NGO). An assignment for the Communications Officer will be to ascertain these rules a few months before the event, while also selecting reporters, closeup TV crews, and photographers for special requirements. While permanently accredited reporters have broad access even after hours, temporary reporters might not. A suggestion is to find a few reporters in Rome, New York, Geneva, and Nairobi in particular who understand the NGOs specific interests and get them permanent accreditation. That way, should the need arise for instant coverage, friendly reporters will be able to achieve the right slant.

## 12.8 Photo Display Opportunities

Before engaging a photojournalist, the Communications Officer needs to make sure they are allowed. Many deliberations, such as those of the G77, do not allow reporters or photographers, definitely not film, in order to preserve the off-the-record

[12] This should give journalists complete access to an NGO's events, but might not to other events the NGO is interested in. For example, a journalist might gain access to a conference being held, but not parallel discussions at the UN Security Council.

nature of meetings. Certain spaces are off limits as well, e.g., the Delegate's Lounge and Dining Room in the UN HQ in Geneva and New York. On the other hand in Geneva, one of the main coffee shops is a congregation point for reporters and diplomats; however, no film is allowed. The point behind this isn't to foster secret deals, though they probably take place, rather to allow delegates to speak in total candor. It happens at every level of diplomacy, from exchanges between two or three in the Delegate's Lounge to negotiations to negotiate a treaty. However, you can often organize film interviews in the hallways and next to the coffee lounges.

Most conferences offer opportunities to display posters, which can be an effective tool to influence diplomats, if the message is simple and direct. Keep in mind however that this might be best done by an ad agency; journalists are not typically good phrase makers, as they are too connected to the facts. Keep in mind though that ad agencies are mainly concerned with the message getting through, not whether it conveys truth.

At the UN HQ in New York, a large display area sits just inside the main entrance, which has a massive amount of space for photographs. The area has to be reserved by a UN official or a mission, but many missions are very willing to accommodate NGOs. Keep in mind that such space is reserved 6 months or more in advance. This is well worth it as every important figure in the UN in New York passes the display space every day! Similar spaces exist in many international organizations.

## 12.9 Negotiating an Unfettered Media: Especially Social Media

War correspondents track stories at the risk of life. It is also a free press that can follow a public diplomacy event as happened when the actor George Clooney informed the US Senate in 2012 of atrocities by the Sudanese regime. Because of his star power, he influenced Senators and the nation. That tactic works because a free press covers his call to arms. This only works however if a free press is operating, a press that show how corrupt leaders exploit victims for personal gain and how incompetence can destroy an economy and highlight the vulnerabilities of these officials so that the public can take action. It must not be forgotten that a free Media is something in its own right for which NGOs should advance, even if the NGO's primary mandate is something else.

Social Media is clearly an emerging and very powerful public diplomacy Tool; NGOs need to be aware that access by targeted citizens won't always be possible. During the Arab Spring, the Egyptian regime tried to shut down Twitter, Facebook, Google, and YouTube, which shared news and were used for organizing demonstrations. Other regimes like China and Saudi Arabia have tried the same thing, and some like that of China want access to accounts like Google's to track and punish political dissidents. In order to maintain market share in China, Google censored its search engine. China wanted that in order to prevent the sharing of information they felt threated political control. In 2010 Google stated that they stopped censoring because of evidence that China was compromising Gmail accounts (Drummond 2010), though there was also huge public pressure on Google as well.

Every year journalists are also targeted, not just the brave ones who covered the crisis in Syria in 2012: crime reporters, political reporters, commercial reporters, etc., who are killed, beaten, jailed, and intimidated. It isn't just dictators who are the problems; organized crime and terrorists feel threatened by an open society. Freedom of expression is seen by the west as the foundation upon which all other rights stand; when working in many fragile environments, however, the regime can push back, fearing the truth will lead to their demise, perhaps fearing cultural taint or that such a media environment can lead to "popular uninformed decisions," even violence, especially when the public reacts to "facts" on blogs. Are the facts accurate and do the decisions make sense? Bloggers are often not restrained by truth.

Note "In some countries like Brazil, the official government actually subsidizes small bloggers who will divulge their good actions to an internet audience. These are almost "fake", propaganda blogs, supported by public incentives to simply extol, praise the government. At the end of his term, President Lula actually held a breakfast at the seat of government, the Planalto Palace, with the so called, "aligned bloggers" in to award their "good work (Augusto 2012)."

Their mission is to achieve a goal, and if a report "goes viral," it can have a dramatic effect; what if it isn't based on science, such as the unfortunate blogger efforts in some quarters to reduce the vaccination of children? Such blogs can endanger the larger population by making the populace vulnerable to epidemics once a certain percentage has gone "unvaccinated." On the other hand, are statements by government officials truthful, or are they propaganda? Any NGO negotiating with the government for an open media or speaking to the UN General Assembly or in an international conference must be conscious of the local culture related to the media.

There is the example already provided of a television anchor who showed astonishing poor judgment when he refused a request to kill a story. That could have led to massive violence, even an invasion by the United States; the authors do not endorse government censorship, just common sense. If the concept of public diplomacy is to take hold, a strong media is required; instead of government censorship, there needs to be an agreement on the role and responsibilities of a free press in a democracy and the creation of a strong self-monitoring media union that develops and enforces standards on itself, essentially promoting professionalism. For example, while freedom of expression means the ability to say nearly anything, publishers like YouTube don't have an obligation to publish "hate speech." In fact, doing so is irresponsible.

With the rise of failed nation-states and rebellions by people looking for political freedom, NGOs will be given the opportunity to advise transitional societies on how to build an effective media system; given the vastly important national security and economic issues at stake in those societies, the government is going to want to control the flow of information, to protect citizens from poor reporters, and to prevent useful stories the public does need to hear. It is imperative that NGOs wanting to help these countries mature do so by arguing against either the legislative or Executive

Branches being able to manipulate public opinion through state-owned media. If broadcasting is not already independent, an early fixed date should be set by the transitional authority by which the print and electronic broadcast media would become independent. Many repressive regimes, like the deposed Mubarak government and its military, own television and radio, as well as newspapers. These kinds of government-owned establishments should be outlawed, though ministries certainly should be able to print informational brochures or maintain internal communications systems.

Newspapers in many countries also own radio and television channels. However, that does not necessarily give them a monopoly, and in many instances of this seeming violation of democratic rules, the principle of competition and avoidance of monopoly may still be applicable. It is a dangerous road on which to travel; if NGOs are given the opportunity, they should argue against control by commercial monopolies; a single individual, company, or political entity should not be allowed to own both radio and television stations in the same city; doing so may place too much power into one hand. Foreign ventures in this sphere should be permitted, although monopoly positions should not be allowed. Similar to public broadcasting in the United States, funding should be found for an educational channel that would teach the average citizen the basics of (free market) economics, business administration, and environmental and occupational safety issues. A good idea might be to place this new channel under the auspices of a local university and convince the university to develop a highly professional journalism school.

## 12.10 Additional Outreach Tools and Partners

When the Iranian revolution began, the Ayatollah Khomeini used the technology of the time to advance his cause by distributing cassette tapes. They would be handed from Iranian to Iranian in markets and other public places, very effectively spreading the word. The corollary today is social media, which has an unlimited audience; also educational videos in schools are used. One of the most effective such videos which I'd offer as an example would be *Solitary Confinement: Torture in Your Backyard* which was done by the National Religious Campaign Against Torture (NRCAT 2010). The film runs for only 20 min but is a powerful piece of public diplomacy, designed to bring a light to the destructive nature of solitary confinement. It also discusses how a religious community in Maine reduced such confinement by 70 %.

NGOs must use such tools as part of their strategic approach to public diplomacy to change the minds of the population so that they might lobby their government to change a policy.

There are also important media NGOs which may be very helpful as partners, such as:

- **Internews Network (USA)**—Internews provides communities the resources to produce local news and information with integrity and independence. With global expertise and reach, Internews trains both media professionals and citizen journalists, introduces innovative media solutions, increases coverage of vital issues, and helps establish policies needed for open access to information (Internews).

- **IREX (USA)—**"We enable local individuals and institutions to build key elements of a vibrant society: quality education, independent media, and strong communities. To strengthen these sectors, our program activities also include conflict resolution, technology for development, gender, and youth. Founded in 1968, IREX has an annual portfolio of over $70 million and a staff of over 400 professionals worldwide. IREX employs field-tested methods and innovative uses of technologies to develop practical and locally-driven solutions with our partners in more than 100 countries" (IREX).
- **Press Now (Netherlands)—**"Press Now is a non-governmental organization that works towards the development of independent media in conflict areas and countries in transition. By supporting existing independent media and initiating its own media projects, Press Now contributes to the development of open and democratic societies. One of Press Now's successful projects is Radio Dabanga/ Radio Darfur, a radio station by and for Darfuri that broadcasts on a daily basis from Hilversum, the Netherlands. Press Now has its office in Hilversum, in close proximity to the Media Park. The organization employs a varied, motivated and enthusiastic team of 18 people" (Press Now).
- **Fondation Hirondelle (Switzerland)—**The Fondation Hirondelle is an organization of journalists which sets up and operates media services in crisis areas. It is part of the Reuters-sponsored Alertnet system which was also an early supporter of Reliefweb.int.

There are also professional news services and related organizations that can be helpful in ensuring the free flow of information:

- **Search for Common Ground**
- **BBC World Service Trust**
- **Voice of America**
- **BBC World Service**
- **Deutsche Welle**
- **France 24**

# Chapter 13
# International Organizations and NGO Associations

**Extract** Chapter 13 introduces the concept of international organizations and NGO associations and how to use them to advance diplomatic initiatives. Several very important examples are provided; but a directory of useful organizations will be provided online in an associated website. Special attention is also provided to the Cluster system, an approach to effectively using international organizations and NGOs during emergencies.

## 13.1 Introduction

There are hundreds of international bodies, especially given that humanitarian relief and development covers everything from protecting culture to the environment, to the economy, and to people's physical security. They roughly fall into two groups, one being major NGO alliances with significant influence on NGO standards or the policy makers in the UN, the Red Cross, the United States government, and the European Commission. The other group would be actual international organizations that focus on emergency management and international law, development, and the international bodies that build sustainable cultures and cities, as well as distribute food, and finally those which focus on the Environment and Conservation; however, this book is not an encyclopedia of organizations. To help, the humanitarian NGO community has listed a few bodies in this chapter that have come up regularly in this book; also the authors have built an online list of many organizations that will be refreshed from time to time. That way, NGOs will always have the freshest information. In addition, readers are invited to recommend organizations that have been missed. The location of the list is at http://internationalorgs.wordpress.com/ (Fig. 13.1).

Every IO has different membership rules. All have governments as members, though NGOs can join some in various capacities, e.g., the ILO. Governments also

L.W. Roeder, Jr. and A. Simard, *Diplomacy and Negotiation for Humanitarian NGOs*, Humanitarian Solutions in the 21st Century, DOI 10.1007/978-1-4614-7113-4_13,

**Fig. 13.1** NGO diplomats headed to the UN ((c) L Roeder 2012)

have rules. As an example, the US government is not allowed to join an IO for more than 12 months without permission of Congress (Borek 2003).

Many organizations mentioned in the online list and some of those that have been inserted in this book are related to or are part of the UN; just what is the UN? Some scholars look at it as a sort of yin–yang. The General Assembly of UNGA (an organ of the UN) is often touted as a positive force since it is sympathetic to underprivileged nations and seeks funding and policies to avert plague, reduce starvation, poverty, etc., and those calls often present program opportunities for NGOs. In other words, if the Team Leader can find a funded UN program, that's an opportunity to be a contractor, using the project itself to support NGO strategic goals. The Security Council or UNSC (another UN organ) is touted as a negative force since it is preventative or punitive. Former US Secretary of State John Foster Dulles once famously said, "Its task is to stop the nations from public brawling" (Dulles 1972). It is a true forum for humanitarianism; all humanitarian NGOs should follow the proceedings of the Security Council, for it is the one organ that enforces international law.

Dulles' generation survived the failures of the League of Nations and gave the next generation the United Nations; of course the world of 2012 is very different from the 1970s when Dulles made his statement. The truth about humanitarianism is that just as the governments that created the UN did not "constitute a true community with common judgments about conduct," the same is true of today's UN and the NGO communities that lobby for change. Keep that in mind when "lobbying" people to alter the conditions under which people live or when "negotiating" agreements to change conditions on the ground. UN organizations, the International Red Cross and Red Crescent Movement, and international organizations outside the UN like the Organization of American States (OAS), the World Bank group, or OECD and OIE all have their own mandates and methods of operations. While they cooperate, they also compete. Exploit those differences and common elements to (a) raise funds and (b) change policies. When doing so, keep in mind the lessons from the early sections on theory, conferences, and protocol.

The term **"international organization (IO)"** is much abused and is one of several non-state entities (international organizations, nongovernmental organizations, and the Red Cross/Red Crescent Movement). With the exception of some emergency management IOs, none do just one thing. UNESCO is a case in point, with opportunities in conservation, disaster management, education, and culture. The same could be said of UNDP, UNHCR, the FAO, and the European Commission, the later which is a potential source of funds for relief operations and development. CMS is another example. On the other hand, the UNEP/CMS Secretariat (Bonn, Germany) is primarily a conservation body and a vehicle for funding for NGOs.

## 13.2 Sample Agencies and Associations

### *13.2.1 InterAction*

InterAction (based in Washington, DC) is the largest alliance of US-based international NGOs that focus on the world's poor; US based does not mean "US owned." Nearly every serious humanitarian and development NGO in the world has an office in the United States and thus qualifies for membership (InterAction Secretariat 2010). InterAction is a powerful networking tool for NGOs with working groups that focus on emergencies, economic development, the Internet, and telecommunications. InterAction is also well connected to USAID, the US Department of State, and the UN Office for the Coordination of Humanitarian Affairs (OCHA). While InterAction is not a source of income, it can influence policy makers.

### *13.2.2 CoNGO: The Conference of NGOs in Consultative Relationship with the UN*

For half a century, CoNGO (based mainly in New York and Geneva) has promoted NGO working with the UN. They have no funds and are poorly staffed; their staff is excellent and influential in New York and Geneva in particular and could lobby for

NGO interests. Today, over 3,500 NGOs have consultative status with ECOSOC alone, in addition to those with only DPI accreditation or that are accredited to a specific specialized agency or fund. All can join CoNGO.

### 13.2.3 ICVA: The International Council of Voluntary Agencies

ICVA (based in Geneva) was founded in 1962 as a global network of humanitarian and human rights NGOs, focusing primarily on refugee policy. ICVA also brings members' ground level experiences to international decision-making forums (ICVA Secretariat 2010).

### 13.2.4 Can One NGO Umbrella Agency Advocate for All?

One staff can't replace all of the other NGOs. Even if possible, that would constipate the industry's thought process. Variety is essential, so InterAction, ICVA, and CoNGO are not there to replace other NGOs. Instead, NGOs should use more than one and see them as enablers capable of bringing any idea to the common table for presentation in a professional and effective manner. A government's envoy to the UN doesn't necessarily agree with his government's point of view nor a Secretary General with the views of his member states once collectively agreed upon, but both will help their clients develop their positions and, once decisions are made, advance them in a positive manner. That's the vision of the umbrellas, to support, never undercut, humanitarian NGO's, even when they disagree on specific policy.

One thing the umbrellas are good at is facilitating coordination between NGOs in development and emergency environments. That's great, since donors actually look for shared advocacy, even when the implementing partners have different skill sets. The umbrellas can also send officers to facilitate field coordination; more likely since there are so many such operations, it will be best if the NGOs themselves coordinate in the field, keeping the umbrellas informed.

### 13.2.5 UN Cluster System: A Tool for NGO Diplomats

On January 12, 2010, Haiti was struck by a massive earthquake that killed many people and flattened cities, especially the overcrowded capital. Humanitarian NGOs were and still are involved, an example being the GARR (the Support Group for Refugees and Repatriated Persons), which runs a human rights monitoring program along the border. They have provided funds to over 200 farmers to replace or care for livestock (ACT Alliance 6/29/2010). To help various NGOs on the ground, Roeder is a member of the FAO Agriculture Cluster, as well as the Health and Shelter clusters. So what is the Cluster System and why should NGOs care about it? How does it link to diplomacy and fund-raising?

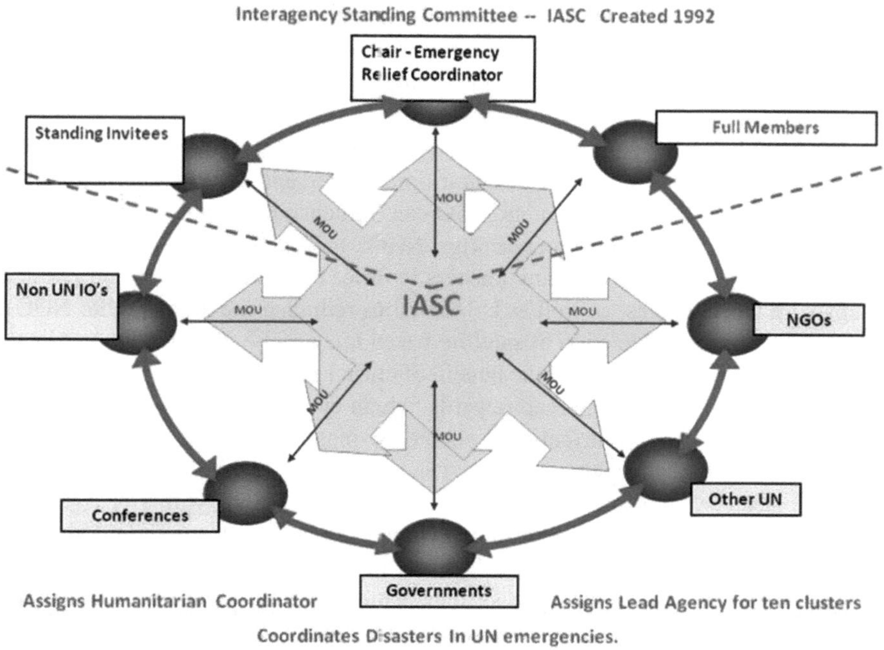


**Fig. 13.2** Coordination of Disasters (© 2010 LRoeder)

The cluster system emerged out of the 2005/2006 humanitarian reform effort, to fill in gaps, strengthen response, ensure accountability, and build partnerships. These clusters are thematic groupings of NGOs, UN agencies, and government agencies, as well as partner corporations which are led by a lead agency and pull together related efforts. That is supposed to avoid duplication. Although they haven't always worked perfectly, the concept is sound and offers significant networking opportunities for NGOs to raise funds through being a project implementing partner or for negotiating changes in rules (Fig. 13.2).

Sitting above the cluster system, every UN disaster has a UN Coordinator who reports to the UN's Emergency Relief Coordinator (ERC) via the UN's Inter-Agency Standing Committee (IASC), which is the interagency body that coordinates[1] how emergencies are managed. Members come from governments, UN agencies, the IFRC, and three humanitarian NGO networks. Because many of those organizations have overlapping mandates and skill sets, to avoid confusion in how assistance is applied as well as gain cost efficiencies, relief bodies operate the thematic clusters. For example, the agriculture cluster is led by the FAO. The mix of clusters in an emergency will depend on the nature of the crisis, and the decision on which one

[1]For some, the word "coordination" is controversial; some NGOs feel it stifles imagination and independence. The authors propose that coordination of emergencies needs NGOs as full partners so collective cooperation can increase effectiveness.

will be activated is made by a UN country team made up of the lead UN agencies in consultation with the host nations and donor nations. The whole idea is to provide predictability and accountability in humanitarian response, which is why it is so very important for NGOs to be a part.

In Somaliland nine clusters are also active: agriculture and livelihood, education, food aid, health, protection, logistics, nutrition, shelter, and water and sanitation. By being part of the cluster system, an NGO can influence relief policy at the ground level, as Roeder discovered representing NGOs in Bangkok during the Cyclone Nargis crisis. Roeder sat on many clusters in order to build synergies and partnerships with UN agencies, as well as USAID, thus reducing the cost of relief NGOs. One example was a collection of satellite-based imagery he was able to coordinate through the US government for the benefit of cluster members. It is a good example of how NGO diplomacy can reap rewards, which even though they don't translate into direct monetary contributions, equate to massive overhead reduction that releases scarce funds for other purposes (Shean 2008).

The cluster system links government agencies like USDA with UN Agencies, NGOs, and other interested parties and becomes a platform for multilateral diplomacy, meaning that around one NGO could be 50 other important players to be influenced at the same time. The system, which recently went through a major review, began as part of an examination of humanitarian practices in 2005. Humanitarians recognized that prior to then, emergency responses were often ad hoc and poorly coordinated, which in turn led to gaps in resources and speed of response. In September 2005, the Inter-Agency Standing Committee (IASC) designated global "cluster leads"—"specifically for humanitarian emergencies—in nine sectors or areas of activity. The IASC Principals also agreed that the cluster approach should be applied, with some flexibility, at the country level." The system has since been strengthened through partnerships with industry, NGOs, and the International Red Cross and Red Crescent Movement, as well as a suite of UN agencies and collaborating governments.

**Recommendation** NGOs should consider joining the cluster system, thus becoming part of a global network of experts who respond to emergencies and reflect on long-term development in ways that reduce the vulnerability of societies to disasters (IASC 2006). In other words, long before a vulnerable society is struck by an earthquake or a hurricane; NGOs can influence policy makers on how to integrate concerns into global humanitarian policy making. Such an effort will strengthen any diplomatic initiative by an NGO.

### *13.2.6 ISDR: International Strategy on Disaster Reduction (Geneva)*

ISDR is the primary body in the UN responsible for coordinating risk reduction policies and is trying to build a global risk reduction culture, so this body, based in

Geneva, is a must organization for the humanitarian community (ISDR_Secretariat 2010). An example of why is the interest of ISDR (along with WHO and PAHO) is promoting earthquake resistant hospitals, though not veterinary clinics, which is unfortunate, as was discovered in Pakistan.

### *13.2.7 IASC: Inter-Agency Standing Committee and OCHA (New York)*

The IASC was established in 1992 in response to UNGA 46/182 which called for strengthened coordination of humanitarian assistance. Led by the ERC (Emergency Relief Coordinator of the UN), who reports directly to the UN Secretary General and is the head of OCHA (Office for the Coordination of Humanitarian Affairs), IASC is made up of the chief executive offices of UN operational agencies, the IOM, World Bank, NGO alliances like InterAction, CoNGO, and the International Red Cross and Red Crescent Movement. It coordinates humanitarian policies and standards and thus will be an invaluable tool for any organization using this book and especially for developing a coordinated approach to relief and recovery operations.

OCHA is the arm of the UN secretariat that is responsible for bringing together humanitarian actors to ensure coherent response to emergencies. OCHA also ensures there is a framework within which each actor can contribute to the overall response effort, and it supports the IASC. Its mission is to *mobilize and coordinate effective and principled humanitarian action* in partnership with national and international actors in order to alleviate human suffering in disasters and emergencies, advocate for the rights of people in need, promote preparedness and prevention, and facilitate sustainable solutions.

### *13.2.8 IFRC and ICRC the International Red Cross and Red Crescent Movement (Geneva)*

The Red Cross Red Crescent association of societies is the world's largest humanitarian movement, far bigger than the UN, and needs to be part of any NGOs thinking about integrating development and emergency management or just as a source of invaluable information. The movement began in 1863 when a group of Swiss men set up the International Committee for Relief to the Wounded. That became the International Committee of the Red Cross most people are familiar with. Each country has one national society, which in turn manages smaller committees, often at the county level. By the end of World War I, American veterans realized that better coordination was needed, so while the League of Nations was being developed so too was the Federation of Red Cross and Red Crescent societies, otherwise known as the IFRC formed in 1919 in Paris. NGOs should develop a relationship with the National Society in each country they operate in; also with the IFRC if they wish to influence global policy. A global NGO might even negotiate bilateral arrangements with national societies in advance of emergencies.

Roeder worked closely with the Red Cross for many years, collaborating on best practices in emergency management, the development of the Tampere Convention on Emergency Telecommunications, general international humanitarian law, and crises like the breakup of Yugoslavia and both Gulf conflicts, in particular both of the Iraq conflicts. The IFRC also sits on the UN's Inter-Agency Standing Committee, which sets UN relief policy. The movement also is part of the SPHERE project that develops relief standards.

### *13.2.9 SPHERE Project and LEGS (Boston, Geneva, New York, Washington, Ethiopia)*

The SPHERE project is a voluntary effort of the IFRC and the NGO community to develop standards of care for water supply and sanitation, nutrition, food aid, shelter and site management, and health services. Although the focus is on humanitarian assistance, many participants in SPHERE have recognized the relationship between their work and livestock care. LEGS is already a partner project with a focus on livestock, and some SPHERE experts have suggested expanding SPHERE to include companion animals and other animals not handled by LEGS, perhaps through a parallel handbook (Feinstein-International-Center 2009, SPHERE_Editors 2010).

## 13.3 Help Is Available

Humanitarian relief takes many, many forms, everything from helping refugees reach safety, to protecting vulnerable children, to protecting the culture, livestock and economy of a fractured society. That's why this book argues for a unified approach to relief that takes into account the impact of any one action on other aspects of relief. The UN Department of Public Information and ECOSOC are two of the most important structures because they are officially a part of the UN apparatus and work hard to help member NGOs gain information, as well as network. In addition, individual international organizations have pathways for nonprofits. It is however true that there is no single system bridging the many multilateral platforms, connecting what happens in UNICEF New York with what goes on in the OAS in Washington or the UN Environmental Program (UNEP) in Nairobi, with the UN High Commissioner for Refugees (UNHCR) in Geneva, with the UN in New York. Further, there are thousands of small, very useful nonprofits that just can't afford the representative staff to each of these bodies. There are however several wonderful associations of NGOs that can bring together the entire sweep of humanitarian NGOs (Fig. 13.3).

CoNGO (the conference of NGOs with consultative relationship with the United Nations) plays an important role in the preparation of NGOs wanting to participate

**Fig. 13.3** Camel caravan in Saudi Arabia ((c) L Roeder 2012)

in EC Ministerials. These are called Civil Society Development Forums or CDDF and can deal with such important issues as "implementing the internationally agreed goals and commitments in regard to education" (CoNGO 2011). For many, InterAction, ICVA (International Council of Voluntary Agencies), and CoNGO can serve as a source of independent, peer-reviewed policy analysis and advice for humanitarian nonprofits, though clearly there are resource limitations. The range of topics covered however is very broad, such as Internet governance, the rights of women, sustainable development, and global health, often in conjunction with major United Nations conferences which need to be attended by civil society. They can present a strategic view of global trends and then frame *private recommendations* for the use of NGOs in order to further their particular interests or the community as a whole. Especially impressive has been InterAction, USIP (United States Institute for Peace), and CoNGO as excellent venues for sharing new thinking. Their value is to provide expertise and counsel to advance everyone. Becoming associated with these bodies or attending their meetings will help Team Leaders and negotiators anticipate emerging problems and opportunities. They can also help NGOs craft professional appraisals of NGO policies and projects and ideas on funding and partnerships and the feasibility of success with government. Money will also be a problem for smaller NGOs and especially indigenous NGOs which often cannot afford to attend meetings of these associations or any multilateral forum. Their absence in the political discussion needs to be addressed.[2]

[2]Many indigenous peoples are represented in United Nations forums, such as Native Alaskans and Native Americans from the United States and First Nations from Canada, but our view is that more should be done to expand participation, especially for poorer populations.

Apart from NGO umbrella bodies and government bodies like USIP, international organizations are also very welcoming platforms for small gatherings of NGOs. UNESCO is a great location to discuss risk reduction, as is OECD, the Organisation for Economic Co-operation and Development. In addition, the World Bank in Washington, DC, is a regular venue. For example, in December 2011, the World Bank hosted a discussion of bank officials and NGO representatives with Randolph Langenbach, an international expert in architecture and building conservation who wanted to propose fresh thinking on earthquake resistant structures essential for sustainable development (Langenbach 2011). Another example of a group that can help NGOs is the Church Center for the United Nations.[3] Despite its name, the Center houses both religious and nonreligious nonprofits and is a terrific location for networking. Many informative briefings are held there.[4] If an NGO can send representatives to such meetings, it needs to do so, because these "umbrella bodies" and "think tanks" to one extent or another can be helpful with policy analysis and training, USIP which trains peace builders in the USA and around the world (USIP 2012). They can also point to effective funding opportunities and strategies, as well as offer policy platforms for smaller NGOs.

## 13.4 Working with Nontraditional NGO: Operation Gwamba, 1964

Not every organization using this book will be a traditional humanitarian NGO, though its activities may help humans, so it is useful to examine animal welfare which is not a humanitarian group of NGOs. They can directly humanitarian issues like food security and jobs. Consider Suriname in 1964. The country's economy largely depended on bauxite, an aluminum ore. In February of that year the Suriname Aluminum Company closed the Afobaka Dam which it had constructed, causing water to rapidly rise over 1,300 square miles of dense rain forest in the Brokopondo Valley of the Upper Suriname River. At risk were more than 5,000 indigenous Saramaka and Auka-Bushnegroes, which were forced to evacuate, as well as uncounted number of wildlife, some endangered. The wildlife included everything from anteaters and deer to spider monkeys, jaguar, and snakes. The snakes were critical to the banana crop because they kept down pests. With time quickly running out, an NGO in Paramaribo wrote for help from the International Society for the Protection of Animals (ISPA) in Boston, USA. Knowing their own limitations, the Paramaribo group figured ISPA would be more successful in garnering money and expert staff

[3] The center is across the street from US headquarters.

[4] For example, The International Health Awareness Network (IHAN) in partnership with PeaceAction invited NGOs from many disciplines in March 2012 to attend a discussion with H.E. Ambassador Chowdhury on the occasion of the 56th Session of the Commission of the Status of Women (CSW).

for what became the largest wildlife rescue operation in history. Many believe this operation gave birth to the modern science of wildlife disaster response (Michels 1964). The massive effort was led by a young animal control officer from Massachusetts who saved 10,000 animal lives and became the subject of a book (Walsh and Gannon, *Time Is Short and the Water Rises* 1967) and a film (Twentieth Century Series Back with Operation Gwamba 1965).

As today, solutions often require an alliance of NGOs (Walsh, *Discussion About Relief Operations* 2010b). When John Walsh was approached to manage the rescue operation, few Americans knew where Suriname (formerly Dutch Guiana) was located, much less Afobaka Dam. Today, the advice is to garner information from allies and the Internet, as well as talk to the FAO and other NGOs that focus on wildlife, as well as those that deal with indigenous peoples; Walsh did not have the luxury. What he did have was training in rescue techniques. He did not have time for much pondering, so he quickly went down to Suriname and successfully recruited Bushnegroes, descendants of slaves. Understanding that a common language would be essential, Walsh also learned their language, so very important not just to manage labor resources but also to learn about the land and the animals. Living conditions were minimal, sometimes sleeping in huts inhabited by vampire bats.

**Study Team and Assessment** The project began with a plea for help from a local NGO who had studied the problem and realized they did not have the proper resources. They then sent a letter of appeal to all of the directors of ISPA, which formed a hybrid study/decision group in Boston, to discuss possible intervention. There wasn't time for an extensive study; some discussion was required to decide (a) if an intervention was warranted, (b) who would go, and (c) what resources would be available. The GO decision was made at the same meeting and Dr. Eric H. Hansen, president of the Massachusetts SPCA (ISPA's first president), offered Walsh's services. A plan of action was also developed, which included sending Walsh and the chief administrator for ISPA's western hemisphere operations to Suriname to conduct a professional assessment. In an emergency today, an NGO probably has much background information at hand, especially with access to tools like ReliefWeb.int, which pull together fresh information every day on every emergency in the world, sourcing NGOs, governments, and international organizations. But even with all of that and Facebook, Twitter, etc., there is still usually a need an on-the-ground assessment. Walsh also had to deal with priorities, e.g., was he to rescue all animals, or leave some out, like the highly dangerous bushmaster. The rules of the road were, if it can be rescued, rescue it. This was also a human tragedy, as one village after another was flooded out, destroying centuries of civilization. The indigenous people were also being moved from riverside villages full of fish to lakeside homes. The water was stagnant, and because the flooded area covered a rain forest, rotted plants consumed the oxygen, leaving no life below 10 feet, other than bacteria. There was also the piranha, which could snap a toe as though a fresh carrot (Walsh, *Time is Short and the Water Rises* 1967, p. 64). Walsh wondered about precedent. The only similar example was a 1964 Rhodesia operation related to Kariba Dam. What was being proposed for Suriname was unprecedented in size and the local NGO had only begun to search for money.

**The Go Decision** Despite doubts, the decision was a Go, with Walsh being asked to design what he needed in terms of equipment and local staff. Another official raised money and it was decided that Walsh would go down for a year, with a mandate to negotiate for support with the local government and private sources. Enough money had been found already to begin, so in short order Walsh headed south again. These are exactly the sort of details that need to be in a decision memo because they give the team an expectation of support.

**The Result** John Walsh's book on the operation is an excellent example of communications and public diplomacy, the later because it inspired people around the world to lobby governments to protect wildlife. Walsh also used the operation to springboard a career of directly negotiating changes in rules with governments.

# Chapter 14
# Creation of the League of Nations and the UN

**Extract** Although a model for NGO diplomatic initiatives has been proposed, not every situation is the same; the model won't always be a perfect choice. In other words, the model is a guideline, not a static approach. Chapters 14, 15, 16, 17, 18, and 19 provide case studies of major diplomatic initiatives that used or failed to use some or all of this book's techniques such as a major initiative by governments, the UN, and NGOs to develop an information management tool in 1995 that is still used today to assist relief operations. Regardless of the model used however, before taking action, NGOs need to gather fact, do a professional analysis, conduct professional negotiating, and report on results in a truthful, clear manner.

When reading these case studies, also keep in mind the many other examples already discussed. Chapter 14 examines the birth of the modern multilateral world through the lens of the League of Nations and the United Nations, two international organizations about which NGOs played a major role in the creation phase. To this day, NGOs play a major role in United Nations life.

## 14.1 Introduction

Woodrow Wilson and Franklin Delano Roosevelt are two of the greatest world leaders of the twentieth century because they brought to practical form a theoretical concept proposed by many NGOs and political scientists of a world authority to advance peaceful commerce, eliminate secret treaties, and foster disarmament and human rights. Some even believe their work has laid the groundwork for a distant day when there will be no nation state, only a global democracy. That said, the path to any form of democracy is full of peril and faltering efforts. Since much of this book encourages NGOs to work with international organizations and especially the United Nations, and because the League of Nations project proposed by Wilson

L.W. Roeder, Jr. and A. Simard, *Diplomacy and Negotiation for Humanitarian NGOs*, Humanitarian Solutions in the 21st Century, DOI 10.1007/978-1-4614-7113-4_14,

failed in the United States,[1] whereas the United Nations has done well, it is useful to see how the methodologies of the presidents tracked with the negotiation model proposed for NGOs and whether it mattered when the two leaders strayed; can lessons from those experiences and other historical examples be instructive in today's diplomatic market?

**Note** *A study group always needs to look at precedence, both to understand what has happened and better understand competing negotiators by learning what documents or instruments have influenced them.* The notion of a League was probably first proposed in 1795 by Emmanuel Kant in *Perpetual Peace: A Philosophical Sketch*. A precursor was also the Inter-Parliamentary Union, formed by William Randal Cremer of England and Frederic Passy in 1889. Theodore Roosevelt also proposed a similar idea in 1914 (World Peace Foundation 1919, April, Vol II, No 2). South African Prime Minister Jan Christiaan Smuts published a book in 1918 called The League of Nations: A Practical Suggestion (Miller, *The Smuts Plan* 1928e); the first formal governmental proposal was the Phillimore Plan presented in March, 1918 by the Committee on the League of Nations, led by Sir Walter Phillimore, later Lord Phillimore (Miller, *The Phillimore Plan* 1928d). *Keep in mind however, when doing such a study that each precedent document has its own unique historical context, politics and circumstances.*

**Reminder** In the model, once an idea starts to percolate, a team leader steps up or is assigned to gauge its value and then, if that officer thinks it is a worthy project, creates a study group to refine the concept and further pokes and prods for potential problems. Once that's done, a decision memo is created for a senior decision maker, usually a CEO, to give a go to the project, send it back for further review, defer to some other organization, or even say no. Assuming the decision is a Yes, a chief negotiator is picked to negotiate the deal, while the team leader and CEO generally stay at HQ to manage the allies, funding, and any other issues required to help the negotiation team in the field.

## 14.2 The Study Group "Inquiry": and the "CSOP"

**Note** Wilson first discussed a League of Nations in a speech before the Committee to Enforce Peace on May 27, 1916, as the beginning of a reorganized international system, but Col House felt he had already moved in that direction in 1914 when he

[1] The League of Nations is still alive today, in the improved model that is the United Nations, as well as in two NGOs. Following the rejection of the Treaty of Peace, Col House met in Paris's Majestic Hotel on May 30, 1919 with American and British delegates. They formed an Institute of International Affairs with a branch in England which became known as the Royal Institute of International Affairs and a second on July 21, 1921 as the Council on Foreign Affairs, HQ'd in New York, with an office in Washington, DC. CFR publishes the prestigious Foreign Affairs Magazine.

accepted House's Pan-American Pact proposal. In the May speech, Wilson denounced America's traditional isolationist foreign policy in favor of multilateralism. We are, according to Wilson "participants, whether we would or not, in the life of the world. The interests of all nations are our own also. We are partners with the rest. What affects mankind is inevitably our affair as well as the affair of the nations of Europe and of Asia." (Seymour 1926, pp. 293–295)

Wilson needed to begin "systematic work to lay out the American position for post-war negotiations" (Cooper, *Woodrow WIlson: A Biography* 2009, p. 419), so a study group was created in 1917 as a secret, free-standing element of the Department of State, first known as the War Data Investigation Bureau, then simply "The Inquiry."[2] As initially proposed by Assistant Secretary of State Breckinridge Long on Aug 4, 1917 in a letter to Secretary of State Lansing, the "board" was to consist of a high naval official, the Naval Instructor; the head of the War College, a State Department official named by Lansing, and an expert on International Law (US Department of State 1942a, p. 9). Breckinridge felt the department should be in charge, but it was led by a team leader named Col Edward House, a White House confidant who then named Sidney Edward Mezes as chairman. Mezes was president of City College of New York and House's brother-in-law. The group enlarged to about 126 with some of the finest minds in the country. One went to become the foremost treaty expert at the Department of State. Following the war, some were part of the US delegation at the Paris peace talks, and some in 1921 formed the Council on Foreign Relations, now one of America's most prestigious independent think tanks with the mission to "afford a continuous conference on international questions affecting the United States, by bringing together experts on statecraft, finance, industry, education, and science" (CFR 2012).

Something similar happened in response to the rise of war in Europe in the 1940s; a number of study groups on both sides of the Atlantic emerged to examine possible improvements on the Wilson model, to include one at the US Department of State called the Commission to Study the Organization of Peace (CSOP), formed in February 1941,[3] generated initial plans for a United Nations by October 1943, though its work continued on by different guises through the Dumbarton Oaks and San Francisco conference. It included some of the best professors, business leaders, and attorneys in the USA. Commission members met regularly with president Roosevelt, and the influential first lady Eleanor Roosevelt took a personal interest in their recommendations (Pasvolsky 1944, Oct 4). Finally with the support of the US Department of State, on September 28, 1944, CSOP invited fifty civil society organizations to meet at the Woodrow Wilson Library in Washington, DC. The job was to build a common strategy for what is now known as the UN (Hillmann 1988). Also, while NGOs were involved with the Wilson plan, Roosevelt included far

[2]The staff members were housed in secret in the basement of the New York Public Library on 42nd Street.

[3]CSOP went by a variety of names and was managed out of several offices. For ease of reading, the term CSOP is used throughout this book.

more. The State Department study group was mainly led by Leo Pasvolsky who wrote much of the UN Charter and was very different from Colonel House. Whereas House was a politician, as Ambassador Richard Holbrooke put it, Pasvolsky "was one of those figures peculiar to Washington -- a tenacious bureaucrat who, fixed on a single goal, left behind a huge legacy while virtually disappearing from history" (Leo Pasvolsky 2009).

Although Roosevelt's work was secret, there was collaboration with the allies, much more so than in the Wilson model. In Wilson's time, in addition to his Inquiry, the British and French also appointed secret committees, the British under Lord Philmore and the French under Leon Bourgeois. Initially, the groups did not know of each other's existence, though eventually both governments sent their plans to Washington; extraordinarily, according to one source, Wilson did not invite the Inquiry to review the British or French ideas or even to create an American plan, fearing his team would become bogged down in details (Walters 1952 (reprint 1965), pp. 22–24). Roosevelt's group by contrast, especially at Dumbarton Oaks, shared ideas with allies. That's the model proposed for NGOs initiating a study group on a major initiative that may be of general interest to NGOs. Find out if other NGOs are examining the same idea and fairly quickly share thinking. This will be invaluable to small NGOs with limited resources and should be the model for any sized NGO. Sharing ideas and knowledge (a peer review) is bound to build a strong, practical product.

## 14.3 The Peer Review

One of the key recommendations in the Model for a study group and then also for the decision memo is to conduct a true peer review that does not assume at the outset that an idea will work, even if the participants agree on the goal. In other words, if the team uses a rigorous intellectual discipline, it will identify potential weaknesses as well as possible solutions. Unfortunately, there is no evidence that the Inquiry studied domestic critics. In other words, there was no "opposition research, meaning research" on the Republican Party. There are probably two answers to that. First, its leaders probably felt debarred from domestic affairs (Cooper 2012b) since the Inquiry was formed to plan for the Paris conference. It might also be that since Wilson and House were experienced politicians, they did not feel opposition research was required; that decision proved disastrous, especially since they included no Senators or prominent Republicans on the delegation (Cooper, *Woodrow WIlson: A Biography* 2009, p. 456). Wilson was an advocate for parliamentary government, so he must have understood the value and weaknesses of coalitions, yet ignored the potential, probably because of personal problems with Senator Lodge and others. The same was not true of the FDR exercise. They did study the Senate very carefully and were fortunate in timing perhaps many understand that the failures of the Paris Peace effort and a weak League helped German extremists.

NGOs like the World Citizen's Association of Chicago[4] were certainly pushing hard to learn from the League and build an effective global parliament to foster peace. So, as already mentioned in the discussion on the potential for a UN Army, it was not too surprising that some Senators on both sides of the aisle support the idea in response to the violence of World War II. The Ball–Burton–Hatch–Hill bipartisan Resolution (S.Res.114) provided specifically for "the assembly and maintenance of a United Nations military force" (Oaks 1943, p. 11). Just as conservatives in Wilson's time worried about a "supergovernment," Roosevelt faced Senate conservatives very worried about becoming entangled in wars of no national interest. For Roosevelt, his lead problem was Republican Senator Robert Taft, son of former president and Chief Justice William Howard Taft who had supported the League of Nations. Robert Taft however disagreed on the purpose of World War II, feeling it was not "to establish liberty throughout the world," nor did he feel it correct to "interfere in the internal affairs of nations" to advance basic human rights (Oaks 1943, p. 27), perhaps one of the reasons why the Universal Declaration was considered a set of goals, not a binding document. Taft could easily have taken over the debate and derailed Senate support for the UN, much as Senator Lodge did to Wilson; Roosevelt was generally in town, so he could manage the debate far more effectively than Wilson when he was in Paris. Working with his own allies in the Senate, Roosevelt avoided a full debate and successfully shepherded the UN Treaty.

## 14.4 The Red Scare: What Does the Other Side Fear?

*A study group should figure out what the other side fears.* From 1917 through the end of the Cold War, fear of socialism and communism, as expressed by the political systems in the Soviet Union and China, colored multilateral negotiations. Their socialism was different from many believed in by American socialists and created a major rift in the American Labor Movement, with Samuel Gompers firmly against socialism, but many in the labor movement were in favor like cigar maker Ernst George Winter, president of the Cigar Makers Union in Saint Louis. The fear of the Russian model, which threatened to overtake Germany and was briefly successful in Bavaria, was so great that it impacted who was picked to be in delegations and even how international organizations were formed such as the International Labor Organization (ILO). Gompers led the labor element at Paris in part because of his hard line against socialists.

In the Paris Peace Conference, NGOs and other members of civil society met with national delegations; all the allies feared socialism politically destabilizing. Though research on the opposition of the Republican Party might not have taken

[4]The NGO existed from 1939 to 1943. Records are in the Special Collections Research Center, University of Chicago Library.

place, there was a clear desire to understand and put down what were termed "the left" partly out of fear of the Bolshevik Revolution, which was very violent, especially in its physical suppression of opponents through mock trials and executions. In fact, following the signing of the Treaty of Brest-Litovsk in March of 1918, Allied, Japanese, and US troops occupied parts of Northern Russia, the Ukraine, and Siberia. This was done to prevent expansion by the German Army and also to support White Russians, who were fighting "the Reds." However, when the World War I ended, allied leaders found it difficult to justify leaving tens of thousands of war-weary troops in Russia. Although Wilson considered himself a Progressive, he distained Socialism, repressing its proponents in the United States and making criticism of the government a crime under the Sedition Act. Ironically, the first Red Scare in America was under his administration, making it hard for NGOs associated with socialists. But in fairness to Wilson, the next generation of multilateralists had similar fears, with the Latin American states suggesting during the San Francisco conference that with the Soviet Union on the Security Council, their security was at risk, a view shared by some on the US delegation like Nelson Rockefeller; he felt that if the Security Council could veto decisions by regional bodies, this gave the Soviets too much power and threatened inter-American unity. The issue was similar to what Manley Ottmer Hudson had feared back in the League days, if regional alliances or bodies could take independent collective action, the power of a multilateral body would be destroyed, or at least seriously weakened, leaving competing regional bodies. Fortunately, despite internal fighting, the US delegation was able to achieve a compromise, which declared that instead of using regional collective security arrangements, states had the right of self-defense if attacked, so long as they first reported it to the Security Council. After some British pushback, this was eventually amended to mean the inherent right of individual or collective self-defense. Crisis averted. A critique might question why the US delegation did not anticipate the Latin issues in advance; you can't anticipate everything, no matter how prepared. Instead, when a crisis does emerge, it is important to remember your own core principles, try to understand the other's fears and move forward creatively, as was done in San Francisco.

During the Paris conference and sponsored by Russian socialists was the Stockholm Peace Conference which was intended to cause pacifists and organized labor to argue for a different approach to peace than proposed by the allies (*Die Stockholmer Friedenskonferenz von 1917* 2012). The allies saw this as a threat. Could the socialists tap into public distain for wealthy or traditional governments? As a result, France would not allow socialists to attend, nor the Wilson Administration, nor the UK or Italy, which caused the Stockholm event to collapse. There was also a worry about allowing domestic political movements like the socialists an opportunity to moderate the common approach (US Department of State 1942, p. 27). By March 1918, the Soviets were seen as even more of a threat, due to their agreement to the Treaty of Brest-Litovsk, which created a separate peace with Germany and opened up resources for Germany to use against the allies. During the Peace Conference, the Col House did consider negotiating a specific accord with the Bolshevists; this was rejected by the delegation legal adviser, thinking that while the

Russians would agree, they could not be trusted to comply (Miller, *My Diary At the Conference of Paris* 1924, pp. 206, Vol 1). Further many allied political forces were working against the Bolsheviks.

The strongest statement about the negotiations on the League of Nations as a counterpoint to the socialists was probably made by president Wilson to the Inquiry study group. "The poison of Bolshevism was accepted readily by the world because it is a protest against the way in which the world has worked."[5] It was to be our business, the legal advisor commented, at the Peace Conference to fight for a new order, in the words of Wilson, "agreeably if we can, disagreeably if necessary (Miller, *My Diary At the Conference of Paris* 1924, pp. 373, Vol 1)."[6] The exception was the labor talks that led the establishment of the ILO (International Labor Organization). While Samuel Gompers, who represented United States labor, was antisocialist, many nations did send socialist representatives. Gompers saw them as obstructing constructive (Gompers 1921) work and when speaking of the agreements reached in Paris on labor said constructive organization was an obstacle to radicalism, which is how he described Bolshevism (House and Seymour, *What Really Happened At Paris* 1921, pp. 486–487). In an essay, Herbert Hoover was of the opinion that during the war the misery of the conflict was fertile ground for Bolshevists and Anarchists and that if allowed to prosper, Central Europe would succumb to chaos (Hoover 1921).

In the late 1950s when negotiating arms control with the Soviet Union, the USA came to understand that the Soviets feared a surprise attack more than nuclear war itself. Understanding Soviet fears was crucial to American thinking for long-term strategic talks (Department of State 1960, p. 1515). But as New Zealand Prime Minister John Key put it in 2012, in the twenty-first century, war between major nuclear powers, while possible, is less of a threat than a surprise attack by a terrorist group or lone wolf (Vance 2012). It is interesting that while many in the labor movement were sympathetic to socialism, Samuel Gompers, America's biggest labor leader, fought it. president Wilson appointed Gompers to the Commission on International Labor Legislation at the Versailles Peace Conference, a position Gompers used to create the International Labor Organization (ILO).

[5] While Peace negotiations were going on in Paris, US diplomat William Christian Bullitt was sent by the US delegation to the Paris Peace Conference on a secret mission to Soviet Russia to broker a deal with the Bolsheviks and end the Russian Civil War, lift the allied blockade, and allow the allies to withdraw the troops they had dispatched to Russia in 1918. Bullitt felt that only a Bolshevik government could be established without the use of bayonets that Lenin was as moderate as any Soviet, and the Russians did make a proposal. However, the allies in Paris rejected the idea in strong, public terms (Office of the Historian 2010).

[6] The authors decided to consult with John Milton Cooper, Jr. on this because the origins of anti-Bolshevism and the Red Scare under Wilson are a fascinating, disputed, and much-written about subject, which, while relevant, are the topics for a different book. Cooper in a discussion on 5/20/2012, opined that Wilson was actually sympathetic to socialism in private, and he did try to put the brakes on allied intervention in Russia. The exclusion of socialist NGOS may also have been more due to Clemenceau and Lloyd George than Wilson, but it's worth looking into further.

## 14.5 Long-Term Impacts

An important function of any study group must also be to consider *long-term impacts of negotiation positions and whether they might undermine core contemporary principals*. Though the Secretary of War under Wilson clearly worried that crushing economic sanctions could lead to a militant Germany in some future time, a point shared by Miller and Keynes and others, what is surprising was that the Inquiry did not develop an effective approach to deal with such demands by foreign allies like France who wanted the industrial Ruhr valley or territorial claims by Japan on China. They were all made as a bargain for recognizing the League, to the point that Secretary of State Lansing eventually felt that Wilson's 14 Points had been betrayed in the president's zeal to seal the deal on the League at all costs. This was also a position made by Keynes, which is that the Germans agreed to attend the conference under the terms of the 14 Points and then found the treaty was not consistent with those assurances (Keynes 1920, p. 49 and 55).[7] This is an important observation because at that time in history, the country was split on the practical value of a global society, despite knowledge of the Interparliamentary Union and the concept of enforced arbitration. On March 18, 1918, the British leader Lord Robert Cecil proposed edits to Article 11 which for some at least implied that the League had an affirmative obligation to respond to acts of war on behalf of its members (Rappart 1931, p. 30). It was agreed without debate by president Wilson that a move his legal advisor felt might prove fatal in the Senate where many conservatives thought the League to be a direct threat to the constitutional prerogatives of the Senate to approve any treaty the president might choose to negotiate or war the president might decide to prosecute. In other words, they saw the League as threatening American sovereignty, perhaps forcing them to agree to an unwanted war, a view held also by some Canadian officials (Miller, *My Diary At the Conference of Paris* 1924, pp. 177–178, Vol 1). Many of those conservatives in the US Senate were also the children of soldiers who fought in the Civil War who believed in state's rights and saw Wilson wanting to be a kind of dictator who brooked no compromise. A century after the negotiations, this discussion of internal Senate debates might sound arcane to an NGO diplomat worried about advancing environmental law or negotiating some change in status for civilians in a war zone; consider that now and then, just because an Ambassador or other government representative agrees to something doesn't mean there won't be opposition back at capital that can reverse the decision. A smart NGO delegation will research for possible opposition and develop a counter strategy, perhaps by asking partner NGOs to engage in Public diplomacy. In the case of Article X, which was the most controversial, the president was firm, offering that the French would see the League emasculated without it or

[7] This attitude by the Germans was probably naïve.

in weakened form, his fear obviously being that absent the French, no League (Miller, *My Diary At the Conference of Paris* 1924, pp. 183, Vol 1). The delegation also proposed that the Canadian fear was overstated.

## 14.6 Assigning the Negotiator

The model proposes that the team or decision maker assign the role of negotiator to a skilled individual[8] and that the team leader remain at HQ to manage the allies and any problem. Unfortunately, president Wilson initially assigned the role of chief negotiator to the team leader (Col House), but then took on the job himself over two extended trips. House was more flexible than Wilson, but the League was the president's idea, so one can understand his desire to be on the scene; going to Paris for the negotiations weakened his ability to manage domestic critics, leaving him out of touch with the public as well or at least weakened his ability to influence them through public diplomacy (Miller, *The Drafting of the Covenant* 1928a, pp. 278, Vol 1). Communications across the Atlantic were not excellent, and by not managing the government on a day to day basis, Wilson couldn't use the inherent power of the Presidency to move the pieces of government to his advantage, especially the "bully pulpit." Allies in Washington did point this out, including House, who wanted the plum assignment for himself (Cooper, *Woodrow WIlson: A Biography* 2009, p. 455). According to Walter Lippmann, then assigned to the Paris team by House,[9] "Wilson was convinced that only he could achieve an equitable peace" (Steel 1980, p. 150), yet other on-site observers felt the president's negotiating skills were weak. It would be uncharitable today to criticize the president's abilities, especially as he was trying to achieve something never done before. Nonetheless, it is noteworthy that in a private conversation with David Miller, the president's right-hand man Colonel House remarked at the end of the negotiations that "the president would not ask for help as he never asked anyone for help" (Miller, *My Diary At the Conference of Paris* 1924, pp. 329, Vol 1). Whether actually true of not, House's observation is an apt alarm bell for any NGO chief negotiator. *No negotiator will know everything, nor is any negotiator perfect. Always be willing to ask for help from your team or friends. That is a sign of strength, not weakness.*

[8]Lansing of the US delegation grew disenchanted with the League's final form and that of the treaty, due to compromises made by Wilson that Lansing felt undermined the moral underpinnings of the American position. Unfortunately statements he made in confidence expressing that disillusionment were leaked to the press, which harmed public opinion and that of the Senate. John Maynard Keyes of the British delegation resigned in anger and wrote a book in 1920 about why he felt the treaty was destructive to future peace.

[9]Lippmann also served as secretary to the Inquiry when he left the staff of the New Republic.

The president's decision to go to Paris was understandable; yet it was highly problematic for the Democratic Party since both houses of Congress reverted to the Republicans just prior to peace talks. However, the CEO's of NGOs are not presidents, and frequently, CEOs do go into the field, such as Jeremy Hume of SPANA, who in a discussion for this book, communicated from his blackberry while sitting on an upturned cart, with his mobile clinic just outside the township of Gweru in central Zimbabwe. Hoover regularly went behind combat lines to advance diplomacy for his Belgian relief NGO; so there is no rule against sending the CEO to conduct negotiations; it should however be done with care, since just as Wilson had to manage a nation, a CEO must manage his or her NGO and not overly fixate on one project. The war was over, and at the end of any war, rules are changed. Measures were needed to bolster the economy, and there were racial tensions, issues of which the Inquiry was well aware, according to a memo of Dec 19, 1917 (US Department of State 1942, p. 39); yet Wilson largely ignored his domestic responsibilities while in Paris and similarly while on his rail tour of America to sell the League. As a result when America was hit by terrible race riots in 1919, Wilson only spoke of them once on his cross-country trip, an awful decision for a president. Don't be out of touch with reality.

## 14.7 Public Diplomacy

A NGO team leader can set up a public diplomacy campaign to convince the people to lobby one or many governments, as WSPA did in support of UDAW.[10] Governments use the technique to gain support of the populace; this wasn't done prior to the Paris Talks by the US government, despite a massive and very successful propaganda campaign to garner hatred of Germans during the war. That said, an NGO did help, the *League to Enforce Peace* (LEP) begun in 1915 by prominent Americans to establish a new world order of collective security led by an international organization (League of Nations) with powers of arbitration (To Hold War Convention 1918).[11] Indeed, despite a plethora of NGOs proposing a wide range of organizational models, as noted already, Wilson's 14 points came with no organizational structure, other than a few ideas proposed by the Inquiry, itself influenced by Smuts and a few world leaders. Wilson's focus was on ideals—not details. Mistake.

Led by former president Taft, the League to Enforce Peace was well funded, very organized, and its public diplomacy efforts rivaled later efforts by FDR to garner public support for the UN (Cooper 2012). The LEP followed in a long line of organizations that now includes Peace Action. Some of the precursor NGOs included the New York Peace Society, which was America's first such NGO.[12] It went out of

[10] See discussions on public diplomacy and declarations.

[11] The NGO's first president was former US president William Howard Taft.

[12] Formed in 1815.

business several times before finally being merged in 1940 with the Quaker-based World Alliance for International Friendship through Religion.[13] Goldsworthy Lowes Dickinson, who founded the League of Nations Society in 1915 is said by some to have coined the term. There was also the League of Free Nations Association, formed in New York and Union of Democratic Control. There were also similar bodies in Germany and Austria–Hungary. The Massachusetts Peace Society was also formed in Boston in 1815 was another anti-war NGO; it merged with the American Peace Society in 1828. Those groups were against all war. In 1816 came the Society for the Promotion of Permanent and Universal Peace, which advocated arbitration and simultaneous disarmament. From there, the number of peace NGOs grew quickly.

NGOs definitely wanted an international organization to arbitrate and enforce peace; they faced some of the same issues as did Wilson. Pacifists did not like the notion of collective security; nationalists like Lodge saw arbitration as weakening sovereignty.[14] They were however able to advance the cause of the League of Nations, though their point of view went beyond what was politically possible in the Senate at that time. Typical criticism was a speech before the Veterans of the Grand Army on May 13, 1918 by noted orator and Republican Senator Alfred J. Beveridge. His attack was that the goals of the LEP and the League of Nations would force America into unwanted conflicts and unconstitutionally restrict the power of Congress to authorize wars (Indianapolis Star 1918).

Today, New York is seen as the font of great humanitarian NGOs like Peace Action; yet a century ago the conflict that erupted in Europe brought to life a number of fascinating NGOs interested in finding multilateral approaches to peace, and their legacies survive. In 1915, the largest of all the NGOs to influence discussions related to global peace was the League to Enforce Peace, led by former president William Howard Taft. He had 34 state governors as vice presidents; it held a lot of influence, but collapsed when the US Senate rejected US membership in the League of Nations in 1919. The call to peace was then taken up by the American Association for a League of Nations, founded in 1922, and similar NGOs like the League of Free Nations Association, founded in 1918, now known as the Foreign Policy Association[15] and the Council on Foreign Relations founded by Colonel House and others in 1919, which now publishes Foreign Policy Magazine. One thing they had

---

[13]Formed in 1914. Records are at Swathmore College.

[14]In the post-World War II period, the best current example of collective security is probably NATO, formed by the North Atlantic Treaty of 1949, which links its members to the UN, but agreeing to collective defense. In addition, as the Security Council has become problematic due to Chinese and Russian votes in creating humanitarian defense operations, NATO has agreed, if controversially, to occasionally fill the gap.

[15]The League of Free Nations Association was started by Paul Kellogg, journalists, and others to support Woodrow Wilson. Some of the prominent American members were later to be Secretary of State John Foster Dulles and Eleanor Roosevelt, perhaps the most influential first lady in multilateral diplomacy.

in common was the pursuit of democracy. The LEP and societies of the League[16] which supported the League of Nations were also often well funded, and they did exactly what all modern NGOs should do; they met with the US National delegation, and certainly the delegations of Britain, France, Singapore, etc., though probably not at the Head of Mission level, with the exception of an Irish group that lobbied the president for independence and was rebuffed. In addition, they engaged in direct talks with government officials like the influential French Diplomat Paul-Henri-Benjamin Baluet d'Estournelles, baron de Constant de Rébecque, who was an advocate for arbitration and European Union (Bartlett 1944, p. 119) and Leon Bourgeois who was spokesperson for Clemenceau, president of France. In addition, the NGO known as the German Society for International Law[17] actually proposed specific language for the League's charter[18] (Miller, *My Diary At the Conference of Paris* 1924, pp. 95 and 187, Vol 1). House also mentioned that "While the accredited statesmen occupied the center of the stage, influential men and women in every walk of life were there in some capacity…They came from the four corners of the earth" (House 1925, December). One NGO called the International Council of Women[19] and Conferences of Women Suffragists of Allied Countries and of the USA demanded officers in the League be split equally between men and women (International Committee of Women 1919). The idea was presented to the negotiators on their behalf by president Wilson on March 24,1919, and the policy was indeed adopted, so this is a triumph of NGO diplomacy.

It is odd, given the public interest in creating a body to end wars, and the existence of influential, well-funded NGOs as well as the nature of public criticism by his political foes, that Wilson did not also push an aggressive, effective public diplomacy campaign of his own while in Paris[20]; his administration conducted a

---

[16] The League of Nations Union was formed October 13, 1918 by joining of the League of Nations Society with the Free Nations Society, the former which had been formed in 1916 to propose practical models of international organizations. That society wanted a permanent peace through a body that settled disputes, provided mutual defense, and published treaties—thus avoiding secret diplomacy. It mounted a massive public diplomacy campaign and continued its work up to 1946 when it merged with the UN Association of Great Britain. One notable achievement was the Peace Ballot of 1935. Eleven million people participated, calling for peaceful resolution of disputes.

[17] The German Society was founded in 1918 (Macalister-Smith 2012).

[18] Many NGO meetings happened at the Cercle de l'Union interalliée or Inter-Allied Club, founded in Paris when the United States entered the war, a club which still exists to this day. The location provided a convivial atmosphere for off-the-record conversations.

[19] The International Committee of Women (ICW) was founded in 1888 and was one of the first women-specific NGOs that operated on an international scale.

[20] Miller was also opposed to some publicity, such as a movie proposed to be made of the conference, which he felt would be highly criticized in the United States, though it is not certain as to why (Miller, My Diary, pg. 96, Vol. 1). It may be because the project was led by William Christian Bullitt, who under Roosevelt would become the first US Ambassador to the Soviet Union. At the time of the conference, Bullitt was a political radical with close ties to the Bolshevik revolution and was even married to the widow of John Reed. Ironically, he became a hardened anti-communist after serving in Moscow. Bullitt—there's a story of spurned love, at least on Bullitt's side. He broke publicly with Wilson when the preliminary terms of the treaty were published, and he later participated in a vendetta against him. His later ambassadorship is a tale in itself.

massive propaganda effort to sell the war through what was known as the CPI or Committee on Public Information (Mock and Larson 1939). In fairness, Wilson did speak on this before the conference began by saying the Inquiry that the United States had to be told the truth about the diplomacy, indicating that he had arranged with the French and British to publish *political news*; in the end Wilson's hands were partly tied by negotiating partners, known as the Council of Ten, who, as Lloyd George observed, did not want "a peace settled by public clamor" (Cooper, *Woodrow Wilson: A Biography* 2009, p. 469) and instead insisted on a restrictive sharing of news. Not following his basic instinct was a mistake; it hindered his ability to directly inform reporters about the controversial Article X. Instead, they had to rely on rumor.

Further, although the president did do a cross country train tour after Paris to sell the League, by then the president was physically exhausted. Indeed, the tour had to be cut short because a stroke partially paralyzed Wilson. This is not to say Wilson ignored the public, and if he hadn't suffered a stroke, likely he would have done a second run; the impression one comes away with is the effort was more about impressing the newspapers than the actual voters, thinking that the papers would then sway the Senate. This analysis is supported by a private note from Secretary of State Lansing to the head of the US Commission in Paris on July 31, 1919 in which Lansing offered, when speaking of the Republican opposition, "I advised him not to arouse resentment by going on a speaking tour on August 4$^{th}$. He seemed disposed to go but some of the Democratic senators gave him the same advice, so he has postponed his trip which is a good thing. He can win more support by talking to individuals than by speaking to arouse the people" (US Department of State 1942, p. 625). A century after the event, it is probably unfair to criticize the president's staff for a possible lapse in political judgment about the voters, the value of public diplomacy, or the Republican Party; the same cable suggested the opposition was in disarray, when the reverse was true. The president went on the tour; it brought on a stroke. Others on his staff were better disposed to public diplomacy, like Col House, who wrote to the president on Aug 30, 1919, while noting the impending tour, "The people throughout the country are tired of the technical controversies into which discussion has lately been drawn in Washington, and will welcome a reassertion of the ideals America fought for and the broad principles upon which the League is based." Hamilton Holt, head of LEP, also wanted to conduct a publicity campaign, which he did through his liberal weekly magazine *The Independent*. Probably the proponents of public diplomacy were right to push for it,[21] and that were Wilson to have had the opportunity for a second tour, he might have made political headway (US Department of State 1942, p. 637). House then went on to remind the president about the sticking point, Article X " ..it seems to me that hostility to the League in America is almost wholly based upon article 10. … It would seem that our people have not grasped the limitations and significance of the external aggression clause" (US Department of State 1942, p. 638). For NGO leaders reading this book, the

[21] We are calling these efforts public diplomacy because a major purpose was to convince the public to convince their senators.

lesson is less about any failures by Wilson or his staff, who were doing something unprecedented, than a reminder that in any negotiation, anything can kill success. Public diplomacy is a crucial tool, so is understanding and respectfully working with your opponents.

This lack of public diplomacy resulted in the public not being totally sold on Wilson's concept, while they might have favored joining a league, with sovereignty reservations proposed by Senator Henry Cabot Lodge, to which Britain and France were mostly prepared to agree (Fleming 2003, p. 442). By 1943, there was an agreement among the Big 4 (the UK, the USA, the Soviet Union, and France) to replace the League of Nations.[22] That then led to the Dumbarton Oaks Conference in Georgetown, Washington, DC,[23] which on October 7, 1944 created a set of proposals that largely laid out the framework of the UN, though it remained for the Yalta Conference to iron out the Security Council and Trusteeship issues. Just as the League was quite a huge chew for the public in Wilson's time, so too was the UN in FDR's, and he did not want to repeat Wilson's mistake of a weak public engagement, so his administration decided in late 1944 to engage in a massive public relations move before VE Day.[24] Roosevelt knew that once victory took place, the public's mood would shift to demobilization and jobs, not world governance. CBS broadcast Commission statements for free across the nation. Regular press conferences were held, and experts were sent across the country to explain the Dumbarton Agreements, and copies of the draft charter were widely distributed. In other words, Roosevelt wanted to leave nothing to chance. The public was going to know the truth about the UN and support it.

## 14.8 The Role of Compromise

From the start, Wilson faced opposition from the Republican Party, which described the League as a threat to US sovereignty. Those objections were led by Massachusetts Senator Henry Cabot Lodge who felt that Article X of the League Compact could force the United States to go to war to defend an attacked nation, even if the Senate objected.

[22] This decision was made at the Third Moscow Conference October 18 to November 11, 1943, in the Kremlin and Spiridonovka Palace.

[23] Formal name was the Washington Conversations on International Peace and Security Organization.

[24] VE Day (May 8, 1945) was the term for Victory in Europe and VJ Day was the term for Japanese surrender. VJ could mean the day of the Japan's initial surrender (querythe afternoon of August 15, 1945, in Japan, or August 14, 1945 depending on the time zone or September 2, 1945, when the surrender document was signed in Tokyo Bay.

**Note: The Final Text of Article X** The Members of the League undertake to respect and preserve as against external aggression the territorial integrity and existing political independence of all Members of the League. In the case of any such aggression or in case of any threat or danger of such aggression the Council shall advise upon the means by which this obligation shall be fulfilled. (Department of State 1942b, p. 83)

Contrast the final text with Wilson's initial draft which ended up by saying regarding aggression against a member that "the Contracting Powers shall also unite in coming to the assistance of the Contracting Power against which hostile action has been taken, combining their armed forces in its behalf" (Department of State 1942, p. 505). There was to be a "uniting of forces against any state that rejected arbitration and went to war" (Miller, *The Drafting of the Covenant* 1928b, pp. 17, Vol 1). In other words, Wilson wanted a collective security system similar to what LEP desired and went in with language akin to a NATO multi-defense pact; ended up proposing something much less, a convention that only called for advice on action, in other words a version of today's UN based collective security, rather than a global system. This happened probably because Wilson came with much experience as a skilled legislative negotiator and wasn't a strict structuralist, meaning he believed in structural evolution. If he gained a level of collective defense one day, eventually the system would evolve to a full NATO-like alliance (Cooper 2012).[25]

Also contrast the final text with the statement by Leon Bourgeois,[26] Technical delegate in the French delegation to the preliminary meeting on February 14, 1919. Mr. Bourgeois felt that a state that attacked a member of the League "must regard itself as being in a state of War, not merely with the state which has been the victim of the aggression, but with the whole world," a statement which would seem to lend support to Senator Lodge's concern. He went on to say that "The State which violates the international Covenant is at war against the remainder. Thus, all the Allied forces will necessarily act in this war which the law of right has sanctioned… It ought to be impossible for a sudden aggression to take place … without the certainty of its being immediately put down." In other words, even if two nations went to war, if the victim was a member of the League, that meant all members were in a state of war with the aggressor and thus obligated to send forces (Department of State 1942, pp. 221–223). However, Bourgeois then moderated this position in his Nobel Lecture, saying "Our American friends have voiced the fear that Article 10 could involve their country in military operations to which it would not have given its consent. To be sure, Article 10 provides a general guarantee preserving the

[25]Miller took a different view, saying that Wilson's initial draft was a negative covenant with no positive guarantee of support, whereas the British insisted on a concept of ipso facto war with all members when an armed intervention took place (Miller, My Diary, Volume 1, pages 333–337).

[26]Winner of the Nobel Prize for Peace, with others, in 1920, was also president of the Council of the League of Nations and president of the French Senate, as well as a former Secretary of State.

integrity of the territories of each nation. But none of the articles that follow permits us to conclude that any nation could find itself suddenly involved against its will in a military operation without the explicit consent of the agencies which embody its national sovereignty" (Bourgeois 1922, December).

The Irony is that the British and French agreed that Article X (in final form) was not a threat to sovereignty; Wilson refused to any further compromise on language and that led to a showdown in the Senate, with Wilson and the League losing. This probably should not have happened; partisan politics played a role, or the president just believed, albeit mistakenly, that the idea of the League was too big, too important to fail. In a letter to then head of the US Peace Commission, Frank Lyon Polk on July 31, 1919, Secretary of State Lansing made the following comment: "...The Republicans have no definite plan as to the treaty and seem considerably disorganized. The president has been very conciliatory and has undoubtedly smothered a good deal of opposition. ... The impression is gaining ground that the opposition is to the president personally and not to the treaty, the public does not like it. I am sure the president is gaining ground every day" (US Department of State 1942, pp. 624–625).

This last element is surprising in the abstract, though true to Wilson's personality, not grasping that compromise on language shouldn't be considered an issue, unless one's core ethical principles are violated. Wilson had already made compromises on territories, which some considered unethical, that might have led him to be stiff on change. Lodge's demands were drafted in a confrontational tone; the substance, which the allies were largely in agreement with, was reasonable, essentially that that League could not commit US forces without US Senate approval that being because only Congress can declare war. The same is true today with the United Nations Charter, which can lay down sanctions (unless the US objects), can't force a war. Wilson made the point in public addresses, such as a speech in Indianapolis when he said while the League is obligated to give advice on how to work against aggressor nations, "there is no compulsion upon us to take that advice – except the compulsion of our good conscience and judgment" (Bridgeport Indianapolis Telegraph 1919).

While an administration often agrees to binding obligations, they have no force, absent Senate approval. What has allowed the UN system to work is that while the UN can't force action, it can "prevent it," such as with sanctions; the power to do that was approved by the Senate. What is surprising is that Wilson, knowing the American system, did not start from that premise, thus undercut his critics' primary objection.[27]

John Milton Cooper, Jr. discussed Article X with us, noting that "Wilson had not committed himself to anything like Article X while the Inquiry was functioning. The moral vs. legal obligation argument is an interesting one, and I have often

[27] Sanctions and the ability to force nations to comply was a big difference between the League and the UN. The League was essentially voluntary, especially as it evolved, but in the UN under Article 25, the Security Council has the power to compel member states. Further Article I of the charter obligates states to support the UN in general.

wondered whether Wilson might not have developed it further if the stroke hadn't put him out of commission during his first speaking tour (he had another one planned for after his return)" (Cooper 2012).

The Republicans overstated the risks to sovereignty by the League and wrongly indicated that the Covenant (in final draft) would force the United States to send armies to the aid of others, thereby subverting the constitutional prerogatives of the US Congress; the early draft showed that Wilson had different aspirations. It is possible that Wilson might have pulled the Republicans along if Senator Henry Cabot Lodge and others had been brought in early and if Wilson had compromised over language and placed protections for sovereignty into the Covenant; Wilson did not understand the value of compromise.[28] Wilson probably did not invite Lodge because he wanted freedom of movement, the ability to make negotiation decisions on the fly; that was a mistake. In a similar situation, an NGO CEO should consider bringing a potential foe to a negotiating event in order to coop and build political bridges. If Lodge had gone to Paris, he would have been in the middle of the biggest negotiations of the modern era, been consulted on language, and have been a player on the world stage. Assuming that Wilson then listened to Lodge's advice, the two might have achieved acceptable, if not perfect language. Especially since Wilson believed in organizational evolution, that was probably his best approach. After all, Lodge was at one time supportive of the League concept and would eventually coin the phrase United Nations. But to be fair to Wilson, congressional elections that had just ended were nasty, and the national political scene was as divisive as 2012 in the United States. Lodge and Wilson also just did not like each other, making compromise by either party tough; also Wilson wasn't a coordinator at heart. For example, his 14 points were never coordinated with the allies and, while popular with European citizens, held little sway with the governments (Steel 1980, p. 136).

## 14.9 Conclusion

It is worth noting however that Woodrow Wilson, despite his tactical failures in diplomatic tradecraft, was the one head of state/government who really captured the idea that the World War I needed to be followed by a new form of world governance, with a League of Nations to look after the political security needs of countries and a League of Red Cross Societies to handle the humanitarian business and

[28]There is some thought that Wilson may not have been entirely believed. Postwar analysis has shown that CPI engaged in true propaganda, the distortion of truth, and the effort was massive, distributing over 75 million pieces of propaganda to the public in 1917–1918. In other words, many statements about the German people were factually wrong, to the point that German-Americans were regularly disadvantaged. The Administration also advanced the Espionage Act and the Sedition Act, which were clear violations of the 1st Amendment rights to free speech, in an effort to tamp anti-war fervor.

specialized agencies like the ILO to build safe jobs. The American Red Cross, under the leadership of Henry Davison, accepted the humanitarian challenge, as did Fridtjof Nansen, and the IFRC is the growth from that dream. The fact that Senator Henry Cabot Lodge denied Wilson the political arm of that dream doesn't dislodge Wilson's prominence as the man who inspired a practical approach to world humanitarian governance. Indeed, the way the American Red Cross and a number of other National Societies were called into action to help combat the ravages of the Spanish Flu epidemic from 1919 is testament to the dream's value. Any criticism of Wilson must be tempered by this observation that the greatness of his humanitarian ideals and the structure he proposed are a legacy to be proud of. To this day, with evolutionary changes, Wilson's dream saves lives and property every day.

# Chapter 15
# The People's Treaties at Rio + 20 – 2012

**Extract** Although a model for NGO diplomatic initiatives has been proposed, not every situation is the same; the model won't always be a perfect choice. In other words, the model is a guideline, not a static approach. Chapters 14, 15, 16, 17, 18, and 19 provide case studies of major diplomatic initiatives that used or failed to use some or all of this book's techniques. Regardless of the model used however, before taking action, NGOs need to gather fact, do a professional analysis, conduct professional negotiating, and report on results in a truthful, clear manner.

When reading these case studies, also keep in mind the many other examples already discussed. Chapter 15 examines People's Treaties, an alternative to the traditional treaty process. While the documents do not have standing in international law, they can be a powerful lobbying tool and thus a fulcrum to enable negotiations.

## 15.1 Introduction

At Rio+20 in Brazil in June 2012, a coalition of civil society organizations proposed 13 "treaties," as an expression of the will of the people on sustainability (Peoples' Sustainable Treaties 2012a). Believing that traditional organizations and government agencies have failed to protect the planet, this effort represents the start of "a coordinated global movement (GCM) which is struggling towards a just and sustainable planetary civilization (Peoples Sustainability Treaties 2012a)." In essence, the People's Treaty effort is a coalition. Organizations that joined the coalition went through some version of the decision-making process proposed in the model, and there are similarities in how the coalition works with this book's model regarding how they approached their diplomacy and lobbying. As an example, they formed several study groups. Does their model offer clues into the future of CSO diplomacy? In the context of Rio+20, CSOs were the UN major groups, including

L.W. Roeder, Jr. and A. Simard, *Diplomacy and Negotiation for Humanitarian NGOs*, Humanitarian Solutions in the 21st Century, DOI 10.1007/978-1-4614-7113-4_15,

organizations representing (a) Business and Industry, (b) Children and Youth, (c) Farmers, (d) Indigenous Peoples, (e) Local Authorities, (f) NGOs, (g) the Scientific and Technological Community, (h) Women, and (i) Workers and Trade Unions. Nonprofits and NGOs were also invited to participate as full members. Private citizens participated as contributors and could endorse or comment on the text. For-profit organizations, IOs, and donor agencies were also invited to contribute with recommendations, even become sponsors.

## 15.2 Eight Steps to Rio

The process involved eight steps up to Rio, plus an understanding that Rio should lead to a broader, global movement (Process: People's Sustainability Treaties 2012a):

1. **Creating a "Treaty Circle,"** with broad geographical representation.
2. **Organizing Dialogues** through meetings, email, and phone conversations.
3. **Writing Draft Texts,** which was done through an appointed Editorial Team.
4. **Consulting Experts,** to make sure that texts were credible.
5. **Editorial Review,** for improvement and integration with other treaties.
6. **Generating Comments,** done through broad dissemination by email.
7. **Finalization of Treaties,** done through the International Editorial Committee.
8. **Lobbying of Treaties** at Rio+20 with governments, IOs, and other stakeholders. This was both lobbying and true diplomacy.

Leading the overall process were five teams (People's Sustainability Treaties 2012a):

(a) **International Advisory Board (IAB),** which managed the effort. These were senior leaders from each of the major groups in civil society. Partner organizations also were invited to guide process. The IAB was a caretaker in other words or guardian of the process, and its role continued after Rio. This is a blending of the study group and HQ team from Chap. 1.
(b) **Media and Advocacy Group (MAG).** This was the communications element envisaged in Chap. 10 on Communications and designed public diplomacy efforts, but also managed the lobbying of decision makers at Rio+20.
(c) **Editorial Review Committee (ERC).** This group was appointed to manage content, and one member was invited to join the Treaties Review Committee to assist the IEC in a final outcome document that reflected input from the treaty circles and the public at large. This is similar to the Model in that any conference has an outcomes document and that NGOs should do their best to negotiate language for inclusion.
(d) **Secretariat.** This was hosted by the Centre for Environmental Development (CED) in Sri Lanka and consisted of representatives from each treaty facilitating partner organization.

(e) **Treaty Circles (TC).** This was where the hard, visionary work was conducted. Each proposed treaty was crafted by a Treaty Circle or network of facilitating organizations. Any CSO could join. The facilitators each appointed someone to a treaty editorial team, to include a subject expert and at least one member each from north and south geographies.

## 15.3 Results

The result of the effort was a collection of "treaties" proposed by NGOs and other civil bodies at the conference, and some did want to influence the actual outcomes documents. But in the case of the ***Radical Ecological Democracy Treaty***, there were different goals: "agree on a CSO treaty....including joint actions post-Rio. The initial draft of the treaty emerged from experiences in India, and was then sent out on a few networks for comments and endorsements....this process took place over 3–4 months before Rio (Kothari 2012a)." That's perfectly proper of course, and a movement generated this way might well garner enough support to alter the view of government leaders as well as new players in civil society downstream. Perhaps without any government regulation, for example, enough companies will be inspired by an initiative like this to do the right thing on their own for the environment. Although not an internationally recognized treaty in the traditional sense, the document is an agreement between partners to improve how they approach the environment and to also influence government to do the same, so it also has some similarities to public diplomacy.[1]

[1] The process started when the lead author (Ashish Kothari of Pune, India) heard about the People's Sustainability Treaties (PST) process and suggested a Treaty on R.E.D., based on ongoing work in India. He then did a rough draft, which was sent out to several NGO networks for comments and endorsements. The draft was further revised a few times, and a final draft for the purposes of discussion at Rio came out just before coming to Rio. Further refinements continued at Rio, taking advantage of access to potentially fresh partners, one of the values of international c onferences (Kothari, *Progress Discussion* 2012a). A graduate in Sociology, Ashish has taught environment at the Indian Institute of Public Administration in the 1990s and been guest faculty at several universities, institutes, and colleges. He has been a Mellon Global Fellow at Bowdoin College, USA. Ashish was co-chair of the IUCN Inter-commission Strategic Direction on Governance, Equity, and Livelihoods in Relation to Protected Areas (TILCEPA) (1999–2008) and in the same period a member of the Steering Committees of the World Commission on Protected Areas (WCPA) and IUCN Commission on Environmental, Economic, and Social Policy (CEESP). He has served on the Board of Directors of Greenpeace International and currently chairs Greenpeace India's Board. He has also been on the steering group of the CBD Alliance.

# Chapter 16
# Rebuttal to an Outcome Document

**Extract** Although a model for NGO diplomatic initiatives has been proposed, not every situation is the same; the model won't always be a perfect choice. In other words, the model is a guideline, not a static approach. Chapters 14, 15, 16, 17, 18, and 19 provide case studies of major diplomatic initiatives that used or failed to use some or all of this book's techniques. Regardless of the model used however, before taking action, NGOs need to gather fact, do a professional analysis, conduct professional negotiating, and report on results in a truthful, clear manner.

When reading these case studies, also keep in mind the many other examples already discussed. The book advises NGOs to try to negotiate the insertion of language into the outcomes documents of conferences, since that creates a moral fulcrum or mandate for future action. But there are times when the outcomes document is so disappointing that NGOs need to join behind a protest statement. While the documents do not have legal standing, if written well and backed by significant public support, that they can be a powerful lobbying tool and thus a fulcrum to enable negotiations.

## 16.1 Introduction

Rio+20 was often very disappointing to civil society, so many NGOs issued a strong rebuttal. One is reminded of a story told by Germans to explain World War II. It has to do with a discussion between a horse, a cow, and ass. Each wanted to know who had done the most. The horse offered "Of course, if I hadn't been there to carry our cavalry across the border and draw our guns, we could never have invaded France and Belgium." The cow scornfully replied "If I hadn't stayed at home and nourished the civil population, we couldn't have carried on for

L.W. Roeder, Jr. and A. Simard, *Diplomacy and Negotiation for Humanitarian NGOs*, Humanitarian Solutions in the 21st Century, DOI 10.1007/978-1-4614-7113-4_16,

three months." Then the ass laughed with the loud obnoxious asses have and said "If I hadn't been in diplomacy, there never would have been a war" (Mcconnell et al. 1942, pp. 135–136).

## 16.2 Statement Opposing the Final Outcome Document

The following statement by Judy Lerner, UN Representative of Peace Action, was presented to the Plenary of Rio + 20 three days prior to completion of the conference in protest to the draft final statement as a tool to argue for a fresh text (Lerner 2012). Ms. Lerner could not make the statement herself, so the presentation was made by Leida Rijnhout, ANPED ivzw, Northern Alliance for Sustainability Brussels—Belgium, www.anped.org.

> Thank you President
>
> I am making this statement on behalf of the NGOs
>
> It feels amazing to be sitting in this room among all the world leaders, and feeling all this power around me that can shape the World. We all know the threat that is facing us, and I do not need to repeat the urgency. Science is very clear. If we do not change in the coming 5–10 years the way our societies function, we will be threatening the survival of future generations and all other species on the planet. Nevertheless, you sitting here in this room have the power to reverse all of this. What you can do here is the dream of each one of us: to have the opportunity to be the savors of the planet. It is all up to you.
>
> And yet we stand on the brink of Rio + 20 being another failed attempt, with governments only trying to protect their narrow interests instead of inspiring the World and giving all of us back the faith in humanity that we need. If this happens, it would be a big waste of power, and a big waste of leadership.
>
> You cannot have a document titled 'the future we want' without any mention of planetary boundaries, tipping points, or the Earth's carrying capacity. The text as it stands is completely out of touch with reality. Just to be clear, NGOs here in Rio in no way endorse this document. Already more than 1,000 organizations and individuals have signed in only one day a petition called "The Future We Don't Want" that completely refuses the current text. It does not in any way reflect our aspiration, and therefore we demand that the words "in full participation with civil society" are removed from the first paragraph.
>
> If you adopt the text in its current form, you will fail to secure a future for the coming generations, including your own children.
>
> To mention a few examples:
>
> In the issue of finding resources to implement sustainable development, there are countries using the economic crisis as an excuse, while at the same time spending 100s of billions of dollars subsidizing the fossil fuel industry, the most profitable industry in the world. The first thing you can do is eliminating the existing harmful subsidies, especially fossil fuel subsidies, which was voted as the number one issue during the civil society dialogue.
>
> Under the oceans section, you have failed to give a clear mandate to even start negotiating an implementing agreement to stop the Wild West abuse of the high seas.

> There are many other failures in the document related to women's reproduction health, missed opportunities to start new global treaties on civil society participation and on sustainability reporting, the extraordinary lack of any reference to armed conflicts, nuclear energy (especially after the Fukushima disaster), and many others.
>
> But it is not too late. We do not believe that it is over. You are here for three more days, and you can still inspire us and the world. It would be a shame and a waste for you to only come here and sign off a document. We urge you to create new political will that would make us stand and applaud you as our true leaders.

## 16.3 Not Everyone Agreed with This Assessment

Margareta Wahlström, Special Representative of the Secretary General for Disaster Risk Reduction, considered the conference to have been very useful for raising awareness of about global disaster risk reduction efforts, a point she made in an in interview with the UN News Centre at the sidelines of the conference: "Our hope is that it will be recognized as a strong strategic issue, and that we need to mitigate for risks in order to be able to achieve all our positive development objectives" (UN-Spider 2012, June).

# Chapter 17
# An NGO Saves Belgium

**Extract** Although a model for NGO diplomatic initiatives has been proposed, not every situation is the same; the model won't always be a perfect choice. In other words, the model is a guideline, not a static approach. Chapters 14, 15, 16, 17, 18, and 19 provide case studies of major diplomatic initiatives that used or failed to use some or all of this book's techniques. Regardless of the model used however, before taking action, NGOs need to gather fact, do a professional analysis, conduct professional negotiating, and report on results in a truthful, clear manner.

When reading these case studies, also keep in mind the many other examples already discussed. Chapter 17 examines one of the first instances of a modern humanitarian NGO and certainly one of the most successful at saving lives in an emergency. The book advises NGOs create Study Teams to develop their initiatives, which will reduce the chance for mistakes, but often there just isn't enough time to create such a team. What then? This chapter explores just such an instance.

## 17.1 Introduction

> Never was a nobler work of disinterested goodwill carried through with more tenacity and sincerity and skill and with less thanks either asked or given (Keynes 1920, p. 256).

For details on the relief operation itself, a good start is George Nash's epic three part series, *The Life of Herbert Hoover*, especially Volume Two *The Humanitarian*. Also recommended is *Landslide: A Portrait of President Hoover*, a film by the Public Broadcasting Service. The film doesn't say much about the Belgian relief effort but does describe Herbert Hoover's mind. There is much that is impressive about the effort that any NGO should examine. In most of the other case studies, there was time for a formal time-consuming study group process before engaging in diplomacy; as so often happens in real emergencies, while people dither, others die.

L.W. Roeder, Jr. and A. Simard, *Diplomacy and Negotiation for Humanitarian NGOs*, Humanitarian Solutions in the 21st Century, DOI 10.1007/978-1-4614-7113-4_17,

Time is the enemy. What Hoover accomplished was unprecedented, creates the world's first private, international NGO dedicated to humanitarian relief, and takes on the salvation of an entire nation. There was no blue print for his task, no filing cabinet full of contingency plans; Hoover did have serious engineering skills and a wealth of management experience, especially the management of large numbers of people, and he saw a real moral issue. It was just wrong, he thought, for so many people to suffer, and he was determined not to let bureaucratic or political niceties get in the way of humanitarian relief. In that sense, he was a very modern NGO CEO. It is probably good to keep in mind as well that Hoover had experience in war. While on his honeymoon and taking up a job as a mining engineer in China in 1900, Chinese nationalists rebelled against the Chinese Emperor and foreign influence. The most famous episode was the 55-day attack on the foreign embassies in Peking, which became the subject of a movie, but in addition, Boxer rebels surrounded 800 westerners in Tientsin. Hoover and his wife led the building of barricades to push back the rebels for a month and thought to have rescued many Chinese children as well, while his wife tended to the wounded, so he already understood the dangers to civilians in war.

## 17.2 Speed Was Essential: No Time for a Study Team

Before doing a diplomatic initiative or a field operation, the model proposes asking if the NGO has the resources to do the job, can they go the long haul. Some of the answers will come from precedent, but Hoover had no precedent other than personal experience. He was in the end a resolute, resourceful person without historical data or contingency plans upon which to fall. Further, he did not know how long the war would go on or if America would join. The problem of trench warfare and how to get through to millions of civilians was also new, and then what about taking care of French civilians across the Belgian border? Today's NGO often faces such challenges on a frequent basis; in Hoover's time, it was new. He did not have the luxury of time to develop contingency plans; a century later small and large NGOs need to examine their mandates before leaping into action and consider contingency plans before a crisis occurs using intelligence gathered by professional services and NGOs alliances, and field staffs then fuse that intelligence into a workable knowledge management tool. If the mandate is to feed indigenous peoples suffering from drought, then that means using websites like the Famine Early Warning Systems (www.fews.net) and ReliefWeb.net to look around the globe, see where indigenous people live, and make plans for geographies prone to famine. Figure out where it is possible to work with success. In other words, even the smallest NGO can build a reasonable perspective on what will be needed, by whom and where, and who the allies and donors are likely to be. Hoover did not have that luxury and had to invent his process each day, which is why the techniques in this book are important and Hoover's accomplishments remarkable.

## 17.3 First Events: Saving Americans

Hoover's humanitarian story began in London in August 1914 as an American crisis. Herbert Hoover was a young, successful mining engineer running projects around the globe, with offices down the street from the American Consul General. Americans were delayed in Belgium between a British blockade and advancing German forces. At first only the wealthy could make their way to London. They stayed at the Savoy Hotel and formed impatient, long lines at the Consulate's offices, which caught Hoover's eye. Working in coordination with the US Consul General, Hoover and his wife Lou eventually took over relief operations on his own with little planning. It was an unprecedented emergency, yet Hoover and his wife set up a system of providing loans to refugees to tide them over pending travel home to America. He also assembled a volunteer Committee of American Residents in London for Assistance of American Travelers, including probably the first system of transatlantic money exchange by cable for refugees. He then set up teams to greet Americans on arrival, especially unaccompanied women and children, so that white slavers and crooks couldn't take advantage. IOM does this now for migrants. Interestingly, the Ambassador arranged for a system to reimburse Americans of means, but left Hoover out of the embassy system, so Hoover's committee had to take care of thousands of less well-off Americans through his own resources and those of his committee members (Nash, *The Life Herbert Hoover, Vol. 2, The Humanitarian 1914–1917* 1988a). Eventually, however, with the arrival of an official relief ship from Washington, Hoover convinced officials that he should take over all operations. His NGO was now semiofficial, sponsored by the Ambassador, in today's parlance similar to an NGO contracted to USAID, under the supervision of a government or UN agency, but doing the real day-to-day relief work.

Hoover's efforts were extraordinary, but not without controversy. His committee faced a common complaint now often made by stranded travelers, expecting their Consulate to provide free travel home, which is not normal. Loans were available, not grants, and wealthy Americans often had to travel third class, because there were not enough funds to accommodate first class travel, nor to accommodate a delay in London until better berths were available. Hoover also made a complaint often heard today from NGOs that the capital sent high-salaried officials who knew nothing of local conditions to stay in expensive hotels instead of relying on local residents with local knowledge. He was also irked by government reporting requirements, another common complaint of today's NGOs. By October, after a wave of less affluent Americans went through, Hoover sat back and saw he had managed a wonderful blending of public and private sector assistance. His was not the only effort, nor even the first that fall, which was Theodore Hetzler, of the Fifth Avenue Bank; Hoover made the biggest impact, largely due to energetic zeal and good organizational and political skills. Seeing the need for further work, he transformed his group into the American Committee and continued relief efforts for the duration of the conflict.

## 17.4 And Then Belgium

Saving Americans led to saving millions of stranded Belgian and French citizens from starvation. Belgium, then perhaps the wealthiest country in Europe and neutral, was between France and Germany, and the Kaiser had to circumvent the fortifications along the Franco-German border, so he invaded little Belgium. That's partly what led to the flood of Americans, and the citizens were truly trapped between a British naval blockade and German land forces. To deal with the potential for massive food shortages, Belgian and American businessmen formed a private committee known as the Comite Central de Secours et d'Alimentation. Politically neutral, the committee understood the value of diplomatic friends and secured the patronage of the American and Spanish missions and then quickly secured the distribution of food for 800,000 needy in Brussels; the crisis was quickly turned national. The Comite then went to London, not only to obtain food but also to gain permission to pass food through the naval blockade. The HMG went along; due to a misunderstanding, a suggestion to use American signage to avoid seizures at sea was thought to be a demand that the US Ambassador become the consignee, an unprecedented development in international humanitarian relief—because it hadn't been done before. At about the same time, the Comite also approached Hoover for help.

Hoover's assessment indicated the priority in Europe was Belgium; other impacted European countries had enough food, but Belgium only had 2 weeks of food, a point also made by the Belgians in a plea direct to President Wilson. Within 48 h, Hoover turned impulse into action by creating a fresh committee made up of Hoover's fellow mining engineers and members of the American Committee. He also realized that there was a plethora of fund-raising drives, so in an action that is remindful of the UN's Consolidated Appeals Process (CAP), managed by the Office for the Coordination of Humanitarian Affairs (OCHA), Hoover suggested creating a consolidated relief Commission in order to avoid waste and improve efficiency of relief delivery. Meanwhile, US Ambassador Paige waited without word from Washington to see if he could be the consignee. That way, relief boxes could bear the American flag; the USA was still a neutral. Hoover was impatient and mounted a massive public diplomacy campaign, causing articles to appear in the New York times and other papers in order to both directly influence the government and convince the American public to do the same, and whereas American Committee press releases were mild, Hoover's were strongly worded, citing the immediate potential for starvation. One press report was titled "US Red Tape Starves Brussels." Hoover patience was thin, and on October 17 he issued a statement that a plan of action had been developed with the US Ambassador for the American Committee to take over the relief effort under US government supervision and was just waiting for Washington's approval. Hoover's intended to pressure the US government, while providing it private sector shipping and distribution experience, and at the same time because this would be a public-private enterprise, convince the Belgians and donors that the relief effort would be efficient and fair. Finally, the German government agreed, as did the Department of state. By October 19, Hoover was offered the lead on relief, his condition being that he be in total control.

The following day, Hoover cabled Brussels on the decision to form an entirely American-based relief operation with as members Americans in Brussels and London and with the mission of facilitating relief supplies under American government protection. Hoover then drafted an operational blueprint, right away also figuring out that there might be a problem with diversion of supplies by the Germans. He also needed, so this required a major communications campaign. At first, the diplomatic effort went well, with the Foreign Secretary agreeing to permit shipments on neutral ships to neutral ports; both he and Prime Minister had spoken too soon. Under the British system, for such an agreement, even from the prime minister, there needed to be cabinet approval; the deal fell through when the cabinet rebelled, demanding that German occupation forces be responsible for feeding civilians. Lord Kitchener of the War Office, Winston Churchill at the Admiralty, Lloyd George at the Exchequer, and the Home Secretary all objected, on political, military, and practical grounds. As Nash reported in his history of the crisis, time was running out for the Belgians. Hoover couldn't wait. He ordered the food, and it was on its way and could have been turned around; he likely realized that this coercive action against the British would embarrass them into submission. After all, they needed American to eventually enter the war. On October 22, the cabinet met and went along with the aid, though not with a subsidy, since England too needed food, but the British agreed to allow already-purchased supplies to proceed.[1]

Hoover then formed the American Commission for Relief in Belgium, making the US Ambassadors to Holland, the UK, and Belgium honorary board members, with himself as chair. A law firm represented them pro bono, and the Spanish Ambassadors in Brussels and London became Honorary Co-chairman. He then dropped the American off of the title to form the CRB, though it would go by various names. An oddity in relief operations, CRB was not incorporated[2] and had no legal standing, nor was it sanctioned by the US government. President Wilson refused to go along, lest America be sucked into the war. To make it all work, the CRB operated through the Belgian Comite, which the German occupational authority recognized to manage Belgium relief.

As any contemporary relief manager knows, without money, there is no relief operation, so Hoover set up a massive public diplomacy campaign by November, seen by many as unprecedented in scope, as well as direct appeals to every state governor. It is important to understand that he was inventing this as he went along. Today, NGOs think nothing of attracting celebrities. Hoover did this as well, enlisting George Bernard Shaw and Thomas Hardy. It is important to note here, as Nash did, that Hoover wasn't just mounting a public diplomacy campaign to garner US government support. The British military opposed sending food to occupied Belgium; so by pulling at American heart strings, Hoover knew their pressure would bring British public opinion around to influence the British government not to get in the way.

[1] Though very dramatic, it may be possible that Hoover, who did push for permits personally, may have waited until he had them before ordering supplies.

[2] Today, NGOs should incorporate as nonprofits to be recognized as NGOs, but we still consider CRB as an NGO.

To wrestle logistical problems, the team of engineers and businessmen under Hoover organized docks, depots, and barges to move food down Belgian canals (Nash, *The Life Herbert Hoover, Vol. 2, The Humanitarian 1914–1917* 1988a, p. 39). And like UNHCR or UNICEF would do today, Comite and Hoover men handled rationing, to avoid discrimination. It is interesting as well that he hid many donations from the public eye, for example, from the Belgian government in exile, for fear that private donations would dry up. Hoover also had to deal with stiff competition from businessmen in New York, including Rockefeller, who wanted to do their own effort with Hoover as junior partner. His was a delicate balancing act; Hoover succeeded because he developed a good relationship with the US Ambassador, and the Belgian government in exile. Through his good offices, Hoover arranged the partnership favorably to himself and thus insured reliable distributions of relief supplies. Hoover was the most influential humanitarian in the world at that moment in time. It just shows what an NGO can accomplish through public diplomacy and traditional diplomacy with governments. Indeed, when Woodrow Wilson made a tour of Europe as part of the Paris peace talks, he brought Hoover with him when in Belgium, because Hoover was clearly the "most beloved American in the country," and it needs to be remembered; Hoover did his work as an NGO leader, not a government official (Cooper, *Woodrow Wilson: A Biography* 2009, p. 502).

# Chapter 18
# The ReliefWeb Project

**Extract** Although a model for NGO diplomatic initiatives has been proposed, not every situation is the same; the model won't always be a perfect choice. In other words, the model is a guideline, not a static approach. Chapters 14, 15, 16, 17, 18, and 19 provide case studies of major diplomatic initiatives that used or failed to use some or all of this book's techniques. Regardless of the model used however, before taking action, NGOs need to gather fact, do a professional analysis, conduct professional negotiating, and report on results in a truthful, clear manner.

When reading these case studies, also keep in mind the many other examples already discussed. Chapter 18 examines the creation of the first disaster website by the United Nations. It was developed in partnership between many NGOs, governments, the United Nations, and the Red Cross movement and industry. As a result, it can be a model for future such partnerships.

## 18.1 History

Relevant, timely reliable information is essential to successful humanitarian outcomes. Reliwefweb.int is the premier disaster information website at the United Nations, especially for response.

This is contributed by Sharon Rusu, International Affairs Consultant, and Strategic Planning Facilitator, UNISDR.

ReliefWeb evolved out of various managed information systems within the UN system. In the 1980s, the United Nations Disaster Relief Organization (UNDRO) was in charge of disaster relief and saw the need for an information system to support the humanitarian response to disaster aid. As a result, UNDRO and the secretariat for the International Decade for Disaster Risk Reduction were responsible for developing the precursors to ReliefWeb: UNIENet and IERIS, among others. Within the UN system, there has always been a need for timely and reliable

L.W. Roeder, Jr. and A. Simard, *Diplomacy and Negotiation for Humanitarian NGOs*, Humanitarian Solutions in the 21st Century, DOI 10.1007/978-1-4614-7113-4_18,

information. Information is central to the coordination of joint humanitarian response. Gathering information, processing it, adding value with easy navigation, maps, statistics, analysis, relevant linkages, filters, and archiving supports informed humanitarian decisions.

Following the Gulf War in 1991, and General Assembly Resolution 46/182, the Department for Humanitarian Affairs (UNDHA), headed by the office of the Emergency Relief Coordinator, was formed. ReliefWeb was a child of this new agency.

In the 1990s, though UN information systems had been developed over many years for disaster relief, they had some way to go to meet the increasing challenges of humanitarian emergencies. It took the Rwandan crisis in 1994, for Member states to acknowledge that early action had somehow been forestalled through the lack of timely and coherent information system. "We need something that is going to work and add value" was the mantra of the stakeholders after Rwanda. Recognizing the need for a global information response capacity that met the emergency preparedness needs of the international relief community, states came together with UN agencies and NGOs. Meetings were held in Geneva, New York, and Washington to discuss how best to develop a robust humanitarian information system that would provide timely and trustworthy information to support humanitarian relief efforts. ReliefNet (as it was then called but later renamed ReliefWeb) was the product of those consultations as was the decision to make its home in UNDHA, and it quickly received media attention for its innovative nature (Economist Staff 1995).

The challenge for the new system was to provide information that would directly benefit relief UN, government, and NGO agencies and operations. This was a tall order, especially when taking into account the number of agencies and their independent and often-overlapping mandates. What was needed was an agreed plan supported by member states with content supplied voluntarily by humanitarian partners. Most important was the need for rapid and sustainable access by users.

In the early 1990s, the Internet was very new and untested by the UN. But it was developed and ready just in time to support ReliefWeb. At the same time, the donors and sister UN agencies responded positively providing support and expertise. Among early developers were Matthias Warnes, Government of Germany; George-Andre Simon, World Food Program; Andy Andrea, Action-Aid; Dennis King, USAid; and Larry Roeder, at that time a career foreign affairs officer with the State Department whose advice and support in the early days was incalculable. UNHCR provided the services of Sharon Rusu on secondment, the designer of the website, Daniel Zalik, was contracted and a talented, and young team of editors and web developers took ReliefWeb forward.

An essential demand was that the clients understand the need for ReliefWeb as a specific product and even the Internet as a general tool. Selling the later proved hard at first because of the newness of the Internet; at a conference of over a 1,000 representatives of NGOs, UN agencies, the IFRC, and officials from many governments at the US Department of State HQ in Washington, DC, a discussion on the plenary floor with ADRA brought into focus the economic benefits, which today are taken for granted, namely that instead of using expensive fax machines to share information, the Internet is essentially free and more efficient, allowing millions of dollars then used for telecommunications to be diverted to food and medical supplies.

Further, it allowed for the potential of updating field-relevant data every day. Field trips to former Soviet republics like Azerbaijan and to Sudan were also used to have direct contact with and experts from NGOs and other relief agencies on the practicality of sharing information in conflicted environments. For example, in workshops in rebel-controlled South Sudan and in the supply camp of Lokichokio in Kenya, experts discussed using ReliefWeb to track mine fields, and changes in potable water and useable roads through reports are submitted to the site by field workers. These discussions were held not only with international relief agencies but also rebel forces and the Government of Sudan to convince them that ReliefWeb was not about sharing military information. This was an entirely new concept, having easy access to maps, twice daily reports, and other operational information, right along with political reporting.[1] Recognizing how new the Internet was, the designers also wanted to be ReliefWeb to be an easy portal to use, so site was tested in high schools in Virginia for ease of use and passed easily (Hudson 1996). In Chap. 1, the authors proposed that study group should often include field assessments as an essential part of deciding on field negotiations. Assessments were also a major feature tested by the UN as a tool to allow more efficient expenditures and deployment of supplies (Warns 1995). Though not study group as envisaged in Chap. 1, the intense interaction between NGOs and other agencies produced an effective peer review of the idea of using the Internet and especially web pages as an operational tool. At the time in history, it was the largest such cooperative study project ever attempted linking the Internet and relief operations.

Within less than 9 months, the system was ready to "go live" on the Internet. To ensure that the content was timely, reliable, and representative of the needs of all stakeholders in relief efforts, agreements with 250 partners were negotiated. An advisory committee was formed comprising experts from ICRC, IFRC, WFP, UNHCR, and others. It was a wonderfully rapid response to a need that had been identified by member states, the United Nations System, and NGOs; the Internet was ready to make it universally available. It was a wonderful time, a seemingly never-to-be repeated time of cooperation.

## 18.2 Coverage and Content

ReliefWeb's stated purpose "to strengthen the response capacity of the relief community through the timely dissemination of reliable information on dangerous natural phenomena and conflict" required 24 h coverage across all time zones. Beginning

[1]Some of the entities that make major contributions and suggestions were UNICEF, UNHCR, DHA (now OCHA), ADRA, American Refugee Committee, CARE, Catholic Relief Services, International Medical Corps, the International Organization for Migration, National Museums of Kenya, CIESIN, Specialized Disaster Systems, Inc., MapInfo, SAIC (Science Applications International Corporation), InterSat, Lutheran World Federation, Operation Lifeline Sudan (OLS), World Food Program. The largest initial donors were the United states, the United Kingdom, Switzerland, Austria, and Finland, as well as the European Union (Lyman 1996, Dec 4).

with Geneva in 1995, the coverage expanded to New York in 1997and Kobe in 2001. Today, global coverage is assured by editors in Nairobi, New York, Greece, Spain, Italy, and Bangkok.

ReliefWeb's content, including documents, reports, maps, and web links, derives from online sources and from a network of source partner/providers. The online editors are responsible for acquiring information from the UN, NGOs, media, academic, and regional sources. Managing editors provide supervision and oversight. The online editors collect information but much now is supplied by partners who submit content. The editors concentrate their efforts on humanitarian disasters and emergencies, sometimes over a long period. A concrete example is potential for flooding in Pakistan 2012. Though the monsoon season is just beginning and the current situation has not been designated a disaster by OCHA, ReliefWeb will be already monitoring to ensure coverage in the event that the humanitarian impact is sufficient to have an OCHA Situation Report sent out. Though this year's flood potential may never "evolve" into a disaster, ReliefWeb will monitor preventively.

The people working in OCHA, other UN agencies, governments, and NGOs, can see which events are being covered. There is a strong commitment among ReliefWeb staff and partners to work cooperatively to support emergency response whether it is for disaster relief or conflicts.

ReliefWeb also follows the evolution of a conflict. This requires a huge amount of work and knowledge. ReliefWeb online and managing editors possess tremendous knowledge about their sources—most importantly, they have to know the provenance of sources because they have to be able to defend what they publish. To ensure that information admits of challenge requires a strong understanding of research methodologies and how these apply to assessing different sources of information. ReliefWeb editors do not just say "I find that interesting. Let's post it." Behind such decisions is a corporate plan and information source standards. The standards ReliefWeb applies to source acquisition derive from the principles that underpin its practice: reliability, timeliness, trustworthiness, integrity, and independence. How do you measure independence? One way is to provide total transparency regarding the methods and criteria you use to acquire and assess information before you publish it. If ReliefWeb cannot defend the origin and nature of the source, it does not use it. If it is clear that the reporting is biased or otherwise unreliable—it will not be published. For ReliefWeb, authority as a publisher rests on its assurance that its information is trustworthy and defensible.

## 18.3 ReliefWeb Today

Today, following two redesigns since 1995, ReliefWeb has a brand new platform that is web based. New features include improved navigation and personalized filtering and soon a ReliefWeb application for mobile phones. Partners can now submit content from anywhere in the world, and editors can manage content from anywhere so long as they have a browser and Internet access. This makes for a highly flexible and versatile system.

The major users of ReliefWeb continue to be humanitarian affairs desk officers in the UN, governments, or NGOs. ReliefWeb's advanced analytics capacity keeps on top of their information needs for financial tracking of donations, maps, briefing kits, updates, disaster coverage, a new vacancy submission system, and linkages to other relevant sites and information.

ReliefWeb today is the decision-support tool that was promised in 1995. Its content, technology, and applications seamlessly provide support to humanitarian decisions makers worldwide with the information they require to take informed decisions.

# Chapter 19
# Die Deutsche Liga für Völkerbund (DLfV)

**Extract** Although a model for NGO diplomatic initiatives has been proposed, not every situation is the same; the model won't always be a perfect choice. In other words, the model is a guideline, not a static approach. Chapters 14, 15, 16, 17, 18 and 19 provide case studies of major diplomatic initiatives that used or failed to use some or all of this book's techniques. Regardless of the model used however, before taking action, NGOs need to gathering fact, do a professional analysis, conduct professional negotiating and report on results in a truthful, clear manner.

When reading these case studies, also keep in mind the many other examples already discussed. Chapter 19 explores an effort by a German NGO that acted in partnership with its government to save its country from political disaster. Though "Die Liga" failed in its goal, it used many of the techniques proposed in the book and provides many useful lessons that might be used in countries emerging from revolution or military occupation.

## 19.1 Introduction

**Note** The authors are especially grateful for the assistance of the staffs of the US Department of State Library; the German Foreign Office Archives as well as the Walther Schücking Institute for International Law at Kiel University; Dr. Jost Dülffer, Professor für Neuere Geschichte, University of Cologne; Dr. Peter Macalister-Smith, Editor, Journal of the History of International Law, Max Planck Institute for Comparative Public Law and International Law; Wolfram von Scheliha, Global and European Studies Institute, University of Freiburg; and Professor Christoph M. Kimmich, former president of Brooklyn University, who wrote one of the premier textbooks on Germany and the League of Nations. Also consulted were declassified manuscripts held in the US Library of Congress and the National Archives which belonged to the US delegation to the treaty of Peace.

L.W. Roeder, Jr. and A. Simard, *Diplomacy and Negotiation for Humanitarian NGOs*, Humanitarian Solutions in the 21st Century, DOI 10.1007/978-1-4614-7113-4_19,

NGOs operate according to a broad spectrum of association with governments. At one end, MSF is totally independent. Others, while legally independent, intentionally reach out to their national authority or other institutional donors for financial or political support. A third group operates in a formal public–private partnership with the government.[1] To illustrate the benefits and dangers of public–private partnering, a good choice is Die Deutsche Liga für Völkerbund (the German League for the League of Nations[2]). Die Liga tried to save Germany from the anger of France, the UK, the USA, and Italy in 1919 by adopting the political message in Woodrow Wilson's famous 14 points in the form of a proposed draft League of Nations Charter. Though their effort failed, Die Liga deserves mention because of its methods and what it tried to do, despite operating in an extraordinarily difficult political environment that included an attempted revolution in 1918–1919. NGOs in today's politically stressed nations like Syria, Cuba, or the Congo could try to do the same thing in order to save their countries, so NGOs need to understand what worked, what did not, and why. Finally, Die Liga was an NGO with a massive public following in its early days,[3] but it was also tightly tied to the German government that emerged from the fall of the Kaiser. This meant that when German membership in the League of Nations was rejected, the popularity of Die Liga plummeted. There are many NGOs operating today that have also been accused of being too close to their donors or to governments. Rather than point to any one of them as an example, which could be sensitive, it was deemed more appropriate to discuss an extinct NGO whose officials are now dead. The lessons are still relevant.

---

[1] GDIN (the Global Disaster Information Network) was another example of a public–private partnership. It was begun by the office of Vice President Al Gore in the 1990s and had two parts. The domestic program was not an NGO and was entirely managed and staffed by the US government, but the international part was an NGO which gained legal nonprofit status and had an Executive Director who was elected by the members, officials from governments (local and national), the UN, the IFRC, NGOs, academic centers, and a few corporations. However, though GDIN was legally independent as an organization, the Executive Director was also a US State Department official who took instructions from the Office of the Vice President and the Department.

[2] A more felicitous translation perhaps is the German League of Nations Union. Die Liga is worth a major monograph in its own right, tracing its origins to the end of life during the Nazi era. We recommend the finding aids "Catalogue of Files and Microfilms of the German Foreign Ministry Archives 1920–1945, Volume II," compiled and edited by George O. Kent, Historical Office, US Department of State. This Catalogue and the microfilms of the files are available in the National Archives, Washington, DC. The Handakten (reference files) von Staatssekretär Simson are kept in the Political Archive of the Foreign Ministry *Auswärtiges Amt* in Berlin. Also relevant is Jost Dülffer's article "De l'internationalism a l'expansionism: la Ligue Allemand pour la Sociéte des Nations," *Guerres mondiales et conflits contemporains*, 39 (1989), pp. 23–39. The most recent German sources are Joachim Wintzer, *Deutschland und der Volkerbund 1918–1926* Paderborn: Ferdinand Schöningh Verlag, 2006, a massive (634 pp.), heavily detailed exploration of Germany's relationship with the League of Nations, which also covers some of the NGOs active in the cause. More specifically on Die Liga is Günter Hohne, "Deutsche Liga für Volkerbund" in Fricke, Dieter et al., eds., *Lexikon zur Parteiengeschichte,* vol. 2 (1984).

[3] Unlike some other national leagues, Die Liga was never a mass, membership organization. It did not conduct membership drives (lest it dilute the influence of the government) and its members were appointed rather than taken in upon application (Kimmich 2012).

**Note** To some experts, Die Liga was primarily a group of well-meaning advocates of a "true" League of Nations, but with a strong legal bent, with compulsory arbitration, and universal disarmament—and thus totally innocent of political realities. That anyone ever hoped that such a scheme would be adopted (or that the allies could be shamed into adopting it) is a sign of that innocence. At the same time, a League of Nations as conceived by Die Liga, were it to have been adopted, would have gotten Germany off the hook after the war, a top priority to the hard-nosed professionals of the Foreign Ministry. Die Liga served a useful purpose, proposing an alternative to the allies' League of Nations formulation while not being identified with official German policy.

## 19.2 Founding

Die Liga was probably started in December 1918 by Ernst Jäckh[4] and Matthias Erzberger (later assassinated for signed the armistice) and had the approval and financial support of the Foreign Ministry (Jäckh and Erzberger had been sounding out sympathetic political parties since the summer months). Die Liga also drew on the ideas/ideals of leading members of Germany's pacifist organizations (e.g., Walther Schücking,[5] Ludwig Quidde,[6] Hans Wehberg[7]) and on the Gesellshaft für Völkerrecht (German Society of International Law), which began the effort, according to its own printed account (Niemeyer, *Draft of a Constitution of the League of Nations* 1919).

## 19.3 Purpose

Die Liga seems to have been a typical association of German dignitaries, a mixture of an NGO, a think tank, an association to advance research, and a public advocate. Its initial aim may have been more about being a popular proponent of pacifism and

[4]Ernst Friedrich Wilhelm Jäckh *(b.1875 in Urach, d. 1959 in New York City)* was a liberal who believed in parliamentary democracy. He was also a consultant with the Foreign Ministry and an enthusiast for Wilson's ideas.

[5]Schücking was a liberal politician and professor of public international law, the first German judge at the Permanent Court of International Justice in the Hague and one of the six German delegates to the Paris Peace Conference.

[6]Ludwig Quidde was a German pacifist (associated with *Deutsche Friedensgesellschaft*, the German Peace Society) and a critic of Emperor Wilhelm II and lived through the Bismarck era, the Hohenzollern Empire, and the Weimar Republic and then escaped to Switzerland during the Nazi era. In 1927 he was awarded the Nobel Peace Prize.

[7]Instructor of international law and a pacifist. Walther Schucking founded the pacifist doctrine of international law. From 1924 until his death, Wehberg was the editor of the *Journal of International Peace and Organization*.

League of Nations thinking inspired by Woodrow Wilson, not a think tank to save Germany; the pressures of the Versailles process and probably government lobbying and funding led them to boldly propose their own draft charter for the yet-to-be-created League of Nations.[8] Die Liga was also founded by some of the prospective members of the German peace delegation, perhaps to strengthen their position within the delegation and within the elite and to give it a broader societal basis. However, they were only a part of the whole apparatus with others of more traditional views, often overwhelmed in their thinking (whether liberal or conservative thinking), with questions of national honor, etc. They were also embarking on multilateral diplomacy, only then coming into its own in its modern form, and like most of the participants were somewhat unprepared. What they found was that gaining agreement from the allies was too steep a hill to climb.

## 19.4 Mistakes in Analysis: Not Understanding the Enemy or the Allies

Germany may have misunderstood that Wilson's zeal for his 14 points was not as strong as his desire to create his League. They also may have misjudged the anger of the allied governments, especially France; perhaps like the inquiry in the states, none of the subcommittees appeared to focus on that point. As a result, not properly studying the allies, one might argue that the work of Die Liga was too legalistic and economic in nature; it did not address the core issues of the combatant nations gathering in Paris. On the other hand, it could also be that they deliberately ignored the probable attitudes in order to promote their own ideas. In the situation of 1918/1919, Wilson's 14 points seemed to be the only suitable lever to change the allied policy towards Germany. What other argument could they have used? The ideas of Die Liga were too legalistic and economic driven, but in fairness, most German diplomats had an educational background as lawyers, and that's the way they thought. Failure was probably inevitable; they stuck to statements by Wilson[9] as a lifeline to a peaceful future, envisaging that the Paris Peace Conference would inculcate a moral climate of fairness.

Wilson envisaged a brilliant idea in the League; even he seemed unprepared for the venom of Paris, which would flatly reject German membership in the League. In fact, one of the major briefing papers brought across the Atlantic by Wilson team from the Inquiry proposed making Germany a member, a position also favored by

[8] A brief analysis of the German proposals is offered by David Hunter Miller in (Miller, *The Drafting of the Covenant* 1928b).

[9] *Papers Relating to the Foreign Relations of the United States*, 1918, Supplement 1, The World War, Vol. I, pp. 12–17, January 8, 1918: Address of the President of the United States delivered at a Joint Session of the Two Houses of Congress

the UK. The paper was developed by Manley Ottmer Hudson,[10] who argued for avoiding a potential alternative League (perhaps fearing something akin to NATO vs. Warsaw Pact?). Hudson suggested that the eight great powers should be members precisely to avoid another balance of power crisis, so this meant including Austria, the British Empire, France, Germany, Italy, Japan, and possibly Russia with the United States (Hudson, Undated).

What the Germans and the United States both faced was the reality that except for the United States, the allies, especially France, were less interested in reconciliation than retribution, and everyone mistrusted the new German government because of its socialist roots, which was linked to fear of the Bolshevists and because Prussian aristocrats were still influential. Although Wilson and his team clearly had a distaste for socialists and worried about events in Germany, the Social Democrats (SPD) was the backbone of the Weimar Republic; many others only supported the republican constitution out of reason, not out of conviction. The allies must have been aware of that, and the leading representatives of the SPD were mostly not radical but quite reasonable, although the party program was still based on Marxism (which was a problem for the allies). Nevertheless, as can be seen in reports in the manuscript collection at the US Library of Congress, the allies mistrusted any German, regardless of his social status or his political views.

Germany probably also did not help its position by initially trying to negotiate directly with the United States, not the UK, France, or Italy. That must have irritated the three European powers, so finally on November 18, 1918, Clemenceau sent a secret message to Wilson demanding that messages from Germany to one of the allied powers had to be shared with all of the powers at the same time.[11]

To be fair, confusion over Wilson's zeal for his own words may make sense. Wilhelm Solf,[12] the Secretary of Foreign Affairs (October–December, 1918), had conducted per-armistice discussions with Washington that led him and the new Die Liga to think the Americans were certain that the allies would support Wilson (American Association for International Conciliation 1919, Nov, #144). This would lead to the German delegation being blindsided on arrival at Paris. Neither the Foreign Office nor Die Liga may have fully examined the political desires of the allies. If true, that's a fundamental mistake any NGO must avoid. If you don't take the time to do this properly, you may assume that the political reality is one thing when it is actually totally different. It doesn't pay to live in an ivory tower, in other words.

[10] Hudson was a US attorney, expert in international law. He became a judge at the Permanent Court of International Justice, joined the International Law Commission, was an international conflict mediator, and gained a professorship at Harvard University. He was also nominated twice for the Nobel Prize. He was also a member of the Law Department of the League of Nations.

[11] *Papers Relating to the Foreign Relations of the United States*, 1918, Supplement 1, The World War, Vol. II, page 17, Message from Col. House to the President on Communication from Clemenceau

[12] Solf's wife Johanna Dotti would become an active member of the German resistance to Adolf Hitler.

Informal contacts between Germans and various liaisons from the French and American side in 1918–1919 led the Germans to assume that opportunities existed for getting the German view accepted at Paris. Did the allies deceive or did the Germans deceive themselves?[13] This is unclear; if the right questions were not asked, perhaps people were just talking past each other. Know the other side as best as you can, what motivates them and what scares them. That is just as important as listening to their public statements, often more so, giving what some call *positional power* because it enables you to position your proposals in a way that will be acceptable to the other side; it only works if your proposals are based on solid analysis.

Thinking Germany was on safe ground, Solf made the case for this approach with representatives of German State governments 2 weeks before the armistice. Although many German diplomats might not have been professionals in today's terms, they certainly had training or exposure to those with it (Dülffer 2012; Kimmich 2012), and actually, given Wilson's pronouncements and the strength of the US Armed Forces in Europe, their posture had a certain sense, though their experts should have understood that their government's ties to socialism was a real problem and that Wilson hated the socialists and was unlikely to deal with a German government in an unsettled political state.

## 19.5 Never Insult the Other Side

This happened when the Germans blundered on the question of war blame. With the distance of time, today's experts can disagree on the real causes of the war, though all agree the issues were complex; France, Britain, and Italy were still smoldering and blamed Germany. As Lloyd George put it, "Critics after the event forget that peace had to be made in an atmosphere still reeking with the fumes of war and still more or less dominated by the military spirit" (Howard-Ellis 1928, p. 44). "That should have been clear; and American government propaganda and that of the other powers during the war also painted the picture of an evil empire, which inflamed the American public. Regardless of the real causes, and even though the government the allies were negotiating with was post Kaiser, the new German government and Die Liga should have also realized that even if they did not believe their country was "to blame," taking that tone with the governments would rub salt into political wounds; yet on Dec 2, 1918, (the month Die Liga was formed), the German government recommended to the allies that a special fact-finding Commission make the actual

[13] There were also all kinds of informal, behind-the-scenes contacts between the allies and the Germans while the peace conference was in session in Paris. There is evidence in the German Foreign Ministry archives on contacts with the Americans and with the French (and probably with the British), many of them by Germans who had no official standing but reconnected with contacts dating from before the war. The information they brought back would end up at the German Foreign Ministry, some to be believed and some not. For the diplomats it was obviously useful to have this kind of backchannel for the latest on what was happening at Paris. We first learned of German NGO participation through the diary of David Hunter Miller; the conversation was probably among these.

determination of blame" (US Department of State 1942, pp. 71–75). The allies decided to not respond to the idea at all, agreeing that guilt had already been proven. Some experts are of the opinion this maneuver was actually an intentional provocation by Foreign Minister Ulrich Graf von Brockdorff-Rantzau (Dülffer 2012) and Brockdorff (who led the German delegation to Paris) was adamant about not admitting guilt for the war, the reasons being both political and legal. If it was an intentional slight, an odd move, it played well domestically.

## 19.6 Did Die Liga Have a Chance?

Realistically, the League being the first such world body to be attempted, agreement to German proposals would have meant asking the European allies to forget fresh wounds and set aside generations of animosity. As a result, Die Liga's efforts in Paris may never had a real chance, and while members of Die Liga were part of the German official peace delegation, their work, in fact, turned out to be quite peripheral to what the delegation was attempting to do. Their proposals were often sound, if overly legalistic, and despite failure at the peace talks, Die Liga continued to advance the League of Nations through the Second World War, unfortunately later being subsumed by the Nazi Party. Indeed, some of their members and friends like Ludwig Quidde would eventually escape Germany during the Nazi period.[14]

One also has to bear in mind that when Die Liga was founded in 1918, the German elite was absolutely divided about how to deal with the situation. One issue was negotiating peace; another was how to push back the actual threat of a Bolshevist revolution in Germany. Except for the Kaiser, who moved to Holland, and the other ruling houses, the personnel remained more or less the same (unlike after 1945 when there was some change). In view of the fact that this personnel had more or less supported the Kaiser and his goals in the war, the conditions of the Versailles peace treaty appeared to be a deep humiliation. But how to deal with it? One group pleaded

[14] Apropos Die Liga after 1933, Dülffer's essay has information on that. Die Liga's near-voluntary adaptation to Nazism early on, its relatively obscure existence after Germany left the League, an official decision to disband it in 1935/36 or so (stayed when Hitler talked, not seriously, about a return to the League), and a subsequent fading from the scene. While this may support the concern about NGOs getting burnt by being too close to the regime, in this case Die Liga was no different from most other organizations and associations in Germany at the time, whether close to the regime or not.

What's significant in the 1920s is that Die Liga was active and usefully employed until Germany entered the League; it pretty much lost much of its usefulness after that. Before then, Die Liga helped make the government's case for a "true" League (which underscored Germany's determination to keep its distance from Geneva), and the diplomats were prepared to tolerate Die Liga's more extreme views/activities. In fact in the summer of 1921, upon the recommendation of the French, Die Liga, led by former German Ambassador to the United States Count Bernstorff, was admitted into the Union of League of Nations Societies (Walters 1952 (reprint 1965). But after 1926, with Germany a member of the League, the tolerance faded and Die Liga lost most of its support from the government; it would be interesting to see on what occasions after that the Foreign Ministry resorted to it again, but it would have been relatively seldom).

not to sign the treaty. But the General Staff made it clear this would certainly have led to a continuation of a war Germany couldn't win. Germany would have been occupied by the allies and the peace conditions would have been even worse. The other group around Erzberger, Ebert, and others argued in favor of signing the treaty. Their strategy was to show compliance with allied demands and to improve the peace conditions from this position. This was the strategy of all governments of the Weimar Republic, and it was called "Fulfillment Policy" (Erfüllungspolitik) and later "Rapproachment Policy" (Verständigungspolitik) which turned out to be, to some extent, successful (reduction of reparations, the seven Locarno treaties, etc.[15]). This kind of strategy was, however, very disputed in the German public and in parts of the elite. Die Liga has to be seen as an organization to promote the "Fulfillment Policy" within the elite and the public; the promotion of the Fulfillment Policy within the elite was considered more important than in the public.

## 19.7 Funding

Funding for Die Liga came from the Rat der Volksbeauftragten[16] (Council of the People's Deputies) through the Legal Department of the Auswärtiges Amt—foreign office, which provided an initial contribution of 100,000 marks and then 450,000

---

[15] Drawing in part on ideas developed by Die Liga at the start of its efforts, these treaties were the result of an effort by the Weimar Republic to rehabilitate Germany politically in the eyes of the rest of Europe and lay down a mechanism for peace management, entry of Germany into the League of Nations, and its own economic resurgence. One was the Rhineland Pact between Germany, France, Belgium, the UK, and Italy in which the first three agreed not to attack each other and the latter two nations were guarantors. An attack on one was an attack on all.

Germany also signed arbitration conventions with France and Belgium and arbitration treaties with Poland and Czechoslovakia, disputes to be handled by an arbitration tribunal or the Permanent Court of International Justice. France also signed treaties with Poland and Czechoslovakia, pledging mutual assistance should Germany attack.

[16] A country in turmoil can be a confusing entity for negotiations or NGO activity. A good contemporary example is post-revolutionary Egypt in 2012 or Germany in 1919, which was close to collapse. In late October 1918 the Navy planned one last big battle with the British fleet, but sailors in Wilhelmshaven and Kiel mutinied, setting up councils similar to Russian soviets. Within days the revolution spread to the Western front and Germany's major cities and ports. This became known as the November Revolution. The Kaiser then abdicated, followed by the King of Bavaria, which was declared a socialist Republic, though not in the Russian mold. Chancellor, Max von Baden, handed power to Friedrich Ebert, the leader of the German Social Democrat Party (SDP). Due to the revolution, the Council of the People's Deputies (*Rat der Volksbeauftragten*) was then government (Nov 1918–Feb 1919). Communists were heavily involved, but unlike in the Russian revolution, an accommodation was made to blend the aristocracy into the new Germany. The Council organized a ceasefire on November 11, 1918, and the election of a National Assembly in December. The leading political party (SPD) also refused to go the route of Russian Soviets because of hatred and mistrust of the Bolsheviks. In addition to all of this was the risk of a full-scale armed uprising, and indeed there was the Spartacist uprising, putdown by right-wing militia or Freikorps. Then on August 11, 1919, the revolution ended with the establishment of the Weimar Constitution.

marks annually in 1919 and 1920, so there was a tight relationship between the League and the government (Kimmich 1976), though its draft charter speaks of political independence. However, as seen with many NGOs of today that receive government funding, Die Liga being funded by the government did not mean it or any of the other similarly funded were just the voice of the government, although they, of course, did not act entirely against it. But nevertheless, they acted quite independently. It is quite usual that such kind of associations were financed by the government or by single ministries. One is reminded of the Society for the Advancement of the Study of Russia founded in 1913, but there are others as well. It is our impression that the members worked hard to develop their own ideas, and they declared ownership, saying that the draft was theirs, not that of the government. It listed some specific purposes: spreading the idea of a League of Nations among the German populace, seeking to influence foreign countries to accept Germany's version of a "true" League of Nations, and do research on League of Nations issues. But they did not do this in isolation; all of this was closely coordinated with the Foreign Ministry, which justified the FM's subsidies. Funds also came from liberal automobile industrialist Robert Bosch,[17] who believed in reconciliation between France and Germany, but rejected the treaty as setting the foundation for future conflict; however, he did invest 300,000 marks into Die Liga in the hope that creating a world organization would build new trust between governments. Die Liga had other corporate members as well—various unions, associations, and political party groups. They too may have made contributions.

However, once Germany was rejected from membership in the League of Nations, subsidies were reduced to 50,000–75,000 a year and Die Liga may have become a mouthpiece for the government at that time. Wintzer's figures are 225,000 M (1920), 400,000 M (1922), 600,000 M (1923), 20,400 M (1924), 25,000 M (1925), and 50,000 M (1925 and 1926). Given the hyperinflation in 1922–1923, the figures are not readily comparable.

## 19.8 Membership of Die Liga

Their first purpose was to pool representatives of different parts of the society, from academia, the industry, media, ministries, etc., which shared the same interest in one particular topic, in this case the idea of the League of Nation, in order to promote this idea to the government and to the public. The members are mostly notabilities, representatives of the elite; they were never designed to be a mass organization. As a result, Die Liga had very powerful politicians as members including various

[17]Bosch would work hard after the Nazis took over to save many people from deportation and death.

Chancellors of Germany. It was also associated with the German Peace Cartel, a loose confederation of most pacifist organizations in Weimar Germany. While most did not agree to Germany admitting guilt for the war, as demanded by the treaty of Versailles, all were opposed to a resurgence of German militarism. The League later admitted right-wing politicians and when the Nazi Party took off was under their control until it faded into obscurity after Germany withdrew from the League. Initially, the roll may have been about 1,000, consisting of some of the nation's best legal minds and influential, liberal political, academic, commercial, and industrial figures.[18] Representing the government was Friedrich Ebert (first president of Germany and head of the SPD), Hugo Haase (acting chairman of the Provisional Government [Rat der Volksbeauftragten]), Prince Max von Baden (served briefly as Chancellor of Germany in Nov–Dec, 1918), Wilhelm Solf (who insisted on direct talks with the United States), Ambassador Count von Bernsdorff (former German Ambassador to the US),[19] Matthias Erzberger (later assassinated for signed the armistice), and Hugo Preuß,[20] Minister of the Interior (Bernstorff 1918). All of the political parties were also represented except the Nationalists and Communists. Eventually, the roll of supporters (not formal members) reached ten million (Kimmich 1976, p. 15). That's perhaps not surprising and something for current NGOs to keep in mind. If it can capture the minds of the population, many will follow, as it did in the UK where at its high point around 500,000 citizens paid to belong to the League of Nations Union[21] and attended rallies (Joyce 1978, p. 164); nominal membership in 1933 rose to one million (Pugh 1974 (dissertation)). Die Liga support however sharply declined after rejection of German membership in the League of Nations. This was a very short period, of course, since Germany was excluded from the League of Nations at Versailles.

## 19.9 The Process

The German International Law Society went to its roots and based their charter on a study of international law, of precedence, and how to apply the results to the facts on the ground in order to design a practical charter—not politics. According to

[18] Might be too high a figure

[19] Count Bernsdorff would later represent the German League of Nations Society to the League of Nations.

[20] Preuß was Jewish, which the Nazi Party used against him, saying that because the Weimar Republic was created by a Jew, it was un-German. He was even mentioned in the 1940 Nazi propaganda film Der Ewige Jude by Fritz Hippler.

[21] The LNU had as members some of the more important figures in the British Empire and membership in 1933 was about one million.

Theodore Niemeyer of the group,[22] the design began even before the armistice, bringing in reputable German international law scholars and other experts with a common conviction that the League of Nations had to be propagated by pacifists.[23] The umbrella body they created was called the German League for the League of Nations (Die Liga). Encouraged by speeches of President Wilson, they figured on receiving a fair peace (as did the German government) and focused on (a) pushing back on traditional German militarism and (b) advancing a structural architecture to enable the philosophy of a League of Nations. Here they made a similar mistake to Wilson's Inquiry. The Inquiry reviewed how to build a League and how to cut up the German Empire; it never examined the political feelings of the US Senate or how to effectively deal with them, a failure which led to the Senate denying accession to the League and effectively ending Wilson's political days. Similarly, Die Liga League failed to fully examine the political desires of the allies, and thus the German delegation to Paris was blindsided.

Today, some argue that NGOs should have no ties to governments; indeed, some argue that if an NGO accepts government at all, it isn't an NGO. That's incorrect. Very likely, most of the German pacifists did not want to wait for the government; and they probably worried about the military class, which hadn't accepted responsibility for defeat. In addition, Europe had just suffered a brutal war, which many blamed on nationalism, imperialism and especially the Germany military. Yet, the people were also loyal Germans, swimming in new and uncharted political waters; they were glad to have the German government as a partner; they ran their own show.

To develop a "practical proposal," the group formed a broad-Study Team, using Wilson's speeches as inspiration as well as a book on a possible League of Nations written by German Secretary of State Mathias Erzberger[24] who became chairman of the League's executive committee. Walther Schücking, later the first German on the

[22]The author, Dr. Theodor Niemeyer, was a good choice, in part because he knew English and the American culture. Niemeyer was a Professor of International Law at Kiel University and in 1914–1915 the Kaiser Wilhelm Exchange Professor at Columbia University. It is interesting to note that he, like many Germans, saw the war as a struggle for the preservation of German culture (Niemeyer, *The Causes of the War* 1915). Niemeyer gained international attention as a defense attorney for his successful defense of Soghomon Tehlirian in 1921. Tehlirian had assassinated the Grand Vizir Talaat Pasha, who many was felt responsible for the slaughter of Armenians. Niemeyer's team convinced the jury that the shooter was suffering from temporary insanity. Niemeyer was also the first Director of the Institute for International Law at Kiel University, later renamed to Walther Schücking Institute for International Law, honoring Professor Schücking who was the successor of Professor Niemeyer and the first German Judge at the PCIJ (Permanent Court of International Justice) (Braasch 2012).

[23]No surprisingly perhaps national societies in Great Britain, Canada, and elsewhere in support of the League teamed with pacifists.

[24]Mathias Erzberger was the leader of the Centre Party in Germany and a member of the armistice delegation. This paragraph appears to be a reference to his paper called "The league of nations: the way to the world's peace," which was reprinted by Holt in English in 1919 and is now a Google book. Erzberger would later be assassinated for signing the instrument of armistice.

International Court of Justice, became vice president and may have written most of the final draft, assisted by Walter Simons, who later became head of the German delegation to Paris and was General-Secretary[25] as well as Chief of the Legal Department of the Foreign Office, and Friedrich Gaus.[26] Most in Die Liga were pacifists, but with a good mix of nonaligned businessmen as well, for example, Huldermann, Director of the Hamburg-Amerika Linie, a huge passenger line for immigrants from Germany to the United States and in general shipping terms at the time the largest maritime company in the world.

Active around the margins of the peace conference were various informal contacts between the Germans, allies, military men, informal advisers, and neutral diplomats. The message that was received was that Wilson had some flexibility and that he was determined to stay with his program. It was only close to the time the Germans were summoned to Paris to receive the peace terms that they began to get bad news, and certainly Brockdorff-Rantzau's reaction at Paris spoke to some of the things they had heard (war guilt, war crimes, and such). But for much of the time, steeped in their belief in a Wilsonian peace, the Germans by and large did not consider alternatives (it is interesting, and puts Die Liga into some perspective, that the main thrust of the German peace strategy was economic: offering Germany's economic power to help rebuild and to restore prosperity for all, with the ulterior thought that this economic power might well boost its own status in Europe) (Kimmich 2012).

According to Niemeyer's "Monographien zum Volkerbund," a draft charter was also working its way through the German Foreign Office and had received little input from legal scholars or parliamentarians, so the German Society of international law did not feel associated with it and even said they had no specific knowledge of the text. This was probably a model charter that was developed in the spring of 1918 for a notional association of nations. Similar to what became Die Liga's draft, the government's paper focused on permanent peace and the pacific settlement of disputes, arms limits, and the development of international law. Member states would also respect each other's territories and refrain from interference in internal affairs. There is uncertainty if this draft was shared with the USA or the allies, but the Germans were willing to make significant concessions in return for a global system based on the Wilson points. Niemeyer's paper indicates that with regard to Die Liga's draft, Dr. Simons, the Director of the Legal Department of the Foreign Office (Geheimrat), told a Dutch journalist that the government intended to submit the draft to the peace negotiations.

For Die Liga, their draft was the only real paper to be considered, especially as it was built from such a large body of contributors from a wide swatch of Germany, including government officials of authority. They then recommended it to the government as a basis for negotiations, and Berlin agreed. Indeed, the government published

[25] Simons was the head of the German peace delegation in Versailles but resigned because he rejected the treaty of Versailles. An interesting side note, in later life, he formed a social club called the SeSiSo-Club, many of who members formed the Solf-Kreis, a group of resisters against Nazi party.

[26] Gaus was Director of the Legal Department in the Foreign Offices in the 1920s and 1930s.

a history of their work and the society actually went to Paris for the peace talks and tried to directly negotiate with the US delegation and others (der Deutschen 1919). Wilson's aide House noted in his memoirs that "While the accredited statesmen occupied the center of the stage, influential men and women in every walk of life were there in some capacity .... They came from the four corners of the earth" (House 1925, December). It is also uncertain if Die Liga itself made a presentation, though they had members on the German delegation. They may instead have been represented by the German Society for International Law[27] (Miller 1924, pp. 95 and 187, Vol. 1).

## 19.10 The German Study Group

The public effort in Germany began at a conference in February 1918 with participants from the empire, the Reichstag, and the staff of the Foreign Office. The conference agreed to create a study group (our term), which then created the formal draft charter, which was not scheduled for completion until September 1919; however, the new German government decided to quickly sue for peace, so the report was completed on September 21, 1918. Germany then communicated to the United States government on November 13, 1918 (Sulzer 1942), that it wished to negotiate terms of peace, arguing in subsequent communications that famine, the lack of food for returning troops, and other economic issues could cause a national breakdown. Some of the basic principles of the German peace proposals proposed by the study group were:

1. Lasting peace.
2. Independence and inviolability of all its members.
3. The common welfare of all peoples.
4. The League was to have central institutions, not only for general compulsory arbitration but also for design and execution of federal legislation, federal administration, and ordinary jurisdiction, the later which was in harmony with pacifist thinking, and did not become part of the final charter, due to governments wanting to preserve sovereignty.

Several subcommittees formed the larger study group or "special committee," none of which apparently focused on allied points of view:

1. **Organization and Frame of the League. Note:** Whereas the Germans spent considerable time thinking about this, the Inquiry did not, leaving that to the allies to some extent. In contrast, the Pasvolsky's CSOP under Roosevelt did pay a lot of attention to structure. The problem for the German's was that they did not pay enough attention to the ethics of the conflict from the perspective of the allies.

[27] At least some NGO meetings happened at the Cercle de l'Union interalliée or Inter-allied Club, founded in Paris when the United States entered the war, a club which still exists to this day. The location provided a convivial atmosphere for off-the-record conversations.

2. **Jurisdiction and Mediation.**
3. **Restrictions on Armaments.**
4. **Development and Economics**, which included free access to the air and sea. One of their main issues was that continuation of the blockade, then of 50 months, and the surrender of their transport ships could cause massive starvation.
5. **Colonial Issues**. Erzberger led this effort and had a long publically stated distain for how Germany treated its African nationals in the colonies.
6. **Federal Execution**, how the government would implement League rules.
7. **Relationship of the States with Each Other**, meaning how the separate German states would relate with a federal system.
8. **Self-Determination and Protection of National Minorities**. This meant protecting ethnic German minorities ethnic Germans in Alsace-Lorraine and in Poland after the World War I, which became one of the excuses for conflict in World War II. That became one area of focus for Die Liga in the years between the Paris Peace Conference and the rise of the Nazi Party, to lobby for German minorities with national Leagues, and in June 1927 at the annual conference of Leagues for the League of Nations, Liga proposed the League of Nations revise its procedures and create a permanent minorities commission (Kimmich 1976, pp. 135, 139).
9. **Social Policy**.
10. **Press:** Public diplomacy and advocacy through the media was a major component of Die Liga's efforts, through handbills, literature, and announcements to press agencies. They had a press service; received widespread overage in the media, except for right wing papers; and published a journal called the Neue Brucken. Die Liga claimed in 1919 that most of what was said or read about the League of Nations was from them (Kimmich 1976, p. 15). **Note**: Pacifists before the end of the war were proscribed, papers seized, and members sometimes arrested (Walters 1952 (reprint 1965), pp. 18–19), but after the end of the war, censorship was no longer a serious concern, and it was significantly modified in the Weimar Constitution (Kimmich 2012).
11. **Additional Members** not associated with any particular subcommittee.

The entire group of experts met again in Berlin on October 27, 1918, and directed the subcommittees to meet on a frequent basis, from which 11 drafts were created for consideration. All of those recommendations were distilled into a final draft in Hamburg on January 8, 1919, and then formally presented to the German government 3 days later. One of the interesting elements of the final effort was a desire to end the occupation of Germany by allied forces, thus allowing the growth of domestic industry; they also proposed the establishment of a global economic covenant and that governments had to agree to allow the League to enforce arbitration. The government did adopt the proposal and charged Die Liga with promoting the idea in Germany and with similar League in other countries, as well as engage in a major Public Relations effort, to include rallies and publications.

## 19.11 Reaction by the Allies at Paris

The allies of course decided not to allow Germany to join the League, not until 1926. The view in Germany as well was that, given the text of the treaty, they also couldn't join the League without reforms proposed by Die Liga in 1919. That became Die Liga's main role and did lobby for issues around Europe and in Geneva; it suffered greatly due to the attitude of the allies. Whereas millions were in its supporter rolls initially, probably in hopes of gaining an organization along Wilson's original dream, support dropped sharply when the League appeared to be alliance of victors or an organ of peace and justice. Die Liga then became a "lobbying NGO" of little importance (Kimmich 1976, p. 27 and 38). In summary, Die Liga was at its most active, with the most powerful support, between the fall of 1918, when Germany sued for peace, and summer 1919, when it signed the peace treaty. It is in this period, and from the very start, that Die Liga was close to the government. It is in this period that Liga committees did much of their work and that their output was considered most useful to the government. Once it was clear that Germany would not be a member of the League of Nations, Die Liga lost standing (though it continued to play a role for the Foreign Ministry).

# Chapter 20
# Epilogue

Who carries the flag of humanitarianism? To understand that, one might remember a conversation some people had with Eleanor Roosevelt in 1948 just a few days before the approval of the Universal declaration of Human Rights. The world was full of totalitarian regimes, all fighting the tenets of the declaration. Mrs. Roosevelt's answer to the question about who would carry the flag of human rights was "a curious grapevine," by which she meant the NGO community (Special to NY Times 1948). That is the future of humanitarianism. Governments are needed, and industry, and international organizations and the media; without NGOs keeping everyone else honest, the world will be in deep trouble. The tools to win this victory will be lobbying and diplomacy.

L.W. Roeder, Jr. and A. Simard, *Diplomacy and Negotiation for Humanitarian NGOs*, Humanitarian Solutions in the 21st Century, DOI 10.1007/978-1-4614-7113-4_20,

# Thanks from Larry Roeder

My parents were diplomats who exposed me to world leaders very early, like Gamel Abdel Nasser who put me on his knee and Golda Meir who incessantly smoked my father's cigarettes. I got a taste for the business and went on to meet people like King Hussein of Jordan, President Ronald Reagan, Ambassador Skip Gnehm, Harold Saunders and Edward Said of Colombia University, the latter with whom I collaborated on a Palestine peace plan. These experiences and their observations informed the book. I could of course have not organized this effort without the many NGO diplomats and operational officers with whom I've had the honor to meet or serve.

**J. Barry Harrelson**, my best friend for over 30 years who had been on many intellectual and fun adventures, and who provided expert analytical advice on the book.

**Al Simard**, my joint author has been a close collaborator on the advancement of disaster knowledge management, for example, on the Global Disaster Information Network (GDIN), which we worked on for Vice President Al Gore.

- John Milton Cooper, Jr., author of *Woodrow Wilson*, who provided significant advice on the Paris Peace Conference, as well as insights Herbert Hoover and his NGO, the 1927 Mississippi Flood and his rescue of millions of starving Russians.
- Hal Fleming, former Deputy Assistant Secretary of State for International Organization Affairs, who was a true inspiration for work on humanitarian issues.
- The Herbert Hoover Presidential Library in Long Branch, Iowa.
- George H. Nash, the world's foremost authority on Herbert Hoover.
- Hal Saunders, former Deputy Assistant Secretary of State for Middle Eastern Affairs, for whom I worked on the Iran Hostage Crisis and the Palestine question.
- Arnold Toynbee, who inspired me to study the reasons for political movements, not simply be swept up in emotions.
- The staff of the Manuscripts Collection, US Library of Congress
- The staff of the Max Planck Institute for Comparative Public and International Law, Heidelberg, Germany.

L.W. Roeder, Jr. and A. Simard, *Diplomacy and Negotiation for Humanitarian NGOs*, Humanitarian Solutions in the 21st Century, DOI 10.1007/978-1-4614-7113-4,

- The librarians of the Ralph Bunch Library at the US Department of State, one of the finest academic libraries in Washington, DC.
- The team that developed and continues to manage ReliefWeb, the UN's first modern disaster information website.
- The Woodrow Wilson Library and Museum in Staunton, Virginia.

**David Hunter Miller.** We wish to honor him because his works on international law have been so influential. When he joined the Woodrow Wilson's Inquiry as legal adviser, he had been an attorney since 1911. Prior to that he had been a lieutenant in the 9th New York Volunteer Infantry during the Spanish American War. Later he became head of the presidential nomination of William Gibbs McAdoo in 1924. McAdoo was also husband to a daughter of Woodrow Wilson. That experience alone is interesting; Miller went on to be the lead lawyer for the Inquiry, often considered a coauthor of the Treaty of Versailles. His knowledge of the new field of multilateral diplomacy was considered so good that the US Congress created the position of Editor of Treaties at the Department, which he filled from 1929 until he retired in 1948. He later led the US delegation to the 1930 Hague Conference for the codification of International Law.

# About the Authors

**Larry W. Roeder, Jr., MS**, (Editor and Co-Author), currently Series Editors for Humanitarian Solution Series, Springer-Verlag, publishing. Former soldier, International Commodities Economist, Bureau of Economic and Business Affairs, and Policy Adviser on Disaster Management, Bureau of International Organizations, the US Department of State, and Civilian Observer, Multinational Forces and Observers. Former United Nations Director, the World Society for the Protection of Animals and Editor-in-Chief of ClimateCaucus Network. Former Executive Director of GDIN, the Global Disaster Information Network, a satellite-based emergency system proposed by Vice President Gore. Led US government's technical team on the development of ReliefWeb.int, the UN's premier disaster response website. Currently an adviser on humanitarian relief and development, with a focus on failed nation states. Lives in South Riding, Virginia, near Washington, DC. Has written over 100 articles, and is an artist.[1]

**Albert Simard, Ph.D**. (Co-Author) Dr. Simard is the Knowledge Manager for Defense R&D Canada, Directorate of Knowledge and Information Management. He coordinated development of two award-winning, automated national forest fire information systems. He also developed knowledge management projects, programs, and strategies for the Canadian Forest Service and Natural Resources Canada, including an access to knowledge policy and a knowledge services framework for government S&T organizations. Internationally, he developed strategic

[1]Disclosure Notice by Larry Roeder: None of the reporting on UDAW in this book comes from records obtained while serving as UN Affairs Director at WSPA 2005–2009. To avoid the possibility of accidently using confidential information, reporting was entirely based on work he conducted in the US Department of State until he left in 2005 and work he conducted after he left WSPA in October 2009. Information in the public domain is an exception. The same general rule was followed for research on WSPA matters. He also relied on interviews of WSPA former and current staff conducted between 2010 and 2012.

L.W. Roeder, Jr. and A. Simard, *Diplomacy and Negotiation for Humanitarian NGOs*,
Humanitarian Solutions in the 21st Century, DOI 10.1007/978-1-4614-7113-4,

plans and frameworks for the "Global Emergency Management Information Network Initiative" and the "Global Disaster Information network." He recently led development of a modeling framework for the Canadian Food Inspection Agency. He has published more than 200 scientific and management articles and given more than 300 presentations on forest fires and knowledge management. Currently, Dr. Simard is developing a knowledge services agenda and architecture that adapts knowledge management to the business strategy of Defense R&D Canada.

# Main Contributors

1. **G. S. Silva Augusto Antonio,** former Country Director of WSPA (World Society for the Protection of Animals) in Brazil, candidate for Master's Degree in Development and International Cooperation, conducting a thesis on how NGOs can influence change in legislation and participate in the creation of public policies.
2. **Jane Ballentine,** Director of Public Relations and Marketing, Public Affairs Officer, AZA, the American Zoological Association.
3. **Dr. Annyssa Bellal,** research fellow at the Geneva Academy of International Humanitarian Law and Human Rights.
4. **Elez Biberaj,** former Director, Eurasia Division, Voice of America, for help on Roeder's exploratory trip to Albania and assistance in book.
5. **James Bishop,** US States Ambassador to the Republic of Niger (1979–1981), then Deputy Assistant Secretary of State for African Affairs until becoming US Ambassador to Liberia in 1987. His next post was Ambassador to Somalia until evacuated by US military forces in January 1991, whereupon he became Principal Deputy Assistant Secretary of State for Human Rights and Humanitarian Affairs, retiring in 1993. He became Vice President of the Congressional Human Rights Foundation in 1994 and a year later VP for Humanitarian Policy and Practice at Interaction, the largest coalition of humanitarian NGOs in the USA.
6. **Jimmy Blas,** Mission of the Republic of the Philippines to the United Nations.
7. **David Bowles,** Head of External Affairs, RSPCA, the Royal Society for the Prevention of Cruelty to Animals.
8. **Mette Boritz,** protocol expert, The National Museum, Denmark.
9. **Patrick Braasch,** University of Kiel, Walther Schücking Institute for International Law.
10. **Sálvano Briceño,** Chair, Science Committee, Integrated Research on Disaster Risk, IRDR, and Senior Advisor, Global Earthquake Model GEM. Former Director International Strategy for Disaster Reduction, UNISDR, 2001–2011.

L.W. Roeder, Jr. and A. Simard, *Diplomacy and Negotiation for Humanitarian NGOs*, Humanitarian Solutions in the 21st Century, DOI 10.1007/978-1-4614-7113-4,

11. **Patricia Clavin,** Professor of International History, Jesus College, Oxford.
12. **Victor Comras,** Attorney/Expert Consultant at Comras and Comras PA, former Minister Counselor at US Department of State, Diplomat in Residence at GSPIA, expert in Economic Sanctions and Law of the Sea.
13. **John Milton Cooper, Jr.,** one of the foremost experts on Woodrow Wilson.
14. **Ollie Davidson,** former Department of State Official and former Senior Advisor, Emergency Services, HSUS, Humane Society, USA.
15. **Glenda Davis,** Director of the Navajo Nation Veterinary and Livestock Program.
16. **De Bruhl, Marshall,** author of *Firestorm: Allied Airpower and the Destruction of Dresden.*
17. **Dr. Jost Dülffer,** Professor für Neuere Geschichte, University of Cologne.
18. **Constance Colding Jones,** Public Affairs Officer, retired, US Department of State
19. **Dr. Johann Georg Goldammer,** senior scientist specializing in forest research, Max Planck Society for Chemistry; Director, Global Fire Monitoring Center; Leader, UN-FAO/ECE/ILO Team of Specialists on Forest Fires.
20. **Jeremy Hume,** CEO of SPANA, London.
21. **Peter Hulm,** Communications Consultant for international organizations including the World Economic Forum, IUCN-The World Conservation Union, The International Trade Centre, and the United Nations Environment Program.
22. **Dena Jones,** Animal Welfare Institute, Washington, DC.
23. **Ashish Kothari,** chair of GreenPeace, India, former Co-chair of the IUCN Inter-commission Strategic Direction on Governance, Equity, and Livelihoods in Relation to Protected Areas (TILCEPA) (1999–2008), and in the same period a member of the Steering Committees of the World Commission on Protected Areas (WCPA), and IUCN Commission on Environmental, Economic, and Social Policy (CEESP). He has served on the Board of Directors of Greenpeace International.
24. **Christopher (Chris) Lamb,** a former Ambassador of the Government of Australia and a former Special Assistant to the Secretary General of the IFRC, as well a highly regarded expert on International Humanitarian Law. He is now an honorary associate professor of political science at the University of Melbourne.
25. **Dr. Peter Macalister-Smith,** Editor, Journal of the History of International, Law/Revue d'histoire du droit international, Max Planck Institute for Comparative Public Law and International Law.
26. **Robert Marro,** Trustee, ADAMS (All Dulles American Muslim Society) Center, Sterling, Virginia, US diplomat, retired.
27. **Michael W. McClellan,** Diplomat in Residence, the Gerald R. Ford School of Public Policy, Michigan.
28. **Wolf Maier,** European Commission, Directorate General for Health and Consumers.
29. **Nancy Mitchell,** CEO, of Protocol Partners.
30. **Valentine Ndibalema,** Special Technical Officer, UNHCR, Geneva.
31. **Claes Lykke Ragner,** Head of Administration and Information, Fridtjof Nansen Institute.

32. **Heather Rice,** Director of US Prisons Policy & Program, National Religious Campaign Against Torture, who was particularly helpful in discussing contemporary efforts to end solitary confinement.
33. **Rebecca Regnery,** Deputy Director, Humane Society, International.
34. **Badaoui Rouhban,** Chief of Disaster Reduction, UNESCO, Paris.
35. **Sharon Rusu**, former Director of ReliefWeb, Geneva.
36. **Pierre-Alain Scheib,** Chief of Future's Program, OECD, Paris.
37. **Wolfram von Scheliha,** Global and European Studies Institute, University of Freiburg.
38. **Nadia Smiecinska,** Chief of Staff, Equality and Opportunity Foundation, San Francisco.
39. **Emmanuel Tronc,** Humanitarian Advocacy & Representation Coordinator for Médecins Sans Frontiers (MSN)
40. **Carl Emil Vogt,** Associate Professor at the University of Oslo, noted expert on Dr. Fridtjof Nansen.
41. **John Walsh,** legendary animal rescue expert.
42. **M. Karen Walker,** Associate, Booz Allen Hamilton.
43. **Trevor Wheeler,** former Near Eastern Affairs Director, WSPA.
44. **Anna Lena Wonnenberg,** M.A. Candidate, Political Science and International Relations, University of South Dakota.
45. **Hans Zimmermann, former** Senior Officer in the United Nations Office for the Coordination of Humanitarian Affairs (OCHA), and former Chair of the UN Working Group on Emergency Telecommunications.

# Definitions/Explanations

**Ambassador:** See Sect. 11.8

**Armed Non-state Actor:** Any armed group, distinct from and not operating under the control of states, and which has political, religious, and/or military objectives. (See discussion on this topic in Sect. 7.5.)

**Bilateral Diplomacy** usually describes negotiations between two governments, but in this textbook it means negotiations between an NGO or coalition of NGOs and one government or international organization, even an armed non-state player.

**Clearances:** People often blanch at the time involved in seeking *clearances*. Sometimes this may be because the drafting official cannot deal with contrary points of view. In other words, the drafting officer may have written the Memo in order to justify a specific action she or he feels passionately about or which the boss has demanded. Think of the clearance process in intellectual terms as a Peer Review, not a confrontation. A constructive criticism by a clearer is not a threat; clearances are actually reflecting a conversation where the memo's question is tested, like an experiment tests a theory. Be neutral on the outcome; otherwise, the paper will prejudice the result, which is why the "subject line" is a question, not a policy statement. Each part of the team can offer opinions, even recommend changes, and challenge assumptions. Doing so builds consensus and a better product.

**Community:** A community of NGOs is defined as anyone associated with a broad political or civil rights movement, such as the humanitarian movement, from private donors and volunteers to staffs in NGOs, private corporations, academic institutions, government agencies, or international organizations

**Compromise:** The ethical editing of a negotiating position to meet another party's needs while at the same time retaining core principles. As John Maynard Keynes put it, "a moment often arrives when substantial victory is yours if by some slight

L.W. Roeder, Jr. and A. Simard, *Diplomacy and Negotiation for Humanitarian NGOs*, Humanitarian Solutions in the 21st Century, DOI 10.1007/978-1-4614-7113-4,

appearance of a concession you can save the face of the opposition of conciliate them by a restatement of your proposal helpful to them and not injurious to yourself (Keynes 1920, p. 40)."

**Consensus:** The decision making process by which offices in an NGO or members of an NGO alliance should recommend diplomatic initiatives. They are also used to describe how the United Nations makes most decisions, with the notable exception of sanctions by the UN Security Council. In both instances, consensus is inherently more difficult than individual decision making because it requires compromise, putting on a single unified plane players with differing value systems and goals. That's never easy; the end result tends to be a strong agreement.

**Convention:** See **Binding International Instruments**

**Civil Society Organizations (CSOs)**: These include NGOs, trade unions, faith-based organizations, indigenous peoples movements, foundations, and many others.

**Covenant:** See **Binding International Instruments**

**Diplomats:** This book takes the position that NGO officers[2] are diplomats with a small "d" when they negotiate agreements (vs. lobby) with governments and international organizations; and they are often as professional as any career government diplomat. However, they do not necessarily warrant the privileges and immunities (P&I) accorded accredited government diplomats, nor should they use the title Ambassador, though some NGO officials have been known to call themselves Ambassadors or "good-will Ambassadors." That practice can be confusing.

Professional government diplomats often say that their roots lie in the French system, which began in the sixteenth century but then was modernized by Cardinal Richelieu's Foreign Ministry in 1626 (*Encyclopedia Britannica*). Richelieu saw the Ministry as a mechanism to protect the interests of the State, interests that stood above any particular King. He also saw diplomacy as a continual process of negotiation and evolution. NGO diplomats tend to be less interested in the interests of the state than of the people or issues like the environment.

Modern NGOs work for civil society constituents, not governments (except as contractors), and they are invaluable as intermediaries in conflict, doing what states could not, and thus have become true descendants of Richelieu's diplomats, even if not government officials. Indeed, humanitarians often work for both NGOs and their governments during their careers, particularly in the USA (Sizer, Roeder, & Marcus, 1982). NGO officials are science advisers to the United Nations, the Red Cross, and governments, but also passionate independent advocates for change, their skills and knowledge on par with any government official, their role in making policy and negotiating agreements essential. Thus, such experts are often called "global diplomats," and some of the best-known NGOs are managed by former

[2] Some organizations use the term "officer" to mean the lowest rank. This book defines the term to mean everyone from the CEO to the lowest official. All delegation members are officers, though in diplomatic jargon, the head of the delegation to a UN conference is usually the delegate, with the other members being called alternative delegates.

presidents but more often by average citizens like the IFAW, the International Fund for Animal Welfare, Climate Caucus Network of New York, the Climate Action Network, Friends of the Earth, and the World Wildlife Fund.

Under the British system, ministers are not diplomats; they are members of the government, and in that system, it is the government, not diplomats, that formulates foreign policy (Roberts 2009). But this is because Britain (as with other governments) merges the executive and legislature into one, whereas Americans and others separate the two branches of government. Under that system, the Secretary of State is the chief diplomat, even though not a member of the diplomatic service. Further, while there often is a formal diplomatic service, members of the civil service are also diplomats where they are assigned tasks like representing the government to an international organization, leading a diplomatic mission or being accredited by a Foreign Ministry. In other words, the definition is about the function, not the job title. NGO officials can be diplomats, especially when negotiating directly with governments, the UN, or the Red Cross to change an international law or a local regulation. Further, officers in the executive branch regularly formulate foreign policy recommendations, everyone from a scientist in the US Geological Survey to the head of a Bureau in the US Department of State. In the end, in the USA, both the legislative and executive branches share responsibility for foreign policy.

**Disasters:** A disaster is an event that overwhelms or nearly so the capacity of a social unit to respond, e.g., a city, province, or nation; a natural disaster is such a crisis when caused by natural phenomena, e.g., a hurricane or storm surge or an earthquake. However, a hurricane is not a disaster unless it causes overwhelming damage. Indeed, a hurricane might bring nourishing water to a drought.

**Explanation of Vote:** Rather than force a change in text, before signing agreements or when voting for or against a resolution, governments often provide an "explanation of vote" which can contain an interpretation of the language, one which might not be shared with every other party. An example of this is provided in Sect. 10.3 in the discussion of the evolution of Kellogg-Briand Pact in which governments like France and the USA let it be known that nothing in the text precluded the right to self-defense (Miller, The Peace Pact of Paris, 1928, pp. 99–111 and 63.). Another example is provided in Sect. 1.2 regarding explanations of Votes regarding the Declaration on Rights of Indigenous Peoples adopted in 2007. These explanations of Yes votes limited the right to self-determination and defined limits regarding individual vs. collective rights.

**The Humanitarian Charter:** It binds humanitarian agencies to basic principles of care and minimum standards, which taken together define the level of service any human should receive in an emergency. The principles are (1) the right to life with dignity, (2) the distinction between combatants and non-combatants, and (3) the principle of non-refoulement (not returning a refugee to a place of harm).

**Humanitarian Diplomacy:** This is defined by the International Federation of Red Cross and Red Crescent Societies as "persuading decision makers and opinion leaders to act, at all times, in the interests of vulnerable people, and with full respect for fundamental humanitarian principles."

**Intelligence:** A meaningful statement derived from information that has been selected; evaluated; taking into account local conditions; interpreted; and finally expressed so that its significance to an NGO's priority issues is clear. Unless otherwise noted, intelligence is NOT used in the context of espionage.

**International Organization:** Diplomatic practice since the founding of the United Nations generally considers an "international organization or (IO)" as a legally chartered association of national authorities. Some experts do use the term IGO, or international governmental body; that can be confusing as a parsing term. Instead, the authors adopted an interpretation of international organizations used by the US Department of State. First, the organization must have a legal personality; otherwise, it does not possess the power to sue, nor can it be sued, contract, or be contracted with. Secondly, its members will be sovereign states or on rare occasion other international organizations (McLeod et al. 2000, June 8).

Examples are IOM, UNHCR, WHO, UNICEF, WFP, the North Atlantic Treaty Organization (NATO), the Association of South East Asian Nations (ASEAN), the Organization of Economic Cooperation and Development (OECD), the Organization of American States (OAS), and the Group of Seventy-Seven Non-aligned Nations (G77), which is also the UN's largest coalition of nations. Humanitarian NGO's, especially small, national and regional bodies, can benefit from collaboration with all of those IOs. National societies of the Red Cross/Red Crescent Movement should also be important for cooperation.

Like any kind of diplomatic practice which changes over time, what defines an IO is also changing. Some experts used to feel that national societies of the International Red Cross and Red Crescent Movement were neither NGOs nor IOs. They certainly have their own set of legal rights defined by international conventions and are accepted by governments as auxiliary partners. What has certainly not changed is that NGOs are not IOs. Many NGOs like CARE are international in nature, and like GOAL take heavy amounts of government funding; they are also not IOs.

Public–Private partnerships may also wish to be considered international organizations, which could be a very helpful phenomenon for NGOs wishing to enhance their stature or access to resources. There is a body of legal opinion that states were the organization to have a mixed public–private/NGO membership, while it might be a public–private organization, that presence would preclude it from becoming an international organization, even if it were to obtain legal personality under national law (McLeod et al. 2000, June 8). Thinking in that way would certainly argue for making a distinction between international organizations in general or international governmental organizations (IGO), and the authors are sympathetic to that taxonomy, when used outside this book. Users are cautioned that the distinction is not universally understood and may need to be explained.

NGOs are not international organizations "under the traditional post UN view," certainly not if an IO must have governments as members, though NGO's sometimes have government members, as in public–private partnerships like GDIN, the Global Disaster Information Network set up by Vice President Gore and the governments of Turkey, Mexico, Italy, Canada, Australia, and others. Its members were a mix of government officials and private sector officials from traditional NGOs, the IFRC, academia, and industry. It should be noted that IOs have privileges and immunities not otherwise granted to NGOs. However, for purposes of this book, the definition of an IO is expanded. Because of their unique nature, the ICRC and IFRC have been seen by many as unique entities, neither NGOs nor IOs; they are now accepted by most national authorities as an IO and also by the UN and the European Union. So too, more recently and in somewhat ambiguous language, is the International Olympic Committee. So an evolved definition of an international organization will be "an organization derived from a treaty or other national level intergovernmental arrangement," – the entity itself does not have to be composed of national authorities, but it does need to have international legal personality.

NGOs need to be aware that there is a rich community of international organizations, some associated with the United Nations, some not associated at all, except perhaps by an MOU. Some are older that the UN going back to the League of Nations like the World Health Organization (WHO), International Postal Union (IPU) and the International Labor Organization (ILO). The League's Nutrition Committee would become the UN Food and Agricultural Organization in Rome. Its Committee on Intellectual Cooperation became UNESCO (United Nations Educational, Scientific and Cultural Organization). In the early days of modern multilateral diplomacy, when the air in Europe still smelled of cordite, most people saw the point of the new international organization known as the League of Nations as peacekeeping or the prevention of war, same just after the San Francisco Conference for the United Nations. In other words the work of the so-called technical agencies to reduce and prevent the spread of disease; develop weather, postal, labor, and maritime standards; protect women; enhance transportation safety; etc., was secondary to the prime directive – "stop war." Not handling such issues properly will set the stage for economic decline, war, crime, and health emergencies. They are all interconnected and inhabit the big stage on which NGOs need to participate.

An historical note: See also the definition of NGO's during the days of the League of Nations.

**Interpretation:** Interpreting is paraphrasing – the interpreter listens to a speaker in one language, grasps the content, and paraphrases his or her understanding. A professional interpreter at an international conference does his or her best to render the words and nuances of the speaker in another language – this is a highly specialized skill, and not the same thing as translating, which is produced in writing. NGO delegates to a conference or participating in a bilateral event are wise to pay attention to which languages will dominate and make sure that if they do not speak those languages, someone on the team does. During the Paris Peace Conference following the armistice of World War I, a summit of four leaders managed things, President Woodrow Wilson of the USA, Prime Minister Clemenceau of France, Prime Minister Vittorio Orlando of Italy, and Prime Minister David Lloyd George of Great Britain. Only Clemenceau spoke both French and English. Wilson only spoke English and Orlando only French and Italian. As for George, his first language was Welsh, English was a second language. So, direct communication was a problem at times (Keynes 1920). This would not usually be an issue in the United Nations where English is the most common language, though not the only official one.

**Lobbying vs. Engagement:** (see Sect. 12.5.3)

**Moral Suasion:** Pressure based on ethics or emotion instead of force or coercion in order to convince a delegation to change its own position to that of the delegation applying the pressure. **Note:** Moral Suasion is also often called "jawboning," in the USA at least.

**MOU: Memorandum of Understanding:** See Sect. 6.6.4

**Multilateral Diplomacy:** This is a creature of the twentieth century. It is usually understood to mean a negotiation conducted between members of a cluster of governments, often through international organizations. This modern form was first associated with the League of Nations, and now is mostly associated with the United Nations, its members are international organizations and regional bodies like NATO, the North Atlantic Treaty Organization, or ASEAN, the Association of Southeast Asian Nations. In the context of this book, the phrase refers to a negotiation between an NGO or coalition of NGOs and a cluster of governments.

**Nation-State:** Though used interchangeably, a state or country is a political and geographic entity, e.g., the Vatican or the USA. A nation is a cultural or ethnic entity, e.g., the Kurdish nation. A nation-state exists when the two concepts coexist. This distinction is dwelled upon in Chap. 6 on Weak and Failed Nation-States; in the everyday of diplomacy, just consider the context. After all, the UN is the United Nations, not the United States, and there they do mean state when they say nation. Quotes have not been altered to reflect the difference, as the context is generally obvious.

**Non-governmental organization (NGO):** This is a term with a variety of definitions. In this book, NGOs are generally legally constituted organizations that operate with a legal independence from governments; there are however many examples where a legally independent entity had close ties to a government, sometimes by doing contracts or working as a public–private entity. Several NGOs mentioned in this book actually made significant contributions to humanitarianism precisely because they had close ties with governments.

Most experts consulted with for this book do not consider public–private partnerships to be NGOs, which is an entity whose members are governments and private sector entities like GDIN, the Global Disaster Information Network which initially was[3]; however, GDIN's international arm certainly did consider itself an NGO and

[3]GDIN (the Global Disaster Information Network) was a White House project under the authority of the Vice President, which aimed to facilitate the flow of satellite data to relief agencies. The project was developed as a partnership of NGOs, academic institutions, UN, and government agencies and then was divided into a domestic and international effort, with the international effort led by a Department of State officer elected by the member entities. Eventually, GDIN international was incorporated as a full 501©(3) non-profit, and at that point, it became an NGO. The original website was GDIN.org. That site went down in 2010 and was replaced by a private disaster entity unaffiliated with the original project.

was a registered non-profit under US law which took its instructions from its international partners, whereas the domestic program took its directions from the White House. The term is understood to have originated in 1945 with the formation of the United Nations (UN); NGOs (just not called that) existed long before and were influential in the formation of the League of Nations as well as promoting better race relations, and many aspects of humanitarianism back into the nineteenth century.

NGOs are always non-profit and today often divided into humanitarian, development, environment, and human-rights specialties; however, that distinction is a distraction to this book, so all types are combined, since in some way all benefit humans. Some NGOs receive no funding from governments, others do. Political parties are not considered NGOs; however, there are NGOs that foster political thought, as well as NGOs associated with parties.

The term INGO for international NGOs is used to distinguish those from local NGOs; the authors are trying to benefit the entire community of NGOs and encourage cooperation, so this distinction is not used. Some sources believe there to be over 40,000 international NGOs, with millions of others operating only at the local and national level. Some NGOs like Citizens for Global Solutions also have Political Action Committees (PAC) that will support political candidates. The lesson in this book should be of value to all categories.

*As an historical note:* it is worth mentioning that prior to the advent of the UN, NGO's were usually called "private international organizations." From the beginning, the secretariat of the League of Nations understood that in order to foment peace, it needed expert advice from its own bodies, as well as private international organizations, sometimes also called "unofficial international associations.[4]" NGOs today fulfill the same function at the UN, as well as advocate for change based on their own mandates. Many existed prior to the League like the **League to Enforce Peace of (LEP),** which is discussed in this book. NGOs at the League worked on everything from Animal Welfare like the Paris based **Bureau International des Fédérations et Sociétés Protectrices des Animaux et D'Antivivisection** (Secretariat 1938, p. 42) to schooling like the London-based **World Association for Adult Education** (Secretariat 1921, p. 126) or the **International Arbitration League**, which advocated for a World Court (Secretariat 1938, p. 9), and many others covering human rights, pacifism, etc. Like today, many were also faith based, such as the Les **Chevaliers du Prince de la Paix**, a Protestant movement to enable Christian nationalists (Secretariat 1938, p. 20), or the **Women's International Zionist Organization (WIZO),** which prepared women for life in the British Mandate of Palestine (Secretariat 1938, p. 100).

**Officer:** Some organizations use the term "officer" to mean the lowest rank. This book defines the term to mean everyone from the CEO to the lowest official.

[4]This term could be confusing. As an example, a popular study of private international organizations published during the time of the League of Nations included the IPU or International Parliamentary Union. Founded in 1889, this is an international organization as used in this book, not an NGO. Its members are Parliaments, and its funding is nearly exclusively governmental (White 1933).

All delegation members are officers, though in diplomatic jargon, the head of the delegation to a UN conference is usually the delegate, with the other members being called alternative delegates.

**Open Diplomacy:** Many experts feel that the existence of secret treaties helped lay the seeds of World War I, so the League of Nations required that all agreements be in public and published. This is also a UN mantra. Open diplomacy also can mean diplomacy that is open to observers and the media.

**Outcomes Document:** Virtually every conference has an outcome document, which is a report on the accomplishments of the conference which may lay out contentious issues, and often sets out proposals for further work. A convention or declaration can be an outcomes document.

**Propaganda:** (See Sect. 12.5.2)

**Public Diplomacy:** (See Sect. 12.5.1)

**Translating:** A translator can write in the target language and understands the culture and can provide an exact understanding.

**Team and Delegation Officer/Functions:** The following officers are mentioned throughout this book. Although in the real world, one person might do more than one task, for purposes of this book, key functions are assigned to specific officers. It is important to also keep in mind that because many NGOs work in alliances, the officers do not need to come from the lead NGO.

Negotiation efforts are also divided between two groups of related officers, together all of whom form one team. One group is the HQ team, usually large, headed by a team leader who manages the whole effort and reports to senior management. This officer's HQ team is made up of officers from the NGO and perhaps the alliance. The other group is the negotiation team, which is usually small, led by a chief of delegation of chief negotiator, also sometimes called a delegate. Each is defined.

- **Team Leader:** (Sect. 1.3, Report to CEO) This is a project manager who pulls together an Study Team of interested parties and decides after intensive debate whether an initiative makes sense to bring to the attention of senior management. This officer also manages the development of a decision memo which is the tool that decides if the project moves forward, and lays out the basic plan and mandate. The team leader also manages the overall effort from HQ.
- **Chief Negotiator:** (Sect. 1.3, Reports to the team leader). Manages the creation of briefing material for the delegation, manages the delegation and creates the Final report after a negotiation showing what happened and why.
- **Legal Adviser:** (Chap. 4). Whether there is a legal adviser in the delegation or in the HQ team or both will largely depend on the nature of the negotiation. For many negotiations, especially involving any aspect of international law and custom, it is important to have an in-house attorney or at least one on-call. This attorney should be an expert in the field. And be able to convey the impact of the

negotiations on local law and customs. It doesn't matter if the attorney is on retainer by the lead NGO or some partner NGO in the alliance. This is totally separate from a lawyer that might be used to provide advice on contracts or hiring, etc. To gain an understanding of how important this matter is, consider the debate over Article 10 of the Covenant in the League of Nations, covered in Chap. 12. Though the debate was colored by politics, questions of domestic and international law were also pertinent.

- **Security Adviser:** (See Chap. 5) For the most part, this officer is a core member of the lead NGO or one of the alliance. The officer then reports to the team leader; this officer might also accompany a delegation to the field, if the city or region is especially dangerous, important since there has been an uptick in attacks on international development workers in recent years. In the latter case, the officer reports directly to the chief negotiator. The role of a security officer is to assess the physical risks to a negotiation and must be an expert at threat assessment and situational analysis, capable of professionally providing solutions to weaknesses and being able to recommend cancelation of a trip, if the risk merits.
- **Administrative and Protocol Officer** (often called the Admin Officer): This officer is limited to the task of furthering an NGO-led diplomatic initiative, not general support for the NGO back home. Also has the function of reporting to the chief negotiator, which might be accomplished by a single person or even a group of people from the lead NGO or allied NGOs, some physically part of the delegation, others perhaps in an HQ, depending on many factors, intra-NGO politics, available resources, etc., the nature of the negotiation. But for purposes of this book, the function of the Administrative Officer is in the following areas: (a) Physical communications, internet, etc.; (b) Matters of Protocol; (c) Knowledge Management; (d) Setting up Meetings, Visa, Currency Exchange, and Transportation; (e) Handling Visa; and (f) Managing the Budget at the delegation level. It is assumed there is a parallel Admin Officer managing budget issues at HQ.
- **Communications Officer (often known as the Spokesperson):** The HQ Team is likely to have a Communication officer, just as will the NGO for general NGO purposes; it is usually best if the delegation also has one that reports to the chief negotiator and (a) coordinates press reports and press statements; (b) works with delegation members to make sure their spoken word comports with the coordinated message; (c) creates a cleared Media Kit (also called a Press Kit) for distribution at conferences and events; (d) informs the team about the opportunities of media assets, as well as the potential hazards; and (e) and manages the delegation-level aspects of the public diplomacy Campaign.

**Technology Transfer:** A term of art covering any kind of information in any format, patented or not, copyrighted or not, which can be used or adapted for use in the design, production, manufacture, utilization, or reconstruction of articles or materials.

**Treaty:** See **Binding International Instruments**

# Appendix A
# Glossary of Acronyms

*Keep in Mind that Some Acronyms have more than one meaning.*

ABCDE – Annual Bank Conferences on Development Economics
ACABQ – Advisory Committee on Administrative and Budgetary Questions
ACLU – American Civil Liberties Union
ACLU – American Civil Liberties Union
ADRA – Adventist Development and Relief Agency
ADRC – Asia Disaster Recovery Center
ANSA – Armed Non-State Actors
AOSIS – Alliance of Small Island States
ARRL – American Radio Relay League
ASEAN – The Association of Southeast Asian Nations
AW – Animal Welfare
AWSD – Aid Worker Security Database
BATNA – Best Alternative to a Negotiated Agreement
BBC – British Broadcasting Service
BWC – Biological Weapons Convention
CAO – Chief Administrative Officer
CAP – Consolidated Appeals Process
CBD Alliance – Convention on Biological Diversity Alliance
CBM – Confidence Building Measure
CBS – Colombia Broadcasting Service
CBW – Chemical Biological Warfare
CCPCJ – Commission on Crime Prevention and Criminal Justice
CEESP – Commission on Environmental, Economic, and Social Policy
CEO – Chief Executive Officer
CERF – Central Emergency Response Fund
CFR – Council on Foreign Relations
CG – Consultative Group
CGPCS – Contact Group on Piracy off the Coast of Somalia
CICC – Coalition for the International Criminal Court

L.W. Roeder, Jr. and A. Simard, *Diplomacy and Negotiation for Humanitarian NGOs*,
Humanitarian Solutions in the 21st Century, DOI 10.1007/978-1-4614-7113-4,

CICG – International Conference Center in Geneva
CITES – The Convention on International Trade in Endangered Species of Wild Fauna and Flora
CMP – UN Capital Master Plan
CMS – Convention on Migratory Species
CND – Commission on Narcotic Drugs
CNES – French Space Agency
CoCom – Coordinating Committee for Multilateral Export Controls
CoNGO – Conference of NGOs in Consultative Relationship to the Economic and Social Council of the United Nations
CPD – The Commission on Population and Development
CPI – Committee on Public Information
CSA – Canadian Space Agency
CSD – Commission on Sustainable Development
CSO – Civil Society Organization
CSocD – Commission for Social Development
CSOP – Commission to Study the Organization of Peace
CSTD – Commission on Science and Technology for Development
CSW – Commission on the Status of Women
CUNR – Campaign for UN Reform
CWC – Chemical Weapons Convention
DESA – United Nations Department of Economic and Social Affairs
Die Liga – German League for the League of Nations
DLFV – Die Deutsche Liga für Völkerbund
DLFV – German League for the League of Nations
DOAF – Daughters of Abraham Foundation
DPI – UN Department of Public Information (UN)
ECHO – European Commission's European Community Humanitarian Office
ECOSOC – Economic and Social Council (UN)
ERC – Editorial Review Committee
ERC – Emergency Relief Coordinator
ERZ – Export-oriented Reconstruction Zones
ESA – European Space Agency
ESI – Endangered Species International
EU – European Union
FAO – Food and Agricultural Organization (United Nations)
FDR – Franklin Delano Roosevelt
FTS – Financial Tracking Service
G77 – Group of Seventy Seven Non-Aligned States
GARR – The Support Group for Refugees and Repatriated Persons
GCC – Gulf Cooperation Council
GCM – Coordinated Global Movement
GDIN – Global Disaster Information Network
GDN – Gender and Disaster Network
GHD – Good Humanitarian Donorship Initiative

GPG – Global Public Goods
GRF – Global Risk Forum
HRC – The Human Rights Council
HSI – Humane Society International
IAB – International Advisory Board
IACP – International Chiefs of Police Academy
IASC – Interagency Standing Committee
IATI – International Aid Transparency Initiative
ICBL – International Campaign to Ban Landmines
ICC – International Criminal Court
ICG – International Contact Group
ICJ – International Court of Justice
ICRC – International Committee of the Red Cross
ICRR – International Committee for Russian Relief
ICVA – The International Council of Voluntary Agencies
ICW – The International Committee of Women
IDP – Internally Displaced Person
IDRC – International Disaster and Risk Conference
IFRC – International Federation of Red Cross and Red Crescent Societies
IGO – Intergovernmental Organization (same as IO)
IHAN – International Health Awareness Network
IHL – International Humanitarian Law
ILO – International Labor Office
IMC – International Medical Corps
IMF – International Monetary Fund
INF – Intermediate-Range Nuclear Forces Treaty
IO – International Organization
IOM – International Organization for Migration
IPCC – Intergovernmental Panel on Climate Change
IPU – International Postal Union
IPU – Interparliamentary Union
IRI – International Republican Institute
ISDR – International Strategy on Disaster Reduction
ISPA – International Society for the Protection of Animals
IUCN – International Union for Conservation of Nature
IWG – Iran Working Group
JUSCANZ – Japan, United States, Canada, Australia, and New Zealand
KIA – Kachin Independence Army
KIO – Kachin Independence Organization
KM – Knowledge Management
LDC – Less Developed Country
LEP – League to Enforce Peace
LWF – Lutheran World Federation
MAG – Media & Advocacy Group
MALU – Media Accreditation and Liaison Unit

MARWOPENT – Mano River Women's Peace Network
MCC – Maine Council of Churches
MDG – Millennium Development Goals
MFO – Multi-National Forces and Observers
MOU – Memorandum of Understanding
MSF – Doctors Without Borders
MSF – Médecins Sans Frontières
NAACP – National Association for the Advancement of Colored People
NASA – National Aeronautic and Space Agency
NATO – North Atlantic Treaty Organization
NCAI – National Congress on American Indians
NDI – National Democratic Institute
NGO – Non-governmental organization.
NRCAT – National Religious Campaign Against Torture
NSC – National Security Council
OAS – Organization of American States
OAU – Organization of African Unity
OCHA – Office for the Coordination of Humanitarian Affairs
OECD – Organization of Economic Cooperation and Development
OFDA – Office of Foreign Disaster Assistance (US/AID)
OIC – Officer in Charge
OIC – Organization of the Islamic Conference
OIE – World Health Organization for Animals
OLS – Operation Lifeline Sudan
OPS – Online Projects System
P&I – Privileges and Immunities
PA – Public Advocacy
PAC – Political Action Committee
PAHO – Pan American Health Organization
PBI – Program Budget Implications
PD – Public Diplomacy
POW – Prisoner of War
PRM – Bureau of Population, Refugees, and Migration
PST – People's Sustainability Treaties
QNMK – Qëndra për Ndryshim dhe Manaxhim Konflikti
RAF – Royal Air Force (UK)
RED – Radical Ecological Democracy Treaty
RFP – Request for Proposals
RSPCA – Royal Society for the Prevention of Cruelty to Animals
SAIC – Science Applications International Corporation
SALT – Strategic Arms Limitation Treaty
SPCA – Society for the Prevention of Cruelty to Animals
SPD – Social Democratic Party
SPLM – Sudan People's Liberation Movement
SRRA – Sudan Relief and Rehabilitation Association

SRSG/VAC – Special Representative of the Secretary General on Violence Against Children
TC – Treaty Circles
TEA – Transitional Executive Authority
TILCEPA – Theme on Indigenous Peoples, Local Communities, Equity and Protected Areas
TNR – Trap, Neuter and Release
UDAW – Universal Declaration on Animal Welfare
UDAR – Universal Declaration of Animal Rights
UDHR – Universal Declaration of Human Rights.
UISE – International Save the Children
UK – United Kingdom
UN StatCom – United Nations Statistical Commission
UN/DPI – UN Department of Public Information
UN/ESA – UN Economic Commission for Africa
UNAMIR – United Nations Assistance Mission for Rwanda
UNCED – UN Conference on Environment and Development
UNDHA – UN Department of Humanitarian Affairs
UNDP – UN Development Program
UNEP – UN Environmental Program
UNEPS – United Nations Emergency Peace Service
UNESCO – UN Educational, Scientific and Cultural Organization
UNFF – United Nations Forum on Forests
UNGA – United Nations General Assembly
UNHCR – UN High Commissioner For Refugees
UNICEF – UN Children's Fund
UNPFII – UN Permanent Forum on Indigenous Issues
USAR – Urban Search and Rescue
UNSC – UN Security Council
UNTAG – UN Transition Assistance Group in Namibia
USA – United States of America
USIP – United States Institute for Peace
VAC – UN Study on Violence against Children
VE Day – Victory over Europe Day
VJ Day – Victory over Japan Day
WCDR – World Conference on Disaster Reduction
WCPA – World Commission on Protected Areas
WFP – World Food Program
WFS – World Food Summit
WHO – World Health Organization
WIZO – Women's International Zionist Organization
WSP – Women Strike For Peace
WSPA – World Society for the Protection of Animals
WSSD – United Nations World Summit on Sustainable Development
ZOPA – Zone of Possible Agreement

# Appendix B
# The Ankara Declaration

The Ankara Declaration: To Establish the Global Disaster Information Network

**Note** At the request of the NGOs, academic institutions, corporations, and governments present, the declaration was drafted by Dr. Albert Simard, one of the coauthors of this book, acting as an official of the Government of Canada. Later, he was elected president of GDIN, considered a Public–Private Partnership and NGO.

Endorsed at the GDIN Annual Conference, Ankara, Turkey, April 28, 2000

The right information, in the right format, to the right person, in time to make the right decision.

## *1.1.1 Executive Summary*

This declaration describes the purpose and scope of a Global Disaster Information Network (GDIN). It outlines the goals of GDIN, as well as guiding principles and its intended benefits. It lists several types of participants as well as describing four broad roles. The declaration outlines management and organizational structures for GDIN. It explains the funding process and financial management for GDIN. It concludes with processes for amending the declaration at the Ankara Conference and at subsequent annual GDIN conferences.

### 1.1.1.1 1 Preamble

1.1 Whereas the human, economic, and ecological impacts associated with disasters are increasing exponentially and these costs and losses pose a systemic risk to society's social, economic, and ecological bases. It is correspondingly difficult, in some cases impossible, for local, national, and global disaster management agencies to cope with the scope, magnitude, and complexity of these disasters.

L.W. Roeder, Jr. and A. Simard, *Diplomacy and Negotiation for Humanitarian NGOs*, Humanitarian Solutions in the 21st Century, DOI 10.1007/978-1-4614-7113-4,

1.2 Additionally, developing countries are particularly susceptible to enormous losses from all types of disasters, due to limited response capabilities, vulnerability of their economies and infrastructures, and migration of people to hazard-prone areas and urban centers.
1.3 Further, as we begin the twenty-first century, a revolution in information and computer technologies is transforming the global community from an industrial to an information society. Use of these technologies could assist in reducing and preventing the considerable impacts of disasters on people, their infrastructures, and their environment.
1.4 Resulting from a meeting in Washington, DC, on July 16–17, 1998 and a meeting in Mexico City on May 11–14, 1999, the international community of disaster experts agreed that there was a pressing need to establish a Global Disaster Information Network, hereinafter called GDIN, to harness rapidly evolving technology and information management processes to facilitate and enhance the global sharing of disaster management information.
1.5 Recognizing this need, a consensus declaration was developed, based on consultations with disaster experts from government agencies, the United Nations, the World Bank, OECD, the EU, private industry, non-governmental organizations, and academic institutions.
1.6 Therefore, the international community of disaster experts have endorsed this declaration at the GDIN 2000 Conference in Ankara, Turkey, on April 28, 2000. This endorsement represents the views of the experts as individuals; it does not necessarily reflect the views of their governments, agencies, organizations, or companies. This endorsement reflects a consensus of delegates at the conference; no signatures are required.
1.7 Notwithstanding any language in this declaration to the contrary, it is understood that nothing in the declaration should be construed to give rise to any international legal rights or obligations for any GDIN participant.

#### 1.1.1.2 2 Description

GDIN is a voluntary, self-sustaining, nonprofit association of countries, organizations, and professionals, from all sectors of society with an interest in sharing all types of disaster information. GDIN makes better use of existing and new technologies and develops institutional processes to promote global sharing of information about all disaster management functions between providers and users. It does this, in part, by providing a primary portal of access and linkage to existing national and international emergency- and disaster-management networks. GDIN also attempts to improve the effectiveness and interoperability of disaster information systems. GDIN also promotes and supports more timely access to disaster information by potentially affected communities and the general public through national and regional networks.

#### 1.1.1.3 3 Scope

GDIN is global in scope. GDIN facilitates the exchange of thematic and organizational content (data, information and knowledge), focusing on natural and technological disasters. (This is not to exclude other types of disasters/emergency situations in the context of which GDIN-facilitated exchanges are feasible/appropriate.) GDIN processes information about all disaster management functions: prevention, mitigation, planning, preparedness, monitoring, warning, response, rehabilitation, reconstruction, and recovery. The range of disaster information reflects what is made available by information providers; GDIN should not be a substantial provider, nor should it limit what is made available.

#### 1.1.1.4 4 Goals

The goals of GDIN are as follows:

- Increase awareness of the importance and value of disaster-related information and best practices for managing it.
- Adapt remote sensing, computer, communication, information, and network technologies to acquire, produce, disseminate, and access disaster data, information, and knowledge.
- Promote the development of national and regional capacity and infrastructures to access, manage, disseminate and use disaster information carried by GDIN in a digital format.
- Foster the sharing of information about all disaster management functions via a primary portal of access to national and international networks.
- Facilitate development and foster adoption of mutually agreed interoperability, metadata, and classification standards to support global sharing of disaster information.
- Provide disaster information and support services as directed by GDIN's governing body.

#### 1.1.1.5 5 Principles

Several principles serve to guide the design, development, and implementation of GDIN:

- The provision of information is voluntary; however, such content should be formatted so as to be compatible with mutually agreed GDIN standards.
- Mandates, decision authorities, and responsibilities remain with local, regional, and national information users.
- Disaster information is managed in accordance with mutually agreed best practices and principles, as endorsed by GDIN.
- Copyright, intellectual property, proprietary information, and security concerns must be respected.

- Disaster information should be provided with no or minimal cost and restrictions.
- Information provided without restriction is shared equally throughout GDIN. Notice of the availability of such information should be disseminated to all participants.
- International agreements, such as the Tampere Convention on the Provision of Emergency Telecommunications, should be fostered to enhance disaster telecommunications.
- GDIN complements and partners with, not supplants, existing disaster information networks to leverage the advantages of new technologies.

#### 1.1.1.6 6 Benefits

GDIN has the potential to reduce the human, economic, and ecological impacts of disasters and the costs of disaster management by the following:

- Making information more readily available when, where, and as needed
- Lowering the cost of producing, providing, and using disaster information
- Leveraging the efforts of existing disaster information and relief networks
- Supporting timelier and better coordinated disaster response
- Creating synergy to enable the production of new kinds of information
- Increasing public awareness of how to plan for and respond to disasters
- Expanding the base of knowledge about disaster and emergency management

#### 1.1.1.7 7 Participation

GDIN is inclusive rather than exclusive. The widest possible participation in providing disaster information is encouraged from emergency management communities. These include the following:

- International organizations, such as the United Nations and its Specialized Agencies, the World Bank Group, Organization for Economic Cooperation and Development (OECD)
- Countries
- National, regional, and local disaster management agencies
- Disaster organizations, such as the International Red Cross and Red Crescent Movement, non-governmental organizations
- Academic institutions, such as universities, training schools, research and development agencies, and institutes
- Private industry, such as companies and consultants that provide disaster-related products and services
- Emergency Associations, such as The International Emergency Management Society, International Association of Emergency Managers, and Emergency Planning Society
- Recognized experts, such as managers, scientists, policy analysts, technical specialists, government officials

#### 1.1.1.8 8 Roles

GDIN and its participants have four roles:

- **Providing information** – All activities undertaken by providers are voluntary and as they deem appropriate. Information providers are responsible for managing information assets, acquiring data, transforming data into information, synthesizing new knowledge, disseminating information products, providing access to content, providing search capability, and adapting content to GDIN standards, as determined by the GDIN Standards Working Group. Providers should assist users by identifying potentially useful information and including source references in the metadata.
- **Using information** – Information users determine what information they need, appropriate formats, and how they use it. Information users are responsible for searching for information, accessing and transferring it to their repositories, interpreting and adapting the information to their needs, using it as they deem appropriate (consistent with restrictions from providers), and all consequences of using the information. The source of all information must be clearly identified.
- **Managing information** – GDIN promotes, facilitates, coordinates, and supports the provision and use of information by providers and access by users. GDIN acts as an information broker and manager to integrate providers and users into a disaster information community, to facilitate information sharing through an information infrastructure, and to assist users in finding and adapting content to their specific needs and capacities The brokering function may include a quality assurance/quality control service for disaster information. GDIN develops, implements, and operates a primary portal of access to all existing national and internal disaster information networks.
- **Linking to information** – GDIN links to and does not replace, duplicate, compete with, or supplant, existing global disaster information initiatives such as that provided by ReliefWeb, HazardNet, the International Federation of Red Cross and Red Crescent, and the Reuters Foundation AlertNet. It should also link to regional, sector, and operational systems, such as the PAHO Supply Management System, the WHO/EHA Health Information Network for Advanced Planning, and the Canadian FireM3 System for Monitoring, Mapping, and Modeling forest fires. GDIN leverages its efforts by supporting and linking to existing global disaster information networks. GDIN focuses on adding value to existing information and networks.

#### 1.1.1.9 9 Management

- **9.1 GDIN** is managed by three bodies – an Executive Committee, the Annual Conference, and a Funding Committee. An overview of the management structure is shown in Annex 1.
- **9.2 The Annual Conference** establishes GDIN goals, and objectives, policies, operating procedures, and the types and providers of GDIN services. The conference is hosted by a country or disaster organization; the host and location should

change each year. The conference is organized and executed by a Conference Committee chaired by the host. It comprises chairs of the immediately previous and succeeding conferences, the chair of the Funding Committee, chairs of GDIN Working Groups, the GDIN Executive Director, and other members, as the Annual Conference or Conference Committee may deem appropriate. Direction from the conference is based on a consensus of attending delegates, in accordance with this declaration. The Conference Committee prepares a report of the conference findings and recommendations. The venue for the year after the next one is selected at the close of each conference.

- **9.3 The Executive Committee** provides oversight for GDIN and a secretariat by ensuring that directions from the Annual Conference and the Funding Committee are implemented. The Executive Committee is presided over by a chair, who is elected by the Committee, for a term of 1 year. It also oversees and coordinates the activities of the various working groups. The Executive Committee comprises eight members: two members each from the Annual Conference Organizing Committee, the Funding Committee, and working group chairs, the Executive Director, and one representative from the NGO/Academia working group. Each representative is selected by the committee or group(s) that they represent. Decisions are based on a consensus of members of the Executive Committee, in accordance with this declaration.
- **9.4 The Funding Committee** oversees and directs disbursements from a fund, to be known as the GDIN Fund. The Funding Committee comprises one representative each from any government or other participants that provides 5 % or more of GDIN core funding, including in-kind contributions or contributions of approved services. Organizations may aggregate their contributions to meet the 5 % threshold and gain a joint representative on the Committee. Committee membership is for the year in which a contribution is made. The Executive Director of GDIN is also a voting member of the Funding Committee, except on the GDIN annual budget. Each representative has one vote. An organization is limited to one vote, regardless of the number of contributions from its component parts. The Committee is presided over by a chair, elected by the Funding Committee, for a term of 1 year. Decisions are based on a consensus of committee members, in accordance with this declaration.

Working group chairs and project leaders are nonvoting observers of the Funding Committee. All funding decisions regarding working groups or projects are taken in consultation with appropriate working group chairs or project participants.

#### 1.1.1.10 10 Organization

- 10.1 **Working Groups:** These are groups of experts established and terminated by the annual conferences to accomplish specific goals and objectives on behalf of GDIN. The expected duration of a working group is included in its terms of reference. Terms of reference for each working group are approved and reviewed by the Conferences. working groups report progress, accomplishments, findings, and recommendations to the annual conference. The conference may appoint a chair or allow a working group to select a chair. Travel expenses are normally incurred by working group members. working groups may, however, request funds from the GDIN Fund or other appropriate organizations to support cash expenditures or to pay travel costs for essential experts.

- 10.2 **Executive Director:** The primary role of the GDIN executive director is to implement directions received from GDIN's governing bodies. The director recommends actions and activities as well as reports on progress and accomplishments to these bodies annually. The director represents GDIN at international disaster fora and at key meetings of international disaster organizations. The director assists host countries in organizing and executing the Annual Conference, as needed. The director supports working groups and special projects to facilitate the achievement of milestones and deliverables. The director coordinates the GDIN secretariat and the information facilitator in fulfilling their roles and responsibilities. The executive director could also serve as a point of contact between participants and the various GDIN committees and groups. The executive director may assist with GDIN fund-raising activities but has no fiduciary responsibility with respect to the GDIN fund. The executive director is selected by the Annual Conference and serves for a term of 1 year; the term may be extended by a consensus of the Annual Conference.
- 10.3 **Information Facilitator:** The information facilitator should be knowledgeable in managing both disasters and information. The facilitator assists users in finding information and adapting it to their specific needs and capabilities. This service is intended to provide assistance with unusual information needs, when normal searches have been unsuccessful. The facilitator is not expected to analyze data or maintain a data warehouse or information repository.

A working group has been established by the Ankara Conference to further refine the role and function of the information facilitator.

- 10.4 **Secretariat:** A minimal staff (not to exceed three positions) monitors and records GDIN decisions and activities. It provides administrative, clerical, and staff support for the management bodies, working groups, the executive director, and the information facilitator. It maintains a GDIN presence on the World Wide Web and loads data and information on to a website as directed by the Annual Conference; it maintains links to approved disaster website around the world; it creates and maintains a database of disaster experts associated with GDIN. The secretariat posts records of GDIN meetings, decisions, and activities on the website.

#### 1.1.1.11 11 Funding

- 11.1 **The GDIN Fund** is established to accept and administer contributions to GDIN. Funding for GDIN is through voluntary grants and contributions.

Any organization – government, private, or other – with an interest in disaster management may contribute to GDIN. Contributors may direct their contributions to specific GDIN activities or may place conditions on the use of their contributions. Contributions may be made to the GDIN Fund or, if approved by the Executive Committee or Annual Conference, directly to any person or organization for approved GDIN services or projects.

- 11.2 **The fund is divided into two parts** – operations and projects. Operations include all recurring GDIN expenses, such as costs of the Annual Conference not borne by participants and the host, costs of running the GDIN secretariat, the executive director and information facilitator positions, travel to GDIN events by a limited number of essential experts, approved GDIN services, and other recurring activities or services authorized by the Annual Conference or the Funding Committee.
- 11.3 **An annual operating budget,** designating the allocation of funds for GDIN operations, is prepared by the executive director, in consultation with the GDIN fund manager. It is submitted to the Funding Committee for review and approval, based on directions from the previous Annual Conference and the availability of operating funds. The Committee evaluates the previous year's expenses for conformity with the budget.
- 11.4 **The GDIN Fund** supports projects and working groups, to the extent that funds are available in excess of those required for GDIN operations. Projects and working groups are not funded on a continuing basis, although they may have a life in excess of 1 year. Project proposals are submitted to the project working group who evaluate and prioritize all proposals and make recommendations to the Funding Committee. Terms of Reference for Work Groups are approved by the Annual Conference. The project evaluation committee is appointed by the Funding Committee, as needed.
- 11.5 **An accredited professional Fund Manager** will be contracted to manage and administer the GDIN fund, as directed by the Funding Committee. Duties of the fund manager include fiscal management, fund raising, and administrative support on financial matters for the executive director and the Funding Committee. The fund manager should also recommend processes for upkeep and growth of the fund.

#### 1.1.1.12 12 Amendments

It is anticipated that this declaration will be changed from time to time, as necessary. The process is as follows:

12.1 Before the GDIN Conferences

- Proposed amendments to the declaration are submitted to the GDIN Executive Committee at least 2 months prior to the conference.

- The Executive Committee considers all proposals. It may endorse proposed amendments, according to their appropriateness, based on the intent of this declaration.
- All proposed amendments, together with the views of the Executive Committee, are posted on the GDIN website at least 1 month prior to the Annual Conference.

### 12.2 The Annual Conference

- Proposed amendments are presented on the morning of day 1 of the conference at a plenary session. This is followed by a plenary discussion.
- A Drafting Committee receives written suggested changes from conference participants until 5 p.m. on day 2 of the conference.
- The Committee considers all suggested changes and may modify the proposed amendments, as they deem appropriate.
- Updated versions of the amendments are provided to conference participants on the mornings of day 2 and day 3 of the conference.
- The amendments are presented at a plenary session on day 3 of the conference.
- A consensus of conference participants indicates endorsement of the amendment.

### 12.3 Between Annual Conferences

- Proposed amendments to this declaration are submitted to the Policy Working Group.
- The proposed amendments are made available to the GDIN membership for comment for a period of 30 days.
- Best efforts to achieve consensus will be made.
- If consensus is not achieved:

  (1) If the amendment is editorial in nature, the Policy Committee will make a determination.
  (2) If the amendment is substantive in nature, the amendment will be referred to the next Annual Conference for a decision.

- Proposed amendments to operational procedures will be submitted to the Policy Working Group for review and determination.

# 13 By-Laws

By-laws will be necessary to guide the management and daily operations of GDIN. The Policy Working Group has been directed to develop a set of By-laws for GDIN and submit them to the 2001 GDIN Conference, where they will be reviewed, modified as necessary, endorsed, and appended to this declaration. Such elements of this declaration as are more appropriate to By-laws will be transferred to the appended document.

L.W. Roeder, Jr. and A. Simard, *Diplomacy and Negotiation for Humanitarian NGOs*, Humanitarian Solutions in the 21st Century, DOI 10.1007/978-1-4614-7113-4,

# Works Cited


*About Us*. (2010). Retrieved August 3, 2010, from ICAPO: http://icapo.org/about.html

Abshire, D. B. (2005). *The character of George Marshal*. Lexington, VA: Washington and Lee University.

Achenbach, G., Rourke, K., & McRuer, D. (2008). *Wildlife center of Virginia education animal policy*. Waynesboro: Wildlife Center of Virginia.

ACT Alliance. (2010, June 29). *SitRep Haiti – 17/2010*. Geneva: ACT Alliance.

Action_Against_ Poisoning. (2010). *Universal declaration of animal rights*. Retrieved from Action_Against_ Poisoning: http://jose.kersten.free.fr/aap/pages/uk/UDAR_uk.html

Ad Hoc Working Group on Informatics. (2010, June 13). *United Nations members states*. Retrieved from Permanent Missions to the United Nations: http://www.un.int/index-en/index.html

Adeniyi, A. S. (2010, March 8–April 6). *Livestock keepers' rights – An important concept for food security?* (FSN Forum Discussion No. 53). League for Pastoral Peoples and Endogenous Livestock Development.

Adler, J. (2005, October 1). The fight against the flu. *Newsweek*, pp. 38–45.

ADRC. (2004, July 16). *ADRC presents GLIDE at GDIN2004*. Retrieved July 26, 2012, from Asian Disaster Reduction Center Biweekly News: http://www.adrc.asia/highlights/NewsNo097.pdf

Aesop. (1955). The fox and the grapes. In M. Martignoni (Ed.), *Illustrated treasury of children's literature* (p. 156). New York: Grosset and Dunlap.

Affairs, N. B. (2010). *UN grounds pass for ECOSOC NGOs*. Retrieved from NGO Branch: UN Department of Economic and Social Affairs: http://esango.un.org/paperless/Web?page=static&content=designation

Agence France-Presse. (2005, October 14). *British aid for Katrina victims blocked by fears of mad cow disease*. Retrieved from TerraDaily: http://www.terradaily.com/2005/051014195302.24p8zrf2.html

Aggression, S. C., & Assembly, U. G. (1974). *Definition of aggression, United Nations General Assembly Resolution 3314 (XXIX)*. New York: United Nations.

Al Jazeera. (2011, February 9). *Syrian activist Suhair Atassi*. Retrieved March 8, 2012, from Al Jazeera: http://www.aljazeera.com/indepth/2011/02/201129135657367367.html

Allee, V. (2003). *The future of knowledge: Increasing prosperity through value networks*. Boston: Nutterworth-Heinemann.

American Association for International Conciliation. (1919). Comments by the German Delegation. *International Conciliation, 144*(November), 1203–1337.

American Group at Dubarton Oaks. (1944, August 10). *Minutes of meeting 8 held by members of the American Group at Dumbarton Oaks*. Washington, DC: American Group.



L.W. Roeder, Jr. and A. Simard, *Diplomacy and Negotiation for Humanitarian NGOs*, Humanitarian Solutions in the 21st Century, DOI 10.1007/978-1-4614-7113-4,

Amman, W. (2006, August). *IDRC Davos 2006 Conference Brochure and Program*. Retrieved from Global Risk Forum: http://www.idrc.info/userfiles/image/PDF_2006/IDRC_2006_Program.pdf
Amman, W. (n.d.). *Goals of the global risk forum*. Retrieved March 14, 2012, from The Global Risk Forum: http://www.grforum.org/pages_new.php/Goals/583/1/236/
Anderson, L., & Anderson, A. (2006). *Rescued: Savings animals from disasters*. Novato, CA: New World Library.
Andiressen, D. (2004). *Making sense of intellectual capital*. Oxford: Elsevier/Butterworth-Heinemann.
Animal Production and Health Division, FAO. (2010). *Home page*. Retrieved from Gateway to Animal Welfare: http://www.fao.org/ag/againfo/themes/animal-welfare/en/
Anklam, P. (2007). *New work: A practical guide to creating and sustaining networks*. Burlington, MA: Butterworth-Heinemann.
Antonio, G. S. (2010a, October 19). *Discussions on NGO diplomacy*. (L. Roeder, Interviewer).
Antonio, G. S. (2010b, October 19). *Review of book discussions*. (L. Roeder, Interviewer).
Assembly of the League. (1938, September 30). *Protection of civilian populations against bombing from the air in case of war*. Geneva: League of Nations.
Associated Press. (1927, April 6). Briand urges world will for peace. *Oakland Tribune*, p. 3.
Associated Press. (2010, September 26). *US: Inverted Philippine flag was 'honest mistake'*. Retrieved 2010, from Yahoo News: www.yahoo.com
Associated Press and Reuters. (2009, June 11). *WHO declares first pandemic in 41 years*. Retrieved July 10, 2010, from FOX News: http://www.foxnews.com/story/0,2933,525804,00.html
Associated_Press. (2010, June 21). *Whaling Commission ponders suspending hunting ban*. Retrieved from MSNBC: http://www.msnbc.msn.com/id/37823784/ns/business
Augusto, A. (2012, April 27). *Media in Brazil*. (L. Roeder, Interviewer).
Ballentine, J. (2001, December 6). *Email: Info from WernerWeb site*. Washington, DC: AZA.
Ballentine, J. (2010, August). *Discussions on events surrounding the Kabul rescue operations*. (L. Roeder, Interviewer).
BallotPedia. (2010, August). *California proposition 4 (1998)*. Retrieved from Ballotpedia: http://ballotpedia.org/wiki/index.php/Main_Page
Baloch, M. F. (2012, April 10). *Call for seminar on woman's rights and acid throwing in Pakistan*. Geneva: PreventionWeb.
Bari, E. (2008, November 12). Memo from Managing Director, Grameen Fisheries & Livestock Foundation to FAO, Regional Office, Bangkok. *Memo to FAO, Regional Office, Bangkok* . Dhaka, Bangladesh: Grameen Fisheries & Livestock Foundation.
Bartholdt, R. (1930). *From steerage to congress*. Philadelphia: Dorrance.
Bartlett, R. J. (1944). *The league to enforce peace*. Chapel Hill: University of North Carolina Press.
Bayvel, A. (2005, August). *Animal welfare: Global issues, trends, and challenges* (Vol. 24). Paris: World Organization for Animal Health.
Belair, D. R. (2009). *Universal Declaration on Animal Rights (UDAR)*. Retrieved from D. R. Belair RTMKB: http://www.dr-belair.com/dic/Medicine/Veterinary/Declaration-en.htm
Bellal, A., & Casey-Maslen, S. (2011). *Rules of engagement*. Geneva: Geneva Academy of International Humanitarian Law and Human Rights.
Bellal, A., Giacca, G., & Casey-Maslen, S. (2011, March). International law and armed non-state actors in Afghanistan. *International Review of the Red Cross, 93*, 881.
Bernstorff, J. H. (1918, December 21). *Bernstorff in favor of League of Nations*. 1. (F. J. Taylor, Interviewer).
Berridge, G. (2005). *Diplomacy, theory and practice*. New York: Macmillan.
Besheer, M. (2009, February 4). *Sudan envoy: UN peacekeepers will be safe if ICC issues warrant against Bashir.* Retrieved from Global Security Reporting on Voice of America: http://www.globalsecurity.org/military/library/news/2009/02/mil-090205-voa11.htm
Bettles, C. (2012, June 7). *Activists overshadow welfare work.* Stock & Land. http://www.stockandland.com.au/news/agriculture/cattle/beef/activistsovershadow-welfare-work/2582373.aspx. Retrieved 1 May 2013.

Blas, J. (2010, September 19). *Discussion on UDAW*. (L. Roeder, Interviewer).
Blitzer, W. (1982, March 11–17). State Department article proposes Palestinian state. *Jerusalem Post*, p. 1.
Borek, J. S. (2003). *Membership in ADRC*. Washington, DC: US Department of State.
Boritz, M. (1998). The hidden culture of diplomatic practice. *Ethnologia Scandinavica, 28*, 48–62.
Boritz, M. (2010, September 21). *Email discussion on diplomatic practice*. (L. Roeder, Interviewer).
Bourgeois, L. (1922, December). *The reasons for the League of Nations*. Oslo: The Nobel Committee.
Bowles, D. (2009, December 9). *RSPCA*. (L. Roeder, Interviewer).
Braasch, P. (2012, June 26). *Discussion on professor Niemeyer*. (L. Roeder, Interviewer). Kiel, Germany: Büro des Kanzlers.
Brakes, P., Butterworth, A., Simmonds, M., Lymbery, P., & Attenborough, S. D. Troubed waters: Review of the welfare implications of modern whaling activities, WSPA, London in 2004.
Breen, R. (1994). Saving enemy children: Save the children's Russian relief operation 1921–1923. *Disasters, 18*, 221–238.
Bridgeport Indianapolis Telegraph. (1919, September 5). President's Indianapolis speech. *Bridgeport Standard Telegram*, p. 4.
Brind, J. (1935, October 26). *SAARFORCE. Report of the commander in chief.* League of Nations, SAARFORCE. Geneva: League of Nations.
British Cabinet. (1925, March 2). *Meeting of the cabinet to be held in the prime minister's room*. London: National Archives.
Brown, V. W., Brown, E. P., Gillnore, J., & Swartzendruber, H. D. (1987). *A.I.D. evaluation special study no. 48*. Washington, DC: USAID.
Bruins, H. J., Akong'a, J. J., Rutten, M. M., & Kressel, G. M. (2005, May/June). Drought planning and rainwater harvesting for arid-zone pastoralists: The Turkana, the Maasai, and the Negev Bedouin. *Arid Lands Newsletter*. http://ag.arizona.edu/oals/ALN/aln57/bruins.html.
Brundtland, G. H. (1987). *Report of the World Commission on Environment and Development: Our common future*. Oslo: United Nations.
Bryant, L. (2010, January 26). *Donors expected to make good on Haiti relief pledges*. Retrieved from Voice of America News: http://www.voanews.com/
Bryce, J. (1927). The morality of states. In J. Bryce (Ed.), *International relations: Eight lectures* (pp. 176–205). New York: Macmillan.
Buchanan-Smith, M., & Davies, S. (1995). *Famine early warning and response– The missing link*. London: Intermediate Technology.
Burdett, W. (1969). *Encounter with the Middle East*. New York: Atheneum.
Bureau of International Organization Affairs. (1996). *Voting practices in the United Nations*. Washington, DC: US Department of State.
Bureau of Public Affairs. (1965). The Soviet Union Document VI-28. In *American foreign policy* (p. 581). Washington, DC: Department of State.
Burke, E. (1790). *Reflections on the revolution in France*. Dodsley, London.
C., P. M. (1975). *The quest for collective security (unpublished)*. Norwich: University of East Anglia.
Cambon, J. (1931). *The diplomatist*. (C. R. Turner, Trans.) Philip Allan.
Cambon, J. (mcmxxxi). *The diplomatist*. (C. R. Turner, Trans.) Philip Allan.
Care2. (2005, December 1). *UN declaration for animal welfare*. Retrieved 2010, from Care2.com: http://www.care2.com/
Castle, S. (2010, September 2). E.U. casts doubt on legality of France expelling Roma. *International Herald Tribune*, p. 1.
CBD Secretariat. (2010). Retrieved July 2010, from http://www.cbd.int/
CCAMLR Secretariat. (2010). *CCAMLR*. Retrieved July 2010, from CCAMLR: http://www.ccamlr.org/
CCSBT Secretariat. (2010). *Commission for the Conservation of Southern Bluefin Tuna (CCSBT)*. Retrieved July 2010, from Commission for the Conservation of Southern Bluefin Tuna (CCSBT): http://www.ccsbt.org/

Cecchetti, R. (2010, July 27). *Email interview: Question on UNGA resolution.* (L. Roeder, Interviewer).

Cecchetti, R. (2012, July 27). *Discussion on the VAC.* (L. Roeder, Interviewer).

Cecchetti, R., & Becker, J. (2006, October 2). *Proposal for the 2006 UNGA resolution on the rights of the Child.* Geneva, Switzerland.

Cecil, R. (1923). *The moral basis of the League of Nations.* Hull: Elsom.

CFR. (2012). *CFR history.* Retrieved April 3, 2012, from Council on Foreign Relations: http://www.cfr.org/about/history/cfr/

CGS. (2008). *One step towards effective genocide prevention.* Washington, DC: Citizens for Global Solutions.

Charny, J. (2012, August 6). *Government funding practices.* (L. W. Roeder, Interviewer)

Chatham House. (2012). *Chatham House Rule.* Retrieved June 25, 2012, from Chatham House: http://www.chathamhouse.org/

Cianfarani, M. (2012, September 17). *LGBTQ and the UN – finally!* (L. Roeder, Interviewer). GDNET.

CICC. (2012, March 14). *Coalition for the International Criminal Court (CICC).* Retrieved March 14, 2012, from The International Criminal Court: http://www.iccnow.org/?mod=home

CITES Secretariat, Geneva. (2010). *Convention on International Trade in Endangered Species of Wild Fauna and Flora.* Retrieved 2010, from Convention on International Trade in Endangered Species of Wild Fauna and Flora: www.cites.org

Clark, E. (2010). *The Gulf oil spill: Lessons learned and lost.* 15th Annual Call of the Wild. Waynesboro. Virginia: Wildlife Center of Virginia an The Virginia Department of Game and Inland Fisheries.

Clavin, P. (2012, June 20). *Role of NGOs and the League of Nations.* (L. W. Roeder, Interviewer).

Clinton, W. J. (2005, August 22). *Invitation to the Global Consortium for Tsunami Recovery.* New York: Office of the Secretary General's Special Envoy for Tsunami Recovery.

CMS Secretariat. (2010). *Convention on migratory species.* Retrieved July 2010, from Convention on Migratory Species: http://www.cms.int/

Cohen, W., & Albright, M. (2008). *Preventing genocide: A blueprint for U.S. policymakers.* Washington, DC: USIP.

Cohn, D. (2001, November 30). U.S. zoos offer aid to Afghan animals. *Washington Post*, p. A26. http://www.gdin.org/news/01nov30_zoo_aid.pdf

Comer, C. C. (2010). *iPetitions.* Retrieved July 20, 2010, from petition to protect zoo animals in war zones: http://www.ipetitions.com/petition/zooanimalsinwarzones/

Confidential. (2008, November 5). *Discussion on Sudanese NGOs.* (L. Roeder, Interviewer).

CoNgo. (2011). *Civil society's essential role in achieving education for all.* Civil Society Development Forum (CSDF) 2011 Geneva Component. Geneva: CoNgo.

CoNgo Conference of NGOs. (2007a, December 14). Retrieved July 2010, from http://www.ngo-congo.org/congo/files/congo_ga_2007__call_for_action.pdf

CoNgo Conference on NGOs. (2007b, September 5). *Session 11a: Human development and climate change development crisis.* Retrieved 2010, from Final Programme 23rd GA CONGO: http://www.ngocongo.org/congo/files/ga_2007_final_programme_english.pdf

Cooper, J. J. (2009). *Woodrow Wilson: A biography.* New York: Knopf.

Cooper, J. M. (2012a, April 9). *Discussion on formation of the League of Nations.* (L. W. Roeder, Interviewer).

Cooper, J. M. (2012b, April 11). *Discussion on formation of League of Nations.* (L. W. Roeder, Interviewer).

Copper Canyon. (2010). *Tarahumara natives.* Retrieved from MexicosCopperCanyon.com: http://tarahumara.mexicoscoppercanyon.com/

*Covenant on Civil and Political Rights.* (1994, July 7). Retrieved March 19, 2012, from Human Rights Web: http://www.hrweb.org/legal/cpr.html

Crutchfield, L. R., & Grant, H. M. (2008). *Sustaining impact.* San Francisco: Jossey-Bass.

CSOP. (1943a). *Annex X: The Drafting Group for the United Nations Charter.* Commission to study the organization, US Department of State, Washington, DC.

CSOP. (1943b, July 23). *International organizations: Permanent international organizations: Functions, powers, machinery, procedure*. CSOP.
Cuno, J. (2008). *Who own antiquities?* Oxfordshire: Princeton.
Currion, P., & Hedlund, K. (2011, January). *Strength in numbers: A review of NGO coordination in the field*. Geneva: ICVA.
Dalkir, K. (2005). *Knowledge management in theory and practice*. Oxford: Elsevier Butterworth-Heinemann.
Dan Lyons, C. D. (2010, June 8 and 9). *History of the Universal Declaration on Animal Rights, UDAR*. (E. i. Larry Roeder, Interviewer).
Danieli, Y., Stamatopoulou, E., & Dias, C. J. (1999). *The Universal Declaration of Human Rights: Fifty years and beyond*. New York: United Nations.
Davenport, T. H., & Prusak, L. (1998). *Working knowledge: How organizations manage what they know*. Boston, MA: Harvard Business School Press.
Davies, P. (2010, October 11). *Email discussion on food policy*. (L. Roeder, Interviewer).
Davis, G. (2004, July 24). *Navajo nation: The OECD study*. Window Rock, AZ: Navajo Nation Government.
De Bruhl, M. (2006). *Firestorm*. New York: Random House.
De Bruhl, M. (2012, July 29). *Discussion of the Dresden attack*. (L. Roeder, Interviewer).
de Mello, S. V. (2001, November). *East Timor: The building of a nation*. (F. C. Millet, & R. Rathinasabapathy, Interviewers). Oxford: Europa Magazine.
Decrey-Warner, E. (2012, May). *Discussion on Geneva call*. (L. Roeder, Interviewer).
Dell, R. E. (1941). *The Geneva racket 1920–1939*. London: Robert Hale.
Delong, D. W. (2004). *Lost knowledge: Confronting the threat of an aging workforce*. Oxford: Oxford.
Denza, E. (2008a). *Diplomatic law, commentary on the Vienna Convention on Diplomatic Relations*. Oxford: Oxford University Press.
Denza, E. (2008b). *Vienna Convention on diplomatic relations, 1961*. Retrieved March 12, 2012, from Audio Visual Library of International Law: http://untreaty.un.org/cod/avl/ha/vcdr/vcdr.html
Department of Public Information, News and Media Division. (2007). *General assembly adopts declaration on rights of indigenous peoples*. New York: UN.
Department of State. (1942a). *The Paris Peace Conference, 1919* (Vol. III). Washington, DC: GPO.
Department of State. (1942b). *The Paris Peace Conference, 1919* (Vol. XIII). Washington, DC: GPO.
Department of State. (1942c). *The Paris Peace Conference, 1919* (Vol. 1). Washington, DC: GPO.
Department of State. (1960). *Documents on disarmament 1945–1956*. Washington, DC: Department of State.
Department of State. (2010). *Humanitarian information unit*. Retrieved August 3, 2010, from HIU: http://hiu.state.gov/
der Deutschen. (1919). *Monographien zum Volkerbuncl Liga fur Volkerbund*. Berlin: Hans Robert Engelmann.
DESA. (2008). *DESA News, 12*(12). Retrieved from DESA News (UN Department of Economic and Social Affairs): http://www.un.org/esa/desa/
DESA. (2009). *Core Publications: Agenda 21*. Retrieved August 22, 2012, from Division for Sustainable Development: http://www.un.org/esa/dsd/agenda21/
DESA. (2012a, May). The voice of civil society at Rio+20. *DESA News, 16*(5), p. 1.
DESA. (2012b, May). Urban population to grow more than ever. *DESA News, 16*
DeYoung, K. (2012, July 12). U.S. lifts ban on investment in Burma. *The Washington Post*, p. A11.
Diamond, L. (2006, December). Promoting democracy in post-conflict and failed states. *Taiwan Journal of Democracy, 2*, 93–115.
*Die Stockholmer Friedenskonferenz von 1917*. (2012, March 12). Retrieved April 10, 2012, from Labour History: http://labourhistory.net/stockholm1917/bilder.php
Direnfeld, E. (2001, December). *Emergency response diets*. The Bronx Zoo and the Wildlife Conservation Society, Bronx Zoo, New York.
Dixon, N. (2010). *The three eras of knowledge management*. Retrieved from http://www.nancydixonblog.com

Drummond, D. (2010, March 22). *A new approach to China: An update.* Retrieved June 8, 2012, from GoogleBlog: http://googleblog.blogspot.com/2010/03/new-approach-to-china-update.html#!/2010/03/new-approach-to-china-update.html

Dülffer, J. (2012, June 19). *Discussion on German League*. (L. W. Roeder, Interviewer).

Dulles, J. F. (1972). The general assembly. In H. F. Armstrong (Ed.), *Fifty years of foreign affairs*. New York: Praeger.

ECHO. (n.d.). *ECHO decisions.* Retrieved August 2, 2010, from European Commission: http://ec.europa.eu/echo/funding/decisions_en.htm

Economist Staff. (1995, May 13). Catastrophe theory in *The Economist*, p. 80.

ECOSOC. (2011). *Working with ECOSOC: An NGO guide to consultative status*. New York: UN.

Edvinson, L., & Malone, M. (1996). *Intellectual capital.* New York: Harper Collins.

Encyclopedia Britannica. (n.d.). *The development of the foreign ministry and embassies.* Retrieved from Encyclopedia Britannica: http://www.britannica.com/EB

Enge, D. (2010, June 10). *Minister counselor for political affairs, Mission of Norway to the UN, New York.* (L. Roeder, Interviewer).

Engelken, S. C., & OSiekman, K. (2010, June 9). *Email interview with US mission to UNESCO*, June 2010. (L. Roeder, Interviewer).

Eppstein, J. (1929a). *Ten years' life of the League of Nations*. London: The May Fair Press.

Eppstein, J. (1929b). The minorities problem. In J. Eppstein (Ed.), *Ten years' life of the League of Nations* (p. 111). London: The May Fair Press.

ESI. (2010). *Saving endemic endangered fish, India.* Retrieved from Endangered Species International: http://www.endangeredspeciesinternational.org/current_projects.html

Estol, L. (2008). *The family violence saga: From animal to children.* Retrieved 2010, from Slide Share.

Estol, L. (2010, July 12). *Professor*. (L. W. Roeder, Interviewer).

FAO: Corporate Services, Human Resources and Finance Department. (2001, November). *The Reykjavik Conference on Responsible Fisheries in the Marine Ecosystem.* Retrieved from FAO: http://www.fao.org/DOCREP/005/Y2198T/y2198t01.htm

Feinstein-International-Center. (2009). *Livestock emergency guidelines and standards.* Warwickshire, UK: Practical Action.

Fenzi, J., & Nelson, C. L. (1994). *Married to the foreign service*. New York: Twayne.

FEWS. (2010). *Famine early warning system.* Retrieved August 2010, from Famine Early Warning System: http://www.fews.net/

Fisher, R., & Ury, W. (2011). *Getting to yes: Negotiating agreement without giving in* (3rd ed.). New York: Penguin.

Fleming, T. (2003). *The illusion of victory*. New York: Basic Books.

French, M. M. (2010). *United States protocol*. New York: Roman and Little Fittlefield.

Funai, G. (2010, August). Working together after a disaster. *Monday Developments*, p. 27.

G7 Secretariat. (1995, February 25–26). Proceedings of the Information Society Conference. Brussels, Belgium: G7 Information Society.

Gaillard, P. J. (2012, May 9). *Discussion on transgender issues*. (GDN, Interviewer).

Gannett Editorial. (1950, July 29). Our greatest need: a UN army. *Portland Press Herald*, p. 7.

George, K. (2010, September 16). *Email discussion with K. George, Programmes Officer – Marine mammals*, WSPA. (L. Roeder, Interviewer).

German Foreign Ministry. (2007, November 26). *Federal Minister Steinmeier: "Refugees in Somalia need our help!"*. Retrieved June 26, 2012, from Reliefweb: www.reliefweb.int

GHD Initiative. (2010). *About good humanitarian donorship initiative.* Retrieved July 28, 2010, from Good Humanitarian Donorship Initiative: http://www.goodhumanitariandonorship.org/

Ghosh, S. (2010, November 19). *Discussion with Kegg Farms executives on humane farming techniques*. (L. Roeder, Interviewer).

Glen, J. H., & Symonides, J. (1998). *The Universal Declaration of Human Rights: a history of its creation and implementation, 1948–1998*. Paris: UNESCO.

Global Portal for Diplomats. (2010). *Gender issues.* Retrieved September 2010, from Social Tips: http://www.ediplomat.com/nd/protocol/social_tips.htm

Gompers, S. (1921). The labor clauses of the treaty. In E. M. House & C. Seymour (Eds.), *What really happened at Paris* (pp. 319–336). New York: Scribner's.

Goodman, S. (2000). *Animal rescue: The best job there is*. New York: Aladdin Paperbacks.
Goodman, S. E. (2001). *Animal rescue: The best job there is*. New York: Aladdin.
Government of Australia. (2007). *Introduction*. Retrieved March 17, 2012, from The Australia Group: http://www.australiagroup.net/en/introduction.html
Gregor, M. (2006). *Bird flu: A virus of our own making*. New York: Lantern.
Group of Military Representatives to the Dumbarton Oaks Conference. (1944, October 3). *Special Military Record 1, Informal Record of the Meeting of the Group of Military Representives of the Delegations*. Washington, DC: US Delegation to Dumbarton Oaks.
Group-of-77. (2010). *About the group of 77*. Retrieved from The Group of 77 at the United Nations: http://www.g77.org/doc/
Gunder, M. A. (1995). *The utility of expanding the United Nations Permanent Military Force*. Quantico: UNITED STATES MARINE CORPS command and STAFF COLLEGE.
Habib (Sudan Red Crescent), M., Al-Hadid (Jordan Red Crescent), M., Cheniti (Tunisia Red Crescent), T., & Al-Hazaa (Saudi Arabia Red Crescent), A. M. (2008, March 20). (L. Roeder, Interviewer).
Hackney, R. (2001, December 7). *Fundraising effort tops $130,000 or Kabul Zoo*. Asheboro, NC: North Carolina Zoological Park.
Haeckel, S. (1999). *Adaptive enterprise: Creating and leading sense and respond organizations*. Boston, MA: Harvard Business School Press.
Hamel, G. (2000). *Leading the revolution*. Boston, MA: Harvard Business School Press.
Hargrove, R. (1998). *Mastering the art of creative collaboration*. New York: McGraw-Hill.
Harrell-Bond, B. (2002). Can humanitarian work with refugees be humane? *Human Rights Quarterly, 24*(1), 51–85.
HCHR. (2004). *Elimination of violence against women: Commission resolution 2004/46*. New York: Commission on Human Rights.
Heifer. (2010a). *Our history*. Retrieved from HEIFER: http://www.heifer.org/site/c.edJRKQNiFiG/b.201520/?msource=TH1E100003
Heifer. (2010b). *Partnerships create sustainable change in the Philippines*. Retrieved from Heifer International: www.heifer.org
Hestermeyer, H. P. (2012, June 11). *Discussion on German NGOs at League of Nations*. (J. G. Goldammer, Interviewer).
High_Contracting_Parties. (1920, January 10). *Covenant of the League of Nations*. Geneva, Switzerland: http://avalon.law.yale.edu/20th_century/leagcov.asp
Hillmann, R. P. (1988 (October–December)). Quincy Wright and the Commission to Study the Organization of Peace. *Global Governance, 4*(4), 485–499.
Hippler, J. (2008, June). Democratization after civil wars – Key problems and experiences. *Democratization, 15*(3), 550–569.
HIU Unit. (2012). *World humanitarian day 2012: Aid workers in Harm's way*. Washington, DC: US Department of State.
Hoffman, J. (2010, August 28). *Email interview*. (L. Roeder, Interviewer).
Hogan, A. E. (1908). *Pacific blockade*. Oxford: Clarendon.
Holmes, K. (2004, March 18). *Need for knowledge management*. Washington, DC: US Department of State.
Hoover, H. (1921). The economic administration during the armistice. In E. M. House & C. Seymour (Eds.), *What really happened at Paris* (pp. 336–348). New York: Scribner's.
Horekens, J. (2004, October 13). *Administrative matters on WCDR*. (L. Roeder, Interviewer).
House, E. M. (1925, December). Paderewski, the paradox of Europe. *Harper's Magazine, 152*, 30–36.
House, E. M. (1926). Conversation with the Chancellor of Germany. In C. Seymour (Ed.), *Intimate papers of colonel house* (p. 142). New York: Houghton Mifflin.
House, E. M., & Seymour, C. (1921). *What really happened at Paris*. New York: Scribner's.
Howard-Ellis, C. (1928). *The origin, structure and working of the League of Nations*. London: George Allen.
Hudson, I. J. (1996, December 12). Website Draws Interest in *Times Community Newspapers*. p. 6.

Hudson, M. O. (Undated). *Tentative suggestion for a General Association of Nations*. Washington, DC: The Inquiry.
Huertas, G., & Murillo, J. C. (2007). *Surviving the flood: A risk reduction process for the cattle industry in Sante Fe, Argentina*. Costa Rica: WSPA.
Hulm, P. (2012, May 28). *Discussion on communications chapter*. (L. Roeder, Interviewer).
Humanitarian Outcomes Project. (n.d.). *The Aid Worker Security Database (AWSD)*. Retrieved October 3, 2010, from http://www.aidworkersecurity.org/and www.reliefweb.int
Hume, J. (2012, March 21). *Discussion about Roeder Book Series*. (L. Roeder, Interviewer).
IANS. (2012, March 7). *China faces huge employment challenges*. Retrieved July 7, 2012, from The Economic Times: http://economictimes.indiatimes.com/
IASC. (2006, 24 November). *Guidance note on using the cluster approach to strengthen humanitarian response*. New York: UN IASC.
IATI. (2011, December 16). *About IATI*. Retrieved December 18, 2011, from The International Aid Transparency Initiative: http://www.aidtransparency.net/
ICBL. (n.d.). *Treaty basics*. Retrieved August 2, 2010, from International Campaign to Ban Landmines: http://www.icbl.org/
ICC_staff. (2010). *ICC*. Retrieved from International Criminal Court: http://www.icc-cpi.int/
ICVA Secretariat. (2010). *International Council of Voluntary Agencies*. Retrieved August 3, 2010, from International Council of Voluntary Agencies: http://www.icva.ch/
IFAW. (2008, May 15). *Volcano eruption in Chile spells danger for animals*. Retrieved from IFAW: http://www.ifaw.org/
IFR. (2010a). *Animal welfare survey*. Virginia: IFR.
IFR. (2010b). *NGO survey*. Virginia: IFR.
IFRC. (2009, October 25). *Humanitarian diplomacy policy*. Retrieved March 23, 2012, from IFRC: http://www.ifrc.org/Global/Governance/Policies/Humanitarian_Diplomacy_Policy.pdf
IGAD. (N/A). *IGAD NGO & Civil Society Forum*. Retrieved May 21, 2012, from IGAD Portal: http://www.igad.int/
ILO. (2012, Undated). *Programme on Safety and Health at Work and the Environment (SafeWork)*. Retrieved July 7, 2012, from ILO International Labor Organization: http://www.ilo.org/safework/lang--en/index.htm
*Potomac River Most Endangered in America*. (2012, May 23). Retrieved May 24, 2012, from Environmental News Service: http://www.ens-newswire.com/ens/may2012/2012-05-23-01.html
Indianapolis Star. (1918, May 13). Laud's nation's unity. *Indianapolis Star*, p. 3 and 14.
Inge, W. R. (1921). *Outspoken essays* (2nd ed.). London: Longmans, Green, and Co.
InterAction Secretariat. (2010). *InterAction*. Retrieved August 3, 2010, from InterAction: www.interaction.org
International Committee of Women. (1919). *The position of women on the commissions and in the permanent secretariats*. International Committee of Women.
Internews. (n.d.). *About US*. Retrieved June 7, 2012, from Internews Network: http://www.internews.org/about-internews
IPSA. (1974, July 31). *Council minutes (31 July 1974)*. London: Archives of the RSPCA.
IPU. (2006). The role of parliaments in good governance of LDCs. *IPU Bulletin*, Article2 2.
IREX. (n.d.). *About us*. Retrieved June 7, 2012, from IREX: http://www.irex.org/about-us
ISDR_Secretariat. (2010). *International strategy on disaster risk reduction*. Retrieved August 3, 2010, from International Strategy on Disaster Risk Reduction: http://www.unisdr.org/
IWC Secretariat. (2010). *International Whaling Commission*. Retrieved from International Whaling Commission: http://www.iwcoffice.org/index.htm
J141 USPACOMINST. (2005). *Pandemic influenza preparation and response planning guidance*. Camp H. N. Smith, Hawaii: USPACOM.
Johnston, C. (2009, April 29). *Egypt considers mass pigs cull over swine flu fears*. Retrieved July 10, 2010, from Reuters: http://in.reuters.com/article/idINIndia-39322220090429
Jones, D. (2005, September 8). *Update on the Kabul Zoo Story*. Retrieved from North Carolina Zoological Society: http://www.nczoo.com/News/archive/20050908154106238
Jones, D. (2010a, October 7). *Discussion on food standards*. (L. Roeder, Interviewer).

Jones, D. (2010b, September 28). *Discussion on funding practices*. (L. Roeder, Interviewer).
Jordan, R. (2012, August 8). *Discussion on security*. (L. Roeder, Interviewer).
Joyce, J. A. (1978). *Broken star*. Llandybie, Wales: Davies.
Kahin, D. R. (2010, July 25). *Interview of president of Somaliland*. (L. Roeder, Interviewer).
Kälin, W. (2008). *Guiding principles on internal displacement: Annotations: Studies in Transnational Legal Policy No. 38*. Washington, DC: American Society of International Law and the Brookings Institution.
Kanter, R. M. (2001). *Evolve: Succeeding in the digital world of tomorrow*. Boston, MA: Harvard Business School Press.
Kegg Farms. (2010). *Background*. Retrieved November 2010, from Kegg farms: http://keggfarms.com/index.html
Kelly, K. (1998). *New rules for the new economy*. New York: Viking.
Kennan, G. F. (1951). *American diplomacy: 1900–1950*. Chicago: University of Chicago Press.
Kennedy, J. G. (1978). *Tarahumara of the Sierra Madre: Beer, ecology, and social organization*. Arlington Heights, IL: AHM Publishing.
Kennedy, R. (2010, July 28). *Email interview with R. Kennedy*, Executive Secretary. (L. Roeder, Interviewer).
Keynes, J. M. (1920). *The economic consequences of the peace*. London: Macmillan.
Kierkegaard, S. (1939). *Kierkegaard: The point of view, etc.* (W. Lowrie, Trans.). London: Oxford University Press.
Kimble, M. (1982, Spring). The economic viability of a Palestinian state. *Open Forum*, 25–26.
Kimmich, C. (1976). *Germany and the League of Nations*. Chicago: University of Chicago Press.
Kimmich, C. M. (2012, June 30). *Email discussion on Die LIga*. (L. W. Roeder, Interviewer).
Koo, R. (2008). *The Holy Grail of macroeconomics – Lessons from Japan's great recession*. Singapore: Wiley.
Kothari, A. (2012a, June 22). *Progress discussion*. (L. Roeder, Interviewer).
Kothari, A. (2012b, June 15). *Radical ecological democracy treaty*. (L. Roeder, Interviewer).
Kotok, A. (2010, June 30). *PublicDiplomacy.Org Editor*. (L. Roeder, Interviewer).
Kotter, J. P. (2002). *The heart of change*. Boston, MA: Harvard Business School Press.
Kraus, D., Salter, H., Pan, L., Stazinski, R., Paul, S., Maceyko, J., Moran, T., & Millar, M. K. (2008). *United nations emergency peace service: One step towards effective genocide prevention*. Washington, DC: Citizens for Global Solutions.
Kurtz, C. F., & Snowden, D. J. (2003). The new dynamics of strategy: Sense-making in a complex and complicated world. *IBM Systems Journal, 42*, 462–483.
Lafarge, H. (1946). *Lost treasures of Europe*. New York: Pantheon.
LaFranchi, H. (2012, February 23). *How the 'Friends of Syria' meeting showcases international weakness*. Retrieved February 24, 2012, from Christian Science Monitor: http://www.csmonitor.com/USA/Foreign-Policy/2012/0223/How-the-Friends-of-Syria-meeting-showcases-international-weakness
Lal, P. (2006). *Discussion with Larry Roeder on Livestock Situation in Kenya and Uganda in 2005 from Prakash Lal, Development Co-operation Coordinator, Fida International*. Helsinki, Finland: Prakash Lal.
Lamb, C. (2012, July 26). *Discussion of area bombing*. (L. W. Roeder, Interviewer).
Lamont, T. W. (1921). Reparations. In E. M. House & C. Seymour (Eds.), *What really happened at Paris* (pp. 259–291). New York: Scribner's.
Langenbach, R. (2011, December 8). *Katcvha is Pucca and Pucca is Katcha*. Washington, DC: World Bank.
Lanier, J. (2010, July 23). *Humane va inhumane slaughter techniques*. (L. Roeder, Interviewer).
Lapointe, E. (1938, September 14). *Remarks by the Chair: Protection of civilian non-combatant populations against bombing from the air in*. In Third Committee of the 19th Ordinary Session of the Assembly (p. 9). Geneva: League of Nations.
Leguey-Feilleux, J.-R. (2009). *The dynamics of diplomacy*. London: Lynne Rienner.
Leki, R. (2007). *Protocol for the modern diplomat*. Washington, DC: Foreign Service Institute.
Leney, J., & Remfry, J. (2000). Dog population management. In C. N. Macpherson, F. X. Meslin, & A. I. Wandeler (Eds.), *Dogs, zoonoses and public health* (pp. 299–301). New York: CABI.

*Leo Pasvolsky*. (2009, February 9). Retrieved June 6, 2012, from Famous Pipe Smokers: http://josephcrusejohnson.blogspot.com/2009/02/leo-pasvolsky.html

Lerner, J. (2012). *[OPs_NGOMG] Statement made by NGOs during plenary*. Rio, Brazil: Organising Partners of the Major Group of NGOs at the Rio+20 Summit.

Lester, P. (1900). *The great Galveston disaster*. Illustrated. Fry, Galveston, Texas.

Lippmann, W. (1933, February 8). Today and tomorrow. *Charleston Daily Mail*, p. 4

Lucchesi, V. (2010, June 15 and 28). *Policy officer, IFAP*. (L. W. Roeder, Interviewer).

Luege, T. (2010, July 6). *Shelter cluster, Haiti*. (L. Roeder, Interviewer).

Lyman, P. (1996 November 25). An information flak jacket in christian.

Lyman, P. (1996, December 4). *An information flak jacket*. Washington, DC: US Department of State.

Lymbery, P. (2003, January). *WSPA policy on humanely produced food*. London: WSPA.

MacAlister-Smith, P. (1995). Non-government organization, humanitarian action and human rights. In H. V. Beyerlin, M. Bothe, R. Hofmann, & E. U. Petersmann (Eds.), *Recht zwischen Umbruch und Bewahrung Festschrift für Rudolf Bernhardt* (pp. 477–501). Berlin: Springer.

Macalister-Smith, P. (2012, June 25). *Discussion on history of Die Liga*. (L. W. Roeder, Interviewer).

MacLeish, A. (1945, June 8). *Letter to secretary of state Stettinius* [Private letter].

Maier, W. (2010a, June 11). *Interview of Wolf Maier on the EC*. (L. Roeder, Interviewer).

Maier, W. M. (2010b, June 11). *DG health and consumers*. (L. W. Roeder, Interviewer). Brussels: European Commission.

Malhotra, D., & Bazerman, M. H. (2007). *Negotiation genius: How to overcome obstacles and achieve brilliant results at the bargaining table and beyond*. New York: Bantom.

Mann, C. C. (2011, June). Birth of religion. *National Geographic, 219*(6), 38–59.

Martin, J. (1996). *Cybercorp: The new business*. New York: American Management Association.

Mas de Xaxàs, M., O'Reilly, K., Evans, C., Higgins, D., Gillies, P., & Jana, S. (2008). *Meeting community needs for HIV prevention and more: Intersectoral action for health in the Sonagachi red-light area of Kolkata*. Geneva: WHO.

Masoner, L. (2010, March 29). *Live animal photography props?* Retrieved September 25, 2010, from Liz's Photography Blog: http://photography.about.com/b/2010/03/29/live-animal-photography-props.htm

McCaffree, M. J., & Innis, P. (1977). *Protocol: The complete handbook of diplomatic, official and social usage*. New York: Prentice-Hall.

McCartney, R. (2012, May 20). Potomac 'most endangered'? Just hype. Metro section, *The Washington Post*, Washington, DC.

McClellan, M. (2004, October 14). *Public diplomacy in the context of traditional diplomacy*. Retrieved from Public Diplomacy: http://www.publicdiplomacy.org/45.htm

McConnan, I. (1998). *The sphere project*. Geneva: Sphere.

McConnan, I. (2000). The humanitarian charter. In I. McConnan (Ed.), *The sphere project* (pp. 5–12). Oxford: Oxfam Publishing.

Mcconnell, F. J., Dulles, J. F., Paton, W., Pasvolsky, L., Shih, H., & Hambro, C. J. (1942). *A basis for the peace to come*. Nashville: Parthenon.

McCormack, M. H. (1995). *On negotiating: What they teach you at Harvard Business School*. Beverly Hills, CA: Dove Books.

McDonald, J. W. (1991). *Multi-track diplomacy, a systems approach to peace*. Grinnell, IA: Iowa Peace Institute.

McLeod, M. E., Everly, R., & Malin, M. C. (2000, June 8). *Global Disaster Information Network (GDIN)*. Office of the Legal Adviser. Washington, DC: US Department of State.

Mezes, S. E. (1921). Preparations for peace. In E. M. House & C. Seymour (Eds.), *What really happened at Paris* (pp. 1–15). New York: Scribner's.

Michels, J. (1964, February 28). *Letter requesting help*. Paramaribo, Suriname: Vereeniging Voor Dierenbescherming in Suriname.

Michigan State University College of Law. (2010, August). Retrieved from Animal Legal & Historical Web Center: http://animallaw.info/

Milburn, C. (2010, October 27). *Discussion on food standards*. (L. Roeder, Interviewer).
Miller, D. H. (1924). *My diary at the Conference of Paris*. Appeal Printing, New York.
Miller, D. H. (1925, March 15). Declares British foes of protocol. *New York Times*, p. 3.
Miller, D. H. (1928a). Meetings with the neutral powers. In D. H. Miller (Ed.), *The drafting of the covenant* (pp. 303–309). New York: Putnam.
Miller, D. H. (1928b). *The drafting of the covenant*. New York: Putnam.
Miller, D. H. (1928c). *The peace pact of Paris*. New York: Nickerbacker Press.
Miller, D. H. (1928d). The Phillimore plan In M. D. Hunter (Ed.), *The drafting of the covenant* (Vol. II, pp. 3–6). New York: Putnam.
Miller, D. H. (1928e). The Smuts plan. In D. H. Miller (Ed.), *The drafting of the covenant* (Vol. II, pp. 23–60). New York: Putnam.
Ministry of Foreign Affairs, New Zealand. (2009). ECLAC. In *United Nations handbook 2008/09* (p. 147). Wellington: Ministry of Foreign Affairs, New Zealand.
MN/HN. (2012, January 4). *UN: 100 s thought dead in South Sudan*. Retrieved May 26, 2012, from PressTV: http://presstv.com/detail/219200.html
Mock, J. R., & Larson, C. (1939). *Words that won the war*. Princeton: Princeton University Press.
Montville, J. (2012, April 22). *Email discussion on track two diplomacy*. (L. Roeder, Interviewer).
Montville, J., & Davidson, W. D. (1981–1982, Winter). Foreign policy according to Freud. *Foreign Policy, 45*, 145–157.
Moon, P. T. (1939). *Imperialism and world politics*. New York: Macmillan.
Morgenthau, H. J. (1968). *The game of nations*. New York: Knopf.
Morrin, J. (2010, July 24). *Interview by Email with Joanna Morrini, Ceremonial Office, Protocol Directorate, Foreign and Commonwealth Office*. (L. Roeder, Interviewer).
MSF. (2011, December 1). *About MSF.* Retrieved March 8, 2012, from MSF: http://www.msf.org/
Murphy, R. (1964). *Diplomat among warriors*. Garden City, NY: Doubleday.
Nanaka, I., & Takeuchi, H. (1995). *The knowledge creating company*. Oxford, UK: Oxford University Press.
Nansen, F. (1923). *Russia and peace*. London: George Allen.
Nash, G. (1988a). *The life of Herbert Hoover, Vol. 2, The humanitarian 1914–1917*. New York: Norton.
Nash, G. (1988b). *The life of Herbert Hoover: The humanitarian 1914–1917*. New York: Norton.
National Gulf and Wildlife Foundation. (2010). *The time to save Gulf Wildlife is now.* Retrieved from National Gulf and Wildlife Foundation: http://www.nfwfgulfresponse.org/?gclid=CNDhtananaICFQuB5QodEjPDzA
NCAI. (2010, September 16). *President Obama signs historic tribal law and order act into law*. Retrieved from National Congress of American Indians: http://www.ncai.org/
Negroponte, N. (1996). *Being digital*. New York: Vintage.
Neuman, M. (2012). *Dear friends*. New York: MSF.
New_Zealand_Ministry_of_Foreign_Affairs_and_Trade. (2008). *United Nations handbook*. Wellington: New_Zealand_Ministry_of_Foreign_Affairs_and_Trade.
Niemeyer, T. (1915). The causes of the war. In: N. Times (Ed.), *The New York Times current history: The European War, VO 1* (pp. 206–207 [1914, August 14]). New York: NY Times.
Niemeyer, T. (1919). *Draft of a constitution of the League of Nations*. Kiel: Deutsche Gesellschaft für Völkerrecht.
Northern Territory Government. (2010, February 19). *Animal welfare gets a funding boost*. Retrieved 2010, from Northern Territory Government Media Release: http://newsroom.nt.gov.au/
Norway, UN Mission. (2006, June 15). *Norway Chairs the International Somalia Contact Group*. Retrieved from Norway: Mission to the UN: http://www.norway-un.org/
NRCAT (Director). (2010). *Solitary confinement: Torture in your backyard* [Motion Picture].
NSW_Government. (2007, January 1). *Animal welfare in drought*. Retrieved from Industry and Development, New South Wales: http://www.dpi.nsw.gov.au/
NZ Ministry of Foreign Affairs and Trade. (2012). *The United Nations handbook.* Retrieved December 5, 2012, from NZ Ministry of Foreign Affairs and Trade: http://www.mfat.govt.nz/UNHB2012/index.php

O'Dell, C. S., & Jackson, G. (1998). *If only we knew what we know*. New York: Fine Press.
O'Regan, F. (2006, January 18). *Urgent: Japanese fleet now killing whales*. Retrieved from Windows Live: http://f77239072.spaces.live.com/blog/cns!6CF6E763675AE727!498.entry
Oaks, U. T. (1943). *Functions, powers, machinery*. Washington, DC: US Government.
OAS Secretariat. (2010). *OAS*. Retrieved August 2010, from OAS Organization of American States: www.oas.org
OCHA: The Consolidated Appeals Process (CAP). (2010, June 11). *Guatemala 11 June 2010 flash appeal*. Retrieved from ReliefWeb.int: www.reliefweb.net
OECD Futures Project on Risk Management Policies in Selected OECD Countries. (2003, June 16). *Background presentation of Phase I*. Paris: OECD International Futures Programme.
Office of the Historian. (2010, December 3). *The Bullitt Mission to Soviet Russia, 1919*. Retrieved July 11, 2012, from US Department of State, Office of the Historian: http://history.state.gov/
Office of the Legal Adviser. (2010). *Circular 175 procedure*. Retrieved from Department of State: http://www.state.gov/s/l/treaty/c175/index.htm
OHCHR. (2012). *Born free and equal: Sexual orientation and gender identity in International Human Rights Law*. New York/Geneva: United Nations.
OIE_Secretariat. (2010). *World Organization for Animal Health*. Retrieved August 3, 2010, from World Organization for Animal Health: http://www.oie.int
Oppenheim, L. (1919). *The League of Nations and its problems*. London: Longmans.
OSOC:US Department of State. (2008). *Animal rights extremists, targets, tactics, business, response & countermeasures*. Washington, DC: US Department of State.
Panaman, B. (2009). *Animal rights encyclopedia*. Retrieved 2010, from Animal Rights Encyclopedia: http://www.zoosavvy.com/about.html
Parties, U. N. (1951, July 28). *Convention relating to the status of refugees*. Geneva: UNHCR: http://www2.ohchr.org/english/law/refugees.htm
Pasvolsky, L. (1942). The problem of economic peace after the war. In B. S. Abernathy (Ed.), *A basic for the peace to come* (p. 83). New York: Abinghdon-Cokesbury.
Pasvolsky, L. (1944, October 4). *Work in International Organization in Department of State prior to Oct 1943*. Washington, DC: Department of State.
Penn Museum. (n.d.). *Cultural heritage (1970 UNESCO Convention)*. Retrieved February 6, 2012, from Penn Museum: http://www.penn.museum/cultural-heritage/232-cultural-heritage-1970-unesco-convention.html
Peoples' Sustainable Treaties. (2012a). *Draft treaties*. Retrieved June 6, 2012, from Peoples' Sustainable Treaties: http://sustainabilitytreaties.org/draft-treaties/
People's Sustainability Treaties. (2012b). *Guidelines*. Retrieved June 6, 2012, from People's Sustainability Treaties: http://sustainabilitytreaties.org/guidelines/
Peoples Sustainability Treaties. (2012c). *Movement*. Retrieved June 6, 2012, from Peoples Sustainability Treaties: http://sustainabilitytreaties.org/movement/
People's Sustainability Treaties. (2012d). *Teams*. Retrieved June 6, 2012, from People's Sustainability Treaties: http://sustainabilitytreaties.org/advisors/
Pevar, S. L. (2004). *The rights of Indians and tribes*. New York: New York University Press.
Phillips C (2011, Jan 15). *Discussion on animal welfare standards* (L. Roeder, Interviewer)
Polanyi, J. (1999). Reflections by nobel laureates. In Y. Danieli, E. Stamatopoulou, & C. Dias (Eds.), *The universal declaration of human rights: Fifty years and beyond* (p. xi). New York: United Nations.
Press Now. (n.d.). *Home page*. Retrieved June 7, 2012, from Press Now. www.pressnow.nl/
*Process: People's Sustainability Treaties*. (2012). Retrieved June 6, 2012, from People's Sustainability Treaties: http://sustainabilitytreaties.org/process/
Protocol and Liaison Service, United Nations. (2010). *The United Nations Flag Code- ST/SGB/132*. Retrieved from Protocol and Liaison Service: http://www.un.int/protocol/communication.html
Project, S. (2010). *Sphere humanitarian charter and minimum standards in disaster response*. Washington, DC: InterAction.
Pugh, M. C. (1974). *The quest for collective security*. Dissertation, Norwich: University of East Anglia.

Rahman, S. (2006, December). Development, democracy and the NGO sector: Theory and evidence from Bangladesh. *Journal of Developing Societies, 22*(4), 451–473.
Rappart, W. E. (1931). *The Geneva experiment*. London: Oxford University.
Rawles, K. (2005). Sustainable development and animal welfare. In J. Turner & J. D'Silva (Eds.), *Animals, ethics and trade: The challenge of animal sentience* (pp. 208–216). Sterling, VA: Earthscan.
Reagan, R. (1983, January 14). *Management of public diplomacy relative to national security (NSC-NSDD-77)*. Retrieved June 19, 2012, from National Security Directives: http://www.fas.org/irp/offdocs/nsdd/nsdd-077.htm
Reagan, R. (1985). Document 208: Current travails of the people of Poland, May 1, 1983. In D. o. State (Ed.), *American Foreign Policy, 1983* (pp. 505–506). Washington, DC: US Government Printing Office.
Reddies, J. (1851). *Inquiries in the science of law* (2nd ed.). Edinburgh: William Blackwood.
Regnery, R. (2010, August and September). *Numerous email exchanges with Rebecca Regnery, HSI*. (L. Roeder, Interviewer).
Representative of the Secretary-General. (1996). *Compilation and analysis of legal norms*. New York: UN Commission on Human Rights.
Rice, H. (2012, May 3). *Program to end solitary confinement*. (L. Roeder, Interviewer).
Roberts, I. (2009). *Satow's diplomatic practice* (6th ed.). Oxford: Oxford University Press.
Roeder, L. (1983, March). US policy option on high-tech exports to the Soviet Union. *World Affairs Monthly Retreat*. Seattle/Washington, DC: World Affairs Council.
Roeder, L. (1991). *Diary of events on May 12, 1991*. Washington, DC: Private.
Roeder, L. (2003, January–February). Hope from on high. *Unmanned Vehicles, 8*, 14–15.
Roeder, L. (2006, August). *Linking animal welfare and human survival*. Retrieved from Archived Presentations of the Global Risk Forum: http://www.idrc.info/userfiles/file/archive/2006/presentations/NYRoeder.pdf
Roeder, L. (2008, March 20). *Protecting animals from disasters: A new humanitarian perspective*. 36th General Assembly of Arab IFRC Societies (p. 7). Tunis, Tunisia: IFRC.
Roeder, L. (2011). *Diplomacy, funding and animal welfare*. Hamburg: Springer.
Roeder, L. (2012, February 15). *Operational space*. Retrieved March 14, 2012, from International Organizations and NGO Associations: http://internationalorgs.wordpress.com/
Roeder, L., & Badaoui, R. (2008). *Protecting animals from disasters*. Paris: International Working Group on Animals in Disasters (IWGAID).
Roeder, L., Marcus, F. C., & Sizer, H. (1982a, Spring). Palestinian autonomy and the Jerusalem question. *Open Forum*, pp. 7–8.
Roeder, L., Marcus, F. C., & Sizer, H. (1982b, June). The Palestine debate: Palestinian autonomy and the Jerusalem question, and can a Palestinian state Be Moderate. *Open Forum Journal,*.
Roosevelt, T. (1910). *International peace*. Oslo: Nobel Committee.
Root, E. (1922, September). A requisite for the success of popular diplomacy. *Foreign Affairs, 1*(1), 3–10.
Ross, I. (2009, November). *Technology (transfer?) – agreement needed at Copenhagen*. Retrieved from Climatico: http://www.climaticoanalysis.org/post/tag/g77/
RSPCA. (1974). *1974 annual report for RSPCA*. London: RSPCA.
RSPCA Australia. (n.d.). *Humane food*. Retrieved from RSPCA Australia: http://www.rspca.org.au/what-we-do/humane-food/
Rusk, D. (1965, December 27). *Reply to question at News Conference, Dec 9, 1965*. Washington, DC: Department of State Bulletin.
Russell, P. (2009, April 3). *Gaza relief aid – Report on progress*. London: DM Office, WSPA.
Ryan, O. (2006). Animal welfare and economic development. In J. Turner & J. D'silva (Eds.), *Animals, ethics and trade: The challenge of animal sentience* (pp. 238–248). Sterling, VA: Earthscan.
Saint-Onge, H., & Wallace, D. (2002). *Leveraging communities of practice for strategic advantage*. Boston, MA: Butterworth-Heinemann.

Samuelson, R. J. (2008, December 13). *Lobbying is democracy in action.* Retrieved from Newsweek: http://www.newsweek.com/2008/12/12/lobbying-is-democracy-in-action.html
Sands, P. (2012, April 8). Disaffection, fear growing among Syria's Alawites. *The National*. http://www.thenational.ae/news/world/middleeast/disaffection-fear-growing-among-syrias-alawites
Schlesinger, S. C. (2003). *Act of creation*. Boulder, CO: Westview.
Schultz, H. C. (1919, February 8). Think it over. *The Capital Times*, p. 4.
Schuze-Gaevernitz, G. (1919). *Peace clauses*. Paris: Papers of David Hunter Miller, US Delegation to Paris Peace Conference.
Secretariat. (1921). *Repertoire des Organizations Internationales*. Geneva: League of Nations.
Secretariat. (1938). *Handbook of international organizations* (Vols. XII.B International Bureaux, 1937.XII.B.4). Geneva: League of Nations.
Secretariat, O. (2006). *OECD studies in risk management: Disaster information needs of ethnic minorities*. Paris: OECD.
Sering, S. H. (2012, September 8). *Gilgit Baltistan's role in promoting interests of regional powers in Afghanistan.* (L. W. Roeder, Interviewer)
Seymour, C. (1926). *The intimate papers of Colonel House*. Boston: Houghton Mifflin.
Sharp, S. W. (1999). *Jus Paciarii: Emergent legal paradigms for UN peace operations on the 21st century*. Stafford, VA: Paciarii International, LLC.
Shean, M. (2008, June 10). *Larry & Dennis, We published a new article concerning Burma today*. Washington, DC: USDA.
Shevelow, K. (2008). *For the love of animals: The rise of the animal protection movement*. New York: Henry Holt.
Simard, A. J. (2005, January 18–22). Disaster information service: A proposal. *UN World Conference on Disaster Reduction* (p. 18). Kobe, Japan.
Simard, A. J. (2012). Knowledge services: A strategic framework. In J. K. Karwowski (Ed.), *Knowledge services engineering handbook* (pp. 1–66). Boca Raton, FL: CRC Press.
Simard, A. J., & Eenigenberg, J. E. (1990). An executive information system to support wildfire disaster declarations. *Interfaces, 20*, 53–66.
Sizer, H., Roeder, L., & Marcus, F. C. (1982, June). The Palestine debate: Palestinian autonomy and the Jerusalem question, and can a Palestinian state be moderate. *Open Forum Journal*,
SMH . (2005, October 23). *NZ reporter fired for fabricating stories*. Retrieved February 24, 2012, from The Sydney Morning Herald: http://www.smh.com.au/
Source, C. (2012a, August 16). *About ICC*. (L. Roeder, Interviewer).
Source, C. (2012b, August 1). *Discussion on ICC*. (L. Roeder, Interviewer).
Special to NY Times. (1948, December 8). Mrs. Roosevelt reveals human rights "grapevine". *New York Times*, p. 13.
SPHERE. (Not listed). *The Sphere Project in brief*. Retrieved October 15, 2012, from The Sphere Project : http://www.sphereproject.org
SPHERE_Editors. (2010). *Sphere project*. Retrieved February 4, 2010, from Sphere Project: http://www.sphereproject.org
Spillane, J. P. (1983, August 9). *To all CoCom delegates and the secretariat, a letter*. Paris: US Mission to OECD.
Spokesman, U. D. (2009, January 14). *Media Note number 2009/051: Contact group on piracy off the Coast of Somalia*. Washington, DC: US Department of State.
St. John, Anne, (2010, August 4), Interview on the participation of NGOs in CITES, Larry Roeder, Interviewer.
Steel, R. (1980). *Walter Lippmann and the American Century*. Boston: Little, Brown and Company.
Steets, J., Grünewald, F., Binder, A., de Geoffroy, V., Kauffmann, D., Krüger, S., et al. (2010, April). *Cluster approach evaluation 2 synthesis report*. New York: IASC.
Stewart, T. (1997). *Intellectual capital: The new wealth of organizations*. New York: Banton Doubelday Dell Group.
Stone, K. L. (2005). *Hurricane Emily Update 10 – July 15, 2005, 2:00 p.m.*. Washington, DC: USAID/OFDA.

Stover, E., & McGrath, R. (1991). *Land mines in Cambodia: The coward's war*. New York: Physicians for Human Rights and Asia Watch.
Stoyko, P. (2010). *Compliance, motivation and engagement*. Retrieved from Fugitive Knowledge: http://www.stoyko.net/fugitiveknowlege/?p=1686
Streit, C. (1940). *Union now*. New York: Harper.
Stroh, P. (2000). *United States participation in the UN: Report by the President to the Congress for the year 1999*. Washington, DC: US Department of State.
Sulzer, H. M. (1942). The Minister of Switzerland to the US Secretary of State (Telegram No. 29), December 14, 1918 to the Commission to Negotiate Peace. In U. D. State (Ed.), *Foreign relations of the United States* (p. 71). Washington, DC: GPO.
Swerdlow, A. (1993). *Woman strike for peace*. Chicago: University of Chicago.
Talbot-Rosevear, D. o. (1991). *History of Kabul Zoo*. London: British Federation of Zoos.
Tanaka, R., DePoyster, J. D., & Roeder, L. W. (2004). US delegation position paper on animals: Interdependence of human and animal species in disaster management. In B. o. Affairs (Ed.), *US position papers for the world conference on disaster reduction* (pp. 3–6). Washington, DC: US_Dept_of_State.
Tanaka, R. T., Roeder, L. W., Mantell, C., Huertas, G., & Davidson, O. (2005). *Intersection of animal and human issues in disasters (Session WS013)*. World Conference on Disaster Reduction: 18–22 January 2005, Kobe, Hyogo, Japan (pp. CD-Rom). Geneva: United Nations.
Tapscott, D., & Williams, A. D. (2006). *Wikinomics: How mass collaboration changes everything*. New York: Penguin Group.
Thorp, W. L. (1947, June 1). United States refusal to request reparation from Italy, 1946, September 11. *Department of State Bulletin*, 1076–1080.
Ticehurst, R. (1997, April 30). The Martens clause and the laws of armed conflict. *International Review of the Red Cross*, p. No. 317.
To Hold War Convention. (1918, March 18). *New York Times*. p. 1.
Toynbee, A. J. (1947). *A study of history*. New York: Oxford University Press.
Trent, N., Edwards, S., Felt, J., & O'Meara, K. (2005, December 31). International Animal Law, with a concentration on Latin America, Asia, and Africa. In D. J. Salem, & A. Rowan (Eds.), *The state of the animals III: 2005* (p. 155). Washington, DC: Humane Society Press.
Tronc, E. (2012, March 22). *Discussion about MSF.* (L. Roeder, Interviewer).
Truman, H. S. (1955). *1945 year of decisions: Memoirs by Harry S. Truman*. New York: Time.
Truman, M. (1972). *Harry S. Truman*. New York: Morrow.
Tuch, H. N., & Kalb, M. (1990). *Communicating with the World: U. S. Public Diplomacy Overseas (Institute for the Study of Diplomacy)*. Washington, DC: St. Martin's.
Twentieth Century Series Back with Operation Gwamba. (1965, December 19). *Arizona Republic*, p. 106.
U.S. Department of State. (2012, January 12). *Fact Sheet: Non-Governmental Organizations (NGOs) in the United States*. Retrieved August 5, 2012, from Human Rights Gov: http://www.humanrights.gov/2012/01/12/fact-sheet-non-governmental-organizations-ngos-in-the-united-states/
UN. (1994, July 7). International Covenant on Civil and Political Rights. http://www.hrweb.org/legal/cpr.html
UN. (2005, May 29). *News and media*. Retrieved July 2011, from United Nations: http://www.unmultimedia.org/photo/detail.jsp?id=769/76989&key=11&query=cattle&sf=
UN. (2008, May 2). *Lesson plans: Refugees*. New York: United Nations: www.un.org/works/Lesson_Plans/WGO/WGO_LP_RT.pdf
UN Mission South Sudan. (2012, January 19). *Pibor County Commissioner backs buffer zones between warring communities*. Juba, South Sudan: UNOCHA.
UN OCHA. (2004). *The guiding principles of internal displacement*. New York: UN, OCHA.
UN Treaty Office. (1990, October 23). *MOU between the Government of the United States of America and the Government of the Federal Republic of Germany concerning air navigation services in Berlin*. Retrieved August 29, 2010, from UN Treaty Collection: http://untreaty.un.org/unts/144078_158780/18/10/9026.pdf

UN. (n.d.). *Universal Declaration of Human Rights*. Retrieved from The United Nations: http://www.un.org/en/documents/udhr/
UN_Information_Officer. (2008, September 4). *DPI/NGO conference holds panel discussion on 'human rights and human security'*. Retrieved June 9, 2010, from Press Release, NGO/652, PI/1852: http://www.un.org/News/Press/docs/2008/ngo652.doc.htm
UN_OCHA. (2010a). *Central Emergency Response Fund (CERF)*. Retrieved July 28, 2010, from Central Emergency Response Fund (CERF): http://ochaonline.un.org/Default.aspx?alias=ochaonline.un.org/cerf
UN_OCHA. (2010b). *Financial tracking service*. Retrieved 2010, from ReliefWeb: http://ocha.unog.ch/
UNDPI. (2010). *UN and civil society*. Retrieved from The United Nations: http://www.un.org/en/civilsociety/index.shtml
UNEP. (2010). *What is CITES?* Retrieved from CITS, Convention on International Trade in Endangered Species of Wild Fauna and Flora: http://www.cites.org/eng/disc/what.shtml
UNESCO. (2010). *Convention for the protection of cultural property in the event of armed conflict – 1954*. Retrieved July 28, 2010, from UNESCO: http://portal.unesco.org/culture/en/
UNGA. (1989, December 22). *UNGA Resolution A/44/225*. New York: UN.
UNGA. (1991, December 19). *Strengthening of the coordination of humanitarian emergency assistance of the UN* (UNGA Resolution A/46/182). New York: UN.
UNGA, C. 5.–. (1954, December 17). *International convention concerning the use of broadcasting in the cause of peace (Geneva, 1936)* (A/RES/841). Geneva, Switzerland: UNHCR.
United States Trade Representative. (2010, August). *Trade and Environment Policy Advisory Committee (TEPAC)*. Retrieved August, 2010, from USTR: http://www.ustr.gov/about-us/intergovernmental-affairs/advisory-committees
UNOG. (n.d.). *Anti-personnel landmines convention*. Retrieved 2010, from The UN Office at Geneva: www.unog.ch
UN-Spider. (2012, June). Rio+20 agreement addresses disaster risk reduction. *UN-SPIDER, June 2012 Updates*, 2.
UNTV. (2006, January 9). *Reforming Somaliland's judiciary* (Programme No. 991). New York: UNDP.
US Department of State. (1942a). Organization and work of "the inquiry". In *Foreign affairs of the United States: Paris Peace Conference, 1919* (Vol. 1, pp. 9–119). Washington, DC: Superintendant of Documents.
US Department of State. (1942b). *Papers relating to the foreign relations of the United States, 1919, The Paris Peace Conference* (Vol. II). Washington, DC: GPO.
US Department of State. (1942c). *The Paris Peace Conference, 1919* (Vol. XI). Washington, DC: GPO.
US Department of State. (1996, October 30). State Department Cable 226284 Draft USG Resolution on ReliefWeb. (L. Roeder, Ed.) Washington, DC, USA.
US Department of State. (2011). *Treaties in force as of January 1, 2011*. Washington, DC: Office of Treaty Affairs, US Department of State.
US Supreme Court. (2010). *Holder, attorney general, et al. v. humanitarian law project et al.*. Washington, DC: US Supreme Court.
US_Department_Of_State. (2010). *About the OAS*. Retrieved from US Permanent Mission to the Organization of American State: http://www.usoas.usmission.gov/index/about-the-oas.html
USAID. (2012a). USAID-funded public opinion research provides valuable information on citizens' views. *South Sudan*, 1.
USAID. (2012b). *Sudan – Complex emergency*. Washington, DC: USAID.
USAID/OFDA. (2011). *Three areas: Displacement and USAID/DCHA response*. Washington, DC: USAID/OFDA.
USC 1 – US CODE 1 – U.S. Code – Title 1: General Provisions. (2004, January). United States: US Government.
USDA. (2010). *Animal Welfare Information Center*. Retrieved from National Agricultural Library (USDA): http://awic.nal.usda.gov/nal_display/index.php?tax_level=1&info_center=3
US-Department-of-State-Press-Guidance. (2001, December 7). *U.S. assistance to the Kabul Zoo*. Washington, DC: US Department of State.

USIP. (2012). *Solving real problems in difficult places*. Retrieved 2012, from USIP: www.usip.org

Valkarie. (2011, April 15). *Time for a UN emergency capacity.* Retrieved May 28, 2012, from Citizens for Global Solutions: http://globalsolutions.org/united-nations

Vance, A. (2012, March 3). *PM tells world leaders to take nuclear threat seriously.* Retrieved April 11, 2012, from Stuff: http://www.stuff.co.nz/national/politics/6648578/PM-tells-leaders-to-take-nuclear-threat-seriously

Virtue, M. (2010, August 3). *Interview with Melanie Virtue, NGO Liaison*. (L. Roeder, Interviewer).

von Neumann, J., & Oskar Morgenstern, O. (1944). *Theory of games and economic behavior*. Princeton: Princeton University Press.

Wadleigh, R. (2004, September 28). *Animal panel at world conference on disaster reduction.* Washington, DC: Email from Wadleigh, then Native American Tribal Liaison to APHIS/USDA.

Walsh, J. (1967). *Time is short and the water rises*. New York: Dutton.

Walsh, J. (2010a, July 13). (L. W. Roeder, Interviewer).

Walsh, J. (2010b, September 23). *Discussion about relief operations*. (L. Roeder, Interviewer).

Walsh, J. (2011, June 12). *Discussion of Kabul Zoo operation*. (L. Roeder, Interviewer).

Walsh, J., & Gannon, R. (1967). *Time is short and the water rises*. New York: Dutton.

Walters, F. P. (1952 [reprint 1965]). *A history of the League of Nations*. Oxford: London.

Walters, R. (2010, May 23). *Government provides more animal welfare funding*. Retrieved from NZNewsUK: http://www.nznewsuk.co.uk/news/

Ward, B. (1962). *The rich nations and the poor nations*. New York: Norton.

Warns, M. (1995). ReliefWeb Project. *DHA Retrospective*, pp. 51–53.

Watzman, S. (1983, October). Economic and business affairs. *State*, p. 78.

Watzman, S. (1984, July). Economic and business affairs. *State*, pp. 52–53.

Webmaster, U. C. (n.d.). *Home page*. Retrieved March 27, 2012, from USNS Comfort: http://www.med.navy.mil/sites/usnscomfort/Pages/default.aspx

Wegner, E., McDermott, R., & Snyder, W. M. (2002). *Cultivating communities of practice*. Boston, MA: Harvard Business School Press.

Wellesley, V. (1944). *Diplomacy in fetters*. Anchor Press: London.

Wheeler, T. (2012, June 3). *About diplomacy*. (L. Roeder, Interviewer).

White, L. C. (1933). *The structure of private international organizations*. Philadelphia: Ferguson.

Wiki contributor. (2010, June 8). *Universal Declaration on Animal Welfare (UDAW).* Retrieved from Wikipedia: http://en.wikipedia.org/wiki/UDAW#cite_note-15

Wilkins, D. (2010, August 26). *Email exchange on OIE*. (L. Roeder, Interviewer).

Williams, J. (1997, November 10). *Nobel lecture*. Oslo: Nobel Committee.

Windfuhr, M. (1998). *NGOs and the right to adequate food*. Rome: FAO.

Windward Environmental Center. (1995). *Earthtrust and driftnets: A capsule history from 1976–995*. Retrieved from EarthTrust: http://www.earthtrust.org/.

Woolf, L. S. (1916a). *International government*. New York: Brentano.

Woolf, L. S. (1916b). *International government*. New York: Brentano's.

World Peace Foundation. (1919, April). Joint debate on the covenant of Paris. *A League of Nations, II*(2), 2.

World_Bank. (2010). *Approach to the World Bank's engagement with civil society.* Retrieved July 27, 2010, from The World Bank: http://www.worldbank.org/

Wright, A. (2010, July 29). *Interview of executive secretary on NGO participation*. (L. Roeder, Interviewer).

WSPA. (2000, June 13). *Universal Declaration for the Welfare of Animals*. Retrieved 2009, from http://www.wetnose.org.za/UniversalDeclaration.pdf

WSPA. (2007a, December 10). *Provision draft UDAW 2007.* Retrieved 2010, from Animals Matter: www.animalsmatter.org

WSPA. (2007b, December 3). *Universal Declaration on Animal Welfare: Proposed route to the United Nations.* Retrieved June 2010, from Animals Matter: http://media.animalsmatter.org/media/resources/en/en_routemap.pdf

WSPA. (2010a). *Animals matter.* Retrieved from Animals Matter: http://www.animalsmatter.org/
WSPA. (2010b). *Animals matter to me.* Retrieved from WSPA, USA: http://www.wspa-usa.org/pages/1706_animals_matter.cfm
WSPA-International. (2010). *UNESCO endorses WSPOA's InAwe Project.* Retrieved 2010, from WSPA.
Yunis, M. (2010). Why social business? In M. Yunis (Ed.), *Building social business* (p. 19). New York: Public Affairs.
Zimmermann, H. (2012, March 4). *Discussion on diplomacy.* (L. Roeder, Interviewer).

# Index



L.W. Roeder, Jr. and A. Simard, *Diplomacy and Negotiation for Humanitarian NGOs*, Humanitarian Solutions in the 21st Century, DOI 10.1007/978-1-4614-7113-4, 

MIX
Papier aus verantwortungsvollen Quellen
Paper from responsible sources
FSC® C105338

If you have any concerns about our products,
you can contact us on
**ProductSafety@springernature.com**

In case Publisher is established outside the EU,
the EU authorized representative is:
**Springer Nature Customer Service Center GmbH**
**Europaplatz 3, 69115 Heidelberg, Germany**

Printed by Libri Plureos GmbH
in Hamburg, Germany